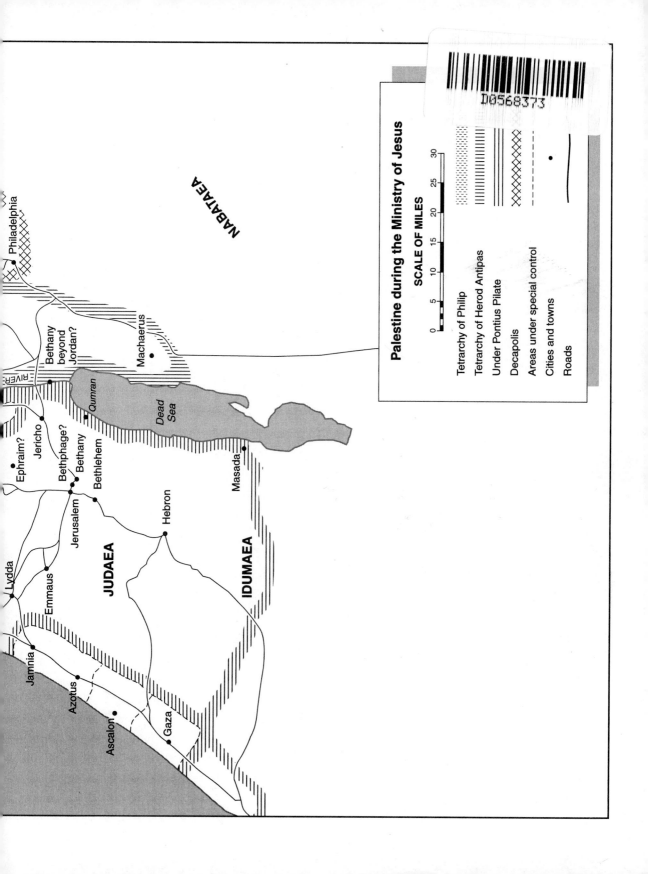

Palestine during the Ministry of Jesus

SCALE OF MILES

0 5 10 15 20 25 30

Tetrarchy of Philip
Tetrarchy of Herod Antipas
Under Pontius Pilate
Decapolis
Areas under special control
Cities and towns
Roads

NABATAEA

Philadelphia

Bethany beyond Jordan?

Machaerus

RIVER

Qumran

Dead Sea

Ephraim?

Jericho

Bethphage?

Bethany

Bethlehem

Jerusalem

Hebron

Masada

JUDAEA

IDUMAEA

Lydda

Emmaus

Jamnia

Azotus

Ascalon

Gaza

Reading the
New Testament Today

Robert E. Van Voorst
Western Theological Seminary

THOMSON
™
WADSWORTH

Australia • Canada • Mexico • Singapore • Spain
United Kingdom • United States

THOMSON

WADSWORTH

Publisher: Holly J. Allen
Religion Editor: Steve Wainwright
Assistant Editors: Lee McCracken, Anna Lustig
Editorial Assistant: Barbara Hillaker
Marketing Manager: Worth Hawes
Marketing Assistant: Andrew Keay
Advertising Project Managers: Bryan Vann, Vicky Wan
Print/Media Buyer: Judy Inouye
Composition Buyer: Ben Schroeter

Permissions Editor: Joohee Lee
Production Service: Matrix Productions
Photo Researcher: Sarah Evertson
Copy Editor: Vicki Nelson
Executive Art Director: Maria Epes
Cover Designer: Yvo Riezebos
Cover Image: W. Perry Conway / Corbis
Compositor: International Typesetting and Composition
Printer: Malloy Incorporated

Printed in the United States of America
1 2 3 4 5 6 7 08 07 06 05 04

For more information about our products, contact us at:
Thomson Learning Academic Resource Center
1-800-423-0563
For permission to use material from this text or product, submit a request online at
http://www.thomsonrights.com.
Any additional questions about permissions can be submitted by email to thomsonrights@thomson.com.

Library of Congress Control Number: 2004103437

ISBN 0-534-54180-1

Thomson Wadsworth
10 Davis Drive
Belmont, CA 94002-3098
USA

Asia
Thomson Learning
5 Shenton Way #01-01
UIC Building
Singapore 068808

Australia/New Zealand
Thomson Learning
102 Dodds Street
Southbank, Victoria 3006
Australia

Canada
Nelson
1120 Birchmount Road
Toronto, Ontario M1K 5G4
Canada

Europe/Middle East/Africa
Thomson Learning
High Holborn House
50/51 Bedford Row
London WC1R 4LR
United Kingdom

Latin America
Thomson Learning
Seneca, 53
Colonia Polanco
11560 Mexico D.F.
Mexico

Spain/Portugal
Paraninfo
Calle Magallanes, 25
28015 Madrid, Spain

To Mary

Her sons rise up and call her blessed;
her husband also, and he praises her:
Many women have done excellently, but you surpass them all.

Proverbs 31:28–29

Brief Table of Contents

Contents

Part One
Introducing the New Testament Today

Chapter One
Introducing the New Testament   2

Chapter Two
Ways of Reading the New Testament Today   23

Chapter Three
The Jewish Matrix of the New Testament   51

Chapter Fourteen

Philippians and Philemon: Two Letters from Prison   394

Chapter Fifteen

2 Thessalonians, Colossians, and Ephesians: The Pauline Tradition   417

Chapter Sixteen

1–2 Timothy and Titus: Pastoral Letters to Guide the Pauline Churches   444

Part Five
General/Catholic Letters and Revelation

Chapter Seventeen
Hebrews, James, 1–2 Peter, and Jude: The General Letters   466

Figures, Maps, and Tables

Preface

This book introduces students to the New Testament as it is actually studied today. New Testament study has changed dramatically during the last generation, and anyone who attends meetings of New Testament scholars or reads their published research knows that "things aren't what they used to be." Change in *method* is perhaps most noticeable to both scholars and students. The time honored historical-critical method, though still strong, is being revised in some quarters and is under attack in others. Newer methods of interpretation have entered the field of New Testament study to supplement or supplant it: feminist, rhetorical, narrative, reader response, social scientific, structuralist, theological, African American, Third World/cross-cultural, and others. Change in the *voices* of those pursuing New Testament study is sweeping through the field as well. For the first half of the twentieth century, male European (especially German Protestant) voices led the field. In the second half of the twentieth century, mostly male American voices of European descent, both Protestant and Roman Catholic, predominated. Now, as the twenty-first century begins, the voices of many other interpreters sound out: American racial and ethnic minorities, Jewish scholars, peoples of the developing world, and most of all, women. New Testament study is now being globalized. Change in the *format* in which research is done and disseminated is beginning to influence New Testament study, as the Internet and electronic publishing increasingly become a preferred avenue of communication. Finally, change in the *results of research* is noticeable as old questions are reopened and new questions are asked. Questions about the person and message of Jesus and the theology of the apostle Paul are particularly prominent. In sum, the "single reading" of historical interpretation in the past is now being replaced in much of New Testament study with multiple readings based on the newer methods.

One would barely recognize this change, however, by perusing current textbooks introducing the New Testament. Most are exclusively oriented to the historical-critical method; only a few of the most recent texts pick up one or two of the newer methods. This book will address this situation by introducing students to a fuller range of contemporary New Testament study and give them a working knowledge of how the New Testament is actually studied today. It began with my efforts to present these methods to my students in a way helpful for teaching and learning. The foundational treatment here remains the historical-critical method, for two reasons: (1) some influential interpreters of the New Testament today still employ it as their sole method; (2) many, perhaps most, interpreters who employ the newer methods use them in some combination with the historical-critical method. In addition to the historical-critical method, each chapter of this book will incorporate four significant newer approaches: feminist reading, social scientific reading, narrative reading (Gospels and Acts), and cross-cultural reading. Although Chapter 1 gives a fuller explanation of these choices, it is helpful to offer a preliminary explanation here.

Feminist criticism is manifestly the leading new method today, practiced by many female interpreters and an increasing number of men. Though traditionally centered in North America, feminist biblical scholarship is now growing in Europe and Asia. Feminist scholarship promises to have a significant impact on biblical study for the foreseeable future, as it will have for the humanities in general. Social scientific criticism is based especially on the methods of sociology and anthropology, and has been fruitful in explaining the social matrix of the New Testament world. Its emphasis on how the New Testament relates to the social structures of its times serves well to overcome the individualistic meanings that have often arisen from the historical-critical method. Narrative approaches to the New Testament are prominent in current research and hold the promise of relating ancient literary forms to modern literary meaning. In the present book, we will largely restrict the narrative method to actual narratives, that is, the Gospels and the Acts of the Apostles. Cross-cultural criticism, especially from African, Hispanic, and Asian biblical scholars in the developing world and in North America, has become prominent in the last two decades as the academy deals increasingly with matters of international cross-cultural and multicultural concerns.

The overall outline of this book is as follows. Chapter 1, "Introducing the New Testament," orients the student to the overall nature and structure of the New Testament. Chapter 2 presents the ways that the NT is read today, by the historical-critical method and the newer methods of reading just mentioned. Chapter 3 presents the historical background to the New Testament in Judaism, and Chapter 4 its background in the Greco-Roman world. Chapter 5 introduces the "Synoptic Problem" and methods of Gospel study as a prelude to the treatment of Mark, Matthew, Luke, and John. Chapters 6 through 9 treat Mark, Matthew, Luke, and John, respectively. Chapter 10 deals with the Acts of the Apostles. Part Four concerns Paul and the Pauline tradition. Chapter 11 introduces this subject, Chapter 12 deals with 1 Thessalonians and 1–2 Corinthians; Chapter 13 with Galatians and Romans; Chapter 14 with the prison letters Philippians and Philemon; Chapter 15 with 2 Thessalonians, Colossians, and Ephesians; and Chapter 16 with 1–2 Timothy and Titus. Part Five treats the Catholic/General Letters and Revelation. It contains Chapter 17 on Hebrews, James, 1–2 Peter, and Jude; Chapter 18 on the letters of John; and Chapter 19 on Revelation. Part Six's concluding Chapter 20 deals concisely with "Christian Origins after the New Testament," especially the views of first- and second-century Christian literature as well as the challenge of Gnosticism.

Chapters 6–10 and 12–19, which treat the individual books of the NT, are structured internally as follows. First, the book's contents are given in a brief outline to orient the student. Second, a Guide to Reading section draws on traditional and newer methods to highlight the important features of the book, stimulating and guiding the student's own reading of the text. Next, matters of historical-critical reading are discussed: author, audience, date, and the like. Finally, the newer methods of narrative, rhetorical, social scientific, feminist, and cross-cultural readings will be introduced and given examples from contemporary NT scholarship.

I have offered a rich variety of pedagogical aids, in this book and especially on its website. These aids are for students as they learn and for professors as they teach.

- The end of each chapter features a list of terms, questions for study and discussion, and briefly annotated bibliography for further reading.
- Sections in the text illustrate the newer methods at work. Short selections from interpretive writings are presented at an appropriate length and level of sophistication for beginning students. In the selections practitioners of these five newer methods apply them to passages under study. These excerpts give interpreters and methods the opportunity "to speak in their own voices" here. Each panel features a brief introduction and follow-up to the reading to help students understand the applications of the different methods and keep them clear and distinct.
- The website built for this book assists students in reaching its pedagogical objectives. It features chapter objectives, chapter outlines, a discussion area, interactive quizzes, and links to important sites for students of the NT. The site also provides access to current biblical study as well as much of the ancient literature from New Testament and post–New Testament times. To visit this site, go to Wadsworth's religion page: *http://www.religion.wadsworth.com.*
- Also on the website is a special area for professors that contains 10–15 Power Point® slides for each of the chapters in this book. These slides contain the basic "least you need to know" information on each chapter. They also feature several photographs for most chapters, courtesy of BiblePlaces.com.

Acknowledgments

I owe many people a word of thanks. The material in this book reflects twenty-five years of studying the New Testament and fifteen years of teaching it on the undergraduate and graduate levels. In these years, I have learned much from my teachers and students, far more than I have taught myself. I would like to thank Lycoming College in Williamsport, Pennsylvania, where I taught a New Testament survey course every semester for ten years and began work on this book; Westminster College in Oxford, England, which hosted me for research on the historical Jesus during a sabbatical in 1997; the New Testament Seminar of the University of Oxford, which kindly invited me to share the results of this research; the administration of Western Seminary in Holland, Michigan, where I now teach, for their strong encouragement of this work; and especially my supportive colleagues in Western.

Brand Eaton, a student of mine at Lycoming College, researched and wrote the first draft of Chapters 3, 4, and 20 of the present book under my direction. Brand is pastor of the York Springs United Methodist Church in Pennsylvania. His contribution of these chapters, and wider advice on this book, has been invaluable. I also thank two former students, Jon Brown and Andrea Phillips, for contributing the first draft of the quizzing material. Finally, I also thank Todd Bolen for his generous permission to use, in this book and on its website, the excellent digital photographs from BiblePlaces.com. The editorial staff at Wadsworth has been a fine partner in developing and producing this book. While they have all done excellent work for me, I especially want to thank my talented editor, Steve Wainwright, assistant editors Anna Lustig and Lee McCracken, technology manager Julie Aguilar, and (not least!) marketing manager Worth Hawes. I also thank my copyeditor Victoria Nelson, and Aaron Downey at Matrix Productions.

Scholars at other institutions offered detailed, insightful critiques at many points along the way: Randall D. Chesnutt, Pepperdine University; Steven D. Driver, Loyola College, Maryland; Charles Emerson, Arizona State University; Nancy A. Hardesty, Clemson University; Stan Harstine, Friends University; Mark Heidmann, Southern Connecticut University; Edwin C. Hostetter, George Washington University; Tod Linafelt, Georgetown University; James R. Mueller, University of Florida; Jeffrey S. Siker, Loyola Marymount University; and Mahlon H. Smith, Rutgers University. Though all these people made this a better book, any errors that remain are mine alone. I would be most grateful if those of you who use this book and the related website would send me your comments and suggestions for improving them. You may reach me by post (Western Theological Seminary, 101 East 13th Street, Holland, MI 49423-3622) or by e-mail (bob.vanvoorst@westernsem.edu).

Finally, I owe an expression of deep gratitude to my wife, Mary, and our two sons, Richard and Nicholas, for all their love and support.

Part I

Introducing the
New Testament Today

Chapter One

Introducing the New Testament

In Toronto, Canada, people crowd into a theater to see the one-person play, Afraid! The Gospel of Mark. The actor Frank Runyeon, a former soap opera star who majored in religious studies at Princeton University, dramatically recites his own translation of the Gospel of Mark into contemporary English on a set made to resemble the Roman catacombs. This recitation of Mark constitutes the whole play. A common comment heard after Runyeon's show is, "I didn't realize how powerful Mark is until I heard it all together."

www * Follow the link for more about Frank Runyeon and this play.

In the slums of Rio de Janeiro, Brazil, members of a Christian base community have gathered for their weekly New Testament study. In their alternative Roman Catholic community with a radical social-justice commitment, the study of the Bible by common people without the leadership of a priest or any educated person is a paramount value. The members hold themselves accountable for understanding and carrying out the teachings of Jesus. Today they are apprehensive because a New Testament scholar from the local Catholic university is coming to converse with them. Bible study among the laity and the scholarly perspective brought by the professor are both fruitful approaches, but there is some tension between the two outlooks.

www Follow the link to a brief description of the process of Bible study in base communities.

In Terre Haute, Indiana, demonstrators gather near the federal prison where Timothy McVeigh is to be executed for killing 169 people when he bombed the federal office building in Oklahoma City. Some protest his execution by carrying signs with words from the Bible, most prominently, "You shall not kill." Some counterprotesters also carry signs with echoes of New Testament words spoken at the crucifixion of Jesus about the two criminals punished with him: "Just punishment for his deeds." This difficult encounter between protesters mirrors the divided mind of American Christianity—is capital punishment sanctioned by the Bible, or is it not?

* Indicates that additional material is found on the companion website for this book at http://religion.wadsworth.com.

www   Follow the link to a pro-and-con treatment of the Bible on this issue.

As these vignettes indicate, the New Testament has a lively role today among Christians and non-Christians alike. The New Testament has shaped the Christian church's teaching, ethics, ritual, and mission in the world. Although Christians differ in language, culture, organization, and the fine points of religious teaching, all believers have the books of the New Testament in common. Indeed, it has often been remarked that the New Testament is the *only* thing that all Christians have in common! Moreover, because the Christian faith has become the world's most widespread religion, and because many people outside the faith are interested in the Bible, it has become the world's most read book and its perennial bestseller.

What exactly is the New Testament? In answering this question, we will first examine the meanings of the terms *testament* or *covenant* and *new testament* or *new covenant* in ancient Israelite and Jewish religion and then discuss the early Christian idea of New Covenant established by Jesus. Second, we will briefly survey the structure and content of the New Testament books. Third, we will introduce the topic of New Testament translations and their variety. Fourth, we will examine using the World Wide Web in scripture study, especially as related to the present book. Finally, we will present suggestions for reading the New Testament more profitably.

What Is the New Testament?

The question, What is the New Testament? seems to have an obvious, simple answer. The **New Testament** is the second, Christian part of the Bible that follows the **Hebrew Bible,** the sacred scriptures of Judaism that Christians often call the **Old Testament.** Early Christian leaders wrote the New Testament's twenty-seven documents, usually called "books," to guide members of what was becoming a new faith in their common life. For almost two millennia, Christians have regarded these twenty-seven books as **scripture,** writings formally accepted as biblical by the church and used as especially sacred and authoritative. Christians also accept the Hebrew Bible as scripture, and the two are most often bound together in the same Bible. (This gets a bit tricky: when Jewish people use the term **Bible,** they usually mean the Hebrew Bible, which Christians traditionally call the Old Testament. When Christians refer to the **Bible,** they mean the Hebrew Bible/Old Testament plus the New Testament.)

When we look more closely at the term *New Testament*, this question becomes more complicated. Our word *testament* suggests a legal will to people today, as in "last will and testament," but this is not an accurate understanding of the Greek and Hebrew words that it translates. Both the Greek word *diatheke* [dee-uh-THAY-kay] and its important Hebrew equivalent *berith* [buh-REET] primarily mean "covenant," a solemn agreement between two parties confirmed by an oath. Both words were also used less frequently to describe arrangements to dispose of one's property at death; here it is indeed similar to our "last will and testament." *Covenant* has a rich background in the ancient Near East, where it was used to describe solemn agreements of many types. The biblical term **covenant** refers to the relationship God has established with particular people, stipulating the conduct of both parties in working out God's purposes for human life. In the biblical covenant relationship, both parties have solemn obligations to each other. The term *New Covenant/Testament* originally signified a new relationship established in the life, death, and resurrection of Jesus—a term soon attached to the collection of Christian sacred documents.

The word *new* in "New Testament" signifies the early Christian belief that in Jesus God has acted in a fresh, definitive way. This is seen as a fulfillment of the promises made by God to the Jewish people. Jesus himself, in his teaching, did not seem to use the term *covenant* explicitly, preferring instead to speak of "the kingdom of God." Early Christians, however, soon latched onto it. The term *new testament* or *new covenant* is found in 2 Corinthians 3, where the early Christian missionary Paul calls Christians a part of the "new covenant" (v. 6). (We are now citing biblical books by their names, chapters, and verse numbers, the technical system of referring to the Bible. If you are not familiar with this form of citation, you should pause here to read Table 1.1 on biblical references.) The books of Moses in the Jewish Bible, on the other hand, are a part of the "old covenant" (v. 14). "New covenant" looks back to Jer 31:31–34, written in the sixth century B.C.E, in which God promises the prophet Jeremiah, "I will make a new covenant with the house of Israel and the house of Judah. It will not be like the covenant I made with their ancestors. . . . I will put my law within them, and I will write it on their hearts. . . . They shall all know me, from the least of them to the greatest." This passage envisions a covenant which is "new" not in content, but in the ability of the people to keep it. The term *new covenant* is not found elsewhere in the Hebrew Bible, but Ezek 36:26–27 alludes to it by promising to Israel a "new heart" and a "new spirit." *New covenant* was regularly used in the early Christian celebration of the ritual of Holy Communion, as its earliest recorded form attests: "In the same way [Jesus] took the cup also, after supper, saying, 'This cup is the new covenant in my blood'" (1 Cor 11:25; see also Mark 14:24; par. Matt 26:28; Luke 22:20). Although the term *new covenant* may imply to us a completely *different* covenant, most first-century Christians did not understand it that way. To them, as to Jeremiah, the new covenant is a continuation and fulfillment of the old covenant. Only at the end of the NT does the idea arise that the New Covenant is fundamentally different from the Old, and replaces it.

A few leading Christians in the second century began to call their basic writings the "New Testament," and by the fourth century it was a name used by all Christians. Christians and others traditionally call the Jewish Bible the "Old Testament," but it is important to note that the Jewish people have never referred to their collection of writings as a "testament/covenant." However, the covenant is a leading theme in the Jewish writings before the first century C.E., and it provides a coherent meaning to the writings as a whole. *Covenant* is the main formal, comprehensive

Table 1.1 *Understanding and Making References to the Bible*

With some careful attention, you can understand and use correctly the scholarly conventions in referring to the Bible. The rules and suggestions followed here are those of the *SBL Handbook of Style,* ed. Patrick H. Alexander and others (Peabody, MA: Hendrickson, 1999). (SBL is the Society of Biblical Literature, the main professional organization in North America for professors of Bible studies and related fields.)

Basic matters, with examples in italics:

- **Colons** appear between chapter and verse numbers: *Luke 1:7 means verse 7 of chapter 1 of Luke's gospel.*
- Use **commas** between verse numbers of the same chapter (and between chapter numbers, but only if no verses are given): *Luke 1:1, 7 means verses 1 and 7 only of chapter 1 of Luke; Luke 1, 3 means chapters 1 and 3 of Luke.*
- Use **semicolons** between references that give chapter and verse numbers from different chapters: *Luke 1:1; 2:2 means the first verse of Luke 1 and the second of Luke 2.*
- Use a **dash** between verses to indicate "from—to" within one chapter: *Luke 1:1–7 means the whole section from verse 1 through verse 7 of chapter 1 of Luke.*
- Use a **dash** also to indicate "from—to" between different chapters: *Luke 1–2 means chapters 1 and 2 in Luke.*
- A **single number** following a book name designates a chapter: *Luke 1 means all of chapter 1 of Luke.*
- Do **not** use periods after abbreviated book names, but do put spaces between the abbreviations and chapter numbers: *Matt 5 begins the Sermon on the Mount.*

General rules, with examples in italics:

- List specific references not only when you directly quote a text, but also when you mention specific biblical passages: *The Gospel according to Mark is the first Christian text that uses the word "gospel" or "good news" (Mark 1:1).*
- Put most biblical references at the end of the sentences in parentheses, but followed by the concluding punctuation, as in the preceding example.
- Use "par." to refer to parallel passages (passages with similar wording) in the other Gospels: *The feeding of the 5000 is in all four canonical Gospels (Mark 6:32–44; par. Matt 14:13–21; Luke 9:10–17; John 6:1–15).*
- Use the standard abbreviations for the names of biblical books in your references, but spell out the full names in your text: *John's Gospel begins with the same two words as the Greek version of Genesis (John 1:1 and Gen 1:1).*
- Note that books with shorter names are not abbreviated: *Mark, not Mk.*
- You can omit the abbreviated name of a biblical book after the first reference if you are obviously still referring to the same book: *The parables of Matthew include the famous parable of the Sower (13:1—9).* If you are dealing with more than one book, include all the book names to make the references clear.

www For more on how to understand biblical book, chapter and verse references like those in Table 1.1 and cite the Bible yourself, see the link on the website.

term for God's relationship to people; the others tend to be more metaphoric (for example, king-nation, parent-children, and shepherd-sheep). Early Christians, drawing on their Jewish heritage, saw "covenant" as an appealing name for their collection of writings. Its comprehensiveness fits the many methods of reading the New Testament today—methods that the present book will employ.

The Early Christians and the New Covenant

Early Christians believed that Jesus' fresh interpretation of Judaism in his teaching and life gave a new, divinely commanded direction for all of Judaism. They also believed that Jesus brought the dawning of a new age, which they expected God would soon send in its fullness. Like other Jewish reformers of the time, early Christians used the Hebrew Bible extensively and reinterpreted it in the light of their own movement.

Jesus offered a radical vision of God's renewal of the covenant. In his preaching, Jesus stressed that the kingdom of God (the reign or rule of God more than a physical place like heaven) was about to come to Israel. Jesus connected the kingdom of God with his own presence and teaching, so that how one responds to Jesus determines one's place in the kingdom. To him, the kingdom of God was not just a "spiritual" or "religious" reality, but a social and political reality as well. The "new covenant in my blood" saying of Jesus preserved in 1 Cor 11:25, Mark 14:24, Matt 26:28, and Luke 22:20 shows that from an early point his followers saw his death as a sacrifice. This sacrifice will establish a covenant between God and the people whom Jesus has called to this new covenant. Several key New Testament texts link God's covenant with Israel to the covenant God inaugurated through Jesus. In Acts 3:25–26, the covenant God made with Abraham is now fulfilled through those who believe in Jesus. Here Peter addresses the Jews, but the text he quotes from Gen 22:18 refers to "all the nations of the earth," thus expressing the universal hope of the covenant, its opening to all the peoples of the earth. Paul contrasts the relationship of Israel to the God of the covenant with the new covenant, promised through the prophets and now fulfilled through Jesus (Rom 11:27). Even though it was obvious to Paul that most Jews do not believe in Jesus, Paul proclaims him as the fulfillment of the covenant promise to Abraham based on simple trust in God (Gal 3:15–17), which takes precedence over the covenant with Israel based on keeping the Law of Moses (v. 17). Even so, in Romans 9–11 Paul views God's covenant with Israel as unbreakable from God's side; even though the people are unfaithful, their unfaithfulness cannot annul God's love (11:29). Paul holds out hope that, in God's mysterious plan, the Jewish people will be saved in the end: "this is my covenant with them, when I take away their sin" (11:27, quoting Jer 31:34).

Later New Testament literature continues this New Covenant theme. The anonymous Letter to the Hebrews extensively contrasts the old covenant with the new. For example, the once-for-all sacrifice of Christ establishes the new, eternal covenant, replacing the continuous sacrifices offered under the old covenant made

Scribe Writing Hebrew A Jewish scribe in Israel writes out scriptures using traditional materials. The devotion of Jews to the Bible has expressed itself in careful traditional copying of Hebrew Bible scrolls for synagogue use. Used by permission of BiblePlaces.com.

by Moses (Hebrews 9–10). Christ is the mediator of the new covenant (Heb 9:15). The last book of the New Testament, Revelation, pictures Israel's Ark of the Covenant as now resting in heaven, where Jesus is enthroned with God (Rev 11:19). This symbolizes that Jesus has made possible an access to God that the old covenant could not maintain. The end of the book of Revelation uses poetic covenant language to describe the consummation of all things: "See, the home of God is among [God's] people. He will dwell with them, and they will be his people; and God himself will be with them" (Rev 21:3). As this evidence suggests, early Christians drew primarily upon the contemporary Jewish understandings of the covenants with Abraham and with Moses and the people of Israel at Mount Sinai. Surprisingly, the New Testament makes no explicit reference to the Davidic covenant passages in the Hebrew Bible, despite strong early Christian belief that Jesus was a Davidic Messiah. In sum, the early Christian writings argue that Jesus has accomplished the original intent of the covenant, to restore the people of God to their Lord so that they can participate with God in shaping God's grand purposes for the world. In this accomplishment the covenant has been, in the words of Jeremiah 31, made new and effective.

It did not take long for "the New Testament" to be formally attached to the collection of books that Christians were beginning to make authoritative. (What books exactly were *in* this collection took some time to work out, as we will see in the last chapter of the present book.) The advantage of "New Testament" as a title for this scripture, aside from the fact that it expresses the religious meaning of its contents, is that it suggests the complexity of the early Christian attitude to its relationship with the Jewish people and their Bible. This relationship has both continuity with Judaism, as expressed by *covenant/testament*, and discontinuity, as expressed by the qualifier *new*. For almost two thousand years, Christians and others have seen "New Testament" as an accurate name for their holy writings. In recent years, some have called the NT the **Christian Scriptures** or the **Christian** or **Second Testament.** These names have some advantages, but they are misleading because they suggest that the Jewish Bible is not a part of the Christian scriptures, and therefore early Christianity can be understood apart from Judaism. This assumption runs counter to the strong consensus of biblical scholarship, which insists on understanding early Christianity in general, and Jesus in particular, in the context of Judaism. Overall, then, it seems best to use the title "New Testament" for the twenty-seven canonical books. This is the commonly accepted label within the academic world and the Christian church, and it is widely used in the media as well.

An Overview of the New Testament

Another way to answer the question, What is the New Testament? is to sketch how and when it arose and the form and contents of its twenty-seven books. At first glance, it might seem that the New Testament (hereafter NT) was written only one or two generations—forty years at the most—after the death and resurrection of Jesus and the birth of the church. Yet modern biblical scholarship has discovered that its writing was not completed until perhaps eighty or ninety years after Jesus' death. The pace of writing was slowed by three main factors. First, the earliest church, which began as a group within Judaism, already had a complete body of scripture—the Jewish Bible. It found this scripture sufficient for its life, because it could interpret the Jewish Bible to bolster its claim that Jesus was the Messiah, the promised deliverer of Israel. Second, the early Christians quite comfortably used the words and deeds of Jesus orally, in the same oral form that he taught them. They did not remember Jesus as a writer (correctly so, it seems, because there is no evidence that Jesus wrote anything), and there was no urgency to write down his words. In ancient cultures, the "living voice" that tells a message orally was more valued than a written message. Third, many early Christians believed that the end of this world order was imminent, within their generation. People who expect the world to end in their lifetime do not generally engage in the lengthy process of composing, copying by hand, and distributing books.

Table 1.2 Books of the New Testament

Book	Standard Abbreviation (if any)	Traditional and/or Given Author	Estimated Date	Genre	Size in Chapters
Matthew	Matt	Matthew (disputed)	80s	Gospel	28
Mark	Mark	Mark (disputed)	70	Gospel	16
Luke	Luke	Luke (disputed)	80s	Gospel	24
John	John	John "the Beloved Disciple" (disputed)	90s	Gospel	21
Acts of the Apostles	Acts	Luke (disputed)	80s	History	28
Romans	Rom	Paul	55	Letter	16
1 Corinthians	1 Cor	Paul	53	Letter	16
2 Corinthians	2 Cor	Paul	55	Letter	13
Galatians	Gal	Paul	55	Letter	6
Ephesians	Eph	Paul (disputed)	90	Letter	6
Philippians	Phil	Paul	61	Letter	4
Colossians	Col	Paul (disputed)	80s	Letter	4
1 Thessalonians	1 Thess	Paul	50	Letter	5
2 Thessalonians	2 Thess	Paul (disputed)	80s	Letter	3
1 Timothy	1 Tim	Paul (disputed)	90s	Letter	6
2 Timothy	2 Tim	Paul (disputed)	90s	Letter	4
Titus	Titus	Paul (disputed)	90s	Letter	3
Philemon	Phlm	Paul	61–62	Letter	1
Hebrews	Heb	Anonymous	80s	Letter-sermon	13
James	Jas	James (disputed)	90	Letter-sermon	5
1 Peter	1 Pet	Peter (disputed)	80	Letter	5
2 Peter	2 Pet	Peter (disputed)	110s	Letter	3
1 John	1 John	Anonymous; John "the Elder"	95	Letter-sermon	5
2 John	2 John	John "the Elder"	96–100	Letter	1
3 John	3 John	John "the Elder"	97–100	Letter	1
Jude	Jude	Jude (disputed)	100	Letter	1
Revelation	Rev	John "the Prophet"	90s	Apocalypse	22

In the process of explaining the life and teaching of Jesus and his continuing community, a variety of writings were produced, some of them based on prior oral and written traditions about Jesus. These documents may be classified by **genre** (overall literary type) as (1) gospels, (2) history, (3) letters, and (4) apocalypse. The NT is organized according to these genres. They will be treated more fully in later chapters, but here we will sketch them out for our survey of the basic meaning of the NT. For an overview of the structure of the NT, see Table 1.2.

www   Follow a link to helpful information about the NT canon, including a presentation of "Eight Tips about the Canonical Arrangement of the NT."

The Gospels

The Greek word translated as **gospel**, *euangelion*, means "good news." In the wider secular world of the first century, it referred to political and economic good news, as for example when the emperor of Rome defeated invaders and peace returned to the empire. The good news about Jesus was oral at first, and then became written down in books called **Gospels.** The word *gospel* occurs in the opening phrase of what we shall see is perhaps the oldest (c. 70 C.E.) writing of the gospel type, the Gospel of Mark. Mark may have invented the formal structure of the written gospel narrative, probably based on the outline of Christian preaching commonly used in missionary work: Jesus' baptism, public ministry, arrest, trial, death and resurrection. (When we call the Gospels "Matthew," "Mark," "Luke" and "John" in this book, we are using scholarly shorthand for the books themselves and do not mean to imply who actually wrote them.) The aim of Mark's author is to show that Jesus is the suffering Messiah of Israel and the savior of the whole world. Mark shows how Jesus befriends, and shares the good news with, those who by the standards of Jewish piety of that time were "sinful" people among the Jews and non-Jews. Jesus' growing conflict with the religious and political authorities over his message and behavior leads quickly to his death. Mark portrays this death not as a meaningless misfortune, but as Jesus' intentional self-sacrifice that expresses the heart of the Good News. Jesus' resurrection validates the power of his death and points to a new age dawning.

The other three Gospels carry on with the basic outline of Mark, adapting its theology to their own situations. Luke expands the theme of the inclusiveness of the new covenant community, describing how the message of Jesus and the community he founded spread across the Roman Empire to the capital itself. Matthew emphasizes that Jesus is the Jewish messiah, whose movement is now spreading into the Gentile world, and contrasts Jesus' principles for the life of God's people with the emerging norms of Pharisaic Judaism. Mark, Luke, and Matthew are so similar in structure and content that they are called the **Synoptic Gospels,** able to be surveyed "in one view" ("synopsis"). The Gospel of John presents Jesus as the eternal Son of God made human for his life, death, and resurrection. In addition to describing some of Jesus' conflicts with his Jewish contemporaries and his openness to wandering Jews and Gentiles, John also symbolically depicts a spiritual participation in God that Jesus has made possible for those who believe in him. For introduction to all four Gospels, see Chapter 5; for treatment of the Synoptic Gospels, see Chapters 6–8; for John, see Chapter 9.

Although these gospel writings share many basic similarities in content and meaning, they also differ from each other in ways that make them distinct works. They write Greek in different styles, which come through in part in our English translations. They also differ in some of their content: about Jesus' family and hometown; the sequence of some events in his public career; the priority among the various themes of his teaching; the presentation of his final days in Jerusalem; and the events following his death. Nevertheless, they agree in their claim that Jesus is the Son of God, the messiah of Israel, and the savior of the world. This claim makes them Gospels, books of the "Good News." Other gospels with similar or dissimilar viewpoints were written in the first century and especially in the second, but the mainstream church eventually recognized as canonical only the four now included in the NT: Matthew, Mark, Luke, and John. (See Chapter 20 for this process.)

Scholarship over the past two hundred years has confirmed what the NT itself suggests, that material about Jesus was used and transmitted orally before our gospel books were written. To put it in other words, the "oral gospel" precedes the "written gospel." Scholars have reconstructed what was probably the first oral source for the sayings of Jesus. This hypothetical source, called sometimes the "Synoptic Sayings Source" or more commonly **Q** (probably from the German word for source, *Quelle*), is analyzed later, in Chapter 5, along with the arguments of those who do not accept its existence. We also have evidence for oral transmission of Jesus' words and deeds in the writings of the apostle Paul. On seemingly crucial issues, Paul appeals to the words and deeds of Jesus. In 1 Thess 4:15 he refers to "the word of the Lord" to explain that both the Christians who have died before the triumphant coming of Jesus at the end of the age will share in the new life with Christ. In 1 Cor 11:23–26, Paul quotes the word of "the Lord" Jesus in laying down basic rules for the celebration of the Eucharist. The author of Acts has Paul quoting "words of the Lord Jesus" about generosity to others in the beautiful maxim "It is more blessed to give than to receive," even though our gospels have no such statement (Acts 20:35). The NT letter of James uses the content of Jesus' sayings extensively, especially as paralleled in Matthew 5–7, but strikingly never attributes them to Jesus. Many Christian writings from the second century contain repeated appeals to the words of Jesus as the oral transmission of his sayings continues. The importance of this oral tradition in the church is evident in an often-quoted statement by Papias, bishop of Hierapolis in Asia Minor (modern Turkey) in the first half of the second century. He regularly asked his teachers what they had heard, not read, of the teachings of Jesus, explaining, "I did not suppose that information from books would help me so much as the word of a living and surviving voice" (*Exposition of the Oracles of the Lord*, as quoted in Eusebius' *History of the Church* 3.39).

www   Read Papias' writings as they have survived in quotations by others.

A History

Unique in the NT is the Acts of the Apostles, the only book of early church history we have from the first century. The opening lines of Acts (as it is known in short) and its general literary style show that it was written as a sequel to the Gospel of Luke by the same author and probably at the same time. The author of Acts skillfully describes how the church spread from its exclusively Jewish origins to reach out across geographical, cultural, and ethnic boundaries until it reached Rome, capital of the Empire and the heart of the Gentile world. This spread was not without internal and external struggle. Although Acts hints about the spread of the Gospel to other places outside the Roman Empire—Ethiopia, for example (8:26–40)—its sharp focus is northeast from Jerusalem, to the city of Rome. Throughout the book, there are repeated claims that what is happening in the spread of the church fulfills the Jewish scriptures. For example, at the beginning of Acts, when the Spirit is poured out on those Jews gathered in Jerusalem "from every nation under heaven," Peter explains, "this is what was spoken through the prophet Joel," foretelling the day when "everyone who calls on the name of the Lord will be saved" (Acts 2:5, 16–21). Throughout Paul's ministry in Acts, he presents the Gospel to Jews and especially Gentiles. Acts ends with Paul's house-arrest captivity in Rome itself, where he is "trying to convince [his hearers] about Jesus from the Law of Moses and from the prophets" (28:23). Like the Gospel of Luke, Acts declares that God has fulfilled God's covenant with Israel by extending it to all humanity. As time goes on, many more Gentiles than Jews are responding positively to this message. We will treat the Acts of the Apostles in Chapter 10.

The Letters

The "letters" of the NT fall into four different categories in modern study: (1) Pauline letters whose authenticity as letters of Paul is not generally disputed by modern scholars; (2) the disputed Pauline letters; (3) letters under the names of other apostles; and (4) letters more or less in essay or sermonic form. The authentic Pauline letters came first, from about 50 to 65 C.E. Paul wrote letters to keep in contact with the churches he founded on his extensive missionary travels. He used them to instruct and exhort his churches, often correcting their problems, as a substitute for his own personal presence. They were read aloud to the whole congregation, probably in a Sunday service (1 Thess 5:26). They reflect the concrete circumstances of his life and of his experiences with the congregations to which he writes. The earliest in this group of letters, with a strong claim of **authenticity** (a document actually written by the person whose name it bears, in this case Paul), are the letters to the Romans, Galatians, Philippians, 1 and 2 Corinthians, Philemon, and 1 Thessalonians. These letters generally accepted today as authentic are also called the **undisputed Pauline letters.** Of course, at this stage probably no one thought that these letters would become a part of a new body of Christian scripture; at least there is no explicit indication of this in Paul's letters. See Chapters 12–14 for analysis of these letters.

Paul's letters gained more standing after his death in the mid-60s. After his death, his co-workers probably wrote letters in his name, sometimes drawing on the earlier letters, to perpetuate and adapt his teachings for a new generation, giving rise to the second of our categories of NT letters. This **pseudonymity** (literally, "under a false name," a writing not in fact written by the person whose name it bears)

Table 1.3 *Authorial Status in Scholarship Today of the Thirteen Pauline letters*

Commonly Accepted as Authentic	Borderline, with No Strong Consensus	Commonly Accepted as Pseudonymous
Romans	2 Thessalonians	Ephesians
1 Corinthians	Colossians	1 Timothy
2 Corinthians		2 Timothy
Galatians		Titus
Philippians		
1 Thessalonians		
Philemon		

was a common practice in the ancient Mediterranean world, including contemporary Judaism. Ancient people considered it a way of honoring a leader from the past. It usually would not deceive the original readers, who would know that the author named was dead. (See Chapter 11 for a treatment of the problem of pseudonymity, which raises qualms for some readers of the NT today.) These **disputed Pauline letters** written in the name of Paul, sometimes called the **post-Pauline letters,** are addressed to an individual or to a community but probably are intended to instruct a wider group of Pauline churches than the genuine letters of Paul. They tend to be more general in content and formal in tone, with little warm personal communication between the authors and recipients. The Letter to the Colossians is attributed to Paul; it more closely resembles his style than the other disputed letters do, so that there is a good deal of disagreement in current study over whether it is genuine or pseudonymous. Current study of 2 Thessalonians also features scholarship sharply divided about its authenticity. However, a strong majority of NT scholars hold that Ephesians is pseudonymous because its style and contents differ significantly from Paul's undisputed letters. 1 and 2 Timothy and Titus also come after Paul's death, according to the strong consensus of current scholarship. Scholars call these three collectively **Pastoral Letters** or **Pastorals** because they deal especially with official leaders ("pastors/shepherds") in the wider Pauline communities after his death. Chapters 15 and 16 treat these letters. For the authorial status of the thirteen letters with Paul's name on them, see Table 1.3.

A third category of letters are those attributed to other early church leaders. Two letters are in the name of Peter, and three of John; one is in the name of James; and one is attributed to Jude. The latter two are traditionally identified as "brothers/relatives of the Lord," who are not among the apostles in the NT. The letter to the Hebrews is usually considered among the General Letters as well. These letters are sometimes called the **Catholic** or **General Letters,** on the false supposition that they were written to the whole church. (Here the term *catholic* is used in its original sense of "universal," not to imply that these letters are particular to the Roman Catholic Church; the term *General* probably arose to get around this misunderstanding.) These letters, along with the Pastorals, were important in the church's life in the last third of the first century as matters of true Christian teaching, patterns of official church leadership, and church organization became more important than they were in the middle third of the first century. Brief letters to churches in seven cities are found in chapters 2–3 of the book of Revelation. The General Letters are treated in Chapters 17 and 18.

A fourth category of "letter" in the NT has only a few of the literary features of an actual letter, typically at the beginning or the end. It may be addressed to a wider audience than other letters. This category is more of an essay on issues that the writer considered important for a wide group of Christian communities. Hebrews, James and 1 John are examples of this type, and we will also examine them in Chapters 17 and 18.

The importance of letters as a means of communication between Christian leaders and their churches is apparent in all the NT letters. Here we will take as an example of this importance the letters bearing Paul's name. As mentioned earlier, in what was probably his first letter, 1 Thessalonians, Paul commands that his letter be read aloud to all the members of the church (5:26), almost certainly when they met for worship. This "sacred setting" for the reading of the letter would give it more weight. In 2 Corinthians, Paul says that his letters exercise authority in his name while he is absent from the Corinthian church. When they read his letter, he is spiritually present with them (2 Cor 10:9–11). Writings that may come from after the time of Paul make even stronger claims for the authority of his letters. In 2 Thess 3:14 the author warns that those who do not obey that letter's instructions are to be excluded from the community of the church. Col 4:16 commands that the letters to one church are to be made available to churches in other cities as well. In what is likely the latest NT book, 2 Peter, the letters of "our beloved brother Paul" are implied to be "scriptures." The audience of 2 Peter has knowledge of these letters, "written to you." However, the author of 2 Peter warns that "some things in them are hard to understand," things that (the author implies) must be interpreted carefully (2 Pet 3:15–16). Thus, although the letters of Paul may have been as controversial in the second century as in the first, the church as a whole kept on considering them useful and authoritative, and they began working their way into the developing NT canon. For example, in *1 Clement* 47, Clement the bishop of Rome refers to Paul's letter we know as 1 Corinthians, saying that it was "truly inspired" and should still be heeded. In Ignatius' *Letter to the Ephesians* 12, Ignatius refers positively to "every letter" of Paul. Finally, Polycarp's *Letter to the Philippians* 3 says that by the study of Paul's letters the readers will be able to increase their faith.

www   Follow a link to these texts of Clement, Ignatius, and Polycarp online.

An Apocalypse

Apocalypse is a symbolic writing about the imminent catastrophic end of the world and the coming of God's kingdom. Although the NT contains short sections of apocalyptic writing in the Synoptic Gospels (Mark 13, Matthew 24, and Luke 21) and in other books, its main apocalyptic document is the Revelation to John, the last book of the NT. In fact, Revelation is known in some Christian churches as the **Apocalypse.**

Revelation (note the singular—the plural "Revelations" is an all-too-common mistake!) resembles closely the unique literary style and theology of the Jewish apocalypses that originated in the last two centuries B.C.E., especially the Hebrew Bible book of Daniel. Daniel encourages Jewish people oppressed by Hellenistic rulers who attempt to force Jews to worship pagan gods, including an idol of their Gentile king, killing them if they resist. Deliverance from this dreadful state of affairs, Daniel insists, can only come by the direct action of God, who expects God's people to be faithful no matter what. This is the message of Revelation as well when Rome demands idolatry from Christians in an attempt to crush this new, seemingly seditious faith. Apocalypses communicate a strong sense of threat from rising powers of evil outside the faith. For the early Christians, the threat came as the Roman emperors began to demand worship as gods from their subjects as a way of guaranteeing obedience to imperial authority. By a revelation of visions and dreams, God enables people to see beyond the impending calamity to a new era of deliverance in which God's purpose for God's people and the world will triumph. Its refrain is, "Here is a call for the endurance of the saints." The author of Revelation sees the faithful people of God, those who follow faithfully in the way of Jesus whatever the price, as the vanguard of God's purpose to recreate the world and bring in divine reign. We will deal with Revelation in Chapter 19.

Conclusion

The second-century Christian designation of the Christian scriptures as the "New Testament" is fitting. The NT bears witness to the ancient covenant relationship between God and God's people that Jesus has made new and fulfilled. The new covenant is the "symbolic world" in which early Christians lived. The main features of the early Christian understanding of this symbolic world as presented in the NT can be "unpacked" as follows (adapted from Kee 1993, 12–13).

1. The NT states and interprets for its readers what Jesus said and did. His teaching introduces his followers to the Kingdom of God, and his life models God's radical love for all people. Although it has other meanings as well, his death is especially significant as the sacrifice that established the new covenant; his resurrection is God's guarantee that what Jesus had begun would be completed in a new world that God will bring in at the end of time, when Jesus will return gloriously to earth.

2. The NT guides Jesus' followers on how to live faithfully in the New Covenant. Not only does the teaching of Jesus as reported in the Gospels give moral guidance, but all other NT documents also have a strong dose of it. Therefore, to believe in Jesus is not just to "talk the talk," but to "walk the walk" of a particular way of life, following his teaching of love for God and other people. Following Jesus means living in a community of believers, the church.

3. The NT articulates early Christian varieties of believers' deep personal and social connection to God. The presence of Christ through the Holy Spirit brings the relationship with God envisioned in the Israelite covenant. This presence is established and mediated by practices such as baptism and the Eucharist as well as by hearing and obeying the word of God given by Christ and interpreted by the Spirit.

4. The NT develops various reasons and plans for spreading the faith in the wider world. Jesus traveled in Palestine to spread his message, and the first Christians spread the message about Jesus by traveling even more widely. Although Jesus had a ministry that was almost exclusively directed to the Jewish people, his followers soon reached out to other ethnic groups with other, non-Jewish religions. This spreading of the faith takes it, as Acts 1:8 says, "to the ends of the earth."

5. The NT outlines various patterns for organizing leadership in early Christian communities. Although one finds different patterns of leadership in the first-century church, some form of leadership is almost always present. The NT lays down a variety of norms for leaders to teach the faith and guide believers to live socially responsible lives. It also warns leaders to keep themselves from hypocrisy, greed, and other forms of serious wrongdoing.

6. The NT develops ways to cope with persecution from outside forces, chiefly local Jewish and regional Roman leaders. This persecution ranged from rumor mongering to dismissal from one's job to execution without a formal trial. Most of these ways of coping with persecution are based upon following the death of Jesus, whose willingness to suffer and die for God became the main model for later believers when they faced persecution.

In sum, despite some disadvantages, *New Covenant* is indeed appropriate as an overarching term for the meaning of early Christian religion, and *New Testament* is fitting as a term for its collection of authoritative literature. The comprehensiveness of the early Christian idea and practice of covenant, encompassing as it does both the divine and human dimensions of early Christianity, is also appropriate for the wide variety of materials in the NT and the wide variety of methods used today to study it. In the next chapter, we will consider these methods.

The New Testament in Translation

As mentioned earlier, the New Testament was written and preserved in Greek. The form of its Greek is called **Hellenistic** or **Koine** (koy-NAY, "common") **Greek,** the language used widely throughout the Roman Empire as the language of commerce and everyday communication. Thus, what most students of the NT read is *not* the original text, but other people's translations of the Bible.

This raises a variety of issues: Which translation is the "best"? Why are there so many different English translations of the Bible, and why can't scholars agree on just one translation? In considering these questions, we must reflect on the following factors.

- *The Greek text from which we translate is very reliable but not perfect.* All originals of the NT documents have been lost or destroyed over the centuries, as have all manuscript originals from the ancient world. We now have copies of copies, most of them produced hundreds of years after the original texts were written, but some copied within a century or two. Moreover, the existing NT manuscripts contain numerous differences in wording. There are thousands of differences in the surviving biblical manuscripts, most of them minor (spelling variations, synonyms, different word orders), but some of them major (words or sentences missing or added). Where the original Greek is uncertain in wording, the English translation will also be uncertain. Nevertheless, the basic text of the Greek NT is highly reliable, the most textually reliable book to come from the ancient Roman world.
- *Important manuscripts have been found in the last hundred years.* Recent discoveries of older manuscripts, especially the Dead Sea Scrolls, the Codex Sinaiticus and many smaller manuscripts, have helped scholars get closer to the original text of both the Hebrew Bible and the New Testament. Therefore, recent translations can be more accurate than early modern ones, or even translations done fifty years ago.
- *The English language is constantly changing.* A good English translation must express the meaning of the original text in current English. Because English is probably the most rapidly changing major language in the world, new English translations are required every generation or so to keep up with the changes. To cite a memorable example, the NRSV avoids the capital-punishment verb "stoned" because of its contemporary implications of drug or alcohol abuse; it now typically says "received a stoning."
- *Every translation is inevitably an interpretation.* All translations have meanings that are at least slightly different from the original. Moreover, different people inevitably translate the same texts in slightly different ways. Greek is both similar to and different from modern English. They are similar in that they are Indo-European languages, but Greek vocabulary, grammatical rules, and other features differ from modern English to varying degrees.
- *Cultural changes require new sensitivities in language.* Awareness of the evils of sexism, racism, anti-Semitism, and other forms of intolerance has shown that certain language in the Greek NT and in older English translations is slanted or biased. Therefore, Bible translators have since about 1970 developed more inclusive language alternatives to avoid the appearance of bias that the biblical authors probably did not intend. For example, ancient Hebrew and Greek typically used the word "sons" to refer to both male and female children. Recent translations change this to "sons and daughters."

Because of these factors, no translation is perfect, because none of them can be completely literal, or 100 percent identical to the original texts. We cannot identify one "best" translation, because all of them have some advantages and some drawbacks. In general, however, the most recent translations (1980s or 1990s), such as the New Revised Standard Version, are better than the older ones such as the King James Version or the Douay-Rheims, both hundreds of years old, or even the Revised Standard Version from the 1950s.

Two styles of translation predominate: formal correspondence and dynamic equivalence. Other popular versions of the Bible in English are not really "translations" but are "paraphrases" instead.

- **Formal correspondence translations** keep as closely as possible to the original wording and word order of the Hebrew and Greek texts. Thus, they may seem more accurate or "literal" but often require detailed explanations in footnotes to avoid being misinterpreted by modern readers. They are good for in-depth academic study of the Bible but may be less suited for public reading aloud, since they can be difficult to understand when read aloud. Examples of the formal correspondence translations are the New Revised Standard Version (NRSV) and the New International Version (NIV).
- **Dynamic equivalence translations** try to put the sense of the original text into the best modern English, remaining close to the ideas expressed but not always following the exact wording or word order of the Hebrew or Greek originals. Thus, they may seem less literal than the formal correspondence translations but can be just as faithful to the original text and are therefore generally well suited for public proclamation or liturgical use. An example is the Today's English Version (TEV).
- **Paraphrases** are not (and do not claim to be) accurate translations, although they are usually still called Bibles. Some of these popular books are intended for children or teenagers, for example the *Living Bible* of 1971 by Kenneth Taylor, still in print. Others are intended for adults, such as Eugene Peterson's 2002 *The Message: The Bible in Contemporary Language*. Not only do paraphrases condense and/or omit much of the material, but they also freely change the wording of the original text to make it easier to understand, more entertaining, and more relevant for their intended readers. A good paraphrase of the NT can help to bring out the hidden nuances of the Greek original; a mediocre or bad paraphrase can obscure it.

www Follow the links to helpful sites dealing with English Bible translations.

Using the World Wide Web to Study the New Testament Today

The last ten years have seen an explosive growth in the World Wide Web, the linked computer system on the Internet. Much information about the Christian religion can be found on the Web; it seems to be one of the leading topics of discussion and inquiry. As a part of this interest in Christianity, many sites on the Web feature presentations and discussion of the NT. This book, as the reader has already discovered, uses the Web to enrich the student's encounter with reading the NT today.

This new opportunity to encounter NT study has many positive features. The access is usually free. The amount of academically appropriate material on the Web is growing rapidly and may someday become a main avenue for researching, teaching, and learning the NT. The Internet is an appealing way for most young, computer-oriented students to encounter NT study. It presents different ways of studying and learning—for example, the ability to search a text electronically. The Internet by its structure encourages exploration and active learning. Some sites are fully interactive, allowing students to ask questions and participate in online discussion groups. Finally, but not least, when students explore a sponsored NT site, the encounter is likely to be more lively than textbook descriptions.

The drawbacks of studying on the Web are also significant. Some sites are not well constructed; they may have poor layout, little eye appeal, or other technical deficiencies. "Link rot," when links are lost or broken for a variety of reasons, is a growing problem in educational use of the Web. Although Internet coverage of NT study is growing, it is still incomplete. Many books and articles posted on the Internet are usually older public-domain works that do not represent current scholarship. Moreover, much of the material posted for the NT is written from a religious, devotional point of view; some of this material is based on sound methods of current scholarship, but much is not. Most significantly, these electronic publications are subject to little or no scholarly control, such as editorial or peer review before publication, so their quality varies greatly.

The result of this mixed situation is that many students need help in finding, using, and especially analyzing critically these Web-based NT sites. For readers of this book, I have designed a special website to further their use of the Web in NT studies. It has links to short, helpful essays on using the Internet in an academically appropriate way. The website also has links to sites that my students and I have found useful in the study of scriptures, including links to all the websites given in this book. This listing cannot pretend to be comprehensive, but it does offer a starting place to surf and learn. The address is: http://religion.wadsworth.com; follow the links to this book's website.

Suggestions on How to Read Scriptures

The NT is indeed for most modern readers, to use the words of a twentieth-century Christian theologian about the Bible, a "strange new world." Sometimes one's preconceived notion of what reading scripture will be like turns out to be quite wrong. It is one thing to read a text like this book and understand its take on the NT, but to encounter scriptures directly—which, after all, is the whole point of a course in the NT—is a challenging process. As Mortimer Adler and Charles Van Doren once wrote, "The problem of reading the Holy Book . . . is the most difficult problem in the field of reading." (Adler and Van Doren 1972, 288). Although any introduction to the NT must discuss methods of study and introduce the NT itself, in the end readers will find it more profitable to wrestle as directly as possible with the texts.

Each reader of the NT must ultimately find an individually suitable method for reading scriptures. However, some or all of the following suggestions drawn from my experience and the experience of others may be helpful for you.

1. Get a basic understanding of the major interpretive methods used here. To have them basically in hand before you begin reading the NT will make this reading more productive. Ask yourself: What questions raised by various people reading the NT text itself do these methods answer?

2. Realize that these methods sometimes complement each other and sometimes conflict with each other. They are so diverse that very few, if any, readers of the NT agree with and use them all. This is perfectly acceptable from an academic point of view—you should *understand* them all and be able to use them in a basic way, but you need not *agree* with them all.

3. Keep your computer logged on to the web page for this book as you read. This will make connecting with the links more efficient.

4. Use your growing knowledge of early Christianity to set the NT in a fuller context, relating the NT literature as fully as possible to the actual people and events in early Christianity. For example, when you are reading a narrative passage, visualize that event taking place.

5. Always take a few minutes to skim the NT book you are studying. Having a general feel for "the lay of the land" will help you when you begin to read in detail.

6. Read the scripture passages with the same intellectual skills as you would any other text, religious or nonreligious. If you remember their holy status in Christianity, don't be intimidated by it.

7. Mark the text as you read. Research on reading shows that students who mark the text, underlining or highlighting as few as three or four items per page, understand and remember more than readers who do not mark their text.

8. Make a personal glossary of unfamiliar terms and names as you go along. You can do this quite easily by circling them in the text and writing them in the bottom margin. (Use circles or other type of marking that will distinguish them from other marked material.) Then you can go back later to make a short note of their meaning, also in the margin.

9. Above all, read this book and the NT actively and critically. Vincent Ruggiero identifies four steps toward effective reading: skim (first glancing, then rapid reading for an overview); reflect (after skimming, examine your own views in conversation with the author's); read (deepen and refine your understanding by reading for detail); and evaluate (judge how well the author writes to persuade you) (Ruggiero 2001, 60–63).

www See the website for more information on active, critical reading.

Key Terms and Concepts

Apocalypse (NT book) • apocalypse (genre) • authenticity
Bible (in both Jewish and Christian definitions) • Catholic/General letters
Christian Scriptures (as a name for the NT) • covenant • disputed Pauline letters
dynamic equivalence translation • formal equivalence translation • genre
gospel, the Gospels • Hebrew Bible • Hellenistic/Koine Greek • New Testament
Old Testament • paraphrase • Pastoral Letters • post-Pauline Letters
pseudonymity • scripture • Second/Christian Testament • Synoptic Gospels
testament • undisputed Pauline letters

Questions for Study, Discussion, and Writing

1. Reflect and comment on this statement about insiders and outsiders in the reading of the NT: "If you are not of the faith . . . you can nevertheless read a theological book well by treating its dogmas with the same respect you treat the assumptions of the mathematician. But you must remember that an article of faith is not something that the faithful <u>assume</u>. Faith, for those who have it, is the most certain form of knowledge, not a tentative opinion" (Adler and Van Doren, *How to Read a Book*, 288).
2. Give your reflection on the Italian proverb, "Translators are traitors." In what sense(s) is it true that English translations of the NT betray its real meaning?
3. If you are familiar with more than one translation or paraphrase of the NT, which one is your favorite, and why?
4. Is it better, in your opinion, to use the title "Christian Scriptures" or "New Testament"?
5. Explain in your own words the idea of covenant and why the Christian half of the Bible is called the "New Testament/Covenant."
6. Explain in your own words the genres in the NT: gospels, acts, letters, and apocalypse.
7. What has it meant for relations between Christians and Jews that they share a large part of the same Bible? How has this fact both improved and complicated their relations?

For Further Reading

Brown, Raymond E. *An Introduction to the New Testament*. New York: Doubleday, 1997, pp. 1–15. Extensive, detailed information on the nature of the NT and its contents, with a moderate scholarly stance.

Coogan, Michael D., ed. *The New Oxford Annotated Bible*, 3rd ed. New York: Oxford University Press, 2001. The New Revised Standard Version text, with excellent study notes that often draw on newer methods of reading.

Guthrie, Donald. *New Testament Introduction*, 4th ed. Downers Grove, IL: Intervarsity, 1990. Exhaustive information on the NT, with a conservative Protestant stance.

Harrelson, Walter, ed. *The New Interpreter's Study Bible*. Nashville, TN: Abingdon, 2003. The New Revised Standard Version text, with fuller, more explanatory study notes than the *New Oxford Annotated Bible*.

Koester, Helmut. *Introduction to the New Testament*, 2nd ed., 2 vols. Berlin and New York: de Gruyter, 1995. Complete coverage of the NT and its cultural background, with a more liberal scholarly stance.

Peterson, Eugene. *The Message: The Bible in Contemporary Language.* Colorado Springs: Navpress, 2002. The contemporary best-selling paraphrase of the Bible.

Ruggiero, Vincent R. *The Art of Thinking: A Guide to Critical and Creative Thought,* 6th ed. New York: Longman, 2001. Chapter 4, "Be a Critical Reader," is an excellent and concise guide to the kind of critical reading skills necessary to read the NT and its contemporary interpretations by different methods.

Senior, Donald, ed. *The Catholic Study Bible,* 2nd ed. New York: Oxford University Press, 1990. An excellent study Bible for both Catholics and others who wish to know more about the contemporary Catholic understanding of the Bible. It contains the text of the New American Bible version, which is similar to that of the Revised Standard Version.

Chapter Two

Ways of Reading
the New Testament Today

Every time we read a text, we use a method of reading appropriate to that text whether we know it or not. Usually we choose a method of reading based on our initial perception of what kind of document we are beginning to read. We read novels in one way, newspaper editorials in another way, personal letters in yet another way, and so on. In this chapter, we will introduce the various ways of reading the New Testament in current study: historical, social scientific, narrative, feminist, and cross-cultural. These methods will be introduced here; later chapters will examine them more fully and put them to use.

The methods listed fall under the general category of biblical criticism, and they are critical methods. Criticism here has nothing to do with making negative comments, as many people assume. Instead, it is derived from the Greek word *krino,* "to discern, to judge." **Criticism** is academically informed understanding whose purpose is to make discerning judgments about literary or artistic productions. Thus, we speak of literary criticism, art criticism, or music criticism as fields of inquiry that carefully study the productions in their discipline in order to understand significant features and discern lasting value, and to communicate observations to others. To put it another way, criticism of a written document is the way we read and explain it with understanding. **Biblical criticism** is careful scholarly study of the Bible that seeks to understand it and reach informed, discerning conclusions about it. Biblical criticism began in the Enlightenment as new ideas in the study of history made their way into the study of Christian origins, and it continues today as new scholarly perspectives and methods are applied to the Bible. All methods of reading the Bible with an academic approach are considered methods of biblical criticism, regardless of whether they have the words *critical* or *criticism* in their name.

www Read a short essay on nonacademic uses and ways to read the NT, such as in public worship and private devotion, and also on the fundamentalist reading of the NT.

The Historical-Critical Method of Reading

When we read literature from the ancient world, especially the scripture of a religion to which we may belong, we often look for its meaning for us today. This response is in line with the standing of such literature as scripture: it continues to speak and guide believers toward life-giving understanding, and even for those who do not believe it is a part of their cultural heritage. We do not think that often about the ancient readers of the text, their language, culture, and historical situation. Rather, we see ourselves as the important audience and today as the important time.

The **historical-critical method** does not ask primarily what the NT means to its readers today. Instead, it seeks to understand what its documents meant *to their original writers and readers*. It seeks the original meaning, which may or may not be the same as our meanings today. The term *historical-critical method* refers to the principles and presuppositions of historical research and reasoning that began in the Renaissance and Reformation, grew in the Enlightenment, and flowered fully in the nineteenth century, when German scholars applied the general principles of natural science methods to historical study. These principles include the following: Human life through time is basically uniform; past reality is accessible to present human research and understanding; past events are comparable by analogy to present events; an understanding of present human experience can provide objective criteria for understanding the past. These principles have often been controversial in the study of the NT, with its claims of supernatural beings and supernatural events in human history. It makes a great deal of difference if these principles are applied in a wooden way or in a way that respects religious experience in the NT. For example, if one rules out the possibility of miraculous healings because they seem to be unknown in modern life and are challenging to ordinary historical interpretation, one's picture of the historical Jesus will be quite different from much of early Christianity's view. This is not to say, of course, that NT reports of miracles—or any other event, for that matter—are beyond historical study.

Like all literature, the documents of the NT arose in a particular historical setting or sequence of settings and were written by particular historical persons for particular audiences. The historical method views the NT documents in their historical and cultural context as ancient works. The methods of analyzing these documents are the same as those other historians use to study nonreligious texts. Readers using the historical method are concerned with historical events, and they use the literature of the NT to reconstruct the history of those events. Actually, the reconstruction has two focal points: the general, wider historical situation in which the text is situated; and the particular historical situation of the author and recipients of the NT books. In the former, attention is given to other contemporary literature and the religious environment. In the latter, attention is given to matters of authorship, date, genre of writing, recipients, and historical meaning. In other words, the purpose of historical reading is to reconstruct as fully as possible the historical situation out of which a document arose and determine how it came to be written and what the author meant to communicate to the audience. Any contemporary meaning of the text, if any is to be construed, derives from this historical understanding. In the sections that follow, we will consider briefly the main parts of the historical-critical method of interpreting the NT: textual criticism, source criticism, form criticism, and redaction criticism.

Textual Criticism

Before we can study closely a copied or printed document, we must be confident that the wording of our copy is a faithful reflection of the author's original. Today, when we read a printed book and notice a mistake—a misspelled or missing word, for example—we mentally correct the text to conform to what we believe to be the original manuscript of the book. We may even write the correct wording in our copy of the book. When we do this, we are engaging in textual criticism on a small, informal scale.

In dealing with the NT, as with other documents from the ancient world, textual criticism is necessary on a much larger, formal scale. **Textual criticism** of the NT establishes as fully as possible the wording of the original Greek text of the NT, first copied by hand almost two thousand years ago. No **autographs,** original copies so called whether the author signed them or not, of the documents written by the NT authors have survived. Instead, we are confronted with over five thousand **manuscripts** (handwritten documents, all copies of the originals), no two of which are exactly alike, ranging from the second century to the fifteenth century, when printing was invented and hand copying of the Bible mostly ended. The beginning student of the NT should know the basic procedures of textual criticism, work that is done by specialists in the ancient languages, especially Greek. The ordinary reader of the NT directly encounters textual criticism only occasionally, when the editors and translators of modern versions note at the bottom of the NT translation that the manuscript evidence is uncertain.

www   For a supplement to the treatment of textual criticism here, go to the excellent "Interpreting Ancient Manuscripts" site.

Six main types of manuscripts are used in NT textual criticism. First, most of the earliest manuscripts are classified as **papyri** because of the material on which they were written. Papyrus is paper made from river reeds—our word "paper" comes from *papyrus.* The earliest extant papyrus is a fragment of the Gospel of John dated around 135 C.E. Second, the major NT manuscripts are called *uncial* ("inch-high") manuscripts because they are written in capital letters; these are usually copied on parchment and circulated in *codex* form, that is, as a bound book, as opposed to scrolls. Uncials date from the third to the tenth centuries. Third, the large body of later Greek manuscripts is called *minuscule* manuscripts because they feature cursive (connected-letter) handwriting with smaller letters. These date from the ninth through the fifteenth centuries. Fourth, ancient *versions* (translations) of the Greek NT into Latin were made as early as the second century. Latin was more widely spoken in the western half of the Roman Empire than in the eastern. Then other versions of the NT were made, for example, Syriac, Coptic, and Armenian, all languages of the western Roman Empire and beyond it. Fifth, early church writers in the second and third centuries frequently quoted the NT in their own writings. These quotations provide text critics with another source of data. Sixth, early Christian *lectionaries,* NT passages written out for reading during Christian services, are also useful in the effort to restore the original text. These come from the seventh century on.

The expert examines the **textual variants,** differences in a word or phrase between the manuscripts, to classify and evaluate the manuscripts. Textual variants arose for a variety of reasons. Unintentional variants are caused by typical visual or auditory mistakes by scribes copying the documents—repeating the same word or skipping to the next occurrence of the word, for example, or confusing words that look and sound alike. (We often make these kinds of accidental mistakes today if we copy another document by hand.) Sometimes variants are intentional: copyists may attempt to correct a text that they think is wrong or improve its theology, grammar, or style. At times interpretive comments consisting of one or two words found their way into the text. Despite curses occasionally put in ancient books against scribes who change wording (see Rev 22:18–22), they continued to do so.

The variant readings, both intentional and accidental, that result are corrected by means of certain principles that apply to all textual criticism of ancient documents. Principles based on **external evidence** (the readings of all the manuscripts considered together) are these:

- The reading in older manuscripts is usually best.
- The more geographically spread reading is best.
- The reading supported by the most families of text-types is best.

When this external evidence cannot determine which textual variant is the likely original reading, internal evidence comes into play. Principles based on **internal evidence** (indications from inside a document) are these:

- The shorter reading is usually best.
- The more difficult reading is best.
- The reading that does not agree with other passages in the NT is best.
- The reading that accords with the author's style and theology is best.

www   For a brief discussion of the history of textual criticism, see the website.

As we consider how the New Revised Standard Version treats text-critical problems in two illustrations, we will show the importance of textual criticism for all readers of the NT and why even beginning students of the English-language NT should be acquainted with basic textual criticism. First, in Matthew 6:13, some manuscripts have the following words in a variant reading at the end of the Lord's Prayer/Our Father: "for the kingdom and the power and the glory are yours forever. Amen." Better manuscript evidence omits these words and so does the main English text of the NRSV, placing them instead in a footnote. In Matthew, Jesus gives this prayer to his disciples as an example of brevity in prayer, which Jesus encourages. The long variant raises an issue: Just how short should this prayer be? The second illustration is John 7:53–8:1, the story of Jesus protecting and forgiving a woman caught in adultery who was facing imminent execution. Many manuscripts omit this whole story; others put it in different places in John or even in the Gospel of Luke; a few include it but mark it as doubtful. Is this well-known passage, with its often-cited words of Jesus, "Let the one among you without sin be the first to cast a stone," an original part of the Gospel of John?

www   To test your knowledge of these principles of textual criticism more fully by an entertaining exercise based on an English-language text, follow the link to the "Exercise in Textual Criticism" section of the "Interpreting Ancient Manuscripts" site.

Source Criticism

Most authors today do not borrow extensively from other recent works for their own books. If they do, they must obtain permission from the copyright holder and note this permission in their books, or legal problems may ensue! In many colleges and universities throughout the world, professors must carefully teach students about what is and is not proper use of sources. Even some famous scholars and professional writers have been caught in controversies about inappropriate use of sources. The Internet has made the problem of plagiarism worse.

In the ancient world, the situation was completely different. Copyright law, and the moral justification behind it, did not exist. The leading writers in almost every field, including several early Christian writers whose works entered the NT, often borrowed heavily and without attribution from earlier, lesser-known written works. No one considered this a moral or legal fault. **Source criticism,** a second part of the historical-critical method, is the study of how some NT documents draw on other sources either inside or outside the NT. Usually this involves written sources, but oral collections of material come into play here as well. Gospel sources are especially important, for two reasons. First, the material in our four Gospels had a long period of oral transmission that certainly featured oral collections and probably written collections. Second, as far as we can tell, none of the Gospels was written by an eyewitness or based *directly* on eyewitness testimony, so the Gospel writers had to use sources. That a later writer could reuse an earlier book is not foreign to the biblical tradition. For example, the author of Deuteronomy in the Hebrew Bible used earlier material from the book of Exodus, and the author of 1–2 Chronicles rewrote material in Samuel and Kings.

From the second century through today, Christians have realized that Matthew, Mark, and Luke are closely related in both structure and content. One common-sense explanation for this similarity, held by many in the church for almost two thousand years and still popular among many Christians, states that they are so similar in wording because they are closely based on similar accounts from eye-witnesses circulating in the early church. Among NT scholars today, this is an extremely small minority position. Almost all scholars in the last two hundred years have argued that the Synoptics are similar because they were drawn from common sources. They have used three theories to explain this common-source relationship: (1) the Gospels depended on sources now lost, such as "Q," which contains sayings of Jesus; (2) the Gospels were somehow literarily interdependent, using each other as sources; (3) the Gospels are based on both lost sources and are interdependent. According to theory 1, the lost sources consisted of oral tradition, a variety of written fragments, or an early gospel now lost. According to theory 2, one of the Synoptics made use of at least one of the others. Various possibilities were suggested, but the two most popular solutions advocated either the priority of Matthew or the priority of Mark. As we will see later in Chapter 5, most historical critics of the Gospels today accept theory 3, arguing that Matthew and Luke both used Mark and other written and oral sources.

Since about 1975, some source criticism of the gospels has run in a reverse direction, with scholars considering whether some second-century noncanonical gospels may contain material that was used earlier as source material by the Synoptics. Most notably, the sayings of Jesus in the *Gospel of Thomas,* discovered in an Egyptian monk's grave in 1945, have been recognized by most scholars as literarily related to Synoptic sayings, especially the sayings in the Q source. Some scholars are so convinced of the importance of the *Gospel of Thomas* that they call it the "Fifth Gospel." To cite another example, John Dominic Crossan argues that a "Cross Gospel" now embedded in the *Gospel of Peter* was a source for Mark (Crossan 1988). With less persuasiveness, Morton Smith argued that the *Secret Gospel of Mark,* referred to and briefly excerpted in a letter of Clement of Alexandria that he discovered in a Jerusalem monastery in 1958, is a literary source of canonical Mark (Smith 1973). This "source-criticism in reverse" is not nearly as important for Gospel study as the main current of source criticism, but it does form a fascinating side current in the field.

Source criticism also applies to other sections of the NT, although not nearly to the extent and significance as in Synoptic Gospel study. For example, many students of the Gospel of John believe that a "Signs [miracles] Source" underlies that Gospel. In the study of Acts, scholars have given attention to the "we" passages, where the author shifts the narration to the first-person plural (Acts 16:10–17; 20:5–15; 21:1–18; 27:1–28:16). These may represent a diary source or perhaps a travel itinerary source. Other scholars detect evidence in Acts of sources dealing with the early history of Christianity in major centers, for instance, Jerusalem and Antioch sources. Source criticism of the NT also deals with how letters sometimes use earlier documents as sources. For example, Ephesians draws upon Colossians, James has strong connections to the teaching of Jesus in Matthew, and 2 Peter draws on Jude. How these sources are used provides an important clue for the meaning of the documents that use them.

Form Criticism

When we read something today, we know how to recognize different types of writing and read accordingly. For example, someone reading a newspaper would recognize and read differently news reports, sports reports, editorials, comics, horoscopes, advertisements, want ads, and the rest. When we surf the World Wide Web and all sorts of things appear on our computer monitors, we know how to sift through the material by discerning its different literary, visual, and auditory forms.

Those reading the Gospels using the historical-critical method also recognize different types of passages in them, and read accordingly. **Form criticism** has two main components: first, it studies the structure and (to a lesser degree) the content of the different types of passages ("forms") of the written gospels; second, it goes beyond these written forms to study their history in the oral tradition. Its German inventors called this approach *history of form,* a name that emphasizes the second component. Form criticism of the Gospels depends on the results of source criticism. Most source critics had already concluded that Mark was the earliest. Wilhelm Wrede and others had shown, however, that Mark was not primarily a historical record of the life of Jesus but more so an expression of the theological confession of the author (Wrede 1901). The quest for the historical Jesus, therefore, would have to go beyond the written material to earlier, oral sources that could be identified and isolated in the existing written sources.

Three German NT scholars working independently in the early 1900s arrived at similar results. Karl Ludwig Schmidt concluded that the gospels had literary frameworks upon which **pericopes** (puh-RICK-uh-peas), small independent units of oral tradition now written down in the Gospels, were hung (Schmidt 1927). Martin Dibelius believed the individual units of oral tradition were shaped in accord with the practical needs of early Christian preaching before they were written down in the gospels (Dibelius 1934). Rudolf Bultmann saw the origin and development of the units of traditions as related to more specific church concerns—worship, teaching, and moral exhortation (Bultmann 1921). Form criticism made its way to America in the 1930s and 1940s by way of England, and the basic contributions of

Schmidt, Dibelius, and Bultmann as outlined here became permanent parts of historical reading of the NT.

www   Follow the link to a general treatment of form criticism, and special treatments of Dibelius and Bultmann, on the excellent Rutgers University religion website by Mahlon Smith.

All form critics agree that the earliest memories of Jesus, his sayings and stories about him, were circulated first by word of mouth. A few leading scholars have argued that the followers of Jesus wrote them down at an early point and used these written accounts to spread the church's message about Jesus. However, the Gospels and Acts preserve no hint of written documents used in early evangelism; in fact, they strongly imply that the spread of Jesus' message was exclusively oral. The earliest witnesses of the words and deeds of Jesus, the twelve leading disciples with many other followers of Jesus, had come to believe in him as Messiah and Lord, and this faith influenced the ways they passed along stories about him. As material about Jesus was circulated, it was shaped into "forms" according to the conventions of oral communication—parables, proverbs, miracle stories, controversy stories, and the like. Most form-critical study analyzes these smaller, paragraph-sized units, but it also studies the larger literary units of the Gospels as well: passion narratives, resurrection appearance narratives, and conception and birth narratives.

As these stories were retold in the early churches, they took on a more refined shape, with additional details and emphases. Some new stories probably arose to meet the changing needs of the believing community. Some form critics, especially those following Bultmann's lead, relate historical authenticity to form; for example, parables tend to be authentic teachings of Jesus, Bultmann argued, while miracles are not authentic. The main intent of the form critic is to find the *Sitz im Leben* ("zits ihm LAY-ben"), the social and religious "setting in life" of the first-century church where such oral forms originated and developed. (This German term has persisted in English-language scholarship, and we will use it here.) This in turn enables us to understand how this setting shaped the oral tradition about Jesus and how the Jesus tradition shaped early church life. The evangelists were viewed by some early form critics primarily as collectors and editors of these traditional units, exercising little authorial creativity. For these form critics, the Gospels are like a string of differently shaped and colored beads—a loose collection and arrangement of traditional data that bore little relation to the actual history of Jesus. We shall examine form criticism of the Gospels more fully in Chapter 5.

Form criticism has been supplemented more recently by **tradition criticism,** the study of how particular forms are transmitted, both orally and in writing. Tradition criticism also analyzes the origin and development of written units of tradition within the literature of the NT. For example, Paul in letters presents older Christian hymns (e.g., Phil 2:6–11), confessions (1 Cor 8:6; 15:3–7), and liturgical formulas (1 Cor 11:23–25). Tradition criticism studies the way NT authors use and adapt the traditional material to their own purposes. Some scholars, most prominently James M. Robinson and Helmut Koester, trace the course of a unit of tradition as a *trajectory* or "line of development" moving from its origin through various stages of writing (Robinson and Koester 1971).

Redaction Criticism

When we read contemporary literature, whether as brief as a short story or as long as a novel, we know that the reading of a *whole* document, and what comes from this reading, is most important. Though some characters or incidents might linger in our minds more than others, it is our impression of the whole work that gives meaning to these parts. The same is true of a play or a Hollywood film—we understand it as a whole. We pass along the final, overall impression of the play or film by word of mouth, which creates success or failure at the box office. Moreover, when a book or film is a remake of an earlier work, we know that the differences introduced in the remake are important for understanding it.

Historical study has developed such an approach to reading the NT. **Redaction criticism** is analysis of the particular religious meaning of the final NT composition as a whole, especially the Gospels. (*Redaction* refers to editorial shaping of a work, usually just before its publication.) It assumes the results of source and form criticism because the meaning of the whole Gospel can only be discerned by reading and interpreting its various parts, but it moves beyond them to view the Gospels as coherent works. To put it another way, form criticism studies each tree individually, whereas redaction criticism studies the forest as a whole. Using form critical results, redaction critics ask how Mark used the oral traditions he had received. Using the results of form and source criticism, redaction critics ask how Matthew and Luke employed Mark and Q, and how the Gospel of John used its Signs Source. Redaction criticism seeks to discern the particular theological point of view of each Gospel, which is known as its **tendency.** Tendency can be discerned most clearly in how the four Gospels shape the source materials they use. Because redaction criticism identifies the overall patterns of a writer's use of sources, it helps specify the particular circumstances, interests, and meaning of each individual Gospel.

As with the development of form criticism, German scholars working independently developed the method of redaction criticism. NT scholars had seen both the promise and the limitations of form criticism and now were working to move beyond it. In the study of Mark, Willi Marxsen concluded that Mark adapted his material to the situation of the church in 66 C.E., when the Jewish revolt against the Roman Empire broke out in Palestine, and used his gospel to support the expectation of the imminent return of Christ (Marxsen 1954). In the study of Matthew, Günter Bornkamm investigated its use of Mark and concluded that Matthew shaped the tradition to present his own particular views of Jesus Christ and the church, which emphasized Jesus as the Messiah of Israel who fulfills and affirms the Law of Moses (Bornkamm 1963). In the study of Luke, Hans Conzelmann believed Luke presented and arranged the traditional material in Mark and Q to depict a history of salvation consisting of three periods: the era of Israel, the time of Jesus, and the era of the church (Conzelmann 1953). Redaction criticism redirected form criticism's attention from the small units of tradition to the finished literary product. As a result, the role of the early church in shaping the tradition was reduced, and the work of the Gospel writers as literary authors and theologians was enhanced. They were seen no longer as cut-and-paste assemblers but as creative, skillful authors in their own right. (In general, it is more difficult to be creative as an author when one is using sources and other traditional material so extensively, but this is exactly what the Gospel writers have done.) The insights of redaction criticism have persisted until today. They are strongly affirmed in many of the newer methods of critical reading we will consider here, even if these methods do not employ redaction criticism itself.

www For a brief treatment of genre criticism, a newer form of redaction criticism, see the website.

Evaluating the Historical Method of Reading

The historical-critical method, from textual criticism through redaction criticism, has several strengths. It has shown the NT to be a collection of diverse writings, many of which have a basis in older oral and written traditions. It has given us an awareness of the historical conditions of NT times and how the NT documents arise from these times and speak the religious message of early Christianity. It freed the NT, especially in the nineteenth century, from the strictures of traditional church teaching, and in the twentieth century it contributed rich new insights on the NT to the church, first the Protestant and then the Roman Catholic. As a method that strives to be culturally and religiously neutral, historical criticism is a tool that scholars of different cultural and religious orientations have used fruitfully. It has shown itself quite adaptable to new times and new interpretive methods and has grown in size and sophistication. Not least, its academic orientation enabled NT study to claim a rightful place in the modern university and its scholarship. Because of these and other strengths, the historical-critical method, now going on two hundred years old, is likely to remain an important method of reading the NT, and perhaps the single most important method, for the foreseeable future.

However, as is often the case in human life, strengths entail weaknesses. The historical-critical method's exclusively *historical* orientation, especially its power to understand the text by way of its origins, has often meant that many researchers using it do not understand the fullness of the text, either its meaning in the ancient world or its meaning for today. Four brief illustrations of this weakness must suffice here. First, the historical-critical method as traditionally practiced seems to many scholars today to focus too much on the development of religious ideas in the NT (e.g., the development of its teaching on the person and work of Jesus), to the neglect of a fuller analysis of how these ideas relate to social and economic realities. Second, despite the corrective efforts of redaction criticism, historical criticism as it is practiced today still seems to shatter the literary unity of many of the NT documents. It is good at analysis, but it is not very good at synthesis. Third, the increasingly complex source-critical labors of many contemporary researchers in not only reconstructing sources of the gospels such as Q, but also reconstructing and analyzing the stages and sources of Q itself, seems excessive to many. Finally, its claim to be objective and scientific, to use accepted rules of historical scholarship in a dispassionate way to produce a universal truth, seems increasingly naïve to many current interpreters, especially feminist and cross-cultural critics. They question if value-free study of the NT is possible, and they charge that this falsely "neutral" study of the NT actually promotes certain religious and political agendas. Despite these weaknesses, the historical method is still by far the most employed approach in biblical study today.

Since about the 1960s, however, scholars have developed and applied many other methods to the study of the NT. Many of these researchers came from other fields of study beyond history, especially the humanities and social sciences. The theory and application of their methods tend to be North American in origin, in contrast to the older components of the historical-critical method, which, as we have seen, are largely German. In this book, we will employ these methods to help us read and understand the NT today. We will consider in turn social-scientific reading, narrative reading, feminist reading, and cross-cultural reading.

Narrative Reading

"Everybody loves a story," a well-known adage states. A good story, whether long or short, draws us in and makes us a part of it as we connect with certain characters and experience the story through them. A story subtly changes our emotions and attitudes as it entertains us. Stories are found in oral tradition, in jokes, in the short story form, in novels, in plays, films and television shows, and in other settings.

Although all ancient cultures had stories and valued them, the NT seems to be particularly rich in story. Not only was Jesus a master storyteller himself, accounting for a large measure of his appeal as a teacher, but the story *of* Jesus—his birth, ministry, death, and resurrection, with an open end for his return at the end of time—was fundamental for early Christianity. **Narrative criticism** or reading seeks to understand the story ("narrative") forms in the NT. Narrative criticism is opposed to the historicizing and theologizing of the text that aims only to reconstruct its "real history" or analyze the development of doctrines. In particular, it intends to restore an appreciation for the narrative features of the Bible. It looks carefully not just at the smooth, consistent story, but also at the text's repetitions, gaps, inconsistencies, and even contradictions. Both the smooth center and the rough edges of the document are important for understanding the text as a whole. The focus is the text itself and the reader's encounter with it; meaning is created in this encounter, not by the author of the text. Seymour Chatman, in his *Story and Discourse* (1978), states that any narrative is composed of story and discourse. "Story" is *what* is told, and it is composed of three elements: settings, characters and events. "Discourse" is *how* the story is told, and it includes such elements as narrator, point of view, implied author, and implied reader. We will consider story and discourse more fully in Chapter 5.

Narrative critics read the Bible in order to understand its stories. The narrative elements of the four canonical Gospels and Acts—in their parts and whole—are plentiful and obvious. Narrative critics have accused historical critics of sacrificing narrative for merely historical purposes—reconstructing the *historical* Jesus apart from the *stories* of Jesus, for example. To take another example, in reading Mark, narrative criticism does not care about whether Mark is the actual author, about his possible sources, about form-critical or even redaction-critical issues. One of the most influential treatments of Mark is the fascinating study by David Rhoads, Donald Michie, and Joanna Dewey, *Mark as Story: An Introduction to the Narrative of a Gospel* (1999). They read Mark as a whole, as it stands now, on its own narrative merits. They present (1) the point of view of Mark's narrator: an omniscient narrator not bound by time and space, giving inside views of the characters' minds; (2) the characters: Jesus, to take the leading character, is presented with authority, integrity, and self-denying service to the point of his own death; (3) the plot and its outcome: the interactions between Jesus and the authorities and between Jesus and his disciples. The narrative works by engaging its readers in its narrative world, thereby transforming the understanding and life of the reader. The more powerfully the *narrator*, the storyteller, engages the reader, the more transformative potential the narrative has. To readers of the NT who are accustomed to reading it in bits and pieces from a historical or religious point of view, narrative reading offers a dynamic way to grasp the meaning of the whole story.

So far, this narrative criticism seems to be rather simple and straightforward in its theory and application. However, narrative criticism often introduces complexity by drawing a distinction between the real author and the implied author, and between the real reader and the implied reader. The *real author* is the person who actually wrote the story, and the *implied author* is the image of the author that readers create in reading the story. The *real reader* is the person who actually reads or hears the story, from the time it was first read until today. The *implied reader* is the reader that the text shapes as it is read, the person who cognitively and emotionally enters the story and responds to it as first the real author, and then the implied author, intends.

Narrative criticism also seeks a broader meaning. For some narrative critics, narrative is not just a story, but a fundamental feature of human existence. People are said to live in a *narrative world*; that is, they understand and value their lives as part of the story-like reality of the world. In other words, seeing their personal story as a part of the world's story gives their lives meaning. This larger meaning indicates that narrative criticism is important not just for NT material in narrative form, but for texts that are not formally a story as well. Thus, some narrative critics argue, the whole NT can and should be read by the narrative-critical method. The letters of Paul, for example, are said to assume a narrative, the story of Jesus. When Paul writes to address the particular problems of his churches, he gives expression to this basic narrative. Paul has a smaller, personal story himself, and the relation of his story to the larger story provides personal meaning. Moreover, each of Paul's letters has an implicit story—a "plot" that involves Paul's previous relation to the recipients of the letter, the writing and reception of the letter, and the readers' response. This process in turn becomes a part of the continuing relationship of Paul with his churches and often of further correspondence with them (Longenecker 2002).

With all this emphasis on the story itself, what does narrative reading have to say about whether these stories ever *happened*? This important question connects narrative reading with historical criticism. Narrative criticism typically does not automatically dismiss the significance of historical events. The narrative substructure of the Gospels presupposes the life of Jesus, and Paul's story is related to his own experience, especially his call/conversion. For the main method of narrative reading, however, the written story is primary and questions of historicity need not be raised. (By analogy, most scholars reading the NT with the historical method hold that the parables of Jesus, remarkable short narratives in their own right, are "true" regardless of whether they actually happened or not.) The writing of history can never be the exact reiteration of the bare facts of the past, but a process that involves selection, plotting, and interpretation. For narrative critics, this process is known to us in and through the written story, not in the history behind it.

In sum, narrative criticism obviously has great potential for NT study. It focuses on the text of scripture itself. Narrative method is well suited to the narrative character of much of the NT. Some NT critics combine it effectively with rhetorical criticism—a story that seeks to convince; others combine it with elements of the historical-critical method, especially redaction criticism. It offers a fresh, exciting way to do NT study and for many readers is very effective in unlocking the transformative power of the text. Nevertheless, many NT scholars see drawbacks in narrative criticism. They hold that narrative criticism does not work so well when applied to nonnarrative or implied-narrative texts, such as the Pauline letters of the NT. Sometimes it appears that narrative critics must strain to construct a "story" from these letters. (In this book we will largely confine our study of narrative reading to explicitly narrative materials, the Gospels and Acts.) Another drawback to narrative reading is that its distinction between the real/implied author and real/implied reader makes its application more difficult and abstract. Finally, some NT scholars given to historical criticism argue that narrative criticism is too subjective, letting the reader inject her or his own meaning, which may or may not coincide with the author's intended meaning. Nevertheless, narrative criticism has demonstrated its value for NT study and likely will continue as an important method for years to come.

Social Scientific Reading

Although we may not recognize it, most of us think to a significant extent in a social scientific way. Not that we collect and analyze scientific data on groups or ponder social scientific theory. Rather, we think about life in general, and our own lives in particular, in terms of how we are shaped by the various groups we live in and by our society as a whole. Although North American society has been criticized for its strong emphasis on individualism, groups are still important to us. We are accustomed to understanding ourselves by our gender, family, race, religion, economic class, and nationality. To do this is to think social scientifically.

Social scientific criticism is the study of the NT by means of sociology and especially cultural anthropology. It seeks to discern how the religious message of the NT and the life of its communities impacted, and was impacted by, its social setting. Those who practice the historical-critical method have paid some attention to the social dimension of the NT, matters such as rich and poor, slave and free, female and male, states and nations, and the interaction of different religious movements. Since the 1960s, however, the more formal, self-conscious application of social scientific methods to the NT has made it a separate method of reading and critical study. Some of its leading current advocates are Wayne Meeks of Yale University, who has analyzed the urban social setting of the apostle Paul's churches (Meeks 1983). Gerd Theissen of Heidelberg University, a leading German social scientific interpreter of the NT, has analyzed the earliest Christian communities in Palestine (Theissen 1978). Bruce Malina of Creighton University in Omaha, now widely regarded as the leading social scientific NT scholar, has applied this method in several NT treatments, such as *The New Testament World: Insights from Cultural Anthropology* (Malina 2001), and his fascinating book for students, *Windows on the World of Jesus: Time Travel to Ancient Judea* (Malina 1993).

Critical of a disembodied historical reading of the NT that produces a "mere history of religious ideas," social scientific interpreters note that most early Christians were not detached intellectuals. Rather, they were ordinary people who lived in families and communities, social organizations that had a great impact on their lives and faith. They were free or enslaved, and insiders or outsiders to Roman citizenship and its privileges. They were males and females in a world with strong differentiation of gender roles. They had jobs and sometimes belonged to

Jewish Man with Sons for the Priestly Blessing An observant Jewish man places his hands on his sons in blessing in Jerusalem. His prayer shawl with its fringes is on their heads. Kinship and honor, prime social values of Mediterranean-Jewish peoples, are reaffirmed in this blessing. Note in the background the fence with the women watching from their area. Used by permission of BiblePlaces.com.

private associations. The Jewish and Hellenistic societies in which they participated and in which Christianity spread were largely urban and marked by social and economic stratification. These social features combine in a powerful mix in early Christianity. Unlike most religions of the Greco-Roman world, Christianity made a wide appeal to various social groups, treating them with a significant measure of equality for the times. For example, Paul wrote: "There is no longer Jew nor Greek, slave nor free, male nor female; for all of you are one in Christ Jesus" (Gal 3:28). Conflict over these social issues often surfaces on the pages of the NT.

The anthropological method so important in the social scientific reading of the NT studies wider cultural aspects as well: language, art, belief, and the rest. It pays attention to comprehensive social values employed in a society, such as the **honor-shame paradigm:** a main purpose of life, it is said, is to bring honor to oneself and family and avoid shame. In the NT, the synonyms of honor include such terms as respect, reverence, tribute, glory, prize, reward, and good reputation; the synonyms of shame include dishonor, insult, disgrace, disregard, and punishment. The social scientific reading of the NT also studies broad patterns of relationships, such as the patron-client relationship, and it examines **kinship** in particular. In general, anthropology seeks to understand the characteristics of different kinds of humans in their social, cultural context, deriving these from the study of contemporary cultures and applying them to ancient cultures. In all its study, anthropology seeks to construct overarching typologies, models that it uses to study a number of cultures. Those who employ it can be divided into two camps. The first camp is those who give anthropology a historical orientation, often calling themselves *social historians*; they integrate sociology and/or anthropology with the historical-critical method. Most NT researchers using the social-scientific method are in this group. The second is those who look upon their work as more purely social scientific, working with models and data without strong reference to historical questions.

www   For an excellent site that introduces social scientific criticism by applying it to the Gospel of Mark, see Daniel Schrock's "Windows into the World of Jesus" site.

Social scientists have delineated the **Mediterranean person,** a figure who is relevant for NT study. Putting the social scientific dynamics of ancient Mediterranean persons in their culture in contrast with our modern North American culture, the main differences can be suggested in Table 2.1.

NT scholars debate the limits of social scientific methods as they apply to the NT. Some say it is not applicable as a truly scientific method because we have so little "hard data" on social institutions in the NT world, and it is difficult or impossible to use a quantified scientific method on the ancient world, let alone apply the experimental method to it. Others criticize the social scientific method for painting with too broad a brush—for example, that all people who lived in the eastern part of the Roman Empire can be characterized as a "Mediterranean" type of person, that there were few significant cultural differences between Jews and Gentiles, and that the maintenance of honor was the prime value for every social transaction. Other issues surround the social scientific method of interpreting the NT. Is this method new and distinct enough from previous historical-critical study to be a method in its own right, as Christopher Tuckett has questioned (Tuckett 1987, 142)? Do the NT documents merely indicate and promote the social realities of the early Christian communities, or could they also work against them, as when Christians subverted the honor-shame typology by their new norm of humility? Finally, does some social scientific reading give too much emphasis to matters of economics and social class, making religious ideas and life secondary? Despite all these questions and criticisms, the application of social scientific theory to NT study is valuable. It provides a comprehensive, fascinating framework to understand both

Table 2.1 A Comparison of Jesus' Mediterranean-Jewish Social World and 21st-Century Mainstream North America

First-Century Palestine	Twenty-First-Century Mainstream North America
Life expectancy is an average 20 years at birth. At age 5, it doubles to 40 years. Only about 5% live to 60 years.	Average life expectancy is about 75–80 years.
"Family" means an extended group of relatives, usually 2 or 3 generations, living together.	"Family" means immediate parent(s) and children. Grown children generally do not live with their parents.
Family life is controlled by **patriarchy** (male power). Husbands are in charge of their wives. Fathers rule family life and have a general authority over their married sons.	Married couples can choose to have a patriarchal marriage, an equalitarian marriage, or something in between. Parents have no formal authority over their married children.
Parents arrange marriages for their children according to social customs, often when they are very young. Virtually all young people marry.	Young people choose on their own whom they want to marry, when they marry, or even if they marry.
The ideal mate is usually a cousin or other relative outside the immediate family.	Laws generally require that first cousins or other close relatives do not marry; custom extends this restriction more widely.
Married children live with the groom's parents and inherit their house.	Married children usually live in a new residence.
All real and personal property is passed on to one's family. The oldest son receives a double portion of the inheritance, other sons a single portion. Daughters when they marry receive a dowry, a financial gift of some substance but much less than the single portion inherited by second sons.	No fixed inheritance rules; parents can, with a legally binding will, dispose of their property inside and/or outside the family as they see fit. Wedding gifts from parents to married children are informal and usually do not represent a significant portion of the parent's wealth.
One's primary identity, social standing, and occupation come from **kinship:** belonging to a particular family and its economic status.	One's primary identity and social standing come from one's chosen occupation, especially the income it generates. One's identity can also derive from a spouse's standing.
The main purpose of life is to accumulate and retain honor for one's group and oneself and keep away shame.	A main purpose of life is individual happiness, which is usually linked to financial success. Honor and shame are more individual than social realities.
This world has **limited goods.** One must keep the goods of one's group	The world has unlimited goods; wealth can be "created." Each individual should

(continued)

Table 2.1 Continued

First-Century Palestine	Twenty-First-Century Mainstream North America
intact to pass them on to succeeding generations. To become significantly richer is to leave one's group (family and social class) and is done to other people's detriment.	have the opportunity to become as financially well off as possible. "Rags to riches" is a prominent and powerful North American ideal.
Ritual purity is an objective matter, and purity rules about matters like eating and sexual activity keep things clean and "in their proper place."	Purity rules have largely disappeared, to be partially replaced by loose social customs and individual preferences.

www See the website for a succinct introduction to four main social scientific paradigms: honor-shame, kinship, social standing and limited goods, and purity-pollution.

the cultural background and the theological foreground of the NT. It enables us to see and understand all the important cultural values (such as the honor-shame mentality) that are hidden from our view because they are simply assumed and shared by all, and rarely spoken of explicitly. "What belongs to the foundation is hidden from sight." There is enough variety among practitioners of this method that good academic disagreement can occur, as for example in John Elliott's recent assertion that Jesus' primary value of kinship in the kingdom of God rules out the increasingly common notion that he led a movement of radical social equality of all persons (Elliott 2003). Social scientific criticism has a growing presence in NT scholarship, and reading the NT today likely will call for more application of social scientific knowledge.

Feminist Reading

One of the largest social changes in the twentieth century, and one that has continued into the twenty-first, is the liberation of women from traditional attitudes and practices that made them subservient to men. Despite the political struggles over feminism, and despite its unfinished state, this movement has already transformed our North American society and is spreading throughout the world. In North America, the aspects of all our lives—men's as well as women's—have radically changed as women have gained freedom: marriage and singleness, family life, business, government, academia, and religion. This movement's methods of reading the NT are in the process of reshaping biblical scholarship.

Feminism identifies a wide social, political, and academic movement that works to understand the structures of society that give women a second-class status and transform these structures. **Feminist criticism** of the NT is the study of gender issues in the NT to promote the equality of women today. It not only *describes* the NT but, more important, *prescribes* a remedy for continuing gender inequality. Just as feminism affirms and promotes the full humanity and equality of women, it rejects anything that diminishes this full humanity and equality. It therefore has an adversarial function, to critique all forms of patriarchy and oppression, and a proactive function, to strive in interpretation and life towards fulfilling a vision for the reform of the world. Feminism is built on the experience of women but is not exclusive to women, except among its most uncompromising practitioners. Male readers of the Bible can also engage in feminist criticism to a certain degree, following the example of women.

The origins of feminism in America (and the world, since feminism is largely American in origin) are directly linked to the earliest feminist reading of the Bible. In 1898, Elizabeth Cady Stanton's *The Woman's Bible* launched a public debate in the United States about the Bible and its authority. Stanton saw how translation and interpretation had broad implications in how the Bible was represented in 1898 and used against women. In this period, it was unpopular for women to read the Bible with a woman's intention and offer, through their interpretations, a critique of society and the church. The practice of feminist criticism has always recognized that understanding the NT is a social activity and that texts have a wide impact that go beyond the purely "religious." How the academy and the church read the NT has profound and concrete religious, political, and cultural implications for women and for men. The issue of how one reads is further shaped by who is doing the reading. Privileging women's experiences, concerns, and interpretations lies at the heart of feminist reading. In some quarters, feminist reading of the Bible is just as controversial today as it was a century ago, but it is without doubt a leading method of biblical study.

> **www**   Follow a link to the Introduction to *The Woman's Bible.*

From its beginnings, feminist interpretation has been concerned with both the theory and the practice of interpretation. Feminist criticism is not a unique method in itself but embraces a variety of methodological approaches and disciplines. Most, but not all, of feminist reading continues to draw on the historical method and recently has made use of the social scientific method. Women reading the Bible as women, and men using feminist methods, represent diverse perspectives. They address diverse issues associated with the theory of interpretation: what one reads, how one reads, and especially how the reading process impacts the reader and the community in which a text is read. The feminist scholar approaches and studies these issues recognizing that the NT is a product of ancient patriarchal cultures. Feminism also practices a **hermeneutic of suspicion,** a belief that the surface of the text is covering up an important truth deeper within it, a truth that the modern interpreter must uncover.

(**Hermeneutics** means "interpretation," in its widest sense the meanings and methods of understanding a text.) The feminist use of the hermeneutic of suspicion goes against the patriarchal grain of most of the NT to uncover a deeper, inclusive meaning that is more in line, feminists believe, with its religious message as a whole. This uncovered meaning is sometimes referred to as the *transcendental framework of reference* and is used as an interpretive tool to correct the patriarchy of the NT.

Some feminists view the NT as so hopelessly and irredeemably patriarchal, and its views of God and/or human life so objectionable, that they do not spend their time interpreting it. A more moderate feminist dissent is offered by Kathleen Corley, who argues in her *Women and the Historical Jesus* that the authentic teaching of Jesus does in fact critique class and free-slave distinctions in his culture, but that his critique did not extend to gender distinctions, either in his teaching or his practice. In other words, Jesus was not concerned about women's liberation (Corley 2002).

Feminists who do research on the NT fall into three main stages, as outlined by Phyllis Trible (Trible 1982). The first stage, beginning about 1970, was concerned with *description*. Feminists first examined the Bible to document its attitude to women, much of which was negative. This scrutiny uncovered abundant evidence of patriarchy, and the resulting inferiority, subordination, and even physical abuse of women in the Bible from its beginning to its end. To some this stage of feminist criticism seemed negative and destructive. The second stage is one of *recovery*. Certain feminists who have moved through the first stage defend that stage as a necessary "clearing of the ground" to recover the liberating inner message of the NT. In the recovery stage of feminist criticism, the Bible's critique of patriarchy is explored and applied. Female imagery for the divine, especially the female figure of Wisdom, and the few leading females from Eve to Mary the mother of Jesus remind us that a voice for women's equality can be found in the biblical tradition, even if the larger, stronger voice is that of men asserting their right to rule. Some feminist scholars examine both ancient extrabiblical texts and the ancient social world. They reconstruct the wider role of women in those times, against which they compare the biblical views of women. In other words, feminist interpretation strives to "recover the female presence and voice." The third stage Trible analyzes is a sympathetic *retelling* of the general role and specific stories of women from a liberating point of view. It entails making the female voice of the NT challenge the male voice. Since about 1980, this stage of feminist criticism has led to gender-inclusive English translations (e.g., "brothers" has often become, where the meaning warrants, "brothers and sisters"). Now, in the current generation of feminist interpreters beyond the range of Trible's essay, we can discern a fourth stage beginning roughly around 1990, which might be called the *holistic* stage. It analyzes entire NT documents, not just the parts that deal with women, in full-scale scholarly studies, using feminist methods of reading on the entire NT.

www   Follow the link to the full text of Trible's essay online.

Another recent development in feminist interpretation is **womanist criticism,** or women's liberationist interpretation by African American women. They have had a very different experience with the Bible and American culture than traditional feminists, who strongly tend to be white and middle to upper-middle class. Womanists generally feel a strong bond to African American male interpreters; bonds of ethnicity have proven as strong, or stronger, than bonds of gender. The word *womanist* was coined in the 1970s by Alice Walker, the noted African American novelist, as a word play on the folk term *womanish.* In traditional African American culture, "womanish" refers to the self-assertive behavior of young black women before they are socialized into patterns of patriarchy. Womanist criticism affirms the assertive interpretation of the Bible by African American women. Hispanic American women have also contributed to feminist reading of the NT. **Mujerista** ("moo-hair-EES-tuh," from the Spanish for "woman") **criticism** of the NT focuses on liberative reading by Hispanic women. Coined by Ada Maria Isasi-Diaz in the 1990s, the word *mujerista* refers to Hispanic or Latina women living in North America who struggle to free themselves from the particular male dominance ("machismo") of Latin American culture.

In sum, feminist reading of the NT, like the feminist movement as a whole, has often been controversial in wider society. However, because of its scholarly passion and productivity, its developing perspectives on the NT that male scholars have neglected, its ability to "bring aboard" male scholars to its aims and methods, and its widespread influence not just in biblical study but in all fields of the humanities, feminism promises to be a leading method of reading the NT for generations to come.

www   Follow the link to a site that features condensed versions of notable works by feminist NT scholars.

Cross-Cultural Reading

Most North Americans today recognize that we live in a culturally diverse time and place. The number of different ethnic groups in North America grows constantly, as does the proportion of ethnic minority groups to the majority European Americans. Some of our cities—New York and Toronto, for example—are the most culturally diverse urban areas in the world. Recently, immigrants have taken to settling directly in our small towns and rural areas as well. The rapid growth of cultural diversity brings social and political challenges, but we experience this growing diversity by working in the same offices, factories, and farms (although often not at the same rates of pay). We increasingly enjoy each other's foods, music, and other aspects of culture. Expressions like "a global village" and "a shrinking world" are overused, but they do speak the truth—our lives are increasingly becoming a cross-cultural experience.

Cross-cultural criticism or reading is the use of contemporary experiences and concepts of non-European and non-European American peoples in the reading of the NT. In a sense, all interpretation of the Bible in the modern world is cross-cultural, because no one today lives in the cultures of the Bible and reads it from its own cultural home. The NT itself shows that much of early Christianity was explicitly cross-cultural, reaching across the large barrier between Jews and non-Jews to many different peoples and expressing its message in their languages and cultures. For centuries, European and European American scholars adopted the historical-critical method and newer methods of reading (such as feminist and narrative readings) using Western experience. In the last half of the twentieth century, scholars from other cultural backgrounds have recognized the limitations of these Western approaches. Moreover, they have begun to develop and employ interpretive methods that are more indigenous (native) to their cultures. These methods are employed in the local indigenous settings, but they also are published and shared more widely with people who read NT from other cultural backgrounds, so that the word *cross-cultural* takes on a fuller meaning. East Asians, Africans, African Americans, Indians, Palestinian Arab Christians, and others have engaged this enterprise. Of the methods of reading the NT considered here, cross-cultural criticism is the newest. Because it is so new, with the first publications in this area coming from the 1990s, it goes by several other names: cultural interpretation, Third World criticism, and postcolonial or decolonial criticism. Within this broader orientation, cross-cultural interpretation pays attention to matters of race, class, and gender. Like feminist reading, cross-cultural reading explicitly promotes liberation. (At this point you may profit from reading the "Story of Mama Africa and the Story of the Healing of the Bleeding Woman [Mark 5:21–43]" in Chapter 6).

Because cross-cultural interpretation is specific to the scholars who write from various cultures, we must sample briefly some important recent publications. This will illustrate the astonishing breadth of cross-cultural interpretation. First, here in North America, African American biblical scholars have contributed books like *Stony the Road We Trod: African American Biblical Interpretation,* by Cain Felder of Howard University (Felder 1991). Two books by Brian Blount of Princeton Seminary have made an important contribution to cross-cultural interpretation with some African American applications (Blount 1995, 2001). Gay L. Byron's recent book on color and ethnic differences in early Christianity examines both pejorative and idealized representations of Egyptians, Ethiopians, and blackness in the NT and other early Christian writings (Byron 2002). Leading NT scholar Fernando Segovia of Vanderbilt University introduces cross-cultural criticism from a Hispanic context (Segovia 2000). The best introduction for students to North American cross-cultural biblical criticism is by Miguel De La Torre of Hope College, *Reading the Bible from the Margins* (2002), which gives cross-cultural readings from several different perspectives.

Armed Israeli Women in Jerusalem Israeli women make their way up Ben Yehuda Street in the New City section of Jerusalem. They are armed with automatic military rifles, a not uncommon sight in Israel, for defense against possible Palestinian guerrilla attacks. The long-standing Palestinian-Israel conflict is a sad example of two liberation movements contending against each other. Palestinian Christians (who typically do not engage in terrorist attacks) have begun to use cross-cultural reading of the NT to struggle for their liberation. Used by permission of BiblePlaces.com.

These studies aim to show how understanding the NT from African American and Hispanic American experience reveals more clearly the underlying message of liberation in the Bible. The readings are typically done with a strong combination of traditional scholarly methods, especially the historical-critical method and methods influenced by social location.

The second area of cross-cultural study is Africa. There the influential New Testament scholar Musa Dube of the University of Botswana has edited *Other Ways of Reading: African Women and the Bible* (Dube 2001), and (with Gerald West) *The Bible in Africa* (Dube and West 2001). She has also written a general introduction to postcolonial feminist interpretation of the Bible (2000). The essays in her edited volumes are by dozens of different scholars from different parts of Africa and the

African diaspora, and they testify to the variety of social locations, reading communities, and approaches to NT study in Africa today. The third area of cross-cultural reading of the Bible is Asia. Among Asian and Asian American scholars, the work of two scholars is notable: Yeo Khiok-khng of Northwestern University and his book *What Has Jerusalem to Do with Beijing? Biblical Interpretation from a Chinese Perspective* (Yeo 1998); and Kwok Pui-lan of Harvard University and her book *Discovering the Bible in the Nonbiblical World* (Kwok 1995). Indian biblical scholars are well represented by the work of R. S. Sugirtharajah of the University of Birmingham, England (1998, 2001). Note that these scholars, while speaking about the NT from their own cultural context, have been trained in and/or have academic positions in Euro-American institutions of higher education. This has led to a rich interplay of academic interpretive methods with the indigenous aspects of the cross-cultural approach. Many scholars who still use Western methods have taken up cross-cultural study. European and European-American scholars have also recently taken up cross-cultural issues such as color and ethnicity. For example, a good deal of current research into the theology of the apostle Paul deals with questions of Jew and Gentile in an ethnic—not just religious—perspective.

However, one must avoid overgeneralizing—not every scholar from the developing world uses cross-cultural methods. Some have received university training in Europe and North America, where there has been little feeling for cross-cultural concerns until recently. Others, regardless of where they took their education, are more attached to other methods. An example is the recent book by the Filipino American scholar Narry Santos, whose book on the Gospel of Mark uses historical, narrative, and reader-response criticism, but not cross-cultural methods (Santos 2003). Moreover, some scholars who use cross-cultural methods are not from the developing world but are Europeans and European Americans.

www   For an example of a European scholar who probes cross-cultural issues, follow the link to Mark Goodacre's thought-provoking essay, "Jesus as a Person of Colour."

In conclusion, cross-cultural reading has made a strong contribution to the globalization of NT study. Although it is the youngest of all the new major methods of reading the NT, it has made an immediate, creative impact. Because it is in part NT scholarship's response to the pluralism and globalization of life and academic study today, cross-cultural reading will likely be a major part of NT study in the foreseeable future.

www   Discussion of methods tends to be abstract. For a brief essay demonstrating how these major historical and newer methods can actually be applied to one NT passage, Matt 12:1–8, see the website.

The leading questions of the main methods of reading the NT are listed in Table 2.2.

Table 2.2 *Leading Critical Methods and Their Key Questions*

The Historical-Critical Method

Who wrote it, and for whom? When was it written?
What is the historical setting of the writer and readers?
Why was the document written?
What is the meaning of the text to the author?
How might the first readers/listeners have understood it?

A. Textual Criticism
   What is the most likely original wording of the text?
   How and why did changes occur?

B. Source Criticism
   Can we detect sources the writer may be using?
   How does the writer use those sources?

C. Form Criticism
   What units of oral tradition ("forms") do the gospel authors use?
   How do these forms reflect the situations of the early churches before the
      gospels were written?
   How does the Greco-Roman letter form influence the writing of the
      NT letters?

D. Redaction Criticism
   Can we detect the words of the final Gospel author, added to his source?
   Are there obvious omissions or changes in the narrative from the source?
   Can we detect the writer's point of view, and the overall presentation of the
      writer's story?

Social Scientific Criticism

   What types of social relationships and worldviews are found in the NT?
   What cultural values do the NT writers accept, and which do they reject or subvert?
   How does the religious message of particular NT documents form and promote a
      "symbolic universe"?

Narrative Criticism

   How do the NT stories function?
   What are the roles of character, setting, and plot?
   What is the distinction in the story between real author and implied author, between
      real reader and implied reader?

Feminist Criticism

   How are female characters portrayed in the narrative?
   When the text does not portray women, why not?
   Can the interpreter detect a certain bias toward women that limits their abilities or
      place in society?
   What elements of the text may be resources for women's liberation?
   Can a more inclusive view be found in the text to guide our understanding of its
      overall patriarchy?

(continued)

Table 2.2 Continued

Cross-cultural Criticism

What is the "social location" of the text?

What is the "social location" of today's reader, and how does it influence the reading of the text today?

What resources for liberation and other human advancement can be found in the text?

Adapted from Selvidge 1999, 48.

www Read a brief discussion of other new methods used less frequently in NT study than these major methods: psychological criticism, the new literary criticism, reader response criticism, structuralist criticism, canonical criticism, and theological criticism.

Conclusion

With all this variety in method, what methods are most appropriate in reading the NT? The choice of method(s) can best be made in response to the questions that the interpreters bring. If they are primarily concerned with the history that the text describes, they will use methods effective for reconstructing history. If they are interested in social meanings of the NT, they will use a social scientific method. If they are primarily concerned with the literary significance of the text, they will use methods effective for literary analysis. However, many contemporary interpreters adopt an eclectic method, combining two methods into one reading. Most often this is a combination of the historical method with another, newer method. Despite the perceived weaknesses of the historical-critical method, it remains a foundational way of reading the NT for most interpreters. The newer methods can also be combined, for example, into socio-rhetorical criticism and narrative-feminist criticism. The variety of critical methods indicates not so much a quest for a new single approach as an acceptance of the necessity of a variety of readings to bring out the richness of the NT.

Key Terms and Concepts

autograph • biblical criticism • codex • criticism • cross-cultural criticism
feminist criticism • form criticism • hermeneutics • hermeneutic of suspicion
historical-critical method • honor-shame paradigm • internal evidence
kinship • limited good • manuscripts • Mediterranean person
mujerista criticism • narrative criticism • papyri • patriarchy • pericope
purity and pollution • redaction criticism • *Sitz im Leben* • social scientific criticism
source criticism • tendency • textual criticism • textual variant • tradition criticism
womanist criticism

Questions for Study, Discussion, and Writing

1. Explain in your own words why textual criticism of the NT is necessary and how it is done.
2. Why have so many different ways of reading the NT arisen in the last twenty years or so?
3. Are the different "advocacy" criticisms (feminist and cross-cultural, for example) an appropriate way to read the text, in your opinion? Is it important for them to be objective?
4. Why has feminist criticism of the NT proven to be so popular and yet so controversial?
5. Can a man be as effective a feminist reader of the NT as a woman? Why, or why not?
6. Why do so many of the other, newer methods considered in this chapter arise from the field of contemporary literature?
7. Some scholars have argued that womanist and mujerista approaches to the Bible are more properly considered cross-cultural than feminist. Why would they make such a claim? What is your conclusion on this issue?
8. Review Table 2.1 on the different social worlds of ancient Mediterranean times and our modern North American culture. What differences impress you most, and why?
9. View the 2002 hit movie, *My Big Fat Greek Wedding*, directed by Joel Zwick, written by and starring Nia Vardalos, and list the characteristics of Mediterranean culture portrayed in the film. For an excellent film that addresses feminist issues in a traditional culture, in this case the Maori of New Zealand, see *Whale Rider*, directed and written by Niki Caro.
10. Reflect on this statement: "Cross-cultural reading of the Bible is not a matter of choice. Since the Bible is a Mediterranean document written for Mediterranean readers, it presumes the worldview of a reader socialized in the Mediterranean world. This means for all North Americans, reading the Bible is always an exercise in cross-cultural communication."

For Further Reading

De La Torre, Miguel A. *Reading the Bible from the Margins*. Maryknoll, NY: Orbis, 2002. The best introduction for students of cross-cultural criticism.

Elliott, John H. *What Is Social-Scientific Criticism?* Guides to Biblical Scholarship Series. Minneapolis: Fortress, 1993. A well-written, authoritative introduction to social scientific criticism of the NT.

McKenzie, Steven L., and Stephen R. Haynes. *To Each Its Own Meaning: An Introduction to Biblical Criticisms and Their Application*, 2nd ed. Louisville, KY: Westminster John Knox, 1999. Excellent coverage of historical-critical methods as well as social scientific, narrative, feminist, and others.

Perrin, Norman. *What Is Redaction Criticism?* Guides to Biblical Scholarship Series Philadelphia: Fortress, 1969. An introduction to this aspect of historical criticism by one of its leading practitioners.

Powell, Mark Allan. *What Is Narrative Criticism?* Guides to Biblical Scholarship Series. Minneapolis: Fortress, 1990. A succinct introduction to this topic.

Rohrbaugh, Richard, ed. *The Social Sciences and New Testament Interpretation.* Peabody, MA: Hendrickson, 1996. Excellent essays by leading scholars on the various dimensions of social scientific study of the New Testament and its world; one of the best resources for beginning students.

Sugirtharajah, R. S. *Voices from the Margin: Interpreting the Bible in the Third World,* rev. ed. London: SPCK, 1995. A collection of important, interesting essays on its topic.

Tuckett, Christopher. *Reading the New Testament: Methods of Interpretation.* Philadelphia: Fortress, 1987. A fine introductory treatment of historical-critical method and newer methods, especially social scientific and structuralism.

Wimbush, Vincent. *African Americans and the Bible: Sacred Texts and Social Textures.* New York: Continuum, 1999. The introductory article and the article by Barbara Holdrege are particularly useful for beginning students.

Chapter Three

The Jewish Matrix of the New Testament

Reading the pages of the New Testament, one becomes aware of a curious fact: the text is immersed in two very different cultures, the Jewish and the Greco-Roman. Pharisees and Sadducees; Jewish priests and common people; Roman emperors, governors and soldiers; and Greek philosophers all have left their footprints on its pages. As historians and social scientists would explain it, Jewish culture is Middle Eastern and Semitic by heritage, Greco-Roman culture is European, and the NT mixes them together. This is true of its religion, politics, family life, economy, and many other cultural aspects. In other words, the NT has two matrices that strongly interact and, to a significant extent, overlap. In this chapter we will examine the highlights of the Jewish matrix of the New Testament. The birth of Christianity cannot be understood without an understanding of Judaism, nor can the New Testament be understood without a basic knowledge of the Hebrew Bible/Old Testament.

A Brief Review of the Essentials of Jewish Religion

By the time of Jesus, the Jewish religion was already ancient. It had undergone a long development: first, a stage in which it is properly called *Hebrew religion,* its very beginnings with Abraham through Moses in the second millennium B.C.E.; then an *Israelite religion* stage in the united and divided kingdoms of Israel in the early first millennium; and finally a stage in which the religion is properly called *Judaism,* from the sixth century B.C.E. until today. At every stage, there was always some internal variety. This is especially true of the **Second Temple period** of Judaism (sixth century B.C.E. to 70 C.E., so called because the second Jewish temple stood in these years). No longer do scholars talk, as they did until about a generation ago, of "normative Judaism," especially as represented by the Pharisees. As we will see in this chapter, the Judaism of the first century C.E. was diverse and dynamic.

Even though the idea of "normative Judaism" has rightly fallen into disuse, first-century C.E. Judaism did have important common features. The main ideas of Judaism, and their antecedents in Israelite and Hebrew religion, can be outlined as follows.

The first is **monotheism**, the belief that only one God exists in and beyond the universe. The *Shema* from Deut 6:4-9 was said daily by most Jews. In the Ten Commandments (Exodus 20), the first and foundational command is to acknowledge the one God alone. God is not depictable in anything but words because God is a purely spiritual and eternal Being. God made the world as a good place, but humans rebelled against God and brought sin and death into the world. But God is still holy, just, and loving, as evidenced by God's establishment of a covenant to bring about the world's salvation. Because God is in fact the only God who exists, those who serve other gods and their idols are worshiping beings that live only in their imagination.

The second important feature of Second Temple Judaism was the notion of the Chosen People. Israel understood itself as chosen by God from among all the nations of the earth to be God's own people. Like monotheism, this belief has roots in the beginnings of Israel but becomes firm in the Second Temple period. It formed the basis of wars of Jewish independence from the second century B.C.E. to the second century C.E., and it gave Jews a desire to maintain their separateness from non-Jews, or *Gentiles*. Ritual purity was important in this separateness, requiring ritual baths, kosher foods, special clothing, and other requirements. The positive side of being the Chosen People gave the Jews an ability to survive and often thrive in a hostile world. The negative side was that it could lead to exclusivism toward Gentiles and a harsh attitude to other Jews who did not seem to measure up to the standards.

The third important commonality was observance of the teaching and law of God, the **Torah.** This practice flows from both monotheism and being the Chosen People: because the one God is radically good ("holy"), and because God has chosen Israel, Israel must be good. God has revealed the Law especially in the Ten Commandments (Exodus 20), and they are worked out in other laws that follow in Exodus, Leviticus, and Deuteronomy. God gave the Law to Israel so that they would know how to live, to serve God in love and obedience, and to treat others justly. Although we today make distinctions between *moral* law and *ritual* or *ceremonial* law, ancient Jews most often did not. Torah observance was so important that when the Roman armies swept away the Temple in the first century C.E., Pharisees survived to reconstitute Judaism into the form that has lasted through today.

This leads us to the fourth and final characteristic, the place of the **Temple,** the sacred complex in Jerusalem where sacrifice was offered to God and God was thought to dwell. Although it was destroyed in 70 C.E., the Temple was the focal point of Jewish life in Judea and the wider world. Indeed, "Jewish" meant "Judean"; the center of Judea was Jerusalem, and the center of Jerusalem was the Temple. The Temple was home to the priesthood and controlled by the high priestly families whose alliance with changing governments gave them a great deal of political power, social standing, and wealth. The Temple was the only place where sacrifice could be offered to God for forgiveness and divine blessing on Israel. Other gods of ancient Mediterranean peoples each had temples in many places, but Israel's God had only one Temple, and this fact served as long as the Temple stood to unify Israel. Of all the places on earth, the Temple was God's home, and therefore the place to encounter God. Although Jews like those at Qumran denounced the Temple's operation, and although Jesus "cleansed" the Temple by physically attacking its moneychangers and animal sellers, "the disputes and denunciations relating to the Temple do not amount to a dispute regarding the fundamental importance of the Temple itself. On the contrary, it was because the Temple was so important that disputes about its correct function were so important" (Dunn 2003, 288).

www   Follow the link to a guide to high-quality websites for the study of Judaism.

Origin, Development, and Structure of the Hebrew Bible

The Hebrew Bible had a long history of formation in oral tradition, transcription in writing, and editorial polishing. Because this process of development is shrouded in the mists of antiquity, scholarly judgments vary, but the following summary description has some consensus. The writing probably began about 1100 B.C.E., after the Israelites entered Palestine, when the oldest sections of poetry and historical narratives were written (e.g., the "Songs of Moses and Miriam" in Exodus 15; the "Song of Deborah" in Judges 5). Under Solomon, the story of his father David began to be written (II Samuel 9—1 Kings 2). One source of the Torah, which told of creation and the **patriarchs** (Abraham, Isaac, and Jacob, the male founders of Israel) as a prelude to the formation of Israel, was written in southern Israel. Another source of the Torah was written in northern Israel from a northern religious and political perspective.

The eighth century B.C.E. saw a flowering of literary effort. The disciples of the prophets Amos, Hosea, Isaiah, and Micah began to write down their words. When the north fell in 721 B.C.E., the sources mentioned earlier were combined into the *Old Epic* narrative to give us much of our present Genesis. In 621 B.C.E., the finding of a law scroll in the Jerusalem temple, a scroll probably containing the substance of Deuteronomy 12–26, gave an impetus for the writing of the rest of that book.

The Exile in Babylon (587–539 B.C.E.) was a fruitful period of literary activity. Jeremiah, Ezekiel, and "Second Isaiah" (chapters 40–55) were largely written by their disciples. The Deuteronomic history (Deuteronomy, Joshua, Judges, I–II Samuel, and I–II Kings) was probably completed at the end of the Exile. Priestly sections of the Torah were completed, and many of the Psalms were written down. After the Exile, Jewish scriptural activity centered on Jerusalem and its temple. More prophetic books were completed: "Third Isaiah" (Isaiah 56–66), Malachi, and Joel were written, and Haggai was edited to its final form. By the year 400 B.C.E., the Torah probably reached its present form as it was finished and edited by the Jerusalem priests, becoming the first and primary section of Jewish scripture. Genesis through Deuteronomy was labeled Torah, and Moses was said to be its author. Around 350 B.C.E., the historical work of the Chronicler, I–II Chronicles and Ezra-Nehemiah, was completed. The later wisdom books, Job and Ecclesiastes, were compiled, and two short stories, Ruth and Esther, appeared. By 200 B.C.E., the eight-book section known as Prophets was complete. The final stratum of the Jewish scripture was in the apocalyptic mode: Isaiah 24–27, Ezekiel 38, and especially the book of Daniel, the last book to be written, in 160 B.C.E. The Writings section was basically collected by about 100 B.C.E., but the canonical status of some books in it (especially Esther and the Song of Songs) was debated later.

The full and formal canonization of the entire Hebrew Bible as we now have it—the **Law (Torah)**, **Prophets**, and **Writings**—took place at the end of the first century C.E. No one disagreed on the books of the Torah and the Prophets; this had been settled for several centuries. The Jewish council at Jamnia (about 90 C.E.) seems to have ruled on the writings as we have them, but it took some years for this ruling to be widely accepted. The main criterion for canonicity was the recognition that God was revealed in these books and spoke to his people in them. Canonization did not *confer* scripturality on a book. Rather, it was the official and formal recognition of a longstanding reception and use of these books as holy and scriptural by the Jewish community itself. Once it was given, canonization helped reinforce their holiness and authority. The structure and content of the Jewish Scriptures are summarized in Table 3.1.

The order of the books of the Jewish Bible more familiar to Christians is based on their Greek translation made before Christianity began, the Septuagint. This order is charted in Table 3.2.

Palestine from Alexander's Death to Roman Occupation

Following Alexander the Great's death in 323 B.C.E., his generals vied for control over parts of the vast territory he conquered. This conflict brought turmoil, hardship, and suffering to the Jews living in their ancestral land. Warfare between Seleucid Syria and Ptolemaic Egypt for control over Palestine raged for a generation following Alexander's death, devastating the land and its people. Egypt finally established its control over the region in about 305 B.C.E.

The Jewish relationship with the Ptolemies was ambivalent. Under different Ptolemaic kings, the Jews were sometimes respected, sometimes tolerated, and sometimes persecuted. Ptolemy I ruled Jerusalem with an iron hand and enslaved many Jews, yet he also extended citizenship to the Jews of Alexandria. The Torah was translated into Greek by order of Ptolemy II Philadelphus. The resulting version of the

Table 3.1 *The Books of the Hebrew Bible*

Division	English Name	Hebrew Name	Chapters
Torah ("Teaching, Law")			
	Genesis	*Bereshith* ("in the beginning")	50
	Exodus	*Shemoth* ("names")	40
	Leviticus	*Wayiqra* ("and he called")	27
	Numbers	*Bemidbar* ("in the wilderness")	36
	Deuteronomy	*Debarim* ("words")	34
Nevi'im ("Prophets")			
	Joshua	*Yehoshua*	24
	Judges	*Shofetim* ("judges")	21
	1, 2 Samuel	*Shemuel*	31, 24
	1, 2 Kings	*Melakim* ("kings")	22, 25
	Isaiah	*Yeshayahu*	66
	Jeremiah	*Yirmeyahu*	52
	Ezekiel	*Yehezqel*	48
	The Twelve:		
	Hosea	*Hoshea*	14
	Joel	*Yoel*	3
	Amos	*Amos*	9
	Obadiah	*Obadyahu*	1
	Jonah	*Yonah*	4
	Micah	*Micah*	7
	Nahum	*Nahum*	3
	Habakkuk	*Habaqquq*	3
	Zephaniah	*Zephanyah*	3
	Haggai	*Haggai*	2
	Zechariah	*Zekaryahu*	14
	Malachi	*Malaki*	4
Kethuvim ("Writings")			
	Psalms	*Tehillim* ("Praises")	150
	Job	*Iyyob*	31
	Proverbs	*Mishle* ("Proverbs of")	42
	Ruth	*Ruth*	4
	Song of Songs	*Shir Hashirim* ("Song of Songs")	8
	Ecclesiastes	*Koheleth* ("Preacher")	12
	Lamentations	*Ekah* ("How")	5
	Esther	*Ester*	10
	Daniel	*Daniel*	12
	Ezra-Nehemiah	*Ezra-Nehemyah*	10, 13
	1, 2 Chronicles	*Dibre Hayamin* ("words of")	29, 36

Table 3.2 *The Books of the Greek Version of the Jewish Bible, the Septuagint*

Genesis	Job
Exodus	Psalms
Leviticus	*Odes
Numbers	Proverbs
Deuteronomy	Ecclesiastes
Joshua	*Wisdom of Solomon
Judges	*Wisdom of Sirach
Ruth	*Psalms of Solomon
1 Kings (1 Samuel)	Isaiah
1 Kings (2 Samuel)	Jeremiah
3 Kings (1 Kings)	Lamentations
4 Kings (2 Kings)	*Baruch
1 Chronicles	*Letter of Jeremiah
2 Chronicles	Ezekiel
*1 Esdras	Daniel
2 Esdras (Ezra-Nehemiah)	*Susanna
*Tobit	*Bel and the Snake
*Judith	Hosea
Esther	Joel
*1 Maccabees	Amos
*2 Maccabees	Obadiah
*3 Maccabees	Jonah
*4 Maccabees	Micah
	Nahum
	Habakkuk
	Zephaniah
	Haggai
	Zechariah
	Malachi

*These apocryphal, or deuterocanonical, books are not included in the canon of the Hebrew scriptures or in the Bibles of most Protestant churches. They are included in the Bibles of the Eastern Orthodox, Roman Catholic and Anglican churches, but the Catholic and Anglican canons exclude 1 Esdras, 2 and 4 Maccabees, Odes, and Psalms of Solomon. Some Bibles used by Orthodox Christians omit 4 Maccabees, Odes, and Psalms of Solomon.

Hebrew Bible is the **Septuagint** (in Greek the number 70, for the legend that seventy scholars did the work; thus this version is often known by the Roman numeral for 70, **LXX**). Under all the Ptolemies, observant Jews on the land in Palestine were exploited and kept down by the favor extended to people of Greek descent and Jews who took on Greek ways. Likewise, the response of the Jews to the Hellenistic culture and rule of the Ptolemies was mixed. In Egypt itself, many Jews held on to their religious identity and observance of the Law of Moses but were Hellenized in all other cultural respects, even though this distinction between religion and culture was much harder to make in the ancient Mediterranean world than it is today. In Jerusalem and its immediate environs, old cultural and religious practices were maintained, but the economic and social pressures to adopt Greek ways were strong.

Since Palestine was exploited as a source of agricultural production and tax revenues, numbers of Jews migrated to Egypt, where the soil was better. Others went to seek the opportunities available to those who were willing to Hellenize and whose talents might be of use to the Ptolemaic administration.

In 201 B.C.E., Antiochus III of Seleucid Syria invaded Palestine and after a three-year conflict wrested control of Palestine from Egypt. At first, the new face of Hellenistic rule over the Jews living in Palestine appeared to be a favorable change. Antiochus III extended benevolence to the Jews in gratitude for their assistance during the war and to make up for the deprivation and suffering the war had caused them. He ordered the restoration of property to Jews imprisoned and enslaved under the Ptolemies. The Jews were allowed to maintain their ancestral customs and to govern themselves according to the Mosaic Law. Antiochus paid for improvements and repairs to the Jerusalem Temple and provided financial support for the cult. He reduced taxes across the board and exempted from taxes Jewish civil officials and religious functionaries. Antiochus III's successor, Seleucus IV, continued his liberal policies. Under the third Seleucid to rule Palestine, Antiochus IV, Jewish fortunes changed.

Under early Seleucid rule, a movement toward full Hellenization among some of the leading Jews in Jerusalem had begun to grow. When Antiochus IV assumed the Seleucid throne in 175 B.C.E., he inherited a large war reparation debt as a result of the Roman defeat of Antiochus III at the Battle of Magnesia in 190. Antiochus IV began looking for creative ways to finance this debt. Jason, a leader of the Hellenistic Jewish group and the brother of the Jerusalem high priest Onias, offered Antiochus a large sum of money in exchange for appointing him high priest in the place of Onias. The agreements seemed good for both: Antiochus discovered a means to raise some of the funds he needed, and Jason received the power he needed to further his group's dreams for promoting the complete Hellenization of Judaism. The sale of the high priestly office proved to be the match that touched off explosive revolt in Jewish Palestine. Jason introduced major religious changes at the Temple and established a gymnasium in Jerusalem, where observant Jews were aghast to learn that other Jewish males were exercising in Greek fashion, naked. (Traditional Semitic society sees nakedness in social settings as deeply shameful.) Intrigue within the Hellenistic party led to Jason's ouster in favor of Menelaus in 172 B.C.E., but Menelaus continued Jason's program of religious and cultural Hellenization that infuriated Jewish traditionalists. In 169, Antiochus IV, still strapped for cash, decided to campaign against Egypt in the hope of defeating the Ptolemies and exacting tribute from them. When he was ordered by the Romans to desist from his military adventurism, he tried to alleviate his shame by sacking Jerusalem, which in its civil and religious unrest had become an aggravation to the Seleucid ruler. He ransacked the Temple and stripped it of its adornments. Two years later, his troops returned, stormed Jerusalem, constructed a citadel there, and established military oversight of the city. He then issued a decree making Greek cultural ways and Hellenistic polytheism compulsory for all his subjects, effectively outlawing Judaism (see 1 Maccabees 1:41–50). The Jerusalem

Temple was dedicated to Olympian Zeus. Pigs—a traditional sacrifice to Zeus but a gross impurity to the God of the Jews—were sacrificed on its altar. Syrians forced the Jews of the city to violate their dietary laws. Circumcision was forbidden upon pain of death. Books of the Law of Moses were destroyed.

The **Hasmonean** family, a priestly clan from the Judean village of Modein, organized a resistance movement under the leadership of Mattathias, the Hasmonean patriarch. In a short time Mattathias died, but his son, Judas Maccabeus (*Maccabeus* = "the hammerer"), led a brilliantly successful campaign against the Seleucid forces sent to crush the revolt and was able to retake the Temple three years after its cult was outlawed by royal decree. The Jewish struggle against Seleucid control did not end with the recapture of the Temple. The decrees of Antiochus IV banning the practice of Judaism were not officially repealed until 162. Judas continued to lead the Jewish revolt until he died in combat in 160. His brother, Jonathan, then took control of the Jewish resistance and was later named high priest. Eventually Jonathan was captured and executed through an act of treachery by a man named Trypho who aspired to the Seleucid throne. The conflict between the Jews and their Seleucid overlords dragged on until 140, when Judas's younger brother, Simon, expelled all Seleucid forces from Jerusalem and claimed the high priesthood.

www   Follow the link to primary texts on these events.

The Hasmonean Dynasty

Simon was the last, and perhaps greatest, of the sons of Mattathias to be leader of the Jews in Palestine. The people in Judea accorded him full political and religious power. According to 1 Maccabees, Simon retained his primary position of leadership under the title of high priest and enjoyed great popularity. But in 134 B.C.E.. he was assassinated by his son-in-law in an act of intrigue that would become all too characteristic for Jewish politics during the reign of the Hasmoneans and beyond. John Hyrcanus, who ruled as high priest for a period of thirty years, succeeded Simon. Hyrcanus extended his territorial control into the neighboring lands of Samaria and ancient Moab, forcing the inhabitants of these territories to observe Jewish customs. At his death, his eldest son, Aristobulus, who became the first Hasmonean to assume the title of King of Judea, succeeded John. Aristobulus continued the expansionist policy of John Hyrcanus, conquering neighboring Itrurea and forcing its inhabitants to proselytize. Aristobulus distrusted his family. He had his brothers imprisoned and is accused by the ancient Jewish historian Josephus of murdering his mother (*Antiquities of the Jews,* 12.11). Aristobulus died after a short reign and was succeeded by his brother, Alexander Jannaeus, who ruled for twenty-seven tumultuous years. Jannaeus' rule was not popularly accepted by many of the Jews, particularly the Pharisees, a group we will hear more about later. He executed many of his domestic opponents, including numbers of Pharisees, and many others fled into exile. Jannaeus continued the expansionist policies of his predecessors and died in 76 B.C.E. on a military campaign into neighboring territory.

Following the brutal Alexander Jannaeus, the political situation in Judea deteriorated rapidly. Jannaeus bequeathed the throne to his wife, Alexandra, who had also been married to his brother Aristobulus. She ruled for nine years. At her death in 67 B.C.E., her sons Hyrcanus II, who was high priest, and Aristobulus II contested the throne. Civil war broke out, with forces loyal to Aristobulus fighting against the forces of Hyrcanus. The Arab King Aretas of Petra joined the fight on the side of Hyrcanus at the urging of the Idumean nobleman, Antipater. Antipater sought to weaken the position of the more capable Aristobulus. This struggle for power might have continued indefinitely had the superior power of Rome not intervened. The Romans had been allies of the Jews against the Seleucids, whose empire fell to the Roman general Pompey in 64 B.C.E. After completing his conquest of Syria, Pompey turned his attention southward. He was greeted by Jewish delegations imploring him to stop the devastating civil war in Judea. He was also met by delegations from both Hyrcanus and Aristobulus seeking to enlist Roman aid. In the end Hyrcanus, in exchange for the high priesthood, threw in his lot with the powerful Roman general, who took Aristobulus prisoner and entered Jerusalem. Aristobulus' troops held the Temple precincts and offered resistance, but after a three-month siege they capitulated, thus putting an end to Judean autonomy and the Hasmonean dynasty. Judea and Galilee became a part of the Roman Empire.

Herod the Great

While Hyrcanus gained the high priesthood by the power of Rome, his old ally Antipater also gained Roman favor and was named governor. Antipater named his son, Herod, governor of Galilee. **Herod the Great** demonstrated a tenacious ability to increase his power in turbulent times. In 40 B.C.E. Antigonus, the son of Aristobulus II, attempted a coup in Jerusalem with the backing of the Parthian Empire, which had invaded Syria. Herod went to Rome, where the Senate named him King of Judea. He returned to Judea and in 37 B.C.E. defeated Antigonus with Roman support. Amid an unstable Roman political situation during the fourth decade B.C.E., with the intrigues surrounding Mark Antony, Cleopatra VII, Julius Caesar, and Octavian, Herod deftly switched his allegiances and remained in favor with Rome. At home in Judea he systematically eliminated the remaining members of the Hasmonean family, including his own wife, Mariamne, and his mother-in-law, Alexandra. With the ascension of Octavian in 27 B.C.E. as Caesar Augustus, Herod was firmly established as King of Judea.

Herod ruled over Judea as a great benefactor. He built whole cities, such as Caesarea, and fortresses, such as Herodium and Masada, as well as a magnificent palace and amphitheater in Jerusalem. Most notably, he expended a great amount of funds on the improvement and adornment of the Temple in Jerusalem. Despite the costs of these monumental architectural projects, he managed to cut taxes twice

The Jerusalem Second Temple In this model of the Second Temple of Jerusalem at the Holyland Hotel in Jerusalem, the main Sanctuary of the Temple, in which is the Holy Place and the Holy of Holies, is seen at the rear. In the foreground, behind the front entrance, is the Court of the Women, then up the steps is the Court of the Israelites (men); the Court of the Priests is in front of and around the Sanctuary building. The pavement surrounding the walls is the Court of the Gentiles. Used by permission of Niel Bierling/Phoenix Data Systems.

and increase the prosperity of many of his subjects. Furthermore, Herod was keenly aware of Jewish customs and religious sensibilities and generally avoided offending his subjects on these grounds. Despite his public works and benevolence, however, Herod remained an unpopular ruler. Many of his subjects regarded him as a usurper—an Idumean (Arab) convert to Judaism who ruled only by virtue of his relationship with the Romans. His ruthlessness increased as he aged, especially toward his own family, as his murder of three of his sons demonstrates. And while Herod's massacre of the children of Bethlehem recorded in Matt 2:16–18 is not attested to elsewhere, such an event indeed reflects the increasing paranoia and cruelty of Herod's later years. For example, when he sensed the imminence of his death, he ordered a group of leading Jews executed when he died, so that if the nation would not mourn *because* he died they would nonetheless mourn *when* he died. In 4 B.C.E., Herod died, but the order was not carried out.

Emperor Augustus then decided to break down Herod's dominions into three smaller administrative areas. He named Archelaus *ethnarch* ("ruler of a nation/people") of Judea proper (Matt 3:19–23); Antipas became *tetrarch* ("ruler of a fourth part,"

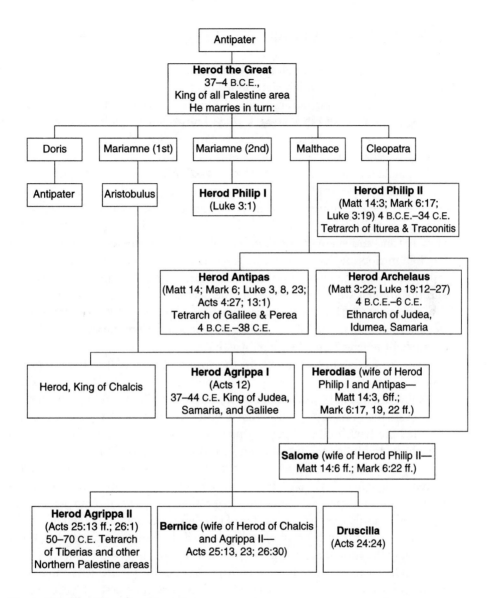

Figure 3.1 The Herodian Dynasty

Names appearing in bold type are those family members who are mentioned in the NT. Dates given are those of reigns.

rather a putdown) in Galilee, and Philip, another of Herod's sons, became tetrarch of Itrurea (Luke 3:1). Archelaus' rule in Judea was brief and intolerable. In 6 C.E., a combined Judean and Samaritan delegation traveled to Rome and requested relief from his tyranny. The Romans deposed Archelaus and exiled him to Gaul (modern France). (For an explanation of the complex Herodian dynasty, see Figure 3.1)

Direct Roman Rule in Judea and the Jewish Revolt

After Archelaus, Judea was ruled by Roman prefects until 41 C.E. Following an interlude from 41 to 44, in which Herod the Great's grandson, Agrippa I, ruled as king, Judea was placed under the authority of Roman procurators until the Jewish revolt of 66. The prefects and procurators, often known simply as "governors," had little sensitivity to Jewish culture and religious particularity. The best known of these men is **Pontius Pilate,** a Roman member of the equestrian class, who began his rule as prefect in 26 C.E. and before whom Jesus stood trial. Shortly after coming to power, Pilate used Temple funds to build an aqueduct for Jerusalem, which led to Jewish protests that were suppressed at the cost of many lives. The emperor removed Pilate from office in 36, after he used excessive force in dispersing a relatively harmless crowd. Time and again, heavy-handed rule and insensitivity by Roman governors resulted in riots and protests by the Jews. Time and again, such protests were brutally put down. The Jews chafed under Roman taxes and Roman military presence, and the Romans were antagonized by the peculiar ways and obstinacy of the Jews. The situation deteriorated into the Jewish revolt of 66–70 C.E., which ended with the destruction of Jerusalem, including its magnificent Temple and the displacement (again) of the Jews from their ancestral land.

This revolt began as follows. In the spring of 66 C.E., the Roman procurator Florus, in an attempt to shore up his dwindling power in Judea, staged a murderous show of force in Jerusalem. As tension escalated, Rome and its Jewish allies lost control of the situation. Jewish rebels quickly organized into an effective army, expelled the Jewish client-king Agrippa, seized the Roman forts in Jerusalem and elsewhere, and killed the pro-Roman high priest. Meanwhile riots broke out in the cities and towns of mixed Jewish-Gentile population, where Jews and Gentiles massacred each other. For example, the entire Jewish population of Caesarea, some twenty thousand people, perished. Later that year, the Roman general Gallus assaulted Jerusalem with a large force of ten thousand men. But when he abandoned the attempt, the Jewish army bravely pursued the Roman army and destroyed it. Gallus and the survivors returned to Antioch, and the Jews established a short-lived independent state that had its own coinage. At first the government remained in the hands of the members of the Jewish elite, whom a popular assembly elected to positions of military leadership. In the spring of 67, Vespasian invaded Palestine from Syria with two legions and his son Titus from Egypt with one. With the addition of auxiliaries, cavalry, and contingents from client kings, Vespasian's army numbered about 60,000. The conquest of northern Palestine, completed by the end of 67, involved no pitched battles and only a few difficult sieges. The most famous of these occurred at Jotapata, where, after losing all of Galilee but a few fortresses, the Jewish commander Josephus defected to Rome and became a protégé of the future emperor.

Meanwhile Jerusalem descended into chaos as the militant Jews purged the city of supposed Jewish sympathizers of Rome and long pent-up religious and class

Table 3.3 *A Basic Timeline of Judaism from the Babylonian Exile to the Mishnah*

Persian Period: 538–334 B.C.E.
    Founding of Persian Empire: 538 B.C.E.
    Jewish return from Exile in Babylon: 538 B.C.E.
    Jerusalem ("Second") Temple built: 520–515 B.C.E.
    Reform led by Ezra and Nehemiah: 450–400 B.C.E.
    Torah (Pentateuch = first division of Jewish Scripture) begins to gain recognition
        as Scripture: c. 450 B.C.E.

Hellenistic (Greek) period: 334–63 B.C.E.
    Alexander the Great conquers Palestine: 331 B.C.E.
    Palestine under Ptolemies and Seleucids: c. 320–168 B.C.E.
    Septuagint: c. 250–200 B.C.E.
    Prophets (second division of Jewish Scriptures) recognized by some as Scripture
        by c. 200 B.C.E.
    Maccabean revolt and end of Seleucid rule: 167–160 B.C.E.
    Qumran community founded: c. 150 B.C.E.
    Jewish independent kingdom under Hasmoneans: 142–63 B.C.E.
    Rome annexes Palestine: 63 B.C.E.

Rule of Rome in Palestine: 63 B.C.E.–400 C.E.
    Herod the Great, Jewish client-king of Palestine: 40–4 B.C.E.
    Herod captures Jerusalem and marries the Hasmonean princess Mariamne I:
        37 C.E.
    Herod and his successors rebuild the Temple in Jerusalem: 20 B.C.E.–70 C.E.
    Rome establishes direct rule of prefects in Judea: 6 C.E.
    Philo of Alexandria, leading Hellenistic Jewish thinker: c. 13 B.C.E.–after 41 C.E.
    Jesus: c. 4 B.C.E.–c. 30 C.E.
    Gamaliel I (Jewish leader-scholar): fl. c. 40
    Paul called and ministers as an Apostle: c. 36–64
    Josephus (Jewish leader, historian): c. 37–100
    Emperor Claudius expels Jews from Rome: 49
    NT writings: c. 50–125

Rabbinic Jewish Period: 70–200 C.E.
    First Jewish Revolt against Rome: 66–73
    Pharisee academy established at Jamnia/Yabneh, becomes the center for
        rabbinic Judaism: 69
    Destruction of Jerusalem and the Second Temple: 70
    Jewish sectarians, including Christians, excluded from the synagogues: c. 90
    Writings (third division of Jewish Scriptures) accepted as scriptural: c. 90–150
    Rabbi Akiba active in consolidating Rabbinic Judaism: 120–135
    Bar Kokhba rebellion (Second Jewish Revolt), with complete devastation of
        Jewish life and property in Palestine: 132–135
    Emperor Hadrian renames Jerusalem Aelia Capitolina and builds a pagan temple
        over the site of the Second Temple: 136
    Mishnah (first written compilation of rabbinical oral law) compiled and edited
        under Rabbi Judah the Prince: c. 200

animosities were violently vented without any restraint. In 68, Vespasian permitted the capital to self-destruct while he conquered the rest of Palestine. The death of Nero in June of 68 interrupted this work except for limited operations in the spring of 69. The Roman army in Egypt declared Vespasian emperor in July of 69, and only after his armies had secured his throne did Vespasian have Titus resume the Jewish war. The capture of Jerusalem took all of the summer of 70 and ended in the utter destruction of the city, including its fortified places and the temple. The Romans destroyed Jerusalem so thoroughly, Josephus reports, that visitors could scarcely believe anyone had ever lived there (*Jewish War* 7.1.1). It became little more than a garrison town. Titus left for Rome, where he and Vespasian celebrated with a triumphal parade, passing through a triumphal arch built for the occasion that still stands today on the edge of the main Roman forum. Titus left the governors of Palestine to capture the last outposts of the rebels, the great fortresses of Herodium, Machaerus, and Masada. Masada fell last, after a short siege, in 73 or 74.

The failure of the revolt changed Judaism permanently. It brought the destruction of the Jerusalem Temple, the end of formal animal sacrifice, the abolition of the priesthood, the disappearance of the Sadducees and Essenes, and the dissolution of the Jewish ruling council. Leadership within Judaism passed to the Pharisee rabbis of Jamnia near the coast west of Jerusalem, who initiated the great transformation of Judaism into rabbinic Judaism that came to fruition in Galilee in the second, third, and fourth centuries.

Jewish Literature in the Hellenistic Age

Life for the Jewish people in the centuries following Persian rule was certainly tumultuous. However destructive the cultural and political turmoil of the Hellenistic and Roman periods were, it proved to be fertile for religious development within Judaism. The flourishing of religious thought among the Jews is reflected in the vast amount of religious literature produced during this time, and we gain a good deal of insight into the New Testament as we consider it within this stream. Three major strands of Jewish literary development from this period merit review in our study of the background of the New Testament: apocalyptic, narrative tales, and wisdom literature.

Apocalyptic Literature

The word *apocalyptic* comes from the Greek *apokalyptein*, which means to uncover or reveal. While the origins of the **apocalyptic worldview** have been debated for decades, it seems to have likely developed from the prophetic tradition in Israel. As the prophets reflected upon the covenant failures and subsequent suffering of the people of Israel, they began to understand more of the cosmic nature of evil. They became less certain that human suffering could be causally linked in every instance with human sin. They came to see evil as more powerful and mysterious than could be explained by the failure of human responsibility. As prophetic thought wrestled with the problem of persistent and universal evil, there developed the hope of a divine intervention into human history that would vanquish evil and usher in a new age free from suffering, oppression, and death. We glimpse the beginnings of this apocalyptic trend in the prophetic tradition in Ezekiel, Zechariah 12–14, Joel 3, and Isaiah 24–27.

The cultural and political upheaval the Jews experienced during the Hellenistic Age helped apocalyptic thought to flourish. A major underlying element in the clash between the Jewish and Hellenistic worldviews was their different interpretation of history. The Greeks generally understood history as cyclical, a process in which similar events were repeated over and over again as the result of fate. Jewish thought, focused theologically, understood history as linear, with a definite beginning in God and proceeding toward a definite goal determined by God. We can easily understand how the apocalyptic worldview, with its central theme of God's revelation of judgment and the establishment of a new order at the end of human history, was a powerful expression of revolt against Hellenistic cultural and religious imperialism.

Perhaps the best example of Jewish apocalyptic writing from the Hellenistic period is the book of Daniel, written during the reign of Antiochus IV. Daniel is not only apocalyptic in *content,* as outlined above, but also in *style*; it features visions, dreams, and time sequences that are all intentionally difficult to understand unless one is "inside" these forms of expression. In chapters 7–12, the book's hero has four visions that cryptically tell of the rise and fall of the four great imperial overlords of Judea—the neo-Babylonian, Median, Persian, and Seleucid empires—as if predicted from a past time. According to Daniel, the progressive evil of these empires only served to demonstrate that history was rapidly leading to God's final overthrow of evil and the establishment of the divine reign. The apocalyptic section of the book of Daniel introduces the "son of man" motif that became increasingly significant in apocalyptic literature of the period and carries over into the Synoptic Gospels. In Hebrew, the expression "son of man" (*ben 'adam*) means simply a member of the human race. But in Daniel this phrase takes on special meaning as it is employed in the phrase "one like a son of man," who is the agent of God's judgment in the end time. Here the son of man figure, one with human form, is contrasted to the evil empires that are portrayed in bestial form. Furthermore, the son of man figure in Daniel comes from heaven, as opposed to the beasts representing the empires that come up out of the chaos, represented by the sea.

Two other significant apocalypses from the Hellenistic Age are the book of Enoch and 4 Ezra. The protagonist of the book of Enoch is the seventh generation from Adam as recorded in Genesis 5. Enoch is recorded by Genesis not to have died, but to have been "taken" by God because he walked with God. The book of Enoch is believed to have developed from oral traditions about the patriarch and reached the form in which it is now extant in the first century C.E. The book of Enoch reports Enoch's visions of the heavenly realm as well as predictive visions of the end times, God's judgment, and the renewal of creation. Its high standing in first century Christianity is seen by the Apostle Paul's informal use of it, and its formal citation in 2 Peter. Fourth Ezra provides a series of visions attributed to Ezra the priestly scribe of the early Second Temple period. As with Enoch, Ezra's visions include the apocalyptic motifs of the coming reign of God established by a messianic son of man figure and God's judgment at the conclusion of history.

Apocalyptic literature sought to inspire faithfulness to historic Jewish traditions and the Torah under conditions of persecution and oppression by assuring readers that everything transpiring on history's stage was under the absolute control of God. Even though the outlook might seem desperate, the outcome was already determined in God's plan for history. The appropriate response was to remain faithful, even in the face of death, knowing that one would be vindicated in the God-determined conclusion of history.

Narrative Tales

Another literary form that inspired resistance to Hellenism was the *narrative story* of heroic faithfulness in the face of religious persecution. Here again the primary example of such a tale is the Old Testament book of Daniel. The first six chapters of Daniel tell several stories in which heroic faithfulness in the face of persecution is rewarded by God with miraculous deliverance from certain death. The most popular are the stories of the three young men in the fiery furnace (Daniel 3) and Daniel in the lion's den (Daniel 6). The stories are told in the setting of the neo-Babylonian and Median empires, but their theme of deliverance from evil rulers resonated with Jews facing forced apostasy during the reign of Antiochus IV. A significant motif of the narrative tales developed among the Jews during this period is the religious heroine. One example is the story of Susanna, a beautiful Jewish woman falsely accused of adultery. The story, which is an addition to the book of Daniel composed during the situation of Seleucid oppression and military occupation, is an exhortation to integrity and courage in speaking truth before power. Susanna is a symbol of resistance against overwhelming pressure. The book of Judith, which is included among the deuterocanonical books, is also set in neo-Babylonian times. Judith is the story of a pious Jewish woman of the same name who saves her city by killing Holofernes, the commander of Nebuchadnezzar's armies. Aspects of the story, such as the worship of Nebuchadnezzar as divine, the desecration of the temple, and the death of the leading general of the enemy's army, reflect events that occurred during the Maccabean revolt in the 160s B.C.E.. The book of Esther dates from the Persian period but was revered by many Jews of the Maccabean revolt. Esther's heroism saves her people from the evil plan of the king's courtier, Haman, to exterminate the Jews.

A deuterocanonical book also dating to the Persian period, Tobit, includes the character Sarah, whose continuing piety and trust in God in spite of the suffering and hardship she experiences serves as a model for others facing difficult times. Tobit and Esther demonstrate that this genre of religious literature probably had its origin in the Second Temple Period preceding Alexander's conquest of the East but fueled Jewish resistance to Hellenism in later years.

Wisdom Literature

In the Jewish **Diaspora,** the spreading or dispersion of the Jewish population from its ancestral home to throughout the Greco-Roman world from the sixth century B.C.E. onward, the need both to maintain Jewish identity and peacefully coexist with the dominant Gentile culture led to expansion upon the long-standing Jewish *wisdom tradition.* **Wisdom literature** in Judaism is represented in the Hebrew Bible by Job, some of the Psalms (such as Psalms 37, 73, 112), Proverbs, and Ecclesiastes. Wisdom thinking in this period, as before, dealt universally with the problems of human existence and the proper approach to life. It did not explicitly comment upon Israel's covenantal relationship with God or divine revelation, although Israel's sages grounded their thought in the Torah as the fountain of all wisdom. Because wisdom is open to the wisdom of other cultures, the Jewish sages of the Diaspora sought to be in dialogue with Hellenistic thought. They worked toward a synthesis of the Hellenistic philosophical traditions and the teachings of the Torah while establishing something of an apologetic for the Jewish religion.

Among the wisdom literature produced by Diaspora writers in the Hellenistic Age, the Wisdom of Ben Sira, sometimes called Ecclesiasticus or Sirach, and the Wisdom of Solomon are perhaps the best examples. Both books personify Wisdom in female form, since the words for wisdom in both Hebrew and Greek are feminine in gender. Both books portray Wisdom as the agent of God in creation, through whom creation is brought forth, ordered, and given a sense of purpose. In Ben Sira, Wisdom is identified as the reward of those who fear God and obey the Law of Moses (1:26). After her work in creation, God gives the people of Israel to Wisdom as her dwelling place on earth (24:8). In Ben Sira 24:19–22, in words that seem to be echoed by Jesus in John 6:35, she extends an invitation to anyone who would receive her:

> Come to me, you who desire me,
>   and eat your fill of my fruits.
> For the memory of me is sweeter than honey,
>   and the possession of me sweeter than the honeycomb.
> Those who eat of me will hunger for more,
>   and those who drink of me will thirst for more.
> Whoever obeys me will not be put to shame,
>   and those who work with me will not sin.

The Wisdom of Solomon is the work of an Alexandrian Jew of the early first or late second century B.C.E., presented as the thought of Israel's king noted for his wisdom. Originally written in Greek, the Wisdom of Solomon presents a synthesis of Hebrew wisdom with Hellenistic thought. As in Ben Sira, Wisdom is personified in female form and is known as God's agent in creation. In 7:25–26, the author blends together the Hebrew concept of wisdom with the Stoic Logos in much the same way that the first chapter of the Gospel of John identifies the Christ with the Logos ("Word") of God:

> For she is a breath of the power of God,
> and a pure emanation of the glory of the Almighty;
> therefore nothing defiled gains entrance into her.
> For she is a reflection of eternal light,
> a spotless mirror of the working of God
> and an image of his goodness.

A notable feature of the Wisdom of Solomon is the writer's presentation of belief in a personal afterlife based upon the Greek notion of the immortality of the soul rather than the Jewish concept of resurrection.

The identification of Wisdom with Logos reached its zenith in Philo of Alexandria, a Hellenistic Jewish philosopher contemporary with both Jesus and Paul. Philo wished to offer an apologetic for Judaism that would secure its respect in the Hellenistic world. He developed this apologetic by identifying the Torah as the real source of Greek philosophy. According to Philo, the Scripture of the Jewish people and the God presented in them were gross and barbaric to many Greek readers because they tried to understand them literally. He proposed that the Bible revealed its true wisdom only when interpreted allegorically. For instance, Philo interpreted biblical characters as personifications of Greek virtues. Philo had precedence for this kind of literary interpretation among Greek philosophers, who had interpreted Greek mythology allegorically. Philo's full identification of Wisdom with the Logos is a key element in his thinking. As the mental power of God, the Logos was God's agent in creation and the natural law of the universe. In Philo the Logos, as an emanation of God, was manifest as wisdom in the lives of the patriarchs. In early Christian thought the eternal Christ incarnate in Jesus of Nazareth was identified with Logos (John 1:1–14).

Judaism's encounter with a radically alien culture, and its revolt against that culture's domination, brought forth a new diversity in Jewish religious thought and literature. In the same way, it brought about divisions among the Jewish people into several parties whose origins are traced to Hellenistic times and who represented or were in some way influenced by that diversity of thought. These parties, or sects, were a part of the Judaism of Jesus of Nazareth, and so we turn now to a consideration of their place in our study.

Religious Groups in Second Temple Judaism

As is often the case with the rise of ideologies or particular party groups in a society, an exact date for the origin of the different groups that characterized late Second Temple Judaism cannot be pinpointed. The Jewish historian Josephus first mentions them in his writings treating Jewish history during the rule of the Maccabean high priest Jonathan during the mid-second century B.C.E. (*Antiquities,* XIII, 1–6). The divisions within Judaism were related to differences in the interpretation of Scripture, especially over differences in the eschatological thought found in the copious religious literature produced during the Hellenistic Age.

Sadducees

The name for the **Sadducees** may be derived from the name of the ancient high priest Zadok, who was the leading figure in the worship of Yahweh during the united kingdom of David and Solomon. They may have been the successors to a priestly group who had to struggle for control of the Second Temple against another group who traced their doctrine back to the patriarchal figure Levi. It has been commonly held that the Sadducees only accepted as authoritative the Pentateuch, the first five books of the Hebrew Bible, also known by its Hebrew name *Torah*. However, this may be an overdrawn conclusion. Certainly both groups maintained the Torah as primary. What is known with some certainty is that the Sadducees did not regard the oral tradition of law that the Pharisees maintained as binding. Since the Sadducees held strictly to what was written Torah, they necessarily rejected those teachings that could not be grounded directly therein, such as a doctrine of bodily resurrection, the existence of a human soul, or the developed eschatology presented in the apocalyptic writings.

The Sadducees followed a policy of compromise with the ruling political powers, whoever they happened to be. From a sociopolitical viewpoint, we can attribute this policy to the fact that the Saducean party was made up mostly of the wealthy and elite class within Judean society. Many, although perhaps not all, of those who held the office of high priest were Sadducees. They had the most to lose in any civil upheaval or struggle with an imperial overlord, such as the Seleucids or the Romans, and therefore sought to preserve their affluent way of life by maintaining the status quo. It would be unfair, however, to assume that the Sadducees operated solely on the basis of economic or political self-interest. The theology they derived from their interpretation of the Torah focused upon the establishment of an elect community who honored the Commandments and the system of priestly sacrifice revealed to Moses as the divine plan for Israel. In order to maintain the holy community in the Promised Land and the continuance of the Temple services, they were willing to collaborate with foreign rulers and even compromise with foreign culture, if need be.

www   Follow the link to a more detailed introduction to the Sadducees, with bibliography.

Pharisees

The most influential group within Second Temple Judaism was the **Pharisees.** Most scholars posit that the Pharisees were the theological and cultural descendents of the **Hasidim** ("separated ones"), who had opposed Hellenism and advocated strict observance of traditional Jewish cultural and religious practices. The Hasidim had backed the Maccabean revolt, but they became disenchanted with the later Hasmonean rulers, who took the title of king while still holding the office of high priest. They were especially abused by Alexander Jannaeus, whom Josephus reports killed many Pharisees who opposed him (*Antiquities*, XII, 13.2).

In their efforts to defend the Jewish religion and Jewish cultural ways, the Pharisees developed an extensive system of oral law. This system, called the **tradition of the elders,** was a method of Torah interpretation that sought to apply the Law of Moses to every facet of daily life. In so doing, the tradition served as a kind of fence around the Torah, which was meant to safeguard Jewish ancestral ways. Because their theological viewpoint included an oral tradition that applied the written law to the changing circumstances of daily life, the Pharisees were theologically able to incorporate later doctrines into their teaching, including the idea of bodily resurrection and the eschatological kingdom of God, established by the coming of a messianic figure.

The Pharisees' strong adherence to the tradition of the elders and their zeal for the Law of Moses caused them to be highly regarded by the majority of common people in Judea. For this reason, they were able to wield an influence in Jewish society that was well out of proportion to their own number. The Pharisees occupied positions on the Jewish Council, called the **Sanhedrin,** and sometimes even held the high priestly office during the Hasmonean era. During the Roman period of rule in Judea, the Pharisees promoted a policy of grudging toleration of Roman rule rather than either collaboration with it, like the Sadducees, or revolt against it, like the Zealots. They did not shy away from contact with Gentiles and even seemed to have sought some converts to Judaism among them (e.g., Matt. 23:15). In the name of purity, however, they maintained, as much as possible, separation from Gentiles. Thus they avoided the ritual contamination that close contact with non-Jews would bring, such as eating and drinking together or going into a Gentile's house.

www   Follow the link to a more detailed introduction to the Pharisees, ancient texts about the Pharisees and Sadducees, and writings by the Pharisees.

Essenes

Although the **Essenes** are not mentioned in the New Testament, it is important to study them in order to arrive at a fuller understanding of Judaism at the time of Jesus. They were not as numerous as the Pharisees, and we do not know for certain what the word *Essene* means. One proposed meaning is "those who do the law." But this gives us no insight into the group because the Sadducees and Pharisees had much the same self-understanding. From Josephus we know that the Essenes practiced an austere communal life (*War of the Jews* 2.8). A long admission process led to becoming an Essene, somewhat in the same way one would go through a trial period to enter a monastic community today. Most Essenes abstained from marriage, although there was an order of the group who did marry.

To identify the Essenes in comparison with the two previously mentioned groups is difficult. Like the Sadducees, the Essenes did not regard an oral tradition of law. However the Essenes seem to have been greatly influenced by the apocalyptic spirit and strove to lead a life of austere righteousness that would merit reward in resurrection at the conclusion of history. They were opposed to the Jerusalem priesthood, which they viewed as defiled and not carrying on the practice of the cult in faithfulness. Because they viewed the Pharisees as being too moderate in their adherence to the Law of Moses, they withdrew into the wilderness to live separately from less observant Jews and the Gentiles in traditionally Jewish cities. The Essenes have come to be generally identified with the **Qumran** community, who produced the **Dead Sea Scrolls.** The remains of the Qumran settlement along the shores of the Dead Sea and the scrolls, which were deposited in a nearby cave, were discovered in 1947. Among the scrolls were complete copies or fragments of all the books of the Hebrew Bible except the book of Esther. The exclusion of Esther may indicate the Essenes' rejection of the Festival of Purim, perhaps because it was a Jewish adaptation of a Persian celebration. Also found were copies of apocryphal writings from the Hellenistic Age and two manuscripts specific to the community: the *War Scroll* and the *Rule of the Community.* The *War Scroll* is an apocalyptic outline of the combat that will occur between the "sons of darkness" and the "sons of light" in the last days. The *Rule of the Community* was a manual of discipline regulating the life of the community and the behavior of individuals.

The Dead Sea Scrolls are an important source for understanding the background of the New Testament, because ideas once thought to be original to the New Testament have been found in these writings. For instance, according to what we find in the Dead Sea Scrolls, the Essenes of the Qumran community understood themselves as a community of a new covenant. Both Qumran Essenes and members of the early Christian community understood themselves as "sons of light;" both interpreted the prophetic writings of the Hebrew Bible in terms of their own experience; both celebrated a sacred meal of bread and wine. Some scholars have proposed that John the Baptist was, or had been, a member of the Essenes, given John's ascetic lifestyle in the wilderness and given that the Essenes are thought to have practiced a form of water baptism for purification. Other scholars have postulated that Jesus may have spent time among the Essenes. But until additional evidence is revealed, this hypothesis remains a conjecture. In any event, the possibility that John the Baptist's movement, and the Jesus movement that followed it, was influenced by the Essenes may explain some limited similarities between them but not the overall differences. As James Vanderkam has written, what differentiates the Essene movement from Christianity is the Christians' view that Jesus was "the messiah and son of God who taught, healed, suffered, died, rose, ascended and promised to return in glory to judge the living and the dead." (Vanderkam 1994, 184).

www Follow the links to two excellent websites on Qumran and the Dead Sea Scrolls.

Zealots

In Judea there may have been a fourth group, known as the **Zealots**, who maintained belief in a radical theocracy. (We say, "may have been," because current scholarship is divided on whether this was an organized group before the Jewish revolt in 66 C.E.) If they were a group, they were akin to the Pharisees, with the exception that they refused to acknowledge any king or ruler other than God and promoted revolution against foreign control of the land of Israel. They were also not opposed to visiting violence upon Jews who refused to support them in their fight against the Romans. The Zealot history goes back to Judas the Galilean (Acts 5:37), who led a revolt in opposition to the census taken under the Syrian governor, Quirinius. Although the Zealots probably were not solely responsible for the Jewish Revolt of 66–73 C.E., they certainly played a not insignificant role in the war's instigation. Another violent revolutionary movement in Judea at the time was the Sicarii ("Dagger men"), named after the short knives they carried and often used against Romans. The Sicarii were more noted for their terrorist tactics of assassination rather than any agitation for open revolt.

Other Groups

Several other groups within Judaism bear mentioning here, although they may not fit the category of religious parties. First among these is the Jewish **Diaspora** or dispersion; Jewish life and thought in the Diaspora is often referred to as **Hellenistic Judaism.** Significant Jewish communities survived in Egypt and Babylonia following the Exile of the sixth century B.C.E. The number of Jews in

Egypt grew significantly during the Hellenistic Age, and through them the Hebrew Bible came to be translated into Greek.

The Diadochi wars brought many Jews into Asia Minor, Greece, and Macedonia as war captives and slaves. Their descendants eventually established Jewish communities in many of the cities of these regions. Following the ascendancy of Rome, trade and new opportunities led to the establishment of a significant Jewish population in the imperial capital.

The chief cultural and religious institution of Diaspora communities was the synagogue. The establishment of a synagogue was incumbent upon every Jewish community where there were at least ten Jewish males. The Diaspora was not unaffected by the religious ferment in Judaism during the Greco-Roman period. Many Diaspora Jews were influenced by the eschatological prophecies of the apocalyptic writers, and many hoped for the coming of the messiah. The presence of Diaspora synagogues throughout the Mediterranean world was significant for the spread of Christianity in the first and second centuries.

A very large group within Second Temple Judaism that merits mention is the common people of Palestine. The Pharisees seemed to have referred to them as "the people of the land." They included artisans, peasant farmers, day laborers and slaves, and constituted more than two-thirds of the population. The common people were exploited by the ruling classes and often excluded from the full practice of their religion because of being ritually unclean. Scenes best known to the life of the common poor were often the context for the parables and analogies told by Jesus to illustrate the nature of the coming kingdom of God (cf. Matt 13:24–30; Mark 4:4–9; 4:26–32; Luke 12:22–31; 16:19–31). According to what we read in the Gospels, it was among the common people that Jesus most often practiced his ministry, and he gathered his leading disciples from among them.

We might also consider Jewish women as a separate group, socially if not politically. Jewish society was strongly patriarchal, even more so than Roman society. Full participation in Jewish religion was the provenance of men only. Women sometimes were held up as models of faithfulness and reverence for God (as we saw earlier in the narrative tales of the Apocrypha composed during the Second Temple period), but they were excluded from significant participation in the public practice of religion. Women were barred from entry into the inner courts of the Temple complex in Jerusalem and instead were forced to offer their prayers from an outer court reserved for them. The same kind of exclusion held true for synagogue worship. Jewish women had somewhat more freedom than Greek women of the earlier Classical and Hellenistic ages did, but less so than Roman women of the first century. Jewish women could not initiate divorce, but Jewish men could on even the smallest grounds (cf. Matt 19:3–9). Widowed women had little provision beyond remarriage to a near kinsman of their husband, according to the Hebrew Bible prescription.

Women Praying at the Western Wall A crowd of Jewish women prays at the women's section of the Western Wall. The segregation of women from men while women are in public is a common feature of traditional Mediterranean cultures and applies to most religious services as well. Note the large stone blocks used in the construction of this retaining wall, the only part of the Second Temple that remains. Used by permission of BiblePlaces.com.

We can see that a broader diversity existed within Judaism and among the Jewish people of the Greco-Roman period than we might at first think. However, three institutions regulated daily life and served as touchstones of identity for most Jews of the first century.

Institutions of Jewish Life

Three institutions gave shape and content to Jewish life and faith during the lifetime of Jesus and for most of the New Testament era. They were the Temple at Jerusalem and its worship, the synagogue with its social as well as religious function, and the Sanhedrin.

The Jerusalem Temple

The first **Jerusalem Temple**, completed about 922 B.C.E., was built under the reign of King Solomon. It was the center of religious life for the people of Israel until its destruction by the invading armies of the neo-Babylonians in 586 B.C.E. Jews who returned to their ancestral homeland after being exiled in Babylon constructed the Second Temple about 516 B.C.E. We have little solid information concerning what the early Second Temple looked like. In Ezra 6 we are given a list of dimensions, but these seem historically implausible since they describe a structure significantly larger than the First Temple. This Second Temple stood for nearly five hundred years. It was adorned by the gifts of foreign kings (Cyrus, Darius, Artaxerxes, Ptolemy II, Antiochus III) but suffered major damage in wars and reprisals (the Seleucid-Ptolemaic wars, the desecration of Antiochus IV).

We know much more about the reconstruction of the Second Temple undertaken by Herod the Great. Beginning about 20 B.C.E., the old Temple was completely torn down and a new one some 150 feet long was built in its place. The construction of the new Temple sanctuary was concluded rather swiftly—in about a year and a half. However, construction of the entire Temple complex went on for many years (cf. John 2:20, "This temple has been under construction for forty-six years"). Other auxiliary structures within the compound were also constructed. The surface area of the Second Temple complex was greatly expanded through the construction of massive retaining walls around the sanctuary and the filling of low-lying ground. The Western Wall in Jerusalem, which was part of this system of retaining walls, is all that remains of the Temple complex today. Most Jews consider it the holiest site in their faith. (For a map of the temple, see p. 156.)

The temple compound included three courts. Columns and porticoes surrounded the outermost court, the court of the Gentiles. The middle court was reached from the outer court via a short flight of stairs. Only Jews could enter the middle court, which was surrounded by a stone wall. All along the wall, inscriptions warned foreigners not to enter upon pain of death. On the east side of the middle court was located the women's court, with the inner part of the middle court reserved for ritually clean men only. The inner court was reached via a short flight of stairs from the middle court. Only the priests could enter the inner court, within which was located the temple sanctuary. Before the doors of the temple sanctuary stood the massive altar of burnt offering, 75 feet square and 22 $^1/_2$ feet high. The sanctuary itself—90 feet long, 30 feet wide, and 90 feet high—was reached from the inner court by another flight of stairs. It was divided lengthwise into the holy place (60 feet long), which contained the bread of the presence, the seven-candled lamp stand, and the altar of incense, and the **holy of holies,** the small room inside the sanctuary where the high priest offered incense on Yom Kippur, the Day of Atonement (30 feet long). While the holy of holies in the temple of Solomon contained the carved cherubim and the Ark of the Covenant, the holy of holies in the Second Temple was empty.

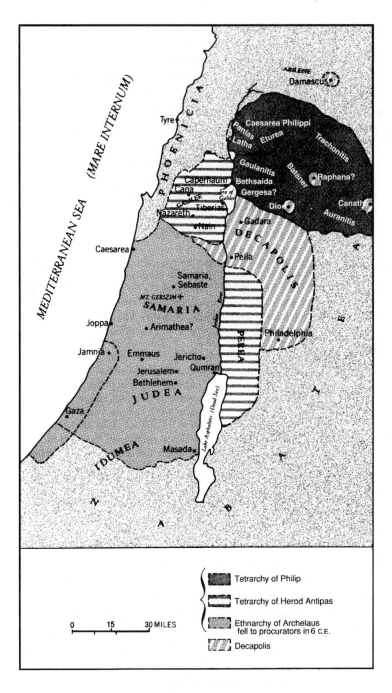

Map 3.1 The divisions of Herod the Great's kingdom, 4 B.C.E.

It took a great deal of money to support and maintain the temple and the sacrifices offered there. A one-half shekel tax was levied annually on all adult male Jews for support of the temple cult (cf. Matt 17:24–27, where Peter miraculously obtains the temple-tax coin), but occasional gifts from wealthy benefactors also helped maintain the sacrificial system. The priests sacrificed a lamb on the altar of burnt offering twice daily, morning and evening. Special offerings and sacrifices were also made on each Sabbath, at each new moon, and on festival days. Besides all these official, regular sacrifices, Jewish people would bring every day a much larger number of animals to be sacrificed for sin offerings, thank offerings, and the rest.

www   Follow the link to an interactive cybertour of the best-known model of the Second Temple.

Feasts and Festivals

The Passover and the Feast of Unleavened Bread commemorated the exodus from Egypt. At Passover, a yearling lamb was slaughtered by each Jewish household on the fourteenth of the first month and its blood sprinkled on the doorpost of the house in remembrance of the actions of the Hebrews in Egypt on the night when the angel of death spared the firstborn of every Hebrew household but struck down the firstborn of the Egyptians (Exodus 12). The related Feast of Unleavened Bread was a seven-day holiday commemorating the making of unleavened cakes by the Hebrews in their haste in leaving the land of their bondage (Exod 12:39). The Feast of Unleavened Bread was a pilgrimage festival, so many people came to celebrate both Passover and Unleavened Bread at the Temple.

Shavuot, or the Feast of Weeks, was a harvest festival celebrated seven weeks after the beginning of the barley harvest. This festival was also a pilgrimage festival. Since it was celebrated fifty days after the beginning of the harvest, it came to be known in the Greek-speaking world as *Pentecost* ("fiftieth"). It was at the Feast of Weeks, or Pentecost, that the New Testament records the outpouring of the Holy Spirit on the Church (Acts 2).

The first day of the seventh month was a day set apart for complete rest, marked by the blowing of trumpets, according to the prescription of Lev 23:23–25. In the third century C.E., this festival day became the Jewish new year's day, or *Rosh Hashanah* ("head/beginning of the year").

The most sacred day in the Jewish calendar is *Yom Kippur,* the Day of Atonement. Yom Kippur is celebrated as a day of repentance in order to receive forgiveness of sins. After the destruction of the Temple, Yom Kippur came to be celebrated in the synagogues with prayer and acts of confession. While the Temple stood, the Day of Atonement was a day for solemn assembly in which atonement was made for both the people and for the temple sanctuary. It was the only day of the year in which the holy of holies was entered, and only by the high priest. The entire ritual for the Day of Atonement is laid out in Lev 16:1–34.

The third prescribed pilgrimage festival in the Jewish calendar was the Feast of Tabernacles, or Booths (Hebrew, *sukkoth*). It was celebrated in the fall, at the conclusion of the harvest season. In the addresses given in John 7–8, Jesus analogizes on the rituals performed during the Feast of Tabernacles. On the first day of the festival, water was brought to the Temple from the Pool of Siloam; on the last day, the court of the Temple was lit with torches. These two ritual actions were the backdrop for Jesus' references to himself as the light of the world and the source of living water.

Hanukkah is a festival from Maccabean times, commemorating the rededication of the Temple after it had been desecrated according to the decree of Antiochus IV. Lasting eight days, this holiday was patterned after the Feast of Tabernacles (cf. 2 Maccabees 1:9). Hanukkah was the only major festival time celebrated in Second Temple Judaism that did not find its basis in the Hebrew Bible, and one of two festivals that do not date back to the time of the First Temple. Jews today celebrate Hanukkah with more emphasis than they did in the ancient world, since it was a "nonbiblical" feast; this increased observance may result from the pressure of the Christian holiday of Christmas, which falls near Hanukkah. The second of the two festivals not dating back to First Temple times was the festival of *Purim* ("lots"). Purim celebrated the deliverance of the Jews from the Persian holocaust planned by the courtier Haman. It was celebrated on the fourteenth day of the twelfth month in the Jewish calendar.

www   Follow the link to a website that provides an Orthodox Jewish explanation of biblical Jewish feasts today.

The Synagogue

Synagogue is from the Greek, meaning "a gathering." It is used to designate the assembly of people, in this case for worship, and also the place where they gather. The word *proseuche,* "place of prayer," was also in use in the Greek-speaking Diaspora. The synagogue probably originated in response to the destruction of the First Temple. However, the construction of the Second Temple did not obviate the need for the synagogue. The synagogue served functions in Jewish life that became imperatives after the exile and dispersal of the Jews that were not fulfilled by the Temple. Synagogues provided localized places for prayer and worship and, perhaps as important, served as centers for the study of the Law of Moses. Synagogues were also centers for Jewish community life, whether in Palestine or in the Diaspora.

In Jewish society, the synagogue combined the functions of the schools and voluntary associations found in Greco-Roman society. The synagogue provided a means of community organization and pooling of resources for such benevolent work as feeding the hungry, caring for the sick, providing for the care and education of orphans, and burying the dead. From an educational standpoint, religious education was the priority in Jewish society, and the synagogue schools taught the reading and writing skills necessary for the transmission and application of the Law of Moses. The Sabbath worship service of the synagogue featured prayer and the reading of scripture. The basic structure of the services has varied little through the centuries to the present time. The service typically opened with a call to bless the Lord, followed by the recitation of the *Shema* (Deut 6:4–9) supplemented with Deut 11:3–21 and Num 15:36–41. Then followed a liturgical prayer. After the prayer, two passages of scripture were read: one from the Torah and one from the Prophets. Following the scripture readings, a sermon was preached. Sometimes alms were collected for the poor, and additional prayers might be asked as the occasion called for.

A synagogue was established in every community where ten or more Jewish males were present to organize one. The chief official position in the synagogue was the "ruler of the synagogue." This official organized and presided over the synagogue services, guarded orthodox teaching, and served as a general overseer of the life of the Jewish community. The development of the synagogue in Jewish life was extremely important for the beginning of Christianity. It was in the synagogue that Jesus began his teaching ministry (see Matt 4:23; Mark 1:21; Luke 4:15), and it was to the synagogue that Paul first went to proclaim the gospel in whatever town he entered. Many aspects of early Christian worship were taken from the synagogue services with which the first Christian converts were familiar. The synagogue provided the early church with a proven model for institutional life in the Roman world.

www   Follow the link to take a closer look at Second Temple synagogues, especially the current scholarly controversy over whether there were synagogue buildings in Palestine during Jesus' day.

The Sanhedrin

Sanhedrin actually comes from the Greek word *synedrion,* which means "council." Sources indicate that there were local sanhedrins organized in many Palestinian towns of significant size. In the early Roman period the Jewish nation was divided into five districts, each with its own sanhedrin. The most important of these, however, was the Jerusalem Sanhedrin, which was regarded as a national body, the "Great Sanhedrin," since Jerusalem was the location of the ancient capital, the Temple and the seat of the high priest. The Jerusalem Sanhedrin, a legislative and judicial body of seventy men comprised of the leading priests, scribes, and Jewish lay aristocracy ("elders of the people"), was presided over by the chief priest. Although the Romans permitted local judicial bodies, such as the Great Sanhedrin, to administer justice in matters of customary local law, they also exercised a good deal of authority over them, too. For example, Josephus quotes members of the Great Sanhedrin as saying that it was unlawful to call a session of the Sanhedrin without the consent of the Roman governor (*Antiquities* 20.9). A good deal of scholarly debate has been expended on the exact nature of the Jerusalem Sanhedrin. Some sources from the early years of the Common Era speak of the sanhedrin, others mention the *gerousia* ("senate"), and still others speak of the **Beth Din.** One view posits that the Beth Din was a rabbinic council comprised after 70 C.E. to replace the Jerusalem Sanhedrin that disappeared with the destruction of the Temple. It was presided over by two leading scholars, the Nasi ("prince") and the Ab Beth Din ("father of the court"). The Beth Din's primary function was the interpretation of the Law for the regulation of Jewish life in the Diaspora in which all Jews found themselves following their expulsion from Judea. Another opinion maintains that there were actually two councils in Jerusalem before 70 C.E.: the Beth Din, whose function was interpretation of the Law of Moses; and the Great Sanhedrin, which was chiefly a political/judicial body. The former view seems the most likely, since no real distinction between matters religious and matters political existed in the Judaism of first-century Palestine.

Another source of debate is the question concerning the authority of the Sanhedrin to execute anyone it found guilty of a capital offense. Although Josephus indicates that the Sanhedrin had this authority during the time of Antipater (*Antiquities* 14.9), the account in John 18:31 seems to indicate otherwise. However, the accusations against Jesus seem to indicate that the official charge against him was a capital offense under Roman law (cf. John 19:7; 19:12; also Matt 27:11; Mark 15:12; Luke 23:2). It may be that in the case of Jesus the Jerusalem Sanhedrin actually served the function of a grand jury rather than a trial court. The testimony to conflicting charges against Jesus—blasphemy under the Law of Moses for claiming to be the son of God and the charge of treason under Roman law for his claim to kingship—perhaps serve theological more than historical purposes in the gospels.

www   Follow the link to a traditionalist Jewish presentation of the Sanhedrin.

Conclusion

Although we have surveyed the historical and cultural matrix of the New Testament as two distinct elements, the Jewish world and the Greco-Roman world, the boundary between those worlds at the time of the New Testament was not sharply drawn. The Jewish people struggled mightily to retain their particular national, cultural, and religious identity against Hellenistic cultural imperialism. Yet despite the ambivalence, and open hostility, between Judaism and Hellenism, there was a significant exchange of thought and ideas between the two cultures during the three and a half centuries immediately before the New Testament. The rise of apocalyptic thinking characterizes Judaism's resistance to the political and cultural pressures of

Greece and Rome, but the writings of Philo of Alexandria and the expansion of the wisdom tradition within Judaism illustrate something of the spirit that sought to accommodate Hellenism without capitulating to it. This cross-cultural exchange was not unidirectional. Many people in the Greco-Roman sphere were attracted to the monotheism and morality of the Jews while being repulsed at the same time by what they saw as Jewish cultural peculiarities.

Christianity and its New Testament in many ways show themselves to be the children of the rocky marriage between Hellenism and Judaism. The tragedy of their encounter figures into the death of Jesus. But in the New Testament one also hears the raucous sound of the apocalyptic tradition and the mellow strains of Logos philosophy played together; the spiritual search of the Greco-Roman world and the messianic expectations of Second Temple Judaism harmonize in the choir. In the resurrection narratives of the gospels, moreover, and in Paul's commentary upon the meaning of Jesus' resurrection, one hears a trumpet note of hope for their complete reconciliation on a cosmic scale. Christians believe themselves divinely charged with the mission of sharing with the world the cosmic hope they believe to be revealed in Jesus. The New Testament expresses the Christians' understanding of Jesus and the divine hope they believe to be manifest in him.

Key Terms and Concepts

apocalyptic • Beth Din • Dead Sea Scrolls • Diaspora • Essenes Hasidim • Hasmonean dynasty • Hellenistic Judaism • Herod the Great holy of holies • Jerusalem Temple • monotheism • patriarchs Pharisees Pontius Pilate • Prophets (scripture division) • Qumran • Sadducees Sanhedrin • Second Temple period • Septuagint (LXX) • synagogue Temple • Torah (the Law) • tradition of the elders • wisdom literature Writings (scripture division) • Zealots

Questions for Study, Discussion, and Writing

1. What factors at work in Jewish society during the Hellenistic Age gave rise to apocalyptic thought and literature?
2. How did sectarian divisions within Judaism develop from Judaism's encounter and conflict with Hellenistic culture?
3. Review the basic causes, course, and results of the Maccabean revolt.
4. How did the Sadducees, Pharisees, and Essenes differ? What characteristics did they all share? Discuss basic doctrines and social-scientific issues, especially purity.
5. Some scholars talk about "Judaisms," not "Judaism." Explain the possible rationale behind this practice.
6. Discuss the status and role of women in Greco-Roman and first-century Jewish society.
7. Describe briefly the role of the Temple in Judaism and its main activities.

8. Besides worship, what functions did the synagogue serve in Jewish society?
9. Why was the first Herod called "the Great"? In your opinion, was he truly great? Why or why not?

For Further Reading

Ferguson, Everett. *Backgrounds of Early Christianity,* 3rd ed. Grand Rapids, MI: Eerdmans, 2003. A clear, comprehensive introduction to both the Jewish and Greco-Roman backgrounds of the NT.

Hayes, John H., and Sara Mandell. *Jewish People in Classical Antiquity: From Alexander to Bar Kochba.* Louisville, KY: Westminster John Knox, 1998. A balanced, well-written introduction to Jewish history from 333 B.C.E. to 135 C.E.

Ilan, Tal. *Jewish Women in Greco-Roman Palestine.* Peabody, MA: Hendrickson, 1996. An examination of both the ideal and real relationships between women and men in Second Temple Judaism by a leading Jewish feminist historian.

Nickelsburg, George W. E. *Ancient Judaism and Christian Origins: Diversity, Continuity and Transformation.* Minneapolis: Fortress, 2003. An analysis of key elements of Second Temple Judaism in recent scholarship, with discussion of how each element may relate to early Christianity.

Saldarini, Anthony. *Pharisees, Scribes and Sadducees in Palestinian Society: A Sociological Approach.* Grand Rapids, MI: Eerdmans, 2001. An excellent introduction to the sociology of these movements.

Vanderkam, James C. *An Introduction to Early Judaism.* Grand Rapids, MI: Eerdmans, 2001. Provides a detailed commentary on the literature of Second Temple Judaism in an accessible style.

Vermes, Geza. *The Dead Sea Scrolls in English,* 3rd ed. Harmondsworth, UK: Penguin, 1984. Translations of the Dead Sea Scrolls in an inexpensive format.

Chapter Four

The Greco-Roman Matrix of the New Testament

What were the political, economic, and social conditions of the writers and first readers of the New Testament books? What were the ambitions and hopes of the people of that time and place? What were the cultural challenges faced by the first Christian communities to which the authors were responding? We can approach these questions more confidently as we understand the Greco-Roman context in which the New Testament emerged. They will form the necessary background for reading the New Testament with the various methods outlined in Chapter 2, methods that relate to history, society and culture, gender, and literature. Although the Jewish matrix of the NT was treated in the last chapter, the reader should remember that in the first century C.E. Jewish and Greco-Roman life are closely intertwined and must be understood together.

The Conquests of Alexander the Great

The documents that make up the New Testament were written during the first and early second century of the Common Era in the lands of the eastern Mediterranean. Occupied by peoples of diverse ethnic backgrounds, they were united under the rule of the Roman Empire. Although united *under* the rule of Rome, these lands and peoples did not experience their greatest degree of commonality *because of* the rule of Rome. The ties that existed between the different peoples of the eastern Mediterranean existed to a greater degree because of the ambitions of Alexander the Great.

Alexander was born crown prince of the ancient kingdom of Macedon (northern Greece) in 356 B.C.E. His personal tutor as he was growing up was the leading Greek philosopher Aristotle. In 336, he became king as Alexander III when his father was assassinated and became known to history as **Alexander the Great.** In 334 B.C.E., Alexander began his epic campaign against Persia, the traditional enemy of Greece. Crossing the Hellespont with an army of 35,000 soldiers, he defeated a larger Persian force near the ancient city of Troy. Continuing his march southward, Alexander engaged the main Persian army, under the command of King Darius III, in northeastern Syria. In 333 B.C.E., Alexander's armies were victorious and Darius fled.

Alexander then turned his sights on Egypt, and by 332 he had conquered Egypt and founded the city of Alexandria at the mouth of the Nile. In the following year he made a pilgrimage to the temple of the Egyptian god Amun-Ra, whom many Greeks identified with Zeus. The ancient Egyptian pharaohs were considered the divine sons of Amun-Ra, and Alexander may have sought this same recognition. Meanwhile, Darius was reorganizing his resistance. Alexander and his armies marched northeastward into the heart of Darius' Persian realm. In 331 B.C.E., the Macedonian invaders defeated the Persians finally and decisively at the Battle of Arbela. Alexander continued his conquest of the entire Persian Empire, leading his armies all the way into northern India. By the spring of 323 B.C.E., he had returned to the city of Babylon, which he intended to make the capital of his vast domains, but he contracted a fever the following June and died at the age of thirty-three without carrying out his administrative plans.

Some modern historians have conjectured that Alexander dreamed of a world empire in which humanity would be united in a "brotherhood of all men." He himself adopted Persian manners, married Persian wives, and encouraged his leading army officers to do likewise. Alexander enrolled Persian youths into his army and trained them in Macedonian military tactics. However, these may be understood as steps toward consolidating his rule rather than as steps toward realization of a politically and culturally united humanity. If not the architect of a universal brotherhood, Alexander sometimes has been hailed as the apostle of Greek culture to the East. Ancient Greek culture is termed Hellenistic culture, or **Hellenism,** after the Greeks' own word for their homeland, *Hellene* (hel-LAY-nay), "the beautiful land." Alexander's conquest of Persia paved the way for the spread of Hellenism into the ancient Near East. However, like all imperial military campaigns and permanent occupations, it came at quite a cost to the local populations and cultures. We now turn to the Macedonian successors to Alexander's empire, the true promoters of Hellenistic cultural imperialism in the Near East.

www Read a lively defense of Alexander the Great.

Alexander's Successors and the Spread of Greek Culture

Immediately upon Alexander's death, his leading Macedonian-Greek generals began quarreling among themselves, vying for control of the empire. Territory was ruled by those who could seize it and maintain control against the others. Eventually, the empire became three kingdoms ruled by the three leading contending generals and their descendants. These rulers and their kingdoms are known as the **Diadochi** (dee-AHD-uh-kee), "successors" of Alexander. Two Diadochi kingdoms are important for us here because they had a major impact upon the history of Asia Minor, Syria, and Palestine—the area where the books of the New Testament were written.

Ptolemy (TAHL-uh-mee), one of Alexander's generals, shrewdly seized power in Egypt upon Alexander's death. In 305 B.C.E., he was proclaimed king of Egypt, and the **Ptolemaic** (tahl-uh-MAY-ic) **dynasty** continued until the self-inflicted death of Cleopatra VII in 30 B.C.E., when Egypt was taken into the Roman Empire. Egypt was relatively isolated from the rest of Alexander's old empire, and its borders were more easily defended than those of the other Diadochi kingdoms. This meant that although the Ptolemies engaged in extended warfare against the other Diadochi kingdoms, these wars were typically fought beyond Egypt proper. This distance from conflict allowed the Ptolemies to pursue the glorification of Greek culture in Egypt, particularly in the capital city of Alexandria. Ptolemy I founded the famous Alexandrian Library and sought to make Alexandria a center of Greek learning and culture. Many of his successors shared this ambition, adding volumes to the library and seeking to draw the finest scholars, poets, and philosophers to the Alexandrian court. Eventually Alexandria became a more important center for Hellenistic philosophy and culture than fabled Athens. Although the Ptolemies sought to make Alexandria the greatest of Hellenistic cities, complete with a library, gymnasium, and philosophic schools, they did not actively seek to found other cities on the Greek model within their realm. They successfully exploited the rest of Egypt in order to fund the enhancement of Alexandria and the Ptolemaic court.

Seleucus, another of Alexander's generals, managed to capture the center of Alexander's empire, and the **Seleucid** (sell-OO-sid) **dynasty** continued to rule most of Syria, Asia Minor, and Mesopotamia for the next two centuries. This Seleucus became Seleucus I, surnamed Nicator ("the Conqueror"). He followed a program of Hellenistic cultural expansion, after the pattern begun by Alexander, by founding Hellenistic-style cities. Seleucus I founded Seleucia Pieria along the Orontes River in Syria. This Seleucia was the seaport for the new Seleucid capital of Antioch. Seleucia-on-the-Tigris, established forty miles northeast of the ancient city of Babylon, became a center of Hellenistic civilization rivaling Alexandria in Egypt. This program of founding Hellenistic cities was continued throughout their empire by succeeding Seleucid rulers, especially in northern Syria and throughout Asia Minor. Likewise, in the pattern of Alexander, these rulers immodestly named their new cities after themselves.

The Seleucid rulers were not the able imperial administrators that the Ptolemies of Egypt were, but they were politically and militarily astute. They typically sought the defense and expansion of their territory through alliance making and military adventurism. They did not take the same view as the Ptolemies regarding the native peoples over whom they ruled as a source of economic exploitation. Certainly the cooperation of their non-Greek subjects was sought as much as possible, in order to maintain internal stability and to provide for a native fighting force in the event of war. But those who did not cooperate or openly rebelled could be regarded as immediately expendable. At times, the native peoples of the Seleucid Empire experienced a disinterested toleration from their overlords regarding the practice of their own religion

Table 4.1 A Timeline of Greco-Roman History in the Eastern Mediterranean

Hellenistic (Greek) period: 334–c. 60 B.C.E.
   Alexander the Great conquers the eastern Mediterranean: 334–323 B.C.E.
   Palestine in Ptolemaic Empire: c. 300–198 B.C.E.
   Palestine comes under Seleucid Empire: 197 B.C.E.
   Antiochus IV forces Hellenization in Palestine: c. 170 B.C.E.
   Maccabean revolt and end of Seleucid rule in Palestine: 167–160 B.C.E.
   Rome conquers Macedonian Kingdom (Greece): 146 B.C.E.
   Jewish independent kingdom under Hasmonean dynasty: 142–63 B.C.E.

Rule of Rome: c. 150 B.C.E.–400 C.E.
   Rome annexes Syria and Palestine: 64–63 B.C.E.
   Herod the Great, Jewish client-king of Palestine: 40–4 B.C.E.
   Herod captures Jerusalem and marries the Hasmonean princess Mariamne
      I: 37 B.C.E.
   Augustus rules as Emperor of Rome: 27 B.C.E.–14 C.E.
   Herod and his successors rebuild the Temple in Jerusalem: 20 B.C.E.–70 C.E.
   Herod's successors rule as client-kings over parts of Palestine: 4 B.C.E.–70 C.E.
   Birth of Jesus: c. 6–4 B.C.E.
   Rome establishes direct rule of Judea with prefects: 6 C.E.
   Pontius Pilate, Roman prefect of Judea, 26–36 C.E.
   Ministry of Jesus: c. 27–30
   Paul called and ministers as an apostle: 36–64
   Emperor Claudius expels Jews from Rome: 49
   Great Fire in Rome and persecution of Christians by Nero: 64–65
   First Jewish Revolt against Rome: 66–73
   Destruction of Jerusalem and the Second Temple: 70
   Second Jewish Revolt in Palestine under Bar Kokhba, hailed as messiah: 132
   Second Revolt crushed by Rome: 135
   Emperor Hadrian renames Jerusalem Aelia Capitolina and builds a pagan temple
      over the site of the Second Temple: 136

and culture. At other times, Seleucids put strong pressure on their subjects to Hellenize for imperial unity. After Antiochus III conquered Jerusalem in 198 B.C.E., making Palestine a part of the Seleucid Empire, an aggressive Seleucid program of Hellenization sparked a Jewish revolt against the Seleucids, resulting in the establishment of an independent Jewish state that remained for nearly a hundred years.

The Decline of the Diadochi Kingdoms

During the history of what has come to be called the **Hellenistic Age**—the Greek-dominated eastern Mediterranean from Alexander the Great until the fall of Ptolemaic Egypt in 30 B.C.E.—the Diadochi kingdoms were engaged in almost endless warfare with each other. The Seleucids and Ptolemaics engaged in no less than six wars for the control of Palestine during a span of 250 years. The nearly ceaseless political turmoil and war steadily damaged the Diadochi states while the power of the Roman Empire in the west and the Parthian Empire in the east continued to mount. By 146 B.C.E., the Macedonian kingdom in Greece was a Roman province. The Seleucid Empire was steadily diminished to little more than the region of modern-day Syria, the interior territories of the Empire being conquered by the Parthians. In 167 B.C.E., the Jewish priest Mattathias launched the Maccabean revolt against the Seleucids. This revolt was subsequently led by his sons, most notably Judas, and it resulted in complete Jewish independence from the Seleucids in 142 B.C.E. In 64 B.C.E., the Roman general Pompey defeated Antiochus XIII, annexing Syria to Rome. In 63 B.C.E., he captured Jerusalem, putting an end to the independent Jewish state in Palestine. Aside from brief periods of Jewish independence won in 66–70 C.E. and again by the messianic pretender Simon bar Kochba in 132–135 C.E., no such state would arise again for two thousand years, until 1947 C.E., when the modern nation of Israel was founded. After a series of intrigues between Roman leaders and Cleopatra VII (dramatized in turn by Shakespeare, John Dryden, George Bernard Shaw, and several Hollywood producers), Egypt fell to Octavian, later known as Caesar Augustus, in 30 B.C.E. Politically speaking, the Hellenistic Age was over. But Hellenistic cultural dominance in the eastern Mediterranean continued to flourish under Roman rule.

www   Read primary texts on the causes, course, and aftermath of the Maccabean revolt.

Roman Rule and Life

With Octavian's defeat of his rivals and the fall of Egypt, Rome was transformed into a true empire. Ruling as Augustus from 27 B.C.E. until 14 C.E., Octavian was able to pursue a policy of imperial consolidation and organization. The eastern Mediterranean, like Rome itself, began to experience a period of stability and peace—something it had not known for nearly three hundred and fifty years. To be sure, it was a peace based on conquest and occupation, but it enabled subject peoples to prosper economically. Augustus set up a plan of imperial administration in which he organized the provinces in two groups. One group was the senatorial provinces, governed by proconsuls. *Senatorial provinces* comprised the more stable interior regions of the empire. Frontier and border provinces were in the second group, called *imperial provinces*. Imperial provinces had governors appointed by, and directly accountable to, the Emperor. Imperial provinces garrisoned Roman troops who guarded the frontier against alien incursions and maintained order among the populace, whose allegiance to the Empire and collaboration with outside enemies could sometimes be suspect. The distrust of provincial loyalty was especially sharp in Syria, Judea, Arabia, and Armenia, since these imperial provinces bordered upon Rome's chief rival in the east, the Parthian Empire.

In order to facilitate the rapid deployment of the Roman army and to improve commerce, Augustus implemented the building of an imperial system of roads. (A famous Roman proverb said, "All roads lead to Rome," but it is just as true that all Roman roads carried armies *from* Rome.) He practically eliminated piracy on the Mediterranean Sea and dramatically reduced highway banditry. Toleration was encouraged in all things not deemed significant for the welfare of the state, but Rome dealt with civil unrest immediately and ruthlessly. Augustus sought peace with nations and peoples outside the Empire, and order inside the Empire. His reign began the **Pax Romana** (pahks roh-MAH-na), Latin for "Roman Peace." Augustus' death in 14 C.E. ushered in a less happy period under a series of emperors with profoundly mixed abilities and accomplishments. Men like Claudius, Nero, Caligula, and Domitian could be able administrators on one hand, but on the other might resort to arbitrary arrest, murder, or persecution to enhance their position or security. Moreover, Rome conquered more rapidly than it could govern—its military prowess was always larger than its administrative—and the bureaucracy needed to administer such a vast empire could never catch up. Justice lay in the hands of local magistrates, although Roman citizens could appeal to higher Roman judicial authority, even to the Emperor's Council. The Pax Romana continued undisturbed for the most part, but frontiers remained fluid and border provinces troubled. Not until the second century C.E., with the so-called "good emperors," was the full fruit of Roman prosperity under the Pax Romana realized.

www   For an excellent web-based treatment of life in the Roman Empire and a listing of Roman emperors in the first century C.E., see the website.

Judea from 40 B.C.E. to 70 C.E.: From Client Kingdom to Failed Revolt

The Roman senate awarded Herod the "Great" the kingdom of Judea in 40 B.C.E. but left him to govern it largely with his own resources. Herod came from a family of Idumean (Arab) nobles who converted to Judaism during the time of Alexander Janneus, the Jewish king who conquered their territory in the second century B.C.E. He was a friend of the early Roman emperors and ruled in Judea and Galilee from 40 until 4 B.C.E., when he died. Herod was responsible for the initial phases of Romanization because of his widespread patronage of Greco-Roman culture and his foundation of cities in the Greek style at Caesarea and Sebaste.

Rome made its influence felt in the eastern Mediterranean primarily through its troops in Syria. This entire force with Syrian auxiliaries came to Judea after Herod died in order to suppress a popular revolt against the Herodians. Meanwhile, Herod's son Archelaus went to Rome to seek confirmation of his succession as King of Judea. Augustus, recognizing the difficulty of governing this area, found attractive the prospect of leaving it in the hands of a client-king who would bear the expense of maintaining order. On the other hand, Archelaus had a poor reputation and considerable opposition in Palestine, and Augustus did not want to give him the kind of power that his father Herod the Great had. So the emperor gave Archelaus the lesser title of *ethnarch* ("ruler of a people") over the southern half of Herod's realm—Judea, Samaria, and Idumea. In 6 C.E., Augustus responded to complaints against the ethnarch by his own subjects and deposed him. Augustus divided the northern regions into two tetrarchies (quarter-kingdoms) for Archelaus' brothers Philip and Herod Antipas. The northeastern tetrarchy remained under the control of Philip until he died in 33/34 C.E. and then became part of Syria until Gaius assigned it to Philip's nephew Agrippa in 37. Herod Antipas ruled the northern tetrarchy from his new capital Tiberias on the Sea of Galilee until about 39, when he fell out of favor with the emperor Caligula (Gaius). The emperor exiled Antipas and awarded his tetrarchy to Agrippa, also a member of the Herodian dynasty. The ethnarchy became the new province of Judea, comprising the districts of Judea, Idumea, and Samaria, and was subordinated to Syria.

As an annex of Syria, Judea had a governor of lesser rank than the senators who governed most provinces, a **prefect** ("administrator"). The prefects fulfilled military, financial, and limited judicial functions. For the most part, Roman officials deferred to Jewish sensibilities. So, for example, Jews did not serve in the auxiliary army units normally recruited from among the native population of a province, nor did they have to participate in the rising imperial cult. Instead, the Jews substituted a daily sacrifice in the temple on behalf of the emperor and the Romans. Pontius Pilate's (prefect 26–36 C.E.) notable lack of accommodation to Jewish laws and customs caused considerable unrest, especially when he tried to introduce images of Tiberius into the city of Jerusalem, which the Jewish people saw as idolatrous. The death of Emperor Gaius Caligula in 41 resolved a dangerous situation after he ordered his governor in Syria to install his statue in the temple in Jerusalem. Now the new emperor Claudius returned Judea and Samaria to Herodian rule, partly to reward Herod's grandson Agrippa (Agrippa I, also called Herod Agrippa), no doubt as an attempt to rule a difficult province by indirect means more effectively than by direct.

The Jews saw Agrippa's short rule as a golden age under a pious king. But at his death in 44, his realm reverted to direct Roman rule, now with a procurator as governor. Roman faith in the Herodians continued, however, and in 53 Claudius detached from Judea its northeastern regions and assigned them to Agrippa II, son of Agrippa I. Agrippa enjoyed considerable influence with the governors of Judea and the Jewish elite in Jerusalem, and indeed the Romans yielded to him authority over the temple and the right to appoint the high priest. Agrippa II proved perhaps the most loyal of all Rome's Herodian clients. The comparative good order that Judea saw under Agrippa I began to break down under the procurators, especially from about 50 C.E., partly because of provocative acts by soldiers and malfeasance by some governors, and partly because of nationalist feelings and terrorist resistance to the restoration of direct Roman rule. Taken together, these threats to the Roman order plunged Judea into anarchy and open revolt against Rome in the mid 60s, related in Chapter 3. The story of the apostle Paul's arrest and long imprisonment at the end of the 50s reflects the general indecisiveness of Rome's agents in this increasingly difficult period (Acts 21–27), and the fact that Agrippa appointed four high priests in as many years attests to Agrippa's inability to govern the Jewish religious leadership.

www   Follow the links for more on the events in Judea from 40 B.C.E. to 70 C.E.

Greco-Roman Culture

Any interpretation of a society or culture alien to one's own experience is risky. One cannot avoid interpreting the nature and character of that other culture through language constructs and understandings that arise from one's own culture. In trying to understand Hellenistic Roman culture, we approach the task as its twenty-first-century cultural heirs with our own analytical outlook and methods. Acknowledging our differences and our distance, in both space and time, from the Greco-Roman world can help us identify our similarities with, and inheritance from it. We can then get inside it well enough to know its basics. That being said, we will attempt our study of Greco-Roman society and culture, and their influences upon the New Testament, by considering different elements and examining each in turn.

The Roman Military

For much of the eastern Mediterranean world, the first and last reminder of Roman rule was the presence of the Roman military. The Roman army safeguarded the peace, not only guarding the borders of Syria and Judea against Parthian invasion, but also by securing highways against banditry. Roman troops acted as a police force as well as a military force. By the end of Augustus' reign, piracy at sea was nearly unheard of, making the Mediterranean truly the "Roman Lake." A strong Roman military policed the Pax Romana, making possible the further spread and development of Hellenistic-Roman culture. Additionally, Roman soldiers performed a number of civil service functions when they were not engaged in direct military or policing activities. Roman armies were responsible for the construction and maintenance of aqueducts and the famous Roman road system. Many Near Eastern and European highways of today follow the course of this Roman system, and some are even constructed over the ancient roadways of Rome.

Military service provided a means of social mobility for men in the lower classes. The Roman **legions** (the largest unit of the Roman army, comprising 6,000 men) were made up of citizen soldiers. Initially this meant that one needed to be a citizen before induction into a legion. However, with the extension of citizenship into the provinces and the expansion of the Roman military, this process became reciprocal—volunteering for military service could become an avenue to citizenship, just as it is in the United States today. Augustus set the length of military service at twenty years; it was later extended to twenty-five years. Part of a Roman soldier's annual pay was withheld as a lump-sum pension to be paid upon honorable discharge, which along with land grants and a generous cash grant made military service an attractive career opportunity.

A Roman legion was made up of ten cohorts; each cohort was comprised of six centuries. As the name implies, a century was a force of one hundred, so a legion numbered six thousand men. A professional soldier promoted from the ranks, the **centurion,** commanded each century. Centurions were typically stationed in one area for a long time and therefore became involved in local civilian affairs. For example, we frequently encounter centurions in our reading of the Gospels and Acts. A centurion appeals to Jesus to heal a household servant in Matthew 8. In Mark 15, the centurion in charge of Jesus' crucifixion bears witness to his identity. In Acts 10, a centurion named Cornelius becomes the first recorded Gentile convert to Christianity. The continuous presence of the Roman military in society also provided ready illustrative material for the NT writers, as in 2 Tim 2:3–4 and Eph 6:11–17. Even though the Roman legions and their local auxiliaries enforced the peace, protected traders and travelers, and provided a vehicle of upward mobility in society, native provincials often regarded their presence as a mixed blessing. This was particularly true in Judea, where the Jewish people correctly viewed Roman forces as occupiers meant to keep them in check as much as to protect them from foreign and domestic threats. The Jews, like most subjugated peoples of the Empire, felt the burden of Roman military presence indirectly as well as directly. Large standing armies require vast financial and material support. Taxation to support the Roman military presence and administration, both monetary and in the form of agricultural products, was a bitter burden for the common people to bear.

Social Classes

Roman society, like most ancient societies, was highly stratified, and the various social classes had their origins in the early Roman Republic. Originally, Roman citizenship was confined to the three classes of Rome proper: the upper, senatorial class called **patricians,** the **equestrians** (the minor aristocracy), and the **plebeians** (the common people). With the expansion of the empire, a notion of expanded citizenship became employed in order to promote unity under Roman law: a man could hold Roman citizenship and still retain citizen status in his home city or country. Citizenship could be obtained in a number of different ways. First, one could be born a citizen by virtue of being the child of citizen parents. Second, freed slaves of citizens of Rome were granted citizen status. Citizenship could also be granted in return for exceptional service to the empire, such as regular legionary or auxiliary military service. Finally, men who were deemed worthy but who did not qualify by these regular means could sometimes purchase citizenship at a substantial cost.

Citizenship granted a person certain legal rights not available to noncitizens. Noncitizens charged under the law were completely under the jurisdiction of the local magistracy. Whether or not they received anything like a fair trial depended on the whim of the judge. For example, Jesus had no legal counsel to represent him at his appearance before the Roman governor Pontius Pilate. A citizen had rights to a fair trial and could appeal his case to a higher court—even to the Emperor's review. Acts 25 tells how the apostle Paul exercised this right of citizenship. Citizens could not be whipped during interrogation or trial, nor were they subject to execution by crucifixion, this form of torture-death being reserved for noncitizens. Some citizens were granted voting rights, but not all; one could only vote in the city of Rome itself. Besides these legal rights, citizenship extended a certain level of status to free people in the lower levels of the social classes.

In the leading towns and cities of the provinces, local aristocracies played a leading role through the **civic magistracies.** Civic magistracies modeled after the Roman Senate were composed of one hundred magistrates, or senators, who were men of means in the community. The cost of the prestige and power of the civic magistracy was high, as magistrates were expected to contribute financially to their cities. They financed the construction of public buildings, funded the costs of circuses and festivals, and provided material relief in times of famine or other emergency. However, power and influence were more a matter of honor than of wealth. Wealth provided a person the opportunity to demonstrate benevolence and thus gain more honor. To be a person of magisterial means and power, but fail to take responsibility for public prosperity and safety, brought shame upon oneself and one's family. These local aristocracies had vested economic and social interests in maintaining the status quo and supporting the empire, so they gained more than they gave away as magistrates. For businessmen, holding public office was a good investment.

Freedmen were a significant social element in Roman society. Freedmen were former slaves who nonetheless retained a close economic and social relationship with their former masters. Through thrift and enterprise, freedmen could amass some level of wealth that lifted their social *status* without altering their social *class*. Freedmen occupied various positions, serving as guardians and teachers to boys in upper class households, and sometimes held high-level bureaucratic positions in the imperial administration. The Roman governor Felix, before whom Paul appears in Acts 23, was a freedman.

Patronage, a type of social contract in which **patrons,** wealthy and powerful individuals, disbursed honors and wealth to **clients** in return for their loyalty, played an important role in Roman society. (Today, a patron is only a wealthy donor to a cause who usually expects little in return except for social recognition.) Patrons had enough wealth to keep one or more clients under retainer. Clients were responsible

Erastus Inscription in Corinth This inscription in the pavement of ancient Corinth reads, "Erastus laid [this pavement] at his own expense in return for his aedileship." The city treasurer of Corinth is identified with the Erastus in Rom 16:23, Acts 19:22, and 2 Tim 4:20. A member of the church at Corinth, he was engaging in patronage to secure a higher position in the city. This illustrates how at least a few early Christians had notable social status. Used by permission of BiblePlaces.com.

for providing a patron with whatever assistance in public or private affairs the patron required; in exchange the patron provided the client with a stipend or other gifts and provided social and financial favors and legal protection to the client. In Rom 16:2, Paul commends Phoebe to his readers as one who has acted as a patron to himself and to others. Patronage was often the basis of the relationship between a freedman and his former master, but it also operated within other classes and groups as well. The patronage system is connected to the stratified nature of Roman society.

At the bottom of the social ladder were the **slaves.** The practice of human slavery began in very ancient times, grew during the Hellenistic Age, and became widespread in the Greco-Roman Mediterranean. Large numbers of war prisoners taken during the ceaseless wars of the time provided a cheap source of slave labor. Many of these slaves were natives of Syria, Palestine, and Egypt. Later, as the Roman Empire expanded westward, the peoples of Britain, Germany, and Gaul (modern-day France) became new sources for slave labor. Of course, female slaves had children, and the number of slaves grew this way as well. Other sources of slavery included abandoned children, debtors, and convicts. In the cities during difficult times, it was common for adults to sell themselves into slavery in return for the means to live. In the first century c.e., one of five people in the Roman Empire was a slave.

Slaves had no legal or social status whatever. They were property under the absolute control of their masters. The actual conditions of slavery varied, and there were thus variations of social status even within slavery. Household slaves typically enjoyed a reasonable level of well-being and autonomy, serving as household administrators, domestic workers, and teachers. Slaves were to be found in every level of economic activity. They worked as skilled craftsmen and artisans, business agents for merchants and traders, farm workers, and temple functionaries. At the bottom of the slave scale were women and men forced to work as prostitutes and the convicts and prisoners sentenced to work in mines and to row in ships. Their conditions were deplorable, and their life expectancy was short. As expansion of the empire slowed, the cost of buying slaves rose so that the institution of slavery did not adversely affect free labor. Incentives, in the form of wages or commissions, were sometimes offered to better-off slaves in exchange for exemplary service. Slaves could often save these funds to buy their freedom. However, since slaves held no legal status, a slave with the funds to buy his freedom had to turn the money over to an intermediary who executed the purchase. A friend or relative with legal status, or an association, could serve as intermediary. Often a slave supplied the funds to a pagan temple in the name of the deity worshiped there, and the deity served as the intermediary. Termed **sacral manumission,** it was one of the more popular forms of buying one's freedom. Freed slaves often entered into a patronage contract as freedman clients to their former masters.

To judge from the NT and other evidence, most churches in the Gentile world seemed to have a good number of slaves in their membership. Slavery is sometimes used in the New Testament as a metaphor for the Christian's relationship with Jesus Christ. In his letters, Paul identifies himself frequently as a slave of Jesus in the performance of his evangelistic ministry (Rom 1:1; 1 Cor 3:5; Gal 1:10). In some passages, the institution of slavery is directly commented upon, with directions given to slaves and masters alike to disregard their worldly status in favor of their status as believers (Col 3:22–4:1). The most notable reference to slavery in the New Testament is undoubtedly Paul's letter to Philemon. There Paul seems to encourage Philemon to manumit the slave, Onesimus, on the basis of the relationship which both Philemon and Onesimus share as Christians. At the end of the NT, in Rev 18:13, the brutal trade in slaves, who are affirmed to be fully human, is categorically condemned. Even though the NT moves in the direction of freedom for slaves, it would take almost another two thousand years, sadly, for this to be carried out in Western societies.

Family Life

The family unit was the basic building block of Greco-Roman society. It consisted of a husband and wife, their children, any extended family or relatives, and slaves all living together. Therefore *family* and *household* may be considered interchangeable concepts in Greco-Roman society. Family life was patriarchal, ruled and directed by male authority, in this case the husband and father of the household. Patriarchy was a far more extensive system of family life in first-century Rome than in Western civilization during the modern era.

Under Greek law, and to some extent during the Roman Republic, marriage between a man and woman was a formal contractual agreement worked out between a prospective groom and the bride's father. During the time of the Roman Republic there came to be three avenues to marriage: a formal religious ceremony (a wedding); the sale of a slave woman to her new husband; and uninterrupted cohabitation in the man's household for one year, what we call "common-law" marriage. All of these practices brought the woman under the rule of a man. The main purpose of marriage was the procreation of legitimate children. Monogamy was the formal norm, but resorting to prostitutes and engaging in adultery were common—common for men, that is, because a double standard applied to women—especially among the privileged classes. Divorce was easy, and therefore also relatively common. Though we might think that in such a patriarchal system divorce would have been a man's option only, this is not the case. By the first century, a Greco-Roman woman could also initiate the termination of a marriage. (This was not the norm in Jewish culture.) A married woman was, to a great degree, confined to her home so that relatively little suspicion might be raised regarding the legitimacy of her children. She managed household affairs and in this role did exercise some degree of indirect influence in society.

Most readers of the NT today typically assume that the life of women in the ancient world underwent little change. Recently, some historians have challenged this notion in their treatment of the rise of "the new Roman woman" in the first century C.E. and its impact on early Christianity, especially in the Pauline churches (Winter, 2003). This "new woman" departed radically from the patterns of modesty in dress and behavior that had typified Roman women for centuries. They went about with no traditional head covering, socialized with men not their husbands, and sometimes even affirmed the value of extramarital affairs. The new Roman woman emerged with changing social mores when the Roman Republic changed into an empire. This label seems to include all Roman women of the first century C.E., but they were probably in the minority, albeit a vocal and visible minority. Winter argues that many NT injunctions about women in churches are directed against the new Roman woman and so must be understood against this historical and social context.

www   Follow the link to Diotima, an excellent comprehensive website on women in the ancient world.

Children in Greco-Roman culture had in some ways a lower status than slaves. In a world that often featured scarcity and famine, children were often viewed more as an economic liability than as beloved offspring, as in Judaism. (The lavishing of love and attention on children to which we are so accustomed in North America did not take hold in Western society until Victorian times.) Under Caesar Augustus, legislation was enacted to provide incentives for couples to have more children in order to increase the Roman population. But the long-established pattern in both Greece and Rome was for small families, with two children or perhaps three in rare instances. Of course, parents were particularly desirous of having a male child as an heir; when this did not happen, people of wealth often would adopt a young-adult relative into their immediate family.

How did such small families arise, given the absence of effective contraceptive measures? Miscarriage and natural infant mortality played the main, sad role. The standard fallback method for controlling family size in Greco-Roman society was **infanticide,** the killing of unwanted newborns by exposure. They were typically abandoned in public dumpsites, under bridges, or in secluded rural places. Infanticide was not considered murder in Greco-Roman culture because of the accepted moral view of family and children. For a child to have any status as a person, it had to be acknowledged as a member of the family by the father. If the father refused such acknowledgement for whatever reason, the child was excluded from the family and was considered a nonentity. Parents seldom exposed firstborn children, regardless of gender. However, families seldom reared more than one daughter, and even male infants beyond the second son were sometimes exposed. Even though exposure was a common practice, the rate of infanticide in the Greco-Roman world was probably far less than the rate of miscarriage and natural infant mortality, which was much higher than in economically developed countries today.

Economic Life

Agriculture was the backbone of the economy in first-century Rome. Egypt and parts of North Africa were the grain belt of the empire, supplying much of its food supply. Winemaking and olive oil production could be found in all parts of the Mediterranean world, but particularly in the east. Agricultural production was the business of large estates in the provinces, typically farmed for the landowners by tenant farmers and peasants (Matt 21:33–44). At peak times of activity, such as at harvest, day laborers might be employed to supplement the workforce of an agricultural estate (Matt 20:1–16).

The towns and cities of the Mediterranean world were usually planned and constructed around a market square called an **agora** (AH-goh-rah) in Greek, or **forum** in Latin. The agora was surrounded by a *stoa* (STOH-ah), a covered porch, and behind the stoa would be located offices and the shops of small businessmen such as artisans and merchants. In general, the agora was not unlike our modern shopping malls. The items sold in the agora came from farm and small industries. Mining, particularly of lead, silver, and iron, was carried out with hand tools, usually by slaves. Textiles of wool, flax, and imported silk were typically produced in small, home-based businesses. Glassware, ceramics, metalwork, and other handicrafts were produced in small shops by independent artisans. These artisans did not consider themselves laborers but rather skilled people of their trade. In every town of any size in the empire, artisans of the same craft would have their shops together on the same street. They organized into trade guilds, not for economic advantage but for the political and social advancement of a guild's membership. The guilds often revered a patron deity. In cities of the Greco-Roman world, the presence of a temple to one of the gods or goddesses was an economic boon to the city's artisans. In Acts 19, the apostle Paul is embroiled in a civil disturbance in Ephesus when the silversmiths of that city become alarmed that his preaching of Jesus might damage the cult of Artemis centered in Ephesus. Since a significant portion of the silversmiths' livelihood was derived from the production of images of the goddess, they had an economic interest in not allowing any rivals to her worship.

The most lucrative business ventures of the Greco-Roman world were in trade, both within and outside the empire. The Pax Romana allowed trade across the empire to flourish, by way of both Mediterranean shipping and overland trade routes. Though Mediterranean shipping was difficult during winter, overland trade could be undertaken on a nearly year-round basis. This method of trade was greatly facilitated by an extensive Roman road system. Most of the overland trade of the Roman Empire was carried on between the provinces, but overland caravans to India and China were not unheard of. Roman coins discovered in the Far East bear witness to trade between this region and the Mediterranean world.

We could not conclude a survey of economic life in New Testament times without mentioning taxation. Taxes in the Roman Empire generally were levied only to produce revenue, not as a means of economic and social policy as well, as today in North America. Those who occupied the land paid tax on agricultural produce, collected on a percentage basis. Taxes on individuals were also collected, as attested by the imperial registration recorded in Luke 2, and as duty on trade goods. A major source of this type of tax revenue were the eastern provinces of the empire, such as Judea, where major trade routes crossed between the Mediterranean world and central Asia. Provincial tax collectors generally were men of some means from among the native population who contracted with Rome to collect the taxes owed to Rome from their particular city or district, a system called **tax farming.** Rome paid them a percentage of what they collected, but whatever they could extort above the regular tax was pure profit. Even without extortion from the collectors, taxes could be excessive. The tax collectors, and their subordinates whom they hired to collect for them, figure prominently in the New Testament. In Mark 2:14, Levi is called from his tax booth to become a disciple of Jesus, and the tax collector Zacchaeus has a life-changing encounter with Jesus in Luke 19. Tax collectors and "sinners" are rather freely associated in the Gospels. The Jews regarded tax collectors with contempt, not so much because of their reputation for corruption or dishonesty, but because they symbolized and cemented Roman control. Since most tax collectors were locals who made a living by taking taxes from their neighbors on behalf of an occupation government, they were often viewed as traitors.

Entertainment

Rome was heir to the Greek theater, but by the time of the New Testament the classical age of the Greek theater was long passed. Students still read the tragedies and comedies of classical Greece, but contemporary Roman theater offered its audiences other fare. Roman theatrical performances for popular viewing were mostly vulgar.

Rome was also heir to the Greek love for games and physical competition. Like the theater, however, sports in the Roman Empire were different from the athletic competitions of classical Greece. The games of the Greek Classical Age were associated with festivals honoring the gods, and athletes were local heroes who competed more for the intangible prizes of personal and civic pride than for material reward. Foot races, wrestling, boxing, discus and javelin throwing, and the long jump were the popular athletic events. Greek athletes competed in the nude, an aspect of Hellenistic culture objectionable to observant Jews that met with resistance from the Romans as well.

The Roman idea of sports was the violence on display that typified the events held in the amphitheaters and circuses. Amphitheaters were large, enclosed arenas where gladiatorial contests were held. Professional gladiators received the kind of acclaim in Rome that professional athletes are accustomed to in our culture today. A gladiator might engage another gladiator in one-on-one combat or fight a wild animal to the death. Criminals were also sent into the amphitheaters, alone or in a group, to face wild beasts and gladiators and provide a spectacle for the crowds. Every significant city of the empire had its own amphitheater for the entertainment of its populace, but the best-known amphitheater is the Coliseum at Rome (dedicated in 80 C.E.), which could seat 50,000 spectators. It had a retractable cloth roof, and its main floor could be flooded to accommodate mock small-scale naval battles. The Roman *circus* (named for its circular track) was an often-enclosed facility dedicated only to chariot racing. Chariot racing became the most popular professional entertainment of the Roman Empire (not unlike the current North American fascination for automobile racing). Local magistrates often sponsored races in a city's circus for the entertainment of the populace and the enhancement of their own prestige. Chariot teams were identified by their colors, with as many as twelve chariot teams participating in a race. Because of the intensity of competition and their "need for speed," chariot races in the circuses were often nearly as violent as the bloody combats waged in the amphitheaters, and people went to the races to see crashes.

www Read a good assessment of the historical accuracy of the 2000 hit film *Gladiator* directed by Ridley Scott, with good links.

Saner and more sedate forms of entertainment could be found at the public baths. These establishments might be compared to the country clubs and health spas of our own time. As might be expected, baths featured a public bath, or swimming pool, and rooms with hot water and steam. By the time of the empire they also included elements of the Greek gymnasia, such as exercise facilities or a lecture hall. The baths were social centers where one could relax, exercise, bathe, get a massage, or even hear lectures by philosophers or readings by poets. The baths were generally the province of the upper classes, whereas the amphitheaters and circuses offered spectator attractions for the common folk.

Education

The Greco-Roman world was generally a literate one thanks to the importance placed upon the education and formation of the young, although the degree of literacy in the Roman Empire is currently debated. It probably varied widely by region, culture, and social class. Not until the nineteenth century, however, did Western Europe experience the level of literacy formerly achieved in the Roman Empire. The pattern of education we find today in Western civilization follows the ancient Greco-Roman model to a great degree. In cities where endowed schools had been established, primary public education existed. However, the vast majority of schools were small, private classrooms established by teachers whose pay came directly from the families of the students they taught. Slaves, of course, were not educated in these schools, and neither were the children of the lower classes, who could not afford it.

Greco-Roman education was a three-stage affair that began for pupils at the age of seven. Primary education continued until about age twelve and was typified by what we call today the "three Rs": reading, writing, and (a)rithmetic. Girls as well as boys were often educated at the primary level. Greco-Roman society acknowledged a girl's need for basic education if she were someday to become a responsible wife and mother in charge of her children and her husband's household affairs. At age twelve, students could continue their education in a secondary program. The Homeric epic and the works of the classical dramatists were the textual basis for an education focused upon grammar and composition. However, given the subject matter, secondary education also schooled pupils in the history and culture of the classical Mediterranean world. For many, particularly females, formal education ceased after the completion of the primary phase. But the sons of the upper class continued through secondary education to the third educational stage, beginning at about age eighteen. This educational phase was associated with the **gymnasium** ("place of naked exercise") in classical Greece. As we saw earlier, gymnasia were more than just health and exercise clubs. Besides space for physical activity, gymnasia also included libraries, classrooms, and lecture halls. Education at the advanced stage prepared one to be a good citizen and civic leader. In the Roman Empire advanced education meant, for the most part, training in *rhetoric,* public speaking for persuading others. Rhetoricians, who were often itinerant teachers in the pattern of the classical philosophers, trained their charges in what was considered the queen of the disciplines. Regardless of what profession one was to engage in during adult life, the art of public speaking was necessary for success.

Another important element in the education of many upper class males was the role of the **pedagogue.** A pedagogue was usually a slave of some learning who was assigned the role of guardian over a male child, or children, in a household. Pedagogues were responsible for seeing these children to and from their locations of formal education, but also for regulating their behavior and teaching them obedience to authority, as well as basic morality. In Gal 3:20–4:5, Paul speaks metaphorically of the Law of Moses as a pedagogue for humanity until the revelation of God in Jesus Christ.

Voluntary Associations

Membership in voluntary associations had been a part of Greek life since the Classical Age. The early voluntary associations were religious in nature, centered upon rites and ceremonies in honor of a particular deity. The trade guilds discussed earlier in the section on "Economic Life" were voluntary associations performing religious rites in honor of a trade's patron deity and providing a means of socialization for the guild's members. As the centuries passed, the religious element in the life of the associations became a secondary feature to social and economic concerns. Dinner clubs were the dominant type of Hellenistic voluntary associations surviving into the Roman Empire.

In the Roman era, law regulated the practice of free association taken over from Hellenistic culture. The Roman voluntary associations were called **collegia** in Latin, from the word for "association" (compare our "college"). They had the same functions as the Hellenistic associations. By the first century C.E., however, some of the collegia had become sources for political intrigue, and so laws requiring them to be licensed were enacted. At times the emperor outlawed them, as when Trajan in the early second century prohibited fire-fighting collegia in certain provinces because they tended to engage in local politics when they were not fighting fires. The only exceptions to licensing were burial associations, which typically were maintained by the poorer members of society as a form of life insurance. Burial associations were permitted to meet monthly, maintain their own burial grounds for members, and provide for the burial expenses of members whose dues to the association had been kept current. Like other collegia, burial associations recognized a patron deity for whom they were often named. It was almost impossible for Christians and Jews alike, who were sensitive to the worship of the gods of the dominant Greco-Roman culture, to maintain membership in social clubs or trade associations, since worship of an association's patron deity was an integral part of its life.

Social Morality

Maintaining a certain level of moral conduct within a society has been a function of law within every significant culture and nation known to history. This was true for Roman law, which was established upon ideas of common sense, fairness, equality, and due process. Our basic notions of law in the Western world are based upon Roman law. But where does a society get these ideas upon which its morality and law are established? For the Romans, morality grew from their understanding of the natural order.

Roman society was highly stratified. Social stratification and the hierarchy of the classes were generally accepted as part of the natural order, because nature was understood hierarchically. What was fitting and right—moral—was the action seen as befitting one's class. This action brought one honor. The natural thing for a deer when threatened by a lioness is to flee, but it is also incumbent upon the lioness to feed her young. Likewise, what was morally imperative for a slave was not necessarily appropriate behavior for an aristocrat. After all, they had different functions and different roles to play in the "natural" order by which society was preserved and enhanced. The responsibilities accorded one's class dictated the moral issues one would need to confront. Furthermore, the amount of personal power afforded one because of his or her place in society profoundly affected one's moral choices. Not wielding the power and authority of one's position was as shameful as pretensions of belonging to a social class above one's own. Roman law reflected this stratification of society. While it maintained a regard for individual rights and equality, these notions were conditioned by acceptance of the social order. Rough equality existed within a social class, but inequality between classes was also assumed. Moreover, as we saw earlier, Roman citizens were assured certain rights under Roman law, but noncitizen subjects of the empire were not accorded these rights.

Roman law was in general a stable system that was adaptable to changing economic, political, or social conditions. However, as power was more and more concentrated in Caesar, this figure also came to be more and more understood as the source of law. Caesar embodied in himself the natural order, his decrees and mandates reflecting that order and thus bringing about the peace and prosperity of his subjects. The increasing concentration of power and authority at the peak of the

Roman hierarchy, and the resultant decreasing civic responsibilities of the upper classes coupled with the increasing leisure and material prosperity afforded them by the Pax Romana, had a negative effect on Roman society. The pleasure-seeking immorality of the wealthy, so often attacked by early Christian writers like the author of Revelation, can be understood as the upper-class reaction to the combination of excessive leisure time, increasing wealth, and political impotency they experienced under the Caesars. From the perspective of the lower class, it became increasingly clear that the only possibility for justice came from being able to appeal to a figure higher than Caesar. The consequence of these historical developments was that law and social morality tended to devolve into matters of power in a might-makes-right equation.

In many societies in the Western and Eastern world, the call for social reform has traditionally been one role of religion. But in ancient Rome the traditional religion did not have an inherent ethical or moral element that would have fitted it for such a task. Religion was more an explanation for, and maintenance of, natural phenomena and "the way things are," rather than a force for change.

Religion in the Greco-Roman World

The religious mindset of the Roman world can be foreign terrain to those of us today whose lives have been lived in a culture with a heritage of ethical monotheism practiced amid secularism. A few words of introduction are therefore necessary if we are to have some idea about what religion meant to most people in the Greco-Roman world, its place in culture, and its practice.

Religion was tremendously diverse in the Roman Empire during New Testament times. Most prominent was the cult of the Roman high gods, adapted to some degree from the Olympian pantheon of ancient Greece. Related to the cult of the high gods was the veneration and worship of a vast number of lesser local gods, spirits, and personified virtues. Related in another way to the cult of the high gods, the Emperor cult developed in an attempt toward a unifying civil religion in the Empire. Though the Emperor cult had its beginning in New Testament times, it did not reach its zenith until about the third century. Alongside the religion of the high gods and associated deities were a number of other cults, Greek mysteries and astral religions imported from the eastern provinces of the empire, which were practiced alongside the religion of the classical pantheon. The polytheistic religious mindset of the Greco-Roman world did not demand any sort of exclusive devotion to a single god or religion. This was the essence of Greco-Roman paganism. Of course, the exception in the first-century Mediterranean world was the Jews of Palestine and the Diaspora, whose exclusive worship of one God, and rejection of the existence of all other gods, was tolerated but disliked. From Judaism, Christianity was born and made its way into the religiously diverse Mediterranean world and beyond.

Pantheon in Rome The Pantheon was built in 27 B.C.E. to commemorate Augustus' victory over Antony and Cleopatra. Domitian restored it after a fire in 80 C.E., and it was rebuilt in 118–125 C.E. by Hadrian. Its most notable architectural feature is the large circular opening at the top of its dome that lets in light and air (and rain). It served as a temple to all the gods ("pantheon") in the Roman Empire—except, of course, the God of Jews and Christians. Today it is a Christian church. Used by permission of BiblePlaces.com.

Table 4.2 *Greco-Roman Gods*

Greek Name for the Deity	Attributes	Roman Counterpart
Zeus	Patriarchal head of the Pantheon. Ruler of the heavens and weather.	*Jupiter
Hera	Consort of Zeus. Goddess of marriage and associated with womanhood.	*Juno
Poseidon	The brother of Zeus and god of the seas; god of horses in early Greece.	Neptune
Hestia	Sister of Zeus and goddess of the hearth.	Vesta
Demeter	Goddess of grain.	Ceres
Athena	Goddess of wisdom and patron of Athens for the Greeks; also the patron goddess of the arts.	*Minerva
Apollo	Identified with youthful manhood; god of wisdom; the patron god of music, shepherding, and archery.	—
Artemis	Apollo's twin sister. Goddess of the hunt; goddess of childbearing.	Diana
Ares	War god—most blood-thirsty character in the Roman pantheon.	Mars
Aphrodite	Goddess of love and fertility for the Greeks; took on a more sexual nature in the Roman pantheon.	Venus
Hermes	Messenger of the gods (particularly in the Roman pantheon); patron of wayfarers (particularly in the Greek pantheon).	Mercury
Hephaestus	Physically disabled deity who served as the blacksmith to the gods.	Vulcan

*Principal Roman deities

The Roman Pantheon

The traditional Roman **pantheon** of gods was a rough adaptation of the Olympian gods of Greece. We look to the epic poems of Homer, the *Iliad* and the *Odyssey*, for their forms and attributes. The Greek gods were highly anthropomorphic (taking human form), in contrast to the gods of early Roman religion, who were without personality. The Romans regarded deity as impersonal force or forces. However, beginning in about the third century B.C.E., Roman deities assimilated the features of the Olympian gods. Because the gods presided over the everyday occurrences of human life, religion was an intensely practical matter. The reality of a spiritual realm paralleling the physical realm was accepted without question. However, the main object of religion was the performance of appropriate rites for the appropriate deity, in order to maintain the kind of relationship with the gods that would favor one's successful endeavors in - this world. In Greece, religion was far more inclusive of the common people. Greece had no priestly class; anyone could offer a sacrifice to a god or to the gods. However, egalitarian access to the cult of the classical pantheon was substantially altered under the Romans, who reserved the performance of rites and sacrifices for official religious functionaries.

The principal gods of Rome were Jupiter, Minerva, and Juno, whose chief temple was established on the Capitoline hill of the Roman Forum. Perhaps the most significant religious functionary was the priest of Jupiter. Other priests were members of the college of priests. The head of the collegium pontificum was the **pontifex maximus,** the "high priest." Later, the emperors took this title, and when the Roman Empire fell it passed from them to the bishop of Rome, the Pope, now called the "Pontiff."

The college of **augurs** (omen interpreters) was involved with the *auspices,* omens interpreted from natural phenomena such as the flight of birds or from examining the internal organs of sacrificed animals. A person or a group before embarking on a major undertaking typically looked for omens or auspices. Although the college of augurs ruled on the propriety of procedure and interpretation of auspices, the actual activity of taking auspices was the function of magistrates, a practice that shows the great extent to which Roman religion was really a state function. The government maintained a calendar of religious observances and activated the College of Priests to perform the appropriate rites. The people were mostly passive in their observance, with the exception of specially proclaimed days of prayer in which all had to participate.

www   Follow the link to an online tour of the Pantheon.

Lesser Deities

Most people understand the Roman pantheon as the full extent of Roman religion, but Roman polytheism allows for the veneration of a wide and ever-expanding variety of gods, spirits, and divine powers. The average Roman invoked different deities to bless particular undertakings. Every aspect of work and personal life had its own minor deity to oversee and direct it, and the common people worshipped local and household gods outside the sphere of activity in the official cult.

The **lares** (LAHR-ace) were spirits venerated in connection with particular places. A stream, a wooded glen, one's home all had their particular *lar*. Similar to the **lares** were **genii** (singular **genius**), the spirits of persons, things, or groups. (This is not to be confused with the word *genie,* which derives from the Arabic *jinn*.) There was the "genius of the Emperor," the "genius of the Senate," and the "genius of Rome." The genii might also be venerated as fortune, or luck, associated with particular people or places. To speak of the "luck of the Irish" expresses in a cliché something of this old Roman religious idea.

Ideals and virtues were also personified and venerated. We understand the blindfolded woman holding in balance a scale as a symbol for legal justice. For the Roman, this was a representation of Justice, the deified virtue. Likewise, Beauty, Mercy, and Truth were understood as goddesses who could be revered, invoked, and worshiped. They could stand alone as independent powers or be brought together to express related conceptions of virtue. The virtues as *numina,* divine powers, enjoyed great popularity to the very end of Roman paganism—and perhaps beyond. Even today, the veneration accorded to those ideals regarded as virtuous can approach worship among certain groups of people. And the continuing representation of justice as a blindfolded woman with her scale demonstrates the lasting informal power in the cult of the Virtues.

The Imperial Cult

The worship of Caesar as a god was a later development in Roman state religion. The divinization of monarchs was an accepted pattern among the peoples of the ancient Near East and Egypt, and Greece had been prepared for the idea in its contact with the Persians. As mentioned earlier, Alexander the Great accepted divine honors upon entering Egypt, and his successors also accepted divinization. The imperial cult was popular in the eastern regions of the Roman Empire as a way to bring about spiritual as well as political unity. The emperors themselves promoted the cult as a means of including a religious element in the quest for political loyalty.

Emperor worship was never intended to replace the classical gods or supplant their worship, but as the imperial cult grew in popularity, it tended to diminish the vitality of the old religion. At the inception of the imperial cult, Jupiter, Minerva, and Juno were seen as expressing their will through Caesar. As time went on, however, the pantheon came to be viewed as something like the imperial bodyguard. The dignity of the gods was somewhat diminished in the presence of the divine Caesar. The popularity and practice of the imperial cult grew steadily, particularly in the provinces. The imperial cult was especially strong in Asia Minor, and its zealous practice there under the Emperor Domitian provides the background for the NT book of Revelation. It grew in the second century, and by the third century it was mandated to all. The imperial cult was reasonably successful as a spiritual program for political unification in the empire. As a religion, however, it did not provide much of an avenue for personal piety, devotion, or individual spiritual aspirations beyond an expression of loyalty to the Emperor. More personal forms of religious expression were becoming available, though, through the growth in popularity of the mysteries and eastern religions.

Mysteries and Eastern Religions

The **mystery religions** were ancient religious movements that featured initiation rites and cult secrets (mysteries), offering hope for a better life after death. Mystery religions were widespread religious movements that existed in ancient Greece and, later, in Rome. Orphism, Bacchism, and the Eleusinian mysteries are the best known of the early Greek mysteries. In later Greece and Rome, these were joined by such mysteries as the worship of Mithras and Isis. The mystery cults varied widely but generally centered on an initiation rite that featured revelation of cult secrets, the mysteries. The mysteries also included some sort of promise for a better life after death, which accounted for much of their popularity. Through the initiation, a worshipper became united with the god and thus shared in divine power and, perhaps, immortality. The different classical mystery religions cannot always be easily distinguished from one another, or from Greek religion in its entirety. They were not, in fact, entirely separate. The mysteries were parts of a larger Greek polytheistic religion, not independent religions themselves. Mystery initiates worshipped the same gods as the rest of the Greeks, though their ceremonies might have a different focus, and their myths also varied. The central feature of their myths featured the physical or metaphorical death of a god or goddess, followed by his or her resurrection. Because of these central myths and the promise for a better life after death, the mysteries have often been compared with Christianity. Christianity also features an initiation rite of a sort, baptism.

These rites are termed *mysteries* because they were secret rituals in which only those who had been initiated could participate. Initiation brought one into a special relationship with a deity and under that deity's divine benevolence and protection. Each mystery had its cult myth. The mysteries may have begun as fertility rites, since the cult myths of the most popular Greek mysteries were agriculture myths interpreting the cycle of the seasons or the growth of plant life from seed. We do not know exactly what happened during initiation rites (after all, they were secret!), but the public rites of the mystery cults often included ritual reenactment of part or all of the cult myth. The most well-known Greek mysteries were the Eleusinian and Dionysiac mysteries. The Eleusinian mysteries were associated with Demeter, the Greek goddess of grain, whereas the Dionysiac mysteries had their foundation in the myth of Dionysus, the divine giver of the vine to humanity.

As Hellenistic culture was introduced into the East, the cults of eastern deities assumed secret rites of initiation in the pattern of the Greek mysteries. Conversely, the cults of these eastern deities were introduced back into Greece and Rome. These included the cult of Isis, Osiris, and Serapis from Egypt; Astarte and Adonis from Phoenicia; the cult of Atargatis from Syria; and the cult of Cybele and Attis from Asia Minor. Like the original Greek mysteries, the cults of these eastern gods and goddesses obviously originated in agricultural and other fertility rites practiced in different regions. The benefits conferred upon initiates by these deities might include the promise of blessed life after death, or freedom in this life from the powers of fate and works of magic. The ceremonies in each cult included ritual reenactment of part or all of the cult's central myth.

An eastern mystery religion of particular interest in the comparative study of Judaism and Christianity to Hellenistic and eastern religions is the Persian cult of Mithras. The chief element in the Mithraic myth is the capture and killing of a wild bull by the divine hero, Mithras. The bull was created by the Persian god, Ahura Mazda. From the blood of the slain bull sprang life and grain as benefits to humanity. Mithras was also associated with Sol, the sun god. The reenactment of a sacred meal of friendship shared between Mithras and Sol was an integral part of Mithraism. Seven grades of initiation were eventually developed in Mithraism as it came to be practiced in the Roman Empire. This cult was limited to men, which is one factor in explaining its popularity among Roman legionaries.

www   Follow the link to an excellent treatment of mystery religions, with many primary sources.

Astrological Religion

Astral religion seems to have developed in Babylonia and was picked up by the Greeks during the age of Hellenistic expansion. The Babylonians understood their gods to be housed in the heavenly bodies. The heavens were also the eternal abode of souls. The soul of an individual descended through the realm of the gods on its way to being born on earth, assuming on its way the characteristics of the astral spheres through which it passed. Likewise, the soul of the deceased ascended back through this realm of the gods after death, with its state of blessedness determined by the manner of its ascent.

From Babylonian astral religion the Greeks developed astrology. Half religion and half "science," astrology postulates that by observing the movement and juxtaposition of heavenly bodies one could predict earthly events and human destinies. Eventually this system of prediction led to a belief in astrological determinism and inescapable fate. Astrological piety entailed surrender to fate and submission to one's destiny. Some of the mystery religions promised escape from fate as a benefit of initiation and identification with their god. Astrology did not disappear with the triumph of Christianity. Forms of astrology survived in Christian Europe during the Middle Ages, and their combination of belief and "science" is still popular among many people.

www   For treatment of the main Greco-Roman philosophical schools, see the website.

Gnosticism

A systematic definition of **Gnosticism** is nearly as impossible as tracing the origination and development of this religio-philosophical movement. It might be described as a syncretistic blend of Greek speculative thought and elements from various religious systems, including Platonism, Neopythagoreanism, and astral religion. Many scholars today posit that Gnosticism arose on the margins of Judaism, where these elements were combined with the faith of Israel. Its key element is reflective of its name—a belief that revealed knowledge (Greek: *gnosis* [NO-sihs]) of the cosmos was the key to human salvation. This salvation through knowledge was strictly an individual matter unmediated by a religious hierarchy.

Another significant element of fully developed Gnosticism was dualism. Gnosticism placed the material and spiritual realms at odds, with salvation seen as the soul's escape from the evil material world by virtue of one's reception of revealed knowledge. This belief led in turn to the dualism of two reigning deities: the higher god the one who was hidden and the source of salvific knowledge, the lower a **demiurge,** a powerful but lesser divinity who created the material world in which ethereal souls were enslaved. The disparagement of the material realm resulted in two opposing ethical responses. For some, the irrelevance of the material world meant freedom to engage in complete libertinism. For others, denial of the material world entailed **asceticism,** denial of the body to improve or free the spirit. The apostle Paul attacks both these tendencies in I Corinthians, a letter to a church where early forms of Gnosticism seem to have been present. Gnosticism became a serious threat to Christianity in the second century, when it developed into two major strains that came to be regarded as abnormal Christian teaching. The first of these, Sethianism, focused upon the third son of Adam, Seth, as the first Gnostic. The second, Valentinianism, named after its chief teacher, presented a more serious challenge to the early church through its development of a systematic and elaborate Gnostic mythology based on the preexistence of Christ.

For years, the only knowledge we had of Gnosticism came to us through Christian writers of the second and third centuries who opposed Gnostic influences. In 1945, however, a large collection of Gnostic writings was discovered in a cave near **Nag Hammadi,** Egypt. The Nag Hammadi collection has greatly enhanced our knowledge of Gnosticism and its relationship to Christianity, but the origins and development of Gnosticism still remain a mystery.

Key Terms and Concepts

augurs • Alexander the Great • asceticism • centurion • civic magistracies clients • collegia (voluntary associations) • Diadochi • equestrian class forum (agora) • freedmen • genii • Gnosticism • gymnasium • Hellenism Hellenistic Age • infanticide • lares • legion • mystery religions • Nag Hammadi patrician class • patron, patronage • Pax Romana • pedagogue • plebeian class Ptolemaic dynasty • pontifex maximus • prefect • sacral manumission Seleucid dynasty • slaves • tax farming

Questions for Study, Discussion, and Writing

1. How do contemporary methods of interpretation help us to understand ancient cultures? How do they prevent us from fully entering into their worldviews?
2. Sketch the most important events in the history of Palestine from 200 B.C.E. to 70 C.E.

3. How did the Jewish revolt of 66–73 resemble the Maccabean revolt? How did it differ?
4. For Jews in Palestine, what were the chief advantages of living under Roman rule? the disadvantages?
5. What were the chief characteristics of Greco-Roman religions?
6. What did the mysteries and Eastern cults offer that made them attractive to people in Roman society?
7. How did Greco-Roman polytheism differ from the religious sensibilities of eastern peoples?
8. Reflect on this statement: "The glory and the downfall of Rome was that it was a militaristic society."
9. What was the status and role of women in Roman society of the first century C.E.? Was the "new Roman woman" phenomenon a form of first-century feminism?

For Further Reading

Ferguson, Everett. *Backgrounds of Early Christianity,* 3rd ed. Grand Rapids, MI: Eerdmans, 2003. A clear, comprehensive introduction to both the Jewish and Greco-Roman backgrounds of the NT.

Hayes, John H., and Mandell, Sara. *Jewish People in Classical Antiquity: From Alexander to Bar Kochba.* Louisville, KY: Westminster John Knox, 1998. A balanced, well-written introduction to Jewish history from 333 B.C.E. to 135 C.E.

Klauck, Hans-Josef. *The Religious Context of Early Christianity: A Guide to Greco-Roman Religions.* Minneapolis: Augsburg Fortress, 2002. A careful study of both official and popular Greco-Roman religions, including mystery religions, the emperor cult, and Gnosticism.

Nilsson, Martin P. *Greek Folk Religion.* Philadelphia: University of Pennsylvania Press, 1987. A readable survey providing insight into the spirit of ancient paganism and the mysteries.

Pagels, Elaine. *The Gnostic Gospels.* New York: Vintage Books, 1989. An interesting and readable study for the beginning student.

Perkins, Pheme. *Gnosticism and the New Testament.* Minneapolis: Fortress Press, 1993. A well-researched account of the interrelationships of Gnosticism and early Christianity.

Robinson, James M. ed. *The Nag Hammadi Library in English.* 3rd ed. San Francisco: Harper & Row, 1988. An excellent collection of Gnostic Christian texts.

Vermes, Geza. *The Dead Sea Scrolls in English.* 3rd ed. Harmondsworth, UK: Penguin, 1984.

Winter, Bruce. *Roman Wives, Roman Widows: The Appearance of New Women and the Pauline Communities.* Grand Rapids, MI: Eerdmans, 2003. A fine study of how rapidly changing roles for Roman women challenged the early church.

Part II

Gospel Portraits of Jesus

Chapter Five

Introducing the Gospels

Before we examine the four New Testament Gospels individually beginning in the next chapter, we must introduce some important introductory questions and methods. First, we will treat the issue of the genre of the Gospels. Second, we will consider why the gospels were written. Third, we will introduce the relationship of the three Synoptics to each other. Fourth, we will consider form and redaction criticism. Finally, we will examine newer ways of reading the Gospels: narrative, social scientific, feminist, and cross-cultural.

What Is a Gospel?

What does it mean that Matthew, Mark, Luke, and John are called Gospels? Why were they given this description, and what would an ancient reader expect of a Gospel book? These questions ask about the **genre** (literary type) to which the Gospels belong, an important question for both historical criticism and narrative criticism. Genre is important for three reasons. First, readers' expectation of a book, even before they begin to read, is shaped by their initial perception of its genre. Just as modern readers expect different things from different kinds of books—we don't pick up a novel with the same expectations as a textbook, for example—so too did ancient readers. As the literary critic Frank Kermode has suggested, genre is a "set of expectations" shared by the writer and the readers (Kermode 1979, 162). Second, establishing the genre of a document can help us understand how the ancient readers or listeners experienced it, if they read for inspiration, instruction, or entertainment. Third, knowing about genre is important for a variety of today's reading methods. Not only do historians of the NT look at genre, but others do as well.

For the first two generations of Christians, *gospel* meant an oral message. The word itself (Greek *euangelion*) means "good news," and both Greek and Romans used it before NT times for political announcements such as the enthronement of a new emperor or a great victory in war. For example, a 9 B.C.E. inscription from Priene in modern-day Turkey gives good news about the emperor Augustus in notably religious language: "Providence . . . created the most perfect good for our lives . . . giving us Augustus and filling him with virtue for the benefit of humankind, sending us and those after us a savior who put an end to war and established all things in order. . . . The birthday of the god [Augustus] marked for the world the beginning of good news through his coming." In the oldest books of the NT, Paul's letters, *gospel* means the oral Christian message about Jesus (e.g., Rom 1:1–4; 1 Cor 15:1). The verb "to proclaim good news" is used for announcing this message orally (e.g., Rom 1:15; 1 Cor 1:17). Only Mark may call his book a "Gospel" (1:1), but he may use the term here to mean the oral message of Jesus' preaching. Matthew uses the term *gospel* four times, but always in reference to the oral message of Jesus during his lifetime and later (4:23, 9:35, 24:14, 26:13). Luke and John do not use the word even once. Also, when the Gospel books of Matthew, Mark, Luke, and John first appeared, they did not have titles, either generically ("Gospel") or specifically (for example, "Mark"). These labels were affixed to the texts in the second century. The second-century mainstream church saw each of them as a representation of the one Christian message about Jesus and called them not just "Matthew," "Mark," "Luke" and "John," as we do now, but "The Gospel according to Matthew/Mark/Luke/John." All this makes our question more intriguing: How *did* a word for an exclusively oral message become both the genre and title of written books? We will answer this question by examining how the Gospel books are both similar and dissimilar to other ancient genres.

The Gospels as Similar to Ancient Genres

Imagine a late-second-century person who is not a Christian believer visiting a house in which a Christian congregation meets. As she looks at the outside of a scroll kept in an open cabinet, she sees the words, "The Gospel according to Matthew." Her first thought would probably be, "A 'gospel'! What sort of book is that?" She would have to begin reading and compare Matthew with other books. (In the ancient world, different kinds of books were written out on the same kind of scrolls, so one could not literally tell a book by its cover!) She would probably consider three particular kinds of genres of her time as possible matches for Matthew.

First, as she read Matthew, she would notice its narratives about a central character named Jesus and might think that Matthew is in the **acts** genre, books giving grand narrative accounts of the deeds of a famous historical figure. For example, Xenophon's *Anabasis* tells about the military campaigns and battles of Alexander the Great, how he conquered most of the Mediterranean and Near Eastern world. Are the Gospels the "Acts" of Jesus? Although they do narrate the story of Jesus and how he does some amazing things, and thus could be considered an act narrative, the evidence on the whole goes against this genre. The Gospels contain few of the heroic adventures that most readers would expect in such a book. Further, Jesus' execution by Rome after founding a movement that still troubled many Romans may have meant that he was too controversial a figure for treatment in a typical acts narrative. These stories treated widely acknowledged heroes, not a controversial figure like Jesus. Also, the Gospels contain much more of Jesus' teaching than the typical acts narrative has of its hero's speeches. A final point against the Gospels as acts narratives comes from the second century: when Christians applied genre labels to their literature, they identified as acts narratives those stories of heroic Christians, such as the NT Acts of the Apostles or the extra-NT *Acts of Paul and Thecla,* but they did not apply this label to their books about Jesus, probably sensing that it did not fit. These books they called Gospels.

As our imaginary reader presses on into Matthew, she may think that this Gospel belongs to an ancient genre called **memoirs.** These were collections of individual stories about famous persons like philosophers and national leaders, which often included some of their teachings. Around 150 C.E., the Christian writer Justin Martyr described an early Christian meeting where "memoirs" of Jesus were read: "On the day called Sunday there is a meeting in one place of those who live in cities or in the country, and the memoirs of the apostles or the writings of the prophets are read as long as time permits" (*Apology* 67.3). He had earlier explained, "The memoirs of the apostles are called Gospels" (*Apology* 66). Justin rightly sees similarities of genre between the Gospels and Greco-Roman memoirs, although he is the only ancient Christian we know of to use this term. He may well use the term because he writes for Greco-Roman readers who are familiar with this genre, explaining the Gospels by way of something they already know. Our Gospels, however, reverse the usual proportion of actions and teachings in the Greco-Roman memoir in that they (aside from Mark) concern teaching as much as actions. Moreover, they contain many elements that the ancients would regard as foreign to ancient memoirs: descriptions of the miracles of Jesus, for example. All the Gospels narrate at length Jesus' trial, death, and resurrection, which would also look out of place in a memoir format. In sum, we can conclude with some confidence that an ancient reader would not recognize a Gospel as a Greco-Roman memoir.

Finally, as she read to the end of Matthew, it might occur to our reader that this belongs to a genre called **lives,** or **biography.** Plutarch, the most famous biographer of the Greco-Roman world, wrote in the first century C.E. a collection of short biographies called *Parallel Lives of Greeks and Romans.* Plutarch describes his "lives" as follows:

> I am not a writer of histories but of biographies. My readers therefore must excuse me if I do not record all events or describe them in detail. I only briefly touch upon the noblest and the most famous. For the most conspicuous [events] do not always necessarily show a man's virtues or failings, but it often happens that some light occasion, a word or a jest, gives a clearer insight into character. . . . Painters produce a likeness by the representation of the countenance and the expression of the face, in which the character is revealed, without troubling themselves about the other parts of the body. So I must be allowed to look rather into the signs of a man's character, and by means of these to portray the

life of each, leaving to others the description of great events and battles. (*Life of Alexander* 1.1)

Plutarch shows here that ancient "lives" focused mainly on a person, while "acts" and "histories" focused mainly on events. "Lives" deal with a single individual, the others with a group or nation. A "life" aims to furnish an example to others by highlighting the person's character. This moral aim and focus on the adult life of its subject, along with other features of ancient biography, distinguish it from modern biographies.

The differences between the Gospels and ancient "lives" are plain: the Gospels do not cover all of Jesus' adult life; they have a strong focus on his death; and they devote much attention to his teaching. These differences have led most scholars to deny that the Gospels are a part of the "lives" genre. However, Richard Burridge has recently made a good argument that the Gospels are indeed an ancient "life" of Jesus (Burridge 1992). He established four key features of Greco-Roman "lives." First, a title and an opening formula begin the story. Second, the subject of the biography gets the vast majority of the treatment and the main focus. Third, the structure of the book and its style strengthen the focus on the subject. Fourth, a "life" features the settings, the topics and content, and the values and attitudes promoted by the work along with the author's intention and purpose. Each of these features is present in the Gospels, Burridge argues, so that an ancient person could identify them as a "life" of Jesus and interpret them accordingly. Against Burridge, we note that the Gospels have no formal title assigned to them in the way that the Greco-Roman lives do. Also, the Gospels focus on the sufferings and death of their subject in a way peculiar for a genre called a "life." *If* the Gospels are modeled after an ancient genre, it is most likely that this was the "life," but the differences are persuasive to most scholars today, who conclude that it probably does not belong to this genre. Strong debate remains, and is likely to continue into the foreseeable future, about the genre of the Gospels.

We return now to our imaginary reader examining a Christian scroll in the ancient house church. She probably started reading Matthew with all these genres in mind. But as she read, she might begin to consider how this "gospel" book is dissimilar to other genres she knew. Perhaps, she might think, it is even a new genre! Her discovery leads us to the next section.

The Gospels as Dissimilar to Ancient Genres

Another approach to understanding the genre of the Gospels has been to study the ways in which the Gospels are unlike ancient types of literature. Form criticism, which arose in the early twentieth century, first stressed that the Gospels are based on oral traditions, not on written genres. These oral traditions were used in the preaching and teaching of the earliest churches. The authors drew on stories and material they had heard from others, rather than researching and writing the Gospels in a fresh manner.

The next step in appreciating the uniqueness of the gospel genre came in the work of the British scholar C. H. Dodd. Following the lead of form criticism, Dodd related the Gospels to earlier Christian oral use in preaching, not to established genres of literature. He studied the evangelistic speeches in Acts in an influential work, *The Apostolic Preaching and Its Development* (Dodd 1936) and concluded that there was a consistent pattern in the sermons in the Acts of the Apostles. Dodd looked especially at Peter's sermon in Acts 10:34–43, identifying six essentials of the speech that formed the pattern of Christian preaching in that passage and in most other sermons in Acts:

- John the Baptizer prepared the way for the coming of Jesus (Acts 10:37).
- These events were promised in the OT Scriptures (v. 43).
- Jesus' ministry was empowered by God (vv. 38–39).
- Jesus was arrested, tried and executed on a cross (v. 39b).
- God raised Jesus from the dead and he was seen by witnesses (vv. 40–41).
- Jesus commands his followers to tell others about him and summon them to faith (v. 42).

Dodd pointed out that these six points correspond to the major sections of Mark and come in roughly the same sequence:

- John the Baptizer appears, fulfilling the OT (Mark 1:1–15).
- Jesus' powerful ministry is described (1:16–8:30).
- After Jesus' movement to Jerusalem, he is arrested, tried, and dies on the cross (8:31–15:47).
- There is a brief mention of the resurrection of Jesus (16:6, perhaps with a lost longer ending).
- Jesus' disciples are to go out and tell others (16:7).

Dodd's outline of the gospel message from Acts does not fit the outline of the Gospels perfectly. For example, Mark 16:7 does not refer to a mission in the world, and John does not have this point at its end. However, the pattern does fit well enough to explain why these books came to be called "Gospels." Dodd showed persuasively that the Gospels are extended written narratives of the oral gospel message that early Christians proclaimed.

www Follow the link to examine Dodd's remarkably succinct book online.

What conclusion can we draw from this debate about how the Gospel genre relates to other ancient genres? On one hand, we see some elements of all three Greco-Roman genres in the Gospels; they are in some ways acts, in other ways memoirs and in still other ways lives. Some recent research into the genres of the Gospels is returning to the position that they most closely resemble the lives. It makes sense that they would have some similarities with other ancient literature, for such similarity would help readers to understand them. On the other hand, something new is present in the genre of the Gospels. They relate the new things that the early Christians believed God did in and through Jesus, and they originated in the oral preaching of the earliest churches. Moreover, they were documents meant not mainly for literate, upper-class people who would be familiar with literary genres, but rather for the lower-class people who predominated in the early church, who would not know or care about genres as they listened to the Gospels being read aloud to them. Dodd argues persuasively that the Gospels give the church's proclamation of Jesus in narrative form.

We can conclude that the Gospels are partially related to aspects of more than one ancient genre, especially the life, but agree in their main contents with none. We cannot categorize them simply and persuasively as an ancient life, memoir, acts, or anything else. Just as the oral gospel message, the "good *news,*" was a new thing, so too the written Gospel message has in some significant measure new features of genre. Our imaginary reader may conclude just that: this written Gospel book she is perusing bears a strong resemblance to the message of the Gospel she has heard Christians relate.

Why Were the Gospels Written?

What caused the oral traditions about Jesus to take written form in the Gospels? In other words, why did the gospel become the Gospels?

First, a *historical* reason has traditionally been put forward. The Gospels were written at a time when the original eyewitnesses to Jesus were dying, and the early church wanted to get the story of Jesus down in writing. For example, many scholars think that Mark was written shortly after the death of Peter during Emperor Nero's persecution of the church in Rome. Luke distinguishes "us" from "those who from the beginning were eyewitnesses and ministers of the word" (Luke 1:2). To be sure, the author does not explicitly mention the death of these "eyewitnesses and ministers," but the passing of this generation may well be implied. In its last chapter (21), the Gospel of John does note the death of the "Beloved Disciple" who was the authority behind its traditions. That this attempt to preserve the knowledge of Jesus for succeeding generations is the main reason for the writing of the Gospel of John is most unlikely, because it explicitly points in another direction, which we will consider shortly. Most NT scholars today, while recognizing the passing of a generation at or near the time the Gospels were written, do not place significant emphasis on this as a reason for the gospel writings.

Second, did early Christians write the Gospels for an *evangelistic* reason, that is, in order to make converts to the Christian faith? After all, as form criticism has taught us, much gospel material was used in the oral proclamation of the faith for conversion; why not also the gospel books that wrote them down? In John 20:30–31, this evangelistic reason may seem to be the case, as Donald A. Carson has argued (Carson 1991). This "first ending" of the Gospel of John reads in the NRSV translation, "Now Jesus did many other signs [miracles] which are not written in this book. But these are written so that you may come to believe that Jesus is the Messiah, the Son of God, and through believing you may have life in his name." This sounds very much like an evangelistic purpose, as Carson maintains. Other scholars, reading the *explicit* reason for writing found in John 20:30–31 in the context of the *implicit* reason for writing found in the whole of John, conclude that it would be most suited to strengthen the faith of those who are already believers, probably in a hostile environment. Moreover, a strongly witnessed textual variant has this verse read, "may continue to believe." Despite the evangelistic way of reading John 20:30–31, the whole of John as it stands today does not appear to be evangelistically oriented, and no other Gospel makes such a seemingly evangelistic statement or calls its hearers to faith as if they had none already. Some scholars have argued that Theophilus may have been someone not yet a convert, and that Luke was written to bring him to full faith (Luke 1:1–4). Again, the Gospel of Luke as we have it is not evangelistic in purpose, and Luke 1:4 actually states to Theophilus, "you have been instructed" (note the past tense). We may safely conclude with the strong consensus among NT scholars that although much of the raw material of all four Gospels was used in Christian preaching to non-Christians, the Gospels themselves were designed for Christians.

Third, most researchers today conclude that a *teaching* reason is the general cause for the writing of the Gospels—that is, to inform those who already believed in Jesus more fully about their faith and to form them in it. The Gospels were both commendatory, to identify and encourage positive things in the life of their audience, and corrective, to identify and ameliorate negative things. If Theophilus was a believer, this was probably one of Luke's aims. If he was not a believer, a teaching reason still applies, as Luke explicitly says that he writes so that Theophilus "may know the truth concerning the things about which you have been instructed" (1:4). Similarly, the major sections of teaching material in Matthew would be useful explaining Christian lifestyle to an audience of believers. As Dodd argued, the written Gospels provide extended narrative summaries of the contents of the Christian proclamation, just the sort of thing to teach believers more fully about their faith.

www See the website for a brief essay on an important question many people ask today: "Why are these four Gospels in the New Testament, and not any of the others written near that time?"

Aerial View of the Temple Mount This view of the ancient Temple area is from the southwest. The Muslim Dome of the Rock mosque complex, the third-holiest place in Islam, is built on this site. Note the Western Wall area below the Dome. The Mount of Olives is at the center right. Used by permission of BiblePlaces.com.

The Synoptic Problem and Source Criticism

What is the literary relationship of the Synoptic Gospels to each other? This issue is known as the **Synoptic Problem.** In NT scholarship over the last two centuries, solving the Synoptic Problem has involved continued source criticism of the Synoptics. When source criticism is so complex, why is it so important? First, source criticism is both a commonsensical and scholarly way to explain historically what actually lies before us in the text of the Gospels, their remarkable similarities and differences. The Synoptic Problem arises from a historical reading of the text of the Gospels themselves, not imposed on it by scholars with nothing better to do than spin hypotheses. Second, recognizing the literary relationships among the Synoptics enables us to see the emphases of each Gospel writer in their use of their material. Third, addressing the Synoptic Problem makes our quest for the "historical Jesus" both richer and more complicated. It becomes richer as we see how the Gospels use their sources and shape their special emphases. It becomes more complicated because it does not solve all historical problems. For example, although we may conclude that Mark wrote first, we should not therefore conclude that his version is *necessarily* a more accurate portrait of Jesus than the others are. Finally, addressing the Synoptic Problem gives us insight not just into Jesus, but into the history of early Christianity.

Developing Your Skills: Using a Gospel Synopsis

An excellent tool for Gospel analysis is a **synopsis***. It displays Matthew, Mark, and Luke (and often John too, although John is not a Synoptic gospel) in parallel columns, passage by passage, to allow you to see them in one view. General and detailed comparisons can easily be made between them. One can find synopses on the Internet (for example, the excellent site by John Marshall of the University of Toronto; use the link on the webpage for this book).*

It is best to make a photocopy of the synoptically portrayed passage you are studying. Then mark the photocopy to identify which words are exactly the same in two or three Gospels. You will easily see the similarities and differences among the accounts. Being able to use a synopsis will greatly facilitate your ability to understand source, form, and redaction criticism.

The Synoptics present two obvious features to any reader: in many sections, they share notable agreements; in many other sections, there are notable differences. First, the agreements are striking. In passages where Matthew, Mark, and Luke tell the same story or relate a teaching of Jesus, they usually agree very closely in how they tell it. Often a majority of the wording is exactly the same in Greek, as is the overall structure of the passage. Agreements are present in the **triple tradition** (the same material told by Matthew, Mark, and Luke), but there are also agreements where only two Gospels have common material. This is called the **double tradition,** especially where Matthew and Luke are the two. For example, the wording of Jesus' healing of Peter's mother-in-law is very close in the triple tradition (Mark 1:29–31; Matt 8:14–15; Luke 4:38–39), and the wording of the Lord's Prayer/Our Father is close in the double tradition (Matt 7:7–11, Luke 11:9–13). Moreover, one finds a general agreement in the sequence of the stories and teachings of Jesus as one moves through the Synoptics. Significant differences in wording also occur. At places throughout the Synoptics, two Gospels agree and the third is different. However, it is rare for the different one to be Mark. Generally, where either Matthew or Luke has a different sequence, the other agrees with Mark's order; cases where they agree with each other against Mark are very rare. Each of the Synoptic Gospels has unique stories or sections. In Mark, however, they are few, since 88 percent of Mark is paralleled in Luke and 97 percent in Matthew.

www Follow the links to two excellent online treatments of the Synoptic Problem. Also see the website enrichment material for a brief treatment of how Luke 1:1–4 relates to source criticism.

How is this remarkable situation, these similarities and differences, to be explained? We will consider first the Griesbach/Two-Gospel Hypothesis, then the idea of Markan priority, next the Two-Document Hypothesis, and finally the Four-Document Hypothesis.

The Griesbach or Two-Gospel Hypothesis

Someone puzzling out the relationship of the Gospels today might begin with the notion that Matthew was written first and used by the others. After all, it is first in the canonical order. This is exactly where scholarship began to attack the Synoptic Problem. According to J. J. Griesbach (d. 1812), the earliest gospel was Matthew; Luke adapted Matthew, and Mark is a shortened combination of Matthew and Luke. This explanation of gospel relationships is traditionally known as the **Griesbach Hypothesis** or, more recently, the **Two-Gospel Hypothesis.** It can be charted as seen below.

W. R. Farmer is the leading champion of this view in recent times (Farmer 1976). A tiny but vigorous minority of scholars today accept this hypothesis and study the synoptic Gospels based on it.

Five arguments are typically used in support of this hypothesis. First, important early Christian writers in the second and third centuries testify that Matthew was written first. Second, Matthew frequently shows the strongest influence of Jewish culture and settings, and since the church became less Jewish and more Gentile as it grew over the years, a strongly Jewish Gospel would likely have come earlier. Third, where Mark says things twice, such as "That evening, at sundown" (1:32), the parallel passages in Matthew and Luke often contain the two elements of Mark's doublet: Matt 8:16 has "That evening"; Luke 4:40 has "as the sun was setting." The Griesbach Hypothesis explains this repetition by arguing that Mark incorporates both phrases into his account because he wants to harmonize them. Fourth, where there are "minor agreements," where Matthew and Luke agree in wording against Mark, Mark is simply choosing to deviate from the wording of his two sources, perhaps because he has independent access to oral tradition. Finally, in a number of places Matthew and Luke appear to "alternate" in agreeing with Mark.

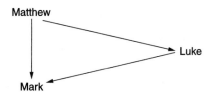

Figure 5.1 The Griesbach/Two-Gospel Hypothesis

Serious, cogent objections have been made against the Griesbach/Two-Gospel Hypothesis. First, although many early church writers say that Matthew wrote first, some imply that Mark came first. Besides, many writers from the second and third centuries seem to rely on guesswork about the origins of the NT, not solid historical information. Second, why should Mark have omitted so much of importance if he is preserving and combining Matthew and Luke? According to the Griesbach Hypothesis, Mark conserves his two sources, Matthew and Luke. However, he omits the birth of Jesus, large amounts of Jesus' teaching, and the resurrection appearance narratives. Third, why should Luke break up Matthew's teaching blocks and rearrange his material? Luke has most of the teaching found in Matthew's Sermon on the Mount, but it is spread around his Gospel. Something similar happens with Matthew's four other teaching discourses (Matthew 10, 13, 18, 24–25). If Luke is using Matthew, this seems most unusual. In the Griesbach Hypothesis, when Luke edited Matthew he systematically moved almost all double-tradition material from its Matthean contexts to somewhere else in his Gospel. Most NT scholars think that an author like Luke, with a self-professed interest in writing an orderly account (Luke 1:1–4), would be most unlikely to do such a thing. Fourth, the Markan redundancies can be explained as Mark's own style without resorting to the more complicated theory that he combined Matthew and Luke. Besides, out of about one hundred Markan redundancies, only seventeen have Matthew take one part of the redundant phrase and Luke take the other; such a low proportion demolishes this argument for the Two-Gospels Hypothesis.

Markan Priority

If someone puzzling over the Gospels today gives up the idea that Matthew is first and Mark is an abridgment of Matthew and Luke, he or she might surmise that Mark, the shortest and simplest Gospel, is first and Matthew and Luke use it. This is what happened in scholarship in the nineteenth century. The arguments against the Griesbach/Two-Gospels Hypothesis gradually gathered strength. The counter theory of **Markan priority**—that Mark was written first and used by Matthew and Luke as a source—eventually gained a wide assent that lasts through today. This can be diagrammed as follows:

Figure 5.2 Markan Priority

Six key arguments, put together, support the view that Mark wrote first and that Matthew and Luke used it independently of each other as a source.

- *Length.* The Gospel of Mark is only two-thirds the size of the Gospels of Matthew and Luke. If Mark is first, the authors of Matthew and Luke added to its material. However, if the author of Mark is using Matthew or Luke, it is hard to explain why he or she omitted so much material, especially things that fit Mark's own distinctive themes and purposes. For example, given Mark's stress on the conflict between Jesus and his opponents in the Jewish religious establishment (already in view in Mark 3), it is hard to explain why Mark would omit so much from Matthew or Luke that deals with this conflict. Also, because Mark constantly stresses Jesus' action as a teacher (1:21–22, 2:13; 4:1–2; 6:2; 8:31; 12:35), it is hard to explain why he would omit Matthew's and Luke's fuller account of the actual teachings of Jesus. The claim that this is explained by the desire of the author of Mark to produce a shortened book is implausible, because even though Mark's overall length is indeed one-third shorter than Matthew or Luke, it often tells each story at greater length. Someone trying to abridge the others to produce a short account would be unlikely to do this.
- *Sequence.* In general, Mark and Matthew agree in the sequential order of their material against Luke, and Mark and Luke agree in order against Matthew. However, Matthew and Luke virtually never agree in order against Mark. This discrepancy is most easily explained by Matthew and Luke using Mark independently and thus independently departing from Mark's order.
- *Style.* Mark's Greek is not smooth or polished. Matthew and Luke, on the other hand, have a smooth, fluent Greek style. For example, Mark overuses both *and* and *immediately*, often starting his sentences with one; Matthew and Luke do not. (Much of Mark's rough Greek is smoothed out by modern English translations, and less noticeable.) Where Mark's sentence structure in a given passage is ambiguous or clumsy, Matthew's and Luke's parallels are clear and smooth. Why Matthew and Luke would improve Mark is easy to explain, but why Mark would coarsen Matthew or Luke is not.
- *Difficult content.* Mark's Gospel has some content that is religiously difficult for Christian readers from the first century and the twenty-first century. For example, it suggests at times that Jesus' power or influence is incomplete, in places where the parallel passage in Matthew and Luke makes no such suggestion. Mark 6:5–6 reports that Jesus "*could* not" do deeds of power in his hometown of Nazareth because of the people's unbelief there, but Matt 13:58 says that Jesus "*did* not" do miracles because of their unbelief, which has a very different implication. In Mark 8:22–26, Jesus' first attempt to heal a blind man is only partly successful and must be followed by a second, fully successful attempt. Matthew and Luke omit the whole story. Moreover, Mark's portrait of the twelve, Jesus' main disciples, is frequently more critical. In most of these cases, it is easy to understand why Matthew and Luke would change Mark's version to be more complimentary to them. However, it is harder to imagine why Mark would change the religiously more acceptable wording derived from Matthew or Luke—unless, of course, he were deliberately devaluing

the Twelve for his own purposes, which is exactly what some have said he is doing (see Chapter 6 for more on this).

- *Theology.* The presentation of Jesus appears "heightened" in Matthew and Luke in comparison with Mark. In their first two chapters they both write about Jesus' supernatural conception, which Mark does not. Also, they call Jesus "Lord" more than Mark in the stories they have in common. This higher Christology is easy to explain if Matthew is using Mark, but it would be difficult to explain if Mark were using Matthew or Luke—he might want to make the Twelve look less impressive, but why would he make Jesus look lesser?

- *Explanatory power in scholarship.* The true measure of any hypothesis in science or the humanities is its ability to explain the data and lead to further discoveries. In Gospel scholarship, the theory of Markan priority has led to results in further scholarship that almost all biblical scholars—especially those using the historical-critical method of reading, alone or in combination with other methods—consider very fruitful.

Therefore, based on these six reasons, the strong majority of scholarship today concludes that Mark is a source of Matthew and Luke, not that Mark is a blending and shortening of Matthew and Luke, as the Griesbach/Two Gospel-Hypothesis contends. Markan priority is still a hypothesis, but it has become almost self-evident today.

The Two-Document Hypothesis and Q

But Markan priority raises another obvious issue in the Synoptic Problem for ordinary readers of the NT who delve into the Gospels: Why do Matthew and Luke also agree almost word for word in many sections not drawn from Mark? Karl Lachmann (d. 1851), who supported Markan priority, helped to solve this problem by proposing that Matthew and Luke used, in addition to Mark, a lost source of the sayings of Jesus, which later scholars called **Q** or the Synoptic sayings source. This source dubbed Q is defined as the material common to Matthew and Luke that is not in Mark. The resulting **Two-Document Hypothesis,** that Matthew and Luke used the two, Mark and Q, as sources, became dominant by the beginning of the twentieth century and remains so today. (Be careful not to confuse the "Two-*Gospel* Hypothesis," which is the Griesbach hypothesis of Matthean priority, with this "Two-*Document* Hypothesis," which posits the priority of Mark and Q). It can be diagrammed as follows:

Figure 5.3 The Two-Document Hypothesis

Most NT scholars today believe that Matthew and Luke drew a significant amount of material from Q. Matthew and Luke share about 235 verses that Mark does not have. These verses in Matthew and Luke are very similar to each other in wording, basically as similar as Matthew and Luke are to each other when they draw on Mark. This similarity has led scholars to theorize that they may be drawing on a single source for this material. This Q source is a **hypothetical document,** that is, a construction by modern scholars; no actual Q document, or even a reference to it, survives from the ancient world.

www   See this website for a chart outlining the content of Q and Burton Mack's presentation of the reconstructed English text of Q.

Four patterns of evidence are typically used to argue that the material common to Matthew and Luke but not found in Mark is derived from Q:

- *Agreements in wording.* This material agrees very closely in wording. Such agreement in Matthew and Luke probably indicates one of two things: either a common source lies behind them, or one of them is using the other's wording.
- *Agreements in sequence.* Q material comes in a roughly similar sequence in Luke and Matthew.
- *Coherence in contents.* The Q material overall has the basically coherent perspective that we expect of a body of material, whether written or oral. Q has a strong eschatological message in much of its contents: the end is near, and God's judgment on the world is coming. Jesus' followers must follow God's law sincerely and fully (Luke 16:17/Matt 5:18), even though they are persecuted (Luke 6:22–23/Matt 5:11–12; we follow here the traditional scholarly convention of citing Q by its Lukan reference first). One notes wisdom sayings (Luke 11:31–32/Matt 12:42); Jesus is a wise teacher, even greater than King Solomon, and expects his followers to live by his wisdom. He is the Son of Man who in his own life will be rejected and suffer (Luke 7:31–35/Matt 11:16–19), and the Son of Man who will come with God's judgment at the end of time (Luke 17:23–27, 30, 37/Matt 24:26–28, 37–39). Jesus is, and asks recognition as, Lord; one must keep his teaching in order to live forever (Luke 6:46–49/Matt 7:21, 24–27).
- *Genre.* Almost all of Q is the teaching of Jesus, rather than stories about Jesus. In the past, many scholars objected to the idea of Q because there was no document in the ancient world containing only the teaching of Jesus. The discovery of the whole **Gospel of Thomas** at Nag Hammadi, Egypt largely ended this argument, because it too contains almost exclusively teaching material. The *Gospel of Thomas* was written in beginning of the second century, but most scholars hold that it is close enough to the mid-first-century Q to make this argument from genre convincing.

The main alternatives to the Two-Document Hypothesis and its Q are that the author of Matthew used Luke and Mark or that the author of Luke used Matthew and Mark. Matthew and Luke each have their unique material, and that means that if one used the other's book, it is surprising (at least to us) that they left out so much. If the author of Luke used Matthew and Mark (the more common view among those who hold to the priority of Mark but reject Q), then he or she broke up Matthew's large teaching blocks like the Sermon on the Mount and distributed this material throughout his or her book. For Luke to disperse Matthew's orderly teaching units into different contexts would be inexplicable, because Luke prizes writing in an orderly way (Luke 1:3). Because the author of Luke follows the ordering of his other source, Mark, much more often than he departs from it, it is unlikely that he would cut Matthew to bits and scatter it all over his Gospel.

www For a short essay on recent scholarly controversies over Q, see the website. See also the link to Dr. Mark Goodacre's "Ten Reasons to Question Q."

The Four-Document Hypothesis

A reader of the Gospels who has puzzled out their interrelationship, accepting first the priority of Mark and then Q, still has one noticeable thing to settle in her mind. There is still a great deal of important material in Matthew and Luke, especially dealing with the teaching of Jesus, that the Two-Document Hypothesis does not explain. Do Matthew and Luke invent this material, draw upon a common oral tradition differently as they write it down, or do they draw upon a written or fixed oral source?

More analysis of the Gospels, assuming the Two-Document Hypothesis, resulted in a supplemental **Four-Document Hypothesis** that answers this question. Four sources were used in the Synoptics. Besides Mark and Q, Matthew used **M,** a source containing material only found in Matthew, and Luke used **L,** a source with material only found in Luke. Many, if not most, NT scholars today do research into the Synoptics on the basis of the Four-Document Hypothesis; they commonly hold that L was a written or oral source, but many doubt if M was either a written or oral collection. (We will consider L and M in Chapters 7 and 8.) The Four-Document Hypothesis can be diagrammed as seen below.

What are we to conclude from this debate over the Synoptic Problem? The strong majority view in scholarship remains the Two-Document Hypothesis: Mark and Q are the two sources used by Matthew and Luke. Most who accept the Two-Document Hypothesis also accept the Four-Document Hypothesis. As we have seen,

Figure 5.4 The Four-Document Hypothesis

good reasons exist for these conclusions, despite debate to the contrary. In general, we assume the Four-Document Hypothesis in the following discussion. However, for the newer methods of reading that do not incorporate historical criticism, that will make no great difference to our methods or conclusions.

Form Criticism of the Synoptic Gospels

Form criticism focuses on the forty- to seventy-year period *before* the traditions about Jesus' words and deeds were set down in the NT sources, the period of oral transmission. Nothing in the NT indicates that Jesus' followers copied down his words as he spoke or recorded his deeds as they happened. The attempt by a few scholars (e.g., Gerhardsson) to show that Jesus required his disciples to memorize his teachings, and that they soon thereafter wrote down these memories, rests on slim parallels gleaned from later rabbinic writings, not from the Gospels themselves. Although small wax tablets for "taking notes" were widespread in the Greco-Roman world, and seem to have been used by later Pharisee rabbis, there is no hint of this practice in the Gospels. Rather, the Synoptics and the book of Acts explicitly say that Jesus commanded his followers to preach and teach his message orally, a circumstance that militates against a written record made during his ministry by his followers that would lead quickly to a written gospel tradition. Jesus was a prophetic teacher, not a writer. His message, especially at first, was passed along in the "living voice" of human speech, to use Bishop Papias' phrase from about 125 C.E., not in books (Eusebius, *History of the Church* 3.39.3–4). So before we analyze the written form of our Gospels, the historical-critical method argues, we must look at the oral tradition behind them.

The Process of Oral Tradition

Form critics have reconstructed the process by which the Jesus tradition was transmitted and shaped during the oral period. The five key elements of this process in a *general* chronological order are:

Independent Units

Form critics have shown that most of the stories and sayings of Jesus circulated at first as single units, not in groups. The reader of the Synoptic Gospels notes that they are largely made up of such short independent units called **pericopes.** Indeed, most paragraphs in the Synoptic Gospels are made up of a single pericope. This made them more usable in the early church, because a single short item is easier to use than a longer collection of items. Acts 20:35 and 1 Cor 7:10 provide examples from outside the written Gospels of the use of such individual sayings. The small units of oral tradition were told singly as needed rather than in larger groups or as one continuous story (just as in most Christian preaching today). The main exception to this rule may be the passion narrative, which most form critics conclude circulated as a unit because it does not seem to make narrative or religious sense when broken into smaller units.

Standard Forms

As the earliest Christians used these individual units of material for similar religious purposes, the stories began to assume standard shapes or *forms*. Some stories take on standard shapes more easily than others. For example, it is hard to tell a healing miracle story differently from the way the gospels tell it, but a "story about Jesus" could be told in a variety of ways. This process led to the particular forms we identify today in the Gospels.

Preservation by Use

As the end of the Gospel of John indicates with a great flourish, Jesus said and did much more than what is written down about him. The stories that survived were probably those the early Christians found helpful in their activities and situations. The German phrase **Sitz im Leben** ("zits im LAY-ben"), meaning "setting in life," is used for the general situation for which a particular story or saying would be relevant. A major concern of form critics is to reconstruct the settings of the stories of Jesus. Actually, form critics speak of three distinct settings in life: of Jesus, if the story is held to be basically authentic, going back to Jesus' life; of the early church, between Jesus and the writing of the Gospel, when the story/saying is used by the church; and of the Gospel writer, when the traditions about Jesus take on new meaning in the literary context of a Gospel book. Form critics maintain that each form had its own type of setting in life. For example, the *pronouncement stories* were probably used as illustrations in the preaching of early missionaries; *parables* were used to teach the Christian message; *miracle* accounts were used in the healing ministries of the church.

Creation by the Early Church

For many form critics, a setting in life might mean a situation that led the early Christians to create a new story about Jesus or saying by him. A new setting in life or new issue in the early church might necessitate such creativity. Material from Judaism and even Greco-Roman philosophy could be adapted for use. Also, sayings of Christian prophets speaking in the name of the risen, heavenly Jesus could find their way into the gospel oral traditions; this is especially true, many NT scholars maintain, about predictions of the future the Gospels present as teachings of the historical Jesus.

Table 5.1 Names of Prominent Forms

Dibelius	Bultmann	Taylor	Examples
Paradigms	Apophthegms	Pronouncement stories	Mark 2:13–17; 6:1–4
Tales	Miracle stories	Miracle stories	Mark 1:29–31; 5:1-20
Exhortations	Sayings	Sayings and parables	Luke 10:7; Mark 7:15
Legends	Historical stories/ legends	Stories about Jesus	Mark 1:9–11; Matt 4:11

Laws of Tradition

Based on studying German folklore such as Grimm's fairy tales, Greek literature, rabbinic writings, the apocryphal and canonical gospels, and actual oral tradition in nonliterate cultures today, form critics identify "laws" about how stories developed as they were orally transmitted. For example, they argue that explanations of Jesus' teaching (such as explanations of parables) are secondary—that is, Jesus did not use them and they arose in the early church's oral tradition. Form critics also argue that where there are shorter and longer versions of the same story/teaching in the Gospels, the shorter stories are probably earlier, because detail was likely to be added in later. For example, the form of the Lord's Prayer/Our Father in Luke is thought to be more authentically from Jesus than Matthew's form, in part because it is much shorter. Using these laws, form critics attempt to reconstruct the earliest form of tradition, stripping away the later additions from the form that they believe was more original. In this process, they hope to get closer to the original, authentic teaching of Jesus.

We can summarize the names of prominent forms according to three leading form-critical scholars in Table 5.1.

The following is a brief description of these main types.

- A **pronouncement story,** like all other forms, is originally independent of its context in the Gospels, a story on its own. It gives minimal information about the participants other than Jesus, who are mainly foils (contrasting figures) to him. It climaxes in an authoritative word of Jesus, the "pronouncement" itself. This pronouncement is the main point used in the preaching and teaching of the pronouncement story in the early church.
- A **miracle story** is also briefly and simply told. It has a basic threefold structure: first, a description of the illness of the person to be healed; second, a statement of Jesus' healing action; third, a description/demonstration of the healed person. Often, but not always, it contains a statement about the faith of the person healed. Miracle stories were probably used in the healing ministries of the early church in addition to its preaching.
- A **parable** can sometimes be as short as a sentence. It is usually a (very) short story drawn from everyday life. Like most short stories, it has a small cast of characters,

often only one, and one plot line. The parable explicitly or implicitly describes one aspect of the Kingdom of God. Jesus used them both to teach the crowds and his disciples and also as a way to attack his opponents. As a story created by Jesus, the parable has a point that is not dependent on whether it happened historically.

- A *"story about Jesus"* is a self-contained short narrative that focuses, as its name indicates, on Jesus. These stories vary in their structure more than other forms.

Developing Your Reading Skills: Identifying Miracle Forms Today

Watch carefully any television commercial in story form that is advertising over-the-counter (nonprescription) medicine. Can you see a typical pattern that resembles the basic threefold pattern of ancient miracle stories? What is the "setting in life" of such commercials? How does the form of modern oral healing stories like television commercials relate to the form of Jesus' healings?

---

www   Follow the link to read and critique the "Form Criticism Timeline."

Criteria of Authenticity

Form criticism confirms what reading of the Synoptics suggests: traditions often change as they move through time. The Jesus tradition was used, gathered, adapted, edited, and sometimes created. How can we discern what in this tradition probably goes back to Jesus himself? Here the **criteria of authenticity,** principles by which one can determine if a saying or story of Jesus actually comes from Jesus or from the later church, come into play. In historical study of the Gospels, positions about how the Jesus tradition was passed down have two extremes: (1) the gospel tradition was so adaptive and creative of Jesus material that what we have in the Gospels is mostly inauthentic, and the burden of proof is on those who argue for the authenticity of a given Gospel passage; or (2) the gospel tradition was basically preservative and conservative, so that what we have in the Gospels is mostly authentic, and the burden of proof is on those who argue for inauthenticity. The truth is likely between these extremes. The careful historical-critical reader of the Gospels will want to examine each pericope on its own merits, without prejudging it one way or the other. What are these criteria of authenticity?

- *Multiple attestation.* Is this tradition in more than one Gospel? Historical study posits that if something is attested by several early writings, then it is more likely to be authentic. Therefore, in Gospel study, the more Gospels (perhaps including works like the Gospel of Thomas) attest to a tradition of Jesus' actions or teaching, the more likely it is to be authentic. However, if a tradition is found only in one Gospel, that may cast some doubt on it but does not automatically rule out its authenticity.

For example, the parable of the Good Samaritan is found only in Luke, but few scholars rule it out for that reason when it is supported by other criteria of authenticity. Many students of the NT Gospels have noted a problem with this criterion: How independent are these "multiple attestations" when the Synoptic Gospels are literarily related? This objection has a point, but it does not cancel out the proposed criterion. Even if it is correct that Matthew and Luke used Mark, the fact that they tell this story is an indication that they agree with it and may have their own independent information about it.

- *Dissimilarity.* This criterion asks whether a saying of Jesus found in the Gospels is unlike the Judaism of Jesus' day and unlike the teaching of the later Christian church. If it is unlike both, then it is more likely a saying of Jesus. This criterion presupposes that the Gospel portrait of Jesus has been influenced both by Judaism and by the early church. For example, in Mark 14:9 the woman who anoints Jesus will have her story "told in memory of her" "wherever the good news is proclaimed in the whole world." Here we see a statement about the life of the early church, which the criterion of dissimilarity indicates is likely not authentic. (The story as a whole is still considered authentic by most scholars, who view the saying at its end as inauthentic.) So if we eliminate all that is possibly "Jewish" or "Christian," what remains has a high claim to authenticity. Broad examples would be Jesus' friendship with notoriously sinful people, which contrasts with the Jewish and early Christian effort to keep their communities pure by socially ostracizing notorious evildoers, and Jesus' reputation as someone who greatly enjoyed eating and drinking, an enjoyment that most of Judaism and early Christianity generally did not appreciate.

This criterion, though widely accepted, is problematic to many researchers. First, our knowledge of early Christianity and Judaism is incomplete, so we sometimes cannot say with certainty if a saying of Jesus has a parallel in Judaism or the early church. For example, Jesus' strict teaching against remarriage after divorce as recorded in Mark and Luke was long thought to be distinct from laxer contemporary Jewish teaching, but the discovery of the Dead Sea Scrolls in 1947 showed that the Essenes were equally negative about remarriage. Second, eliminating all that Jesus had in common with Judaism, and all that he had in common with the church that followed him, may not leave us with the heart of Jesus' teaching, but with only those teachings that happen not to have been shared by the church and synagogue. Third, the strict application of this criterion will leave us with a non-Jewish Jesus, or at least a Jesus who has little in common with his Jewish environment. This interpretation goes against the grain of contemporary scholarship on Jesus, which strongly affirms his Jewish identity.

- *Contradiction of redactional purpose.* A saying or story of Jesus that is contrary to a Gospel writer's own particular interests or tendencies is likely to be a tradition that is being passed on, not something coming from the writer. (Of course, more work must be done to determine if this goes all back to Jesus or arises in the oral tradition between Jesus and the Gospel writer.) One clear indication of nonredactional material is things that do not reflect the evangelist's own concerns. For example, Matthew's Gospel was written by someone who was strongly committed to the Gentile mission of the church, as is clear from its ending (Matt 28:16–20). Therefore, the sayings in Matthew's Gospel that restrict the mission of Jesus and his disciples to Jews, particularly to the "lost sheep of the house of Israel" (10:5; 15:24), are a probably received tradition, not originating in Matthew's redaction.

- *Embarrassment.* Some features of the Gospel narratives seem highly unlikely to have been invented by the early Christians, because these elements could have been embarrassing to them and impeded their life and mission. Probable embarrassments include: the baptism of Jesus by John the Baptizer; the negative things said about the disciples' faults and failures; the prominence of women disciples in Jesus' movement; and especially the death of Jesus on a cross as an executed criminal. Some teachings of Jesus also could have been embarrassing, such as the failure of the Kingdom of God to come in its fullness as soon as Jesus seems to have said it would.

- *Coherence.* If any of the other criteria allow us to identify some sayings or stories of Jesus that are probably authentic, then we may build on that by accepting other sayings and stories that fit in coherently with the emerging picture of authentic material. For example, the "kingdom of God" is a theme that coherently permeates all sorts of gospel material (parables, miracle stories, etc.) and is seen therefore as having a very high degree of authenticity. So too is Jesus' calling himself the "Son of Man," a title that was not used of him by the early church, to judge from the letters of the NT.

Although these criteria are generally accepted and widely applied, continuous refinement and even debate surrounds them. Two leading Gospel scholars illustrate this ongoing effort. First, E. P. Sanders is skeptical about establishing anything with regard to the sayings of Jesus by using the received criteria, and proposes instead a historical approach built on the *events* of Jesus' life more than the *teaching*. He argues that there are certain basic events that are indisputable—for example, that Jesus was baptized by John the Baptizer, that he had disciples, that he taught his disciples and the crowds his basic message, that he was crucified—and that the way to historical reconstruction is through those events, seen in the Jewish context of Jesus' day (Sanders, 1993/1996). However, we may ask whether it is possible to reconstruct any details of Jesus' teaching from the events of his life. Second, N. T. Wright is basically positive about the value of the sayings traditions and the careful use of the criteria of authenticity to discern them. But he is skeptical about the minute judgments made by scholars about individual sayings, calling their approach a way of "frustration and tears." Like Sanders, Wright suggests that the proper method is to look at the Jesus tradition as a whole in the context of first-century Judaism in Palestine and to see if sense can be made of it. He advocates what he calls a double similarity and dissimilarity approach: a historical account of Jesus must explain Jesus in a way that makes sense in the context of first-century Judaism and first-century Christianity (the double similarity), but in a way that also explains how Jesus got crucified and why he had such an impact (the double dissimilarity) (Wright 1996, 133).

www   Follow the link to another, succinct treatment of the criteria of authenticity. For a minimalist reconstruction of the body of authentic Jesus teaching, follow the link to the "Authentic Sayings of Jesus" site.

Redaction Criticism

Redaction criticism assumes the results of source and form criticism, then carries them a step further to read the historical meaning of the text. It arose as a reaction to a too-thorough application of form criticism to the Gospels, which looked at the individual "trees" (pericopes) so completely that it lost sight of the "forest" (the written Gospels). The name of this school of criticism comes from the German *Redaktionsgeschichte,* meaning "redaction (editing) history," and it focuses on the editing of the tradition by the Gospel writers. Günter Bornkamm, one of the founders of redaction criticism, explains it this way: "The synoptic writers show, . . . each in his own special way, by their editing and construction, by their selection, inclusion and omission, that they are by no means mere collectors and handers-on of the tradition, but are also interpreters of it" (Bornkamm, Barth, and Held 1963, 11). Redaction criticism studies the Gospel writers' own theology and the situation from which each writes. Redaction critics argue that the emphases of each Gospel reflect and address the church to which the evangelist wrote. They speak of "Matthew's church," "the community of the Beloved Disciple," or similar phrases, and identify the problems of that church with the issues the Gospel writer addresses. In other words, redaction criticism sees the Gospels as corrective writings and the Gospel writers as shaping this corrective message while they redact their sources.

How Is Redaction Done?

A unit of gospel tradition could be edited in a number of ways by the author of the Gospels. In general, the evangelists selected material, arranged it, added their own contributions, and shaped it all to proclaim their own version of the "good news" about Jesus. Specifically, these include (assuming Markan priority and the Two-Document Hypothesis, as we will throughout this book):

• *Expanding a source.* Redactors can shape their material by lengthening their source with their own material. For example, Matthew's version of the Lord's Prayer/Our Father from Q is longer than Luke's drawn from Q, and most scholars agree that Matthew has added wording (*"Our* Father *in heaven,"* for example) to the form in Q.

- *Changing the temporal or geographic setting of a story or saying.* Changing the time or setting can alter a pericope's nuance and sometimes its basic meaning. For example, Luke moves the story of Jesus' rejection in his home town of Nazareth from Mark 6:16, near the midpoint of his Galilean ministry in Mark, forward to Luke's very beginning of the Galilean ministry (Luke 4:16–30).

- *Omitting parts of the story.* Matthew and Luke often omit parts of the passages they use from Mark, mainly in order to create more space for their own special material but also to streamline Mark's wordiness. Luke also omits larger sections of Mark's material (Mark 6:45–8:26 and 9:41–10:12).

- *Adapting Jesus' teaching to a particular audience.* Jesus was a Jewish teacher who taught a Jewish message to an almost exclusively Jewish audience. As the gospel message spread to Gentiles, his teaching often had to be adapted to fit their situation. For example, Luke says that the wise builder puts down a foundation, typical of Greco-Roman houses, but Matthew's more original form talks about building directly on rock (Luke 6:46–49; Matt 7:24–27). Matthew changes Mark's phrase "the kingdom of God" into "the kingdom of heaven." Even though Jesus used "the kingdom of God," Matthew and his audience have pious Jewish feelings against using the word "God" so directly and often. (This is an example of later Christians being more pious than Jesus!)

- *Adding explanations.* Many scholars conclude that the explanations attached to a few parables and other forms are redactional, or at least originated in the oral tradition.

- *Repeating source material.* Occasionally a writer will duplicate source material in the same Gospel. For example, Matthew gives Jesus' saying on divorce and remarriage twice, in 5:31–32 and again in 19:9. Although it is possible that Matthew repeats material because it comes from two different sources, we may assume that he does so knowingly, and perhaps for emphasis.

- *Drawing on a special source.* Both Matthew and Luke have their own unique materials, which as we saw earlier go by the shorthand initials M and L. Although scholars may dispute if these are actual *sources* of Matthew and Luke, and how closely Matthew and Luke followed their order and content it they were indeed sources, this special material went through some redactional process. They give Matthew and Luke some of their distinctive flavor; we will consider them later in Chapters 8–9. The Gospel of John has probably its special source as well, which we will discuss in Chapter 9.

- *Preserving source material.* What the evangelists preserve unchanged from their sources is important historically and theologically. Where an evangelist reproduces wording from his source without significant change, we may safely assume that he agrees with the source. Matthew and Luke pick up far more words directly from Mark than they change. The words of Jesus typically show closer agreement between the Gospels than the wording of their narrative settings, which the Gospel writers evidently felt freer to change.

Scholars using the redaction-critical method study parallel passages to identify the redactional activity of each evangelist. They ask whether changes are *stylistic,* simply part of the evangelist's style of wording things, or *substantial,* done with a theological purpose showing the evangelist's own theological perspective. Once this has been done for the parallel passages, the results are assembled to see if patterns appear across whole Gospels. This is how major themes of each evangelist can be identified, for example Matthew's theme of the fulfillment of the OT by Jesus, or Luke's theme of the Holy Spirit. When these major themes are put together, the overall picture of Jesus that each Gospel writer portrays comes clear. By looking at the overall redactional structure of a Gospel, its overarching themes important to its author, we can also make educated guesses about the community to which they are written.

> ### Developing Your Reading Skills: Redaction Criticism at Work
>
> *Matthew, Mark, and Luke all report the story of Jesus stilling the storm (Matt 8:23–27; Mark 4:35–41; Luke 8:22–25). We will examine Mark's and Matthew's versions. First, copy or print out the synopsis page with these passages displayed in parallel. Next, read Mark's account carefully; then read Matthew's; finally, compare them. How does Matthew redact Mark?*

www   See this website for a short essay on a book edited by the prominent NT scholar Richard Bauckham that argues that the common assumption that each Gospel book is written for an individual church or group of churches may be mistaken.

Since the heyday of the historical-critical method in the first half of the twentieth century, scholars have developed a number of other approaches to reading the Gospels. Many of these methods come from other academic disciplines in the humanities and social sciences. Some are more interested in the ancient setting; others are particularly focused on using models and methods from today's world. Some are descriptive, others prescriptive. In Chapter 1 of the present book, we introduced these models as they apply generally to the whole field of NT reading. In this section, we will examine briefly these newer approaches as they apply specifically to reading the Gospels.

Narrative Reading

Narrative criticism is a text-centered approach that reads the story of the text in its present, final form. Narrative critics first read the Gospels as a narrative whole. What arises from this reading is an encounter with its **implied author.** This is not the real, historical author from almost two thousand years ago, but a picture of the kind of person who would write this text. (Even from a historical-critical point of view, we know the authors of Matthew, Mark, Luke, and John mainly by what they reveal of themselves through their books, as implied authors, because we have so little independent information about them.) This leads us to consider the **implied reader.**

Just as the implied author is not the actual/real author, the implied reader is not an actual reader in the past or present, but a composite picture of the kind of person who would understand and respond to this text fully. For this reason, some call the implied reader the *ideal reader*. Of course, no reader is ideal or perfect, but narrative criticism constructs this figure to bring out the full meaning of the narrative, as if there were someone who could perfectly read the text. However, the assumption of a perfect reader does challenge us to read the text carefully today, because doing so will put today's reader in touch with the kind of response the implied author seeks from the implied reader. For example, the repeated explanation of Jewish customs by the author of John means that the writer's implied reader was Gentile rather than Jewish. Because Matthew's implied reader needs no such explanations, we can safely deduce that his audience was either from a Jewish background or was knowledgeable about Judaism.

Narrative critics of the Gospels frequently discuss their characters, plot, point of view, and settings. We shall now look at each of these elements in turn.

Characters

Although many elements combine to make a story, it is usually the *people* in the story who draw our attention. In the Gospels, the focus is almost continually upon Jesus as the main character. In narrative reading of the Gospels, characters are the human agents who move the story on. Some scholars speak of *actants* in the Gospels when these characters are not human: demons, Satan, or angels. **Characterization,** how characters are portrayed in their words and actions, is important in a narrative, because authors often show their point of view by which characters they present positively. In considering characters, we need to ask whether they agree with the implied author's point of view; if so, they are "reliable," and we identify with them as they go through the story. The author of Matthew regards John the Baptizer as generally reliable. By contrast, that writer disagrees with the Pharisees' view of Jesus as working miracles by the power of Beelzebul (Matt 12:24). He shows this partly by Jesus' critical answer (vv. 25–32), and partly by his overall characterization of the Pharisees, who are consistently Jesus' opponents in Matthew (e.g., 9:11, 34; 12:1, 14). The same is true of the two Herods and Pontius Pilate.

The text leads the reader to make various responses to characters. Sometimes they are expected to feel **empathy,** to identify strongly with the character, perhaps because they see their own likeness in them or want to be like them. In the Gospels, Jesus is the sole "main character," and the focus stays on him almost continuously, which leads to a strong empathic identification of the ideal reader with him. The implied author can also shape the reader to a lesser degree of empathy. For example, the disciples as they are depicted in Matthew invite a tempered empathy: they have a small faith (6:30; 8:26; 14:31; 16:8); they fail in their tasks (26:36, 40–41, 43); but they do grow in understanding (16:5–12), believe in the risen Jesus despite some lingering doubt (28:17), and are called to spread the Gospel after his resurrection (28:16–20). Alternatively, the reader may be invited to feel **sympathy**, to identify less intensely with certain characters, by recognizing an equal mixture of good and bad traits in them. Mark's portrait of the disciples seems harsher than Matthew's and Luke's; he regularly points out their mistakes and lack of understanding (e.g. Mark 6:37; 7:17–18; 8:4, 31–33; 9:18). Nevertheless, they remain Jesus' disciples, and he is confident that they will become faithful witnesses to him (Mark 13:9–13). Thus, the reader is being encouraged to sympathize with them as characters. Sometimes the reader is asked to show **antipathy** to characters, to feel hostile to them and thus not identify with them at all. The authors of all four Gospels shape the reader to have antipathy to Jesus' opponents and to Judas, who betrays Jesus.

www   Follow the link to an interesting online treatment of the "Christ figure" (one who suffers for doing good and in the process brings positive change to others; prominent examples are the main character in the novella *Billy Budd* by Herman Melville, Neo in the *Matrix* films directed by the Wachowski brothers, and especially Superman in the screenplays by Mario Puzo) in literature and Hollywood film.

Plot

Narrative critics examine **plot,** the way the story begins, develops, climaxes and finishes within the text. Careful structure of plot makes the story of Jesus more understandable and more powerful. Not just the progress of the story in a plot is important, but the *pacing of narrative time* in the plot is also significant. Slowing down narrative time by telling a story at much greater length and in more detail than in previous parts of the story suggests that the slower material is particularly significant. For example, the Synoptics tell the passion narrative at much greater length than the earlier parts of the story. Time slows down as Jesus suffers, and the careful reader feels the effect of this slower pacing as well. The *sequence* of narrative plot is important. A story told out of chronological sequence has a particular effect. Mark's **"sandwiches,"** one story told inside another, fall into this category, as their two interwoven events increased the narrative effect of each. Mark also presents the death of John the Baptizer as an out-of-chronological sequence flashback (Mark 6:14–29). Luke tells of the removal of John from the scene before Jesus' public ministry begins (Luke 3:19–20) because from that point on he can focus upon Jesus. Finally, because no story can tell everything about the plot—if it did, it would be terminally boring—the readers/listeners must "fill the gaps" with their own understanding, thus drawing them into the plot more deeply.

The reader should carefully note **conflict** within the story: battles of wills, actions, characters, or ideas. In any story, the plot carries on by means of conflict. In the Gospels, conflict is usually overt and carried out in people's actions; only Jesus has any significant internal conflict, and that only occasionally. Jesus as the main character is the focus of conflict. He both gives and receives trouble: with the Jewish leaders, who increasingly oppose him; with his disciples, who often misunderstand and sometimes oppose him; with demons he casts out; with nature when it storms; and even with himself on the night before his death as he wrestles with his acceptance of his own death (internal conflict). Most conflicts are resolved within the narrative, but some are left unresolved, often as unfinished business for the reader to deal with. Jesus came to defeat the forces of evil, and the Gospels affirm that he did so, but his followers found themselves still engaged in this conflict. So the story of Jesus continues in them, and the Gospels guide this struggle.

Point of View

In the making of films, the angle of the camera is a key element in the shot. A high shot from above makes the subject look smaller and more vulnerable; a shot from below makes the subject loom larger and appear more powerful. The angle from which a writer looks, called **point of view,** is also crucial. Point of view is a key way the implied author guides the implied reader to see the narrative from the desired perspective. Point of view encompasses the worldview, values, and standards of the implied author. The evangelists present a world in which supernatural beings conflict on the world stage, a world we step into when we read. In their narratives, the Gospels are all written in a *third-person omniscient* point of view, meaning that their narrators stand apart from the story (third person) and know all about it (omniscient). For example, they present Jesus' private thoughts, his opponent's hidden motives, and events that have no human witnesses, for example, Jesus' temptation by Satan in the wilderness. The effect of the omniscient narrator is to impress on readers the narrator's wide authority to tell the story, thus inspiring a confident response in the reader.

Point of view can be *evaluative,* in which the writer shapes the reader's point of view about the story. The Gospel authors give us what they believe to be God's perspective. This happens in two ways. It comes explicitly in statements about characters or situations: for example, the statement that Judas Iscariot would betray Jesus, made almost every time Judas appears, or that Jesus' disciple Nathanael is a "true Israelite in whom there is no deceit" (John 1:47). Evaluation more frequently occurs implicitly in the plot itself, where it is more powerful than explicit evaluation because it carries out the evaluation in the story—for example, the evaluation of Jesus' disciples in their tendency to misunderstand and sometimes oppose him. The values of the author come out as they are dramatized in the plot, an effect that is usually more subtle and powerful than a simple evaluative comment.

Settings

Locations give a mood or meaning to a scene in a story in a remarkable way. They help to reveal characters, shape conflict, and provide a geographic structure for the story. The Gospels tend to be sparing in their descriptions of settings, telling the reader only what is necessary, when it is necessary. For example, in Luke 2:1–7, the author describes the birth of Jesus against an impressive setting of world history but then finishes the story by remarking that Jesus was laid in a manger, an animal feed trough, because there was no room for his family in the local inn. Readers of the Gospels should keep in view whether the narrative takes place in Jewish or Gentile areas. These settings may be symbolic, literal, or both. For Mark, Galilee is the place where Jesus and his followers are "at home"; in Judea, Jesus works no miracles, and finally dies. Thus, these literal locations assume the symbolic value of good places and bad places. When Jesus rises from the dead in Jerusalem, Mark has an angel tell the women visiting the empty tomb to look for the risen Jesus not in Jerusalem or Judea, but back in Galilee. Luke, on the other hand, has all of Jesus' resurrection appearances in and around Jerusalem, and Jesus explicitly commands his followers to remain in Jerusalem until the Holy Spirit descends on them.

Evaluating Narrative Reading

Narrative reading has much obvious strength. First, it enables us to encounter each Gospel as the story it is. The Gospels are narratives, and well-constructed ones at that, so narrative criticism fits the Gospels. Second, narrative reading also enables readers to focus on the Gospels as they actually exist in their final form, not in their sources, forms, or redaction. As an approach focusing on the present form of the Gospels, narrative criticism contrasts with historical criticism. Historical criticism looks through a passage to its original real author and the original real audience. By contrast, a narrative reading of a Gospel passage relates it to the other parts of that Gospel and assumes a consistent, coherent development within the book. Narrative reading thus provides insights into the text where historical reading is not certain. Third, even though it puts historical issues to the side, narrative criticism can be combined with historical criticism and other, newer forms of reading to enrich them. Fourth, because it uses a method of reading that many students have already learned in literature classes, narrative criticism is not as unfamiliar as other methods of reading.

Narrative criticism also has some potential drawbacks. It developed out of the study of modern fiction and early modern folktales, and therefore some of it may not be appropriate to the Gospels as ancient literature. For example, its distinction between *flat* (undeveloped, unchanging) and *round* (developed, changing) characters may not fit ancient Greco-Roman literature like the NT, because the NT is not as interested in personality and personal development as we are. Even Jesus is not a round character in the Gospels! Narrative reading's concern with the way that stories work as stories also puts some limits on its value when narrative criticism is combined with historical criticism, as it frequently is in NT study. Many narrative readers of the Gospel conclude that it needs other, complementary approaches in order fully to understand them, but narrative criticism is also a valid way on its own of reading the Gospels.

> **Developing Your Reading Skills: Narrative Pacing**
>
> *Read the different accounts of Jesus' early life until the coming of John the Baptizer in Matt. 1:18–3:1 and Luke 1:26–58; 2:1–3:2. As you read, identify the speed at which narrative time is moving in different sections of these narratives. Which elements of the narratives are slowed down by details, and which are passed over quickly? What do your discoveries suggest about the particular emphases of Matthew and Luke in telling these stories?*

Social Scientific Reading

Social scientific readers analyze the social and cultural context(s) of the Gospels and their environment by using theories and methods from the modern social sciences. Malina and Rohrbaugh outline several important presuppositions of social-scientific reading of the Gospels (Malina and Rohrbaugh 2003, 15–17). First, the focus of each Gospel is the in-group of Jesus' continuing movement; it speaks to them and is meant for them, not for outsiders. This may not be evident to many modern Gospel readers, because the Gospels themselves do not explicitly refer to their own audience and may look on their surface like they may be meant for anyone who reads them, in the ancient world and today. Second, the Gospels are *occasioned* writings, for a specific Jesus group in specific circumstances, written to keep the in-group intact. Third, the Gospels articulate Jesus' "political" faith, his proclamation of the kingdom of God with God as patron (father). Later Jesus followers formed *fictive kinship* groups, being "brothers and sisters" to each other; they are the audience of the Gospels. Fourth, the Gospels are narratives meant to make sense of the experience of those hearing them. By telling the deep meaning of Jesus' story in a particular way, the Christian faith and life of the audience is strengthened. Finally, the Gospels were written by and for third-generation Jesus-group members who wished to know more about the first-generation experience that accounted for their own fictive kinship groups. This is common to new movements, where the well-known *third-generation principle* applies: the third generation (the Gospel writers and their audiences in 70–100 C.E.) wished to articulate what the second generation (Paul, James the brother of Jesus, Peter, and the rest in 50–70) did not need to articulate or even ignored about the experience of the first generation (Jesus and the earliest church in the 30–50).

In considering the social contexts that the Gospels reflect and assume, social scientific reading highlights important elements of the Gospels not dealt with competently by other methods. For example, Gerd Theissen draws parallels between Jesus' group and the traveling Cynic teachers by examining the Jesus movement and sketches the Palestinian social, economic and cultural setting in which Jesus lived. (The Cynics, a Greek philosophical school, maintained that civilization entangled one in unnecessary affairs and hampered the virtuous life. They advocated a radical return of humankind to nature, "natural reason," and a simple lifestyle.) Although this parallel is controversial in recent scholarship, the social scientific approach does effectively highlight Gospel material concerned with family ties, possessions, and homelessness that other approaches may miss (e.g., Matt 8:19–22; Luke 14:26; Mark 10:28–31). In using models (larger explanations) from modern social sciences, scholars consider how a modern social movement can provide a grid through which to understand an ancient movement. For example, John Gager compared aspects of the early Christian movement—the Gospel of Mark, for example—to modern millenarian cults that expect the end of the world any day. Gager gathered modern studies of modern millenarian cults, noticing that they often grow out of a strong sense of social alienation among their members. Accordingly, Gager then considered the early church as a group that was marginalized within the power structures of the Roman Empire and for which Jesus became a prophet who promised a better world. However, Gager argued, the eventual realization that the return of Jesus was not going to happen quickly caused the Christians to make adjustments to their beliefs and led to accommodation with the Roman state and its social structures (Gager 1975).

Luke 7:36–50, the story of how a "sinful" woman pours precious ointment on Jesus' feet during a banquet, provides an excellent example of the importance of understanding cultural differences between the modern West and the ancient social setting. Our picture of eating a meal involves sitting at chairs around a table, with feet underneath the table. In Luke we should see a low table of food in the middle of a large room, surrounded by low couches on which the diners reclined with their heads nearest the central table, heads propped up on hands and elbows. That was why the woman found it easy to anoint, wash, and kiss Jesus' feet—they were on his couch or mat (v. 38), not underneath the table! Further, the important custom of hospitality in that culture is to greet a visitor to one's home with a kiss and to have a servant pour a small amount of oil on the visitor's head and wash the visitor's feet. (Our modern equivalent is to kiss/embrace or shake hands, to take their coats, and to offer them a drink.) But Simon fails to do these things, thus insulting Jesus; since the feast was in Jesus' honor, this may have been unintentional. By contrast, the woman demonstrates her welcome and love for Jesus by her actions (vv. 44–46).

Evaluating Social Scientific Reading of the Gospels

Social scientific reading brings great gains to the study of the Gospels. It is increasingly practiced in NT study, both on its own and combined with other methods. It enables us to see that social customs and mores so important that they rarely need to be explicitly mentioned, such as the importance of honor, are always present. At times the text itself—if it is carefully attended to!—gives us cues that inform us of these differences. For example, in the preceding story the fact that the other people at the banquet see the woman anointing Jesus indicates that she is not under a table, but somehow more visible; this detail would lead us to question the way we automatically picture this scene in our mind's eye. Social scientific reading enables us to notice other differences between the NT's cultures and ours. For example, terms for family relationships have a rather fixed meaning for us; "father/husband" "mother/wife," "child," "brother/sister" and the rest bring definite ideas to our mind, based on our cultural background and experience. But we must not assume that because the *words* in the English NT are the same, that the *relationships meant by these words* are also the same. The "biological construction" of gender and procreation are everywhere the same, but the aspects determined by "social construction" are often quite different. A careful study of the social background of the NT world can help to alert us to the differences.

The limitations of social scientific reading of the Gospels are debated. Some scholars see a danger of reductionism, the attempt to explain everything in early Christianity as a result of, or reaction to, the social environment. Sociological models, furthermore, often come with built-in ideas about what is most important in social life, ideas that may or may not "fit" the NT; Marxist social models stress the determining significance of economics and class, for example. Another criticism that can be leveled against the way social scientific reading is used is that it does not take historical change and variation into account, assuming that culture is much more stable than changing. This criticism asks: Is the ancient Mediterranean person really the same as the modern Mediterranean person? Finally, some scholars argue that modern models of groups may not always fit the ancient world, and models like "sectarianism," "cult," "millenarian movement" and others need to be corrected with what we know of the ancient settings from more traditional historical and archaeological studies.

> **Developing Your Skills: Social Scientific Reading**
>
> *Often the text itself gives careful readers important clues about social setting that they should notice. In Matthew 5:15, Jesus tells his disciples, "No one after lighting a lamp puts it under a bushel basket, but on the lampstand, and it gives light to all in the house." Read between the lines: What does this statement clearly imply about the size of a typical Palestinian house? Knowing the size of the house, what can you say about the social class of the majority of Jesus' followers, or at least the ones presupposed in this passage?*

Feminist Reading

In this section and the next, we will treat feminist and cross-cultural approaches to the Gospels. Before we begin, however, we should look at the shared aims of these two approaches. Both have a commitment to reading a text from a particular point of view in order to find resources for the struggle for liberation. They are both forms of **advocacy criticism,** which "privileges," makes primary for interpretation, certain ways of thinking and seeing things, and certain questions to be asked. Often such approaches stem from the experience of a group who are marginalized by the mainstream of life and scholarship. Hence liberationist approaches that privilege the experience of poor people historically stem from poor communities in South America. They read the Gospels through their experience and understanding. Similarly, feminist readers concentrate on the experience and the situation of marginalized women from economic, social, and political perspectives. They seek to read "under the text" to hear the suppressed voices of women in written works that came out of an ancient world where women were not powerful in the ruling classes.

In feminist and cross-cultural approaches to the Gospels, groups of readers see their experience as a context for the way they read meaning in the four stories of Jesus. They are reading within their *interpretive communities,* and the values of their communities are important in the reading. This is one reason that books by feminist and cross-cultural readers tend to be collaborative works with several authors, rather than just one. (In other methods of reading such as historical, narrative, and social-scientific, interpretation is more individualized and one sees little reflection on interpretive communities.) Important for feminist and cross-cultural reading of the Gospels is their insistence that reading "from the margins" fits the Gospels better than some other forms of interpretation. That is, they maintain that the aims of feminist and cross-cultural readings align more fully than other methods with the aims of the Gospels themselves.

Feminist approaches to the Gospels vary according to the type of feminism. Feminists who view the Gospels as hopelessly patriarchal do not read them at all, despite the fact that in the opinion of all scholars the Gospels are as positive toward women as the NT gets. On the other extreme, some feminists view the historical Jesus as a force for women's liberation and radical egalitarianism, even if the four Gospel writers do not completely share this view. Most liberationist scholars fall somewhere between these two extremes. They argue that Jesus' overall message was just as liberating for women as for men. Whether Jesus' teaching was centered on eschatology or wisdom, it serves to free women from patriarchy, or at least start that process. A recent book by the Australian NT scholar Margaret Beirne, *Women and Men in the Fourth Gospel: A Genuine Discipleship of Equals,* is indicative of this approach. Beirne looks not just at women in the Gospel of John to discern John's attitude to women, but at how women and men are literarily paired by the author of that book. She finds six such pairings in John: The mother of Jesus and the royal official (chapters 2 and 4), Nicodemus and the Samaritan woman (3–4), the man born blind and Martha (9 and 11), Mary of Bethany and Judas (12), the mother of Jesus and the Beloved Disciple (19), and Mary Magdalene and Thomas (20). She concludes that this Gospel treats women and men equally on the nature and value of their discipleship. Equality, Beirne says, does not mean sameness; rather, it incorporates difference rather than contradicting it (Beirne 2003).

> **Developing Your Skills: Feminist Criticism**
>
> *Feminist thought and practice can be controversial for both males and females. Examine your own preconceived notions of feminism. When you hear this word, what do you first think of, and why? What do you like, and don't you like, about the feminist treatment of the Gospels, as outlined here, and why? Finally, examine one of the key passages in the Gospels and give your own feminist reading of it.*

Cross-Cultural Reading

Cross-cultural readers of the NT focus more on the Gospels than on any other part of the NT. The story of Jesus in itself, of course, is not inherently cross-cultural, because he was a Jew who ministered predominantly to Jews. By the time the Gospels were written, however, the gospel had gone out into the wider world, crossing several cultural boundaries. The main boundary was that between Jewish and non-Jewish (Gentile); this distinction predominates in much of a movement that came from Judaism but by the end of the first century found itself to be predominantly Gentile. The whole variety of Gentile life was encountered: different religions, different races, and different cultures. This variety makes a cameo appearance on the pages of the Gospels, for example, in Jesus' few encounters with Gentiles in his ministry. In a sense, reading the Gospels is itself a many-layered exercise in cross-cultural understanding: we read a Mediterranean culture from our modern cultures; we read a basically Jewish type of religion from our mostly Gentile perspective; and most important, we read the Gospels alongside peoples of other current world cultures who see in them sources for their own self-understanding and liberation.

This leads us to a brief consideration of cross-cultural reading's roots and aims. It was born out of the postcolonial experience of Christian readers of the Gospels. They were searching for a different way to understand the story of Jesus apart from the ways that the colonial powers had taught them to read. Although these colonial ways of reading largely sprang from the historical-critical method, and as such were supposed to be "neutral" and "objective," the way they were carried out was in service of colonial power and ways of thinking. Postcolonial non-Western Christians built a way of reading the text from the postcolonial experience. Jesus was now one who suffered *with them,* and brought them through to freedom in his suffering and resurrection.

Richard Horsley's *Reading Mark in Context* pays strong attention to Mark as a cross-cultural book. He argues that Mark's story is addressed to the ancient equivalent of Third World peoples subjected by empire and should be read as good news in this context. Mark presents Jesus as engaged in the prophetic renewal of the people of Israel by proclaiming and showing the kingdom of God, which brings conflict with Jewish authorities who finally prevail upon Roman power to execute him. Mark's abrupt, open ending vindicates Jesus and implies the continuation of his movement in Galilee. Mark's apocalyptic chapter 13 indicates that it focuses on opposition to Roman imperial order and oppression, an opposition that continues whenever Mark is read carefully (Horsley 2002).

Developing Your Skills: Cross-Cultural Criticism

One of the most misused sayings of Jesus is, "The poor you have with you always." Examine this statement in its context in either Mark 14:7, Matt 26:11, or John 12:8, using a cross-cultural perspective as fully as possible. What does this saying of Jesus mean for someone oppressed by others who use it? How might a correct understanding liberate it from being a tool of economic exploitation?

Evaluating Cross-Cultural and Feminist Methods

Feminist and cross-cultural readings are appealing to many NT scholars. They place a high emphasis on Synoptic Gospel study, with study of the Gospel of John rising now to match. Here they find the most powerful resources for human liberation. They also challenge readers to be self-reflective about their own **preunderstanding,** the personal perspective shaped by one's assumptions, knowledge and bias one brings to the text, which every reader has to a significant degree. Ideologically based approaches, despite their continued controversial nature in society and in higher education, have highlighted issues that would not otherwise have been seen and that relate powerfully to today's readers. In times when the globalization of economic life is a controversial reality, cross-cultural reading of the Gospels can bring their values and world view to bear on the life of the poor in nations that continue to be marginalized. To read the Gospels self-consciously from particular perspectives is a valuable addition and/or corrective to the classic historical approaches. Finally, feminist and cross-cultural ways of reading the Gospels remind us that reading and interpretation of the Jesus tradition is to be judged by the results it achieves in life. Theory and praxis cannot be separated. For example, Luke's emphasis on Jesus' concern for the poor can easily be treated as relatively unimportant by the affluent in the West, for whom cross-cultural reading of the NT presents a great challenge to their wealth and comfort. Moreover, the lingering patriarchy of the NT was overlooked or accepted by male readers until feminist readings challenged it, and this process still continues.

Feminist and cross-cultural readings have been negatively criticized as well. First, their controversial nature as a form of advocacy criticism makes it difficult to engage in, especially for beginning students and laypeople in some Christian churches. Of course, this does not mean to most people that feminist and cross-cultural reading should not be done at all. Second, the precise degree of liberation ideology that can be found in the Gospels is under debate. For example, some scholars have challenged the idea that Jesus was a believer in radical social equality on the grounds that such a concept was unknown in Jesus' day and runs counter to his idea of the kingdom of God (e.g., Elliott 2003). Third, although these two methods are valid in themselves, many interpreters feel that they should be used in tandem with other methods. Many feminist and cross-cultural critics also use other methods, both historical-critical and some of the newer methods, in interpreting the NT. This range of perspectives enables the student of newer methods to grapple with one common scholarly complaint about them: that sometimes their reading is simply a reflection of their own ideology and do not show enough sympathy for the text itself. Reading, when all is said and done, is at its best a conversation with the text. As in any good conversation, each party must listen and respond carefully to the other.

Key Terms and Concepts

acts (Greco-Roman genre) • advocacy criticism • antipathy • apocryphal gospels
authorial intent • criteria of authenticity • double tradition • empathy
Four-Document Hypothesis • genre • Gospel of Thomas • Griesbach Hypothesis
hypothetical document • implied author • implied reader • L
lives (Greco-Roman genre) • M • Markan priority
memoirs (Greco-Roman genre) • miracle story • narrative criticism
narrative characterization • narrative conflict • narrative plot
narrative point of view • parable • pericopes • preunderstanding
pronouncement story • Q • redaction criticism • sandwich • *Sitz im Leben*
synopsis • Synoptic Problem • triple tradition • Two-Document Hypothesis
Two-Gospel Hypothesis

Questions for Study, Discussion, and Writing

1. What is your own conclusion on the genre of the Gospels? Why?
2. List the differences and similarities between ancient biographies/lives and the modern biography.
3. If you were writing a modern Gospel to explain the story and significance of Jesus, what form of literary presentation (modern genre) do you think would be most appropriate, and why?
4. What might it mean for the modern reading of the Gospels that one of the main meanings of "good news" in the Roman world was political?
5. What are the strengths and weaknesses to the two-document solution to the Synoptic Problem?
6. Read the parable of the laborers in the vineyard (Matt 20:1–16). What significant gaps are left in Jesus' telling of this parable at each stage of the story? What effect do these gaps have on how you read the parable at each stage? How might the gaps help the parable be effective in getting its point across?

7. If you were to rank the criteria of authenticity in order of their importance, what would that order be, and why?
8. Pick any section of the "Overview of Current Scholarship on the Historical Jesus" on the website and compare it with a reading of material in one of the Synoptic Gospels dealing with that section (e.g., the material on John the Baptizer). What similarities and differences do you find between them?

For Further Reading

Anderson, Janice C. and Moore, Stephen D. *Mark and Method: New Approaches in Biblical Studies.* Minneapolis: Fortress, 1992. The essays by Elizabeth S. Malbon on narrative criticism and Janice Anderson on feminist criticism are particularly valuable for the study of the Gospels.

Bauckham, Richard, ed. *The Gospels for All Christians.* Edinburgh, UK/Grand Rapids, MI: T & T Clark/Eerdmans, 1997. Argues that the Gospels are aimed at a wide audience and not merely at individual Christian communities.

Borg, Marcus. *Meeting Jesus Again for the First Time.* San Francisco: HarperSanFrancisco, 1995. Borg's most accessible book for beginning students; presents Jesus as a "Spirit person," subversive sage, social prophet and movement founder who invited his followers and hearers into a transforming relationship the same Spirit.

Crossan, John Dominic. *The Historical Jesus.* San Francisco: HarperSanFrancisco, 1993. Jesus presented as a displaced Galilean artisan who preached a radical message, an egalitarian vision of the Kingdom of God manifested in the teaching and healing of Jesus.

Dunn, James D. G. *Jesus Remembered.* Grand Rapids, MI: Eerdmans, 2003. A magisterial introduction to Jesus and the Gospels; students can read the main text, quite intelligible on its own, and leave aside the extensive discussion in the footnotes.

Fredricksen, Paula. *Jesus of Nazareth, King of the Jews: A Jewish Life and the Emergence of Christianity.* New York: Vintage Books, 2000. Presents Jesus as a prophet who preached the imminent apocalyptic Kingdom of God.

Malina, Bruce, and Rohrbaugh, Richard. *Social-Science Commentary on the Synoptic Gospels*, 2nd ed. Minneapolis: Fortress, 2003. An excellent guide to a social scientific reading of the Synoptic Gospels.

Meier, John. *A Marginal Jew: Rethinking the Historical Jesus* (in three volumes). New York: AnchorDoubleday, 1991, 1994, 2001. The first volume is the most helpful for beginning students. Meier presents Jesus as a miracle-working eschatological prophet.

Theissen, Gerd, and Merz, Annette. *The Historical Jesus: A Comprehensive Guide* Minneapolis: Fortress, 1998. A clear, full introduction to all aspects of historical Jesus study, and the best overall recent survey of its topic.

Tuckett, Christopher M. "Introduction to the Gospels," in J. D. G. Dunn and J. Rogerson, eds., *Eerdmans Commentary on the Bible.* Grand Rapids, MI: Eerdmans, 2003, pp. 989–999. A succinct, sensible introduction to many important issues of Gospel study.

Chapter Six

The Gospel of Mark: Following Jesus, the Suffering Messiah

We begin our examination of the Synoptic Gospels with Mark. Mark is the briefest, yet in several ways the most powerful, of all the Gospels. With its fast-paced narrative and a strong focus on Jesus as a powerful healer and teacher, Mark presents Jesus as the Son of God and the long-awaited Messiah of Israel. Mark moves very quickly to Jesus' conflict with his opponents, suffering, and death, with the message to readers that following Jesus means suffering for God as Jesus did. Half of Mark presents Jesus' movement toward the last week of his life, and a quarter of it focuses on this last week. Mark's message that Jesus is a suffering Messiah brings good news to a church probably undergoing suffering itself. Although Mark ends with some text-critical difficulties, the message of the whole book as "Good News" comes through clearly. Both the church and the academy neglected Mark until the nineteenth century, but now it has pride of place in Gospel study. It is a leading Gospel for both historical-critical reading and reading by the newer methods, which have often been applied to Mark before the other Synoptics. Narrative, social scientific, feminist, and cross-cultural methods of reading have been applied extensively and fruitfully to Mark. For many professional interpreters, Mark is the Gospel par excellence, and it is an excellent point of entry for our study of the Synoptics.

Mark in Brief: Outline of Structure and Contents

I. Jesus' public ministry of healing and preaching in Galilee (1:1–8:26)
  A. Beginning of the Gospel; John the Baptizer baptizes Jesus (1:1–15).
  B. Jesus teaches and heals in Galilee; initial conflict and opposition arise; he chooses the Twelve as his special disciples (1:1–6:6).
  C. Jesus sends out the Twelve to preach and heal; he continues to work miracles; controversy and misunderstanding increase (6:7–8:26).
II. Jesus' predictions of death and resurrection; travel to Jerusalem, death and resurrection (8:27–16:8)

A. Jesus predicts his death and resurrection; Peter confesses Jesus' identity; Jesus is transfigured; he continues teaching on discipleship (8:27–10:52).
B. Ministry in Jerusalem: triumphal entry; temple actions and encounters; apocalyptic discourse (chapters 11–13).
C. Jesus is anointed; Last Supper; Jesus' arrest, trial, crucifixion, and burial; the empty tomb and angelic testimony to the women on Jesus' resurrection (14:1–16:8).
[D. Two other endings by later copyists: resurrection appearances (16:9–20).]

Developing Your Skills: *Reading a Gospel as a Whole*

The first step in studying any NT book is to read it in one sitting, concentrating on the shape and general contents of the entire document, not the details. So before you go any farther in the present book, read the Gospel of Mark quickly in one sitting and form an initial impression of Mark as a whole.

A Guide to Reading

The Guide to Reading section throughout this book introduces the basic content of the NT books in a way that touches on the raw material of all the methods. It will deal with the wording and meaning of the story for the real author and first-century readers (historical reading), note the shape of the story (narrative reading), note the social groups and dynamics (social scientific reading), mention the presence and absence of women in the story (feminist reading), and suggest its meaning for different peoples (cross-cultural reading). Students should watch for these materials, but also realize that all these methods of reading can be applied to all of the NT, not just what we can point out here. They should also open their NT text and read it in tandem with this section. This "guide to reading" cannot substitute for the direct reading of the New Testament itself!

Mark opens with a simple but weighty statement, "the beginning of the gospel/good news of Jesus Christ, the Son of God" (1:1). This beginning of good news is thus grounded in Jesus' social status: he is Christ/Messiah, the promised deliverer of Israel, and he is also the Son of God. This beginning of Jesus' activity is prepared by John the Baptizer, the messenger who himself is a fulfillment of OT prophecy. John carried out a prophetic ministry in Judea, proclaiming in the wilderness for his fellow Jews to prepare the way of the Lord. That preparation consists in calling the Jewish people to **repentance** (change of mind and both personal and social behavior to conform to God's will), and announcing Jesus, who will bring

God's Spirit and fully accomplish that reform (1:2–8). When John baptizes Jesus, a voice from heaven calls him God's beloved Son, using the words of Ps 2:7 and Isa 42:1. The Spirit of God descends to be in Jesus; this Spirit drives Jesus into the wilderness where Satan tempts him. King Herod arrests John the Baptizer, and this arrest of Jesus' precursor at the beginning of Jesus' ministry indicates from the start that Jesus' ministry will also meet strong opposition. Mark gives a summary of Jesus' upcoming message in Galilee: "The time is fulfilled, and the kingdom of God has come near; repent, and believe in the good news/gospel" (1:9–14).

The Galilean ministry begins when Jesus calls four men to be his followers. They will become "fishers" who will catch people for God, implying that these four, with Jesus' other followers that he will call later, will have a key role in ministry with Jesus (1:16–20). Jesus thus starts a social movement, not just an individual ministry. In describing a day—in the narrative, seemingly the first full day—of Jesus' ministry, Mark introduces the readers to the things Jesus does in this ministry: teaching with authority and healing many people with different maladies. Jesus works **exorcisms** (casting out evil spirits) on oppressed people, commanding the spirits to keep quiet about him, the first instance of the secrecy motif in Mark. He also works different sorts of healing miracles on many people. Jesus seeks a place to pray on the following morning, only to be urged by his disciples to resume his activity (1:21–38). The word of the gospel and deeds of restoration are united in Jesus' ministry to introduce God's kingdom.

In 1:40 through 3:6, Jesus' ministry begins in Capernaum and quickly extends to all of Galilee. The silence/secrecy motif now extends to a healed leper (person with any sort of skin disease), perhaps because widespread excitement about Jesus would make it more difficult for him to travel and minister openly, which is exactly what happens (1:39–45). In this town on the Sea of Galilee, which is now Jesus' base of operations, Mark places a series of incidents where scribes, Pharisees and others raise objections against Jesus (2:1–3:6). In these incidents, they oppose (1) his forgiving sins (2:1–12), (2) his friendship and especially his social table-fellowship ("commensality") with "sinners" (2:15–17), (3) the failure of his disciples to fast (2:18–22), (4) Jesus and his disciples violating **Sabbath** (the Jewish holy day of rest, the last day of every week) law by picking grain (2:23–28) and (5) Jesus' violation of Sabbath law by healing on the Sabbath a man who could just as well have been healed on another day (3:1–6). In these incidents, Jesus bases his ministry on his own authority and does not fit into the religious expectations of some of his Jewish contemporaries, especially those in power. This opposition results in 3:6 with the Pharisees and Herodians plotting to destroy Jesus—the reader/listener is scarcely into Mark, and already Jesus' death is in view! Mark closes the previous section and begins a new narrative section with a summary stating that Jesus was now attracting people from a widening region beyond Galilee, including Gentile territories (3:7–12). (Summaries in the Gospels often mark a transitional point in the narrative.) This is Mark's first mention of the Gospel's crossing a cultural barrier.

As the next section of narrative begins, Jesus appoints twelve of his disciples to be **apostles,** "ones sent out" to proclaim his message and work exorcisms. These Twelve are named in a roughly descending order of prominence, from the famous Peter to the infamous Judas Iscariot. In the mention of Judas as Jesus' betrayer, the reader learns here how Jesus is to be arrested. In 3:20–35, we encounter for the first time in Mark a narrative arrangement in which the text tells two stories at once: the author initiates one story, interrupts it by another event that is fully told at once, and then finishes the initial story. The formal name for this is **intercalation,** but scholars usually call it the **Markan sandwich.** On one side of the first Markan sandwich is the approach of Jesus' mother and brothers, who do not understand his actions and want to "restrain him," perhaps to restore the family's social honor. In the middle of the sandwich is a story about scribes who come from Jerusalem and accuse Jesus of getting his power from the Devil. Jesus states clearly the cosmic dimensions of the struggle now going on, that Satan's kingdom opposes the kingdom of God that is coming with Jesus. He states that it is an "unforgivable sin" to ascribe Jesus' works to Satan rather than to the Holy Spirit—the worst hostility to God. On the other side of the sandwich, the mother and brothers of Jesus finally arrive. Jesus gives them a startling message about new kinship in the kingdom of God: "Whoever does the will of God is my brother, and sister, and mother." At the end of the sandwich, Mark's teaching in this intercalation is clear: following Jesus and his teaching brings one into a new family and a new kinship system, one that recognizes that Jesus does his ministry out of God's blessing and power.

The next section (4:1–34) is a collection of parables on the kingdom of God, the first in Mark's narrative. (The only other collection will come in chapter 13). Even though Jesus' ministry now centers in a city, Jesus takes the material of these parables from villages and farms familiar to his listeners. In the Markan sequence, three seed-growth parables (the Sower and the Seed in 4:1–20, the Seed That Grows on Its Own in 4:26-29, and the Mustard Seed in 4:30–32) explain what has begun to happen in Jesus' ministry—the seed symbolizing God's kingdom is sown, and the kingdom is beginning to grow. The parable of the Sower and the Seed, and its private interpretation by Jesus to his disciples, explains that only some accept the proclamation of the kingdom, and even among them there are failures. Despite the failures of sowing and growing the seed of Jesus' message, God will give an abundant harvest. The presence of an interpretation of this first parable in the chapter invites the reader/listener to interpret the other parables that follow. Mark 4:11–12 says that Jesus uses parables to those outside in order that they may not understand or be converted. Mark touches here on the growing negative results of Jesus' teaching among his own people, the majority of whom did not understand and follow Jesus' way. Jesus' parables are both inviting and off-putting; they both reveal and conceal the Good News. Yet Jesus' purpose in using parables was not to make God's message altogether too difficult to understand and accept. This is made clear in three ways: these parables all indicate that remarkable growth will occur; the parables about the lamp and the hidden things say once again that Jesus' message will be successful; and Mark's summary at the end of this chapter has Jesus speaking his message to the crowds in parables "as they were able to understand it," and giving his disciples private explanations.

Mark now resumes the action. The reader encounters four miraculous deeds in 4:35–5.43. First, Jesus astonishes his disciples by calming a raging storm on the Sea of Galilee (4:35–41), where the question of Jesus' identity becomes sharp. Second, Jesus struggles with, and is powerful over, the demonic when he heals the (probably Gentile) Gerasene man, by driving out his "Legion" of demons (5:1–20). The pattern of this miracle form resembles the demoniac story earlier in 1:21–28; however, the narration is more detailed and dramatic here, showing Mark's narrative abilities. At the conclusion of the exorcism, the man wants to follow Jesus as his disciple, but Jesus declines this request and in a reversal of the secrecy motif tells the man to return to his friends and tell them "how much the Lord has done for you," a command the man more than obeys as he spreads the message through the Decapolis area, the "Ten Cities" founded by Alexander the Great and his successors. The second and third miracles, in 5:21–43, are another instance of a Markan sandwich, here concerning two women. Jesus sets out to heal Jairus' daughter, then (in the middle of the sandwich) unintentionally heals a woman with a flow of blood when she touches his clothing in bold faith, and finally arrives to raise Jairus' daughter, who had died in the delay. Jesus' declaration to the woman and many others whom he heals, "Your faith has saved you" (5:34), shows that the power of Jesus to heal connects with the willingness of people to believe in him as God's agent of healing. His miracles are neither mechanical nor magical. The section ends with another command to secrecy (5:43).

In 6:1–6, Jesus returns to Nazareth, his hometown. His teaching about his own person and mission in the synagogue generates doubt and then violent opposition, but Jesus avoids death at this point. In 6:7–33, we encounter yet another Markan sandwich: Jesus' sending out of the Twelve is narrated in 6:7–13 and their return to him in 6:30–32, with a lengthy flashback narrative of King Herod's murder of John the Baptizer at the behest of his wife and step-daughter in the middle (vv. 14–29). In this flashback, women and men cooperate in opposing good in a complex social situation of gender, sexuality and politics. John shows himself a faithful forerunner to Jesus even to the point of suffering and death. On their mission trip, the disciples preach repentance, drive out demons, and cure the sick "with oil" (which Jesus does not use), all an extension of Jesus' own mission. Jesus miraculously and compassionately feeds five thousand men (implying that there were women and children there as well, but not counted) who have come to hear him. Jesus then walks on the waters of the Sea of Galilee. That Jesus is the Son of God (1:1) is suggested not only by his walking on water, but also by his answer in 6:50, "I am," reminiscent of God's name "Yahweh" in the Hebrew Scriptures. (This "I am" is obscured in the NRSV, which renders it "It is I.") However, the disciples misunderstand this miracle and the multiplication of bread, because their hearts were hardened (6:52). Next comes another Markan summary of the previous narrative (6:53–56), this one relating the enthusiasm of Galilean villagers for Jesus' many healings. Some are accomplished simply by the sick touching his garments, a narrative glance back to the healing of the bold woman in chapter 5.

Despite all these miracles, the Pharisees and scribes who come from Jerusalem are upset because Jesus and his disciples do not observe their stricter forms of ritual purity (7:1–23), purity that Mark explains to the readers in vv. 3–4. Jesus condemns their understanding of God's law as only human traditions of outward purity that block the true inner purity that God demands. Mark makes clear that Jesus abolishes kosher regulations by this teaching: "Thus he declared all foods clean" (v. 19). As Jesus moves on, the unnamed Syrophoenician (Gentile) woman in the Tyre area, outside the Jewish homeland, shows what true faith is. Jesus initially rebuffs her by insulting her as a Gentile "dog," but the woman responds in bold, persistent faith that she is still worthy of some of Jesus' mercy. Pleased at the woman, Jesus heals her child at a distance (7:24–30). The next miracle, the healing of a deaf man who likely is also a Gentile, describes an unusual (for Jesus, that is) amount of contact between Jesus and the afflicted person, including Jesus putting his spittle on the deaf man's tongue (7:31–35). Mark then indicates that people's growing enthusiasm about Jesus' power leads them increasingly to disregard his command to secrecy (7:36–37).

Next, with the memory of Jesus' feeding of five thousand in Chapter 6 still fresh in the readers' minds, Jesus miraculously feeds a crowd of four thousand people (evidently now including women and children), showing his amazing power in Gentile territory (8:1–10). Jesus' follow-up conversation with his opponents and his still uncomprehending disciples dramatizes the growing doubtfulness that Jesus will be understood during his lifetime; if his own disciples cannot understand him, certainly others will not (8:11–21)! The healing of the blind man that follows is unique among Jesus' miracles in Mark (and elsewhere); the first action by Jesus gives him blurry vision, and only when Jesus tries again does the man see clearly (8:22–26). This shows in narrative form how unseeing people come to faith in stages, a theme in this section of Mark.

The second half of Mark begins at 8:27. Peter's perceptive confession that Jesus is the Messiah, the Son of God (8:27–30), the turning point in the Gospel, shows the truth about Jesus against positive but inadequate popular evaluations of Jesus as John the Baptizer come back to life, as Elijah come back to life, and as a prophet. However, Jesus responds with the command to silence we have often seen before, silence now about Jesus' identity as Messiah. Jesus then predicts his own passion and resurrection for the first of three times, showing what sort of Messiah he is (8:31). Peter rejects this portrait of the suffering Son of Man, and Jesus rebukes his rejection as Satanic. Not only will Jesus have to suffer and die, but so too eventually will those who would follow him. This understanding of Jesus as the suffering Christ/Messiah lies at the heart of Mark's portrait of Jesus and the life of those who follow him (8:34–37). In 8:38, the language of honor and shame rises to the surface as Jesus warns that those who are ashamed of him, perhaps to avoid this suffering, will receive a shameful judgment when the Son of Man comes in the glory of his Father with the holy angels at the end of time.

All this is followed by Jesus' **transfiguration,** or change in the nature of his body from earthly to heavenly (9:2–13). This shows Jesus' identity, and the heavenly voice confirms that Jesus is God's Son; it also anticipates Jesus' glorious destiny in his resurrection. But the disciples, especially Peter, who speaks from sheer emotion when he "does not know what to say" (v. 9), react in yet another display of their inadequate faith. When they come down from the mountain, they meet a boy possessed by a demon, whom Jesus' disciples were not able to cure while he was on the mountain. Jesus himself cures this boy but expresses his sharp disappointment that his disciples could not drive out the demon. He reprimands them for their lack of faith (9:14–29).

A tour through Galilee begins with Jesus' second prediction of his passion and resurrection (9:30–32), which once again the disciples do not understand despite Jesus' transfiguration. Their lack of understanding of the way of the cross is then dramatized in their argument with each other about which of them will be first in the kingdom of God (9:33–37). In Capernaum and eventually as he begins an ominous journey to Judea, Jesus gives his disciples varied instructions about life in the kingdom (9:33–10:31), important last instructions before he dies. The theme of these instructions is set in its opening: Jesus warns the Twelve, and through them all his followers, not to seek to be the greatest in the kingdom but to be a slave, who is least of all on the social scale of honor and importance. Jesus illustrates this teaching by receiving a child, also a lowly person on the social scale (9:33–37). Next comes a dispute about in-group and out-group social concerns, when Jesus' disciples attempt to stop a person not among Jesus' followers from using Jesus' name to heal. Jesus commands them to let such a person continue to use Jesus' name (9:38–41). This incident is followed up with teachings about discipline within the community of Jesus' followers. Its negative aspect is to avoid behavior that drives people away from the faith; its positive aspect is to live in peace with each other (9:42–50).

As Jesus begins his journey to Judea, opposition rises as the Pharisees test Jesus by asking him about divorce. Jesus goes beyond the Law of Moses to God's creation of humanity, and he forbids divorce and especially remarriage for God's people, whether the divorce is initiated by husbands or wives (10:1–12). Then Jesus returns to the issue of those who enter the kingdom. Once again he welcomes children in 10:13–16, correcting an error that demands that only those with social honor should enter the kingdom. For Jesus, the kingdom/rule of God requires only human receptiveness, which the child's low, humble status symbolizes. How adults can have—or lack—this receptiveness is shown in the account of the rich man that follows (10:17–27). When this man says he has observed all God's commands, Jesus challenges him to sell all his possessions and give the proceeds to the poor. Although the man cannot do this, perhaps because it would lead to disgrace for his entire family, the point is clear: following Jesus requires the ability to give up everything else for him. Those who make great sacrifices for Jesus will be rewarded both in this age and the age to come (10:29–31), but once again Jesus speaks about suffering— they will undergo persecution because they follow him. James and John, not understanding Jesus' teaching, want the prime positions in the kingdom of God for themselves (10:35–45). Instead, Jesus challenges them to follow him in "drinking the cup" and "being baptized," both symbolically a challenge to share Jesus' suffering. The journey toward Jerusalem nears its conclusion when Jesus heals the blind Bartimaeus in Jericho, the city closest to Jerusalem (10:46–52). This is the last healing miracle that Jesus will work in Mark.

The next section of Mark features Jesus' entry into Jerusalem, ministry and increasing conflict there, and eschatological teaching (11:1–13:37). All this points toward Jesus' death and resurrection. On the first day, Jesus sends two disciples to obtain a young donkey, and all is as he foretold in obtaining it. Jesus enters Jerusalem triumphally, but on this symbolically humble animal (11:1–11). Another Markan sandwich narrates Jesus' next actions: cursing the fruitless fig tree, cleansing the Temple, and finding the fig tree withered (11:12–25). The fruitless fig tree is those Jewish authorities who have become fruitless, whose corruption of the Temple into a "den of thieves" has frustrated God's intent for it to be a house of prayer for all the peoples of the earth. The miraculous element in the cursing/withering becomes in 11:22–25 a "teachable moment" for Jesus to give the disciples a lesson in faith and the power of prayer when one is confronted by conflict.

Jesus' attack on the Temple leads to heightened opposition, as the powers that be challenge Jesus' authority (11:27–33). This is the first of several "traps" against Jesus, where Mark shows Jesus' superior wisdom when confronted by opponents who are trying to lure him into saying something that they could arrest and punish him for. Social scientific reading explains these exchanges as *challenge and riposte*— Jesus' opponents challenge his honor and authority, and Jesus responds by parrying the challenges and then defeating his enemies completely, thus solidifying his honor and shaming his opponents. Traps are also laid in the questions of the Pharisees and Herodians about taxes for Caesar (12:13–17) and of the Sadducees about the resurrection (12:18–27). These hostile encounters show the wide-ranging hostility to Jesus among the leaders of all the Jewish groups in Jerusalem (no Roman authority is in view yet, however). But not all Jewish leaders are opposed to Jesus: a scribe asks about the greatest commandment (12:28–34) and wins Jesus' approval for being near to the kingdom of God. Then, in response to so many hostile questions, Jesus springs his own trap for his opponents with a question about the messiah's identity as David's son, which they are unwilling to answer (12:35–37). This section ends with Jesus teaching his followers about faithful conduct. Faithful conduct is illustrated negatively in Jesus' criticism of the scribes' love for social honors, which masks economic oppression of widows and false public piety, and positively

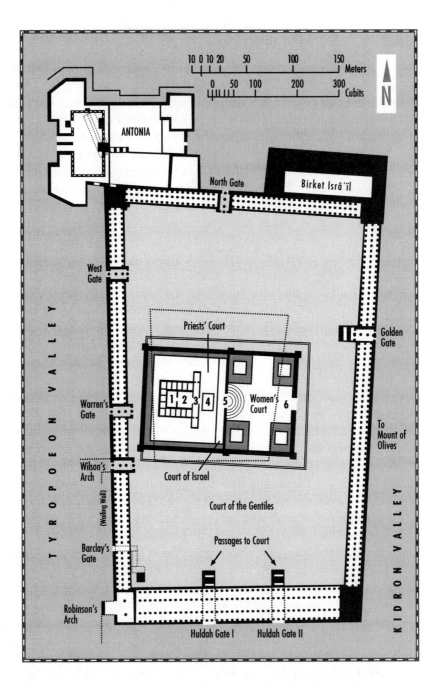

Map 6.1 The Jerusalem Temple in Jesus' Day. Floor plan of Herod's Temple and courts: (1) Holy of Holies, (2) Holy Place (Nave), (3) Porch, (4) Altar, (5) Nicanor Gate, (6) Beautiful Gate?

(Based on Vincent-Steve [W. F. Stinespring, *IDB* R–Z, p. 556] and C. L. Meyers [*Harpers Bible Dictionary*, p. 1028, Maplewood NJ: Hammond Incorporated]).

in the story of the widow's generosity in giving her last small coins to the Temple, perhaps the only possessions left after possible oppression by scribes (12:38–44).

The eschatological discourse of Chapter 13, the second of only two discourses in Mark, is strongly negative in tone. It features three types of material: first, dire prophetic warnings on the destruction of the Temple, second, teaching on the future persecution of the disciples, and third about being watchful for the end of time. The last item is followed up with more detailed apocalyptic signs to be watchful for: messianic deceivers claiming to be Jesus come back in glory, wars between nations, the idolatrous "desolating abomination" standing where it should not be, and signs in the sky. Despite all the teachings about the end of time in this discourse, and the signs of the end given in it, the end will come unexpectedly for all people, even followers of Jesus. Only God knows the time of the end; angels and even Jesus himself do not, so the final message of this chapter is that the disciples must "keep awake," be alert and expectant, for it.

Now the narrative action resumes. Mark's gospel climaxes and concludes with a plot against Jesus, his anointing, his Last Supper, arrest, trials, crucifixion, burial, and the women disciples' discovery of the empty tomb (14:1–16:8). This section begins with another Markan sandwich formed by the chief priests' and scribes' plot to kill Jesus, a woman's extravagant anointing of Jesus, and Judas' joining the plot against Jesus (14:1–11). Jesus' extravagant anointing is "for my burial," a procedure that Jesus' body will not receive when he is buried; this tells the reader in the middle of the sandwich that this particular plot will succeed. The preparations for Passover (14:12–16) not only supply a context for Jesus' action at the Last Supper, but may also illustrate Jesus' ability to foretell what will happen. At the Last Supper (14:17–25), Judas' predicted giving of Jesus to his deadly enemies offers a dramatic contrast to Jesus' self-giving in the bread and wine as his body and blood, offered in his death.

In the Garden of Gethsemane on the Mount of Olives opposite Jerusalem, the setting for the next section (14:26–52), Mark's **passion narrative** proper begins, the story of Jesus' physical, emotional and spiritual suffering extending from his arrest through his burial. Jesus' predictions of the disciples' desertion of him, and of Peter's denials of him, set a fateful tone (14:26–31). Jesus then wrestles with the prospect of his death and asks God to spare him. But when his Father is silent to Jesus' repeated pleas, and after Jesus finds his disciples asleep three times, Jesus accepts what he knows to be God's will and proclaims that his arrest is now here (14:32–42). With a mocking kiss, a greeting usually given by kin or close friends, Judas betrays Jesus to the armed crowd that has come from the chief priests and the scribes. After slight violent resistance, all the disciples flee. Then an unnamed young man who had been following Jesus runs away naked after escaping an arresting officer who had hold of him only by his one piece of clothing (14:43–50).

Those who arrest Jesus now bring him before the Jewish authorities for trial (14:53–65). Jesus is condemned by a **Sanhedrin**, a Jewish religious court, although

Mark makes it clear that Jesus is innocent of all charges, particularly the charge that Jesus promised to destroy the Temple. In the face of false witnesses and hostile judges, Jesus courageously confesses that he is the Son of God and thereby seals his death for blasphemy. Then Mark movingly recounts a contrasting scene in which Peter curses Jesus in a cowardly way and denies knowing him in order to save his own life (14:66–72). After the guilty verdict by the high priest, Jesus is treated shamefully. The Sanhedrin then sends Jesus to Pontius Pilate, the Roman governor (15:1–15). After a brief hearing (Jesus is not entitled to a formal trial because he is not a Roman citizen), Pilate tries to free Jesus. When he encounters popular resistance to that plan, instigated by the Jewish leaders, he hands Jesus over to be crucified, and Roman soldiers mistreat him in the process. Mark draws a clear parallel between the two judicial scenes, Jewish and Roman. In both, Jesus is shown to be innocent. The false witnesses in the Jewish trial show that Jesus' opponents are in the wrong, and Pilate knows that Jesus is innocent. This innocence is important, for it allows Jesus' death to have a sacrificial meaning. At the end of each trial, Jesus is condemned to death, spit on, and mocked—as a prophet by some Jewish Sanhedrin members and the Jewish guard and as "the King of the Jews" by Roman soldiers.

On the way to the place of crucifixion grimly named Golgotha ("Place of the Skull"), Jesus is exhausted, and a bystander named Simon from Cyrene is compelled by the Roman execution squad to carry Jesus' cross (15:21–24). Jesus' crucifixion is narrated quickly (15:25–39), more quickly than his trials. The details that Mark mentions do not describe the crucifixion directly because most of his readers would be familiar with how it was done. Rather, he draws from Old Testament descriptions of innocent sufferers, the two wine drinks, with myrrh at the beginning and vinegary wine at the end (Prov 31:6–7; Ps 69:22) and the distribution of Jesus' clothes—all of them, resulting in Jesus' nakedness—by gambling (Ps 22:19). Three groups speak at Jesus' cross: passersby, the chief priests and scribes, and two criminals crucified with him. They all heap shame on Jesus, adding insult to his deadly injuries. Near the end of the horrific process, Jesus speaks from the cross for the first and only time. Jesus expresses his deep lament that "My God" has abandoned him, drawing again on Psalm 22. Yet in a stunning reversal, the moment he dies, God demonstrates Jesus' innocence. First, the veil that marked off the Temple sanctuary is torn, depriving that place of its holiness and alluding to its destruction to come (chapter 13). Second, the Roman centurion in charge of the execution finally understands what the Jewish council and Pilate could not see, that "Truly this man was God's Son."

Mark now introduces the women who had followed Jesus in Galilee and accompanied him to Jerusalem (15:40–41). The women are the only followers of Jesus to observe his death, but only from a distance, perhaps because of social constraints about unescorted women keeping away from men. After Jesus' death on the cross, Mark narrates the successful effort of Joseph of Arimathea to bury Jesus—ironically the only one who assists Jesus is one who, so far as the reader of Mark knows, had no previous contact with him (15: 42–47). Faithful to the end, the women now follow him to his burial in a tomb with a rolling-stone door. In Chapter 16, they go to the tomb on Sunday morning. Their touching rhetorical question about moving the stone (to open the tomb and finish his formal burial by anointing him) anticipates the divine intervention in the scene that awaits them. The tomb is already open; a young man to be understood as an angel is there, but not the body of Jesus. The ringing proclamation, "He has been raised . . . he is going before you to Galilee where you will see him," tells Jesus' eternal triumph over death that he himself had predicted three times (8:31; 9:31; 10:34). The reaction of the women in 16:8 is astounding. They disobey the angel's command to report this good news to the disciples and Peter. They flee in fear, and out of fear say nothing to anyone. At the end, and with great irony, secrecy about Jesus seems to prevail! (The different endings of Mark will be treated below, in the section on textual criticism.)

www   For a chart geographically situating the narrative flow of Mark, see the website.

Historical Reading

In dealing with the historical-critical interpretation of the documents of the NT, we begin by discussing matters of **NT introduction:** the identity of the real author, what can be known about the real audience and its situation, the date of the Gospel, the purpose for writing, and possible sources. Then we will discuss other issues in historical interpretation.

Mark in Brief: Summary of Historical Reading	
Author:	Anonymous. Traditionally, John Mark of Jerusalem (Acts 12:12, 15:37; Philemon 1:24). Today, most scholars hold the author to be an unknown Christian of the second generation, perhaps a Jewish convert to Christianity.
Date:	Probably in the late 60s or very early 70s.
Audience:	Gentile Christians, probably in Rome, perhaps in Syria or Alexandria, facing persecution.
Sources:	Although some scholars argue for extensive pre-Markan written sources (e.g., an entire but shorter gospel such as a *Secret Gospel of Mark*), most conclude that Mark used at most a few shorter sources such as parable or miracle collections.
Purpose:	To encourage Christians undergoing difficulties and persecutions by relating the sufferings, death, resurrection and return of Jesus.

Author

The Gospel of Mark is **anonymously authored,** that is, it provides no author's name in its text. ("Mark" is *on* it, not *in* it.) The author never gives any direct information about herself/himself, being careful to keep the narrative in the third person. Therefore, we must puzzle out the author's identity in two ways, by **external evidence,** statements by later Christians about who wrote this Gospel, and by **internal evidence,** what can be inferred from the book itself as we "read between the lines" about its author. We will begin by examining the external evidence for Mark. In the mid-second century, the important Christian writer named Justin (*Trypho* 106.3) refers to a book he calls "Peter's memoirs," citing a passage that is found only in Mark 3:16–17. Eusebius (*History of the Church* 3.39.15–16) records an early second-century tradition about Mark that Papias received from "the elder": "Mark, having become the interpreter of Peter, wrote down accurately, but not in order, all Peter recalled of what the Lord either said or did." The title *The Gospel According to Mark* was probably attached to this writing by the end of the second century, to judge from the evidence of surviving manuscripts and church writers. No early church evidence for any other author besides Mark has survived.

Who is this Mark? The name Mark was common at the time, and this complicates the NT references to this person. Acts speaks of a Jewish man in the early church whom it calls "John whose surname was Mark," i.e., **John Mark,** but only once calls him simply "Mark" (15:39). It associates him with Peter, Paul, and Barnabas. In verse 24 of Philemon, a letter sent around 60 C.E., Paul mentions a Mark as a fellow worker who was with him in the place from which he writes. Col. 4:10, which assumes the same situation as Philemon and may be dependent on it, informs us that this Mark is the cousin of Barnabas. First Peter, probably written from Rome around 80, identifies Mark as Peter's "son" who is with him there (5:13). Most scholars conclude that Papias was indeed referring to this (John) Mark as the one who wrote down what was said and done by the Lord. However, was Papias correct? Although what he says about Mark and Peter seems plausible enough, on other matters of which he speaks Papias was known even in the ancient world as a collector of both fact and rumor, with not enough ability or interest to distinguish between them. The internal evidence of the Gospel supplies little to support Papias' idea and much to call it into question. First, that Peter is the most important of the Twelve in Mark need not mean that Peter was the Gospel's source, as Papias may have deduced. Peter is the lead apostle in Matthew and Luke as well, but that does not lead to a Petrine origin for those Gospels. Second, that the author of this Greek Gospel was John Mark, a presumably Aramaic-speaking Jew of Jerusalem who had early become a Christian, is hard to reconcile with the impression that it is not a translation from Aramaic. The Gospel of Mark seems to depend on traditions and perhaps sources received in Greek. Third, the Gospel of Mark seems confused about a few points of Palestinian geography, which one would not expect from someone who grew up there. Therefore, for these reasons and others, most scholars today do not conclude that John Mark was the author of this book. The author has chosen to be anonymous and still succeeds in that intent.

www   Read an excellent overview of historical-critical approaches to the study of Mark at the PBS Television website, "From Jesus to Christ."

Date

We begin by considering the earliest possible date of writing. Those scholars who trust Papias' statement that Mark wrote down Peter's memories usually argue that Mark wrote near Peter's death in the mid- or late 60s. Irenaeus also places it shortly after the death of Peter and Paul, and Clement of Alexandria looks to a date near the end of their lives. Internally that dating is supported by the failure of Mark to show any knowledge of the details of the First Jewish Revolt against Rome in 66–70 C.E., particularly about the fall of Jerusalem. As Martin Hengel has shown in a careful study of Mark 13, it is most likely that Mark was written in the early stages of the Jewish revolt against Rome, that is, from 66 to 70 C.E. This chapter reflects the beginning of the war, not its culmination or aftermath: a time of rumors of war (vv. 7–8), increasing persecutions for those who follow Jesus and therefore perhaps refuse to join in revolt (vv. 9–13), and false prophets holding themselves out as Jesus himself (vv. 5–6, 21–22). Flight from the city of Jerusalem when the Temple is desecrated is urged, but Jesus' instructions to pray that flight would not be necessary in winter conflict with the actual timing of the fall of the Temple, which happened in the summer of 70 C.E. (vv. 14–20) (Hengel 1985, 14–28). This date at the beginning of the revolt also agrees with the historical situation of Nero's persecution of the Roman church in 64–65 C.E. So the earliest beginning point for Mark is around 65.

As for the latest possible date of writing, Hengel's analysis suggests 70. Synoptic relationships also furnish some evidence. If Mark was used independently by both Matthew and Luke and they were written in the 80s or early 90s, as most scholars believe, a date beyond 75 seems unlikely, because there would not be enough time for Mark to circulate and gain the standing necessary for Matthew and Luke to use it as sources. When all this evidence about dating is put together, it leads to wide scholarly agreement that Mark was written in the late 60s.

Audience

Beginning again with external evidence, at the end of the second century Clement of Alexandria (*History of the Church* 6.14.6) cites Rome as the place where Mark wrote the Gospel. This assertion is supported by a large number of scholars today,

The Arch of Titus in the Roman Forum After Emperor Titus died in 81 C.E., Domitian raised a triumphal arch to honor Titus and Vespasian for crushing the Jewish revolt. The arch is 15.4 meters high, 13.5 meters wide, and 4.75 meters deep. In this panel Roman soldiers are depicted carrying the Temple table of the showbread, menorah and trumpets in the triumphal parade of 71 C.E. The Jewish war forms a key part of the setting of Mark; it was probably written to Roman Christians, many of them from a Jewish background. Used by permission of BiblePlaces.com.

who would add that Mark's audience is also the Roman church(es). However, since there was a strong tradition that Peter was killed for his faith at Rome, this location may have been an imaginative derivation from the connection that Papias made between Mark and Peter. To judge from internal evidence, the presence in Mark of **Latinisms**, Greek loanwords derived from Latin and expressions reflecting Latin grammar, may suggest a locale where Latin was spoken. Many of the Latinisms are common commercial or military words and could be found anywhere in the Roman Empire, but the presence of so many of them in Mark may indicate a Roman locale. In addition, parallel ideas have been detected between Mark and Paul's letter to the Romans, which was written in the middle 50s. For instance, Mark's "[Jesus] declared all foods clean" (7:19) resembles Rom. 14:14: "I know and am convinced in the

Lord Jesus that nothing is unclean in itself." To most interpreters, the strongest argument for placing the audience in Rome connects an important theme of Mark and the historical situation of the Roman church. Mark's strong emphasis on the sufferings of Jesus, the necessity for followers of Jesus to suffer for him, and on the disciple's flight when Jesus was arrested, suggests to many interpreters today that Mark addresses a community that had been persecuted and failed in order to correct and encourage them. Although Christians were under duress in various cities during the first century C.E., only the church in Rome endured deadly Roman persecution, namely, under Nero in 64.

A main alternative to Rome is Galilee, or close to Palestine in Syria or in the northern Transjordan. W. Marxsen points to a contrast between Galilee and Jerusalem in Mark; Galilee is where the church sees Jesus (Mark 16:7), where its future lies (Marxsen 1969). It may also serve as a geographical symbol of the Gentile world, because Jews in Judea often called it "Galilee of the Gentiles." Most scholars are not convinced by these reasons, largely because they find so little solid evidence to support them. The fact that Jesus came from Galilee and actually had most of his ministry there may explain Mark's interest in that area without any further implications. (Matthew and Luke center Jesus' ministry in Galilee just as much as Mark does, and this fact has not led modern scholars to conclude that they are written to Galilee.) Recent research has shown that Galilee in Jesus' day was overwhelmingly Jewish, despite a Gentile presence in certain cities (Chancey 2002). Some Semitic language terms are translated as if the audience does not know that language (3:17; 7:34; 10:46; 15:22, 34), and that would scarcely be true if Mark were written for Galilee. Therefore, Rome is the more likely site than Galilee as the location of Mark's audience. That we cannot know precisely the locale addressed by Mark—the original "real audience," as narrative critics say—leads us now to what can be detected from a careful reading of Mark about the addressees, the "implied audience."

The Gospel's implied audience is Greek-speaking Christians who did not know Aramaic. Most of them were not Jews, since the author had to explain Jewish purification customs to them. Yet he could assume that they would know or at least appreciate the most important religious terms stemming from Judaism (he uses without explanation the terms *Satan, Beelzebul, Gehenna, rabbi, hosanna,* and *amen*), so they were probably Christians who had been converted by evangelizers familiar with Jewish Christian tradition. Most likely, they had heard a good deal about Jesus before Mark's Gospel was read to them; the main outline of Jesus' story was doubtless known to them before they heard this Gospel. Almost certainly, they were members or attendees of a Christian church, where Jesus would be worshipped as the Son of God (1:1). They had recently (64–65 C.E.) undergone persecution instigated by the Emperor Nero himself, during which a disappointing number of Christians may have, like Peter, denied knowing Jesus or simply fled like the twelve disciples did. The community as a whole did not realize that following Jesus meant following in his suffering before one enters glory with him.

www Follow the link to a website with a careful reading of Mark against its Jewish background.

Textual Criticism

Overall, the Greek text of Mark is reliable, that is, we can be confident that our critical Greek text of Mark today faithfully represents the original text. However, one of the knottiest textual problems in the entire NT occurs at the end of Mark. In the opinion of most textual critics and other NT scholars, the original Gospel probably ended with Mark 16:8, "So [the women] went out and fled from the tomb, for terror and amazement had seized them; and they said nothing to anyone, for they were afraid." It may seem strange to end a book about "good news" (1:1) on a note of disobedience and fear. Some scholars argue strongly for an ending now lost, perhaps a final page that became detached before Mark was published. This is an intriguing idea but cannot be proven with the evidence at hand. Their main argument is that Mark would surely have narrated the appearance in Galilee promised in 16:7. However, to claim that Jesus' promised appearance in Galilee *necessitates* a narration of that event is presumptuous. We must expect that an intentionally abrupt ending will leave some "unfinished business." Moreover, to argue from a parallel issue, Mark's repeated mention of Jesus' mother did not move him to include a birth narrative like the other Synoptics have.

Our manuscript copies of Mark witness to two main different endings beyond 16:8, both of which are printed as part of the text of Mark in many modern Bible versions. The best attested ending is called the **Markan appendix** or more commonly the **longer ending** (the longer of the two *added* endings, that is). It mentions briefly three appearances of the risen Jesus (to Mary Magdalene, to two disciples in the country, to eleven at a meal) and the ascension of Jesus to heaven. The women were afraid to speak in 16:8; now, however, the appearance of Jesus to Mary Magdalene brings her to confident belief. She shares the news with Jesus' disciples, but they do not believe her. Nevertheless, when Jesus appears to two of them, they too come to believe. Finally, Jesus appears to the eleven, rebukes them for not having believed the news about his resurrection, and sends them into the whole world to proclaim the gospel and baptize believers. The longer ending concludes with the Lord working with missionary disciples through miraculous signs. On the whole, the longer ending is textually doubtful. It looks like a summary based on knowledge of the other Gospels and contains many non-Markan words. The so-called **shorter ending** of Mark is two sentences long, also coming at the finish of 16:8. It relates that the women did speak "to those around Peter" what the angel at the empty tomb commanded them to say and that Jesus himself sent out through them "the sacred and imperishable proclamation of eternal salvation." This overblown language obviously is not Markan. In sum, although it is *possible* that the final page of Mark was lost, textual evidence indicates that the abrupt ending at 16:8 is indeed "the earliest ascertainable [ending] of the Gospel of Mark" (Metzger 1994, 105).

Sources

Recent scholarship is nearly unanimous in concluding that Mark was an actual author who created an effective whole from his material. But did Mark use written sources, and if so, what were they? To begin with the more unlikely sources, Morton Smith has argued that the *Secret Gospel of Mark* is a source for canonical Mark, and John Dominic Crossan has proposed that a source of the *Gospel of Peter* is a source for the Markan passion (Smith 1973; Crossan 1988). These complicated and highly controversial arguments have not gained wide assent. If Mark corrected the *Secret Gospel of Mark* or the *Gospel of Peter* as he used them as sources, Mark would have been omitting the statement that Jesus felt no pain on the cross, or the picture of a gigantic risen Jesus accompanied by a cross that moved and spoke (*Gospel of Peter*), or the scene where Jesus spent the night with a virtually naked young man whom he had raised from the dead (*Secret Gospel of Mark*). If Mark is correcting Gnostic gospels, his references to the Twelve and his description of the women as failing to speak about the resurrection could be meant to support a patriarchal form of Christianity against more egalitarian Gnostic-Christian groups in which women had a more equal role and received postresurrectional revelations. However, Mark's often-unflattering depiction of the all-male Twelve coupled with his more positive over-all depiction of women argues in the opposite direction. Although scholars like Crossan and Koester suppose Markan dependence on early versions of apocryphal works written down in their present form later than Mark, the evidence for this seems so slim to most scholars that they reject this approach. Most of the evidence indicates that Mark did not know or use the supposed sources of these gospels.

Continuing with more likely sources, a larger number of scholars maintain that a written pre-Markan passion narrative (or narratives) can be detected in Mark's passion narrative, but there is little consensus about what its wording would be (Soards, in Brown 1997, 1492–1524). This lack of consensus makes redaction criticism difficult, if not impossible. Sources for smaller blocks of material have also been proposed, especially where Mark has the same kind of forms grouped together. For instance, researchers debate whether the five pronouncement stories in 2:1–3:6 were taken over by Mark from a source. More widely accepted is some source (oral and/or written) for the parables in chapter 4. Several theories about sources attempt to explain the Markan miracle stories, sometimes grouped together in Mark (Achtemeier 1970, 1972). Considerable debate assesses whether a pre-Markan apocalypse underlies Mark 13. For a bold attempt to reconstruct an outline of an entire pre-Markan gospel, see Michael Goulder's essay "The Pre-Markan Gospel" (Goulder 1994).

Purpose

The author does not tell the reader explicitly why he or she is writing, so it is left for us to puzzle this out. The purpose for Mark may be suggested at the beginning of the gospel, "The beginning of the Gospel of Jesus Christ, the Son of God." This implies that Mark's purpose is to tell the story of Jesus as good news and that his writing will bring good news to its readers/hearers. What precisely this good news may be is found in other suggestions regarding the purpose of Mark's Gospel: (1) to show that Jesus as Messiah was innocent of Jewish charges and that his sufferings were a part of the plan of God, thus encouraging readers who suffer for their faith; (2) to explain why Jesus did not publicly declare himself to be the Messiah (i.e., the Messianic secret; see later); and (3) to present the works of Jesus as a triumph over the works of the devil, thus empowering the readers in their struggle against evil. Any—or all—of these could be the purpose of Mark.

Werner Kelber and Theodore J. Weeden have argued that the author of Mark shaped his material editorially to deal with a conflict within the Christian community. In their analysis, the references to "false Messiahs and false prophets" in 13:6, 21–23 refer to Christians who have come into the author's community from outside, advancing claims that appeal to people facing severe difficulties. These "false Christs" claim such a close spiritual relationship with the risen Jesus that it enables them to claim an "identity" with Christ, saying "I am he" (13:6). Corresponding to this is a specific type of christology: these "false Christs" emphasize Jesus' breathtaking power, understanding him in light of a particular type of Hellenistic wonder worker known as a "divine man," which some scholars think was a popular figure at the time (Weeden and Kelber 1983). Most interpreters have termed this type of view of Jesus as **triumphalist christology** because it stresses Jesus' power to use miracles to solve his problems and to triumph over death, and it understands the life of discipleship as so powerfully filled with Spirit that it overcomes virtually all human problems. Weeden and Kelber believe that Mark was written to correct these views, which its author saw as detrimental. Mark promotes instead a **theology of the cross** that emphasizes the necessity of suffering with and for Christ. The first part of the Gospel does indeed present Jesus as a miracle-working Son of God; from 8:27 on, however, this triumphalist understanding gives way to the image of a Jesus on his way to suffering and death, calling his followers to a similar lifestyle.

Mark clearly links both christology and discipleship to the "way of the cross." Many scholars doubt, however, that the notion of the divine man was clearly developed and widely accepted in the Hellenistic world. Here we can cite the work of three scholars in reaction to this corrective christology. Jack D. Kingsbury has argued that while the christological view of Mark's early chapters is developed and deepened in the later chapters, it is by no means corrected, as Weeden and Kelber argue (Kingsbury 1983). Mary Ann Tolbert contends that attempts to interpret

Mark in light of a *specific* historical setting do less than justice to the character of this work as narrative. Such a format would have been a poor choice as a vehicle for the correction of a theological view, Tolbert argues, but it was a powerful way of offering encouragement to Christians facing persecution (Tolbert 1989). Ernest Best has persuasively shown that Mark presents the failings and restoration of the Twelve to encourage those in his audience who have also failed in recent persecutions (Best 1983). Despite the predominant conclusion in scholarship that Mark is not correcting a divine-man christology, Mark does criticize two views about miracles. Jesus refuses to work miracles to show off or prove his authority, and this *could* function in Mark to warn its readers in their communities to stay away from showy miracles. Second, Mark's picture of Jesus as a man who does mighty works is combined with a view of him as an authoritative teacher and especially as one who suffers. In Mark, there is no power in word or in deed without suffering for those who follow Jesus.

We now must discuss in some depth the **messianic secret** in Mark. In 1901, the German scholar Wilhelm Wrede argued that a secret about the Messiah was a key thematic feature of Mark. In Mark, although Jesus is the Messiah (or Son of God, which Wrede considered the rough equivalent for Mark), he hides this fact and tells his disciples not to reveal his miraculous healings to others, with the result that only demons recognize his identity. For example, in the early chapters of Mark Jesus regularly commands people and demons to say nothing about what he has done to them, or who he is (e.g., 1:25, 34, 44; 3:12; 5:43; 7:36). At times he tells them not to tell others about their new-found knowledge of his identity (8:30; 9:9). Further, he appears to tell parables in order to prevent people outside the disciples' group from understanding him (4:10–12, 33–34.). The Gospel may even end in 16:8 with ironic secrecy: when the angel commands the women at the empty tomb of Jesus to speak the news of his resurrection to his other disciples, they keep silent!

Wrede regarded this as historically doubtful. He argued that the Messianic secret had been invented before Mark but was made central by him, as a clever way to bring early traditions that were nonmessianic into a proclamation of Jesus as the Messiah. Wrede argued that the secrecy theme was an attempt to explain how the Jesus whom the early Christians worshipped as Son of God and Messiah had not been recognized as such during his lifetime. Wrede's thesis gained wide acceptance in Germany and became a key factor in showing that Mark was a religious composition rather than simply a historical account. This realization helped to pave the way for form criticism. Today, although Mark is seen clearly as a theological work, many scholars argue that the rudiments of this "secret" goes back to the early traditions about Jesus' life and teaching, and perhaps even to Jesus himself. For example, Mark's secrecy motif may have its roots in Jesus' historical rejection of some messianic aspirations of his own time, such as the triumphalist Davidic expectations rejected in 12:35–37. Many in his audience may have had nationalistic ideas about what the Messiah would be; Jesus did not, Mark is intent to say, and so may not have wanted to use the label "Messiah" too openly. Moreover, it is entirely possible that Jesus himself did use enigmatic stories and sayings in part to avoid being understood too quickly in public. It may have been Jesus' way of giving his teaching without saying things so blatantly that the crisis came too early, before he could train his disciples and before his full understanding of God's purpose for his life, as N. T. Wright argues (Wright 1996, 79–82, 236–237). To sum up: many scholars are still intrigued by the Messianic secret motif, but the majority no longer think of the Messianic secret as the crucial issue in interpreting Mark. Overall, Wrede highlights a key theme, one that any reader today using any method will want to note and deal with, but draws conclusions from it that many today find problematic.

www   Follow the link to a careful historical consideration of crucifixion in antiquity by the prominent Israeli archaeologist Joe Zias.

Doing Historical Reading Yourself

1. *What do you make of the Messianic secret in Mark? Choose any two passages in Mark in which the "secret" appears, and test your theory on them. Take into account at least two settings in life: the situation of Jesus and the situation of the Gospel writer and audience.*

2. *What is your conclusion about corrective christology in Mark? Give your reasons.*

We must now consider how newer methods of reading approach this Gospel. A brief introduction to each method will be offered, followed by examples of these methods in actual practice in the voices of leading interpreters. The treatment of each method concludes with a section called "Practicing Feminist/Social Scientific/Cross-Cultural/Narrative Reading for Yourself."

As a brief preface to this section, we will introduce the recent work by Richard Horsley, *Hearing the Whole Story: The Politics of Plot in Mark's Gospel* (Horsley, 2001). Horsley uses narrative, sociological, cross-cultural, and other methods to help readers see how Mark's Jesus challenged the dominant order of his day. He summarizes these approaches in nine steps. (1) Since Mark was composed as a story, we should read the whole story, getting a sense of its overall drama. (2) Mark's story is addressed to the ancient equivalent of Third World peoples subjected by empire and should be read as good news in this context. (3) Mark was performed orally to whole communities of people. (4) This community orientation makes it unlikely that Mark is concerned primarily with individual discipleship. (5) Mark presents Jesus as engaged in the prophetic renewal of the people of Israel by proclaiming and showing the kingdom of God, which brings conflict with Jewish authorities who prevail upon Roman power to execute him. Mark's abrupt open ending vindicates Jesus and implies the continuation of his movement in Galilee. (6) Mark's apocalyptic chapter 13 indicates that it focuses on opposition to Roman imperial order and oppression. (7) The conflict between Jesus and the Pharisees must be understood based on "social location": Pharisees represent the official Jerusalem version of Judaism, Jesus the popular Israelite tradition. (8) Mark presents Jesus as reforming and renewing the covenant of Israel, especially the Mosaic covenant, as the basis of economic and political equality. (9) The Twelve become negative examples of leaders who resist equality, but the women in Mark's story emerge as examples of those who accept it.

Mark in Brief: Summary of Newer Readings

Narrative: The implied author of Mark is a masterful storyteller, using his characters, settings, plot, and thematic point to communicate his meaning. Mark is characterized by loosely connected episodes, some told in interesting detail, put together to give the impression of quick action. It presents Jesus as a person of powerful saving action.

Social Scientific: Mark speaks of diverse groups. Jews and Gentiles are a particular concern, this Gospel being firmly in the Gentile-Christian camp. Mark constructs a powerful symbolic universe. Jesus' opponents are everywhere, provoking controversy that will harden as it goes along. In the end Jesus will triumph, and his message will be vindicated and spread.

Feminist: Mark is generally positive toward women disciples, portraying them as a better example of faith than male disciples. Jesus' promises and moral commands extend equally to men and women.

Cross-Cultural: Mark shows Jesus crossing cultural boundaries, sometimes not without difficulty for himself and others. The Jewish-Gentile crossing involves ethnic, religious, and social boundaries. This Gospel is, as Horsely remarks, written to the ancient equivalent of Third World peoples; it should be understood this way by all who read it today.

Narrative Reading

David Rhoads and Donald Michie, in their influential 1991 book *Mark as Story* (revised edition 1999, with Joanna Dewey), make a persuasive case that Mark is a masterfully written, powerful narrative. Mark is a narrative world with many features: conflict and suspense, surprising reversals and strange ironies, riddles and hidden meanings, subversive actions and political intrigues. Jesus, the protagonist, is the most surprising figure of all. Mark's is not a simple story in which virtue easily triumphs over vice, nor is it a collection of moral instructions for life, two common misconceptions among those unfamiliar with the Gospels. Rather, the narrative offers difficult challenges full of irony and paradox: to be most important, one must be least; nothing is hidden except to become known; those who want to save their lives must lose them. Within the story, characters may think they understand their situation only to discover their expectations overturned. Several people whom Jesus heals go out immediately to tell others about it with the command of Jesus to keep silent still ringing in their ears. The disciples follow Jesus expecting glory and power, only to find a call to serve and the threat of persecution. The Jewish authorities judge Jesus in order to preserve their traditions and authority, only to bring judgment on themselves. The women come to anoint the dead Jesus, only to discover he is among the living. The author has told the story in order to transform the reader and to be a means to help bring about the kingdom of God. He (or she!) has used sophisticated storytelling techniques, developed the characters and the conflicts, and built suspense, telling the story to generate certain insights and responses in the reader. The ending has a surprising twist that leads readers to reflect on their own relation to the drama. As a whole, the story seeks to shatter the readers' way of seeing the world and invites them to embrace another, thus impelling them to action (Rhoads, Michie, and Dewey 1999, 1).

Narrative Reading at Work, 1
The Desert in Mark 1

In this first reading, after Jesus' baptism by John, the Spirit that he received from God drove him into the desert/wilderness to be tested by Satan before he begins his ministry. Mark relates this temptation in a remarkably terse way, and readers often pass over its significance in the narrative. This reading suggests the connotations of wilderness to the readers of Mark and shows how this notion of wilderness *prepares the careful reader today to look for a new message in Mark.*

In this story, the desert/wilderness has a hostile and threatening atmosphere; it is desolate and barren. It is important to the story as a place of preparation. John prepares there for Jesus, and Jesus is driven there to encounter Satan in preparation for his messianic role. In the opening lines of the story Isaiah's prophecy invites recollections of Israel's past. The prophecy was originally proclaimed for people to "prepare" the way for God to lead the Israelites back across the desert from exile in Babylonia. The desert also has an association with the earlier event in Israel's history when the people wandered for years in the desert in preparation for entering the land of Israel. Both of these journeys were associated with new beginnings. Thus, early in the story, the desert settings "prepare" the reader for the new activity of God that is to follow.

Source: From David Rhoads, Joanna Dewey, and Donald Michie, *Mark as Story: An Introduction to the Narrative of a Gospel,* 2nd ed. (Philadelphia: Fortress Press, 1999), pp. 69–70.

Questions

1. *If you did not know the Hebrew Bible background of the desert, what clues are there in Mark itself, especially in this passage, to indicate the geographic symbolism of the desert?*

2. *How does the desert/wilderness symbolize both positive and negative things, both in Jesus' day and today?*

Narrative Reading at Work, 2
Jesus and His Opponents in Mark

In this second reading from Rhoads, Dewey, and Michie, another important aspect of narrative criticism is shown by looking at the characters and conflict in Mark. This reading shows how careful analysis of Mark's narrative as a whole is crucial to its interpretation.

The narrator has carefully structured Jesus' conflict with the opponents to create tension and suspense. In the five initial clashes between Jesus and the authorities in Galilee, this is clear. The opposition against Jesus widens. The groups opposing Jesus expand in number. One by one, each new group is introduced into an association with a previously introduced group of opponents: first the local legal experts, then the legal experts of the Pharisees, then the Pharisees, then the Pharisees with the Herodians. Similarly, the narrator creates suspense by gradually intensifying the opponents' efforts to get Jesus: first the opponents accuse Jesus in thought only; then they question the disciples about Jesus' actions; next, they query Jesus directly about an offense against a custom; after that, they ask Jesus about the illegal behavior of the disciple; then they watch Jesus in order to get charges against him; and finally they go off and plot to destroy him.

As opposition propels the action forward, Jesus' responses intensify. At first, he tries appealing to the authorities by action and explanation, but he soon becomes angry and saddened by the hardening of their minds. By the end of the five conflict episodes, the sides are clearly established. . . . Consequently, throughout, the reader wonders just how Jesus will deal with the widening and intensifying opposition against him [Jesus]. Nevertheless, the reader sees that Jesus is firmly in control. He regularly evades indictment, wins in debates, and, except at his trial, he always has the last word. The authorities are unable to obtain evidence against Jesus unless he gives it to them. At the trial, Jesus himself volunteers the evidence they need. He thus controls when his opponents will win the indictment, as well as the specific charge they level against him. . . . Jesus, not the authorities, determines his fate.

Questions

1. *Using this passage as a template of conflict in Mark, what is the pattern of Jesus' conflict with his own disciples?*

Source: From David Rhoads, Joanna Dewey, and Donald Michie. *Mark as Story: An Introduction to the Narrative of a Gospel,* 2nd ed. (Philadelphia: Fortress Press, 1999), pp. 86, 88.

2. *Examine the disciples' lack of understanding and unwillingness to share Jesus' suffering; how does the narrative shape these characteristics of theirs?*

Doing Narrative Reading Yourself

1. *Joel Marcus notes that already in chapter 2 the opponents of Jesus turn up seemingly everywhere (Marcus 2000, 240). From a historical point of view, it is unlikely that such opposition happened so early in Jesus' Galilean ministry. What might the narrative-critical point of such early opposition be?*

2. *Consider how Mark uses his sandwiches. Do the parts of the sandwich help to interpret each other, or is there a contrast between them? Is one part of the sandwich more important than the other—e.g., is the "meat" in the middle? Consider 5:21–43 and 14:1–11 as examples.*

3. *Examine the probable original ending of Mark (16:1–8) from narrative perspective. The angel at the tomb commands the women to tell the other disciples that Jesus has risen from the dead, and will meet his disciples in Galilee. But the women "said nothing to anyone, for they were afraid." What do you as a reader think about this ending? What does it mean to end this story of "good news" (1:1) with the words, "for they were afraid"?*

Social Scientific Reading

Social scientific reading of Mark lags a bit behind its study of the longer Gospels of Matthew and Luke but is still substantial. Mark, like all the NT literature grounded in everyday life, speaks of diverse groups. Jews and Gentiles are a particular concern, this Gospel being firmly in the Gentile-Christian camp. Jesus and his disciples have identity and interactions that can be studied in a social scientific way, especially their kinship relationships in the kingdom and reign of God. Jesus defends his honor successfully in arguments against his opponents, and this outcome intimates that he will also prevail against them even though he dies. Even though it is the first Gospel, Mark constructs a powerful symbolic universe. Jesus' opponents are everywhere, provoking controversy that will harden as it goes along. In the end, Jesus will triumph and his message will be vindicated and spread.

The social scientific method is increasingly combined with other methods. The sociohistorical and sociorhetorical study of Mark is a growing feature of scholarship and is proving to be a particularly fruitful path of research.

www   For an excellent introduction to the cultural world of Jesus, primarily using a social scientific reading of Mark, follow the link to the "Windows into the World of Jesus" site by Daniel Schrock.

Social Scientific Reading at Work, 1
Jesus Heals a Man with Skin Disease (Mark 10:40–45)

Probably the feature of social life in the Jewish Mediterranean world most different from our own is the drive to maintain religious purity, to be "clean" rather than "unclean." In Jewish life, purity and impurity often have some connection with sin, but not always; a person can be impure and ostracized without having a moral fault. In this reading, Jesus heals a man with skin disease to restore him to full social standing.

We are to think of this man as having an apparently incurable disease who is driven by desperation to violate the social codes in order to find a cure. According to Levitical law (Lev. 13:45), such a person was to go about crying "Unclean, unclean" so that no one would approach him and be contaminated. He knew of Jesus' power, for he says, "If you will, you can make me clean." Notice that the primary concern is with being clean so that he can become a whole person and reenter Jewish society. This is a very Jewish way of looking at disease, by focusing on its ritual effects, whereas a pagan would have simply said, "If you will, you can make me well . . ."

In this story, we see a definite contrast between Jesus, who can make someone clean, and the priest, who can only declare someone clean. Clearly, Jesus is seen as superior. Later rabbinic literature suggested that such skin diseases were as difficult to get rid of as raising the dead was to accomplish. Thus, this miracle takes on significance as a deed of great power. The seriousness with which Jews took this disease is clearly shown by the fact that they believed that someone who met a person with such a disease might as well have touched a corpse. A man with this disease was among the living dead—untouchable. . . . Jesus heals the man anyway, and we are told quite specifically that he touched him. . . . This would certainly render Jesus unclean. . . . What Mark will suggest in chapter 7 is that Jesus believed that with the inbreaking of God's dominion these rules about clean and unclean, and indeed also various Sabbath rules, were obsolescent. Such rules had fulfilled their purpose, but now the Holy One of God had appeared and a new state of affairs was at hand.

Questions

1. *Explain how this passage in Mark, as explained by Witherington, shows a different concept of disease and healing than most North Americans have today.*

2. *How does this reading show a sociorhetorical (social-persuasive) approach?*

Source: Ben Witherington, *The Gospel of Mark: A Socio-Rhetorical Commentary* (Grand Rapids. MI: Eerdmans, 2001), pp. 102–104.

Social Scientific Reading at Work, 2
Jesus and Kinship (Mark 3:31–35)

Jesus' message and movement posed a challenge to human kinship (family relationship) structures because his movement cut across family and gender lines. The most direct indication of this position in Mark is Jesus' rejection of his own family when they come to take him home, saying that he has a new family with those who follow him.

Jesus' statement in 3:33 is tantamount to a slap in the face, because one of the highest cultural values in the first century was maintaining respect for one's parents. For us in the twenty-first century it is hard to imagine how insulting this was to Jesus' mother and brothers. They may well have been so shocked they did not know how to respond. Very likely Jesus' behavior has now publicly shamed them.

This passage is silent about the role and function of families in the new kingdom of God. Jesus clearly implies that since relationships among his followers make the "true" family, they are more important than relationships in one's family. . . .

As Christian communities spread throughout the Mediterranean world . . . this passage probably provided a great deal of comfort to new Christians who were rejected by their families when they became Christian. Even if their family rejected them, they have a new family in the Christian church.

Notice that no father is mentioned in this passage, probably because Mary is single. In fact, the book of Mark never speaks of Jesus having a father. The figure of Joseph is found only in Matthew and Luke.

Questions

1. *What does Jesus' teaching of family in the kingdom of God mean for human families today? Is it the end of human families, or a qualification of their value? Use other passages in Mark to study this issue.*

2. *Anthropologists call new family arrangements like this* fictive *kinship. In your opinion, is this a good term? In what sense is it "fictive," in what other sense real?*

Doing Social Scientific Reading Yourself

1. *Examine the women in Mark who appear together, in a group. How do they relate to other groups (Jewish authorities, the crowds around Jesus, his male disciples, and the rest)? How would you describe them as a group?*

Source: From the "Windows to the World of Jesus" website by Daniel Schrock.

2. In Mark, Jesus heals directly, by word sometimes accompanied by touch. But when he sends his disciples out ahead of him in Mark 6:7–13, Mark reports that the disciples healed by anointing people with oil. What is Mark's point about the relationship of Jesus and his disciples as healers?

3. In Mark 5:1–20, Mark tells at some dramatic length the story of the exorcism of a demon whose name is "Legion." Explain the significance of this Roman army term. Do you think that Mark is making an anti-Roman point here?

Feminist Reading

Mark has been a rich document for examination by feminist critics. Women have a significant presence and place in this gospel. First, although this fact is frequently overlooked, the many crowds in Mark evidently contain both men and women, perhaps as family groups. In Mark 5, for example, a woman emerges from the crowd when she touches Jesus and is healed. In the feeding of the (Jewish?) five thousand in chapter 6, the number includes only males, but in the feeding of the (Gentile?) four thousand in chapter 8, the number indicates "people." Women like Mary Magdalene, Mary, and Salome were "followers" of Jesus, and ministered to him—*followers* is a word Mark uses particularly for disciples, male and female (Mark 15:40–41). These named women are not alone—many other women, Mark says, followed Jesus (v. 41). When we realize that the original circle of disciples (although not the Twelve) included women, we should position women in among Jesus' disciples when they receive Jesus' teaching and instructions.

In Mark's narrative, women disciples appear more positively than most of their male colleagues. The Twelve, all men, increasingly misunderstand Jesus' person, mission and message, are disrespectful to their teacher (4:38, 5:31, 8:4, 14:4), and disobey him (7:36). One of the males (Judas) betrays Jesus, and another (Peter) denies him. On the other hand, Mark's women are models of faith. The Syrophoenician woman not only bests Jesus in an argument—the only time this happens in Mark!—but also reveals the extent of his mission to the reader, and perhaps even to Jesus himself (7:24–30). An anonymous widow exemplifies radical self-giving (Mark 12), and an anonymous woman anoints Jesus in Bethany shortly before his death (14:3–9). (Lest the reader suppose that unnamed women may indicate a lesser view of women, one should remember that most men in Mark who encounter Jesus are anonymous as well.) The three women disciples witness Jesus' death when all the male disciples have fled (or worse), follow to see where his body is buried, and on the first day of the week go to the empty tomb and are called to be witnesses to the resurrection of Jesus although, explicitly in the narrative at least, they disobey this command and say nothing to anyone (15:40–16:8).

Jesus' teaching in Mark is typically gender neutral, aimed at both men and women. Jesus came to call all Israel to repentance and faith, including its women. Mark's interest in how Jesus' teaching affects the life of women is most clearly illustrated in his treatment of the divorce and remarriage pericope in 10:2–12. Most readers of this text who use the historical-critical method conclude that against its cultural backgrounds, this prohibition of easy divorce is a protection of women. Divorced women were usually in a very difficult social and financial situation, much more so than today in North American society. Although many people today do not agree with Jesus' negative attitude here to remarriage after divorce, they do agree with the general principle in Mark: women are under the same moral obligation as men to keep this teaching (v. 12). The standard is strong (some might say wrong), but at least it is not a double standard.

Feminist Reading at Work, 1
Greatness and Equality for Women and Men (Mark 9:33–37)

In her analysis of Mark 9:33–37, Judith Gundry-Volf of Yale University argues that Jesus models the greatness of the kingdom of God by a feminine image, that of welcoming little children and caring for them.

In this pericope Jesus defines greatness in a "feminine" way in terms of receiving little children and that the female disciples in Mark's passion narrative are presented as the "greatest" disciples. This form of "status seeking" leads to true knowledge of and solidarity with Jesus and reshapes the community through radical love.

Two critical responses might be offered. First, one might try to relativize the significance of the women's actions by saying that they simply conform to gender stereotypes. Nevertheless, what matters is not whether the women's behavior is stereotypical, but that it is taken to exemplify genuine greatness and appropriate reception of Jesus.

A more difficult question, however, is whether the woman's actions might be viewed as merely an imprint of suffering experienced or a reflexive response to oppression. Do not the "feminine" definition of greatness and the social scheme on which it rests perpetuate injustice rather than alleviate it? And does not the idea of receiving Jesus as the one who identifies with the little child because of his role as the suffering Son of Man legitimate the suffering of the powerless, including women? Does this model of community really represent a discipleship of equals? . . . What I have called "feminine" greatness—loving and serving the least—may indeed be partly a product of the patriarchy that reinforces such behavior in women. Still, I would contend that this "feminine" greatness has creative potential. The kinds of actions that women, living under the condition of patriarchy in the first century, showed toward children and others who counted as the "least" reveal significant aspects of what it means to be truly human in the world of conflict and imbalance of power and to

Source: Judith Gundry-Volf, "Discipleship of Equals at the Cradle and the Cross," *Interpretation* 53 (1999): pp. 60–61.

live in a community that fosters life and wholeness. And though Jesus' advocacy of this "feminine" greatness might appear simply to reinforce social inequities, it in fact challenges and begins to dismantle them, for it requires the first to love and serve the last. That is, not only are women called to self-sacrificial service toward the very least, but those who occupy the highest positions of power are to put themselves below the lowest through radical love. . . .

In Mark the female disciples who practiced "feminine greatness" did not thereby become further entrenched in oppressive structures, but experienced liberation in a new community around Jesus the Crucified and Risen One that is anticipated by their radical love. They went down with Jesus to the depths and they rose with him to new heights. The ones who looked on, sharing his pain when he was crucified, who came to the tomb and saw where the body was laid, were the first to see the empty tomb, hear the angel announce that he was risen, and become his witnesses. Their mourning turned to joy. Their insignificant roles—in comparison with the Twelve—were exchanged for the most significant of all roles; the first witnesses to the good news that "he is risen" (16.6).

Questions

1. *Does Gundry-Volf persuade you to accept her position? Why, or why not?*

2. *What would a social scientific reading make of these issues of kinship (mothers and children) and honor (significant/insignificant roles)?*

Feminist Reading at Work, 2
Women at the Last Supper? (Mark 14:12–25)

Christian understanding of the Last Supper that Jesus celebrated with his disciples on the night of his arrest, including famous artistic depictions of it, have only males at the table or even in the room. This reading challenges that assumption with a close reading of this passage in the literary and social context of Mark.

The notion that Jesus had only twelve *male* disciples is reinforced by the church's frequent use of the phrase, "the twelve disciples"; but this phrase is never used by Mark, and it is only used four times by Matthew (Matt. 10:1; 11:1; 20:17; 26:20). Instead, Mark uses the word *mathetes* (disciple, pupil, and follower) forty-two times. Furthermore, Mark uses "Twelve/The Twelve" only eleven times, while he uses "followers/following" Jesus more than forty times. So the way that Mark uses this phrase is to denote a sub-group of disciples.

While Mark often explains Jewish things to his Gentile audience (Mark 14:12; 7:3), the fact that Mark remains silent about the Passover preparations may mean that Mark probably considered this intelligible to Gentiles on the basis of a social given in both

Source: Written for this book by Karen Fitz LaBarge, a graduate of McCormick Theological Seminary, Chicago.

Jewish and Gentile culture—that women prepared food for a meal. In cultures where women have the specific duty of preparing meals, not only do men not participate in this, but they also have no developed skills in preparing meals. If preparing ordinary meals would be difficult for them, especially sophisticated meals like a Passover celebration would be almost impossible for them to prepare. Specific evidence in Mark that women generally provided for meals is found in 1:31, where Simon Peter's mother-in-law serves them food after Jesus heals her, and in 15:40–41 where Mary Magdalene, Salome, and Mary the mother of James are described as providing for Jesus in Galilee. These three or the other women disciples who came to Jerusalem (Mark 15:41) would have been the most experienced candidates when the two disciples were sent ahead to prepare the Passover Feast. Thus in Mark 14:12–17 there is evidence that the two disciples who prepared the Passover Feast were most likely women.

Questions

1. What does the fact that the "two disciples" are seemingly there in the upper room when Jesus and the Twelve arrive (14:17) mean for the possibility that these two disciples are women?

2. Read the Mark passage again with a view to this social issue: could two women have arranged a meal with the (male) owner of the room?

3. If women were present in the room when the Passover meal was eaten, what could their forms of participation be?

> ### Doing Feminist Reading Yourself
>
> 1. What is the symbolism behind the Twelve as all men? Does this symbolism reinforce or restrict patriarchal values in the text? Point to specific places in Mark that support your position.
>
> 2. Read the story of Jesus' "anointing" by a woman in 14:3–9. Note the mention of three marginalized groups: Simon the leper, women, and the poor. How do these three interact in the narrative with the main character, Jesus, who is becoming increasingly marginalized as one marked for a criminal's death?
>
> 3. Discuss the feminist implications of Jesus' teaching on divorce and remarriage in Mark 10:2–9. Follow the link to a short electronic version of the book *Divorce and Remarriage in the Bible*, with a discussion of Mark's text on this topic.

Cross-Cultural Reading

Readers from other cultural perspectives today find Mark to be a fertile field. As Richard Horsley writes, Mark was written for a cross-cultural, Third World audience and can be read most faithfully today in this same way. Mark is not only the first Gospel, but the first Gospel to cross important cultural barriers, especially the basic barrier between Jews and Gentiles. The inner and outer conflict that Jesus has as he crosses cultural barriers is forcefully portrayed, probably as a model for readers crossing their own boundaries.

Those who read Mark from "developing world" cultures see this culture crossing, and work from it. This perspective often challenges the common interpretations of European and European-American scholarship, but the dialogue on Mark is often just as fruitful as it is pointed.

Cross-Cultural Reading at Work, 1
The Poor Widow of Mark 12:41–44

Cross-cultural reading of the NT done by the marginalized, when addressed to those at the center of society's power, often presents a challenge. In this cross-cultural reading of the familiar story of the poor widow and her one coin, Miguel De La Torre presents a striking cross-cultural interpretation that reverses the traditional understanding of this story.

A colonialized Bible tends to romanticize the plight of the poor, even to the point of making the condition of the oppressed the model for victims of racism, classism, and sexism. In Mark 12:41–44 we are told the story of a poor widow who gives all that she has to the Temple. . . . The widow is generally idealized by the dominant culture as an example of Christian behavior for those who are poor, with her self-sacrifice compared with that of the self-indulgence of the religious leaders. . . .

This interpretation maintains societal power relationships that are detrimental to the oppressed. In Mark's account, the story of the widow's offering is preceded by Jesus' outrage toward the religious leaders who devour the possessions of widows. . . . In Luke's account, Jesus concludes the story of the widow's offering with his prediction of the Temple's destruction. . . . Reading Mark and Luke together, we discover that Jesus is not praising the widow's offering as a paragon to be imitated by those who are marginalized; rather Jesus is denouncing a religious social structure that cons the widow out of the little she has.

To side with the widows of the world becomes the appropriate action for *minjung* . . . an untranslatable Korean word . . . [that] refers to all people who are marginalized and oppressed. When the poor are overburdened by economic structures designed to benefit the rich, then they belong to the *minjung.* Jesus too belongs to the *minjung.* A *minjung* reading of the Bible has its foundations in the life events of Jesus, events based not on power but powerlessness, events that sought justice for the disenfranchised. These events become the foundation for rereading the history of Asians and understanding what biblically based actions are required for liberation.

Source: Miguel A. De La Torre, *Reading the Bible from the Margins.* Copyright © 2002 by Miguel A. De La Torre. Published by Orbis Books, Maryknoll, New York. Used by permission of the publisher.

Questions

1. De La Torre states correctly that his interpretation goes against the traditional one. Do you agree with this reading of his reading of the passage, or do you think that the traditional one is more correct? Why, or why not?

2. How would reading Mark and Luke together to interpret this story differ from the way in which historical criticism would work?

Cross-Cultural Reading at Work, 2
The Story of Mama Africa and the Story of the Healing of the Bleeding Woman (Mark 5:21–43)

The experience of a culture has an influence on how that culture reads the NT; it forms a sort of cultural preunderstanding. In this evocative essay, Musa Dube gives a cross-cultural reading of Mark 5:21–43, with a feminist flavor.

Once upon a time, there was a beautiful princess called Africa. . . . Africa, a tall and bouncy girl, walked freely from one end of her land to another, visiting the shrines, offering sacrifices to the Divine, fighting and surviving disasters, but always bringing enough food for her household. . . . Africa blossomed in self-sufficiency, survival, health, and peace . . . [A recounting of colonialism follows]

But in the year 1939, Africa woke up severely ill. She felt walls had entered into all of her body. She felt fenced, bound. Africa cried out, saying, "Take this thorn of suffering away from my flesh! Take it away!" And as she spoke, she began to bleed nonstop. Just then Dr. Colonial Master appeared, saying, "I am the healer of all diseases. But in order to heal this kind of disease, I have to take you into my hospital. I have to watch you very closely, teach you what you need to learn and what you need to know. Basically, what you need most is the medicine of civilization."

Africa entered Dr. Colonial Master's hospital, and she was put to sleep with heavy medication. . . . But in the year 1949, Dr. Colonial Master seemed preoccupied by his homeland. He no longer had enough time to treat Africa in the mornings. Picking up her clothes and still bleeding, Africa escaped into the bush. This is how she came to meet her new physician, Comrade Dr. Struggle-for-Independence. . . .

The pain of the capture of her children, people, land, and property was excruciating. Africa cried out from her anguish, saying, "Take this thorn away from my body! Take it away . . ." Seized by anger, Africa called out, "Talitha cum" which means "Little girl, arise!" And behold, the bellies of the earth opened. UTentelezandeleni jumped out. She was followed by all the beloved old women and men. Miriam Makeba emerged with her new song: Mozambique (*a luta continua[the song continues]*), Botswana (*a luta continua*), Zimbabwe (*a luta continua*), Namibia (*a luta continua*), South Africa (*a luta continua*).

Source: From *The Ecumenical Review* 51.1 (Jan 1999), pp. 11–17. Reprinted by permission of the World Council of Churches.

As she sang, the ground shook and broke open again. And there came from the ground the many handsome sons and daughters of Africa: Kwame Nkrumah, Nehanda, Julius Nyerere, Hastings Banda, Chinua Achebe, Kenneth Kaunda, Ngugi wa Thiong, Milton Obote, Seretse Khama, Joshua Knomo, Buchi Emecheta, P.G. Matante, Samora Machel, Robert Mugabe, Winnie Madikizela, Nelson Mandela, and others. There was much joy and weeping as they saw each other again after such a long time. They told each other the stories of how Dr. Colonial Master had captured and confined them. Yet many more daughters and sons were missing or dead. Africa wept. She wept for the lost children of her womb . . .

Kwame, her firstborn son, turn to her and said, "Mama Africa, stay right here in this infertile land with the young children and the old people. Take care of them while we fight for independence. It is the struggle for independence that will give you healing. It is the only solution to your suffering . . ." From that day on, Africa became Mama Africa: the strong black woman who carries us all on her back . . .

The years of the struggle dragged on. Blood flowed from her body until all the rivers of Africa were red and the land began to stink with the stench of death. That is when Mama Africa stood up and shouted, "Take this thorn away from my body! Take it away!" Just then a horn sounded, and liberty was announced throughout the land. Viva! Victory was certain! And that is how Mama Africa came to meet her new physician, Dr. Independence . . .

Weak and still bleeding, the heart of Mama Africa rejoiced in hope. Independence was here! Power to the people! Healing was certain. She rejoiced at the prospect of getting all her children back again, getting back her power, her honor, and her share in the struggle for independence. Mama Africa was ready for the healing of her own body . . . Weak and still bleeding, Mama Africa struggled and toiled in the hospital of Dr. Independence. Again there were wars. Now the sons of Mama Africa were fighting among themselves . . .

Still sick and bleeding, Mama Africa heard about the miracle of external aid, which would bring an end to the poverty that had befallen her land and children. The qualified players and planners were numerous, among them the International Monetary Fund and the World Bank. . . . Still bleeding, Mama Africa partook of the prescribed medicine of developmental projects. But aid turned to debt. Africa had received millions of dollars and now owed billions of dollars. Her economies had been bad, but now they were ruined . . .

Shaking and still bleeding, Mama Africa was visited by a new physician. Dr. Global Village offered a different medicine. "I can heal you, Mama Africa, just like I can heal the world of all its pains. My prescriptions are simple: I will do away with national boundaries. I will strengthen regional trade. I will prescribe unlimited trade across the globe. I will require competition, and my multinational corporations will create jobs for you." . . . Mama Africa made her last bet—taking the prescriptions of Dr. Global Village . . .

Mama Africa realized that Dr. Global Village was a twin brother of Dr. Neo-Colonialism and a grandson of Dr. Colonial Master. Africa's currencies suffered major devaluations. And while Asian economies were catching the flu from the impact of globalization, Africa caught a more deadly disease: HIV/AIDS. And Mama Africa had no more money to buy prescriptions from the doctor . . .

She is now a nurse. . . . Mama Africa was burying this morning, and this afternoon she will bury again. And tomorrow morning she will bury yet another of her gems. In the afternoon she will bury again. . . . When she called out, "Who is there? Who is there?" she was told, "Jesus Christ, the healer of all diseases, is passing by." She heard that Jesus was on his way to heal a little child already dead, the daughter of Jairus.

Mama Africa is standing up. She is not talking. She is not asking. She is not offering any more money—for none is left. Mama Africa is coming behind Jesus. She is pushing through a strong human barricade. *Weak and still bleeding but determined, she is stretching out her hand. If only she can touch the garments of Jesus Christ.*

Questions

1. *How does this story combine the story of Africa and the story of Jesus' healings?*

2. *Explain how this reading combines a cross-cultural and a feminist approach.*

3. *If you were to press for more connections between the story of Africa and the story in Mark 5:21–43, what would they be?*

Doing Cross-Cultural Reading Yourself

1. *Put yourself into the experience of a person from another culture, if possible someone you know. Then, rethink a passage from Mark using this perspective. What ideas might come to you that are different from hers or his?*

2. *What resources for the freedom of oppressed (and oppressing) peoples does Mark contain?*

Key Terms and Concepts

anonymous authorship • apostles • exorcism • external evidence (for authorship)
intercalation • internal evidence (for authorship) • John Mark • Latinisms
longer ending • Markan appendix • Markan sandwich • Messianic secret
NT introduction • passion narrative • repentance • Sabbath • Sanhedrin
Shorter ending • theology of the cross • transfiguration • triumphalist christology

Questions for Study, Discussion, and Writing

1. What is your conclusion about the meaning of the opening of Mark (1:1)? Is it the beginning of the gospel story, the beginning of this gospel book, or the first gospel book to be written?
2. Why does Mark tell his overall story so briefly and rapidly yet provide detail in many pericopes that Matthew and Luke choose to drop?
3. What do you think are some of the strengths and weaknesses of the author of Mark as a narrator?
4. Compare the positive things said or implied about the disciples in Mark with the negative things. How consistently strong is the author of Mark against the disciples? What possible reasons could he have for portraying Jesus' disciples as he did?
5. Examine the tension between Jew and Gentile in Mark. Is the author's unflattering portrait of Galileans (male disciples, Jesus' family, people in his hometown, and the rest) a part of his preference for Gentile Christianity? Draw on social scientific reading for your answer.
6. How does Mark use Jesus' parables to both reveal and conceal God? How might this use of parables fit in with other themes and purposes of his Gospel, such as the messianic secret, the growth of faith, and the importance of suffering with Christ?
7. How can Mark be read as an anti-Roman protest?
8. Do you think that the different methods of reading Mark presented here present a more or less unified picture of that Gospel? Explain your answer.
9. Why is it that Mark does not depict Jesus as working any healing miracles in Jerusalem, but only in Galilee?

For Further Reading

Anderson, Janice C. and Stephen D. Moore, eds. *Mark and Method: New Approaches in Biblical Studies* (Minneapolis: Fortress, 1992). Analysis of Mark from several new reading methods; the essays by Elizabeth S. Malbon (narrative reading) and Janice Anderson (feminist reading) are particularly good.

Blount, Brian. *Go Preach! Mark's Kingdom Message and the Black Church Today* (New York: Orbis, 1998). An application of black liberationist reading to the Gospel of Mark.

Collins Adela Yarbro, *The Beginning of the Gospel: Probings of Mark in Context.* Minneapolis: Fortress, 1992. Studies of different readings of Mark.

Horsley, Richard, *Hearing the Whole Story: The Politics of Plot in Mark's Gospel* (Louisville, KY: Westminster John Knox Press, 2001). A study of Mark combining historical reading with several new methods, especially social scientific and cross-cultural.

Levine, Amy-Jill, and Marianne Blickenstaff, eds., *A Feminist Companion to Mark.* Sheffield, UK: Sheffield Academic Press, 2001. Eleven essays on various passages in Mark, with a diversity of reading approaches and results.

Malbon, Elizabeth Struthers. *Hearing Mark: A Listener's Guide.* Harrisburg, PA: Trinity Press International, 2002. A brief, helpful guide to hearing Mark as a narrative whole, both in the original situation of Mark's audience and for readers today. An online study guide can be found at this book's page at the publisher's website.

Malina, Bruce J., and Richard L. Rohrbaugh. *Social-Science Commentary on the Synoptic Gospels,* 2nd ed. Minneapolis: Fortress, 1992. For each passage in Mark, a brief social scientific commentary drawing largely on cultural anthropology is offered; an excellent resource for students.

Marcus, Joel, *Mark 1-8*. Anchor Bible Commentary 27A. New York: Doubleday, 1999. The best recent overall commentary on Mark; a second volume covering the second half of Mark is forthcoming.

Mitchell, Joan L. *Beyond Fear and Silence: A Feminist-Literary Approach to the Gospel of Mark*. New York: Continuum, 2001. An excellent feminist study of Mark.

Rhoads, David. *Reading Mark, Engaging the Gospel*. Minneapolis: Fortress, 2004. Uses narrative, social-scientific, and ethical reading in a fascinating study.

Rhoads, David, Joanna Dewey, and Donald Michie. *Mark as Story: An Introduction to the Narrative of a Gospel*, 2nd ed. Minneapolis: Fortress, 1999. An influential introduction to narrative method applied to Mark, clear to beginning students.

Tolbert, Mary Ann. *Sowing the Gospel: Mark's World in Literary-Historical Perspective*. Minneapolis: Fortress, 1989. Clear analysis of Mark from a combined narrative and historical point of view.

Chapter Seven

The Gospel of Matthew: Following Jesus, The Lord of a Diverse Church

Matthew has been known as the "church's Gospel" from ancient times until today. Because of its full and orderly presentation of Jesus' teaching, Matthew was the most often used Gospel by the second century; it was cited by church leaders more than twice as often as Mark, Luke, or John. Even today, Matthew's Sermon on the Mount is among the most widely known treasures in the Christian tradition. For example, almost all Christians use the Matthew's form of the Lord's Prayer, not the shorter form in Luke. Matthew's careful organization and clarity, coupled with thematic content that has been useful to the church through the ages, have assured its continuous priority as the church's chief Gospel for teaching. Especially striking is a pattern of five long discourses or sermons, followed by sections of narrative action. Much of the historical-critical study of Matthew concentrates on its historical situation in early Christianity and the likelihood that Matthew's audience is a group of churches with diverse and divided congregations of Jewish Christians and an increasing number of Gentile Christians. Narrative criticism shows that the author of Matthew is a skilled writer, able to weave a complex, compelling narrative in tandem with well-constructed sections of teaching. Feminist and cross-cultural readings of Matthew are very pointed, because Matthew is both more patriarchal and more Jewish than the other Synoptic Gospels, even as it wrestles with the more inclusive message of the Christian faith. In all the methods of reading, the point of Matthew comes through: Jesus is both the Jewish Messiah and the world's Savior.

Matthew in Brief: Outline of Structure and Contents

I. Introduction: Conception and birth of Jesus the Messiah (Chapters 1–2)

II. Jesus' Galilean ministry (Chapters 3–18)
   A. Narrative: Ministry of John the Baptizer, baptism and temptations of Jesus; beginning of the Galilean ministry (3–4)
   B. Discourse 1: Sermon on the Mount (5–7)

C. Narrative: Nine miracles in which Jesus heals the sick, calms a storm, exorcises demons (8–9)

D. Discourse 2: Mission Sermon (10)

E. Narrative: Jesus and John the Baptizer, woes on opponents, thanksgiving for revelation, Jesus' authority over the Sabbath, Jesus' family (11–12)

F. Discourse 3: Sermon in parables on the kingdom of God (13:1–53)

G. Narrative: Rejection at Nazareth, feeding 5,000, walking on water, controversies with the Pharisees, healings, feeding 4,000, Peter's statement of faith, first prediction of death and resurrection, transfiguration, and second prediction (13:54–chap. 17)

H. Discourse 4: Sermon on life in the church (18)

III. Journey to Judea and ministry in Jerusalem; passion and resurrection (19–28)

A. Narrative: teaching on marriage and money, parables of judgment, third prediction of death and resurrection, entry into Jerusalem, cleansing the Temple, clashes with authorities (19–23)

B. Discourse 5: The end of time and the coming of the kingdom (24–25)

C. Conspiracy against Jesus and the Last Supper (26:1–30)

D. Arrest, Jewish and Roman "trials," crucifixion, death (26:30–27:56)

E. Burial, with guard at the tomb; opening and discovery of empty tomb, bribing of the guard, resurrection appearances (27:57–28:20)

Developing Your Skills: Reading Matthew as a Whole

After you have studied the preceding outline, read Matthew in one sitting, concentrating on the main contents and shape of the whole document, not the details. Read through this Gospel quickly and form your initial impression of it as a whole. If you have read Mark recently, try to put it out of your memory as you read Matthew.

A Guide to Reading

Chapters 1–2 of Matthew present the genealogy, conception, and birth of Jesus, and are called by scholars the **infancy narrative.** The genealogy opens this Gospel, tracing Jesus' descent from Abraham and thus emphasizing his Jewish lineage and identity. The **virginal conception** of Jesus in his human mother, Mary, is by the supernatural action of the Holy Spirit. (The phrase "virgin birth" is more common in later church tradition, but this is not what Matthew is primarily concerned about here.) Jesus is Emmanuel, "God with us," and his virginal conception shows that he is God's Son. After the birth of Jesus at the opening of chapter 2, Gentile **magi,** priests with astrological knowledge, from eastern lands outside the Roman Empire, come to pay homage to the "King of the Jews" (2:1–12). King Herod (the Great), ruler of the Jews, tries to kill Jesus, thinking to protect his dynasty, and "all Jerusalem" is disturbed about this power shift as well. This attempt prefigures Jesus' eventual death, in which the son of Herod the Great plays a part. God thwarts the plans against the infant Jesus by directing Joseph to flee with his family to Egypt. When they return, it is in Nazareth in Galilee that they live (2:13–23). In this section, male characters predominate (Luke will feature a predominance of females). Matthew weaves into his account five **fulfillment quotations,** "This fulfills what the prophet X said . . ." showing that God planned for and guided Jesus' conception, birth, and rescue.

As the Galilean ministry of Jesus (chapters 3–18) begins, Jesus' ministry is introduced by John the Baptizer's ministry (3:1–12). John preaches in the wilderness as Isaiah had foretold and baptizes with water to prepare the way for Jesus, who will baptize with (give) the Holy Spirit. John condemns the Pharisees and Sadducees and threatens that God will destroy them (3:7–10). When Jesus comes for baptism, John states that Jesus should be baptizing him; how can "God with us" need a baptism for forgiveness? Nevertheless, Jesus desires baptism from John as part of God's plan for the kingdom; Jesus' baptism fulfills, in one of Matthew's favorite thematic words, all "righteousness." All people there hear the heavenly voice say, "This is my beloved Son" (3:13–17).

Matthew's narrative of the temptations features three testings to corrupt and betray Jesus' ministry (4:1–11). Satan tempts Jesus to turn stones into bread for his personal ease at the end of his fasting, to test God's supernatural care for him by flinging himself from the top of the Jerusalem temple and trusting God to catch him, and to gain all power on earth from Satan by worshiping him. In each case, Jesus phrases his refusals to distort his ministry from Deuteronomy 6–8. This whole section of Matthew brims with Hebrew Bible connections: in his baptism, Jesus represents Israel passing through the Red Sea waters in their exodus from Egypt; in his temptations for forty days, he repeats the experience of Israel in the wilderness for forty years; and in his turning away temptations, Jesus succeeds at the points where ancient Israel in the wilderness failed.

After his temptations, Jesus goes to Galilee to begin his ministry. He makes Capernaum his new home, and Matthew summarizes Jesus' message with exactly the same words as it summarized John the Baptizer's message: "Repent, for the kingdom of heaven has come near." To emphasize that Jesus begins a movement, Matthew relates Jesus' call of his first four disciples to become "fishers of people." All this takes place in "Galilee of the Gentiles," as Matthew quotes the Bible, showing once again that Matthew may well be addressed to a church mixed with Jews and Gentiles (4:12–22).

Jesus' **Sermon on the Mount** (chapters 5–7) is the longest and most influential grouping of Jesus' teaching in Matthew. The narrative placement of this long teaching section is remarkable—until this point, the only direct words of Jesus' teaching are in one verse, 4:17! Jesus teaches this sermon with divine authority and wisdom, empowering a new life for those who follow his words. On a "mountain" (the "mountains" of Galilee are more like hills, actually) reminiscent of Mount Sinai, where Moses received God's law, Jesus teaches his followers about the duties of discipleship. He begins with eight **beatitudes,** sayings about God's blessing that approve and empower God's people, and that succinctly express Jesus' values (5:3–12). Jesus dubs his disciples the "salt [preservative and flavoring] of the earth" and the "light of the world," and calls on them to act accordingly.

Next, Jesus strongly affirms the Law of Moses. God gave the Law, but Jesus now demands a deeper observance of its inner, original intent as well as in one's outer behavior. In this way, his followers are to be "perfect as your heavenly Father is perfect" (5:48). In the series of six **antitheses,** sayings that express opposite ideas in the "You have heard it said X, but I say to you Y" pattern, Jesus boldly deepens, modifies, or even corrects what God said through Moses about murder, adultery, divorce and remarriage, retaliation, and hatred of enemies (5:21–48). In 6:1–18, Jesus reshapes the exercise of piety (religious feelings and behaviors, including almsgiving, prayer, and fasting) for those who follow him. Jesus does not forbid these or other pious practices in themselves, but rather any public use of them. This public display of piety leads to hypocrisy, a deadly spiritual fault in the eyes of Jesus. Gifts to others, especially gifts to the poor ("alms"), are to be kept secret. This is a direct attack on the public character of the patron/benefactor system of the Greco-Roman world, including its Jewish forms. Prayer must also be offered secretly, and the **Lord's Prayer/Our Father** is given here as an example of short, to-the-point prayer, which Jesus commands. This prayer asks God to bring the kingdom definitively and to enable God's people to live in it.

Further instructions on behavior for the kingdom (6:19–7:27) touch on total dedication to God instead of worrying about the things of everyday life in this world, which were much more uncertain in ancient Judea than in modern North America! Jesus again strongly cautions his followers about the dangers of hypocrisy. The ending of the sermon turns explicitly toward the end of time, with warnings about the difficulty of entering the kingdom or reign of God and the coming danger of false prophets (religious leaders) among Jesus' followers who misuse "my name." The praise of those who hear Jesus' words and do them (7:24–27), who build a well-founded life, is coupled with a judgment against those who reject him. The phrase, "When Jesus finished all these words," formally ends this sermon, and Matthew will use it again when he ends Jesus' other discourses. All Jesus' listeners are astonished at the strong, self-derived authority of his teaching. Although this sermon began by saying that it was taught to Jesus' disciples (5:1–2), it ends by saying that it was taught to the crowds (7:28–29).

In the Sermon on the Mount, Matthew relates Jesus' powerful words. Now the Gospel proceeds to concentrate on the powerful deeds of Jesus, especially on Jesus' miraculous power. Matthew organizes a section of nine varied miracles consisting of healings, calming a storm, and exorcism (chapters 8–9). These are interspersed with some dialogues (but no speeches), mostly pertaining to discipleship and the beginning of opposition to Jesus. First, Jesus performs three healings involving a Jewish leper, a slave of a Roman army centurion who shows a faith greater than Jesus' Jewish followers do, and his disciple Peter's mother-in-law (8:1–17). In the faith of the centurion, Matthew tells his diverse audience that Gentile Christians can and often do have a stronger faith than Jewish Christians have. A Jewish scribe's desire to follow Jesus leads Jesus to state the difficult requirements of discipleship; it is not easy or always happy (8:18–22). Following Jesus brings a higher demand than even burying one's father, a critical social obligation of the time. Next in this narrative panel is another grouping of three miracles that show the range of Jesus' divine authority. First, he calms a sea storm, showing power over nature; second, he drives out demons who recognize and oppose him as Son of God; and finally he heals a paralyzed man to demonstrate his power over sickness and to forgive sins (8:23–9:8). Jesus then calls the tax collector Matthew as his disciple (9:9), defends his eating and drinking with notorious sinners like Matthew (9:10–13), and defends the refusal of people in his movement to fast as long as he is leading it (9:14–17). Three miracle stories round out this panel of narrative action: the healing of the synagogue leader's daughter with another healing of a bold woman sandwiched inside it; the healing of two blind men who acclaim Jesus as the "Son of David"; and the healing of a mute man. This last healing provokes a charge from the Pharisees that Jesus' power to exorcise comes from the devil, not from God (9:18–34). A final summary of Jesus' ministry at this time speaks of Jesus' compassion for the crowds that followed him, and instructions to the disciples to pray for "laborers" to reap this "harvest" (9:35–38).

Jesus' mission sermon in chapter 10 is set in a context of sending out the Twelve as laborers into this harvest, with authority over unclean spirits and the power to heal as they proclaim the reign of God as Jesus' "advance team." Matthew lists the names of the twelve disciples, whom he now calls **apostles** (from the Greek, "ones sent out on a mission"), before Jesus sends them out ahead of him to help him in his ministry. This mission sermon has some teaching meant for the mission to Israel in Jesus' time and shortly thereafter and other teaching meant for the mission of the church in the world after Jesus is gone (recall the probable setting for Matthew, a mixed community of Jews and Gentiles). The sermon begins in 10:5–6 with the sharp instruction not to go to Gentiles, thus crossing religious and cultural barriers, but only to "the lost sheep of the house of Israel." Jesus commands near-poverty in the provisions and clothing of these preachers. In describing the reception they are likely to get, Jesus stresses God's condemnation of those who refuse them and their message (10:12–13, 15–16). He warns that they will be persecuted by both Jews and Gentiles because they follow Jesus and speak his message. Although the Spirit of God will enable those on trial to speak bravely, strong divisions will come as some accept the message and others reject it; even families, the most cohesive social unit in the ancient Mediterranean, will be divided by trials (10:17–25). Jesus then gives encouragement assuring divine care to motivate the disciples in the face of this opposition (10:26–33). Then Jesus says again that his coming brings division as well as challenging choices of life and death (10:34–39). As he did at the end of the Sermon on the Mount, Jesus again makes people's reaction to his person and his message the basis of their judgment at the end of time (10:40–42).

The next block of material, chapters 11–12, is usually construed as narrative, but it contains a good deal of teaching material. Jesus travels around Galilee and teaches in its synagogues. Matthew's next treatment of John the Baptizer and Jesus begins with John the Baptizer, now in prison, hearing about Jesus' deeds (11:2–19). Jesus says that John the Baptizer is more than a prophet; he is God's agent to lead Israel to the Promised Land and a type of Elijah sent to prepare Israel for God's action in Jesus. However, just as the people as a whole did not repent when John asked them to, so too they do not respond positively to Jesus. Because they did not accept Jesus' mighty works and words, some Galilean cities and villages will meet a terrible fate in the judgment at the end of time (11:20–24). Despite all this harshness, Jesus calls himself the divine Son to whom the Father has given all things. He invites all who are heavy with the demands of religion to come to him, "take up his yoke [way of life]," and receive rest (11:25–30).

Then, in chapter 12, Jesus teaches in a sequence of controversy stories. The first involves the disciples' plucking grain on the Sabbath and has christological significance: Jesus claims the right to do what David did and proclaims that he as the Son of Man is lord of the Sabbath (12:1–8). The next controversy is over Jesus' healing on a Sabbath. In a synagogue Jesus heals a man with a withered hand by asking him to stretch it out in faith. These two controversies end in a menacing tone—the Pharisees are now planning to kill Jesus (12:9–14). A third controversy is over a demon-possessed man healed of blindness and muteness. Aware of growing deadly opposition, Jesus withdraws, followed by large crowds; he continues to heal many, as the prophet Isaiah predicted (12:15–21). Just as a previous section (11:28–30) ended with talk of Jesus' winsome invitation, here Matthew quotes Isaiah 42:1–4 to reiterate the tenderness of Jesus, who does not break a bruised reed or quench a smoldering wick. In hostile reaction, the Pharisees again attribute Jesus' power over demons to Satan himself, implying that they are in league together to deceive God's people. This time, Jesus sharply disproves this charge by comparing his expulsion of demons to plundering the realm of Satan. He then warns in the strongest possible terms that attributing the power of God in him and his movement to the devil will not be forgiven (12:22–32). The tone of the condemnation becomes sharper in 12:33–36, when Jesus calls the Pharisees a "brood of vipers" whose evils deeds will condemn them on judgment day. When the scribes and Pharisees demand a sign from Jesus, a definitive deed that will prove beyond question his right to act and speak as he does, Jesus gives them only the signs of the Bible: Jonah who preached repentance and the queen of the South who came to King Solomon (12:38–42). Jesus has driven out demons, but they will return to make this generation even worse than before (12:43–45). At the arrival of Jesus' mother and brothers, Jesus explains that with the nearness of the kingdom, a new kinship system has come—those who do the will of the heavenly Father are now Jesus' brother, sister, and mother (12:46–50).

Chapter 13 is Matthew's parable collection and the third of Jesus' speeches in the Gospel. It contains seven parables dealing with the mixed reception that the reign of God receives in this world and its surpassing value. In the parable of the Sower, Matthew deals with the types of difficulties and failures encountered by the reign of God, but he emphasizes the astounding growth that will come (13:1–23). The next parable, the Weeds in the Wheat and its interpretation (13:24–30, 36–43), raises another concern for the life of the church after Jesus departs. As the church grows, some who seemingly do not belong to God (the "weeds") will be among those who do (the "wheat"). Some in the church will say, Why not get rid of evil people among the people of God? Because this would harm the good people, Jesus teaches, and such judgment belongs only to God at the end of time. The paired parables of the Mustard Seed and the Leaven contrast the small beginnings of the kingdom and its certainly vast future by using everyday examples of extraordinary growth familiar to men (the mustard seed) and to women (the leaven) (13:31–33). Then comes another pair of parables, the Hidden Treasure and the Expensive Pearl, emphasizing that people must enter the immeasurably valuable kingdom at all human costs (13:44–46). Another parable, the Net and its interpretation, deals with the great numbers of people that God will separate at the end (13:47–50). The sermon ends with a summary important to Matthew's overall purpose (13:51–53). When Jesus asks his disciples if they have understood this sermon, they answer, "Yes." Jesus responds with a saying that may be a key to understanding this Gospel: the scribe trained for the kingdom of God can appreciate both the new (in Jesus) and the old (in Moses), and can combine the best of both into one harmonious whole.

The next, lengthy section of narrative (13:54 through chapter 17) illustrates and develops the theme of chapter 13 on the mixed reaction to Jesus. In this new section, both faith in Jesus and opposition to him mount. It features Jesus' rejection at Nazareth, his miraculous feeding of the five thousand and soon thereafter four thousand, walking on the water and assorted healing miracles, increasing controversies with Pharisees, Peter's confession of faith in Jesus' identity, Jesus' first prediction of his death and resurrection, his transfiguration, and finally a second death and resurrection prediction. Jesus' rejection at Nazareth (13:53–58) explains in a narrative way why Jesus must now focus on his disciples: if the people of his hometown do not accept him, others in Israel will not, either. This is followed by a long narrative flashback about the cruel and superstitious Herod Antipas killing John the Baptizer and becoming suspicious of Jesus (14:1–12). Herod is more concerned about social conventions of honor and power than he is about doing God's will. Jesus at first withdraws when he hears this, but then returns to his ministry to miraculously feed "five thousand men, besides women and children" (14:13–21). On the Sea of Galilee, Jesus walks on the water and summons Peter to come to him by walking on the water; when Peter begins to sink from his doubt, Jesus rescues him. At the end of this episode, Jesus' disciples worship him as "the Son of God" (14:28–33). The boat carrying Jesus and the disciples arrives in Gennesaret, where Jesus heals all their sick (14:34–36). Then Pharisees and scribes from Jerusalem debate with Jesus about what ritually defiles a person. Jesus sharply responds to their attack, especially to teach his disciples about what true purity is (15:1–20). Moving on to the Gentile territory north of Galilee, Jesus heals the daughter of the Canaanite (Gentile) woman. Her steadfast faith shows once again that Gentiles can be equal in faith to Jews (15:21–28). Then comes a miraculous feeding of four thousand men, again "besides women and children" (15:32–39).

However, hostile disagreements with the Pharisees and Sadducees (16:1–12) follow these miracles and the trust in Jesus that they show. After criticizing his disciples for not understanding fully the feeding miracles, Jesus warns them against the "yeast" or corrupting teaching of the Pharisees and Sadducees, whom he calls evil and spiritually adulterous. That the disciples are not infected by this yeast is shown in 16:13–20, where Peter now confesses that Jesus is the Son of the living God—a revelation that is from the Father in heaven, not a result of human thinking. Peter is the rock on which Christ will build his church, a church against which even the "gates of hell" (death from satanic persecution) will not prevail. This positive attention to Peter is immediately followed by Jesus' sharp rebuke of Peter when he rejects Jesus' prediction of his suffering. Jesus goes so far as to call this "Rock" a "stumbling stone" and "Satan." This reproof of Peter leads into Jesus' directives to all the disciples about the suffering that true discipleship entails (16:24–28). They should be encouraged that the suffering of the present will be replaced with future glory. Jesus, as the Son of Man, is to be the key figure in that glory by bringing with him the kingdom in which his disciples will have a role. After that, Jesus is transfigured, or shown in his heavenly glory (17:1–13), as the voice from the cloud repeats what the voice from heaven said at Jesus' baptism (3:17) and echoed most recently in Peter's confession (16:16–19), that Jesus is God's Son. After the story of the epileptic boy (17:14–21), which challenges Jesus' disciples to have "faith to move mountains," Matthew presents a second prediction of the passion and resurrection (17:22–23). Then comes another scene featuring Peter, this time about the moral question of paying taxes. Peter and all Jesus' followers are to pay their taxes as obedient citizens, even if they have moral objections (17:24–27).

Chapter 18 is the next teaching discourse, Matthew's "sermon on the church," a collection of mixed materials about community life and discipleship mostly after Jesus is gone. The sermon begins with the disciples' conflict over honor ("greatness") in the kingdom of heaven (18:1–5). Jesus teaches that the humble and marginalized are more important than the powerful, for dependence on God is what makes one open to God's rule. Of this, a little child, the least valuable part of the social structure of the time, is held up as an example. Jesus harshly condemns scandals and temptations, poetically called "stumbling blocks," that cause believers to fall away from faith (18:6–9). A parable of the one Lost Sheep commands the disciples to search after these fallen believers (18:10–14). Those who have fallen away must be dealt with encouragingly and forgivingly, because this is how God treats people. People who argue in the church must reconcile to each other, but those who refuse reconciliation are to be treated as "Gentiles and tax collectors" (18:15–20). Peter then gets instruction from Jesus on the extent of forgiveness in the church, that is, on how soon one who refuses to be reconciled should be ostracized. "How many times must I forgive someone?" he asks, thinking that the upper limit would be seven times. Jesus gives a remarkable answer: seventy-seven times, symbolic of limitless forgiveness. To illustrate the importance of unlimited forgiveness, Matthew relates the parable of the Unforgiving Servant that sternly warns believers about God's judgment on people who receive God's abundant forgiveness but refuse to forgive others for comparatively small sins (18:23–35). The end of Matthew's sermon on the church ends with a statement anticipating the promise of Jesus' presence found at the end of the Gospel: "Where two or three are gathered in my name, I am there among them" (18:20).

As the reader now expects, Matthew's next panel of material is a narrative. It features conflict stories and parables, a third passion and resurrection prediction, Jesus' entry to Jerusalem, his "cleansing" of the Temple, and clashes with Jewish authorities (chapters 19–23). In this section Jesus experiences more and more opposition that will lead directly to his death, and his teaching to his disciples about how to follow him becomes more challenging as well. The narrative of the trip to Jerusalem begins with Jesus' high standards for life in the kingdom. The question about divorce (19:1–12) is set in the context of the Pharisees' testing of Jesus. In criticizing easy divorce and remarriage, Jesus repeats material found earlier in 5:32. This highly unusual repetition of the same material probably indicates the importance Matthew placed on it. When the disciples express their dismay about this, Jesus speaks even more radically, suggesting that some of his followers become "eunuchs" (i.e., **celibate,** not engaging in sexual intercourse) for the sake of the kingdom of God. When the disciples reject the children, Jesus corrects their false social and spiritual values (19:13–15). The low status that children have is dramatized in the following story of the rich young man who could not give up all that he had to follow Jesus and gain eternal life (19:16–26). Only by God's power can salvation come to any human, Jesus remarks, let alone a rich one. The parable of

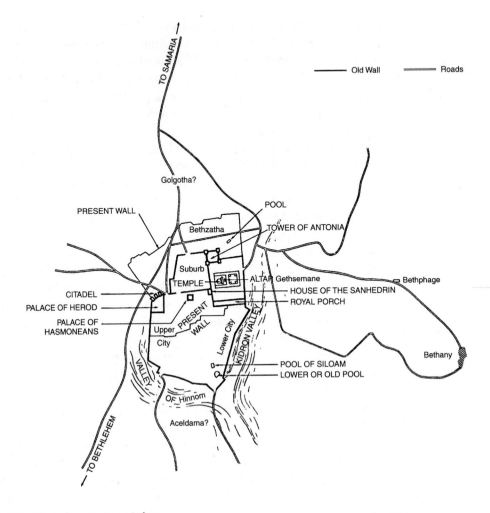

Map 7.1 Jerusalem in Jesus' day.

Reproduced from *The Westminster Historical Atlas to the Bible*, Revised Edition, by George Ernest Wright and Floyd Vivian Wilson. Used by permission of Westminster John Knox Press.

the Workers in the Vineyard vividly illustrates that in God's grace-full value system, the first will indeed be last and the last first (20:1–16). The third prediction of Jesus' passion and resurrection follows (20:17–19), showing how this reversal of values is grounded on the willingness of Jesus to be "last." When Jesus predicts that the Twelve will rule with him in his kingdom, the disciples misunderstand this statement, and some request the most honored places in the kingdom (20:20–28). Jesus has indeed promised the Twelve that they will sit on thrones of judgment when Jesus as the Son of Man returns in glory; that does not entail sitting at his right or left, the prime social positions, in the kingdom. The continuing journey to Jerusalem brings Jesus to Jericho, where Jesus heals two blind men who hail him as the "Son of David" (20:29–34). In chapter 21, Jesus enters the city of Jerusalem. Matthew uses fulfillment quotations from Hebrew prophets to emphasize the humility and peacefulness of the Messianic king. To underscore the completeness of this fulfillment, Matthew construes the ass and colt (meant in the Hebrew Bible as poetic designations of one animal) as two animals, so that Jesus sat "on them" and rode them both into Jerusalem (v. 7)!

After the whole city is agitated and recognizes Jesus as an important prophet when he enters Jerusalem (21:10–11), Jesus fiercely "cleanses" the Temple by chasing out the moneychangers and sellers of ritually pure sacrificial animals (21:10–17). The cursing and withering of the fruitless fig tree follows, a symbolic prophetic action expressing God's judgment on those who are disobedient (21:18–22). After the priests and elders challenge Jesus' authority to do these striking things (21:23–27), Jesus effectively counterchallenges and silences them by asking about the authority of John the Baptizer. Although this seems like a victory, the allusion to John fills an ideal reader with foreboding: Matthew has reported that John was martyred for his ministry even though the people applauded him; despite his current popularity, Jesus will soon meet a fate similar to John's. There follows in this narrative section a group of three strongly reproving parables of judgment. In the parable of the Two Sons (21:28–32), Jesus matches the religious authorities in Jerusalem to the son who says he will obey the father but does not. The tax collectors and prostitutes who repent and believe, who initially are disobedient but then obey like the other son, will enter the kingdom of God before the authorities do. In the parable of the Wicked Tenants (21:33–46), the chief priests and the Pharisees correctly understand themselves to be the target of the parable. They are its wicked tenant farmers, and Jesus warns that God will take away the kingdom of heaven from them and give it to other peoples such as Gentiles who will produce fruits (Matthew's recurrent theme). Next comes the parable of the Wedding Feast, which contains in a different story the same point as the Wicked Tenants: God will take away from God's disobedient people their place in the joyous messianic feast of heaven, and give it to strangers. The short parable tacked on, about the man without a Wedding Garment (22:11–13), deals with a sad reality in Matthew's churches. With the diverse population of the church, both bad and good people are in it, and the church must deal wisely with the task of judging itself.

After hearing this series of scathing parables, Jesus' opponents rouse themselves to reply. They pose a series of three trap questions: Pharisees and Herodians ask about taxes for Caesar (22:15–22); Sadducees ask about the resurrection (22:23–33); and a Pharisee "lawyer," an expert in the Law of Moses, asks about the great commandment (22:34–40). Jesus repels all these challenges to his honor and authority with ripostes of counter-questions and arguments, and then turns the tables, asking one trap question of his own about the Messiah as David's son (22:41–46). After Jesus entraps his opponents with just this one question, none dares to challenge him again. But Jesus will not be silent; he engages in a lengthy, caustic denunciation of the scribes and Pharisees throughout chapter 23. Considering the negative content of the whole chapter, it begins rather oddly with an order to obey whatever the scribes and Pharisees teach, because of their authoritative position, but not to follow their example (23:1–3). Earlier the Matthean Jesus criticizes their teaching (for example, 15:6; 16:11–12; 23:16–22). The hostility of these authorities in the trap questions of chapter 22 is returned by Jesus' assault on their proud behavior and love for titles. In addition, Jesus thunders seven (symbolic of completeness) *woes* or eschatological condemnations against their hypocrisy. The harsh criticisms in this chapter are directed primarily to Jesus' opponents but implicitly warn his own followers again about their own hypocrisy.

Jesus' fifth and final discourse in this gospel is on the end of time (chapters 24–25). When Jesus leaves the temple (24:1), it has already begun to be desolate (23:38). On the way out, his disciples remark about its glorious buildings, but Jesus solemnly predicts that it will soon be destroyed (24:2). This leads to a discussion of the end of time, which Matthew separates from the destruction of Jerusalem. Jesus emphasizes at the end of chapter 24 that one cannot know when the Son of Man is coming, despite attentiveness to the signs that he explains. Thus, the best thing his followers can do is wait expectantly for the end so that it does not surprise them. This command to watchfulness continues in the parable of the Ten Maidens (25:1–13). The judgment theme grows stronger in the parable of the Talents (25:14–30). Its point is not earning a reward from God, but using God's gifts in a creative, productive way. The discourse ends with the enthroned Son of Man judging the sheep, those who are righteous because they are loving, and the goats, those who are unjust because they refuse to show love, at the end of time (25:31–46). The verdict at this Last Judgment on each individual is based on one's treatment of the marginalized, especially those within the church.

Jesus predicts at the onset of the next narrative section that he would be given over at this Passover. Judas' disloyalty and the anointing of Jesus for his burial (26.1–16) frames the plot against Jesus by the high priest Caiaphas, thus anticipating the setting of the Jewish trial later. The preparations for Passover (26:17–19) are briefly told, leading into the Last Supper (26:20–29). Judas is named as Jesus' betrayer, and he dishonors Jesus by calling him "Rabbi," the title Jesus had forbidden his disciples to use (23:7–8).

In 26:30–27:56 the panel of narrative action continues, with Matthew now presenting the passion narrative. In the Garden of Gethsemane (26:30–56), Matthew emphasizes Jesus' praying three times by giving the content of all three prayers. In the arrest (26:49–50), Judas once more addresses Jesus as "Rabbi," and he identifies Jesus further with a kiss. Bravely impetuous Peter cuts off the ear of the high priest's servant, but Jesus strongly forbids such violence. The Jewish council tries Jesus first, where he is condemned by this Sanhedrin and mocked while Peter denies him (26:57–27:1). Jesus accepts the title "Messiah, the Son of God," and for this the council condemns him as worthy of death After treating Jesus shamefully, the council sends him to Pontius Pilate, the Roman governor, for another trial. Matthew prefaces the Roman trial with the story of Judas' reaction to the Jewish decision against Jesus (27:3–10). Judas does not want to be accountable for Jesus' innocent blood. After Judas hangs himself, his thirty pieces of silver are used to buy a burial ground for foreigners, but his own burial is not mentioned. One way to read this account is that he was buried in this burial ground for foreigners and thus excluded in death from the people of God (27:3–10). After Jesus' trial begins, Pilate's wife reports to her husband that she has received a dream revelation that Jesus is a just man (27:19). After a short hearing, Pilate washes his hands to signify that he wants (like Judas) to be considered innocent of any responsibility for his unjust punishment. When "all the people" say, "His blood is on us and our children" (27:24–25), Pilate orders the crucifixion of Jesus.

After Roman soldiers mock and then crucify Jesus, the Jewish authorities also mock him as he dies (27:26–43). At his death, two things happen: the curtain of the Temple is torn; at the same time, an earthquake opens tombs around Jerusalem, and some dead members of God's people arise from them and appear to many. These two events signify that human relationships to God are now changing, and the defeat of death has begun. The burial account (27:57–61) introduces Joseph from Arimathea, who gives Jesus a tomb; he is a rich disciple of Jesus. The placing of the guard at the tomb (27:62–66) rebuts later Jewish polemic against the resurrection, that Jesus' disciples stole his body. In the story of discovering the empty tomb, the angels tell the women disciples about Jesus' victory, and they run with joy to tell the other disciples. Jesus himself appears to these women on their way (28:1–10). The alternating pattern of the narrative calls attention to the bribing of the guard by the chief priests and their lie that the disciples stole the body (28:11–15).

The finale of Matthew comes when Jesus appears to the Eleven on a mountain in Galilee and sends them on their mission to the world, a passage called in church tradition the **Great Commission** (28:16–20). These eleven disciples greet him with a mixture of worship and doubt. The resurrected Jesus claims "all power in heaven and earth," given to him by God. He instructs his disciples to go through the entire world, teaching and baptizing people from "all nations" into the Father, Son, and Holy Spirit, the triadic name for God's fullness. Thus the covenant with Abraham is fulfilled as the followers of Jesus take his Jewish light into the world and Israel becomes a blessing to all the nations. This command implicitly cancels Jesus' earlier command to the Twelve to go only to the people of Israel (10:5–6). Jesus' instruction to teach new converts "all that I have commanded you" refers to all the commands of Jesus that Matthew has narrated. This "Great Commission" ensures a basis of unity in the church: the same moral code or "moral universe" is to be shared by all Jesus' followers. The final verse of Matthew is a grace-filled promise on which these commands can be obeyed: "I am with you every day, until the end of the age."

Historical Reading

Matthew in Brief: Summary of Historical Reading

Author: Anonymous. Traditionally, Matthew the tax collector, one of Jesus' twelve main disciples (Matt 9:9, 10:3), is identified as the author. Today, some keep to the traditional author, but most conclude that the author is an unknown Jewish Christian of the second Christian generation, perhaps the "trained scribe" of 13:52.

Date: Probably in the 80s.

Sources: Mark, Q; a few scholars also posit an oral or written M source containing Matthew's unique material.

Audience: A church of Jewish Christians and a few Gentile Christians, perhaps in Antioch.

Purpose: To teach a church committed to mission among all peoples but with internal divisions over Jewish Christianity and Gentile Christianity, and facing external persecution.

Author

Like all the Synoptics, the first Gospel in the canon is anonymous—no author is named in the text. The title "According to Matthew" was added to manuscripts of this writing sometime after the second century and indicates that many ancient Christians thought that this Gospel was written by one of Jesus' twelve main disciples. Around 125, Papias wrote, "Matthew arranged in order the sayings in the Hebrew [or Aramaic] language" (as reported in Eusebius' *History of the Church* 3.39.16). Significant debate has occurred over whether "sayings" meant that Matthew wrote a Gospel, as later writers in antiquity thought. The context in Papias probably indicates that he did mean a full Gospel; because he had just referred to the *Gospel* of Mark, Papias would probably have been referring to a Gospel when he says that Matthew arranged in order the sayings in Hebrew/Aramaic. One piece of internal evidence that might support the traditional view that the apostle Matthew wrote this book is that both Mark 2:14 and Luke 5:27–28 speak of the calling of "Levi," whereas Matthew 9:9 calls him "Matthew." Only the first Gospel calls Matthew "the tax collector" in its list of apostles (chapter 10). A possible and reasonable explanation for this was that the author knew personally about this. Thus he could either be Matthew himself or an associate who later compiled the work. These bits of evidence indicate to some scholars today that Matthew may be the author of this book, but most are not persuaded by them.

Most scholars today conclude that Matthew was written in Greek by someone now unknown to us, but probably not an eyewitness of Jesus' ministry. The author depended on sources like Mark and Q, which an eyewitness would not need to do. Today a more difficult issue is whether the author was a Jewish Christian or a Gentile Christian. Current scholarship favors a Jewish Christian, but some scholars support Gentile authorship on the basis of some statements in Matthew that arguably could not have been made by a Jew. On the other hand, the author's use of the OT shows that he knew it in Hebrew, unlikely (but not impossible) for a Gentile. That the author is Jewish in background is also supported by the many Jewish touches that are found in Matthew:

- Positive comparison of Jesus with Moses, as in the Sermon on the Mount overall (5–7) and in detail (5:17–48)
- Knowledge and experience of contemporary Jewish polemic against the church, for example that Jesus' resurrection was bogus (28:11–15)
- Knowledge of persecution of the church by Jewish authorities (10:17; 23:34)
- Command to obey the teaching of Pharisees (23:2–3)
- Implications that Matthew's church is keeping Jewish practices like fasting (6:16) and Sabbath rest (24:20)
- The statement in 13:52 about a Jewish scribe who can combine the best of Judaism and faith in Jesus.

Taken all together, the evidence strongly favors a Jewish Christian identity of the evangelist. As stated earlier, the author of Matthew's knowledge of Hebrew suggests that he is from a Jewish background, but his excellent Greek indicates that he may be a Jewish Christian from the Diaspora. Theologically, the evangelist was likely a Jewish-Christian "moderate." He may have favored the admission of uncircumcised Gentiles to Christian communities, often a volatile issue in the first-century church (see 28:19, where there is no mention of circumcising converts, but this is an argument from silence, which are always slippery). But he held that the law of Moses as interpreted by Jesus had an important continuing role in the church until the end of time (5:17–20, "until heaven and earth pass away, not one letter or stroke of a letter will pass from the law until all is accomplished"; 28:19, "teaching them [Gentile converts] to observe all I have commanded you"). In sum, he seeks to combine the best of traditional Judaism and the best of Jesus' teaching, the "treasures new and old" that he is bringing out of his treasury for the use of his churches (13:52).

Date

As for the earliest possible date, strong arguments indicate a date after 70 C.E. For instance, the omission in Matt 21:13 of Mark's statement that the Jerusalem Temple is "for all the nations" (Mark 11:17), and the reference in Matt 22:7 to the king burning the city, probably reflect the destruction of Jerusalem by the Roman armies in 70. In terms of theological development, the triadic formula in Matt 28:19 ("the name of the Father and of the Son and of the Holy Spirit") is the most advanced NT step in a Trinitarian direction, coming after Paul and the practices witnessed in Acts, where baptism is only in the name of Jesus. The controversies with the Pharisees in Matthew and the condemnation of Christian use of the title "Rabbi" fit well into the atmosphere after 70, when the Pharisees consolidated their sole leadership of Judaism in its synagogues. Probably the best argument for a post-70 date is the dependence of Matthew on Mark, a Gospel commonly dated to 68–73. Most scholars date Matthew within the rather wide period of 70–100.

As for the latest possible date, Papias (as we saw before) may have known of canonical Matthew as early as about 115, so an early second-century date is unlikely. In a less persuasive argument, despite its close contact with Judaism, Matthew does not show any knowledge of the Jewish decision around 90 to expel believers in Jesus from the synagogue, as the Gospel of John does. (Of course, there may be other reasons why Matthew shows no knowledge of this event.) When all these factors are put together, the latest possible date for Matthew is about 100. In sum, 80–90 is the most plausible dating, in the middle of the broad 70–100 period. This dating, approximate as it is, is accepted by a strong majority of scholars today.

Sources

The Gospel of Mark is Matthew's first and main source for wording and organization. Mark made Jesus intelligible to a Gentile audience; and Matthew, in order to communicate with a church that was becoming more and more Gentile, found Mark a useful source, and adaptable for his own purposes. Overall, Matthew is remarkably faithful to Mark's order and wording. Nevertheless, in the redactional changes to what is taken over from Mark, one can detect Matthean distinctives in style and content.

- The author of Matthew writes Greek in a much better style than Mark's. For example, it streamlines Mark's wordiness and fixes its clumsy or difficult expressions, especially in narratives.
- Matthew is more reverent to Jesus than Mark, correcting what Matthew's audience may have seen as Mark's lessening Jesus' person or authority. For example, Matthew omits completely the healing of the blind man (Mark 8.22–26), where the first action by Jesus gives him blurry vision, and the second clear sight. Matt 9:22 drops the implication in Mark 5:30–31 that Jesus did not know who drew healing power from him by touching him.
- Matthew occasionally (but not at all regularly) heightens Jesus' power in working miracles found in Mark. For example, Matt 14:35 says that Jesus healed *all* who were sick, not just Mark's "some."
- Matthew omits or tones down some Markan passages unfavorable to leading figures in the church. For example, it omits Mark 3:21, where Jesus' family thinks he is mentally deranged. Matthew changes the socially ambitious questioner from the two disciples who are sons of Zebedee in Mark 10:35 to their mother in Matt 20:20.

Q, the Synoptic sayings collection, is Matthew's second main source, and it emphasizes Jesus as a teacher. Many would discern Matthew's distinctive teachings by studying the changes the Gospel writer makes in Q. However, because Q is a hypothetical construction derived in roughly equal measure from Matthew and Luke, it is difficult to avoid circular reasoning about what the precise wording of these changes in Q might be. We can say with some certainty that the order of Q is carefully adapted to Matthew's more systematic order. For example, Matthew rearranges the Q material into sermons or discourses. Matthew can also fill out the slim wording of Q, as Matt 6:9–13 expands the Lord's Prayer/Our Father with wording lacking in Luke 11:2–4.

A third possible source of Matthew is called M, the material found only in Matthew, especially the teaching material. Since this possible Gospel source is unique to Matthew, we will look at it in a bit more depth here. Three main efforts have been made to isolate an M source. First, B. H. Streeter defined M as all teaching material peculiar to Matthew, including Q material different enough from Luke to postulate a different form of Q influenced by Matthew. Streeter isolated a modest source: discourse material from Matthew 5–7, 10, 18, and 23; two parables from Matthew 13; and short sections of miscellaneous material from 12, 15, 16, and 19. This source is Jewish-Christian, but not from the first generation of Christianity; instead, it shows a negative reaction to the Pauline mission with the law-free Gospel (Streeter 1924). The second source-critical study is by T. W. Manson (Manson 1935). Manson shared most of Streeter's method but proposed a more extensive and developed M than Streeter. He dated M between 65 and 70 C.E., placing it also in the Jewish community of Jerusalem. The third main study of M is by G. D. Kilpatrick (Kilpatrick 1946). He organized his M material into four sections: discourse, missionary charge, a collection of parables, and polemic against Jewish religious leaders. Kilpatrick argued that this was a written source that contained only teaching material. Although a single portrait of Jesus does not emerge from this material, it does seem to characterize him as an authoritative leader of the church. Jesus reinterprets the Law to fulfill its original intent, and his teaching of righteousness will be the criterion of judgment at the end of time.

www   See the website for Kilpatrick's reconstructed M.

Current scholarship is correct in concluding that the special material of Matthew most likely does not reflect a single source. This material simply varies too widely in style and content to reflect a single document, which we would expect to have some common literary style and religious message. A more recent study of the special sayings material of Matthew by Stephenson H. Brooks tends to bear out this conclusion on M as a whole. Brooks isolates and reconstructs the shorter sayings of M and shows that it reflects the history of the Matthean community. He concludes that a single written source of M sayings is untenable because (1) we can detect few editorial connections in the collected M sayings; (2) the minor narrative touches in transitional sentences and phrases show little evidence of pre-Matthean origin; and

(3) the style and vocabulary of the isolated M sayings material does not show the kind of unity that suggests a written source. So although some material may have been written, most seems to have existed in oral tradition alone (Brooks 1987). We may conclude that even though *some* of the special material of Matthew may well have come to him from various sources, the evidence does not establish the probability that he used an M source containing most of his special material. As Udo Schnelle writes, "The Matthean body of special materials is not a unified complex of tradition, is without discernable theological organizing motifs, and is hardly to be assigned to a single circle of tradition bearers" (Schnelle 1998, 174).

www   Follow the link for a concise outline of the historical criticism of Matthew.

Audience and Purpose

By the end of the second century, church writers placed Matthew in Palestine. Probably that was a deduction based on the well-known Papias tradition that Matthew wrote in Hebrew as well as on the internal evidence of controversies with, and persecutions by, Jewish authorities. However, the majority view today gives this Gospel a Diaspora setting, placing Matthew in Syria and specifically in the city of Antioch. Matt 4:24 adds "Syria" to Mark's description of the geographic scope of Jesus' activity, perhaps hinting about a basis in Jesus' ministry for the foundations of Matthew's church. The leading influence that Matthew had in antiquity suggests that it was the Gospel of a Christian church in an important city like Antioch, the third largest city in the Roman Empire. (Matthew, like Mark and Luke, seems to have an urban audience; for example, it uses the term *city* twenty-six times, compared to only four times for *village*. The possible Galilean setting of Matthew, either as the place of its origin or its destination, has few, if any, areas that are large cities.) The *Didache* shows an early second-century knowledge of Matthew, and the *Didache* is associated with Antioch.

A plausible interpretation of Matthew is that it was addressed to a once strongly Jewish Christian church that had become increasingly Gentile in composition, and this assumption fits well what we know of the church in Antioch. W. D. Davies has made a strong case that Matthew was written in Antioch as a Christian response to the Judaism that was emerging after 70 C.E. at Jamnia in Palestine, where the rabbis consolidated the survivors in Palestinian Judaism and became its sole leaders (Davies 1977). Perhaps the Matthean Christians lived in the shadow of a larger Jewish community that opposed them. The two groups would have come from the same Jewish background, shared the same scriptures and many of the same religious convictions, so their differences would have provoked all the more dispute. (Social science and common experience remind us: there is no fight like a family fight!) John Meier has also shown how the history of Christianity at Antioch features

Synagogue in Capernaum This synagogue, built sometime after the first century C.E., is the grand-
est in Israel. Built on the model of a Roman basilica, it faced Jerusalem. Jesus taught and
healed in the synagogue of Capernaum (Mark 1:21–27; 5:22; Luke 4:31–37; John 6:35–59),
Used by permission of BiblePlaces.com.

Jewish Christianity and Gentile Christianity in close proximity and conflict (Brown
and Meier 1983, 45–72). When Hellenist Jewish Christians were scattered from
Jerusalem after the martyrdom of Stephen (Acts 8:1) and came to Antioch, they
spoke of Christ to Gentiles there as well (Acts 11:19–20). Paul's Law-free mission
to the Gentiles was with the support of the Antioch church, his "home base." It
was at Antioch that Paul, Peter, and men from Jerusalem disagreed sharply over
how Jewish food laws affected the table relationships of Jewish and Gentile
Christians. Christianity in Antioch would have been dominated by a more conservative outlook than Paul's on how the Law impacted Gentile converts; the
Antioch churches may have carried out the decree from James and the Jerusalem
"council" in Acts 15:28–29, whereas Paul in his churches did not. In the post-70
period at Antioch, Gentiles probably became the majority among Christians, perhaps leading to the conservative wing of Jewish Christians separating from the main
church as things they saw as essential, such as circumcision for all the people of
God, was no longer demanded.

How does Matthew offer advice to this diverse and divided community? First, it recognizes that this mixed community is intentional, a part of God's plan. Jesus' ministry, a ministry he shared with his disciples, had been purposefully restricted to the Jewish people in Jewish areas. However, all through Matthew, from the magi of chapter 2 to the Great Commission in the last chapter, there are strong hints that Jesus' message and ministry will eventually go out into the whole world. Second, Gentiles like Roman centurions and "Canaanite" women sometimes encounter Jesus in his travels within Palestine, with happy results. They become models of faith for all in Matthew's church, even for Jews. Third, at the end of the Gospel Jesus tells his eleven disciples to make disciples from "all the nations." The Gospel once restricted to Jews is now to move out into the world, and into the entire world at that. But the way that disciples are made is the key to unity: they are to obey all that Jesus commanded the eleven disciples, so that all share the same outlook on the faith and its practice. (In social scientific terms, they all inhabit the same symbolic universe, that is, have the same view of the world.) Finally, Matthew pulls this all together with his strong emphasis on discipleship. The word *disciple* occurs sixty-five times in Matthew, of which forty-five are unique to Matthew. All Christians are disciples, not just those who followed Jesus on the dusty roads of Palestine. They must be continuous "students" in the church to learn how to believe and live a Gospel that combines Jews and Gentiles in one community. They are to become the wise scribes who can combine the best of Judaism with the best of Christianity (13:52).

www Follow the link to a treatment of the teaching discourses in Matthew with good reference to the aims of its author.

Doing Historical Reading Yourself

1. *Matthew 23 is strong, even vitriolic, against the Pharisees. Does the more nuanced and positive teaching about the Pharisees in 23:1–3 serve in any way to frame a context for the rest of this chapter?*

2. *Matthew is the only Gospel that presents the tradition about the guard at the tomb of Jesus and the Jewish explanation of Jesus' resurrection (27:62–66, 28:11–15). Use the criteria of authenticity to study the historicity (whether it actually happened) of this story.*

Newer methods of reading have typically been applied to Mark first, but Matthew was soon to follow. Narrative analysis has dealt with the alternating action/teaching structure of most of this Gospel. Social scientific criticism has been fascinated by the conflicted issue of Jewish and Gentile identity, and feminist reading by Matthew's more patriarchal tendencies. Matthew is rich in material on social scientific themes: kinship, honor and shame, and economic life. Matthew's text and subtext have much on ethnic identity (Jews and Gentiles as ethnic groups), about religious identity (Jews and Gentiles as religious groups), and about insiders (Jews, Jewish Christians, males) and outsiders (Gentiles, Gentile Christians, females). Cross-cultural criticism of Matthew is in its beginning stages and deals with an issue raised by historical criticism: the lively combination of Jew and Gentile in this writing.

Matthew in Brief: Summary of Newer Methods

Narrative: Most of Matthew is characterized by alternating panels of teaching and narrative, but the narrative panels do not follow up on the themes of the teaching panels. In this way, Matthew stresses that Jesus is both a teacher and a doer. Matthew has a fully developed infancy narrative, passion narrative, and resurrection-appearance narratives.

Social Scientific: Matthew's foremost concern is relating two diverse groups, Jew and Gentile, in one church. Despite his attachment to his Jewish heritage, Matthew gives social priority to Jesus and his movement.

Feminist: Matthew's continuing devotion to Judaism may temper his advancement of women. A fuller, freer role for women is present, but with less attention and less force than one finds in Mark and Luke.

Cross-Cultural: As stated, Matthew's foremost concern is crossing the cultural barrier between Jew and Gentile but in such a way that the best of Judaism is brought over, and one church combining Jew and Gentile results.

Narrative Reading

One of the first books on narrative in Matthew was *Matthew as Story* by Jack Dean Kingsbury, a Gospels scholar known for his historical-critical studies (Kingsbury 1988). Kingsbury argues that Matthew's plot is built around the dual conflict Jesus engages in with his disciples and the Jewish leaders. The principal conflict is the latter one, and the resolution of this part of the plot is the death of Jesus. Jesus' conflict with the disciples basically concerns his attempt to guide them to a greater understanding of their own mission of servanthood, which entails a rejection of society's honor system. Kingsbury's controlling thesis for characterization is that Jesus is the central character who represents God's system of values to the reader, namely, total obedience to God's will. The baptismal scene (3:13–17), where God declares that Jesus is the Son of God, becomes the normative one for the reader. From this point on in the narrative, the reader will measure all other characters by Jesus' obedience, compassion, and saving actions as the Son of God.

Narrative Reading at Work, 1
Matthew 12:46–50

Here is a reading of the story of Jesus' rebuff to his immediate family that uses a narrative approach. Allen calls on us to put ourselves into the mind of the implied reader, which has been shaped by a continuous reading of everything in Matthew before this passage and to reflect carefully on its meaning to us as the implied reader.

Since we are attempting to understand and identify with the experience of the implied reader, we begin with the assumption that the implied readers are reading the gospel of Matthew from beginning to end. By the time they come upon 12:46–50, they have already read 1:1–12:45 and carry impressions from this material with them into their reading of this passage. On the other hand, they have not read any of 12:1–28:20 and have only expectations (based on their prior knowledge of the non-Matthean story of the Christ event) of what is to come.

Because of the way the Gospel of Matthew uses scripture and because of the heavy concentration on the conflicts between traditional Jewish life and the new Christian way of life, many scholars argue that Matthew's implied readers were Jewish Christians. Having submitted to the identity of the implied reader, we are ready to begin the process of reading while constantly taking our pulse. We take stock of ourselves as we ingest each movement of the passage:

"While he was still speaking to the crowds": The narrator introduces the scene by connecting it with the preceding scenes where (as we have seen) Jesus has been in conflict. Reading these opening words, the implied reader might expect that conflict to continue.

"His mother and his brothers were standing outside, wanting to speak to him": The expectation of conflict would lessen with the introduction of Jesus' family into the scene. Although this is Matthew's first mention of Jesus' brothers, the reader has already been introduced to Mary in the infancy narrative. The fact that an angel of the lord defended Mary to Joseph and described her giving birth to Jesus as a fulfillment of scripture gives the implied reader a strong positive image of her (and thus of her children with her).

Question

Compare this treatment of Matthew 12:46–50 with the treatment of Mark 3:31–35 as presented in the social scientific reading section of the previous chapter. What are their similarities and differences?

Source: O. Wesley Allen, Jr., Reading the Synoptic Gospels: Basic Methods for Interpreting Matthew, Mark, and Luke (St. Louis: Chalice, 2000), pp. 129–130.

Narrative Reading at Work, 2
Making Sense of a Flashback in Matthew 14

Flashbacks, interruptions of an ongoing narrative to tell a story of what happened earlier, may be common in literature and film today, but they are rare in the Gospels. In this reading, Terence Donaldson explicates the long flashback in Matthew 14 on the death of John the Baptizer. Unlike Mark, Matthew does not return to the narrative present when the flashback is finished; the next event follows in temporal sequence with John's death.

While Chapter 13 . . . contains little in the way of mighty works that would have accounted for Herod's comment about Jesus, the episodes immediately following the retrospective account of John's death are quite different. This material—part of an extended flashback—is replete with accounts of Jesus' mighty works: the feeding of the multitude (14:14–21); the walking on the sea (14:22–33); and, in particular, widespread healing activity in . . . Herod's own territory (14:34–36). Our hypothetical reader could easily take this as confirmation that the narrator's guidance at 14:3 is to be taken at face value: after John's death, Jesus carried out a series of mighty works that eventually brought him to the attention of Herod himself. That is, because of its content, our reader is encouraged to see the remainder of Chapter 14 as part of an extended flashback, and thus to expect the closure of the flashback to come with the reappearance of Herod at some subsequent point in the narrative. Despite this auspicious beginning, however, the experiment in reading is doomed to failure. Herod himself does not reappear in the narrative at all. The only hint of his presence is the reference in 22:16 to the Herodians who accompany the Pharisees in an attempt to trap Jesus. While this action of Herod's followers is fully in keeping with what the reader expects of Herod himself, by this point it is clear to even the most docile and trusting reader that the flashback has not been explicitly resolved. Jesus' departure from Galilee for Judea (19:1) represents the last possible point at which the temporal lanes might merge. By the time the Herodians are confronting Jesus in Jerusalem, it is clear that the narrative time clock has advanced well beyond the point reached by 14:1. But while the project inevitably fails, it nevertheless has an effect on the experience of reading that makes the attempt worthwhile. Herod himself might not reappear, but other elements in the passage do, or at least are echoed in ways that our expectant reader would find highly suggestive. My point, then, is that although the reader's expectations are ultimately disconfirmed, the desire to look for closure serves to draw attention to several elements in the subsequent narrative and to increase their impact on the overall reading experience. . . . Included here are references to Jesus' spreading fame, speculations about his identity, similarities with John the Baptizer, and (less forcefully) opposition to Jesus on the part of ruling authorities in general. The presence of any of these elements would cause our reader's ears to prick up, alert to the possibility that the narrative is heading back into the thematic territory from which the flashback took its point of departure.

Source: Terence L. Donaldson, "'For Herod had arrested John' (Matt 14:3): Making Sense of an Unresolved Flashback," in *Studies in Religion/Sciences Religieuses* 28, 1 (1999), pp. 35–48.

www   You can read the whole article online.

Questions

1. *Explain in your own words how Donaldson urges us to read this flashback in its narrative context.*

2. *Explain in your own words how this flashback is to be understood, and how it operates in the narrative of Matthew.*

> ### Doing Narrative Reading Yourself
>
> 1. *Note that the Sermon on the Mount begins by saying that Jesus was teaching his disciples (5:1–2), and at its end says that Jesus was teaching the crowds (7:28–29). Can both be true? If they cannot be reconciled, how do you explain this, with either narrative or historical reading?*
>
> 2. *Read closely the last pericope in Matthew, 28:16–21, and explain the veiled conflict in characterization and plot that comes with "they worshipped him, but some doubted." What does this mean, and how might verses 18–20 point to a resolution of this conflict?*

Social Scientific Reading

The social scientific reading of Matthew confirms what historical criticism suggests: this is a community that is coping with change as Gentile "outsiders" believe in Jesus and become "insiders." One key to understanding this dynamic is found in Matthew's interpretation of women's "insider/outsider" status. They are insiders because they share in the Jewish tradition and heritage, but they are outsiders because they are not socially recognized in the same way as men. Nor do they participate in the key areas of church power that would enable them to help shape the tradition and make its values for women visible. Women are also both victims and survivors. This is especially evident of the women in the genealogy (chapter 1). In their stories from the Hebrew Bible, these women experienced danger, loss of relationships, and damage to their reputations, yet they managed to prevail over the most trying circumstances and contribute to the future of Israel. In a move that parallels their role in the history of Israel, Matthew's Gospel shows the way that "outsider" women begin to move to the inside and begin to make a contribution to the future of the church. Victims become survivors. This same movement takes place with Gentile men and women, who begin to move from the margins onto the main page. In addition to this social scientific critique of women, Warren Carter has shown that Matthew keeps up a running criticism of Roman power and offers a vision of God's reign that seeks to replace it (Carter 2000).

Social Scientific Reading at Work, 1
The Role of Class and Social Status and its Reversal (Matthew 20:25–28)

In this imaginative and informative work, Malina depicts fictional interactions between modern North Americans and first-century Jews in Palestine who share the basic social values of Mediterranean culture. Although these stories are fiction historically, they are nonfiction social-scientifically. Malina utilizes these interactions to demonstrate the sociocultural differences between our modern world and the world of ancient Palestine. The following "window on the ancient world" informs our understanding of class and social status and how this social background makes Jesus' teaching more radical than it might seem at first to modern North Americans.

Lauren Boulay's husband had been working in first-century Palestine for about five years. The couple bought a house and . . . she had a maid come in to clean and do the washing and ironing. Lauren treated the maid as a friend and paid her well.

Each morning she would leave out the clothes she wanted cleaned and ironed. When she returned, however, she discovered that her Mediterranean-Judean maid would only do certain dresses or blouses. When Lauren inquired why this was so, the maid replied that she didn't think a certain dress was attractive or that it was too early to wear sleeveless blouses. Lauren was very angry.

Why did the maid act this way?

The maid is testing Lauren to see what she can get away with. In first-century Palestine, maids generally have relatively low status. Many are slaves, the lowest status in the social system. As a result, they more or less expect that their owner will be formal with them. By treating the maid like a friend and thus not maintaining the needed distance between her and the maid, Lauren gave the impression that her own status was also relatively low. As a result, the maid began to disobey Lauren and was in effect trying to see how far she could go. . . .

The Synoptic tradition has the following: But Jesus called them to him and said, "You know that the rulers of the Gentiles lord it over them, and their great men exercise authority over them. It shall not be so among you; but whoever would be great among you must be your servant, and whoever would be first among you must be your slave; even as the Son of man came not to be served but to serve, and to give his life as a ransom for many" (Matt 20:25–28).

Questions

1. *What does the passage from Matthew say about the reversal of the social structure found in this story?*

2. *Is this definition of "first" and "last" workable in everyday life?*

Source: Bruce J. Malina, *Windows on the World of Jesus: Time Travel to Ancient Judea* (Louisville, KY: Westminster John Knox, 1993), pp. 39–40.

Social Scientific Reading at Work, 2
Jesus and Purity Rules in Matthew

In this more formal work than his Time Travels, *Malina lays out Jesus' opposition to purity rules as portrayed in Matthew.*

Just as God really has no need of sacrifices, so too God does not need purity rules to confine and hedge God in from the dishonor and outrage of human beings. God is perfect because God is open to all Israelites, both the good and the bad. Relative to God's distinctive people in God's holy land, "he makes his sun rise on the evil and on the good, and sends rain on the just and on the unjust" (Matt 5:45). Since God is open to all the covenanted people of Israel, to do God's will is to be open to one's fellow Israelites, whether good or bad, just as God is open to them. God's will, then, is the welfare of this people. Hence any interpretation of the purity rules should be in the direction of the welfare of Israel, not in the direction of simply maintaining the system in some mechanical way–at the level of hands and feet only. The purpose, the heart, must enter the picture.

For example, "Moses said, 'Honor your father and your mother'; and, 'He who speaks evil of father or mother, let him surely die'; but you say, 'If a man tells his father or his mother, What you would have gained from me is Corban' (That is, given to God)–then you no longer permit him to do anything for his father or mother" (Mark 7:10–12; also Matt 15:4–6, where God rather than Moses commands respect for parents). Jesus' contention is that this sort of interpretation, with parents' rights being reversible and overruled by a person's decision for God and the Temple, indicates lopsided priorities. The same holds for priorities in Temple sacrifice: "So if you are offering your gift at the altar, and there remember that your brother [fellow Israelite] has something against you, leave your gift there before the altar and go; first be reconciled to your brother, and then come and offer your gift" (Matt 5:22–23). Consequently, if purity rules are to facilitate access to God, and if the God to whom one wants access has human welfare as the main priority in the divine will for the chosen people, it follows that proper interpretation of purity rules must derive from giving primary consideration to relationship with one's fellows. This is what righteousness is about. For righteousness means proper interpersonal relationships with all those in one's society, between God and covenanted human beings and between human beings and their fellow human beings.

Questions

1. *Explain how Jesus' interpretation of purity rules leads to greater human "access to God," as Malina puts it.*

2. *What might this reading about Jews entail for Gentiles?*

Source: Bruce J. Malina, *The New Testament World: Insights from Cultural Anthropology* (Louisville, KY: Westminster, 1998), pp. 188–189.

Doing Social Scientific Reading Yourself

1. *Reflect on the love-hate relationship between Matthew's church and its Jewish neighbors in Matthew 23, particularly in regard to its positive opening and its negative "woes."*

2. *Critique this statement: "Matthew is more critical of purity rules than he is of other social scientific features such as kinship and honor/shame."*

Feminist Reading

Women in Matthew's Gospel do not seem particularly significant, especially when compared to the other Synoptics. This lack of prominence is often related to Matthew's real and implied audience; with its strongly Jewish identity, readers usually suppose that Matthew will not be as open to women as the Gentile-Christian Gospels of Mark and Luke. With a few notable exceptions, women in Matthew do not have speaking roles, and they usually appear as background personalities or in often silent association with men. The five discourses Matthew arranges to carry the weight of Jesus' teaching contain only a few references to women, even though they do not seem to be addressed only to men. One might conclude that Matthew expresses a traditionally patriarchal view of women who have little importance in the church or the life of Jesus. However, a closer examination of the roles they do play reveals a somewhat more complex picture. Matthew features women moving from the periphery to greater public involvement and from being victims and survivors to being disciples and leaders. From the genealogy of chapter 1 through the women at the empty tomb, Matthew presents women moving from the margins to the center.

Feminist Reading at Work, 1
Women in the Sermon on the Mount

The Sermon on the Mount (Matthew 5–7) is Matthew's longest and most influential collection of Jesus' teaching. Here Jane Kopas examines briefly what is explicitly said about women in the Sermon and traces an echo of its teaching in Matthew 22.

There is no mention of women again [after chapter 2] until chapter 5 in the Sermon on the Mount (5:27–32). While women are mentioned merely as an example, the example is significant because it involves a cultural criticism of the status of women. When the Gospel presents Jesus' discussion of divorce and adultery, the dignity of women (and perhaps even their rights) is clearly implied. Jesus says that anyone who looks at a woman lustfully commits adultery in his heart. Clearly the entire discussion of the collected sayings is geared toward the relation of action and faith.

Source: Jane Kopas, "Jesus and Women in Matthew," in *Theology Today* 47, 1 (1990), pp. 13–21.

But, at the same time, it undeniably insists that women are not to be regarded as objects to be discarded at will.

When Jesus discusses divorce in the same discourse (5:31–32), he says that a man who divorces his wife is responsible for putting her into a compromising situation, and that his relationship to her continues beyond any unilateral decision of his own. This is not as surprising as a parallel statement in Mark's Gospel. Mark states that if a man divorces his wife and marries another, he commits adultery, but also if she divorces him and marries another, she commits adultery (Mark 10:10–12). These intimations of equality pave the way for a more pervasive equality. They also invite the hearer to consider unexamined forms of violence, sexism, and racism that underlie the need for conversion. A later reference in the Gospel deals with a similar situation in which sexual prejudice is dissolved in light of an ultimate equality. The Sadducees, questioning Jesus about life after death in order to discredit belief in the resurrection, receive an added lesson (22:23–33). When asked to whom a widow, childless after seven marriages, will be married in heaven, Jesus replies that they do not understand the Scriptures or the power of God. The social and economic power of men and the derivative identity of women fall into new perspective in light of the Kingdom of God. "At the resurrection men and women do not marry; no, they are like the angels in heaven." That is to say, not only ideas about heaven but also the unexamined ideas about the roles of women and men must become subject to the new vision of the reign of God. Women no longer receive their identity from their subordination to men.

www   Follow the link to read the whole article online.

Questions

1. *Why do you think that Kopas looks to Mark's treatment of divorce in this essay on Matthew?*

2. *At the end of this reading, the author relates a (supposedly) single existence of all God's people in heaven to equality between men and women on earth. Do you think that equality on earth is necessarily dependent on singleness in heaven?*

Feminist and Cross-Cultural Reading at Work
A Third World Feminist Perspective on Matt 14:21–28

Matthew does not often highlight women, but when it does they are usually positive examples of faithful response to Jesus. In this excerpt, Ranjini Rebera offers a Third World feminist perspective on the Gentile woman in Matthew 14 who persists in asking Jesus to heal her daughter even after Jesus insults her as a "dog."

Source: Report of the Programme on Women and Rural Development of the World Council of Churches. In We Cannot Dream Alone, ed. Ranjini Rebera (Geneva: WCC Publications, 1990), pp. 72–76.

The woman came from somewhere near the cities of Tyre and Sidon and this made her a non-Jew, a Canaanite woman. To Jews, therefore, she was a second-class person. She was also a woman, and women had no standing in Jewish society. . . . Only the mother, who was closely involved with her sick daughter, knew the trauma, the anguish, and the need for healing for her child. This gave her the selfless courage needed to face Jesus.

- At the first confrontation Jesus is silent. To us, this is out of character for Jesus, who went about ministering to people's needs. One wonders if Jesus was reacting in a traditionally male manner by being silent in the face of confrontation.
- The disciples attempted to send her away by giving Jesus negative advice: "Send her away! She is following us and making all this noise." A typical reference to women who become too insistent and forceful even today.
- When Jesus finally speaks to the woman, he seems to be on the defensive: "I have been sent only to the lost sheep of the people of Israel." It is hard to know what Jesus meant by this statement. He could have reverted to his Jewish traditions by stating his mission within the context of the Jewish race. The woman was an outsider in this situation.
- The commitment of the woman to gain healing for her daughter and her tenacity in the face of opposition gives her the wisdom to use other means. She appeals to the compassionate side of Jesus' nature: "Lord, help me!"
- Jesus continues to speak as an elitist Jew: "It isn't right to take the children's food and throw it to the dogs."
- The woman does not give in. Her resourcefulness leads her into the realm of debate: "Yes, Lord, that's true, but even the dogs eat the leftovers that fall from the master's table." Her argument is strong and forceful and she has a valid point. Jesus may belong to a superior race, but even dogs have rights and will not be denied scraps from the table.
- Jesus seems to capitulate. The woman's commitment, forcefulness, and intelligence seem to have triumphed. Jesus sums up: "What you want will be done for you." Her daughter is healed.

Questions

1. *How has Rebera combined feminist reading and cross-cultural reading in this excerpt?*

Doing Feminist Reading Yourself

1. *Comparing Matthew's treatment of women to Mark's, what are the important changes Matthew makes, and why? Look in particular at Matthew's divorce texts compared to Mark's, as outlined by Kopas here and more fully by David Instone-Brewer (via the website).*

2. *From any main section of the Sermon on the Mount, indicate how Jesus' teaching for all his disciples might impact specifically on women, in his time and today.*

2. Compare Matthew's telling of this story to Mark's (7:24–30). Does the different material in Matthew have any bearing on feminist criticism? How?

Cross-Cultural Reading

Of all the canonical Gospels, Matthew wrestles the most with cross-cultural barriers and how to overcome them. To read between its lines, this Gospel moves with some struggle from an exclusively Jewish following of Jesus, then to an originally exclusively Jewish-Christian church, and finally to a widening of this identity to include Gentiles in all the nations. In this process, Matthew is concerned that the unity of the church be preserved by everyone's following together the same basic gospel message and its moral implications.

Cross-cultural reading has looked first to Mark and Luke, because these Gospels are obviously Gentile-Christian, and have successfully crossed cultural and religious barriers. Now cross-cultural readers are turning to Matthew. Because it shows a community struggling with matters of culture and faith, Matthew could prove to be the most fruitful Gospel for showing how cross-cultural reading of an ancient Christian text can enable modern peoples of faith to cross their own cultural divides.

Cross-Cultural Reading at Work
Divine Justice in Matthew 7:21

Cross-cultural reading has taught us the importance of knowing one's own social location and how it impacts the way we read the Bible. This treatment of Matthew 7:21 from the location of African American slaves shows how a reading of Matthew's strong ideas of righteousness can help oppressed peoples cope.

The theme of divine retributive justice for the oppressor . . . sounds in other spirituals. For instance, in the spiritual "All God's Chillun Got Shoes," after making the claim to having those resources which are presently illegitimately denied to us here on earth,

> *I got shoes, you got shoes,*
> *All God's Chillun got shoes,*

and after affirming the claim to receiving those resources at a future time,

> *When I get to Heb'n*
> *I'm gonna put on my shoes*

there is the disclaimer that,

> *Everyone talkin' 'bout Heb'n isn't goin' der!*

Source: Randall C. Bailey, "The Danger of Ignoring One's Own Cultural Bias in Interpreting the Text," in R. S. Sugirtharajah, ed., *The Postcolonial Bible* (Sheffield, UK: Sheffield Academic Press, 1998), p. 69. Reprinted by permission of the Continuum International Publishing Group.

I can imagine my fore-parents standing outside the white folks' churches with the horses and carriages, not allowed into the church of their slave-owning oppressors. "You may be inside the church praying to your God, but in the end you ain't goin' to Heb'n, cause of de way you treatin' us." . . . This is a faith affirmation in the spirit of 'Not everyone who says to me, "Lord, Lord," will enter the kingdom of heaven' (Matt 7:21).

Questions

1. *How might this affirmation of divine justice at the end of time affect the relationship of slaves and slaveowners in NT times and today?*

2. *Can the other-worldly orientation of many oppressed Christian peoples, here African American slaves, illustrate for us the eschatological orientation of most early Christians? Give your reasons.*

Doing Cross-Cultural Reading Yourself

1. *Perhaps the most affirmative statement on crossing cultural barriers is the end of Matthew (28:16–20). Give it a close reading, and state how this "final word" of the Gospel relates to what goes before in terms of cross-cultural reading.*

2. *Outline what for you are the main opportunities for, and impediments against, cultural liberation that come from Matthew.*

Key Terms and Concepts

antitheses • apostles • beatitudes • celibate • fulfillment quotations
Great Commission • infancy narrative • Lord's Prayer/Our Father
magi • M • Sermon on the Mount • virginal conception of Jesus

Questions for Study, Discussion, and Writing

1. To judge from the contents of Matthew, why might it be appropriate as the first book of the Christian Testament, the first to follow the Hebrew Bible/Old Testament?
2. Discuss what we can know about the author of Matthew. Why do most scholars conclude that this Gospel was not written by one of Jesus' twelve disciples?
3. Could Matthew have been written by a woman? Give your reasons.
4. Express as clearly as you can how Matthew's Gospel advocates a combination of the best of Judaism and of Jesus. In particular, how does Matthew offer advice to a divided (Jewish and Gentile) community? How might this advice be applicable to other, analogous situations today (over today's ethnic, racial, or even gender orientation issues)?

5. Explain in your own words the narrative impact of Matthew's alternating panels of teaching and action. For example, why is the teaching panel first? Why is the narrative action unrelated to the themes of the teaching panels?
6. Do you think that Matthew is overall a positive or negative resource for the liberation of women today? Defend your answer.
7. What does Matthew's vision of the Kingdom of Heaven/God as a social reality embracing all dimensions of life have to say to our contemporary North American society, which is based on a much more individualistic notion of religion and spirituality?
8. Look again at the passages in the Sermon on the Mount in which Jesus warns against hypocrisy. Why does Jesus condemn it so strongly and so often? How could this have been a continuing problem in the church?

For Further Reading

Aune, David E., ed. *The Gospel of Matthew in Current Study.* Grand Rapids, MI: Eerdmans, 2001. An excellent introduction to Matthew. The essay by the Jewish scholar Amy-Jill Levine, "Matthew's Advice to a Divided Readership," is particularly good.

Carter, Warren. *Matthew and the Margins: A Sociopolitical and Religious Reading.* Maryknoll, NY: Orbis, 2000. A lively study of Matthew that combines cross-cultural and social-scientific methods.

Gallardo, Carlos B. "Matthew: Good News for the Persecuted Poor," in Leif E. Vaage, ed., *Subversive Scriptures: Revolutionary Readings of the Christian Bible in Latin America.* Valley Forge, PA: Trinity Press International, 1997, pp. 173–192. A cross-cultural and historical reading of Matthew on this important topic.

Kingsbury, J. D. *Matthew as Story.* Philadelphia: Fortress, 1986. An influential narrative analysis of Matthew.

LaGrand, James. *The Earliest Christian Mission to All Nations in the Light of Matthew's Gospel.* Grand Rapids, MI: Eerdmans, 1998. A study of how Matthew presents the change from an exclusive mission to Jews to embracing a mission to all nations.

Levine, Amy-Jill, ed., with Marianne Blickenstaff. *A Feminist Companion to Matthew* Sheffield, UK: Sheffield Academic Press, 2001. A collection of essays on feminist issues.

Luz, Ulrich. *The Theology of the Gospel of Matthew.* Cambridge: Cambridge University Press, 1995. Nine chapters, succinct and readable, based on the author's commentary on Matthew.

Malina, Bruce J., and Richard L. Rohrbaugh. *Social-Science Commentary on the Synoptic Gospels,* 2nd ed. Minneapolis: Fortress, 2003. For each passage in Matthew, a brief social scientific commentary drawing largely on cultural anthropology is offered; an excellent resource for students.

Senior, Donald. *Matthew.* Nashville, TN: Abingdon, 1998. A concise commentary on Matthew, especially good on the historical context of the Gospel.

The Gospel of Luke: Following Jesus, the Savior of the World

The third Gospel of the NT canon, traditionally called the Gospel of Luke, is the first half of the two-volume work by the same author that concludes with the Acts of the Apostles. The longest of the four Gospels, Luke is also the most literarily polished. It contains more parables than any other Gospel, and half of its contents are unique to Luke. It presents Jesus as Messiah ("Christ") of Israel and shows a good knowledge of and appreciation for Judaism. Luke also portrays Jesus as a humble servant of God for all people, modeling values of humility, prayerfulness, and spirituality. At the same time, Jesus is the divine Lord of the world who will send his message into the whole world. For narrative readers, the author weaves a well-developed theology into the carefully structured story, which stretches in Luke-Acts from the conception of Jesus in the Gospel to the imprisonment of Paul in Rome in the Acts. For feminist readers, Luke has been seen as highly positive toward fuller roles for women, but some recent feminist criticism has questioned this reading. Luke has a special concern for the marginalized, which makes it a favorite resource for cross-cultural criticism, and offers a treatment of different social groups than the other Gospels, which endears it to social scientific criticism. Luke has probably shaped the view of modern people to Jesus, both Christians and those not Christians, more than any other Gospel.

Luke in Brief: Outline of Structure and Contents

I. Prologue (1:1–4)

II. Conception, birth, and childhood of John the Baptizer and Jesus (1:5–2:52)

    A. Conceptions of John and Jesus (1:5–56)

    B. Births of John and Jesus (1:57–2:40)

    C. The boy Jesus in the Temple (2:41–52)

III. Preaching of John, Jesus' baptism, Jesus' genealogy, temptations (3:1–4:13)

IV. Galilean ministry (4:14–9:50)

A. Rejection at Nazareth; ministry around Capernaum (4:14–5:16)
B. Wider teaching, controversies, miracles; naming the Twelve; two passion predictions; transfiguration (5:17–9:50)
V. Journey to Jerusalem, the center section (9:51–19:27)
A. The first mention of Jerusalem; ministry and teaching about discipleship on the way (9:51–13:21)
B. The second mention; more ministry on the way (13:22–17:10)
C. The third mention; ministry until arrival in Jerusalem (17:11–19:27)
VI. Ministry in Jerusalem (19:28–21:38)
A. Entry (19:28–21:4)
B. Teachings on the end of time (21:5–38)
VII. Conspiracy against Jesus; Last Supper; arrest, Jewish and Roman trials, death and burial (Chapters 22–23)
VIII. Resurrection
A. Women disciples at the empty tomb (24:1–12)
B. Appearances of the risen Jesus on road to Emmaus and in Jerusalem; ascent to heaven (24:13–53)

Developing Your Skills: Reading Luke-Acts as a Whole

Read rapidly through Luke in one sitting, concentrating on the overall contents and shape of the whole document, not the details. If you have read Mark or Matthew recently, try to put them out of your memory as you read Luke. After you have read Luke, skim through the Acts of the Apostles.

A Guide to Reading

The **prologue** (1:1–4) tells the audience about the purpose and general organization of both Luke and Acts. The author states that many writers have set down "the events which have occurred among us," and now he too will write it. The source for this material is a previous generation: the original "eyewitnesses and servants of the word." These events include not just the story of Jesus in the Gospel, but the story of the early church in Acts. The author has traced these events with care and ordered them more carefully, both historically and theologically. The goal is spelled out to "most excellent Theophilus," perhaps the author's aristocratic patron: assurance that the Christian instruction that had been given him is true.

The first main section of Luke's gospel is the **infancy narrative**, dealing with the conception, birth, and childhood of both John the Baptizer and Jesus (1:5 through the end of chapter 2). Luke begins his narrative at 1:5 with the conception of John

the Baptizer, who will play the role of a new Elijah (1:17), the one who according to the last prophetic book of the Hebrew Bible, Malachi, will be sent before the coming Day of the Lord. An unnamed angel brings good news of a baby to the aged Zechariah and his wife Elizabeth, a baby who will grow up to be John the Baptizer, but the angel Gabriel brings the truly Good News to the virginal Mary who is astonished by the idea of her impending pregnancy. This conception will not come by human reproduction, as John's conception did, but by the action of the Spirit of God. Gabriel says two things about the child to be born of Mary. First, the expectations of Israel will be fulfilled in him as the Messiah. Second, the expectations of Israel will be far exceeded, for he will be the unique Son of God in power through the Holy Spirit. When Mary visits Elizabeth and these two relatives share their news with each other, Elizabeth reacts to Mary's news by blessing her as the mother of the Messiah and as one who has believed the Lord's word. (Note how Luke's cast of characters in these opening two chapters features women prominently and positively.)

Four moving **canticles** (religious songs of praise to God) are a part of this section, punctuating the narrative with music as in a modern opera or musical. The Magnificat ("[My soul] magnifies") is spoken by Mary (1:46–55) to her cousin Elizabeth. This canticle is especially meaningful because having heard who her child would be, she speaks about good news for the lowly and the hungry, and bad news for the powerful and the rich. This will be a favorite Lukan theme in his presentation of Jesus' ministry. The "Blessed be the Lord God" is spoken by Zechariah the father of John (1:67–78). The short "Glory to God in the highest" is sung by the angels at Jesus' birth (2:13–14), and the "Now let your servant depart" is sung by the priest Simeon in the Temple when he sees the baby Jesus (2:28–32). Their christology is implicit, proclaiming that God is now fulfilling his promises but never explicitly revealing Jesus' upcoming work.

In chapter 2, a broad setting for the birth of Jesus is supplied by the decree of Caesar Augustus for a census of the whole world. To comply with the census, Joseph and Mary travel from their home in Nazareth to Bethlehem, the ancestral town of King David and his descendants. While they are there, Jesus is born and laid in a humble feed trough (2:1–7). Angels appear to lowly shepherds, calling them to visit the newborn Jesus, which they do with joy (2:8–20). On the eighth day after his birth, Jesus is circumcised and formally named (2:21); Jesus' parents faithfully observe the Jewish law of circumcision and the angel's command to name their son Jesus ("God saves"). These same two themes are also seen in the presentation of Jesus in the Temple when his mother undergoes the ritual for purification after childbirth (2:22–40): Jesus' parents were faithful to the Law, and Jesus was accepted as Messiah by the priest Simeon and the prophet Anna, representatives of devout Jews waiting for the fulfillment of God's promises to Israel. Nevertheless, the coming of Jesus will be a mixed blessing, because the light that is "a glory for Israel" and its "rising" will also cause the fall of many in Israel (2:32, 34). Even the mother of Jesus is not exempt from this mixed blessing, as Simeon ominously says to her that "a sword shall pierce your own soul also." By placing the story of the precocious boy Jesus in the Temple (2:41–52) between his infancy and ministry, Luke has bridged them in a way that focuses on the identity of Jesus as the Son of God. Jesus is the Son who "must be in my Father's house." Already his sense of special connection to God is loosening his social kinship with his family, and this loosening of traditional kinship bonds and forming of new kinship will accelerate for Jesus and his followers in his public ministry.

Chapters 3 and 4 present Jesus' preparation for his ministry in baptism and temptation. We see Luke's feel for history and theology in the transitional section used to mark the beginning of the period of Jesus and the Gospel (3:1–2). It is dated (in our chronology, about 29 or 30 C.E.) by the reigns of the Roman emperor Tiberius, the Roman governor Pontius Pilate, the Jewish client kings and the Jewish high priests. John the Baptizer's preaching ministry (3:1–20), which introduces the period of Jesus, fulfills Gabriel's prediction to Zechariah in Luke 1. John's teaching in 3:7–14, with its emphasis on sharing goods, justice for the poor, and kindness, anticipates a Lukan theme in the ministry of Jesus and in the earliest Jerusalem church. Luke 3:15 raises the issue of whether John the Baptizer was the Messiah, introducing John's preaching about the one to come, who is Jesus (3:16–18). Then 3:19–20 reports that Herod imprisoned John the Baptizer, thus finishing his ministry before Jesus' ministry begins, which serves to differentiate them. When John baptizes Jesus, Jesus prays, the first mention of a favorite Lukan motif, and the Holy Spirit descends "in bodily form" as a dove, probably a Lukan expression to stress actuality (3:21–22). Luke pauses here to recount Jesus' genealogy, which is traced all the way back to Adam to suggest that all humanity will be impacted by Jesus (3:23–38). The testing of Jesus by the Devil, the chief evil spirit also called Satan (4:1–13), is introduced by the statement that Jesus was "full of [God's] Spirit," an emphasis on the prominent role of the Spirit in the ministry of Jesus and in Acts. Over a forty-day period in the wilderness, Satan tempts Jesus to betray himself and his mission–by performing self-serving miracles, by making a deal with the Devil to share power, and by testing God to rescue him–but Jesus is true to God. The rejection of these three temptations shows what kind of ministry Jesus will have: one that refuses to use his miraculous power merely to impress others; one that makes no compromise with evil, but fights it consistently; and one that faithfully relies on God. Luke concludes that when Satan's effort to get Jesus to betray himself failed, he left Jesus "until an opportune time," tipping off the reader to look for Satan's return later, when others will betray Jesus.

With its strong sense of narrative setting, Luke calls attention to Jesus' return to Galilee to start his ministry (4:14), which lasts until Jesus' departure for Jerusalem (9:51). Between these two points, Luke places most of his account of Jesus' public ministry. Jesus has a powerful ministry of healing and teaching, especially directed to the socially and religiously marginalized. Luke uses repeated short summaries to keep the reader focussed on Jesus' bringing of God's kingdom in his words and

deeds (4:14–15; 4:44; 5:15; 7:17; 8:1–3). He also weaves into this section the beginnings of conflict, as Jesus' message and deeds encounter opposition (4:14–30; 5:17–21, 30; 6:7; 7:31–35, 44–49). Luke begins this Galilean ministry section on a pessimistic note, the rejection of Jesus at Nazareth (4:14–30). Jesus comments on the scroll of the prophet Isaiah, portraying himself from then on as the anointed, Messianic prophet promised in Isa 61:1–2 who will bring justice and peace. However, Jesus is rejected as a prophet by his own hometown. The fury of the people against Jesus, even to the point of trying to kill him, is an early sign of what eventually will befall Jesus at the instigation of his own people, how at the end of this long section Jesus will go to Jerusalem to meet his fate. Jesus' implication that God will transfer his favor away from the covenant people becomes definitive for the entire Luke-Acts work, in which the other peoples and nations of the world will gradually take the place of those Jews who reject the covenant.

Luke narrates four activities connected with Capernaum (4:31–44), which now becomes Jesus' home and the base of operations for his Galilean ministry. Jesus' first miracle is an exorcism; even though Jesus has turned away the temptations of the Devil, he still must struggle against many demons. The healing of Peter's mother-in-law (4:38–39) shows Jesus' care for his disciples and his respect for the social life of the family. After Luke offers a summary of Jesus' deeds at Capernaum (4:40–41), Jesus goes to a deserted place, looking for rest and prayer, a typical move in Luke (4:42–44).

Luke then narrates a miraculous catch of fish granted by Jesus and Jesus' call to the disciples to follow him (5:1–11). Impressed by the catch of fish and Jesus' divine power, Simon confesses himself an unworthy sinner in a dramatic presentation of divine calling to Jesus' disciples to become "catchers of people," that is, those who bring people into Jesus' movement. The theme of the disciples' leaving "everything" to follow Jesus illustrates Luke's stress on indifference to possessions (5:11). Luke then narrates the healing of a leper, emphasizing his theme of the importance of prayer (5:12–16). Next comes a series of five controversies in which Pharisees play a role, largely by criticizing Jesus' actions (5:17–6:11). The controversies involve (1) Jesus' forgiving the sin of a paralyzed man whom he healed, (2) Jesus' table fellowship (**commensality**) with notorious sinners like Levi the tax collector, now a disciple of Jesus, (3) Jesus' refusal to make his disciples fast while he is with them, saying that they will fast when he is gone, (4) picking grain on the Sabbath and (5) healing on the Sabbath. After the call of Levi, the anger of the Pharisees is also directed against Jesus' disciples (Luke 5:30); the whole movement has come into conflict with the religious establishment. The controversies about the Sabbath—picking grain and healing—show Jesus' command over the Sabbath. This controversy leads Jesus' enemies to begin actively plotting against him (Luke 6:11).

Luke now turns to the favorable side of the reaction to Jesus. He begins with Jesus' choosing of the Twelve, whose names are given (6:12–16). The Twelve are with Jesus when he heals all the sick among the crowds on a plain (6:17–19). Four Lukan

beatitudes (divine blessings upon faithful people) open the short **Sermon on the Plain** in the rest of chapter 6. This sermon is addressed not to the crowds, who have come from Jewish and Gentile areas to hear Jesus, but to Jesus' disciples. These beatitudes address those among Jesus' followers who are physically and socially (not just "spiritually") poor, hungry, mournful, and socially rejected. The accompanying **woes** warn of condemnation at the last judgment for people who are rich, full, happy and socially respected. Luke 6:27–36 emphasizes Jesus' disciples must love and forgive those who hate and abuse them. The command not to judge others is an illustration of this love (6:37–42). The demands are not met by those who simply say "Lord, Lord" to Jesus and do not obey his instructions, as illustrated by a concluding parable of the Wise and Foolish Builders (6:43–49).

This sermon is followed by healing miracles. The healing of the Roman centurion's slave contrasts a Gentile's faith in Jesus with the Jewish authorities' rejection of him (7:1–10). The next miracle, the raising of the son of the widow of Nain (7:11–17), is a breathtaking manifestation of power that shows his compassionate care for a mother deprived of her only son. Luke then portrays a scene with John the Baptizer that clarifies his relationship to Jesus (7:18–35). Perhaps as a continuation of Jesus' response to the objection to his fondness for eating and drinking (7:34), Luke skillfully narrates, in the context of eating at the table of Simon the Pharisee, a moving story involving a penitent sinful woman who weeps over and anoints Jesus' feet (7:36–50). After the story of this woman, Luke portrays the women followers of Jesus, who had been cured of evil spirits and diseases. Three of them are named: Mary Magdalene, Joanna, wife of King Herod's steward, and Susanna (8:1–3). Mary Magdalene and Joanna will reappear at the empty tomb on Easter morning (24:10). Luke reports that they generously served the needs of Jesus and the Twelve out of their financial resources, evidently considerable. A short collection of parables and teaching about parables follows. Luke first recounts the parable of the Sower and the Seed, the purpose of all the parables, and the interpretation of the sower (8:4–15). A hundredfold yield is mentioned, and this yield is those who hear the word, hold it fast in an honest and good heart, and bring forth fruit with patience (8:15). Parabolic sayings centered on the lamp (8:16–18) also end on the theme of hearing in understanding and faith. This leads into the arrival of Jesus' mother and brothers, who do not understand or believe at this point, which Jesus takes as an occasion to redefine kinship in the new social order he is constructing (8:19–21).

Luke now gives a series of four remarkable miracle stories (8:22–56): Jesus calms a storm at sea, heals a Gerasene demoniac, brings Jairus' dead daughter back to life, and heals a woman with a long-term flow of blood. Then Jesus sends out the Twelve, giving them his authority to preach the gospel and heal (9:1–6), activities that will dominate the narrative of Acts. While the Twelve are away, we are told briefly of Herod's beheading of John the Baptizer (9:7–9). When the Twelve return and Jesus feeds the 5,000 (9:10–17), the Gospel writer reports flawed popular conclusions about who Jesus is and gives Peter's accurate conclusion about him as Messiah (9:18–20). Peter's profession of Jesus as Messiah is greeted by Jesus' first prediction of his death and resurrection, showing what sort of Messiah he is (9:21–22). Since Jesus must suffer before God will resurrect him to glory, his followers must also "take up their cross daily" if they hope to share in his glory (9:23–27). The **transfiguration** of Jesus, or change in his normal appearance into a heavenly, glorified body (9:28–36), is set in the context of Jesus' praying, just as his baptism was. This transfiguration describes that glory as already present in Jesus' earthly career (9:32). Yet it also affirms the suffering that is to come, for Jesus talks to Moses and Elijah about his "exodus," that is, as the reader already understands, his departure to God through death and resurrection. This death and resurrection will be a new exodus for Israel that will bring salvation to the whole world. In the story of a demon-possessed boy, Jesus heals the boy after his disciples could not (9:37–43). Jesus then predicts his passion and resurrection a second time (9:43b–45), and Luke implies that the disciples did not understand it because God had hidden it from them. This failure to understand leads to a dispute over which of them was the greatest; Jesus points to being like a child, with its low social status, as the way to true greatness (9:46–48). Not only is the most humble person inside Jesus' disciples the greatest, but even an outsider who uses Jesus' name in healing has a place in his mission to the world (9:49–50).

Now Luke's long **center section** begins, extending from 9:51 to 19:27. The time is coming for Jesus to be taken up to heaven, and so he "sets his face" for Jerusalem, where he is to die, and travels steadily there. Even though Jesus' face and Luke's narrative is "set" for his death, this section often talks about other things not directly related to his journey to death and resurrection: the coming of God's salvation in Jesus to the marginalized; regular strong conflict between Jesus and Jewish authorities; and teaching for the disciples to be faithful and effective, now with the time after Jesus is gone in view. In the first subsection of this center section, from the first to the second mention of Jerusalem as Jesus' destination (9:51–13:21), Luke first portrays a hostile encounter with a Samaritan village (9:51–56). Jesus refuses to take vengeance upon the Samaritans, as urged by James and John. A conversation with three would-be followers highlights the absolute new kinship demands imposed by the kingdom (9:57–62). Luke then introduces a second mission to follow up the first in 9:1–10, Jesus' sending of seventy-two disciples (10:1–12). The need for a second mission of a much larger group is explained by the large size of the harvest. It also indicates Luke's strong interest in having all of Jesus' disciples carrying on his ministry, not just the Twelve; this will resurface in Acts. The proclamation that "the kingdom of God has come near" has an implication of judgment, following as it does Jesus' woes to cities that refuse to accept him (10:13–16). When the seventy-two return, Jesus rejoices at the defeat of the demons (10:17–20). Then Jesus thanks the Father for revelation (10:21–22). That the disciples have been chosen by the Son to receive the revelation is shown in Jesus' blessing of the disciples (10:23–24), a blessing that acknowledges what they have seen. Luke's next episode involves a lawyer's question about eternal life and Jesus' response about the love of God and neighbor (10:25–28). Although the lawyer is posing a test, Jesus likes his answer; and that leads into the parable of the Good Samaritan (10:29–37). Jesus chooses a Samaritan outsider, despite the earlier incident of unbelieving Samaritans in chapter 9, to illustrate fulfillment of the Jewish law in unlimited love for others. In the story of Martha and Mary (10:38–42), hearing and heeding the word of Jesus is the only important thing, far more important than a woman's serving food and other material needs, which counteracts Luke's typical portrait of women serving Jesus. Another question comes from an inquiring disciple about prayer, and the Lord's Prayer (11:1–4) is given as an answer. This encouragement to pray is illustrated by the parable of the insistent friend (11.5–8), a story that envisions a socially humble family in a single-room house. Jesus again urges persistence in prayer (11:9–13).

After this happy section where Jesus has been teaching his disciples, Luke shapes an unhappy controversy passage and sayings about Satan (11:14–26). The struggle between the strong man (Beelzebul, or Satan) and the stronger one (Jesus) has been going on all through Jesus' ministry, but 11:12–23 anticipates the climax of this struggle soon to take place at Jerusalem. Jesus then corrects the socially traditional blessing on him from the Jewish mother in the crowd, because Jesus has his own system of "family values" (11:27–28). The warning signs for this generation, parabolic sayings about light, and woes to the Pharisees follow (11:29–12:1). Jesus' exhortation to his followers to speak fearlessly about him promises reward for those who proclaims the truth, but warns of judgment for one who does not (12:2–12). Although Luke emphasizes God's forgiveness, he warns of the unforgivable blasphemy against the Holy Spirit (12:10). Jesus assures his disciples that the Holy Spirit will show them what to say when they face hostile synagogue and secular authorities (Luke 12:11–12), a recurring event in Acts. Next, the pericope warning against greed and the parable of the Rich Farmer (12:13–21) are typically Lukan. Jesus' followers are to live by his proverb, "Life does not depend on what one possesses." A passage denouncing cares about earthly things (12:22–34) shows how freedom from such cares leads to a richer, more fulfilled life in God's kingdom, which has abundance to spare.

Luke now changes the topic to eschatology. Jesus explains the necessity of faithful watchfulness for the end of time (12:35–48). That distinction leads into a frightening description of the diverse results of Jesus' ministry (12:49–53). In eschatological language Jesus speaks of the fire he is to bring on the earth and about the baptism of being tested that is his destiny and the destiny of his disciples. Division, not peace, will be the result, and even families will be split—in the ancient Mediterranean, the worst form of social division. Jesus then expresses indignation at people's inability to read the signs of the times, an indignation meant to encourage them to develop this ability (12:54–56). Examples of destruction are then given to persuade the listener to repent (13:1–5). The parable of the Fig Tree (13:6–9), in which the tree is given one more chance to bear fruit before being cut down, suggests that repentance is still possible as the end nears. Jesus teaches in a synagogue and compassionately heals a crippled woman on the Sabbath (13:10–17), a deed whose timing makes the head of the synagogue angry. Although the healing causes rejoicing among the people, it shames the authorities and in this context of Luke illustrates that some will not repent as their end approaches. Nevertheless, the twin parables of the Mustard Seed and the Leaven (13:18–21) assure Jesus' followers that the kingdom will ultimately be great despite its small beginnings.

Between the second and third mentions of Jerusalem in this Center Section (13:22–17:10), opposition to Jesus intensifies as Jesus gets closer to his destination. Luke opens this subsection with a question about how many will be saved. This question leads to Jesus' teaching on exclusion from and acceptance into the kingdom (13.22–30), the ultimate "outsiders" and "insiders." Typical for Jesus' teaching is a reversal of human social values: many who may claim to know Jesus, supposedly "insiders," will be shut out, while "outsiders" from all over the world who follow Jesus' way will get in. The report of some Pharisees about Herod's plot against Jesus' life and his answer to this report (13:31–33) dramatize the reason for Jesus' going on to Jerusalem: to meet his death there. Jesus' thoughts about this lead to his lament over Jerusalem (13:34–35). Jesus will die there as a prophet, but the city will be severely punished for what it does to the prophets and to Jesus. The next three episodes are set in the home of a prominent Pharisee: the Sabbath cure of an ill man, two instructions about conduct at dinner, and the parable of the Great Banquet (14:1–24). The first instruction about table conduct—on not taking the privileged place at dinner—comes close to shrewd social manners, especially if one's goal is enjoying greater honor at table (Luke 14:10). Yet it does urge humility instead of self-honor, a notable theme of Jesus' teaching in Luke. The second instruction, to invite the disadvantaged rather than one's privileged peers, agrees with the reversed values of the kingdom or reign of God, where the poor are more important than the rich. The eschatological outlook is explicit in Jesus' promise of due reward at the resurrection. The parable of the Great Banquet rejects those who were first invited, because they had priorities that they put before the invitation to the kingdom. Then Luke shows Jesus talking to the great multitudes who accompanied him about counting the cost of discipleship (14:25–35), with wisdom parables about the need to calculate the cost as a wise person does before building a house or waging a war (14:28–32).

The next chapter consists of three parables about finding lost things: the Lost Sheep, the Lost Coin, and the Lost Son (15:1–32). Despite the traditional titles of these parables, they are really about God, who finds and rescues the lost. We see here how Jesus' parables of God's love were aimed at some humans' lack of love for the lost, and how these parables about love are narrative-within-the narrative attacks on Jesus' opponents. In the first two, Luke features a man and woman, respectively (shepherd, housekeeper), who leave the normal tasks of life to find what has been lost. The parable of the "Prodigal" (squandering, not wandering) Son stresses that repentance is always possible, and that the self-righteous elder brother should not object to the father's forgiving treatment of the repentant younger brother. The picture of the father running to the younger son and kissing him in welcome before the son can finish his statement of repentance is one of the most moving scenes in the parables of Jesus. The parable of the Unjust Steward that follows seems to commend crooked business practices; but what is praised is the steward's prudent, energetic initiative, not his dishonesty (16:1–15). Luke attaches diverse sayings about wealth to the parable, perhaps in an effort to interpret it. These sayings serve Luke's theological theme that material abundance corrupts human life and that the right way to use wealth is to give it away. At the end of the pericope, vv. 14–15 shift to challenging the Pharisees, who are "lovers of money" and who honor themselves before others. In his sayings about the Law and divorce (16:16–18), Jesus contradicts OT legal codes, appealing to Genesis to show God's original intent in the creation that marriage be permanent. The theme of the evil influence of wealth returns in the parable of the rich man and Lazarus (16:19–31). Their different fates after death are not based on the rich man's having lived a life of vice and Lazarus' having been very virtuous. Rather, they are based on the rich man's having had a comfortable and well-fed life with no concern for the poor at his gate, whereas Lazarus was hungry and miserable (16:25). This attack on the Pharisees' love of money is made sharper at the end of the parable: if they do not listen to Moses and the prophets, they will not listen to someone come back from the dead. To Luke's audience, this would appear prophetic, for Acts will show that people did not listen even after Jesus himself came back from the dead. The topic changes as Jesus addresses to his disciples four unrelated warnings on behavior (17:1–10). Cautioning against alienating others, these warnings stress forgiving fellow disciples, the power of faith, and the distinction between great achievement and duty. The disciples who have followed Jesus might get the idea that they had done something great, but they are to "keep themselves humble" by reminding themselves that they are like slaves who have only done their duty.

We now enter with Jesus the last stage of his journey to Jerusalem in the center section of Luke (17:11–19:27). It begins with the cleansing of the ten lepers, including the thankful Samaritan (17:11–19). Jesus is passing near or through Samaritan territory, and there is a Samaritan among the Jewish lepers, perhaps an example of acceptance among fellow outcasts. He becomes the only leper healed by Jesus who shows gratitude and thus receives a salvation beyond physical healing. Jesus now gives to the Pharisees and then to his disciples a short eschatological teaching (17:20–37) that anticipates the longer eschatological discourse to be presented in chapter 21. The teaching warns against being deceived by spurious claims that the full reign of God has visibly arrived or by believing and living as if there will never be a judgment. Both of these were temptations in early Christianity known to the author of Luke-Acts. Luke stresses that the reign or kingdom of God cannot be observed and is already present in some significant sense; God's judgment is unpredictably selective, choosing one person and sparing another (17:31).

In face of this judgment, the parable of the unjust judge (18:1–8) encourages the disciples to be persistent in prayer. If continued petitioning persuades a totally amoral, uncaring judge to do the right thing, how much more will God hear their persistent, confident prayer. The theme of prayer leads into the Lukan parable of the Pharisee and the Tax Collector (18:9–14). Although his moral superiority condemns him, the Pharisee has indeed lived faithful to God's commandments as he understood them. This example of God's graciousness to the tax collector leads Luke to recount Jesus' kindness to little children (18:15–17), who again serve as a model of complete dependence on God for entering the kingdom. In turn this leads to the rich ruler's question of what is necessary for eternal life and the obstacle offered by riches (18:18–30). Even those who observe the commandments must be challenged to go farther to enter the kingdom. As an incentive to this sacrifice, Luke 18:30 promises that those who sacrifice in following him will receive "many times as much" in this life in many different ways. Jesus then restates his own sacrifice in the third prediction of the passion (18:31–34).

As Jesus comes near Jericho, the last city before Jerusalem, his ministry continues as he heals a blind man (18:35–43). Then Jesus befriends Zacchaeus, a tax collector and sinner, and brings him to repentance (19:1–10). The story dramatizes Luke's attitude toward wealth: Zacchaeus is a rich man, and in this world riches are immorally gained at the expense of others. But salvation can come to his house because he gives half his possessions to the poor as an act of repentance. The theme of correct use of wealth continues in the parable of the Pounds (19:11–27). The nobleman goes away and gives each of ten servants a pound; one of the servants turns it into ten pounds, another into five pounds, and a third simply preserves it. This challenges the disciples to make profitable use of all that Jesus has revealed to them about the kingdom, so that the promised growth of the kingdom will materialize. Set in this parable is a story about a nobleman who goes to a far country to receive a kingship (vv. 14–15, 27). His citizens hated him and sent an embassy to prevent his being appointed king, only to have him come back as king and slay them. This story, drawn in part from an actual event of the times, is a parabolic prediction regarding Jesus. He will be rejected as the "King of the Jews" by crucifixion, he will return in his resurrection, and Jerusalem will someday be destroyed for its disobedience.

At the end of his long journey to Jerusalem that began in 9:51, Jesus arrives at Jerusalem itself, where he will depart and go to God. At night, he will stay at Bethphage and Bethany in the "suburbs" of Jerusalem, but during the days his activity will be centered in the Temple area. The royal entry into Jerusalem (19:28–38), although mentioning the crowd's acclaim of Jesus, emphasizes the disciples' praise of Jesus as king. When the Pharisees want Jesus to rebuke his exuberant disciples,

Jesus refuses and instead sadly predicts once again, but now in detail, the destruction of Jerusalem (19:39–44; see earlier, 11:49–52 and 13:34–35). That Jesus wept when he uttered this prophecy shows Luke's readers that Christians should not rejoice vindictively over that destruction when it occurred in 70 C.E. On the same day, Jesus forcefully "cleanses" the Temple of its corrupt businesses (19:45–46).

Jesus now takes his rightful place as a teacher in the Temple, provoking his opponents to question his authority. They look for ways to kill him, but Jesus is held in such awe as a teacher that they cannot move against him (19:47–20:8). Frustrated by his popularity among "all the people," the most his opponents can do publicly is to challenge his authority—a challenge offset by his own riposte about John the Baptizer. The parable of the Wicked Tenant Farmers (20:9–19) judges these authorities, because they have not given God the fruit from God's vineyard. The authorities react by spying on Jesus and seeking to trap him with a question concerning the tribute to Caesar (20:20–26), which he deftly avoids. A final fruitless attempt to impeach Jesus' teaching authority is made by the Sadducees with their question about the resurrection (20:27–40). Then Jesus goes on the offensive against his opponents with a question about David's son (20:41–44). These confrontations end with Jesus' sharp condemnation of the scribes for loving social honor while being hypocritical and morally corrupt (20:45–47). The charge that they "devour widows' houses" leads into the story of the widow's offering (21:1–4), which favors the poor over the ostentatious rich. It may illustrate one last time in Luke the value of giving away all that one has.

The disciples' admiration of the Temple buildings sets the stage for Jesus' prediction of the destruction of the Temple (21:5–6), which leads to a long discourse on the last things (21:5–38). Luke places the discourse in the Temple itself, as an extension of Jesus' daily teaching there. Jesus warns against Messianic pretenders and cautions that despite seeming signs of the end, the end itself is not soon. In the meantime, the disciples will certainly endure persecution because they follow Jesus (21:7–12). He promises a powerful wisdom when his followers on trial must bear testimony (21:13–15); even though they die, not a hair of their head will perish (21:16–18). Then his talk turns to Jerusalem specifically: he speaks of Jerusalem surrounded by armies, between the destruction of Jerusalem and the final times; Jerusalem will be trampled "until the times of the Gentiles are fulfilled," perhaps a long period of time in Luke's scheme (21:19–27). Not even Jesus himself knows when this will happen (21:28–33). The discourse ends with Jesus' warning about judgment to come on the entire earth, and Jesus tells his disciples to pray to endure faithfully until the end (21:34–36). Humble faithfulness, not special knowledge of the end, will bring them through to the kingdom of God.

Luke's Gospel has shaped his narrative toward this point, and now it presents here a narrative about the suffering and death of Jesus in chapters 22–23 that is carefully ordered and skillfully told, both in narrative and theology. First, it relates a conspiracy against Jesus (22:1–6). Satan entered into Judas to resume his attack on Jesus, discontinued after Jesus' temptations at the beginning of the Gospel. Human forces are also arrayed against Jesus: the chief priests and the captains or officers of the Temple. In the lengthy, detailed account of the Last Supper (22:7–38), Jesus links a cup used in this Passover meal with his upcoming death: "This cup is the new covenant in my blood which is poured out for you." Luke's stress on the body and blood of Jesus given or poured out "for you" stress the saving purpose of Jesus' death and of this continuing Supper. Then Jesus predicts his betrayal by one of his disciples (22:21–23). Although the reader knows which disciple it will be, the disciples do not. Even though they discuss which of them is about to betray Jesus, they then argue over which of them is the greatest! Jesus praises them for their faithfulness to him in his trials and promises them places at table in his kingdom and thrones from which to judge the twelve tribes (22:24–30). Similarly, in Luke 22:31–34, Jesus predicts Peter's threefold denial of Jesus and his restoration.

On the Mount of Olives opposite Jerusalem, Jesus awaits his arrest (22:39–53). With calm composure, he first kneels to pray. He prays once and finds the disciples sleeping once. If 22:43–44, the appearance of a ministering angel to Jesus, was written by the evangelist rather than added by a later copyist (and textual criticism has difficulty deciding which), Jesus' prayer is answered. Jesus' words during the arrest show that he knows the evil intention behind Judas' kissing him (22:48). When the disciples ask about violent resistance, Jesus commands nonresistance to evil, now and in their future. To dramatize this, he heals the right ear of the servant of the high priest who came to arrest him, an ear that one of his disciples had just cut off with a sword. The chief priests themselves come to the Mount of Olives to see Jesus arrested; Jesus reminds them of his daily teaching in the Temple area as a challenge to the armed force being used to arrest him as if he were a revolutionary. Jesus knows that "this hour" belongs to his opponents, who are allied, although they do not realize it, with the power of darkness (22:53).

Peter's denials of his relationship to Jesus (22:54–62) come before Jesus' Jewish trial, so that Jesus is present in the courtyard while Peter is denying him. Also in the night courtyard setting is the Jewish mockery of Jesus by those who were holding him captive (22:63–65). Luke presents a simple Jewish trial and sets it all in the morning (22:66–71). After this trial, Jesus is transferred to Pontius Pilate, the Roman governor. In the Roman "trial" (actually an appearance before a judge, because as a noncitizen of Rome Jesus is not entitled to anything like a formal trial), Jesus' opponents put a mixed set of charges to Pilate: Jesus is misleading the nation, forbidding taxes to Caesar and claiming to be a messianic king (23:1–25). Three times Pilate finds him innocent (23:4, 14, and 22). In the middle of Jesus' appearance before Pilate, Pilate sends Jesus to Herod Antipas, the Jewish tetrarch of Galilee who Luke explains was in Jerusalem at that time. Herod questions and then mocks him (23:6–12). After Jesus comes back from Herod, Pilate tries twice to release him, saying that he and Herod have found no crime in him, but finally he capitulates to pressure from some Jewish leaders and orders Jesus crucified.

Immediately before Jesus is crucified, three compassionate groups come into view to ease somewhat the narrative grimness: Simon from Cyrene in Africa, who carries Jesus' cross; a passing mention of a large multitude of people who sympathetically witness the procession; and women from Jerusalem who weep for Jesus. He tells them to weep instead for Jerusalem, which will be punished for its unbelief (23:26–31). Luke groups together the Roman centurion, the crowds, and his women disciples from Galilee (23:47–49). Surrounded by these groups, Jesus dies by crucifixion as a triad of mockers add verbal shame to Jesus' physical shame: first, the rulers who mock Jesus and exult in their victory over him; second, the soldiers who mock Jesus while killing him; and third, one of the other two criminals crucified with Jesus, who mocks Jesus' miraculous power (23:33–46). The so-called "good thief" rebukes the mocking thief, puts his faith in Jesus, and is rewarded with a promise of eternal life: "Today you will be with me in Paradise." Jesus makes a trusting and confident final statement, "Father, into your hands I place my spirit" (23:46). Luke now relates the reaction of three sympathetic groups to the death of Jesus (23:47–56). The Roman centurion testifies that Jesus was a just man and did nothing wrong. The crowds express sympathetic sorrow as they return home. The women disciples stand at a distance looking on, and follow Jesus' body to its burial by Joseph of Arimathea. As faithful Jews, they observed the Sabbath law by resting on that day.

Describing events at the empty tomb on Sunday morning (24:1–12), the quick narrative pace of Luke's narration stands in sharp contrast with the deadly slow narrative pace of Jesus' death. (Joy moves faster than sorrow!) When the women enter the rolling-stone tomb, they do not find the body that they had seen laid out there on Friday afternoon; instead, two men in "dazzling clothes" suddenly appear. These interpreting angels ask a challenging question to the women: "Why do you seek the living among the dead?" and they remind the women of Jesus' prediction of his death and resurrection. When they leave the tomb, the women "[tell] all this to all the rest." Luke names the women as the first witnesses of the resurrection, specifically of the empty tomb and the angelic interpretation. The other disciples do not believe these women, but Peter examines the empty tomb for himself.

Jesus' first resurrection appearance is on the road to Emmaus (24:13–35). Luke employs good narrative techniques: plot tensions such as the disappointed hopes of the disciples and Jesus' pretending to want to go on farther; strong emotions such as the disciples' hearts glowing when Jesus opened to them the meaning of the scriptures; and a sudden, dramatic ending with Jesus vanishing right in front of them. Just as on the long journey to Jerusalem Jesus revealed these events and journeyed toward them, so now on the other side of them Jesus reveals himself to his disciples, building their faith by explaining how what he has accomplished relates to the scriptures. The appearance to all the disciples (24:36–49) is set in Jerusalem on that Sunday evening. Jesus stands among them and blesses

The Garden Tomb This tomb outside the ancient walls of Jerusalem is thought by some to be the burial place of Jesus. It is beloved by modern tourists and pilgrims for its serene garden setting, much different from the bustling Church of the Holy Sepulcher, which has a better archaeological claim to housing the real tomb of Jesus. Note the low door and the channel for the rolling stone cover. Used by permission of BiblePlaces.com.

them, shows the terrified disciples the identifying wounds in his hands and feet, and gives them a mission "to all the nations." Luke emphasizes the physical reality of Jesus' appearance, for Jesus shows his wounds, invites his disciples to touch him, eats food, and affirms that he has "flesh and bones." Jesus explains the Scriptures to these disciples too, as he also did on the road to Emmaus, saying that there was a divine plan and necessity in his death and resurrection. Jesus commissions his disciples to be witnesses of these things that have happened to him in fulfillment of scripture, and promises them for their mission the coming of the same Spirit that empowered him for his ministry. This final appearance ends with a disappearance, Jesus' **ascension** to heaven (24:50–53). Then the disciples return "with great joy" to Jerusalem and the Temple, praising God there and waiting for the Spirit soon to come. The reader is left to anticipate Luke's second volume, the Acts of the Apostles, in which the Spirit will take up where Jesus left off.

Historical Reading

Several issues in the historical study of Luke have been important: its use of sources; the author of Luke as a historian; its relation to Acts; how the author of Luke uses history to advance his own religious vision of Christianity. Historical study has also noted issues that are now important in other methods of reading, such as Luke's narrative sophistication and its attention to women and other marginalized groups. In a word, the author of Luke-Acts is both a historian and a theologian. His aims in writing history and his religious themes must be taken into account in reading his two-volume book.

Luke in Brief: Summary of Historical Reading

Author: Anonymous. Traditionally, Luke the physician and co-worker with Paul (Col 4:14, 2 Tim 4:11, Phlm 1:24). Today some keep to the traditional view, but most view the author as an unknown Gentile-Christian convert of the second Christian generation, well educated in Greek literature. Perhaps he is a client of Theophilus (1:1–4).

Date: Probably somewhere in the 80s.

Audience: Gentile Christians, probably in an urban setting; the precise city cannot be determined.

Sources: Mark, Q, and perhaps L (material found only in Luke but not by the author).

Purpose: To challenge and enable believers to be more devoted to the faith, especially its growth among the marginalized.

Author

Like the Gospels of Matthew and Mark, Luke-Acts is anonymous. No author's name is given in the text, and the name on the text dates from the second century. As for the external evidence about the author, traditions in the second century unanimously identify this person as Luke, a physician and co-worker with the apostle Paul. The oldest Greek manuscript of this document, Papyrus Bodmer XIV from about 200 C.E., uses the title "Gospel according to Luke." The Muratorian Canon in the late second century also identifies Luke as this Gospel's author. This identification is also found in the mid-second-century writings of Irenaeus (*Against Heresies* 3.1.1; 3.14.1) and in later writings (e.g., Eusebius, *History of the Church* 3.4.1–7; 3.24.14–15; 5.8.3; 6.25.6). As for internal evidence, almost all scholars conclude for good reasons that the Gospel of Luke and the Acts were written by the same person. They share a common prologue (Luke 1:1–4, renewed in Acts 1:1–2), and the literary style and theological aims indicate that the same person certainly wrote them.

But was this person really Luke? The name "Luke" appears three times in the NT, in Col. 4:14, Philemon 24, and 2 Tim. 4:11, all clearly with reference to the same person, an associate of Paul. Because the NT links Luke with Paul, puzzling out the authorship of Luke-Acts proceeds more from the direction of Acts, which features Paul, than from the Gospel. The reference in 2 Timothy has little to offer about Luke himself beyond highlighting his faithfulness to Paul in comparison with others. In Philemon, Luke is identified as a "fellow worker," a term that designates one of Paul's traveling companions and colleagues. Col. 4:14 refers to Luke as a "beloved physician." Because Col. 4:10–11 refers to Aristarchus, Mark, and Justus as the only Jews present among Paul's co-workers, it appears that Luke is a Gentile. Some who see evidence in Luke-Acts of an author with a notable Jewish background debate this last point. The level of scriptural and Jewish knowledge in Luke-Acts does not indicate that the author is a lifelong Jew (as Matthew's does), but is compatible with a Gentile author who has had a significant knowledge and appreciation of the Jewish origins of the Christian faith.

Although it may be *possible* that Luke was the author, we can describe the author from Luke-Acts itself, with information that is far more useful in understanding Luke-Acts than just a name. The author was highly educated, especially in literature and rhetoric. This education means that the author likely came from the upper classes of society. Knowledge of Israel's scriptures may indicate that the author was a "God-fearer" before becoming a Christian, or (less likely) a convert from paganism directly to Christianity who then learned much about Judaism. The author was a Gentile Christian of either the second or third generation and so most probably never met Jesus or had a firsthand witness about him. Though it is likely, given the culture of the times, that the author was a man, we cannot exclude the possibility that a woman authored Luke-Acts.

Date and Audience

A strong majority of scholarly opinion holds that Luke-Acts was written after 70 C.E., when the Romans destroyed Jerusalem and its Temple. When Luke has Jesus predict this destruction, he uses detailed knowledge of the actual event. In 19:34–44, Jesus gives details, speaking of siege-works, full encircling of the city, and complete destruction ("not one stone standing on another"). Later, he says, "But when you see Jerusalem encircled by armies, then be sure that its destruction is near. Then you who are in Judea must flee to the hills; those that are in the city itself must leave it . . . because this is a time of retribution. . . . They will fall by the sword; they will be taken captive into all countries; and Jerusalem will be trampled down by foreigners until their time is gone" (21:20–24). Another piece of the dating puzzle is that Luke used Mark, so it must be written some length of time after Mark, to account for Mark's spread and standing as a Gospel.

If 70 C.E. is the earliest possible date, the latest possible date is not quite so precise, but most scholars would date Luke before 100, primarily because the pattern of church organization in Acts is earlier than the more developed patterns we begin to see around 100. Within this broad 70–100 period, the consensus today is that Luke probably comes from the 80s or early 90s. Its place of origin is uncertain, but Ephesus seems to be the place of composition and destination favored by many scholars today. It was a large, Greek-speaking city in Asia Minor and an early center of Christianity. However, this is just an educated guess, as very little specific information ties Luke-Acts to any particular place. Indeed, it could originate from, and be directed to, many Greek-speaking Gentile churches in major cities in the western Mediterranean.

Sources

The intriguing introduction to the Gospel of Luke reads, "Since many have undertaken to set down an orderly account of the things that have been fulfilled among us, just as they were handed down to us by those who were eyewitnesses and servants of the word from the beginning, I too decided, after investigating everything carefully from the first, to write an orderly account for you, most excellent Theophilus, so that you may know the truth about the things you have been taught" (Luke 1:1–4). This prologue implicitly raises the issue of sources.

The writer of the Gospel of Luke (and Matthew) used two main sources. (See Chapter 5 for more detail.) First is the Gospel of Mark, which is about one-third of Luke. Luke uses Mark in the following ways:

- Like the author of Matthew, the author of Luke writes Greek in a much better style than the author of Mark.
- With only a few exceptions, especially the omission of the material in Mark 6:45–8:26 and 9:41–10:12, Luke follows Mark's order and takes over large portions of his material.
- Luke omits or softens Markan passages that reflect negatively on Jesus' family (Mark 3:21, 33–34 [omissions]; Mark 6:4 and Luke 4:22 [softenings]). It omits many passages portraying the ignorance and unbelief of Jesus' disciples (e.g., Mark 8:22–26, 8:33).
- Luke adds an explicit journey motif to his Gospel, Jesus' long journey to Jerusalem in the center section, a motif he will richly employ in Acts.
- Finally, many scholars hold that Luke tones down Mark's portrayal of Jesus' death as sacrificial, emphasizing instead how Jesus' death is a radical pattern for service.

The second source Luke used is Q, teaching material that forms about one-fifth of Luke. Luke seems to have followed the order of Q more carefully than Matthew, and scholars believe that overall Luke has preserved the wording of Q in a more original form than Matthew has.

Luke may also have used an oral or written collection of material peculiar to his gospel, a source named **L**. Since we have not encountered this source yet, we will examine it more closely here. The material unique to Luke forms a large portion of this gospel, variously estimated between one-third and one-half. Most of it is the teachings of Jesus, containing some of his most memorable parables: the Good Samaritan, the Prodigal Son, and the Rich Man and Lazarus. It also contains memorable narratives: the repentance of Zacchaeus, the disagreement between Mary and Martha over true service to Jesus, and the grateful Samaritan leper. Researchers into the historical Jesus have typically given the distinctive contents of Luke a high degree of authenticity, much higher than the special material in Matthew.

www   Follow the link to a helpful, color-coded presentation of Luke showing the various sources Mark, Q, and L.

Recent scholarship has not formed a consensus on the existence of L. Helmut Koester argues that an L source does not exist, pointing to the large size and formal diversity of the material (Koester 1995, 336–37). The most thorough and careful source-critical work on L is Kim Paffenroth's 1997 study, *The Story of Jesus according to L*. He concludes that the L material has enough dissimilarity from Lukan style, form, and content to make it probable that it forms a coherent, unified L source. L was written by Jewish-Christians in Palestine sometime between 40 and 60 C.E. It views Jesus as the authoritative teacher and agent of God's radical, free grace. He came to "seek and find" the lost and restore them to the covenantal people of God. This grace is first directed to Israel, but the bounds of Israel proper are broken when Samaritans are brought into the fold. Jesus also acts to bring women into a freer state in God's kingdom. In sum, L sees Jesus as a "powerful ethical teacher who substantiated and revealed the authority of his teaching by acts of healing" (Paffenroth 1997, 158).

www   See the website for the contents of L according to Paffenroth.

Purpose

In the prologue (Luke 1:1–4), the author states that he or she writes so that Theophilus, and implicitly readers like him, may be more carefully and accurately informed about the story of Jesus and the early church. This leads us to ask, what exactly did Theophilus and the audience at large need to know that they did not know already? To answer this question, we must look at the special themes of this book. The author presents a powerful vision of Jesus that almost certainly is the key part of Theophilus' need for knowledge. Luke portrays Jesus as originally the Messiah of the Jews, but now the Savior of the world. Jesus came to save the lost, including persons that societies and religions marginalized. Jesus journeys from Galilee to Jerusalem, and then the church grows into the whole world. All of this is based on Jesus' life and death for others as an example of humility and service. Jesus did not break Roman law but suffers as an innocent. Presumably, some of these characteristic emphases of Luke's Gospel were needed in the church(es) to which this Gospel was written, for their instruction and growth in faith. According to the influential work of Hans Conzelmann, Luke-Acts' purpose was to set forth his scheme of salvation history in which a long "period of the church" comes between the period of Jesus and the end of time (Conzelmann 1960). I. Howard Marshall sees Luke-Acts as a witness to salvation itself (Marshall 1998). Others have seen an apologetic purpose to defend Christianity against Roman suspicions or a theological purpose, for example, to specify the identity of the new people of God. In conclusion, Joseph Fitzmyer's caution against interpreting Luke's theology in terms of one's own thesis about the purpose of Luke is wise (Fitzmyer 1981).

Doing Historical Reading Yourself

1. *Compare Matthew 1–2 to Luke 1–2. What are the common features between both, and what are the unique features in each? How does Luke 1–2 show Luke's particular themes and interests?*

2. *In the death of Jesus, Luke reports that one thief crucified with him shamed Jesus, but the other honored him (23:39–43). Mark and Matthew both report that both thieves dishonored Jesus. Why might Luke make such a change?*

The author's knowledge of both the Jewish and Gentile cultures, and special views of poverty and riches among the people of God, enriches social scientific reading. He seems to be an advocate of significantly greater freedom for women, especially when compared to Matthew and Mark. His insistence that the Gospel is meant for all people, and thus must cross cultural barriers, makes him a favorite Gospel for cross-cultural readers.

Luke in Brief: Summary of Newer Methods

Narrative: Luke tells its story consummately, weaving together different sources into an almost seamless tale with consistent story line and theological themes. Its style is highly literate, and it often employs the journey motif. Moreover, many of the narrative features of Luke are echoed and repeated in Acts.

Social Scientific: The author of Luke is an astute observer of society; although he views it from the top, he knows and writes sympathetically about all social groups. The author is well acquainted with patronage (and may be a client), the honor/shame paradigm, matters of (Jewish) ritual purity, and kinship. Luke's view of money and possessions in life is a key theme in this Gospel.

Feminist: Luke features women in prominent roles more than any other Gospel. It is generally positive toward greater freedom for women. Many feminist readers appreciate Luke's aims, but some doubt if they are truly liberating.

Cross-Cultural: Like all the canonical Gospels, Luke crosses cultural barriers. Although a Gentile, the author of Luke has a positive appreciation for Judaism but holds it to the past. Because its concern for marginalized people is highest among the Gospels, Luke is a rich field for cross-cultural reading.

Narrative Reading

Narrative reading of Luke encounters a particularly skilled storyteller. The author's Greek style is highly literate, and this comes across in most English translations. For those who do narrative-historical reading of Luke, the author's ability to combine and adapt three sources (Mark, Q, and L) into one almost seamless whole is no small feat for any writer! His center section and passion narrative show skill in writing that far surpasses Mark and Matthew. Luke is also skilled at narrative rhetoric, so he tells his stories to convince and persuade his readers, not just to inform them. He deftly weaves many subthemes into his main theme about Jesus as the Savior of the world: the importance of the Holy Spirit and prayer, God's love for the marginalized, and an understanding of eschatology that opens a wider time between the resurrection of Jesus and the end of the world. Moreover, much of his narrative skill does not become apparent until one reads carefully the Acts of the Apostles, in which the author builds parallels to his Gospel that shed light on its meaning. The author of Luke has said in his preface that he aims to write a careful, orderly account, and readers today can conclude that he has largely succeeded in this intent.

Narrative Reading at Work, 1
The Annunciation to Mary (Luke 1:26–38)

Luke 1:34 and its context have been vexing to several recent interpreters. Mary asks the angel who has just informed her that she will bear an important son, "How can this be, since I do not know [in the "biblical sense," have sexual intercourse with] a man?" Here David Landry works through the narrative of

Source: David T. Landry, "Narrative Logic in the Annunciation to Mary" (from *http://personal1. stthomas. edu/dtlandry/mary.html.*).

Luke 1 to respond to the feminist scholar Jane Schaberg, who has argued that the narratives of Jesus' conception in Luke and Matthew attempt to cover over that Jesus' conception was the result of ordinary intercourse, and thus that Jesus was an illegitimate child.

From a literary perspective, Schaberg's interpretation [that Jesus is illegitimate] is preferable . . . She focuses on the dynamics of the narrative rather than Luke's theological purposes and insists that her reading make sense in terms of the story's logic. However, there are problems with Schaberg's reading. Her translation of Mary's question in 1:34 is unlikely, and she has great difficulties dealing with both the angel's response in 1:35–37 and Mary's final acquiescence in 1:38.

I have attempted to show that it is possible to preserve the narrative logic of the passage in another way. Luke mentions the fact that Mary is a virgin twice in his introduction of her character precisely because this will become important for the reader's understanding of the plot. When Mary questions the angel's announcement, she understands that this pregnancy will occur immediately and she objects on the basis of her virginity, in effect saying, "How can I become pregnant now, since I will not have relations with my husband for some time?" The angel's response naturally answers Mary's question, explaining to her how she will become pregnant even though she is a virgin, that is, by God's agency. Mary accepts her fate, showing that she believes that the promises made to her will be fulfilled, and in fact confirms this belief by aligning herself with other women who have been so blessed, calling herself God's "handmaid," as did Hannah in 1 Samuel 1. In the next scene Elizabeth congratulates Mary for believing that there would be a fulfillment of what was spoken to her from the Lord, and Mary goes on to celebrate her extraordinary pregnancy in a long speech. Nothing in the text precludes understanding it in this way.

Question

How well does Landry's explanation explicate this narrative?

www Follow the link to read Landry's entire article on line.

Narrative Reading at Work, 2
Reading Luke 5:1–11

This excerpt from McKnight's essay combines reader-response criticism with narrative criticism. As in all narrative and reader-response criticism, one must pay very close attention to content as one goes along, because the meaning of a given passage is shaped by what precedes it.

The reader reads until some minimal unit of meaning presents itself (can be discovered or created). Luke 5:1–3 makes up a minimal unit of meaning as it is read

Source: Edgar V. McKnight. "Reader-Response Criticism," in *To Each Its Own Meaning*, ed. Steven L. McKenzie & Stephen R. Haynes (Louisville: Westminster/John Knox, 1999) 241–242.

in light of lexical and grammatical information. This unit begins with the press of the people upon Jesus to hear the word of God–and the consequent inability of Jesus to teach the word–and concludes with the successful teaching of the people from a boat. The major actor in the episode is not identified in this unit (pronouns are used instead of the name "Jesus," so the reader must identify this actor as Jesus by moving either backward or forward in the text to a place where the proper name is used). The reader knows that Jesus is the personal name of Jesus of Nazareth (Luke 24:19), the son of Mary (Luke 1:31), the prophet (Luke 7:39, 24:19), who is "a Savior . . . Christ the Lord" (Luke 2:11).

From the words and deed in the unit itself, a reader constructs an image of the Jesus of this unit. He is popular and is the speaker of the word of God. He is ingenious (he uses a boat to solve the problem presented by the press of the people), and his authority is compelling. The unit shows that Jesus has a mission and indicates that the mission involves being sent by God for the purpose of teaching the word of God. This indication is confirmed and made more explicit by a movement to the earlier pericope, which has a quotation from Jesus himself indicating that he has been sent to "preach the good news of the kingdom of God to the other cities also."

Questions

1. What does McKnight mean by saying that Jesus' "authority is compelling"?
2. How does narrative reading remind us here that one must read a pericope (passage) in the light of its context, especially what goes before it?

Doing Narrative Reading Yourself

1. Read Luke 4:16–30 as closely as you can. Does Jesus "pick a fight" in this narrative?
2. Read Luke 16:19–31, the parable of Lazarus and the rich man. How might the end of this parable refer to the resurrection of Jesus? What does it imply about how the proclamation of Jesus' resurrection will be received by the Jewish people?

Social Scientific Reading

The reader of Luke encounters a key social relationship in the ancient world at the very beginning of this Gospel: the author may be a client of Theophilus, his patron (social and financial supporter) who is being schooled in the Christian faith. The rest of the Gospel bears out this picture. The implied author is someone from the top echelons of society, but nevertheless has a strong message—the strongest of the four NT Gospels—of indifference to possessions and the dangers of building wealth. He emphasizes the role that money and the lack of it play in human life, but this emphasis is richly nuanced. Although God is about to reverse the situations of poverty and wealth, the author shows us a Jesus who ministers in a gracious yet challenging way to rich and poor alike. In this way, the author of Luke is in tune with social values in the ancient Mediterranean about limited goods but reforms it with his/her own particularly Christian values. The author is well acquainted with, and can be read by, other social scientific paradigms: the honor/shame paradigm, matters of purity and pollution, and kinship.

One example of how Luke uses the Good News for the poor to address the rich is in his table/banquet scenes. All the Synoptics present Jesus as one who enjoyed eating and drinking and who made a point about God's kingdom while doing so. Willi Braun has argued that the writer of Luke, especially in Luke 14, presents Jesus in the familiar role of the "dinner sage," one who uses conversation at formal banquets to persuade others of the need for change. In this banquet scene, Jesus presents Luke's vision of a society that mirrors the values of God's kingdom. Luke 14 is directed especially at the wealthy urban elite, who are most in need of transformation to become a part of this society (Braun 1995). Braun's study confirms what most scholars have concluded about Luke: although its literary style reveals the author to be a member of the aristocracy, its theology identifies Jesus with those who are not wealthy.

Social Scientific Reading at Work, 1
The Temptation of Jesus as a Test of Kinship (Luke 4:1–13)

In their commentary on the Synoptic Gospels using the social scientific perspective, Malina and Rohrbaugh give this explanation of the testing/temptation of Jesus. Not just an event that sets the course of Jesus' ministry, it is a testing of his kinship with God and of his client relationship with God as his patron.

It is important to recognize that this test occurs at the cosmic level where false hearts are inexorably exposed and no secrets can be hidden. . . . This is first and foremost a test of kinship loyalty. Note carefully how the devil frames the first challenge: "*If you are the Son of God* . . ." Note also how carefully Jesus answers when his lineage is questioned. He does *not* answer in his own words, as if his honor derives from what he is in himself. To do that would be to grasp honor above that of his own Father and turn honor into dishonor. So he answers as a loyal Middle Eastern son would always answer—with something from his family tradition. He offers the words of his true Father in Deuteronomy and by such laudable behavior he gains honor as virtue.

Source: Bruce J. Malina and Richard L. Rohrbaugh, *Social-Science Commentary on the Synoptic Gospels* (Philadelphia: Fortress, 1992), pp. 240–241.

The second challenge asks Jesus to worship—the term should be translated "honor"—the devil rather than God. Here terms from the semantic field of honor-shame abound: authority, glory, worship. . . . It is thus clear that this time [in this temptation], kinship is not the issue, patronage is. The devil makes the audacious claim to be God's broker, saying that both the kingdoms of the world and the right to dispose of their resources in whatever manner he wishes have been given to him. . . . Here Jesus' client-loyalty to his Patron (God) is being fundamentally challenged. Since the test involves a counterclaim in which the devil asserts his own priority over Jesus in the patronage chain, if Jesus acquiesces in the devil's request, Luke's claim that Jesus acts by the power of God's Spirit (4:1) would be effectively refuted. But a true and honorable client would never switch patrons in this way or try to serve two masters at the same time (16:13). So the loyalty challenge is thrust aside once again with the words of God, the true Patron of all.

Social Scientific Reading at Work, 2
Hospitality and Purity Systems in Luke 11:37–54

The ancient Jewish/Israelite values of hospitality (welcoming strangers) and purity (staying ritually clean) could come into conflict. In this treatment of Luke 11:37–54, which you should read before you read this excerpt, Jesus implicitly claims that inner purity causes outer purity. Luke as narrator creatively utilizes Jesus' rejection of the cultural expectations of hospitality (which includes both honor and purity concerns) to illustrate how his new system of purity and honor replaces the purity system of the scribes and Pharisees.

Luke 11:37–54 is a confrontation not only between Jesus and the scribes and Pharisees, but also between Jesus' revolutionary understanding of purity/virtue and the purity system of the specifically Jewish culture of the Lukan scribes and Pharisees. This clash takes place in the reflective context of hospitality, which graphically illustrates societal norms of purity and honor that Jesus seeks to transform. Note how the narrator defends the purity of Jesus, even when Jesus crosses the Pharisees' purity/impurity boundaries. In fact, Jesus remains a figure of unsurpassed holiness: holy in pedigree (e.g., 1:5–6, 27; 2:4; 3:23, 31–32), observances (e.g., 2:21–24, 41; 4:16, 33; 19:45–47), and evaluations by reliable characters (e.g., 1:35; 2:11, 25–32, 38; 3:22). Therefore, the narrator sincerely classifies Jesus as an insider, although a reforming insider. . . .

To further this point, the narrator portrays Jesus as not only unaffected by contact with impurity, but Jesus actually imparts purity and wholeness to the impure. As a limit breaker Jesus possesses the authority to cross boundaries of purity/impurity, and he can also invest others with that power to cross purity boundaries. For example,

Source: David B. Gowler, "Hospitality and Characterization in Luke 11:37–54: A Socio-Narratological Approach," in *Semeia* 64 (1993): 213–251.

the exhortation to give alms implies Jesus' belief that [it] would generate purity. Ironically, according to the scribes and Pharisees' purity regulations, if you offer alms from the inside of an impure vessel, then the alms you give become impure. The result is that you transfer impurity to the receiver of the alms. Yet Jesus proclaims that giving alms has the same effect as ritually cleansing that impure vessel. In other words, Jesus transposes the question of ritual purity into the wider spectrum of moral behavior. He interiorizes the purity code, and in that context can declare that true purity/virtue is antithetical to rapacity and the other vices of the scribes and Pharisees. . . . Jesus and his followers, obeying the dictates of God and the Holy Spirit, initiate a modified purity system based on a new set of inner values. . . .

Persons of social prominence, notably the scribes and Pharisees, reject Jesus' interiorized purity system and designate Jesus as a *deviant*. The portrayal of Jesus in Luke, however, exhibits Jesus as in fact a *limit-breaker* and a *prominent*. In Luke 11:37–54, those persons who have prominence in society dictate the terms of the encounter in a hospitality framework of testing a stranger, but the narrator vividly portrays the Pharisees and scribes being bested by Jesus. They fail in their roles as brokers because they actually block access to God, instead of facilitating it. They are the true deviants, according to the narrator. The reader who identifies with the narrator's ideological point of view will also identify with Jesus, the hero of the story. Thus, because of the narrative's characterization of Jesus and his opponents, when Jesus defies cultural expectations, even one so dear as the law of hospitality, the reader happily goes along.

Questions

1. *Describe how this passage from Luke and Gowler's essay relate ritual purity to moral purity.*

2. *Explain in your own words what* deviant, limit-breaker, *and* prominent *mean here.*

www   Follow the link to read the whole article and/or its abstract.

Doing Social Scientific Reading Yourself

1. *What might it mean for social scientific reading of the Gospel of Luke if Theophilus were the patron of its author (Luke 1:1–4)?*

2. *Luke 6:20–26 presents not only blessings (beatitudes) on those who follow in God's way, but curses ("woes") on those who do not. Use in-group and out-group thinking to explain a social dimension of these sayings.*

3. *Discuss the social scientific dimensions of the parable of the Good Samaritan.*

Feminist Reading

Luke's Gospel features women playing prominent roles at key points in its story of Jesus. Women are prominent at Jesus' conception and birth; note how Matthew's cast of characters is predominantly male in Matthew 1–2 but predominantly female in Luke 1–2. They are present with Jesus more noticeably during his ministry and are the only witnesses at Jesus' death and burial. They are at the empty tomb, and Jesus appears to them first after they visit the empty tomb. Affluent, influential women and poor, unempowered women both figure in Luke's account. His narrative carefully builds the picture of women as disciples, believers, repentant sinners, and finally credible witnesses.

Feminist scholarship disagrees, however, on the significance of all this prominence. The prominent feminist NT scholar Jane Schaberg has argued that Luke is "an extremely dangerous text, perhaps the most dangerous in the Bible." Because it contains a great deal of material about women that is found nowhere else in the Gospels, many feminist readers insist that the author is enhancing or promoting the status of women. However, even as this Gospel highlights women, Schaberg claims that it deftly portrays them as models of subordinate service, excluded from the power center of the movement and from significant responsibilities. Claiming the authority of Jesus, this portrayal is an attempt to legitimate male dominance in the Christianity of the author's time. Nevertheless, Schaberg says that a close reading of Luke is promising because it has insights valuable for the building of an egalitarian society and of a theology that preserves and respects women's experience, but freeing them from the harmful elements of the tradition is a difficult task (Schaberg 1999). Which view of women in Luke is correct can only be determined by careful reading of its treatment of women in the context of the whole Gospel.

www   Follow the link to examine a chart of "Women in Luke's Gospel," by Professor Felix Just.

Feminist Reading at Work, 1
Mary Magdalene in NT and Western Tradition

The recent bestselling book by Dan Brown, The Da Vinci Code, has raised new interest in Mary Magdalene by suggesting she was Jesus' wife. She did travel with Jesus (Luke 8:2–3) and was one of the key witnesses to his death, burial, and resurrection (Luke 23:49–24:10). However, early church tradition also identified her as the prostitute of Luke 7:36–50, and this identification passed into Western culture and Brown's book.

Source: Carolyn Osiek, "Mary [Magdalene]," in Carol Meyers, ed., *Women in Scripture* (Grand Rapids: Eerdmans, 2001), p. 122.

For the most part, Western tradition developed a very different perspective on Mary of Magdala [than that found in the NT and later antiquity]. Onto her was projected the male fascination with the sex object. In spite of a total lack of evidence in the canonical Scriptures or early church tradition, Mary became identified with the woman who "was a sinner" in Luke 7:36–50, who washed the feet of Jesus with her tears and dried them with her hair (perhaps this is because the story occurs immediately before Luke 8:2–3, where she is first named). In the male imagination, only one sin could require such dramatic repentance: she had to be a reformed prostitute. . . . In the West, the figure of Mary Magdalene has connoted suppressed eroticism. In circles wherein such can be contemplated of Jesus, a sexual liaison between him and her is suggested. She is represented as young and alluring, yet at the same time she is said to have spent her reformed life in penance and monastic asceticism. In the modern period, paintings of Mary Magdalene usually reflect male fantasies and are intended to titillate. In spite of the ascetic context, such depictions usually include sensually flowing hair and enough clothing carelessly out of place to be provocative. Her name has become synonymous with barely repentant sensuality.

How can Mary Magdalene be restored to her original image as prominent disciple and spokeswoman of the gospel? She is thought . . . to have had the economic means and social freedom to spend her income and time the way she chose, she is likely to have been widowed or divorced at the time of her encounter with Jesus. To have acquired her reputation for closeness to Jesus, there must have been a certain intimacy in their relationship, which may just as well have been motherly or patronal as anything else. Her unquestioned presence at both the cross and at the tomb on Easter morning . . . points up her preeminence as disciple. At the darkest and most uncertain moments, when others had withdrawn—even Jesus' mother, according to the Synoptic Gospels—Mary Magdalene faithfully remained in Jesus' presence. This was a strong woman.

Questions

1. *Why, according to Osiek, did the picture of Mary Magdalene become that of a scarcely reformed prostitute?*

2. *Why, in your opinion, does that picture persist today in spite of good NT evidence to the contrary?*

www Follow the links for a critique of Brown's *Da Vinci Code*.

Feminist Reading at Work, 2
Martha and Mary of Bethany (Luke 10:38–42)

In this feminist examination of the sisters Martha and Mary of Bethany (not Magdalene), Jane Kopas shows the most liberating message that Luke has for women.

Source: Jane Kopas, "Jesus and Women: Luke's Gospel," *Theology Today* 43, 2 (1986): 193–202.

In the great journey up to Jerusalem . . . women are mentioned in a number of episodes that are highly significant. First, there is the story of Martha and Mary, which is reported exclusively in Luke's Gospel (10:38–42). Though it stood for a long time as evidence for the superiority of the contemplative over the active life, it has more recently been understood to demonstrate Jesus' serious acceptance of the education of women. Even beyond these possible meanings, however, when we take this story in the context of all the other stories about women on the journey, we find that it reveals to us a fuller picture of the thoroughness of women's commitment to discipleship and Jesus' acceptance of their participation.

Martha does many things and worries about many things. She is not faulted for this, but for failing to root her actions in a basic awareness of why she does what she does. It seems not to be her actions, but her intentions (and her comparisons) that create her dissatisfaction. Mary, on the other hand, listens to Jesus to appreciate and develop the single-mindedness that integrates the diverse activities of life. She lays the groundwork for a spirituality of wholeness, integration, and reconciliation. . . . Lest one think that Mary's attentiveness to Jesus implies passive listening, in the next chapter a brief encounter of Jesus with a woman clarifies the way discipleship is rooted in relationship. As he was speaking, a woman in the crowd cried, "Happy are the womb that bore you and the breasts you sucked" (11:27–28). In response, Jesus corrects two erroneous notions. One is that mere association imparts some kind of blessedness, either through physical descent or even by virtue of being part of a group around Jesus. The other notion he corrects is that women derive their status or worth from their relationship to their husband or children. Important as these relationships may be, in the last analysis one's fidelity to the responsibility of being a child of God by acting as such confirms the value of the person and motivates discipleship.

Questions

1. What might it mean, as Kopas implies, that Jesus' most significant encounters with and teachings about women come in his journey to Jerusalem?

2. How does the analysis of 11:27–28 shed light on what Luke means by holding up Mary as an example?

Doing Feminist Criticism Yourself

1. Is there a tension in Luke between women as servants and women as liberated, between traditional and more liberated roles? Give reasons for your answer.

2. Is it possible or likely that some of the seventy-two disciples Jesus sends on a preaching and healing mission are women (Luke 10:1–12)? Could the pairs sent out be male-female?

Cross-Cultural Reading

Like all the canonical Gospels, Luke crosses cultural barriers. Though a Gentile, the author of Luke has a positive appreciation for Judaism but holds it to the past. Perhaps the only Gentile writer in the NT, his reading and re-presentation of the Jesus tradition is itself a cross-cultural move. Because its concern for marginalized people is highest among the Gospels, Luke is a rich field for cross-cultural reading.

Luke presents Jesus as strongly prophetic, perhaps even revolutionary, in his words and actions crossing cultural barriers and inviting his followers to go with him in crossing them. He did not allow the religious and ethnic prejudices of the time to hinder his movements among all classes of people. He gave hope to men and women alike, to those powerful and marginalized in society, and to the ritually clean and unclean. Although he was not an egalitarian in our modern sense, Jesus rejected the social and religious structures that contributed to the oppression of the poor.

Cross-Cultural Reading at Work, 1
Black African Women and Anna the Prophet (Luke 2:36–38)

This essay deals with the post-apartheid era in South Africa, investigating how the black churchwomen of South Africa survive. Their strategies of reading the Bible empower them to resist the patriarchal domination that continues. The following question and response indicates how black women from Mankweng, a black community in South Africa whose women are among the most impoverished in that country, read the Bible and its culture in light of their own Northern Sotho culture.

Some of the women see Anna as an independent woman. Anna is independent because she chooses not to be married again. Some women hold that Anna is a trustworthy woman because of her godly life: she never leaves the temple. Anna is also perceived as an empowering figure in their lives in general because she has great faith in God, and she does everything that is pleasant in the eyes of God and in the eyes of fellow human beings.

The prophet Anna is seen as an exemplar for other women. These women maintain that her character and role inspire them to serve God ardently. The prophet Anna is seen as empowering and encouraging other women to live their lives in the community, as God wills. She is also seen as a good exemplar to married women because she is faithful and loyal in her marriage. This group of respondents believes that

Source: Gloria Kehilwe Plaatjie, "Toward a Post-Apartheid Black Feminist Reading," in Musa W. Dube, ed., *Other Ways of Reading: African Women and the Bible* (Atlanta: Society of Biblical Literature, 2001), pp. 116, 128, 129. Copyright © 2001 Society of Biblical Literature. Used by permission.

prophet Anna remains single because she does not want to forget her late husband. These women point out that Anna encourages them to be independent as women, to trust in themselves, and to be trusted by other people in the community.

Some respondents specifically read Anna's choice in reference to Sotho-Tswana rituals. They speak of the difficult and degrading widowhood rituals to which women are subjected. They hold that Anna could have married a male relative of her deceased husband, but that she probably did not wish to undergo the rituals of widowhood twice. For these women, not all cultural rituals concerning women are "good" or acceptable. Nonetheless, the married women of this group consent that they will undergo the ritual of widowhood when their time comes, for they feel forced by circumstances beyond their control to submit. . . .

Some women interpret Anna's choice to remain single in relationship to her children, believing that she may have wanted to protect her children from abuse in a second marriage. These women hold that if they were in Anna's position they would not marry again in order to protect their children from the possibility of an abusive stepfather.

Questions

1. *Do you think that the African women come from a culture closer to Anna's than yours? Why, or why not?*

2. *What does this essay contribute to your understanding of Anna?*

Cross-Cultural Reading at Work, 2
The Yielding Son (Luke 15:11–32)

In this essay, a prominent Indian NT scholar examines an indigenization of the parable of the Prodigal Son in the light of Indian-Hindu culture.

Palakeel's story "The Serpent and the Master," in keeping with the Indian way of storytelling, is full of plots and subplots and is inhabited by a whole host of characters. It is essentially a primordial parable that retells the tale of a young person's failed attempt to leave home and lead a life of his own, free from parental control and the pressures of the extended family. It is about a Christian family in Kerala in South India who fast and pray during Holy Week and brood about the death and resurrection of Jesus. It points out the futile effort of the son, Appu, to live literally and imaginatively away from home and his father's expectation. The son's desire is to study Malayalam literature and become a writer, but his father's plan is to send him to medical school and make him the first medical doctor in the family. As a way of counteracting the resistance of the son, the father sends him to spend time at a secular monastery run by a master whose fame included, among other things, producing a fake Bible.

Source: R. S. Sugirtharajah, "Son(s) Behaving Badly: The Prodigal in Foreign Hands," in A. K. M. Adam, ed., *Postmodern Interpretations of the Bible: A Reader* (St. Louis: Chalice, 2001), pp. 198–199.

Eventually, when the father and the master urge him to undertake the self-quest he is pining for, and offer money, the son, unlike the son in the Lukan story, becomes frightened of the impending journey. When he thinks about the prospect of hazardous long rail rides, deserts, and strange languages, he decides to return to the family, much to the joy of his father. Whereas, in the Lukan narrative, taking the money is seen as the son's right, in Palakeel's story it is seen as a failure. In the eyes of his grand uncle, the moment Appu took the money, he had come a cropper: "You took money. You failed." The son—egotistical, insecure, and under-confident—realizes that stargazing alone is not sufficient. He starts hearing voices: "Turn back. Go home. Return to your beginnings. Go home."

These retellings [of the story of the Prodigal Son/Welcoming Father] acknowledge the background and the influence of Judeo-Christian elements, but, at the same time, they redirect that influence by opening and nativising or Hinduising it. Indigenization is achieved either through writing in additional materials or excising awkward elements in the texts.

Questions

1. In your opinion, how well does Palakeel's story succeed as a retelling of Jesus' parable?

2. Explain Jesus' parable and this retelling as closely as you can using social categories of kinship and honor/shame.

> ### Doing Cross-Cultural Reading Yourself
>
> 1. Luke 10:29–42 presents two parables about marginalized people. Compare them for insights into what it means to be marginalized.
>
> 2. If you were to retell the parable of the Prodigal Son/Welcoming Father for a North American cultural minority group that you know, how would you do it?

Key Terms and Concepts

ascension • beatitudes and woes • canticles • center section/Jesus' journey to Jerusalem
commensality • L • infancy narrative • Jesus' genealogy • prologue
Sermon on the Plain • transfiguration

Questions for Study, Discussion, and Writing

1. State and analyze Luke's major theological themes and aims.
2. Describe the evidence for and against the authorship of this gospel by Luke the companion of Paul.

3. Compare the Lord's Prayer/Our Father in Luke and Matthew. Which version is likely to be more authentic? Do the two Gospels' concerns come through in these prayers, and how?
4. Explain the persistent connection in Luke between the Holy Spirit and prayer.
5. Compare Mark 13 to the parallel passage in Luke 21. How does Luke alter Mark to say that the end of time is not near? What role might the presence of Acts play in this?
6. Some scholars have suggested that Jesus' parable of the lost/prodigal son is autobiographical of Jesus, dealing with an incident in his life before his ministry began. Is there any evidence to decide on this hypothesis, and what might it be? Compare this suggestion with the argument of Kenneth E. Bailey in his *Jacob and the Prodigal,* which argues that this parable is a retelling of the story of Jacob.
7. Show how Luke portrays the elder brother of the parable of the Prodigal Son as the truly "lost" son.
8. Describe Jesus' attitude on poverty and wealth in Luke. Is this applicable to North American society generally today, or is it practicable only for devout—and very countercultural—Christians?

For Further Reading

Blount, Brian K. *Then the Whisper Put on Flesh: New Testament Ethics in an African American Context* (Nashville, TN: Abingdon, 2001). Contains excellent treatment of Luke-Acts from an African American perspective.

Conzelmann, Hans. *Theology of St. Luke.* New York: Harper & Row, 1960. An influential redactional study of Luke, accessible to beginning students.

Fitzmyer, Joseph. *The Gospel According to Luke.* Anchor Bible 28, 28A. Garden City, NY: Doubleday, 1981, 1985. The best English-language commentary.

Green, Joel B. *The Gospel of Luke.* Grand Rapids, MI: Eerdmans, 1997. An excellent commentary on the narrative dimensions of Luke.

Green, Joel B. *The Theology of the Gospel of Luke.* Cambridge: Cambridge University Press, 1995. A fine study of Lukan theology.

Kurz, William S. *Reading Luke-Acts: Dynamics of Biblical Narrative.* Louisville: Westminster John Knox Press, 1993. Shows how literary criticism illuminates the Gospel of Luke and the Acts of the Apostles, reclaiming them as biblical narrative.

Levine, Amy-Jill. *A Feminist Companion to Luke.* London/New York: Sheffield Academic Press, 2002. A collection of essays on key feminist passages and themes in Luke.

Malina, Bruce J., and Richard L. Rohrbaugh, *Social-Science Commentary on the Synoptic Gospels:* Philadelphia: Fortress, 1992. For each passage in the Synoptics, a social scientific commentary drawing largely on cultural anthropology is offered; an excellent resource for students.

Powell, Mark A. *What Are They Saying about Luke?* New York: Paulist Press, 1989. An excellent general introduction to issues in current scholarship.

Chapter Nine

The Gospel of John: Following Jesus, the Eternal Son of God

When we read the opening words of John's Gospel, "In the beginning was the Word, and the Word was with God, and the Word was God," we sense that we are in a much different kind of Gospel than the Synoptic Gospels. As we read through to the end of John, this sense is confirmed. Ninety percent of John does not appear in the Synoptics. John has a different order of events for Jesus' ministry, a literary style in which both the narrator and Jesus speak in very similar ways, and above all a higher view of Jesus and his teaching. Jesus' words and acts point to his own identity as the eternal Son of God, the one in whom eternal life and light are found. Following Jesus means to live continuously in him and to live and love as Jesus did, by the power of the Holy Spirit sent to replace Jesus. Historical criticism and other methods of study have contributed much to our knowledge of the Fourth Gospel. Narrative reading studies the long chapters of John and the narrative structure of the whole Gospel. Social scientific criticism focuses on how the primary kinship relationship of God as Father and Jesus as the eternal Son affects other kinship ideas in John. Feminist readings of John study how the women of the Fourth Gospel are key to its portrayal of the followers of Jesus. Cross-cultural reading deals with the leading division between the followers of Jesus and "the Jews."

John in Brief: Outline of Structure and Content

I. Prologue: Hymn to the Eternal Word, testimony of John the Baptizer to Jesus (1:1–18)

II. The Book of Signs (1:19–12:50)

    A. John the Baptizer and Jesus' new disciples bear witness to him (1:19–51)

    B. Jesus changes water to wine in Cana (2:1–11)

    C. Jesus cleanses the temple (2:13–25)

    D. Dialogue with Nicodemus (chap. 3)

    E. Dialogue with a Samaritan woman; healing the royal official's son (4)

    F. Jesus fulfills Judaism: Sabbath, Passover, Tabernacles, Hanukkah (5–10)

    G. Jesus raises Lazarus from death, and is condemned by a Jewish court; Jesus anointed for burial; enters Jerusalem; ends his public ministry (11–12)

III. The Book of Glory (13:1–20:31)

    A. Last Supper and Farewell Discourse (chaps. 13–17)

    B. Jesus' passion, death and burial (18–19)

    C. Jesus' resurrection: empty tomb, resurrection appearances in Jerusalem (20:1–29)

    D. First conclusion of the Gospel (20:30–31)

IV. Epilogue: two resurrection appearances in Galilee; second conclusion (21:1–25)

Developing Your Skills

Read the Gospel of John rapidly, in one sitting. Use the outline to guide your reading. Notice especially the overall structure of the book, with its long chapters often thematically organized.

A Guide to Reading

Positioned as a theological introduction to the Gospel, the poetic **prologue** succinctly but comprehensively introduces John's view of Christ as the eternal Word (John 1:1–18). God's Word is a divine being, the **Logos** (1:1, 14). This Logos is the creating and sustaining light of the world (1:5, 9), and God's only Son (1:14, 18). This Word comes into the world and becomes human. He shows God's glory and retains his own glory as a human being (1:14). Although rejected by his own people, he empowers all who do accept him to become God's children, so that in him they participate in God's grace and truth (1:16–17). This hymn to Christ is interrupted twice to deal with the Baptizer, first to mention John the Baptizer before the light comes into the world (1:6–8) and second to record John the Baptizer's testimony to Jesus after the Word becomes flesh (1:15). Here the author works to bring John inside the Jesus movement, although the author may know of others who see John as the messianic head of a competing movement. These words about John seem not to belong in a hymn to Christ, but they do tie the prologue and beginning of the narrative together. The prologue itself ends on the grand note, "From his [the Word's] fullness we have all received, grace upon grace. . . . God the only Son, close to the Father's heart, has made him [God] known" (vv. 16, 18).

As the narrative of the Fourth Gospel begins, we see the **Book of Signs,** the name often given to the first twelve chapters of John because of the prominence of Jesus' miracles in it. John the Baptizer explains his ministry, rejecting honor for himself and predicting the coming of one of whom he is unworthy (1:19–28). Much of this language echoes and reinforces the prologue of John. A new phrase appears in 1:19, "the Jews." The writer of John uses it to denote (as here) official Jewish leaders, but it is unusual not least because most everyone in the Gospel is Jewish, including John the Baptizer, Jesus, and his disciples! On the next day, this honorable one comes, and John the Baptizer introduces Jesus, but there is no explicit mention of Jesus' being baptized (1:29–34). John proclaims Jesus as the sacrificial Lamb of God, as one who existed beforehand, and as God's chosen one/Son. On the next day, Andrew and an unnamed disciple of John follow Jesus (1:35–42). Andrew hails Jesus as teacher and Messiah, and Andrew's brother Simon is brought to Jesus, who names him "Cephas" ("rock"), the Aramaic equivalent of the Greek-based "Peter." On the next day, Peter finds Philip, who in turn finds Nathaniel (1:43–51). These new disciples of Jesus identify him as the one promised in the Mosaic Law and the prophets as the Son of God and as the King of Israel. Despite their initial understanding of Jesus' greatness, the Gospel writer has Jesus promise that they will see even greater things, an explicit use of the narrative technique of anticipation.

The Cana scene is "the first of his signs" (2:1–11; the second sign, also in Cana of Galilee, will come at 4:46–54). In the Fourth Gospel, a **sign** is a miracle by Jesus that points to Jesus' identity as God's Son. In this first sign, Jesus miraculously replaces the large amount of water approved for Jewish purifications with wine so fine that the headwaiter wonders why the best has been kept until last. The mother of Jesus, who is never named in John despite her important roles, asks Jesus to help. Her request, made on behalf of the hosts who are about to be socially shamed because their supply of wine has run out, is rebuffed by Jesus because his "hour had not yet come." Yet his mother's persistence in telling the headwaiter to "Do whatever he tells you" paves the way for Jesus to honor her original request. She thus becomes a model of persistent faith in Jesus. This first sign has, like many episodes in John's narrative, two levels: the historical-literal (Jesus turns water to wine) and the eternal-symbolic (Jesus replaces the water of Judaism with the fine wine that is himself). In 2:12, we learn that Jesus' mother and brothers followed him to Capernaum, but when his public ministry begins they disappear from view, and John does not mention them until Jesus' death. Jesus' disciples, however, "believe in him," seeing in his miraculous action a sign that he is the fulfillment of a significant aspect of Jewish messianic expectation, that the Messiah will bring a fullness of fine wine (Isa 25:6, Jer 31:12, Amos 9:13–14). From the first mention of the Baptizer (1:19) to this point of the Cana wedding (2:12) is framed as one week. This one-week period at the beginning matches the one week at the end of Jesus' life, in chapters 12–20. In Jerusalem near Passover,

Jesus cleanses the Temple of its impurities by making a whip and driving out the animals and the money exchangers (2:13–22). Jesus puts moral purity ahead of ritual purity. Two special Johannine theological themes surface here. First, the antagonism of "the Jews" from the very beginning illustrates the incompatibility between Jesus and his own people, who did not receive him (1:11). In social scientific terms, he is supposed to be an insider with them, but he is really an outsider—a cosmic outsider, at that. Second, the new sanctuary that replaces the Jerusalem temple is Jesus himself; he will be destroyed by "the Jews" but raised from death by his own power. According to 2:23–25, many in Jerusalem believed in Jesus because of signs he was doing. However, he did not trust their faith because it centered on the miraculous aspect of his signs and not on Jesus himself as the Son of God.

Next, the conversation with Nicodemus is the first of the Johannine dialogues (3:1–21). This Pharisee, a member of the Sanhedrin, comes to Jesus at night, probably because he does not yet belong to the light. He knows that Jesus is a "teacher who has come from God" because of his miracles. To judge from the rest of the conversation, Nicodemus means by this only that Jesus is "sent by God," but Jesus has personally come from God. Nicodemus represents inadequate faith, as becomes clear when Jesus explains that only conception and birth "from above" enables one to enter the kingdom of God. This birth takes place when one is baptized in water and receives God's Spirit. Nicodemus misunderstands, thinking of natural birth from a Jewish mother that makes one a member of the covenant people. Jesus redefines here who will be considered the children of God, challenging any privileged status stemming from natural parenthood. He explains the need for being reborn "from above" (or "again"—the Greek word means both), connected to Jesus' own origin in God. The dialogue now becomes a monologue as Nicodemus fades into the narrative background at 3:15 until he reappears as a hidden follower in 7:50–52, and finally as an open follower in 19:39–42, an example of one who comes to faith gradually. What is more, in 3:16–21 we are unsure who is speaking: is Jesus continuing the monologue, or does the Evangelist add his own words to explain it? This section continues the prologue's basic Johannine theology of **incarnation,** or God coming "into the (human) flesh." He is God's Son come into the world with God's own life. Therefore, everyone who believes in him has eternal life in the here and now, and has already been judged and acquitted by God.

John the Baptizer's final witness to Jesus (3:22–30) comes as Jesus is first said to be baptizing and then said not to be baptizing—note how the narrator makes an explicit self-correction. When the Baptizer's disciples are opposed to Jesus because his movement is eclipsing the Baptizer's movement, John clarifies one last time that he is not the Messiah and speaks of the greatness of the one for whom he has prepared the way. The style of the monologue about earthly and heavenly testimony in 3:31–36 is the same as Jesus' style in his talk with Nicodemus, and it reiterates things said in the Nicodemus dialogue. For the second time in chapter 3 we are uncertain about who is speaking, the narrator of the Gospel or (here) John the Baptizer.

When Jesus learns that the Pharisees have heard about his growing popularity, Jesus and his disciples go from Judea toward Galilee (4:1–3). On the way, Jesus stops in Samaria at the well of Sychar. The dialogue with the Samaritan woman and its aftermath (4:4–42) is the first example of John's narrative portrayal in one episode of a particular type of encounter with Jesus. This chapter portrays how one comes to faith despite the many obstacles that stand in the way. The dialogue portrays Jesus as the "living water," that is, the water that gives eternal life, and the Samaritan woman takes many twists and turns as she finally arrives at this truth and believes fully. Another key Johannine theme present here is the replacement of Judaism, specifically Jesus as the replacement in his own person of temple worship, whether Jewish or even Samaritan. Worship at the Temple yields to worship "in spirit and truth" as revealed in Jesus. By placing side by side the narratives of the more open faith of the Samaritan woman and the inadequate faith of Nicodemus (chap. 3), John points the reader to this open faith.

The second sign at Cana, the healing of the royal official's son (4:43–54), resembles the first Cana story in that the one who requests a miracle is initially rebuffed by Jesus but persists in faith and has the request granted. This official probably served Herod Antipas, the tetrarch (minor king) of Galilee. The transitional 4:43–45 speaks of an inadequate faith that gives no honor to a prophet in his own country. This contrasts with the faith illustrated by the royal official who believes that Jesus' words will come true and returns home on the strength of it. He then reaches a fuller faith, and in that fuller faith he leads his whole household to faith in Jesus.

Now we enter a section of John, chapters 5–10 in the "Book of Signs," in which Jesus fulfills and replaces the holy days and feasts of Judaism: Sabbath, Passover, Tabernacles, and Dedication or Hanukkah. This fulfillment-replacement is accomplished in each narrative subsection first by what Jesus does, and then by what he says in a monologue or dialogue. Two themes from the prologue will be developed here: the theme of Jesus as life in chapters 5–7 and the theme of Jesus as light in chapters 8–10.

On the Sabbath, Jesus gives life by healing. This action leads to a short hostile dialogue and a much longer monologue (5:1–47). Jesus cures a lame man who has been waiting to be healed at the pool of Bethesda. His healing action along with his instruction that the healed man take up his mat violates the Sabbath law forbidding all work. The explanation that Jesus offers to "the Jews" does not appeal to human-itarian grounds, but to his supreme authority. Although people should not work on the Sabbath, God continues to work on that day by causing birth and death on the Sabbath. God is Jesus' Father, and the Father has given to the Son a power based on this cosmic kinship that he uses appropriately on the Sabbath. "The Jews" recognize what Jesus is claiming, that "he was calling God his own Father, making him-self God's equal," and they sought to kill him for this (5:18). Thus a lethal hostility toward Jesus appears early and consistently, especially associated with "the Jews." In 5:31–47, the follow-up monologue, Jesus advances five witnesses as testimony for him: God the Father ("another"); John the Baptizer; the works that Jesus is doing (probably his signs); scripture in general; and Moses in particular, who wrote about Jesus.

Next, Jesus multiplies the bread and fish, and presents himself as the Bread of Life, as he fulfills and replaces the Passover (all of chapter 6). This is the second Passover mentioned in John, and the talk in this chapter about Jesus' death anticipates the final Passover. Moses has just been cited as a witness to Jesus, and this long chapter will develop the prophet-like-Moses presentation of Jesus. Jesus explains that Moses did not give the true bread from heaven after the Hebrews left Egypt, because those who ate the manna died (6:32, 58). The crowd finds and puts demands on Jesus the next day, showing again that most people did not really see beyond the miraculous signs to what they signified. Jesus did not come simply to satisfy earthly hunger but to give "bread" that would nourish people for eternal life. Jesus is the "bread of life" in the sense that his revelation constitutes teaching by God (6:45), so that one must believe in the Son to have eternal life. Jesus' eternal connection with his Father is the basis of his becoming the "bread of life" for the whole world. In John 6:51–58 Jesus is nourishment in another sense, for one must feed on his flesh and blood to have eternal life. The themes of 6:35–51a are duplicated in 6:51b–58, but now in language suggestive of Jewish sacrifice, which Jesus replaces with the sacrifice of his own life: "The bread that I shall give for the life of the world is my own flesh." The language seems to be Eucharistic; if so, John's teaching on the Eucharist is as "high" as his Christology. The monologue in John 6 reveals that Jesus feeds his followers through both his revelation and his flesh and blood, both in his words and deeds. In response, some of Jesus' disciples object to this striking teaching and leave Jesus (6:60–61), even as "the Jews" objected in 6:41–43, 52. Simon Peter and the rest of the Twelve are among those who do not go away, for they recognize that Jesus has the words of eternal life. Although most of them follow Jesus in true faith, Jesus already knows and tells his disciples that Judas is the "devil" who will betray him (6:70–71).

The next Jewish feast, Tabernacles (also known as "Booths"), seems to cover the long section of 7:1 to 10:21, until the Feast of Dedication/Hanukkah is mentioned in 10:22. Usually the feast of Tabernacles is associated with living in "booths" (tents), but here John probably draws on local Jerusalem color. On this eight-day-long pilgrimage-feast on which Jews went up to Jerusalem, a daily ritual procession from the pool of Siloam in Jerusalem brought water to the Temple, according to later Jewish writings. There the Court of the (Jewish) Women was lit by immense torches—thus the themes of water and light in this section. This section begins when Jesus refuses a request of the brothers in his human family that smacks of disbelief, and secretly goes up to Jerusalem at his own initiative (7:1–10). Opinions about Jesus produce a division (7:11–15); again Jesus indirectly but inevitably causes people to judge themselves. Jesus' dialogue with "the Jews" recalls previous hostility over the Mosaic Law, and culminates with a warning that soon he is going away to God who sent him, the first mention of Jesus' departure in John (7:16–36). His opponents misconstrue this announced departure as a sort of cross-cultural mission, that Jesus might go to the Jews in the Diaspora and teach them (7:35–36). The theme of water emerges on the last day of Tabernacles in 7:37–39, as Jesus announces that from within himself shall flow rivers of living water that reach those who believe in him. Rising opposition to Jesus leads to a botched attempt to arrest him, bringing Nicodemus back on the scene as he defends Jesus. He still does not believe in him, but he is moving closer (7:40–52).

In 8:1–11 we have the well-known but textually uncertain passage about Jesus' rescue of a woman about to receive a stoning for adultery. Although it seems to be an authentic incident in Jesus' life, it has no particularly Johannine literary style or themes and it interrupts John's treatment of Jesus and Tabernacles. Then 8:12–59 presents Jesus as the "light of the world," the replacement for the lights of the feast. The legal atmosphere of defensive testimony against Jewish charges returns, and the situation becomes very hostile with suggestions of (Jesus'?) illegitimacy, and Jesus' countercharges that the devil is his opponents' father. It ends with a remarkable chris-tological statement, "Before Abraham was, I am" (8:58), which brings about an attempt to kill Jesus by stoning.

Chapter 9 describes dramatically how the man born blind came to sight, first physically and then spiritually. "The light of the world" motif (9:5) and the refer-ence to the pool of Siloam (9:7, 11) provide a loose relationship with the Tabernacles feast. He exemplifies one who truly believes at the first encounter with Jesus but can come to see the deeper significance of Jesus only later, after undergoing trials and being cast out of the synagogue. The intensifying series of questions to which the man born blind is subjected, the increasing hostility and blindness of the inter-rogators who finally eject him from the synagogue, the blind man's growing faith in Jesus even while under pressure to abandon it, and his parents' pathetic attempt to avoid taking a stand for or against Jesus—all these events are developed masterfully into a drama to illustrate how, with the coming of Jesus, judgment has come into the world with him. Those who claim to see (the Pharisees and perhaps the par-ents) have become blind, and those who were blind (the healed man) have gained sight (9:39).

In the narrative sequence, the monologue on the good shepherd (10:1–21) has a certain independence within its context, but is directed to the Pharisees whom Jesus accused of being blind in 9:40–41. A **mixed metaphor** (using two unrelated metaphors in close proximity to describe the same thing; in our usage considered poor style, but typical of good Hebrew Bible/Jewish expression) offers two different ways of looking at the same reality. Jesus is metaphorically the gate of the sheep pen by which the shepherd goes to the sheep and the sheep come and go to pasture. He is also the ideal shepherd, who knows his sheep by name and lays down his life for them. When 10:16 refers to "other sheep not of this fold" and expresses Jesus' goal of one flock and one shepherd, this suggests that division among Jesus' followers would become a problem. Since the readers do not know of these divisions from

The Pool of Siloam This famous pool is at the lowest point in the City of David area, 400 feet south of the Temple Mount. The Pool of Siloam today is significantly different in size and shape now than in the NT period, when it was much larger. The Jewish historian Josephus frequently referred to Siloam as a fountain and said that its waters were sweet and abundant. The Gospel of John presents Jesus as the living water to replace the water like that of this pool. Used by permission of BiblePlaces.com.

the narrative to this point, they may be led to think of "other sheep" outside the text, perhaps in the situation of the author.

The next Jewish feast is Dedication or Hanukkah (10:22–42), which celebrates the rededication of the Jerusalem Temple by the Maccabees in 164 B.C.E. This feast is replaced when in the Temple colonnade Jesus claims to be the one whom the Father dedicated and sent into the world (10:36). Jewish authorities object to Jesus' claim to be the Messiah and consider it blasphemy that he said he was God's Son. Faced with attempts to arrest and stone him, Jesus defiantly reasserts the deepest truth of his identity, "The Father is in me, and I am in the Father." Jesus now goes back across the Jordan to where the story began in 1:28 (10:40–42).

Chapter 11, although a part of the "Book of Signs," serves as a bridge between it and the **Book of Glory,** the second half of the Gospel of John, because the Book of Signs' last miracle will lead to Jesus' death and his glory. Jesus gives life to Lazarus (11:1–44) and thus performs the most effective and dramatic of his signs, yet ironically the gift of life leads to the decision that Jesus must die (11:45–53). In the raising of Lazarus the dialogue precedes the sign that it explains and heightens its narrative tension, a reversal of the usual structure that signals its importance to the reader. In this dialogue, Martha states her belief that Jesus is the Messiah, the Son of God, and that her brother will rise on the last day; but Jesus characteristically leads her to an even deeper faith. Jesus is himself the resurrection and the life, so that whoever believes in him will never die. Lazarus's miraculous return to life is still only a sign, for Lazarus will die again, as his emerging from the tomb still bound with burial clothes implies. So great is this sign that even "many of the Jews" present believed in Jesus (11:45). This large number of Jews who now believe in Jesus provokes a Sanhedrin session (11:45–53). They fear that if the Jewish nation follows Jesus, the governance system would be challenged, and the Romans might intervene and destroy the nation and the Temple. Caiaphas, high priest in that year, unintentionally utters a prophecy that will come true, the Gospel narrator says. Caiaphas says cynically that Jesus should die instead of the nation, but John sees this to mean that Jesus will die sacrificially *for* the nation and even more "to gather together even the dispersed children of God." Jesus' fate is sealed by this Sanhedrin, and he prepares for his arrest at the upcoming Passover (11:54–57).

At Bethany outside Jerusalem six days before Passover, Mary, the sister of Lazarus, anoints Jesus' feet (12:1–9), preparing Jesus for burial. On the next day, Jesus triumphantly enters Jerusalem on a young donkey (12:12–19). The end of his public ministry is signaled by the arrival of Gentiles (12:20–50), which causes Jesus to exclaim loudly that the hour of his glorification, his death and resurrection, has come. Jesus explains his death as that of a grain of wheat that dies in order to bear much fruit. Jesus' soul is troubled and sorrowful, but he refuses to pray that he might be saved from his destiny. Instead, kinship and honor prevail: he prays that his Father's name be glorified in what is about to happen. The crowd mistakes the voice from heaven affirming Jesus as the voice of an angel (12:28–29). The failure of the crowds to accept this as the voice of God is a fulfillment of Isaiah's prediction that they will never believe (12:37–41). Although some even in the Sanhedrin believe in Jesus, they fear the Pharisees and so are not willing to acknowledge their faith openly (12:42–43). The last word of Jesus in his public ministry forms an impressive inclusion with his first monologue in 3:16–21: Jesus the light has come into the world and has led those who believe in him from darkness into light; but those who reject him are even now being condemned to wander in darkness (12:44–50). Jesus has struggled with his fate, but his inner struggle is over now, and he will face his suffering with calm confidence.

The theme of chapters 13–20, the Book of Glory, is introduced in 13:1: Jesus passes from this world to the Father. In the five chapters (13–17) set in Jesus' Last Supper, only his own disciples are present with Jesus and hear his farewell teaching. Chapters 18–20 describe the passion and resurrection of Jesus as a glorification and ascent to his Father that bring life and the Spirit to them. Chapter 21 forms a second ending to the Gospel, dealing with the death of the Beloved Disciple and the community crisis it causes. The Book of Glory begins with the Last Supper (chapter 13). It is not a Passover meal, as in the Synoptics. Jesus knows of his betrayal by one of his own disciples, setting a somber tone. John then portrays Jesus' washing of the disciples' feet, a loving act of extreme humility typically done by a slave, which serves as an example for his disciples to serve each other humbly. When Jesus tells them of his betrayal by one of his own, the **Beloved Disciple**, the special "disciple whom Jesus loves" in this Gospel, leans against Jesus' chest to ask the identity of the one who will betray him. Mentioned explicitly only in the Book of Glory (here and in 19:25–27; 20:2; 21:7; 21:24), the Beloved Disciple is often contrasted with Peter, as here.

After Judas has gone out into the night (symbolic of the realm of Satan), John supplies a short introduction (13:31–38) to his longest discourse, the Last or **Farewell Discourse** (chapters 14–17). Jesus speaks once more of his coming glorification and issues his new commandment: "As I have loved you, so you too must love one another." This is "new" not because the OT was lacking in love, but because there are now two Christian modifications to the love command: The love is to be empowered by and modeled on the way Jesus loved his disciples by dying and rising for them, and it is a love to be extended especially to one's fellow believers.

In the body of Jesus' Farewell Discourse (chapters 14–17) he speaks to "his own" as he anticipates his departure. This monologue presents diverse material in one final message. The Johannine Jesus speaks here as still in the world and as no longer in it (16:5; 17:11), making his message of timeless value. It resembles a **testament** or farewell speech, where a dying speaker makes a long, stylized goodbye to loved ones, first with comfort and then instruction to them. Jesus offers this comfort and instruction, but in a highly mixed-together way. (Note how so much of the first half of the Farewell Discourse in chaps. 14–15 is echoed in the second in chaps. 16–17.) He explains the nearness of his departure (13:33; 14:2–3; 16:16), eliciting expressions of sorrow in himself and others (14:1, 27; 16:6, 22). He recalls his past life, words, and deeds (13:33; 14:10; 15:3, 20; 17:4–8), urging the addressees to emulate and even surpass them (14:12). He urges them to keep his commandments (14:15, 21, 23; 15:10, 14); he urges them to stay united after he is gone (17:11, 21–23). He wishes them peace and joy (14:27; 16:22, 33), prays for them (17:9), and promises them that as they abide in him as the "vine" they will bear much fruit as his "branches" (15:1–11). He predicts that they will be persecuted (15:18, 20; 16:2–3) and assures them of the coming of the Spirit to take his place among them when he goes. This Spirit goes by the Johannine term **Paraclete** (PEAR-uh-kleet), whose dual role is suggested by the two main ideas in this Greek word, "helper" and "advocate/attorney" (14:16–17, 26; 15:26). The divine Word became incarnate in one human being, whose stay in this world with his followers was temporary. The Paraclete does not become incarnate but dwells forever in all who love Jesus and keep his commandments (14:15–16), to defend them against the world and to explain the implications of what Jesus said. Emphasizing his departure, Jesus consoles his disciples by a promise to return to take them to himself so that they may be with him. The flow of the Farewell Discourse is initially interrupted by the disciples' distress at what is about to happen, and they misunderstand Jesus' explanation of it. Thomas' interruption (14:5) leads to one of the most memorable proclamations by Jesus in the Gospel: "I am the way and the truth and the life." Philip's interruption (14:8) leads to Jesus' "Whoever has seen me has seen the Father . . . I am in the Father and the Father is in me." This mutual divine indwelling—in social scientific terms, kinship among divine beings—leads to how the Spirit/Paraclete, Jesus himself, and the Father will all dwell in the Christian (14:15–24).

As the Farewell Discourse seems to end, Jesus gives his gift of peace, accompanied by a warning that the Prince of this world is coming (14:27–31b). Jesus' final words in chapter 14, "Get up! Let us leave here and be on our way," give the impression of signaling the formal end of the discourse (v. 31). Surprisingly, three chapters of discourse follow 14:31, apparently in the same room! 16:4–33 treats many themes of the first part of the Farewell Discourse and yet seems to suppose that the audience knows nothing of them. Earlier in the Supper Jesus spoke of being with his disciples only a little while; 16:16–22 will restate and develop that theme. In 16:23–24, with the issue of asking and receiving, we have once more a theme found earlier in the Farewell Discourse (14:13–14). The section 16:25–33 also has some themes that we have heard before: "The Father loves you because you have loved me" in 16:27 is found earlier in 14:21, 23; "I am going to the Father" in 16:28 and in 14:12; the promise of peace in 16:33 and 14:27. Some new items also appear: the contrast between Jesus using "figures of speech" and his speaking plainly, and the prediction of the scattering of the disciples.

The conclusion to the Last Discourse in chapter 17 is Jesus' final prayer, often called in later Christian tradition the "High Priestly" prayer. In the first section (17:1–8) Jesus prays for his glorification (i.e., with the glory that he had before creation) on the grounds that he has completed all that the Father has given him to do and revealed God's "name," that is, God's very being. The goal of the glorification is that the Son may glorify the Father properly. In the second section (17:9–19) Jesus prays that those whom the Father has given him may be kept safe. He refuses to pray for "the world," a social-spiritual entity that by rejecting Jesus has become even more the realm of evil. Jesus does not ask that his disciples be taken out of the world, but only that they be kept safe from the Evil One, who is the ruler of this world. Praying that they will be consecrated as he consecrates himself, Jesus sends them into the world to bear witness to truth. In the third section (17:20–26) Jesus prays for those who believe in him through the word of the disciples—a prayer that they may be one just as the Father and Jesus are one. A unity among believers will be convincing to the world. Honoring statements about these believers are addressed to the Father: "I have given to them the glory which you have given to me"; "You loved them even as you loved me"; and "They are your gift to me".

The passion of Jesus comes next in chapters 18–19. In it, Jesus is arrested, interrogated by the Jewish high priest, tried before Pilate, crucified and buried. Before Jesus' arrest (18:1–12), he leaves the upper room and crosses the Kidron brook to a garden. There Jesus is eager to drink the cup the Father has given him. Jesus is in charge at his own arrest, as he will be in charge throughout his passion. This control is expressed here in three short dramatic incidents. First, knowing that Judas is coming, Jesus goes out to meet him and initiate what happens next. Second, when he identifies himself by saying, "I am," the arresting party, both Jewish Temple police and Roman soldiers, fall back to the ground before him at these words for the divine name Yahweh. Third, he commands the arresting party not to arrest his followers, a command that they obey.

The Jewish priest Annas then interrogates Jesus about his teaching, as Peter denies him simultaneously (18:13–27). The Sanhedrin already met to condemn Jesus in 11:45–53, so Jesus' fate is already sealed. Although Caiaphas is the High Priest at the time, Annas conducts the hearing. Peter's denials are prefaced by the mention of the presence of another, unnamed disciple who is known to the high priest (the Beloved Disciple?). The lengthier hearing before Pilate (18:28–19:16) is a highly developed drama. John supplies careful stage setting, with "the Jews" outside the praetorium and Jesus inside. Seven short episodes describe how Pilate shuttled back and forth trying to resolve the difficult situation to his own political advantage. John explains clearly why the Jewish leaders brought Jesus to Pilate (18:31: the Jewish authorities were not permitted to put anyone to death) and why Pilate expediently rendered a death sentence even though he knew that Jesus did not deserve it (19:12). Jesus challenges Pilate as to whether he belongs to the truth (18:37), and thus the scene becomes a "trial" of Pontius Pilate before Jesus, over whom Pilate has no real power (19:11). The whipping by the Roman soldiers is at the mid-point of Jesus' trial so that Pilate can present him shamed and bleeding to "the Jews," naively hoping that they will give up their demands for Jesus' death. However, it is Pilate who yields in the end, and he gives Jesus over to crucifixion.

After this long, slow trial scene, the narrative pace quickens, and the crucifixion, death, and burial of Jesus advance rapidly (19:17–42). Jesus dies in control of the situation and his own destiny. Pilate refuses the Jewish request to change the wording on the placard on Jesus' cross identifying him as the "King of the Jews," and so Jesus dies as a king. John notes two other figures at the cross whose names he never gives us: the mother of Jesus and the disciple whom he loved. Jesus brings them into a new kinship, a mother-son relationship. This done, Jesus is able to make his final utterance from the cross, "It is completed," and to entrust his spirit to God (19:30). When a Roman soldier pierces the dead Jesus' side, it fulfills both Jesus' statement that from within him would flow living water (7:37–39), and, since his bones like the bones of the Passover lamb were not broken, that he was the Lamb of God (1:29). Nicodemus, a **secret disciple** who has not yet openly admitted that he believes in Jesus, now reappears and together with Joseph from Arimathea publicly gives an honorable burial to Jesus.

Chapter 20 in John places all the appearances of the risen Lord in Jerusalem. Four different types of faith response to the risen Jesus are dramatized in the four resurrection-appearance narratives: two in episodes that take place at the empty tomb and two in a room where the disciples are hiding. At the tomb (20:1–3), an introduction consisting of Mary Magdalene's coming to the tomb, finding it empty, and reporting this to Simon Peter and the Beloved Disciple prepares for the two appearances of Jesus at the tomb. Then Simon Peter and the Beloved Disciple run to the tomb (20:3–10). Both enter and see the burial wrappings and head cloth, which the risen Jesus has left behind in the tomb. However, only the Beloved Disciple understands and comes to faith. He knew that Lazarus came out of the tomb bound head and body in his burial clothes, symbolizing that he will die again (chap. 11). Jesus, on the other hand, gives true life, symbolized by leaving his burial clothes behind.

The second scene (20:11–18) has Mary Magdalene return to the tomb where now two angels are present. Neither their speaking to her nor the sudden appearance of Jesus, whom she mistakenly identifies as a gardener, brings her to faith. That is accomplished when Jesus calls her by name (see 10:3–4: the good shepherd calls his own by name, and they know his voice.) Mary is sent to proclaim all this to the disciples, whom Jesus now calls his "brothers." These two scenes at the tomb relate resurrection faith to intimate knowledge of Jesus; now the Gospel turns to scenes of a more traditional character, where faith and doubt greet the appearance itself.

The next resurrection appearance takes place on Easter Sunday night in a place where the doors are locked for the disciples' fear of "the Jews" (20:19–25). After extending peace, Jesus gives to the disciples (minus Thomas, who is inexplicably not there) a mission that continues his own. In an action reminiscent of God's creative breath that gave life to the first human being (Gen 2:7) and of the human need to be begotten of water and Spirit (John 3:5–8), Jesus breathes on them and gives them the Holy Spirit. The third scene is located in the same place a week later, now with the disciple Thomas present (20:26–29). The proof Jesus offers Thomas, examining Jesus' hands with his fingers and putting his hand in Jesus' side, presents a touchable image of the risen Jesus, but one should note that John does not explicitly say that Thomas touched Jesus. Rather, his seeming willingness now to believe without touching is genuine faith. The one who had embodied disbelief—"I will not believe that he is alive unless I see and touch him"—now utters the highest christological confession in this Gospel, "My Lord and My God." "Doubting Thomas" has become an example of the highest sort of faith. In response, Jesus blesses all who will believe in him without having seen him (20:29); this action shows an awareness of the Gospel audience for whom John had been writing. Last in this chapter comes the first of **two endings of John.** The audience comes explicitly into play as John now states his reason for writing, which he has saved until the end. In selecting material for this book, the author's goal has been to have people either come to faith or increase in faith (a disputed reading) in Jesus as the Messiah, the Son of God, and through this faith to possess eternal life in him.

In 21:1–25 John presents a sort of epilogue. Although the Gospel concludes at the end of chapter 20, another chapter of resurrection appearances follows in 21, this time in Galilee, with another conclusion modeled on the first. This chapter contains two episodes dealing with the continuing roles of Peter and the Beloved Disciple. The first scene (21:1–14), in which the disciples do not recognize the risen Jesus standing on the shore even though they have recognized him twice in chapter 20, involves a miraculous catch of fish. Since Simon Peter hauls the 153 fish ashore and the net is not torn, the catch probably is symbolic of the Johannine community's missionary success in bringing people into the one community of Christ. Characteristically for John, the Beloved Disciple recognizes the risen Lord first. Jesus has fish on shore before the catch is brought ashore, and he has the disciples bring some of their own fish to put on the fire as he prepares a meal of bread and fish for them. The second scene (21:15–23) shifts symbolism abruptly as the talk turns from fish to sheep. Peter's shepherding flows from his love for Jesus; the flock still belongs to Jesus ("my sheep"). Peter must be willing, like Jesus, to lay down his life for the sheep. Peter is to take charge of the sheep, but the Beloved Disciple has an honor that Peter does not have—the Disciple may last until Jesus returns. The concern for the exact implication of this statement (21:23: "did not say he was not to die"), which had circulated as a misleading tradition in the Johannine community, suggests that the Disciple has died before Jesus returned, a particular "delay of the Parousia" problem. The Gospel's second ending in 21:24–25 identifies the Beloved Disciple as the witness who stands behind the Gospel narrative and certifies the truth of his testimony. It also challenges the readers/listeners to reflect at the end of their reading about how well any single book can tell the whole story of Jesus.

Historical Reading

What is the historical value of a Gospel that is so different from the others? From the ancient world until the nineteenth century, John's Gospel was seen as a surer guide than Mark or Luke, neither of which was thought to be authored by an eyewitness. The differences between John and the Synoptics were explained by the idea that the apostle John decided to supplement them with his own more "spiritual" memories. With the rise of historical criticism, the pendulum swung to the opposite extreme. The majority of scholars shifted toward the position that John was not written by an eyewitness, is not a supplement to the Synoptics, nor can its material fit with the Synoptics. The material in John was now judged to have little or no value at all in understanding the historical Jesus.

By the middle of the twentieth century, the pendulum swung back, this time stopping in the center of these two positions. The theory gained credence that John, despite its obvious differences from the Synoptics, underwent three stages of development just as they did. First, memories of what Jesus did and said arose in what would become the Johannine tradition. Some memories overlapped with the Synoptic tradition, but most are unique to John. The difference stems from the fact that John's memories were not of apostolic origin in the Twelve, but in another early disciple, as the Beloved Disciple tradition seems to indicate. In the second stage, these memories were influenced by the experiences of the Johannine community that preserved, supplemented, and used them. Third, an evangelist, who was probably a leader of the Johannine church with his own literary ability, shaped the tradition from the second stage into a written Gospel. In current scholarship, especially through the influential research of Raymond E. Brown, John is widely viewed as a mostly independent witness to Jesus. Its material on the life and teaching of Jesus must be weighed carefully to determine its authenticity for the historical Jesus, but it does have much to offer historical study of Jesus.

John in Brief: Summary of Historical Reading

Author: Calls himself "the disciple whom Jesus loved," or "the Beloved Disciple" for short. Traditionally, and for a minority today, he is John the son of Zebedee, one of Jesus' main disciples. Today, most view the author as unknown. The "we" of 21:24 may suggest that another person is responsible for the Gospel's final form (the "redactor").

Date: Probably in the 90s.

Audience: Gentile Christians, probably in an urban setting; the precise city cannot be determined.

Sources: Many interpreters recognize a "Signs Source" behind the miracles of Jesus in chapters 2–11. Whether this Signs Source also included passion and resurrection narratives is less certain.

Purpose: To deepen the audience's faith in Jesus as Son of God and the giver of life, and to encourage them to confess this faith more openly.

Author

The Gospel of John calls attention to its author but, characteristically of John, in a mysterious way that challenges the reader. John 21:20, 24 asserts that an anonymous Beloved Disciple "has written these things." But who was this mysterious "Beloved Disciple"? In the second century, we find the assertion that John, one of the Twelve disciples/apostles of Jesus, wrote this Gospel on his own eyewitness memories in the 90s, at the end of his long life. Irenaeus (c. 180) wrote that John was indeed this author, and put him at Ephesus in the late 90s (*Against Heresies* 3.1). This identification is based in part on Irenaeus' personal chain of tradition: as a boy he had known Polycarp, bishop of Smyrna, who in turn said that he knew John and that John wrote this Gospel (*History of the Church* 5:20) The identification of the Beloved Disciple and evangelist as John received universal church acceptance, and it lasted until modern times. Some contemporary scholars make this conclusion as well. In its favor, beside this second-century witness, are two factors: (1) the disciple John is not mentioned by name in the Fourth Gospel, making it possible that his identity has been taken over by the Beloved Disciple; (2) the Beloved Disciple is often mentioned with Peter, and in the Synoptics no one fits this association better than John. Nevertheless, in recent times this identification has fallen into disfavor among most scholars.

Scholars now pursue three approaches to solving the mystery of the Beloved Disciple. First, some propose a known NT figure. In addition to John, the son of Zebedee, other proposals have included Lazarus, John Mark, and Thomas. Although there may be a passage or two to support each identification, all involve much guesswork. Second, some scholars have evaluated the Beloved Disciple as a pure symbol, created to model the perfect disciple. He is never given a name, and he appears alongside Peter in scenes known to us from the Synoptic Gospels, where no such figure is mentioned. However, the other unnamed Johannine figure who has a symbolic role and appears where she is absent in the Synoptics was certainly real: the mother of Jesus (2:3–12; 19:25–27). The Beloved Disciple's presence at the foot of the cross when all the Twelve had fled need indicate only that he was neither one of the Twelve nor an apostle—a term never used in John. Third, some posit that the Beloved Disciple was a minor figure during the ministry of Jesus, not one of the Twelve. However, this figure became so important in Johannine community history (perhaps the founder of the community) that he became the ideal believer in its Gospel picture.

Did the Beloved Disciple actually write this Gospel? This seems to be directly stated by John 21:20, 24, that the Beloved Disciple "has written these things." However, this could be a simplification by a redactor who may have added chapter 21. This statement *could* mean that the Beloved Disciple was not the actual writer of the gospel but the source of most of its contents. The evangelist who wrote that passage could have been a follower or disciple of the Beloved Disciple (whom he describes in the third person) and not himself an eyewitness of the ministry. Indeed, a member of the

Johannine School—that is, various disciples employing both a style and gospel contents that were traditional in this community and can be seen as well in the three Epistles of John—could have been the redactor (editor) of this book, its final "author."

The thesis that a close actual disciple of the historical Jesus but not one of the Twelve is the source of John plausibly explains how the implied author of the Gospel knows so much about Jesus' life and ministry, but also has grown distant from how that ministry is understood in the Synoptics. First, he is familiar with Palestine. John knows the location of Bethany (11:18), the garden across the winter-flowing Kidron brook (18:1), Solomon's porch in the Temple (10:23), the pools of Bethesda (5:2) and of Siloam (9:7), and the Lithostrotos (19:13). These sites are not mentioned in the other Gospels, and external evidence often supports Johannine accuracy. However, other Johannine geographical references (Bethany beyond the Jordan in 1:28; Aenon near Salim in 3:23) have not been identified. Second, he is familiar with Judaism. Jewish feasts are mentioned in 5:9b; 6:4; 7:2; and 10:22; these show knowledge of Jewish theology behind the feasts. Jewish customs are mentioned both explicitly (purity regulations in 2:6; 18:28; Paschal lamb in 19:36) and implicitly (perhaps the makeup of the high priest's tunic in 19:23). Third, he has knowledge of Jesus' ministry itself that supplements the Synoptics. For example, he knows that some of Jesus' disciples were members of the John the Baptizer's movement before they followed Jesus (1:35–42). The presentation of Jesus' life and teaching in John has moved considerably beyond the Synoptics. Some who confess Jesus have been expelled from the synagogue (9:22; 12:43). The particularly Johannine use of the expression "the Jews" reflects attitudes probably developed in the history of the Johannine community and is not at all reflected in the Synoptics. Unlike the Jesus of the Synoptic Gospels, the Johannine Jesus speaks explicitly of his divinity and his preexistence (8:58; 10:30–38; 14:9; 17:5). The basic argument with "the Jews" is not just about Jesus' violation of the Sabbath rules but much more about his making himself equal to God (5:16–18; 19:7). Traditional deeds of Jesus like healing, multiplying bread and fish, giving sight to the blind, and raising the dead have become the subject of long speeches involving theological reflection and debate (probably debate with Jews about how Jesus' teachings relate to his life and the Scriptures [5:30–47; 6:30–51; 9:26–34]). Indeed, the author herself or himself acknowledges this (2:22) and defends such development as guided by the Spirit-Paraclete (16:12–14).

www See the chart of Johannine community history on the website.

Date

Some critics once thought that John's Gospel was composed in the middle to late second century, just before Christian authors first mention it. This is in line with the older view of John as the last and more "spiritual" (some would say "Hellenizing," or making Greek) of the Gospels. However, manuscript fragments of John discovered in the Egyptian desert have been dated at about 125 and 150 C.E., making them the oldest surviving part of a New Testament book. Allowing time for the Gospel to have circulated as far as Egypt (assuming as most NT scholars do that it was not written in Egypt), the work could not have originated much later than about 100 C.E. John's references to believers being expelled from Jewish synagogues (9:22, 34–35)—a process that began about 85 or 90 C.E.—suggest that the decisive break between church and synagogue was already in effect when it was written. Hence, most scholars today date this Gospel between about 90 and 100 C.E. This dating is shared by those who see John the Apostle as its author, because they trust a second-century tradition that says that John lived to an advanced age, into the last decade of the first century.

Audience

Recent studies indicate that John's Gospel is deeply rooted in Palestinian tradition. As we saw above, John often shows a greater familiarity with Palestinian geography than the Synoptics. He also reveals close connections with first-century Palestinian Judaism, particularly some main concepts prevailing in the Essene community at Qumran. Essene writers and the author of John use a remarkably similar vocabulary to express the same kind of cosmic and ethical dualism, dividing the world up into two opposing groups of people: those who walk in the light (symbolizing truth and goodness) and those who walk in darkness (symbolizing deceit and evil). In this dualistic cosmos, the devil (synonymous with "liar") and his "spirit of error" oppose Jesus' "spirit of truth" (compare John 8:44; 12:35; 14:17; 15:26 with the Qumran *Rule of the Community* 1QS 3.13 17–21). The Qumran and Johannine communities also are apparently based ultimately on the teachings of a single founder, now deceased. As the mysterious Teacher of Righteousness had earlier brought the light of true understanding to the Essenes, so the Johannine Jesus—"the light of the world"—illuminates humanity's spiritual darkness. The unidentified Essene Teacher, of course, received nothing comparable to the exaltation the Johannine writer accords Jesus. Given the two groups' claims to exclusive knowledge, it is inevitable that their literature expresses a rigorously sectarian attitude. Both the Dead Sea Scrolls and the Johannine writings view their respective groups, small as they were, as the only guardians of light and truth in a benighted world.

Before the Dead Sea Scrolls were discovered, many scholars believed that John's Gospel—with its seemingly Platonic dualism and use of Greek philosophical terms such as Logos—originated in a Hellenistic environment, perhaps in Ephesus, the traditional home of the apostle John in his old age. The many similarities between Essene and Johannine thought, however, now incline many scholars to fix the Gospel's place of composition (at least its first edition, minus chapter 21 and other shorter parts of the present Fourth Gospel) in Palestine or Syria. Although it originated in Palestine or Syria, it seems to be written for another area, because the author not only knows Palestinian geography, but has to explain it to the audience.

Many contemporary historians place it in Ephesus, a traditional center of Johannine Christianity. This is a guess, but most scholars seem to regard it as a good guess.

Sources

Perceptive readers note that the Fourth Gospel seems to have two endings. The first, John 20:30–31, speaks of the "signs" or miracles of Jesus, which the author has written to convince his readers that Jesus is the Messiah. The second, John 21:24–25, is modeled after the first. It asserts the truth of the Beloved Disciple's testimony contained in the Fourth Gospel and states with eloquent hyperbole that the world could not contain the books that should be written about the things Jesus did. The first ending's emphasis on signs, and the accounts of the signs that form much of John 1–11 have suggested to some that the Fourth Gospel has embedded within it a "Signs Source," sometimes called a **Signs Gospel.**

Two recent studies of this source are Robert Fortna's *The Gospel of Signs* (Fortna 1970) and Urban von Wahlde's *The Earliest Version of John's Gospel* (von Wahlde 1989). We will describe and examine Fortna's hypothesis as the leading and most influential recent contribution to source criticism of John; von Wahlde's differs in some ways but confirms the main lines of Fortna. Fortna gives a brief discussion of the "Gospel of Signs" as a "gospel" in the same sense that Matthew, Mark, Luke, and even John are gospels: it presents a connected story of Jesus from the beginning of his ministry through his passion to its end in resurrection. In its style and theology, the Signs Source is close to the Synoptics. All this is presented as a message to be believed, a "gospel," which its conclusion makes explicit. Because it has no developed teaching of Jesus, it is a "rudimentary gospel but a gospel nevertheless." The Signs Gospel is determined to be Jewish-Christian because of its Greek style and content. Not concerned with the Gentile question, it has no controversy about keeping the Law of Moses. Moreover, although Fortna does not make this explicit, its purpose indicates that the community that produced it was in active missionary contact with the wider Jewish community. Its social setting and geographic location are hard to determine. Fortna cannot date the Signs Gospel with any precision; it could have been written before or after the first Jewish revolt in 66–70 C.E. According to Fortna, it was designed as a missionary book with the sole intent of showing that Jesus is the Messiah, presumably to potential Jewish converts. Fortna explicates its theology as thoroughly christological. Jesus' miracles are signs of his messianic status, and the passion account is "christologized" by the addition of sayings of Jesus that call attention to his messianic standing. It has a singular, strictly executed purpose: to convince its readers that Jesus is the Messiah in whom they should believe.

www   For a chart outlining the contents of Fortna's Gospel of Signs, see the website. Follow the link for the full text of the reconstructed Signs Gospel in English.

Purpose

The Gospel of John states that its purpose is to call forth belief in Jesus Christ as he is presented in this Gospel (20:30–31). As we saw above, this purpose may be drawn from the Signs Source of this Gospel. Although there is some debate about whether the purpose of this Signs Source is to call unbelievers to faith, there is no such debate about the present Fourth Gospel as a whole—it is not an evangelistic tract. In short, he writes to strengthen the faith and resolve of his community of churches, to offer "encouragement to believing Christians, Gentile and Jew" (Brown 2003, 180). They are under pressure from "the world," especially from the Jewish synagogue authorities in their areas. This echoes the hostility that grew after 70 C.E., when relations between the church and synagogue became much more difficult. John's claim of Jesus' divinity, and pre-existent divinity at that, must have increased the antagonism.

Some scholars have inferred other purposes. First, John may also have been written to counter a growing Gnosticism (salvation by special knowledge), particularly in the form of **docetism,** the belief that Christ only seemed to be human. John insists on the physical reality of Jesus' humanity (1:14, "the Word became flesh."). After his resurrection, Jesus convinces his disciples of his identity and risen life by showing them the wounds in his hands and feet, and he eats ordinary food in front of them (chapters 20–21). Interestingly, John uses typically Gnostic terms to explain Jesus in a way that counters Gnosticism. For example, he states that knowing the Father and the Son leads to eternal life (17:3). This use of Gnostic terms led to its popularity in Gnostic circles in the second century and may have been a factor in the wider acceptance of this book in the Great Church. Second, others have argued that the strong anti–John the Baptizer polemic at the beginning of this Gospel indicates that it may be directed against a continuing Baptizer movement that opposes John's churches. Third, still others have argued that the struggle with Judaism mentioned earlier relates to the main purpose of this Gospel, to equip its readers to deal with hostility and persecution from the synagogue authorities in their areas.

John and the Synoptic Gospels

A comparison of the Fourth Gospel to the first three Gospels shows both important similarities and obvious differences. The differences (here we name only the most notable) include *material found only in John:*

- An explicit **preexistence christology,** with Jesus conscious of having lived from eternity with God as God's eternal Son.
- A public ministry mostly set in Jerusalem rather than in Galilee and lasting three years rather than the one year that the Synoptics seem to present.
- Jesus dies on Thursday, the 14th of Nisan, not Friday.
- Jesus' teaching centers on eternal life as found in him, rather than on the kingdom of God (only in John 3:3, 5).

- Jesus' teaching is given in long monologues and dialogues rather than in shorter units.
- There are no healings of people possessed by evil spirits.
- A very restricted number of miracles (seven?), including some unique to John: changing of water to wine at Cana, healing a man born blind, and the raising of Lazarus.
- Jesus' opponents are called "the Jews."

We also note *differences in material important in the Synoptics but not in John:*

- Jesus is baptized by John the Baptizer in the Synoptics but in John only receives the Baptizer's testimony.
- "The Twelve" are Jesus' leading disciples, but in John are not named as such or listed by name.
- Jesus institutes the Eucharist/Lord's Supper at his Last Supper, but not in John.
- Jesus teaches extensively through parables, but in John uses only "figures of speech."

We must also note important but often overlooked *similarities to the Synoptics:*

- Overall, their narratives are similar in the beginning with John the Baptizer and at the end in the narratives of the passion and empty tomb. Thus, John is recognizable as a Gospel.
- More particularly, the closest similarities are with Mark, for example in the sequence of events shared by John 6 and Mark 6:30–54 and 8:11–33; and in such verbal details as "genuine nard of great value" (John 12:3), 300 denarii (12:5), and 200 denarii (6:7).
- Parallels with Luke are more of characters, for example, Martha and Mary, Lazarus (parabolic in Luke), and Annas. There are some differences in events: lack of a night trial before Caiaphas; the three "not guilty" statements in the Pilate trial; postresurrectional appearances of Jesus in Jerusalem to his male disciples; the miraculous draught of fishes in John 21.
- Similarities with Matthew are few. Compare John 13:16 with Matt 10:24; and John 15:18–27 with Matt 10:18–25.

www   For a fuller statement of differences, see the website.

A variety of solutions has been suggested to explain this complex relationship. At one end of the spectrum, some argue for John's knowledge and use of Mark or even of all three Synoptics. (Such proposals may disagree about whether John *also* had an independent tradition.) At the other end, some say that the fourth evangelist did not know any Synoptic Gospel; occasional similarities between John and the others are explained in terms of the Synoptic and Johannine traditions independently reproducing with variations the same deeds or sayings. In between the extremes, a median position maintains that Mark and John shared some pre-Gospel traditions, oral or written. Although the fourth evangelist had not seen the final form of Luke, he was familiar with traditions incorporated later into Luke. This median position is the more common in scholarship today, and as we saw in the preceding section, it is a plausible explanation.

www For a short essay on an important historical topic, the meaning and use of the term "the Jews" in John, see the website.

Doing Historical Criticism Yourself

1. *Compare the feeding of the five thousand in Matthew, Mark, or Luke with John 6. What are the similarities and the differences? How does John follow up on the miracle with Jesus' teaching?*

2. *Many historians have held that John's way of speaking of "the Jews," and his supercessionist theology, have contributed to anti-Semitism in Europe and North America. Give your reflections on this controversial matter, trying to sort out the responsibilities of John from the responsibilities of its later readers.*

3. *Read Jesus' first sign, changing water to wine at the wedding reception in Galilee, on two levels: what does it say about Jesus' miraculous action, and what does this mean for the relationship of Judaism and Christianity?*

As with the historical-critical method, the newer methods of reading the Gospels were applied first to the Synoptics. They are thought to give more insight into the historical Jesus and so attracted more attention. John was often reduced to the status of poor stepchild of Gospel research. Now these newer methods are being applied to the Fourth Gospel. Unlike historical-critical reading and research, which habitually is "looking over the shoulder" of John to the Synoptics to discern their relationship, the newer methods of reading deal with John on its own terms. No longer is John the stepchild of the Synoptics.

John in Brief: Summary of New Methods

Narrative: John is characterized, like Matthew, by long sections of Jesus' teaching. John often introduces these sections with "signs" by Jesus that dramatize the meaning of the teaching. The narrator's style of theological explanation is so close to the way Jesus talks that it is sometimes hard to distinguish them. Both the narrator and Jesus are omniscient. Finally, John's narratives can sometimes be read on two levels: the level of the historical Jesus and the level of the Johannine church.

Social Scientific: John's preexistence christology gives an added dimension to its social reading. The world of heaven is as real as the world of earth, and Jesus' kinship relation with his divine Father directs how he is their leader. Other social scientific paradigms such as honor-shame and patron-client are also richly represented in John.

Feminist: John features women prominently as Jesus' followers. Conversion of a Samaritan village is done as a result of Jesus' transformative encounter with a Samaritan woman. Women often appear when Jesus is transitioning to a new area or phase of his ministry. Jesus' mother and especially Mary Magdalene serve as examples of faith for all readers.

Cross-Cultural: John crosses the cultural barrier with Gentile life so completely that he seems to leave Judaism completely behind. He also warmly embraces missions to "mixed" cultures like the Samaritans.

Narrative Reading

The Gospel of John has a narrative style unique to the Gospels. First, even as it begins with a long prologue of highly developed teaching on Jesus, it features long monologues by Jesus throughout. Once, in the Farewell Discourse of chapters 14–17, there is no accompanying action. Most monologues are preceded by a narrative action of Jesus, either in a miracle ("sign") or controversy story, which the monologue then develops. Sometimes a dialogue serves as a transition between the narrative and the monologue. At times the style of the Gospel writer is so close to the style of Jesus' speech that we cannot tell for certain when the narration ends and Jesus' words begin (in chapter 3, for example). In the Gospel of John, both Jesus and the Gospel writer are omniscient; Jesus is both a human and divine character throughout.

Narrative Reading at Work
The Implied Reader in the Gospel of John

Jeffrey Staley, a creative employer of several newer methods of reading, describes how the narrator calls forth an "implied reader" first to deceive the reader and then to correct her or him, bringing understanding in the process.

When we looked at plot development in the first three chapters of the book, we noted that whenever the disciples were mentioned, they were with Jesus; and from the perspective of the implied reader, they seemed to instantly believe in him. . . . Furthermore, as we mentioned earlier, the narrator and implied reader appear to share the same perspective: Like the disciples, the implied reader was led to faith quite quickly and seemed "to know all things." In chapter 4, however, there is a change in the relationship between Jesus and the disciples. Now, not only is there physical distance between the two, but there is also a certain tension which will become obvious to the implied reader.

Source: Jeffrey L. Staley, *The Print's First Kiss: A Rhetorical Investigation of the Implied Reader in the Fourth Gospel* (Atlanta: Scholar's Press, 1988), pp. 97–98.

The distance and tension between Jesus and his disciples, which the implied author will go on to reveal to the implied reader in chapters 4 and 6, is exactly the same sort of tension that he creates at a different level between himself and the implied reader by the juxtaposition of 3:22, 26 and 4:2. In 3:22—a section of the gospel that presumes a high degree of collusion between the implied author and implied reader—the narrator tells the implied reader that Jesus was baptizing. The implied reader has no reason to doubt the narrator's reliability, especially when this is confirmed by the characters in 3:26. But then at 4:2, in response to the rumor the Pharisees had heard, the narrator says that Jesus was not baptizing–only his disciples were. Just as the disciples will be forced to reassess their relationship to Jesus (6:60–71), the implied reader is forced, by the tension between 3:22 and 4:2, to reevaluate his relationship to the narrator and the story . . .

Yet the implied reader cannot accuse the narrator of being unreliable, for he sets accounts straight with 4:2 and quickly wins back the implied reader's allegiance with his subtle and whimsical parody of the ancient Hebrew betrothal type-scene (4:7–38). The kind of implied reader which the implied author of the Fourth Gospel forms is thus like some of those real readers whom McKee describes as "inexperienced in reader-victimizing irony . . . [who do] not become aware of the ironist's intentions toward [them] until late in the game, after they have committed [themselves] to several conclusions which are later shown to be invalid." The rhetorical purpose of the implied author's "reader-victimization strategy" is therefore to "reeducate [his] audience," to force the implied reader to realize that in spite of his high degree of knowledge, he still does not know everything. The gospel, as well as being an aesthetic whole, is a "learning program."

Questions

1. Review from Chapter 1 of the present book what "implied author" and "implied reader" are and define these concepts in your own words.

2. What is your opinion on the "ethics" of an implied author's "reader-victimization strategy"?

Doing Narrative Reading Yourself

1. Read carefully the story of the "Adulterous Woman" in John 8:1–11, "filling the gaps" in the story. To do this, you will have to think intentionally about what is "between the lines" rather than what is said.

2. Why does the narrator make an explicit self-correction at 3:22 and 4:1–2? Why not just rewrite the section to edit out the need for self-corrections?

3. Pick one of the Fourth Gospel sections where it is uncertain whether earlier speakers are continuing their remarks, or if the narrator of the Gospel is speaking (3:17–21; 3:31–36). What does it mean that the style of the narrator is possibly—depending on how one reads these sections—so close to the style of the speaker?

Social Scientific Reading

The Gospel of John is becoming a rich field of study for social scientific reading. It features much grist for the mill of social science: religious and ethnic groups like Jews, Samaritans, and Gentiles; the poor and the rich; women prominent in encountering and following Jesus; kinship on a divine plane (Jesus the Son of God the Father) and a human plane (Jesus' relationship to his unnamed mother, for example); and language about honor and shame.

John's presentation of group dynamics is particularly important in recent scholarship. Its seemingly negative attitude to "the world" and "the Jews" has led to the argument that John is **sectarian.** Of course, much depends on how one defines this term; few scholars interpret it along the lines of a "cult." Rather, the history of the Johannine community has called forth and reinforced a wariness and hostility to the outside world, including perhaps other Christian churches, that John's church could be cut off (the Latin root of "sect") from others.

Social Scientific Reading at Work
Two Perspectives on Jesus' Encounter with the Samaritan Woman (John 4)

Thomas Buford is a leading philosopher of personalism, and his study of the parables is based on a combination of personalism and social scientific reading. Jerome Neyrey is a prominent social scientific interpreter of the NT, and his article reflects a rigorous social scientific approach.

[**Buford**] As Jesus waited, a woman came to the well. He did something against the custom of the day; he asked her for a drink. She was surprised that a Jew would speak to a Samaritan or much less ask a woman for water. She knew that the Jews felt repugnance toward the Samaritans. . . . Jesus was talking to a person who was considered an outcast in Jewish society. When the disciples returned they "marveled he was talking with a woman." It was improper for a man to be alone with a woman, to look at a married woman, or even to give her a greeting. That Jesus was talking to a woman was bad enough but that he was talking to a Samaritan woman was simply unheard of. . . . [T]hough the disciples marveled about what he was doing, none of them said anything to Jesus about it.

The marvel of the disciples is understandable. No honorable person associated with dishonorable people or social outcasts. The Samaritans were dishonorable, at the bottom of the social ladder, and it was a sin for a Jew to associate with them. Those who were sinners were unable to participate in the covenantal blessings. Thus, the honor of a full-fledged Jew was at stake if he had anything to do with people such

Source: Thomas O. Buford, *Ambushed on the Road to Glory: Finding the Way Through Jesus' Parables* (Macon, GA: Smyth & Helwys, 1991), pp. 116–117; Jerome H. Neyrey, "What's Wrong with This Picture? John 4, Cultural Stereotypes of Women, and Public and Private Space" *Biblical Theology Bulletin* 24 (1994): pp. 77–91.

as the Samaritan woman. This behavior of Jesus must have been difficult for his disciples to understand. He seemed to be preaching against sin, but he was doing the very things that were considered sinful by the average Jew. How perplexed they must have been. . . . How were they to follow a man whose behavior was so anomalous?

[Neyrey] Of what might the Samaritan woman be a "representative"? Looking at 4:6–26, we argue that the narrator has concentrated in this one figure many of the characteristics of marginal persons with whom Jesus regularly deals in the synoptic gospels. She is an amalgam of cultural deviance. In terms of stereotypes, she is a *non-Jew,* who is ritually *unclean;* she is a *"sinner,"* a publicly recognized *"shameless"* person, even someone with whom Jesus has *commensality* [sharing of food or drink]. As a *shameless* woman, she embodies most of the social liabilities which would marginalize her in her society. At a minimum, she represents the gospel axiom that "least is greatest" or "last is first." Ultimately, she represents inclusivity into the Christian group in a most radical way. The stereotype of gender expectations serves to portray her precisely as the quintessential deviant, the last and least person who would be expected to find favor with God (see 1 Cor 15:8–9). Her status transformation in 4:6–26 is basically that of a person moving from "*not* in the know" to "in the know," and from *outsider* to *insider.*

Does it matter if we note "what's wrong with this picture"? Throughout the story, she violates the cultural expectations of her society. But this intentionally and continually casts her in a deviant role as the most unlikely person on the cultural horizon to be welcomed into Jesus' kinship network. The initial violations of gender expectations (4:6–17) as well as the latter ones (4:27–30) consistently stereotype the Samaritan woman as a deviant, but this deviance does not matter to the narrator, which is the rhetorical point of the story. The gospel goes to unlikely people; it might even be spread in the gossip network by unlikely persons (see Acts 4:13; see John 4:36–38). By noting "what's wrong with this picture?" the Samaritan woman becomes that much stranger and that much more unlikely a candidate for inclusion. Then how much more extraordinary is she as an example of God's inclusivity and Jesus' reform of social conventions!

"What's wrong with this picture?" Gender stereotypes, then, initially work in the narrative to label the Samaritan woman as the ultimate outsider: non-Jew, unclean, sinner, shameless. The author, then, has created a stereotype of the ultimate *outsider* and the quintessential *deviant,* only to have the stereotype broken, but basically in the direction of the inclusivity of *outsiders* and *deviants.*

Looking at 4:27–30 and 39–42, however, we are told more about the Samaritan woman. Here she functions as a mediational figure in the spreading of the news about Jesus to the Samaritans. Although Mary Magdalene may accurately be said to have a formal role as the bearer of a sacred formula to specifically designated persons, we saw that her role still conforms to the gender expectation of that culture and it occurs within the "private" world of the kinship group.

www   Follow the link to read the entire article online.

Questions

1. *Compare these two readings in terms of their approach and results.*

2. *Summarize in a paragraph all that you can learn about social-scientific reading from Neyrey's essay, looking particularly at the terms that Neyrey italicizes.*

Doing Social Scientific Reading Yourself

1. *Much of the kinship talk in the Fourth Gospel deals with divine relationships—Jesus as the eternal Son of God his Father. How might human kinship and divine kinship relate here? Look at John 3:1–21 to suggest some possible answers.*

2. *Read the Sign at Cana (John 2:1–11) in a social-scientific way. What is going on here in matters of kinship (Jesus and his mother), honor and shame (running out of wine at a wedding reception), and purity (all the Jewish ritual water changed to wine)?*

3. *In John 21:1–8, Peter is "naked" in the boat with other disciples, but when he is about to jump into the water to see the risen Jesus, he "puts on his clothes." From your knowledge of cultural body-modesty in Semitic cultures, explain (1) if Peter is literally naked; (2) how it is that Peter puts on clothes in order to go swimming!*

Feminist Reading

Feminist treatments of the Fourth Gospel as a document of significance for women tend to focus on Jesus' encounters with women. John has a significant number of these: with his mother (2:1–11); with the Samaritan woman (4:1–42); with the adulterous woman (8:1–11, but not originally in John); with Mary and Martha (11:1–45); with Mary of Bethany (12:1–8); with his mother and other women at the cross (19:25–27); with Mary Magdalene, the first person to whom the risen Jesus appears (20:11–18). Women's inclusion in John's narrative, especially in conversation with Jesus, gives them an importance beyond their status in the cultures of the first century, where "honorable" men did not talk alone, or even at all, to "honorable" women. Each woman appears at a point in the narrative where the author is bringing Jesus ministry to a new level. For example, the conversation with the Samaritan woman becomes the occasion for Jesus' own revelation that he is the Messiah. Women are given a unique place in the Johannine community, as exemplary disciples in a Gospel that often portrays people as personifying different types of faith. Mary Magdalene is the premier example. John 20:17–18 presents Mary Magdalene as the one person in John who most closely fits the portrait of a leading disciple. Further, she makes the prototypical apostolic announcement of the resurrection:

"I have seen the Lord." Finally, the mother of Jesus has a prominent role in John, often as an example of persistent faith. Recently, Margaret Beirns has argued that John features six "gender pairs" of a man and woman in which women are characteristically shown to be equal to men as disciples: the Mother of Jesus as the royal official (chaps. 2 and 4); Nicodemus and the Samaritan woman (3 and 4); the man born blind and Martha (9 and 11); Mary of Bethany and Judas (12); the Mother of Jesus and the Beloved Disciple (19); Mary Magdalene and Thomas (20). Beirn's book has the advantage of looking not just at women in the Fourth Gospel, but at women and men together.

Probing feminist criticism has also argued for a deeper significance for women in John's Gospel. Some readers argue that Jesus takes on, in deeply symbolic fashion in this deeply symbolic Gospel, the roles of birthing mother and midwife. One striking example occurs in the raising of Lazarus, where Jesus employs the formula used by a midwife to complete a particularly difficult birth: "[Name], come forth!" Thus in John 11:43, Jesus commands, "Lazarus, come out!" and a man is "born again" as he comes alive from the tomb. The inclusion of such an image in the Gospel makes the allusion highly pointed, particularly in view of the importance of John's theme of new birth.

Feminist Reading at Work, 1
A Man and a Woman Literarily Paired in John 9–11

In her book the Australian Roman Catholic nun Margaret Beirne studies the gender pairing of male and female characters in John. This selection shows how the pairing of the "man born blind" in chapter 9 with Martha in chapter 11 shows how they come to faith in Jesus, and become models for male and female disciples in the Johannine church.

The Man Born Blind and Martha thus form a third Johannine gender pair. Their stories are narrated within the context of two passages (9:1–41; 11:1–54) which have a parallel structural pattern. The significant variation in the pattern is that the 'sign' in the second story occurs at the end of the account, precisely because Martha is already a disciple of Jesus. . . . The Man Born Blind, on the other hand, meets the Johannine Jesus for the first time, so that, as with all other instances in the Fourth Gospel, the 'sign' functions to draw him towards belief in Jesus' word and commitment as a disciple. In both cases, the evangelists present them in the setting of an encounter with Jesus in which they act as a foil for Jesus' continuing self-revelation, given both in work (9:35b, 37; 11:25–26, 40) and action (9:6–7, 41–44). In him they find the fulfillment of all their Jewish expectations and respond by believing in his word of revelation as far as they can comprehend it at this stage of their respective faith journeys.

Source: Margaret M. Beirne, *Women and Men the Fourth Gospel: A Genuine Discipleship of Equals* (Sheffield, UK: Sheffield Academic Press, 2003), pp. 137–139.

If the twin concerns of these "paired" stories are once again Jesus' self-revelation and the faith response of his dialogue partners, the twin symbols of "light" and "life." The gift of sight is given to the blind beggar by the one who proclaims "I am the light of the world" (9:5b); the gift of life is restored physically to Lazarus as a symbol of eternal life given to Martha by the Johannine Jesus who revels himself to her: "I am the resurrection and the life" (11:25a). A man and a woman respectively receive these gifts and respond in faith; to this extent, they are representative for every reader of the Fourth Gospel. But their very power to thus involve the readers and draw from them a like response, is in the vitality and strength of their individual portrayal as Johannine characters. Like Martha, the man has become a disciple, one of Jesus' "own" (10:3; cf. 11:5), who receives him as she does (11:20) and responds with full acceptance to his challenge, "Do you believe?" (9:35–38; 11:25–27). [Jesus'] assurance given to Martha [is] that "whoever lives and believes in me" (11:26a), which she does (11:27), will have eternal life and "see the glory of God" (11:40).

The dual symbols of "light/darkness" and "life/death" are embodied in the characters of the respective chapters 9 and 11. By their open confession of faith in the Johannine Jesus, the Man Born Blind and Martha are identified with him whose "signs" demonstrate that he is Lord of "light" and of "life" (10:27). But this necessarily separates them from those who remain in "darkness" (9:39–41) and deal in "death" (11:53) . . . By contrast, this gender pair of disciples are gifted even now with "eternal life" (10:28a), made possible by Jesus' freely giving his own life for their sake and for that of all those who believe in him (10:11, 15b, 17–18; cf. 15:13).

Feminist Reading at Work, 2
Father-Language for God in the Fourth Gospel

The Gospel of John uses "Father" for God extensively, even as it calls Jesus the "Son." The use of male-oriented language for God is a difficult issue for many women today. In this excerpt, Gail O'Day critiques the Gospel of John's use, finding significance and justification for it.

The question of the appropriate language to use for God is an important and painful one for many women. Until recently the church almost exclusively used male pronouns and images for God, overlooking both the rich variety of names and images for God in the biblical and historical material and the political and theological assumptions that lay behind this language. The exclusive use of male language for God is not a neutral or objective act. . . . Father language for God is particularly painful for many women because of the burden of patriarchy it frequently carries. . . .

God is called Father more times in John than in any other book in the New Testament (over one hundred times), and to attempt to eliminate that term in the interests of

Source: Gail R. O'Day, "John," in Carol A. Newsom and Sharon H. Ringe, eds., *Women's Bible Commentary, Expanded Edition.* (Louisville, KY: Westminster John Knox, 1998), pp. 392–393.

inclusive language would destroy the particularity of the Johannine vision. Just as it is false to the richness of the Christian tradition to use father language as generic language for God, it is equally false to the tradition to speak about God in general terms that flatten the vitality and depth of biblical metaphor and language. God is Father in John and the church's job is to move beyond the assumption that Father is simply a synonym for God and discover what father language in John contributes to a fuller understanding of God and the Christian life.

Father language in John is essentially relational: God is Father because Jesus is God's Son. This language, then, is not primarily the language of patriarchy but is instead the language of intimacy, relationship, and family. From the very beginning of the Gospel, the explicit purpose of Jesus' ministry has been to create a new family of God: "But to all who received him, who believed in his name, he gave power to become children of God, who were born, not of blood or of the will of the flesh or of the will of man, but of God" (1:12–13). . . . People who have no families, who come from destructive families, or who are alienated from their birth families can belong to a new family by virtue of becoming children of God. This promise of a new family received its most poignant expression in Jesus' words in John 14:18: "I will not leave you orphaned." All who believe are offered a family and a home. The language of birth and family continues throughout the Gospel: e.g., 3:3–10; 8:31–47; 14:1–3; 18–24; 16:20–24; 19:25–27; 20:17. Moreover . . . , many of the pivotal events in Jesus' ministry occur in the presence of those whom he loves. Jesus' announcement to Mary of the good news of Easter is couched in the language of family: "But go to my brothers [and sisters] and say to them, 'I am ascending to my Father and your Father, to my God and your God'" (20:17). At Jesus' ascension, the creation of the new family is fully under way.

Questions

1. *Give your analysis of Beirne's treatment of John 9–11.*

2. *Do you agree with O'Day's assessment of patriarchal language in John? Does it appear accurate to you, or is it "too kind"?*

Doing Feminist Reading Yourself

1. *Could the Beloved Disciple have been a woman? Give your reasons for or against. After you have done this, read an online article that argues that Mary Magdalene was the Beloved Disciple (linked on the website of the present book).*

2. *Compare the male characters in chapter 3 (Jesus and Nicodemus) with the male and female characters in chapter 4 (Jesus and the Samaritan woman).*

3. *What might be some reasons why John refers to "the mother of Jesus" without ever mentioning her name? Examine John 2:1–11 in particular for clues.*

Cross-Cultural Reading

Cross-cultural reading of John has lagged behind its reading of the Synoptics but now is beginning to pick up pace. John crosses the cultural barrier with Gentile life so completely that it seems to leave Judaism completely behind. It also warmly embraces missions to "mixed" cultures like Samaritans.

The more other-worldly orientation of Jesus in this Gospel than in the other Gospels has probably been a main factor in its previous disuse. Strikingly, it is now this very orientation that is providing a fruitful path of reading John cross-cultur-ally. Peoples of the Third World look to John's incarnational christology to show how a figure from another world, the heavenly world, makes all humans equal and draws people of all cultures together.

Cross-Cultural Reading at Work
Jesus' Healing in Batswanan Perspective (John 5:1–18)

This essay compares Jesus as a supernatural healer with ritual healers in Batswana, Africa, with attention to post-colonial integration of Christianity and traditional African religion.

In John 5:1–18 healing takes place in Bethesda. The restoration of the lame man at the pool, who has been ill for thirty-eight years, is an account of a man healed by the word alone. Jesus said to him, "Rise, take up your pallet, and walk." And at once the man was healed, and he took up his pallet and walked. What is required in this healing is the desire to be healed, and act of commitment to express readiness to accept in faith the gift that God offers. In most healing cases it is an advantage if the patient has faith. . . .

Jesus' role as a divine healer is similar to the *Ngaka's* [ritual healer] role among the Batswana. When we look at Jesus' healing and his world, there is a lot that he shares with the *Ngaka's* role among the Batswana. The belief that the causes of illness are more spiritual than physical, and that these spiritual causes take people beyond the physical world to the supernatural, to God, to *Modimo*. The person who takes respon-sibility for combating illness as a problem of evil occupies an important place in his or her society. She or he is believed to have some special relationship with the Divine power. To the Christian, the power is directly from "God," but for the Batswana it comes through the ancestors–those liberated from physical disabilities–to the *Ngaka*. The *Ngaka* becomes an intermediary between the Divine and his/her people. The underlying belief is that for the *Ngaka* to be successful in the struggle against evil there has to be a source of good to help him–*Modimo*/God. The role of a healer in his/her society is a saving role, a life giving role, a struggle against evil.

Source: Gomang Seratwa Ntloedibe, "Ngaka and Jesus as Liberators," in *The Bible in Africa: Transactions, Trajectories, and Trends,* ed. Gerald O. West & Musa W. Dube (Boston: Brill Academic, 2001), pp. 507–508, 509–510.

The role of Jesus in the Jewish society is similar to the role of the *Ngaka* in the Batswana society. Yet, when colonial Christianity was introduced to Batswana, the role of the *Ngaka* in his/her society was condemned. The same Jesus who built his reputation of healing in the Jewish culture was made to be indifferent to Batswana culture by the missionary enterprise. In spite of the attempt to denigrate the role of the *Ngaka*, his/her role remains indispensable. In this post-colonial era, it is just and right that some of us who are undeniably both African and Christian read for ourselves from both religious testaments—from both African Traditional Religion and the Bible. As I have expounded, my reading shows that both the *Ngaka* and Jesus are sacred agents that serve God's creation.

Questions

1. *What light does this cross-cultural parallel shed on Jesus as a healer?*
2. *What contribution might John's portrait of Jesus as a healer make to Christians in Batswana?*

Doing Cross-Cultural Reading Yourself

1. *Do you think that the heavenly/earthly dimensions of the story of Jesus are properly called "cross-cultural"? Why, or why not?*
2. *Reflect on the various cross-cultural connections of the Fourth Gospel: the Samaritans (chapter 4), the "Greeks" (chapter 12).*

Key Terms and Concepts

Beloved Disciple • Book of Glory • Book of Signs • docetism • Farewell Discourse
incarnation • Johannine School • Logos • mixed metaphor • Paraclete
prologue • preexistence christology • secret disciple • sectarianism
sign • Signs Gospel • testament • two endings of John

Questions for Study, Discussion, and Writing

1. Often the comment is made that John is the "most theological" or "spiritual" of the Gospels. Evaluate this claim: is it true, and if so, in what sense?
2. What are both the similarities and differences between the Holy Spirit/Paraclete in the Gospel of John and the Holy Spirit in the Synoptic Gospels?
3. What is your view of the historical value of the Gospel of John for understanding the life and teaching of Jesus? Defend your answer.
4. Analyze the history of the Johannine community as laid out by Raymond Brown (on the website). What in it is plausible, in your view, and what is not? Why?
5. Explain the differences and similarities between the miracles of the Synoptics and the signs in John.

6. Using both social scientific and historical methods, explain John's concept of full humanity as *belonging*, both in terms of initial salvation as coming into God's family and following Jesus as abiding/remaining in him. Why does John have such a strong emphasis on belonging?

7. Explain the significance of the story of Thomas's doubt and faith in chapter 20. In light of this, do you think that his nickname, "Doubting Thomas," is accurate?

8. Comment on this statement: "John is told from an *explicitly* postresurrectional perspective, the Synoptics from an *implicitly* postresurrectional perspective."

9. The 2004 film directed by Mel Gibson, *The Passion of the Christ*, was highly controversial when charges of anti-Semitism were leveled against it. View this film if you haven't already, and give your own conclusion and reasoning on this difficult debate.

For Further Reading

Beirne, Margaret M. *Women and Men in the Fourth Gospel: A Genuine Discipleship of Equals*. Sheffield, UK: Sheffield Academic Press, 2003. An excellent study of six Johannine "gender pairs" arguing that John has a discipleship of gender equality.

Brown, Raymond E. *The Community of the Beloved Disciple*. New York: Paulist Press, 1979. A readable study of the Christian community that produced the NT Johannine literature.

Brown, Raymond E. *The Gospel According to John*. Anchor Bible, vols. 29 and 29A. Garden City, NY: Doubleday, 1966, 1970. The best historical and theological commentary on John.

Brown, Raymond, E. *An Introduction to the Gospel of John*, ed. Francis J. Moloney. New York: Doubleday, 2003. When Brown died in 1998, he left a manuscript updating his commentary on the Gospel of John. Francis Moloney has edited this for publication.

Dube, Musa, and Jeffrey L. Staley. *John and Postcolonialism: Travel, Space and Power*. London: Sheffield Academic Press, 2002. A cross-cultural, postcolonial interpretation of John from Hispanic, African, Jewish, Chinese, Korean, and African American perspectives.

Kopas, Jane. "Jesus and Women: John's Gospel." *Theology Today* 41 (1984), pp. 201–205. A concise overview of feminist interpretation of the Gospel of John, available online (follow the link).

Levine, Amy-Jill. *A Feminist Companion to John*. Sheffield, UK: Sheffield Academic Press, 2003. Two volumes of essays on key themes and passages in John, from a variety of feminist perspectives.

Martyn, J. Louis. *History and Theology of the Fourth Gospel*, 2nd ed. Nashville, TN: Abingdon, 1979. A luminous study of John, focusing on John 9.

Painter, John, and others. *Word, Theology, and Community in John*. St. Louis: Chalice, 2002. Twelve essays covering historical, narrative, and cross-cultural methods.

Smith, D. Moody Jr. *Johannine Christianity: Essays on Its Setting, Sources, and Theology*. Columbia, SC: University of South Carolina Press, 1984. Accessible essays by a leading interpreter of John.

Stibbe, Mark W. G. *John as Storyteller: Narrative Criticism and the Fourth Gospel*. Cambridge: Cambridge University Press, 1992. This study contains a literary analysis of the final form of John (themes, irony, characterization, etc.), a sociologically based redaction criticism, and a narrative-historical component.

Part III

An Early Christian History

Chapter Ten

The Acts of the Apostles: the Church from Jerusalem to Rome

The Acts of the Apostles (called more briefly "Acts") is unique in the NT for several reasons. Acts contains the only narrative of events involving Jesus' followers after his departure. It alone relates the life of the earliest community, its unity and growing diversity. It testifies to the growth of new Christian centers like Antioch and Ephesus. Acts provides detailed, lively accounts of Paul's missionary journeys and of his final journey under arrest to Rome. It provided an eschatology that the church has employed for almost two thousand years, in which the church stands in the "middle of time," not at the end of time, as in most other parts of the NT. In sum, our knowledge of early Christianity—including how that name came to be!—would be much poorer without Acts.

The Gospel of Luke and the Acts of the Apostles are united at several levels, including authorship, literary style, narrative techniques, social views, and theology. The most conspicuous lack of unity between them is their present canonical location. By the second century, the Synoptic Gospels were already usually put together because of their similarities, with John at the end. When John came to be lodged between Luke and Acts, Luke's story of Jesus was separated from his account of the early church. Still, without Acts' historical narrative, it would be more difficult in some respects to understand the other major figures of the church apart from Paul: Peter the apostle, James the brother of Jesus, or Stephen and the Hellenists. Although the present canonical order does allow Acts to frame for the reader what follows it in the NT, it is important to read Acts in tandem with Luke, not with John inserted between them.

Acts in Brief: Structure and Contents, with approximate traditional chronology according to Acts

I. Prologue: Departure of Jesus and the coming of the Holy Spirit
(Chapter 1; *30 c.e.*)
   A. Jesus instructs his disciples and ascends to heaven (1:1–11)
   B. Believers await the Spirit, appoint a new apostle (1:12–26)

II. Mission in Jerusalem (Chapters 2–7; *30–33* C.E.)
   A. The Spirit comes at Pentecost; Peter's sermon (2:1–36)
   B. Large response to the message; Jerusalem communal life of the church (2:37–45)
   C. Activity, preaching, and trials of the apostles (3:1–5:42)
   D. The Hellenists; Stephen's trial and martyrdom (chapters 6–7)
III. Mission in Samaria and Judea (Chapters 8–12; *32–44* C.E.)
   A. Persecution, dispersal from Jerusalem; Philip and Peter in Samaria (8:1b–40)
   B. Saul converted; he returns to Jerusalem and Tarsus (9:1–31)
   C. Peter at Lydda, Joppa, Caesarea, and back to Jerusalem (9:32–11:18)
   D. Events in Antioch, Jerusalem; Herod persecutes; Peter departs (11:19–12:25)
IV. Mission of Paul to the ends of the earth (Chapters 13–28; *47–62* C.E.)
   A. Antioch sends Barnabas and Paul: Mission to Cyprus and southeast Asia Minor (traditionally called the "First Missionary Journey") (Chapters 13–14; *47* C.E.)
   B. Jerusalem conference; return to Antioch (15:1–35; *49* C.E.)
   C. From Antioch through Asia Minor to Greece and return ("Second Missionary Journey") (15:36–18:22; *49–52* C.E.)
   D. From Antioch to Ephesus and Greece; return to Caesarea ("Third Missionary Journey") (18:23–21:14; *52–57* C.E.)
   E. Arrest in Jerusalem; trials in Caesarea (21:15–26:32; *57–59* C.E.)
   F. Journey to Rome as a prisoner (27:1–28:14a; *59–60* C.E.)
   G. Paul at Rome (28:14b-31; *60–63* C.E.).

Developing Your Skills: Reading Acts for the Big Picture

In one sitting, skim Luke to refresh your memory of it. Then read quickly the Acts of the Apostles to grasp its overall structure. Note especially the geographical progression of the narrative, how the cast of characters and the plot change with the shifting locations, and how the author punctuates the narrative with speeches.

A Guide to Reading

At the opening of Acts, a short prologue (vv. 1–2) alluding to the prologue of Luke's Gospel makes a formal beginning to this "second volume" of Luke's work. As the narrative of Luke-Acts resumes, the risen Jesus appears to his disciples in Jerusalem for forty days (1:3–7). This period allows Jesus to give physical proofs of the resurrection, important to Luke, and to present clearly his notion of the kingdom. The apostles are to wait in Jerusalem for their baptism with the Holy Spirit. Jesus also tells them that the end of the world is not soon, so they are to embark on a mission to the world when the Spirit comes. Jesus supplies the **geographic outline** of Acts in Acts 1:8: "You will be my witnesses in Jerusalem, all Judea and Samaria, and to the end of the earth." The Acts story that begins in Jerusalem will end in Rome (chap. 28). Having thus prepared his disciples for the future, Jesus is taken up to heaven, his **ascension** (1:9–11). Two men in white are suddenly standing with the apostles, and they interpret this event to them. Those who await the coming of the Spirit are listed and numbered in 1:12–15. The disciples choose Matthias a replacement for Judas (1:21–26), and the number is complete at twelve for the mission to Jews and Gentiles.

At the beginning of chapter 2, the Holy Spirit comes upon the whole community of believers when they are gathered for the Jewish feast of Pentecost. The sound of a mighty wind and tongues like fire represent the renewal of God's covenant, once more calling a people to be God's own. The **Table of Nations** in Acts 2:9–11, with its broad sweep from the eastern borders of the Roman Empire (Parthians, Medes, and Elamites) to the city of Rome itself, describes the nationalities that at Pentecost observe and hear the effects of the Spirit. As the gospel goes "to the end of the earth," they too will become believers in Jesus and share in his Spirit. Reaction to the Spirit-filled disciples speaking in tongues—ecstatic behavior that looked to observers like drunkenness—causes Peter to deliver the first sermon in Acts (2:14–36). Peter interprets the action of the Spirit at Pentecost as the fulfillment of the signs of the last days foretold by the prophet Joel in the Hebrew Bible. Prominent in this quotation from Joel is that the Spirit comes upon *all the community*: male and female, young and old, free and slave. Peter tells what God has done in Jesus: a brief statement of his mighty works, crucifixion and resurrection, culminating in scriptural evidence that he was—and is—Lord and Messiah. Having presented this first and fundamental proclamation of the gospel, Acts 2:37–41 now dramatizes in question and answer form the fundamentals of accepting the gospel. Peter makes two specific demands and then gives a promise. The first demand is that people "repent," the second is that they be baptized for the forgiveness of their sins. Peter specifies that baptism must be "in the name of Jesus Christ." Then Peter makes a promise: "You shall receive the gift of the Holy Spirit, for the promise is . . . to as many as the Lord God calls" (2:38–39). That God will give the same Holy Spirit to all believers is a continuing theme in Acts; the whole church will be empowered and directed by God's

Spirit as it reaches to different peoples and cultures. These first years in Jerusalem are idealized as a time when the followers of Jesus were fully united, as Acts characteristically states in its early summaries (1:14; 2:46; 4:24; 5:12). Unity was seen and built up in four important items: fellowship/community (Greek *koinonia* [coin-oh-NEE-uh]), prayers, breaking of the bread, and the apostles' teaching. These four features show both continuity with Jewish institutions, practices, and new features that were beginning to mark off Jews who believed in Jesus from other Jews. For now, the emphasis is on continuity and compatibility with Judaism. Acts will later present how believers in Jesus become a religious group distinguishable from Judaism.

The public ministry of the apostles begins with the dramatic account of the healing that takes place when Peter and John go up to the Temple (3:1–10), in the same Temple areas where Jesus taught in the final days of his public ministry (Luke 19–21). They heal "in the name of Jesus Christ of Nazareth" (Acts 3:6), that is, through the power of the heavenly Christ, and not by their own power. The Lukan account of Jesus' ministry combined healing and teaching; here Peter's act of healing is followed by a sermon (3:11–26). This sermon illustrates the presentation of Jesus to Jews. In 3:19, the demand to "repent" or "change one's mind" appears once more, but now with detail. The Jews of Jerusalem delivered up and denied Jesus, but they acted in ignorance, as did their rulers. However, with the apostolic preaching, ignorance is no longer an excuse, and they must repent if they are to enter God's kingdom (Acts 3:19–21). The apostles' preaching results in five thousand conversions, which stirs up anger in the Jewish rulers and leads to the arrest of Peter and John by the Temple authorities (4:1–22). This illustrates a pattern to be followed in the rest of Acts: some Jewish people did change and believe in Jesus, but most of them, especially Jewish leaders, did not.

The priests and the Sadducees are disturbed that Peter and John have been proclaiming Jesus' resurrection from the dead. They convene a meeting of a Sanhedrin to examine them, just as a Sanhedrin was convened against Jesus (Luke 22:66). Annoyed at their message that salvation is now only in Jesus, and at the boldness and persuasiveness of the apostles who were not formally educated in religious matters, the authorities order Peter and John not to speak in the name of Jesus (4:18). Peter and John emerge steadfast from the Sanhedrin to report to their fellow believers what has happened—a report that consists of a triumphal prayer of praise to God comparing the forces in Jerusalem against Jesus to the forces now against his followers (4:23–31). All the believers are filled with the Holy Spirit and continue to speak the word of God boldly.

To demonstrate that Jesus' followers were of "one heart and soul," a summary emphasizes their "holding things in common" (4:32–35). Two contrasting stories illustrate the author's point. The first is short and positive: Barnabas sold a field and brought the money to the apostles to contribute to the common fund (4:36–37). (Later in Acts, he becomes a missionary with Paul.) The other example, a dramatic narrative involving Ananias and his wife Sapphira, illustrates severe divine punishment of those violating the purity of the early community by lying and deceptive practices that break unity. Peter's judgment on this impurity brings about the action of God in the deaths of Ananias and Sapphira (4:36–37).

The second confrontation of the apostles with the Sanhedrin (5:12–42) has a balanced narrative structure. The apostles do many signs and wonders in Jerusalem, and even people from the surrounding villages begin to bring their sick to the apostles for healing, especially by Peter. To curtail their growing popularity, the high priests and the Sadducees have the apostles arrested again but are frustrated when an angel of the Lord frees them and the apostles return to the Temple. The Sanhedrin session called to discuss the apostles has to have them arrested a third time. Peter expresses his defiance of the high priest with a powerful declaration that has echoed through history: When human authority and divine authority conflict, "We must obey God rather than human beings." When he preaches to his prosecutors, their fury reaches the point of wanting to kill the apostles (5:33) but is interrupted by the intervention of the leading Pharisee Gamaliel I, a Sanhedrin member. Gamaliel's advice to be tolerant toward this new movement carries the day. They beat the apostles as a warning to stop preaching and then release them. However, the apostles continue to preach Christ publicly and privately (5:42).

After all the emphasis on the church as completely united, the author now reveals a rift among Jerusalem Christians that threatens to divide them permanently (6:1–6). Two groups of Jewish believers within the Jerusalem community are fighting over the common goods. The designation of one group as **Hellenists** ("Greeks") whose leaders all have Greek names (6:5) suggests that they were Jews who had Greek as their main language and were more acculturated to Greco-Roman civilization than other Jews. The other group, called the **Hebrews,** had mostly Semitic names and would have been more culturally Jewish/Semitic in outlook. At any rate, they are at odds with each other. The Hebrews are shutting off common funds from the Hellenist widows, who apparently were dependent on this support. Why they are doing this is not stated, but we may presume that it is connected to their differences. To deal with this situation, the Twelve (who of course are in the "Hebrew" group) summon the whole body of the church to settle the issue. They appoint seven Hellenist leaders as administrators of the common goods.

A summary (6:7) about the spread of the word of God in Jerusalem sets the stage for a conflict centered on Stephen (6:8–8:1), and the resulting spread of the movement beyond the Jerusalem area. The leader of the Hellenists, Stephen, stirs up opposition at a Jerusalem synagogue attended largely by foreign Jews. They bring him before a Sanhedrin and level a false charge about the message he is preaching, in general his words against Moses and the Law, and specifically that he intended to destroy the Temple. At the end of his long speech in which he does oppose (but not threaten violence against) the Temple (7:2–53), Stephen accuses his hearers of causing the death of Jesus even as their fathers persecuted the prophets. Not surprisingly, this accusation provokes rage against Stephen, and the council takes him out of the city and stones him to death (7:54–60). Not only does Stephen become the first Christian martyr, but also Acts matches his death to the death of Jesus in Luke by shared narrative touches. Observing this death is a young man named Saul (7:58). He consents to Stephen's death (8:1), but soon he will carry on the work of Stephen.

Acts 1:8 laid out the divine plan of evangelizing: "You shall be my witnesses in Jerusalem and in all Judea and Samaria, and to the ends of the earth." Ironically, the early church's first move outside of Jerusalem is the result of persecution—God's planning, in other words, not the church's. (Later, Paul will also travel farther and farther afield when he is persecuted from town to town.) Luke says that "all except the Apostles" flee from Jerusalem, but from the wider context, it appears the "Hebrews" could stay in Jerusalem, while only the "Hellenists" fled. Those who are expelled and become the missionaries to other areas are the Hellenists, the more radical Christians in terms of their relation to Jewish Temple worship. In 8:5, the Hellenists go to the Samaritans and begin preaching Jesus to non-Jews. Their success attracts Simon Magus, a religious charlatan whom Peter will confront later. More Hellenist evangelizing takes place in the southern part of Judea, showing more geographical spread according to Acts' geographic outline. The nameless Ethiopian eunuch who appears is probably not from modern Ethiopia, but Sudan or Nubia to the south of Egypt—outside the Roman Empire, from "the end of the earth." He had been castrated to qualify for service in the queen of Ethiopia's court and was a powerful official. (Males who regularly came in contact with the king's harem generally had to be incapable of having sexual intercourse with them.) Although Deut. 23:21 prohibited the admission of castrated persons into the community of Israel, Philip has no hesitation about meeting the eunuch's request to be baptized into the community of the renewed Israel. With his simple but powerful narration of this event, the author notes to the careful reader that the early church has crossed three traditional boundaries: racial-ethnic (the inclusion of an African), political (someone outside the Empire), and ritual purity (a eunuch).

Acts pauses in the narrative of the Hellenist mission here to tell us about the Hebrew Saul/Paul, who would become the great missionary to the Gentiles. Because of all that Paul will accomplish later, Acts is very interested in recounting his dramatic conversion, and will tell it twice more, in chapters 22 and 26. The reluctance of Ananias (a different Ananias, of course, from the Ananias in chapter 5—it was a common name) to have anything to do with Saul despite the Lord's instruction highlights the change in Saul from the most fearsome persecutor to the most fearless—and effective—preacher. Acts carefully reports that Saul received the Holy Spirit (9:17), for Paul will preach as powerfully as those who received the Spirit at Pentecost. Barnabas supports Saul against those in Jerusalem who could not believe that the persecutor had now changed. Saul goes back to Tarsus (9:30); the author will describe his great mission after he tells us more about Peter. The narrative overlapping of the two figures helps to show that both men preach the same gospel, despite the differences that will arise between them.

With the church at peace (9:31, a transitional summary), Peter returns to the narrative's foreground. Peter cures Aeneas at Lydda (9:32–35) with a simple command to rise. Next, Peter restores Tabitha/Dorcas to life at Joppa (9:36–43). These are cures of Jewish believers in traditionally Jewish territory, but what Peter does next will, like the Hellenist mission just narrated, also take Christianity outside Judaism to Gentiles. In 9:1–48 Peter is led by the Spirit to baptize Cornelius with his entire household, a Roman army officer. He is a **God fearer,** a Gentile who participates in synagogue prayers and accepts the moral demands of Judaism. In 10:1–18 Peter repeats what happened with a first-person report as he defends his behavior before the mother church in Jerusalem. (As usual in narratives, duplication signals that this is an account of special importance.) Peter preaches a sermon, and the Holy Spirit comes upon the Gentiles present, so that Peter commands them to be baptized. Returning to Jerusalem, Peter has to account for baptizing Gentiles. Acts 10:44–48 describes the acceptance of Cornelius' baptism by the Jerusalem church as a major step, accompanied as it was by an outpouring of the Spirit manifested through speaking in tongues. Comparable to Acts 2's Pentecost, this outpouring of the Spirit is the beginning of the church among the Gentiles. The radical character of what Peter has done is challenged by "conservatives" in the church of Jerusalem: "Why did you go to the uncircumcised and eat with them?" (11:2–3). This commensality (table fellowship) is a social indication of full acceptance, which the conservatives regard as a breach of Judaism. Peter answers them by telling about his visions and the coming of the Spirit upon Cornelius' household. This argument temporarily silences the **Circumcision Party,** those Jewish Christians who argue for circumcision for all non-Jewish converts, and leads to the acceptance of Gentiles into existing Jewish Christian groups (11:18). Nevertheless, the issue has not been resolved; Acts 15 will revisit it in an even more dramatic way.

The focus now turns from the church in Jerusalem to the church in Antioch (11:19–26). The narrator notes that here the followers of Jesus were first called "Christians." Although he does not mention it, this label probably originated as a negative nickname meaning "those Christ-people." (This is also a reminder of a social scientific axiom that the identity of individuals and groups is formed socially by others, especially in Mediterranean society.) As part of his technique of simultaneous narration, the author resumes the Hellenists' story he had suspended in chapter 8. The Hellenists went to Phoenicia, Cyprus, and Antioch (in Syria), preaching at first only to Jews but then gradually to Gentiles as well. Luke seems to imply here, despite what he just narrated about Peter taking the Gospel to Cornelius, that the effort to convert Gentiles actually began with the Hellenists. When the Jerusalem church heard this, they sent Barnabas to Antioch to check on the development, and he approved it (11:22–23). Saul also comes to Antioch (11:24–26). Just at this time Jerusalem and Judea are hit particularly hard by a famine foretold by the Christian prophet Agabus (11:27–30), and by a changed political situation where direct Roman rule had been replaced in 41–44 C.E. by a Jewish client-kingdom ruled by Herod Agrippa I, who persecuted Christians (12:1–23). James, son of Zebedee and one of the Twelve, is put to death. Peter is arrested; but God intervenes again through an angel to release him (5:19). Acts finishes the colorful story of the unsuccessful persecution by describing (12:23) the grisly death of Herod Agrippa, who was eaten internally by worms at God's command because of his extreme pride. This section ends on a positive note with another Lukan summary (12.24–25): God's word grows and multiplies, and Barnabas and Saul bring John Mark back to Antioch.

From this point until the end of Acts, the focus is mostly on Paul. This section begins with a short description of the church of Antioch (13.1–3). Barnabas is listed first there and Saul, last; only during the mission will the Roman name "Paul" begin to be used consistently in place of "Saul" and the order reversed to Paul and Barnabas (e.g., 13:13, 43). This change of name is symbolic of his new identity as a missionary to the Gentiles; in ancient Semitic culture, one's name is the most important thing one has. After prayer and fasting, the church lays hands on Barnabas and Saul, commissioning them for a mission we now call the first Pauline journey, typically dated to 46–49. Barnabas and Saul go to Cyprus with John Mark (13:4–12). This is Barnabas' home area, and they speak in the Jewish synagogues. Saul encounters and defeats the Jewish false prophet and magician, Bar-Jesus. Their move from Cyprus to Antioch of Pisidia in Asia Minor (13:13–50) is perhaps what caused John Mark to depart and go to Jerusalem (13:13). Paul gives a synagogue sermon (13:16–41), the first time we hear the content of his preaching. Its appeal to the OT and summary of what God did in Jesus is similar to the sermons earlier preached by Peter. It meets with success then but 13:44–49 shows that on the following Sabbath there was so much hostility from "the Jews" that Paul and Barnabas shifted their appeal to the Gentiles. The Jewish hostility at Antioch continues so that Paul and Barnabas are driven from Pisidia and have to move on to Iconium, but they are still "filled with joy and the Holy Spirit" (13:52). In Iconium they preach and form a church, but once again they have to move on, now to the Lycaonian cities of Lystra and Derbe (14:6–21). In Lystra Paul heals a man crippled from birth. The Gentiles react foolishly to this healing by hailing Barnabas and Paul as the Greek gods Zeus and Hermes in human form, which of course they reject. Paul receives a stoning and is left for dead, but he recovers and goes on with Barnabas to Derbe. The two disciples retrace their path through the Asia Minor cities by which they came, and then sail back to Syrian Antioch (14:21b–28), appointing **presbyters** (elders) as leaders in every church. The first journey ends with a report to the church of Antioch that had sent Paul and Barnabas: "God opened a door of faith to the Gentiles" (14:26–27).

What Paul has done disturbs the "circumcision party" at Jerusalem, who now send people to Antioch (15:1) to challenge once again the acceptance of Gentiles without circumcision (recall chapter 11). This time, they do not give up their opposition as quickly as before. Paul's opponents attack the principle that Gentiles may be admitted to the church without becoming Jews as well (i.e., being circumcised). They cause so much trouble that Paul and Barnabas go to Jerusalem (15:2–3) to debate the issue. There follows a report of a momentous meeting, the **Jerusalem Council** or conference (15.4–29), to decide how closely this rapidly growing movement would remain related to Judaism. Four main participants are involved: the circumcision advocates (identified only by the name of their group), Paul, Peter, and James the brother of Jesus. One needs to read between the lines of this account, because even here Luke stresses the unity of the church, saying as little as possible about the deep, enduring nature of the problem. The issue under discussion was what Paul and Barnabas had done in their missionary activity, and thus the conference focused on Paul. Paul recounts deeds done among the Gentiles and the gospel he proclaimed to them, which surely means an account of how they had come to faith and received the Spirit but were not circumcised. Peter also argues from his experience: God had sent the Holy Spirit on the uncircumcised Cornelius. James finally settles the matter by observing that the prophets foretold that the Gentiles would come to the faith of Israel, and the Law of Moses allowed uncircumcised Gentiles to live among the people of God provided they abstained from certain listed pollutions prohibited by Leviticus 17–18 for aliens living in Israel. These forbidden things are meat offered as a sacrifice to idols or sold in meat markets; the eating of blood; the eating of animals "strangled," or improperly slaughtered; and "fornication," sexual intercourse outside marriage. Then Paul and Barnabas return to Antioch (15:30–35), carrying a letter with the council's ruling. The Jerusalem conference, under the guidance of the Spirit, preserved the unity of the church about the essentials for conversion: Gentile believers do not have to become Jews but should respect the scruples of Jews.

Paul's next journey begins adversely: he quarrels with Barnabas over Mark's reliability (15:36–39) so that they can no longer travel together. Paul takes a new main partner, Silas, as he sets out on another mission (15:40). First, he goes through Syria and his native province of Cilicia. Next Paul revisits Lystra and Derbe (16:1–5), where he circumcises Timothy, a Christian believer with a Jewish-Christian mother and Gentile father. Paul moves on through Phrygia and Galatia to Troas (16:6–10). In Troas, he sees a vision of a man of Macedonia pleading for help, causing him to cross over to Greece. The "we" form of narrative begins at Troas and continues through the crossover to Philippi. So the Christian faith spreads to Macedonia (northern Greece), and thus to Europe. Acts does not highlight the fact that Christianity is crossing a continent, probably because such geographic divisions were less important in the unified Roman Empire, but 16:9–10 does give it some dramatic importance. The evangelizing at Philippi (16:11–40) features stories of two women, in Luke's typical style one positive and then one negative: the openness and support of Lydia, a model for the Christian household; and an encounter with a young woman who had "a spirit of divination." City authorities put Paul in prison, but the miraculous opening of the prison shows that God is with his missionary to the Gentiles, just as he was with the imprisoned Peter earlier in Acts. Paul is acquitted after a brief hearing under Roman law. The "we" form of narrative ceases as Paul leaves Philippi. At Thessalonica, Paul encounters the same kind of Jewish opposition that marred his mission in Asia Minor before the Jerusalem conference (17:1–9). Forced to leave, Paul goes on to Beroea and finds a more welcoming Jewish audience (17:10–14). Yet some Jews from Thessalonica follow him to Beroea and stir up trouble, and so Paul continues on to Athens (17:15–34). There, Epicurean and Stoic philosophers try to fit Paul's new "teaching" into their philosophical ideas (17:18). Paul's sermon to them offers a cultured Greek approach to the message about Christ, in tone and content quite unlike the other sermons in Acts, and meets (for that reason, does Luke imply?) with slim results. Paul's stay at Corinth (18:1–18) has an added appeal: he meets Aquila and Priscilla from the city of Rome. We can see Paul forming a wider circle of colleagues as his "co-workers," as he calls them in his letters. Again, we see Jewish hostility when local Jews bring Paul before the tribunal of the Roman proconsul Gallio, whose presence at Corinth supplies a key fixed point for the chronology of Paul, dating his mission there to 51–52. The return from Corinth to Antioch (18:19–22) is narrated very briefly, as Paul passes through Ephesus, Caesarea, and Jerusalem on his way.

The so-called "Third Missionary Journey" begins now, as Paul sets out from Antioch through Galatia and Phrygia (18:23). While Paul is en route, we are told of the presence at Ephesus of Apollos of Alexandria, Egypt, another leading Christian missionary (18:24–28). At the beginning of Paul's stay at Ephesus in chapter 19, Luke tells of some there who believed in Jesus but had received only the baptism of John the Baptizer and knew nothing of the Holy Spirit. The reader of Acts is led to puzzle about this—was the Baptizer's movement still alive, and in the Gentile world? True to form, Luke says as little as possible about this potential diversity in the faith. Paul remains at Ephesus about three years, a long time for one who keeps moving on. Acts 19:11–19 piques our interest with portraits of Paul the miracle worker and of Jewish exorcists attempting to drive out evil spirits using the name of Jesus (cf. Luke 9:49–50). That "the word of the Lord grew" in Ephesus (19:20; cf. 6:7; 12:24) implies that alongside Jerusalem and Antioch where the word also grew, Ephesus is now another major center of the new faith. Acts 19:21 is the first indication of Paul's plan to go to Rome by way of Greece and Jerusalem, an anticipation of how the book will end. A colorful account of the silversmiths' riot protecting Artemis/Diana of the Ephesians follows (19:23–40), ending Paul's stay in Ephesus. Briefly told are Paul's travels through Macedonia to Greece (20:1–3a), especially to Corinth, where he stays three months. Then he goes back through Macedonia and Philippi (20:3b–6). The "we" form of narrative resumes as Paul crosses from Philippi to Troas where he raises a dead person to life, a demonstration that he is fully endowed with Jesus' divine power (20:7–12). Hurrying on to be at Jerusalem for Pentecost, Paul sails along the Asia Minor coast to Miletus, bypassing Ephesus (20:13–16). At Miletus, he gives an eloquent but sad farewell sermon to the elders/presbyters of the church of Ephesus (20.17–38), Paul's final directives to those whom he will never see again (20:25, 38). In this poignant context Paul admonishes the presbyters he is leaving behind to be shepherds of the flock in which the Holy Spirit has made them leaders. The most pressing danger to be faced in the future is false teaching; there are unnamed others "who speak perverse things so as to draw away disciples" (20:30). After this farewell at Miletus, the return journey to Palestine continues, bringing Paul to Tyre (21:1–6) and another dramatic farewell, and then goes on to Caesarea (21:7–14). There at the home of Philip the Hellenist and his four daughter-prophets, the prophet Agabus reappears in the narrative, warning Paul of imprisonment in his future.

A turning point that will shape the rest of Acts is reached when Paul goes up to Jerusalem (21:15–17), the city where Jesus, Stephen and James the son of Alphaeus died in the Luke-Acts story so far. The "we" form of narration ends at 21:18, to be resumed six chapters later. Paul is received by James the brother of Jesus and the elders (21:18–25) and reports to them his success among the Gentiles. Not to be outdone, they match his claims with reports of their own successes among the Jews. Acts cannot disguise the negative feelings raised among the Jerusalem Christian authorities by (false) rumors about what Paul has been teaching. The well-intentioned plan to have Paul show his loyalty to Judaism—and implicitly to Jewish Christianity—by going to the Temple to perform a special Jewish ritual fails when Paul's opponents in Judaism start a riot, claiming that Paul has defiled the holy place by bringing Gentiles into it (21:24–30). Paul is saved from the crowd only by the intervention of a Roman tribune with soldiers (21:31–40); after being arrested, however, Paul protests in Greek that he is a Roman citizen and should be accorded his right to speak. He is allowed to speak in Aramaic to the crowd. Paul's speech of defense (22:1–27) recounts his conversion and its aftermath with some variants from the original account in 9:1–30. The speech produces conflict: the crowd reacts violently, but Paul's Roman citizenship wins him the tribune's protection for a fair, Roman trial (22:22–29). The next day Paul is brought before a Sanhedrin (22:30–23:11). He cleverly creates dissent between the Sadducees and Pharisees in the Sanhedrin over the resurrection. Even though the tribune again rescues him from the violent clash, a vision of the Lord warns Paul that he will have to testify in his own defense in Rome. Paul's nephew frustrates a Jewish plot to kill Paul (23:12–22), and Paul is sent to Caesarea and the Roman official Felix (23:23–35).

Paul's trial before Felix (24:1–27) has parallels to the trial of Jesus before Pilate. The high priest and the Jewish elders present Felix with a list of charges (24:5–6) resembling those presented by a Sanhedrin against Jesus (Luke 23:1–2). The author says that Felix knew about the **Way,** the continuing name of the Christian movement (24:14, 22; see 9:2; 18:25; 19:9, 23; 22:4). Felix angles for a bribe, but Paul does not cooperate, so he waits in prison at Caesarea for two years until the end of Felix's time in office. Paul is interrogated by Festus (25:1–12), the next Roman procurator, who ruled from 60–62 C.E., but Paul refuses an offer to be tried in Jerusalem and "appeals to Caesar," that is, demands a trial in Rome. The parallelism to the

The Appian Way Built by Appius Claudius in 312 B.C.E., the Via Appia was the oldest and most well known of the Roman roads. It became a model for the Roman roads built throughout the Empire to hasten military and commercial travel. The apostle Paul traveled on this road near Rome at the end of Acts. Parts of it are still used today for modern traffic. Used by permission of BiblePlaces.com.

Lukan trial of Jesus is heightened, because Festus passes Paul to the Herodian king Agrippa II (25:13–26:32) to be heard, even as Pilate sent Jesus to Herod (Luke 23:7). For a third time in Acts, Paul relates his conversion on the road to Damascus (26:9–20).

The final part of Acts narrates Paul's journey to Rome for his day in court. Using the "we" format again, Acts tells of a long sea journey: up the Syrian coast, past Cyprus, along the southern coast of Asia Minor, across to Crete, to Malta where the boat is shipwrecked in a storm, then to Sicily, and up the west coast of Italy to a landing at Puteoli, near Neapolis (Naples). This journey probably began in the late summer of 60 and ended in 61, and Luke describes the ship and navigation in lengthy but colorful detail. Paul's survival from storm and poisonous snakebite illustrates God's providential care for Paul, who must arrive in Rome safely. Paul's arrival there after a journey from Puteoli on the Appian Way is described in a portentous understatement, "And so we came to Rome" (28:14). This is the final destination of Acts' "geographic outline," foreseen by the risen Jesus in 1:8: "You will be my witnesses in Jerusalem, all Judea and Samaria, and to the ends of the earth." Christian churches had been founded at Rome already; that Acts does not hint how, when it has given every other church an apostolic foundation, is significant. Paul meets local Jewish authorities in Rome, which had a sizeable Jewish community. After he explains the gospel to them, they reject it, leading Paul to conclude weightily, "Let it be known to you then that this salvation of God has been sent to the Gentiles; they will listen" (v. 29). This makes explicit and confirms as the divine plan what the narrative of Acts has been implying—the Jewish response to the gospel is limited, and the movement is becoming increasingly Gentile. Luke closes by relating that Paul lived there under "house arrest" for two years at his own expense, openly proclaiming the gospel to all who saw him (vv. 30–31). To the last, Paul is an apostle of Jesus Christ.

Historical Reading

Many historical treatments of Luke-Acts begin with Willem van Unnik's statement, "Acts is one of the great storm-centers of New Testament scholarship" (van Unnik 1966). This observation is as true today as it was when it was made. Almost every aspect of historical criticism—textual, source, form, and redactional—is controversial. Here we will introduce the main elements of these controversies.

www   Follow the link to an online concise treatment of introductory matters. See also the link to Professor Craig Koester's well-constructed virtual tour of the journeys of Paul.

Acts in Brief: Summary of Historical Reading

Author Traditionally, Luke, the physician and coworker of Paul (Col 4:14, 2 Tim 4:11, Philem 24). Today, a minority keep to traditional view, but most view the author as an unknown Gentile-Christian convert of the second Christian generation, well educated in Greek literature; perhaps a client of Theophilus (1:1–4).

Sources There is wide agreement on a "we" source in 16:10–17; 20:5–21:18; chapters 27–28, so called because it is written in the first-person plural. A much smaller number of scholars hypothesize other sources: a "Jerusalem" source in parts of chapters 1–5, 8, 9–11, and 12; a "Hellenist" source perhaps from Antioch used in 6:1–8:4, 11:19–30, and chapter 15; or a "Pauline" source covering parts of chapter 9, 13–14, and 15:35–28:31.

Date Probably somewhere in the 80s.

Audience Gentile Christians, probably in an urban setting; the precise city cannot be determined.

Purpose To challenge believers to be more devoted to the faith, especially its growth and defense.

Textual Criticism

Acts presents a special difficulty because of the conflicting evidence of two primary groups of manuscripts called the *Alexandrian* and the *Western*. This problem in the Greek text is so significant that occasionally it has to be noted in the footnotes of English versions like the NRSV. The Western text's extra material ranges from a word to a whole verse; for example, see 13:27, 15:29, 18:27, and 28:31. The book of Acts in the Western family is almost 10 percent longer than the Alexandrian, and at many points the character of each of these two textual types is quite distinctive. Most scholars believe that the Western text is secondary, and most scholarly study is based on the shorter Alexandrian text. Still, questions remain: Does the Western text bear witness to an ongoing process of emendation? Does it display a mixture of more or less original and secondary readings that must be considered on a case-by-case basis? A long-standing solution suggests that the author of Luke was responsible for two versions of Acts and that this explains the existence of the two major text types. This view has gained new momentum since the onset of redaction criticism in the twentieth century, when text critics found that the Western text sometimes displayed Lukan style and theological themes. Nevertheless, most scholars conclude that the witnesses of the so-called Western tradition do not contain the original text of Acts and that therefore the author of Acts did not write two versions. Most study of Acts is based on the Alexandrian text type.

Author

We dealt with the introductory matters of Luke-Acts in the treatment of the Gospel of Luke in Chapter 9. We will assume the same results for Acts, especially in the matters of author, date, and audience; it is most likely that the same author wrote these two books together for the same audience. Here we will look more in depth at one issue of authorship particularly significant for the interpretation of Acts, the three so-called "we" sections. (Our conclusion from Chapter 4 will not change, but evidence about the author particular to Acts will be considered.)

Until recently, the view that Luke-Acts was authored by a companion of Paul drew additional support from the so-called "we" sections in Acts (16:10–17; 20:5–21:18; chapters 27–28). Did a specific companion accompany Paul and therefore know the comparatively rich details of these sections, or is "we" simply a literary convention? Examples can be found of "we" used in sea travel accounts in contemporary Greco-Roman literature. However, Joseph Fitzmyer has recently weighed these examples closely and found them wanting, concluding that they do not explain satisfactorily the usage of Acts (Fitzmyer 1998). For example, why does this pronoun not appear throughout *all* the sea-journeys in Acts instead of in only a few sections, if it is a literary convention? In addition, why is Paul on land at Philippi in the first "we" passage (16:10–17)? A simpler explanation of the "we" holds that it comes from an autobiographical diary written in the first-person plural. This diary describing moments when the writer was with Paul came into the hands of the author of Acts. In this case the writer of the diary was not the author of the whole book of Acts but is one of his sources. Nevertheless, scholars who cannot reconcile the picture of Paul in Acts with the picture of Paul in his own letters have proposed a more complicated source theory—that the author got the diary of a true companion of Paul and used it selectively, including sections at appropriate moments in his own narrative. However one decides this issue (and the issue is by no means decided in current scholarship), the "we" passages do little or nothing to alter the anonymity of the author of Acts and bring us closer to the real author. The "we" of his narration contributes to his focus on Paul, rather than on himself.

Sources

In his prologue to Luke-Acts, the author speaks of many accounts of "what has been accomplished among us." We saw that the Gospel of Luke uses sources; does the same author use different sources in Acts?

Scholars using the historical method have proposed several written sources, mainly because Acts covers such a diversity of groups and geographic areas, as well as such a spread of time, that the author would be unlikely to know about them first-hand or even know people who did. The first is a "Jerusalem" source covering events in that area as recorded in parts of chapters 1–5, 8, 9–11, and 12. The second is a "Hellenist" source perhaps from Antioch used in 6:1–8:4, 11:19–30, and chapter 15. The last is a "Pauline" source covering parts of chapter 9, 13–14, and 15:35–28:31, the last main section of Acts. We have already considered the possibility of a "we" source within this "Pauline" source. Although there is some general scholarly consensus that the author of Acts probably used sources, what wording they contained is unascertainable. We can certainly say that although scholars share a wide agreement that Luke uses Mark and Q, and somewhat less agreement that Luke uses a written L source, they share no such agreement about Acts' sources.

Purpose

The most apparent theme in Acts—the emphasis of the implied author—is the spread of the gospel into the world, the "mission" of the church. The geographic outline; the prominence given to mission activities and missionaries like the Philip, Peter, and Paul; and the missionary speeches all point to the central theme: the gospel goes to the end of the earth according to the plan of God, the command of the risen Christ, and the empowering of the Holy Spirit.

Within or apart from this large theme, others have been proposed. F. F. Bruce, following H. J. Cadbury, argues that Acts is written to defend Christians from rising charges that Christianity is politically subversive to Rome. It does this by repeatedly showing Paul to be innocent of charges pressed against him (Bruce 1954). J. C. O'Neill has argued that Acts itself has a missionary purpose, to present the Christian gospel to outsiders in order to encourage them to become Christians. Hans Conzelmann has argued that Acts deals with the problem of the delay of the Parousia (Jesus' return in glory at the end of time) by constructing a theology of **salvation history** focused on the church as the continuing **middle of time.** The time of Israel is the first period, the time of Jesus is the middle, and the time of the church is the third, end period. Conzelmann does not deny that Luke presents an end of time but argues that Luke supposes that the church will extend indefinitely, thus toning down the apocalyptic emphases of Mark and Paul (Conzelmann 1960). R. Maddox has argued that Acts is written to defend the legitimacy of a predominantly Gentile Christian church against the original and now waning Jewish Christian church (Maddox 1982). Of these proposals, Conzelmann's is by far the most influential, probably because it seems to be the most explanatory of Luke's theology in Acts.

www   See the website for an essay on a special historical issue, Luke as a historian in Acts.

Newer methods of reading Acts may not yet be the storm center that it is for historical research, but it is a center of liveliness. Because this book follows in the attention paid to the Gospel of Luke, and because it is the only book of church history in the NT, Acts has attracted lately a good deal of reading with new methods. Here we will sample a few examples.

Acts in Brief: Summary of Newer Methods

Narrative Luke is a well-written historical narrative focused on Jesus, but Acts focuses first on the Twelve Apostles headed by Peter, then on Peter himself, and finally on Paul. The author regularly employs the journey motif, as in Luke. Acts punctuates its narratives with speeches, some furthering the plot and others providing thematic theological details.

Social Scientific Acts is appropriately treated by cultural anthropology and social description: the cultural world of its author, the nature of early Christianity as a utopian movement, based on kinship, the honor involved in Paul's social location, and the cities which he visits or resides.

Feminist Acts continues to be generally open to a wider role for women in the church and society, but seemingly less so than the Gospel of Luke. More scrupulous feminists might argue that the author's true colors come out in Acts.

Cross-Cultural Acts crosses more cultural barriers than perhaps any other NT book. As the gospel goes into the world, people of other religions,

> ethnic status, cultures, races and nations engage the gospel and become a part of the Christian movement. This crossing of cultural barriers is done with great difficulty, however, and not without cost to church unity. While most cross-cultural critics appreciate the story of Acts, many fault Acts for not being cross-cultural enough in its focus.

Narrative Reading

Acts is a historical narrative, the only history of early Christianity that we have in the NT. As the author of the Gospel of Luke was a skilled teller of the story of Jesus, the Acts of the Apostles is skillfully written as well. First, it has notable points of connection with Luke. The Gospel of Luke focused on Jesus, but Acts focuses first on the Twelve Apostles headed by Peter, then on Peter himself, and finally on Paul. Luke has Jesus journeying to Jerusalem, where he will die and be raised; Acts has the church journeying toward Rome, the "end of the earth." Second, Acts punctuates its narratives with speeches, some of which further the plot and others of which provide thematic theological perspectives. These speeches form a sort of interlude in the action. Third, some of Acts is written skillfully in the first-person plural. This device puzzles the reader at times because the narrative shifts from third person ("he/she/they") to the first-person plural "we," but it also creates a renewed interest as the story goes along. Finally, Acts has touches of the ancient Greek romance novel in its telling of Paul's journeys, especially his sea journeys. Acts may not be written to entertain, as Pervo argues (Pervo 1987), but it certainly is entertaining!

Narrative Reading at Work, 1
Conflict with Jewish Authorities (Acts 3–4)

In this reading on Acts' earliest conflict with Jewish authorities, William Kurz describes the struggle for authority: Who is going to lead the Jewish nation? The church loses this struggle over the course of Acts, but here in its first appearance the outcome is still an open question.

Chapter divisions in [the NT] are not original but were added to later manuscripts. In few places are these divisions more misleading than the division in Acts between chapters 3 and 4. The action of chapter 3 flows without interruption into chapter 4, as the narrator shows priests, captain of the Temple guard, and Sadducees interrupting Peter and John "[w]hile they were still speaking to the people" (Acts 4:1). With his omniscience, the narrator explains their inner feelings and reasons for

Source: William S. Kurz, Reading Luke-Acts: Dynamics of Biblical Narrative (Louisville, KY: Westminster John Knox, 1993), pp. 80–81.

confronting Peter and John: they were "disturbed that they were teaching the people and proclaiming in Jesus the resurrection of the dead" (4:2). He juxtaposes the scene of their throwing Peter and John into prison with the conversion of many who heard Peter's speech and the growth of the believing community to five thousand (4:3–4).

He thus sets the stage of confrontation and competition between Jewish authorities and the apostles over who shall teach "the people [of God]," which continue through most of Acts 4-5. He shows a series of arrests and confrontations in their assembly between them and the apostles. In sharp contrast to the apostles' failure to support Jesus effectively during his passion, and especially to Peter's denial of Jesus before even a servant, Peter and the apostles always overcome the Sanhedrin's challenges and threats, even escaping from prison and resuming their teaching of "the people" in the Temple in defiance of the helpless authorities.

In effect, the narrator is showing that the apostles will judge the twelve tribes of Israel, as Jesus prophesied at his farewell supper (Luke 22:30). Though the primary meaning of this prophecy probably refers to the final advent of God's kingdom, the verb *judge* in scripture can also refer to contemporary authority over Israel, as in the biblical book of Judges. As the apostles teach the people of God in the Temple and the authorities prove helpless to stop them, the narrator is depicting the transition of authority over God's people from the Sanhedrin to the Twelve.

Questions

1. *Trace out in Acts the ways that Jewish conflict with Christianity impacts on Paul's activity.*

2. *How might the last statement of Paul in Acts 28:28 confirm this reading of Jewish-Christian conflict?*

Narrative Reading at Work, 2
The Ending of Acts (28:16–31)

The end of any literary work, as literally the author's "last word," possesses a peculiar power. The end of the book of Acts is intriguing, and here Daniel Marguerat explains this effect in terms of narrative suspension, intentionally ending a document abruptly, seemingly before a proper, expected end has been reached.

It has become clear that this enigmatic character [of the end of Acts] does not result from the exegete's incapacity [to understand it today]. A rhetorical procedure noted in Greco-Roman culture, "narrative suspension," allows the author of Acts consciously to use silence and ambivalence in editing the end of his monumental work. This astonishing narrative choice concretizes the theological challenge that the

Source: Daniel Marguerat, "The Enigma of the Silent Closing of Acts (28:16–31)," in David P. Moessner, ed., *Jesus and the Heritage of Israel* (Harrisburg, PA: Trinity, 1999), p. 304.

author of Acts has imposed on himself: to assign to Christianity a new place that the Pauline mission has gained–the Roman Empire–but at the same time to lead Christianity back to its Jewish roots. This intention fits into the conduct of the Pauline heritage. Luke wants to reinterpret the memory of the apostle's martyrdom by inverting the scheme of expected procedure (Acts 27–28), and to assure the perpetuation of his missionary work in the present.

For Luke, Paul's final theological debate with Judaism ends neither in the curse of Israel nor in a trivialization of its refusal. By the apostle's arrival in Rome, a new step is taken in the history of salvation, which marks the failure of a hope in conversion for the entire Jewish people. But the account is voluntarily ambivalent, achieved by a theology that refuses to decide on the future of the relation between church and synagogue. The same disposition of openness characterizes the final scene of Paul evangelizing Rome (28:30–31). This portrayal of the ideal pastor points to the men and women, with Luke or those close to him, who by their missionary engagement perpetuate the memory of the apostle to the Gentiles. In this way, they were associated with the witness of the Risen One "to the ends of the earth" (1:8). The summary offers expectation and remains to be rewritten in the life of the reader at the moment he or she finishes reading the book.

Question

What kinds of rewriting of the end of Acts do you suppose this book's original audience would make?

Doing Narrative Reading Yourself

1. *Read the passages in Acts 2:43–47, 4:32–5:11 on the sharing of goods in the first Jerusalem community. From a narrative perspective, what exactly is going on in the sharing of goods, and how does it work? What are the "gaps" that the reader must fill in? Why is it so important to Luke that the early community be united in this practice, and later in his narrative he drops all mention of radical sharing?*

2. *Read and analyze the two accounts of Jesus' departure from earth (Luke 24:44–53 and Acts 1:1–11). What are the similarities and differences, and how can you account for them in the overall narrative of Luke-Acts?*

Social Scientific Reading

When scholars study the relationship of Acts to the rest of the NT, they tend to work from either a strictly historical or a historical-rhetorical framework. Because Acts is the only "history" document in the NT, historical questions loom large and dominate the discussion. But social scientific reading brings to the study of Acts questions treated appropriately by cultural anthropology and social description. What is the cultural world of Luke? How does the early church gather honor and turn away shame, especially as it proclaims in the Roman Empire a founder who was crucified in shame by Rome? What value is given in terms of honor to Paul's social location or to the cities that he visits or in which he resides? Such social and cultural questions require historical scholars to supplement their traditional methods of inquiry and bibliography. New questions warrant new methods of investigation, and the materials used here are increasingly being employed by traditional scholarly investigation.

Acts is a rich mine for the work of social scientific criticism. Its many groups, different social settings, and developed conflicts have much to offer those who study the birth and spread of the Christian church. On the other hand, as we will see in the readings, the thematic and geographic focus of Acts has come under fire from social scientific critics for its limitations and potential distortions. All in all, readers of Acts from ethnic minorities and decolonializing cultures have a rich field before them in the Acts of the Apostles.

Social Scientific Reading at Work
Ideology of Individuals and Groups (Acts 8:26–40)

Here Vernon Robbins, a leading sociorhetorical interpreter of the NT, gives an appreciative review of Clarice Martin's essay on the Ethiopian eunuch.

Martin begins with past studies of inner texture of the story in the Acts of the Apostles where an Ethiopian eunuch, riding back on his chariot after his visit to Jerusalem, converts to Christianity as a result of Philip's interpretation of a scriptural passage to him. The past studies Martin cites proceeded thematically. Many observed the role of the Holy Spirit in the preaching and evangelism in the story of the conversion of the Ethiopian eunuch itself (8.29, 39) and in the broader narrative of Luke-Acts (Luke 4.18; 24.44; Acts 1.8; 4.8–10; 7.55; 10.11–12; 13.4–10; 16.6–7). Others observed Philip's "witness" to the death and resurrection of Jesus in the story and the theme of witness throughout Luke and Acts (Luke 1.1–4; 24.48; Acts 1.21–22; 4.33; 10.39–41; 22.14–15). Still others observed the "joy" of the Ethiopian at the end of the story in (8.39) relation to the theme of joy throughout Luke and Acts (Luke 1.44; 2.10; 15.4–7; 19.6, 37; 24.41; Acts 2.47; 8.8; 11.18; 16.33) . . . .

Since the eunuch has, according to the story in Acts, gone up to Jerusalem to worship and is now returning home in his chariot (8.27–28), the story enacts the "social reality" of the temple at Jerusalem becoming a "house of prayer for all peoples" as Isaiah 56.4, 7–8 predicted, since the eunuch has just worshipped at the Temple and

Source: Vernon K. Robbins, *The Tapestry of Early Christian Discourse: Rhetoric, Society and Ideology,* London: Routledge, pp. 216–220. Reviewing Clarice J. Martin's "A Chamberlain's Journey and the Challenge of Interpretation for Liberation," *Semeia* 47 (1989): 105–135; reprinted in Norman K. Gottwald and Richard A. Horsley, eds., *The Bible and Liberation: Political and Social Hermeneutics,* Maryknoll, NY: Orbis Books, 1993.

is now returning. But the eunuch is not simply a eunuch; he is an Ethiopian. In Psalm 68.31 it says that Ethiopia will "stretch out her hands to God." This social reality also has been fulfilled in the story. Without saying that Psalms also are considered to be fulfilled in the activities in Luke and Acts, Martin has expanded the intertexture of the story beyond the specific issue of eunuchs in biblical culture. Her interest lies in an aspect of his identity that extends beyond his being a eunuch. He is an Ethiopian, an issue of special importance for an African-American interpreter of scripture. This story enacts the inclusion not only of eunuchs but also of Ethiopians in worship in the Jerusalem temple. . . .

Martin . . . returns to Luke and Acts to exhibit a thicker texture for its ideology of promise and fulfillment. In Luke there is reference to "all flesh" seeing the salvation of God (Luke 3.6), to repentance and forgiveness of sins being preached to "all nations" (Luke 24.47) and to people coming from "east, west, north and south" to sit at table with Abraham, Isaac and Jacob (Luke 13.29). At the beginning of Acts there is a proclamation that the mission in Acts will reach to the "end of the earth" (Acts 1.8c). From this thicker picture of the ideology of Luke and Acts, she moves to Mediterranean cultural ideology about "the end of the earth" and concludes, using Homer, Herodotus and Strabo, that Ethiopia lies on the edge of the "Ocean" at the southernmost limit of the world. Her conclusion, in turn, suggests that the identification of the eunuch as Ethiopian should be significant, because in its context of culture this baptized Ethiopian is returning to his home at the end of the earth. . . .

Martin . . . observes that these two volumes participate in a cultural ideology that focuses on Rome as the center of the Mediterranean world. As a result of this ideology . . . the darker races outside the Roman orbit are circumstantially marginalized by New Testament authors and the socio-political realities of this tend to dilute the New Testament vision of racial inclusiveness and universalism.

Question

How does Martin's reading combine social scientific, rhetorical, ideological, and liberationist readings?

www   See the website for another Social Scientific Reading at Work on honor attached to certain cities featured in Acts.

Doing Social Scientific Reading Yourself

1. What are the social implications of the more or less radical sharing of property found in Acts 4–6?

2. How is humor used in Acts 28:1–6 to poke fun of Gentile superstition? How might Jewish attitudes toward polytheism have contributed to the Christian attitude? How is this typical of an in-group's making sport of an out-group or the honor-shame paradigm?

Feminist Reading

Women have prominent mention but a limited role in the accomplishment of the author of Luke's purposes in Acts, unlike his Gospel, where women are mentioned prominently and have a prominent role. The author frames Acts around the ministries of Peter and especially Paul because they embody for him the movement of the gospel from Jews to Gentiles, a part of his main theme. The ministries of all other teachers and leaders, male and especially female, are probably diminished as a result of this emphasis. Therefore, Acts does not contain a representative picture of church leadership. In addition, Luke's likely desire to present a picture of Christianity that would win favor in the Roman Empire and keep suspicion at bay, a possible secondary purpose in writing, led to a further diminishment of women's roles in Acts. Women were second-class citizens in the Roman Empire; public leadership roles were all held by men. The author of Luke shapes his treatment of women in Acts to conform to this Roman model.

The author of Luke includes women in Acts' story of the church as a whole (e.g., Acts 3.14). He also draws continuous attention to the participation of women in the emerging church. We read of women praying (Act 1:14, 12:12, and 16:13), prophesying (2:17 and 21:9), repenting and being baptized (5:14 and 8:12), carrying out missionary activity (18:2, 26), and being persecuted for the faith (8:3, 9:2, and 22:4). Acts narrates five stories that feature prominent individual women: Sapphira in Acts 5:1–11; Tabitha/Dorcas in 9:36–43; Rhoda in 12:12–17; Lydia in 16:11–40; Priscilla in 18:1–4, 18–28. These stories balance the general references to women by providing the reader of Acts with a concrete glimpse (albeit one determined by the author's purposes) of what life was like for some women in the early church.

Feminist Reading at Work, 1
Roles and Class of Women in Acts

Here is a sympathetic yet critical feminist reading of women's leadership roles in the early church as presented by Acts.

The most positive portraits of women in Acts, those images that Luke may be offering as models for his female readers, are of wealthy women and women who learn from apostles and disciples. Wealthy women who function as patrons of the developing Christian communities were obviously of critical importance to the early success of Christianity. The church depended on the economic largess of women, particularly widows. Luke explicitly draws these women to the community's attention. With the exception of Rhoda (a wealthy woman's maid) and Mary (Jesus' mother), all the women named in Acts are wealthy. Even Priscilla and Aquila had the economic resources to sponsor a house-church. The anonymous women in Acts are those without economic means.

Source: Gale R. O'Day, "Acts," in Carol Newsome and Sharon H. Ringe, *Women's Bible Commentary* (Louisville, KY: Westminster John Knox, 1992), p. 401. Used by permission of Westminster John Knox Press.

Luke's picture of women in the church thus fits with the conventions of the Greco-Roman world. Women can be ministered to and women can give money to support the churches. Because of Luke's theological and apologetic concerns to win acceptance of Christianity as a factor in world history and a participating institution in the Roman Empire, Luke ignores the leadership roles held by women in the church. This amounts to a *de facto* silencing of many of those women . . . .

The reasons for Luke's narrowing of women's roles are twofold. First, as mentioned earlier, Acts is the story of Paul, who embodies the movement of the gospel to the world stage. All characters are secondary to Paul. Second, and more significant for the picture of women in Acts, propriety and decorum are essential virtues for Luke. Luke's sense of decorum means that women in the early church cannot be portrayed in ways that would be embarrassing or threatening to men in the Roman Empire. Men occupied public leadership roles, not women. The importance of decorum is evident also in the civility that characterizes Paul's relationship to the Roman state in Acts. Luke is above all a "gentleman's gentleman," and Acts is his book.

Questions

1. *Do you agree with O'Day's two reasons explaining Luke's narrowing of women's roles? Why, or why not?*

2. *Would there have been some way for Luke-Acts' author to be as encouraging to women in Acts as he is in the Gospel of Luke?*

Feminist Reading at Work, 2
Women at Pentecost (Acts 2)

In this reading, Rosemary M. Dowsett explicates the presence and role of women at the coming of the Holy Spirit on the church on Pentecost day.

While some assumed the worst—that the disciples were drunk, early morning though it still was (Acts 2:15)—Peter, bold with the dynamic life of the Spirit, seizes the opportunity to explain the true meaning of these momentous events. "This is that!" he says, quoting Joel's prophecy (Joel 2:28–32). Joel had prophesied that women and men, young and old, slave and free, would experience such an overwhelming outpouring of the Spirit of God that all would prophesy, see visions of dreams; no one would be excluded by gender or age or civil status. There would be signs in the sky and on the earth. All this would be a prelude to "the coming of the Lord's great and glorious day" (Acts 2:20), a day when "everyone who calls on the name of the Lord shall be saved" (Acts 2:21).

The emphatic inclusion of women on equal terms with men is especially instructive. For prophecy was less to do with prediction of the future and more to do with acting as the mouthpiece of God. Prophecy was a teaching ministry in which the prophet declared the word of the Lord. Women, equally with men, are equipped

Source: From "The IVP Women's Bible Commentary" edited by Catherine Clark Kroeger and Mary J. Evans. © 2000 by InterVarsity Christian Fellowship/USA. Used by permission of InterVarsity Press, P.O. Box 1400, Downer's Grove, IL 60515. www.ivpress.com.

by the Spirit in this new phase of the kingdom for prophetic teaching ministry. And here at least there is no hint that this ministry must be exercised only among women, any more than men only among men.

Questions

1. *Compare the general feminist approach of these two "women's Bible commentaries." Do they read Acts the same way in its depiction of women's roles?*

2. *What is the meaning for women that not only they, but also the young and the enslaved, receive the Spirit equally with men?*

Doing Feminist Reading Yourself

1. *Study the story of Ananias and Sapphira (Acts 5:1–11). How does this present a grimmer picture of equality in the early church?*

2. *Compare the treatment of women in the Gospel of Luke and the Acts of the Apostles. What are the similarities? How can you account for the differences?*

Cross-Cultural Reading

Of all the documents in the NT, Acts crosses the most cultural barriers. As the gospel goes into the world, people of other religions, ethnic status, cultures, races, and nations engage the gospel and become a part of the Christian movement. This crossing of cultural barriers is done with great difficulty; Acts itself shows the struggles over this cross-culturalism, especially the religious-ethnic barrier between Jew and Gentile. Although most cross-cultural critics appreciate the story of Acts, many fault Acts for not being cross-cultural enough in its focus. Be that as it may, those who read Acts "from the margins" have a great deal of resources for cultural liberation.

www See the website for a cross-cultural reading of Acts that compares Paul's speech in Acts 17 to the Chinese concept of the Dao ("way").

Cross-Cultural Reading at Work
Questioning the "Missionary-Tour Pattern" of Acts

A widely-held notion is that Acts explicitly and intentionally presents a missionary-tour pattern for all three of Paul's journeys. Here a leading Indian NT cross-cultural interpreter challenges this notion, arguing that it is a product of modern colonialism.

Source: R. S. Sugirtharajah, "A Postcolonial Exploration of Collusion and Construction in Biblical Interpretation," in R. S. Sugirtharajah, ed., *The Postcolonial Bible* (Sheffield, UK: Sheffield Academic Press, 1998), p. 91. Reprinted by permission of the Continuum International Publishing Group.

A rereading of the textual evidence in Acts raises a serious challenge to the accepted view that the author conceived a triple journey plan for Paul with Antioch or Jerusalem providing the base for departure and return. Of the three journeys, only the first (chapters 13–14) has some semblance of a missionary tour, originating from Antioch . . .

Why, then, was a missionary pattern imposed on the Acts [by Western scholars] during the colonial period? The likely answer is that the commentators were swayed by the momentous territorial changes taking place at the time, and were reading these events back into apostolic times. . . . The story of the expansion of the church as it is told through Paul's journeys in Acts is selective and partial. It documents only the spreading of the church in the West and totally ignores the Eastward movement of the church . . .

It is a surprise to most people to learn that there was a large and widespread Christian community throughout the whole of Central Asia in the first centuries of the present era and that such countries as Afghanistan and Tibet which are spoken of today as lands closed to the gospel message were centers of Christian activity long before Mohammed was born or the Krishna legend had been heard of . . .

The imposition of a missionary-tour pattern on Acts has other hermeneutical implications in addition to bolstering a westward expansion of the church. It reinforces the view that the churches in Asia and Africa have been recipients of the gospel as a gift from a benevolent West to enlighten the heathen. It largely ignores the Christian presence in these parts of the world before the arrival of the modern missionary movement.

Question

How would you evaluate the author's claim that Acts does not present three missionary tours and that this structure is imposed by modern Western interpretation?

Doing Cross-Cultural Reading Yourself

1. *Pick a passage in Acts where the gospel crosses a cultural boundary. What are the groups and issues involved? What conflict results, and (how) is it resolved? Look at your passage from your own point of view, then from the point of view of another cultural group.*

2. *Analyze the first inner-church conflict based on diversity, the Hebrew-Hellenist conflict in Acts 6. How does it arise, and how well, in your opinion, is it resolved?*

Key Terms and Concepts

ascension • Circumcision Party • geographic outline • God fearer • Hebrews Hellenists • Jerusalem Council • middle of time • presbyters • salvation history Table of Nations • the Way

Questions for Study, Discussion, and Writing

1. Argue either for or against this proposition: "The Acts of the Apostles should immediately follow the Gospel of Luke in the canonical arrangement of the NT today."
2. Some researchers have claimed that the Gospel of Luke is a story about Jesus and that the book of Acts is about the Holy Spirit. Evaluate this statement.
3. Imagine that you are a Christian living outside the Roman Empire in the year 100. If you were to write an "Acts" that told your story and that of the church in your country, what would its basic shape look like?
4. Why is it that Peter's and Paul's speeches are so much alike, and Stephen's speech in Acts 7 is so different from them?
5. How does the author of Acts emphasize that Christianity is a universal and missionizing religion?
6. Give a summary of Paul's typical method of operation for starting a church in Roman cities.
7. How does the early Jerusalem church in Acts carry out Jesus' teaching on wealth and poverty? Why do you think this is mentioned with such emphasis at the beginning of Acts but then is not mentioned again?
8. Give your own understanding of what happened at the Council of Jerusalem in Acts 15. Why would this meeting continue to be important in the ancient church?
9. Despite the author's concern to depict the unity of the early church, its growing diversity comes through. Summarize briefly what these diverse movements in Christianity in Acts were.

For Further Reading

Fitzmyer, Joseph A. *The Acts of the Apostles*. Garden City, NY: Doubleday, 1998. One of the finest recent commentaries on Acts.

Gaventa, Beverly. "Towards a Theology of Acts," *Interpretation* 42 (1988): 146–57. An excellent, succinct treatment of its topic.

Jervel, Jakob. *The Theology of the Acts of the Apostles*. Cambridge: Cambridge University Press, 1996. Concise, stimulating introduction to its topic.

Klauck, Hans-Josef. *Magic and Paganism in Early Christianity: The World of the Acts of the Apostles*. Minneapolis: Fortress, 2003. A fascinating reading of Acts against the background of the religious views and practices in the Roman-Hellenistic world.

Lüdemann, Gerd. *Early Christianity according to the Traditions of Acts*. Minneapolis: Fortress, 1989. A leading revisionist treatment of history and theology in Acts.

Marshall, I. Howard, and David Peterson, eds., *Witness to the Gospel: The Theology of Acts*. Grand Rapids, MI: Eerdmans, 1998. Contains a variety of essays on the theology of Acts.

Pervo, Richard I. *Profit with Delight*. Philadelphia: Fortress, 1987. Argues from the "entertainment value" of Acts that it is largely a fictional account.

Powell, Mark A. *What Are They Saying about Acts?* New York: Paulist Press, 1991. An excellent brief introduction to recent scholarship on Acts.

Soards, Marion L. *The Speeches in Acts: Their Content, Context and Concerns*. Philadelphia: Westminster John Knox, 1994. Clear, concise treatment of the speeches.

Vielhauer, Philip. "On the 'Paulinism' of Acts," in Leander Keck and J. Louis Martyn, eds., *Studies in Luke-Acts*. Philadelphia: Fortress, 1980. A seminal, thought-provoking article.

Part IV

Paul and the
Pauline Tradition

Chapter Eleven

Introduction to Paul and the Pauline Tradition

Paul is second only to Jesus in his contribution to the development of Christianity. Formerly a staunch persecutor of the church, Paul had a dramatic confrontation with the risen Christ and became the greatest missionary the church has ever known. For nearly two decades, Paul traveled the eastern Mediterranean, spreading the good news about Jesus and founding small (by today's standards) but strategically located churches. To these churches he wrote letters that form an important part of the New Testament.

In this chapter we briefly introduce Paul and the Pauline letters as a framework for understanding Chapters 12–16. We begin by considering the sources that give us our knowledge of Paul in the NT. Next is a treatment of Paul as a letter writer and a brief discussion of the Pauline letter format. Third is "Seeking the Historical Paul." This section reviews his life and includes a chronology. Fourth is a brief consideration of Paul's major teachings, followed by a discussion of the "new perspective" on the study of Paul. Finally, we treat the Pauline tradition and especially consider why some NT letters that bear Paul's name have been assigned to other, anonymous people after his death.

Our Sources for the Study of Paul

The reader of the NT knows Paul especially through his own authentic letters, through his disputed letters, and through the Acts of the Apostles. Second-century documents, such as the *Acts of Paul* and the *Acts of Paul and Thecla,* do not contribute a significant historical understanding of Paul, in the opinion of most NT scholars. Rather, they show us the way in which Paul and his message were understood in later times. From these three types of sources, Paul's own authentic letters are most significant because they are primary source material. Paul's disputed letters occasionally provide some information about the historical Paul and about how Paul was understood in the two generations after his death.

www   Follow the link to second-century writings about Paul.

A good deal of the material in Paul's letters is difficult to reconcile with Acts. Where discrepancies occur, scholars usually prefer Paul's firsthand version of events. The author of Acts seems unaware of Paul's correspondence with churches, his steadfast defense of his apostleship, and his distinctive teachings. Acts says comparatively little about Paul's essential gospel, only that people are saved by faith in Christ, not by obedience to Torah commands. The writer of Luke-Acts is concerned primarily with his own theological/historical purposes, and he fits Paul into that picture. Acts provides some biographical details that Paul never mentions in his letters: his birth in Tarsus; his Roman citizenship; his original name, Saul; his study under the leading Pharisee scholar Rabbi Gamaliel; and his supporting himself by tent making. These items of information from Acts do roughly fit our picture of Paul from his letters. With Acts' reliability in question here and Paul's autobiographical information so sparse, scholars are unable to reconstruct a full life of Paul. We do not know when he was born, how his family gained Roman citizenship, if he was once married, the precise course of his travels, where or when he wrote many of his letters, or the date and precise circumstances of his death. Nevertheless, Paul's letters that survive in the NT clearly show us his personality, missionary practice, and religious thought. We do not have a full picture of Paul, but what we have is clear enough.

www   Follow the link to an excellent overview of current Web resources for Paul.

Paul as a Letter Writer

In contrast to Jesus, who apparently wrote nothing, Paul wrote extensively. No fewer than thirteen NT letters have Paul's name on them, in total length nearly one-third of the NT. Many scholars regard only seven as genuinely Pauline, but the presence of other works attributed to him shows in what high esteem he was held. He so captured the imagination of later Christian writers that they paid tribute to Paul by writing in his name and perpetuating his teachings in his churches. In the NT canon, the thirteen letters that bear Paul's name are listed roughly according to their length. Letters to churches, such as Romans, appear first. Those addressed to individuals (in reality with a wider audience), such as Philemon, Timothy, and Titus, appear second. The letters to churches seemingly are ordered by length; then those to individuals likewise come in order of length. Because of this organization, the letters are not in any thematic, chronological, or geographic order.

Paul probably dictated his letters to a scribe or secretary, sometimes called an **amanuensis,** who could write quickly and well. Most people in the ancient Roman world would hire a scribe for such a purpose, but it is probable that one of Paul's co-workers acted in this role. Explicit mention of a scribe is found only in Rom 16:21–22, where the name "Tertius" is found. In other places, the one dictating/authoring the letter took the pen personally and wrote final greetings without mentioning a scribe (Gal 6:11; Col 4:18; Philem 19; and 2 Thess 3:17; see also 1 Pet 5:12).

From what we can tell, one of Paul's co-workers delivered his letters personally; the Roman Empire had no public mail system. This co-worker would probably see to it that the letters were read aloud to the whole congregation, likely at its next Sunday service. He or she would be able to answer questions and concerns about the letter, shaping its first interpretation and application. Sometimes letters would be copied and shared with other churches, becoming **circular letters.** Thus, the first and main contact with Paul's letters for almost all his addressees would be a community and auditory experience. Moreover, they experienced the letter as a whole, which modern readers of NT letters should keep in mind.

Paul's Letter Format

Since we know of Paul primarily through his letters, and since his letters are written in a standard literary pattern, we should introduce the main lines of the letter format. This discussion applies to both the genuine and disputed letters.

The internal structure of the Greco-Roman letter must be kept in mind when we study the structure of NT letters. Like secular letters of the time, Paul's consist, with some variations, of the following parts in the following order.

Introduction

Like letters today, Paul's have a brief introduction. It consists of four items, always in the following order.

- *Sender*: Paul as the author of the letter puts his name first. Because ancient letters did not have an envelope and the author's name was usually not written on the outside of a rolled-up letter, it was wise to put the author's name first. Sometimes other people are listed in this section (for example, 1 Thess 1:1: "Paul, Silas and Timothy,") but it is doubtful that they had a significant role in composing the letter.
- *Audience*: Paul then names the intended recipients of the letter, those to whom it is "addressed" (for example, 1 Thess 1:1: "to the church of the Thessalonians"). Because Paul meant all his letters to be read out loud to his intended recipients, they are literally his audience, and their reading is an act of oral performance.
- *Greeting*: Paul greets his audience briefly. In most NT letters, including all of Paul's, one finds the formula "grace and peace to you" (1 Thess 1:1). With this greeting, the author blesses the audience. It is a fuller and more religious greeting than the

usual Greco-Roman letter's generic expression, "greetings" (as we find in James 1:1). This blessing at the beginning of a letter is often called a **salutation.**

- ***Thanksgiving:*** The greeting is typically followed by a thanksgiving to God for the readers. The thanksgiving section is so called from its first words in most Pauline letters, "I give thanks." It sometimes concludes with a prayer on behalf of the intended reader. It is a short paragraph in length. Often Paul hints gently and positively about the more difficult themes to come in the body of the letter, thus making his first rhetorical move. Secular letters of the time have a short wish for health or a short prayer in this section.

Body of the Letter

Following the introduction, the author would deal with the matter for which he is writing. Of course, this is by far the longest part of the letter, varying from less than one page (Philemon) to many pages (Romans, 1 Corinthians). The form the letter body takes depends on how Paul is writing but often includes two main sections. Usually they are in this order; sometimes they are intermixed:

- Teaching on religious ideas, issues, and problems. This teaching was meant to instruct and persuade its audience. Sometimes it replies to issues the audience has written to Paul about, but more often it deals with matters that have come to Paul's attention through other means such as visits by members of his congregations and news from his co-workers.
- **Parenesis,** or moral exhortation urging the audience to live in a manner pleasing to God. This part often begins with a direct appeal such as, "I beseech/urge/exhort/ask you." The main parenesis is usually in developed form, with treatment of various themes such as sexual morality, mutual love among believers, or moral duties to the outside world. At the end of this section, Paul likes to pile up short, even staccato commands.

Conclusion

This is often the shortest of the three sections, in both Pauline and secular letters of the time. The conclusion section has more variety in its internal structure and contents than the other sections but most often comes in this order:

- The conclusion echoes and reinforces major concerns of the body of the letter. At times this is obvious (Gal 6, 1 Thess 5), at other times subtle.
- The author may send his own greetings. Because Paul used a secretary, this part of the letter closing would often be in his own hand for a more personal touch (Gal 6:11). This resembles our practice today of penning a note at the end of a computer-printed letter to make it more personal.
- The author conveys greetings from people known to both him and the reader(s), if applicable.
- In Pauline letters one usually finds a **benediction** (blessing from God upon the audience) at the end. In secular letters, one finds the simple word "farewell."

> ### Developing Your Skills: Identifying Parts of the Letter
>
> 1. Here is an example of a private letter from the second or third century (Oxyrhynchus Papyri CXVII). Identify its main parts:
>
>   *Chaerus to his brother Dionysius, greetings. I have already urged you in person to have the horoscope in the archives prepared, to prepare for the sale of the slaves' children, and to sell the wine that comes from both the near and the far vineyard, keeping the money in a safe place until I come. I send you some good melon seeds through Diogenes the friend of Chaereas the citizen, and two strips of cloth sealed with my seal, one of which please give to your children. Greet your sister and Cyrilla. Rhodope and Arsinous greet you. I pray that you would fare well.*
>
> 2. Next, name the different parts of Paul's letter to Philemon (Paul's shortest).

www Follow the link on the website for more on the NT letter structure.

Seeking the Historical Paul

As a missionary for his new faith, Paul never forgets his Jewishness. Although he fights to free Gentile believers in Jesus from Torah observance, Paul consistently stresses the continuity between Judaism and what we call "Christianity." (Paul never uses this term, and perhaps it would have puzzled him.) For him, the new religious movement is revealed through Jesus' ministry but shaped and largely defined by the Hebrew Bible. It carries on the best features of Second Temple Judaism. Throughout his letters, Paul quotes selected parts of the Hebrew Scripture to add strength to his message. Despite Paul's strong belief that observance of the Mosaic Torah is not necessary for Gentile believers in Jesus, much of the Hebrew biblical tradition retains its teaching authority for him.

Paul's letters repeatedly stress his Jewish heritage. He describes himself as a circumcised Jew from the Israelite tribe of Benjamin (Phil 3:5–6). He states that he outdid his Jewish contemporaries in strict observance of "the traditions of [his] ancestors" (Gal 1:13–14). A member of the Pharisee sect, he obeyed the Torah completely. "In legal rectitude"—keeping the Torah commandments—Paul judges himself "faultless" (Phil 3:6). What is more, Paul still saw himself after his conversion as a Jewish rabbi, only one who now proclaimed Jesus as the Messiah not just of the Jews, but of the Gentiles as well.

Paul's life falls into two completely different parts. In the first part, he was a devout Pharisee who zealously persecuted the first Christians, even to the point of their death. Paul rarely wrote about this, perhaps because he remained deeply sorry for it ("I am the least of all the saints, because I persecuted the church of God," 1 Cor 15:9). The little that we know of this period comes from Acts 8–9 and so must be used with some caution. In the second part of Paul's life, he was a Christian missionary who successfully founded new churches in key Gentile cities in the western Mediterranean and perhaps was the first to found churches on the European continent. The event that so radically transformed Paul from persecuting Christians to resolutely promoting Christianity was nothing less than "a revelation of Jesus Christ" to him (Gal 1:12). Acts depicts this revelation as a vision of the risen Jesus on the road to Damascus, which both "converted" Paul and called him to his apostolic task. (Contemporary scholarship most commonly refers to this event as a "call.") "God set me apart before I was born and called me through his grace, and was pleased to reveal his Son to me so that I might proclaim him among the Gentiles" (Gal 1:15–16). This event probably occurred around 36 C.E., to follow traditional dating. The author of Acts emphasizes the importance of this event by narrating it completely three times (Acts 9, 22 and 26), repetition rare in a narrative. Paul alludes to his experience much more briefly but with just as much meaning, speaking simply of being called by God's grace (Gal 1:15), of having an "abnormal birth" into the faith, and of witnessing an appearance of the risen Jesus (1 Cor 15:8–9).

After a time of preparation that may have lasted for several years, which probably involved a good deal of rethinking his life and beliefs, Paul began his missionary travels. The traditional method of dating Paul's chronology places this around 40 C.E. Paul had a great deal of physical vigor to pursue his constant travels and endure many physical hardships (which he catalogues in 2 Cor 11:24–27). He carried on despite the mysterious "thorn in the flesh" that often hindered him (2 Cor 12:7). Paul's physical strength was exceeded only by the strength of his mind and emotions. His letters reveal a person of great intellect, who can structure an intricate, persuasive argument. Paul also has a good deal of emotional intensity. He expresses, and leads his readers to share, great joy (Philippians) and great sorrow (2 Corinthians). He expresses profound affection and gentle tact toward his audience (1 Thess 1–3; 1 Cor 13; Phil 1:3–9; 2:1–4; 4:2–3). He uses these emotions in a careful way, to persuade his readers to think like him and do what he says. On the other hand, it must have been a withering experience for his churches to be on the receiving end of his negative emotions. In one letter, he calls his own people "stupid" and "bewitched" (Gal 3:1). In the same letter, he urges those who are persuading his Gentile Christians to be circumcised—his opponents who were likely there as the letter was read!—to castrate themselves (Gal 5:12). In another letter, he counters criticism of his conduct with wild boasting, wounded anger, and biting sarcasm, all for careful persuasive effect on the reader (2 Cor 10–13). Even within letters Paul can quickly switch his emotional tone. As he writes one letter to a church he did not himself found, in Rome, Paul is respectful and emotionally restrained. Some modern readers value a more restrained expression of emotions and may look negatively upon Paul for "wearing his heart on his sleeve." Here we must recall here that in Mediterranean cultures, including ancient Jewish culture, fuller expression of one's emotions is the norm.

Table 11.1 *Pauline Chronology*

Traditional Dating	Event	Revisionist Dating
34–36 C.E.	Conversion to Christ/call to be an Apostle on the road to Damascus, Syria	30–34 C.E.
36–39	Travels to "Arabia" (Nabatea), return to Damascus and preaching there	31–33
39	Visit to Jerusalem to meet Peter and James	33/37
40–44	(First) missionary journey, preaching to Gentiles in Syria and Cilicia; return to Antioch	After 37
49	Jerusalem "conference" on admitting Gentiles into the church without circumcision	47/51
50–52	(Second) missionary journey, beginning in Antioch, through southern Asia Minor to Galatia, Macedonia, Athens, and Corinth (1 Thessalonians written); return to Jerusalem and Antioch	48–55
54–58	(Third) Missionary Journey, beginning from Antioch through N. Galatia to Ephesus. Paul stays in Ephesus for three years, possibly imprisoned for some time (Galatians [?] Philippians [?], Philemon, 1 Corinthians written)	Indistinct from second journey (48/55)
	Paul returns to Macedonia and Corinth (2 Corinthians, Galatians [?] written). He winters at Corinth (Romans written), and returns to Jerusalem	(After 54)
58–61	Arrested in Jerusalem; imprisoned two years in Caesarea (Philippians?). Finally sent to Rome under armed guard in a long sea journey	52–55 or 56–58
61–63	Prisoner in Rome for two years (Philippians [?] Philemon [?] written)	61–61
After summer 64	Death in Rome in Neronian persecution after the Great Fire	64

Pauline Chronology

One of the most difficult aspects of studying Paul's career and message is its **chronology**, ordering sequentially and dating it. Having a basic grasp of chronology is important not only for historical understanding, but also for grasping the possible

The Roman Forum Excavations began at the end of the eighteenth century and continue through today. Most of the buildings were dismantled after antiquity and used in churches and private residences, but the glory of Rome can still be seen and felt here. The Arch of Septimius Severus is on the left, the Arch of Titus is at the center rear. On the upper right is the Palatine Hill, where the emperors had their palaces. Rome is Paul's destination in Acts, and his most influential letter was written to Rome. Used by permission of BiblePlaces.com.

development of Paul's thought. For centuries, Pauline chronology was understood by way of Acts and discrepancies were somehow made to fit its picture. Within the last generation especially, some NT scholars have taken their chronology from Paul's undisputed letters themselves. The results of these two methods are laid out in Table 11.1, adapted from Raymond Brown (Brown 1997, 428). Most dates are approximate.

References in the NT to three historical figures or events help to determine key dates in Paul's life and give some external framework for his chronology. The first figure is a mention in 2 Cor 11:32–33 of King Aretas IV, the ruler of the Arab kingdom of Nabatea (southeast of Palestine). Paul says that an agent of Aretas forced him to flee Damascus, in the Roman province of Syria. Since Aretas ruled between 9 and 39 C.E., we can conclude that Paul was involved in his missionary work during the decade of the 30s. The second historical reference is in Acts 18:11, where Gallio is the Roman governor of Greece while Paul visits Corinth. Gallio was governor of Greece only between 51 and 53 C.E. Since Paul had been in Corinth about eighteen months before he was brought up on charges before Gallio, Paul probably arrived in Corinth about 50 C.E. Third, Acts tells us that when Emperor Claudius expelled the Jews from Rome, the Jewish-Christian husband-and-wife missionary team of Aquila and Priscilla had recently arrived in Corinth from Rome and met Paul (Acts 18:1–2). Since the expulsion took place in 49 C.E., it furnishes evidence that Paul arrived in Corinth about 50. This external evidence, when joined to internal evidence, enables us to be relatively sure about the main timeline of Paul's life.

www   Follow the link for a succinct presentation of Pauline chronology.

Paul's Major Teachings: A Very Brief Introduction

Paul's thinking and ways of expressing himself are often complex, making it difficult for scholars today to achieve a consensus about the apostle's views. Paul's letters were also challenging for the people in his churches, and one later NT writer said explicitly about them, "There are some things in them that are hard to understand" (2 Pet 3:16). Paul's conviction that Jesus had revealed himself to Paul and given him the foundations of "his gospel" means that Paul's teaching is grounded in an intensely personal experience. Moreover, because his presentation of theological issues is secondary to his missionary-pastor task, letters do not represent a complete or systematic statement of Pauline belief. They are **occasional writings**, that is, letters addressed to a specific situation and occasion. Therefore, what we have in Paul's letters is not strictly a theology in a sense of a systematic, comprehensive treatment, and a theology cannot fully be extracted from them. In addition, readers will find Paul's thoughts changing and developing from one letter to another. Nevertheless, in studying Paul's undisputed letters, it helps to keep in mind several of his basic beliefs about Christ, the Spirit of God, and the life of the believer.

Paul's Jewish theological heritage is central to his "Christian" belief. There is only one God. This one God is the creator of the cosmos, the redeemer of God's people, and the one who guides human history to its conclusion. This God chose Israel as his own people, and through Israel would bless all the nations of the earth. In the Pharisee side of his Jewish heritage (especially the apocalyptic portions of the Hebrew Bible and other Jewish literature) Paul also saw glimmers of the future. Although evil is strong, God will triumph over it at the end of time. God will send a Messiah, a promised deliverer; God will come to establish God's rule, judge all peoples according to their deeds, and give eternal life to the righteous.

The Centrality of Jesus Christ

Central to Paul's belief is his firm conviction that God saves the world in Jesus Christ. Jesus is not just the Messiah of the Jews, but he is Christ the Lord of all peoples. Indeed, Paul regularly refers to "the Lord Jesus Christ." Although Paul's letters show little concern for Jesus' earthly ministry or teaching (referring to it less than ten times), his belief does center on the death, resurrection, heavenly reign, and coming of Jesus. Therefore, Paul's Christology has a past, present, and future aspect. The past aspect focuses on the death and resurrection of Jesus; although Paul most probably knows of Jesus' preexistence as the divine Son before his earthly life, he does not develop this narrative or make it an important part of his thought (Phil 2:6–11). The present aspect focuses on the heavenly Christ in two main roles: the divine Lord by whom God rules all things (Phil 2:11; Rom 10:9; 1 Cor 15:24–28) and the means by whom God's Spirit dwells in believers (Rom 8). As for the future aspect of Paul's Christology, all of Paul's undisputed letters, from 1 Thessalonians to Romans, express a strong orientation toward the coming of Jesus in glory at the end of time, when through the work of Christ "God will be all in all" (1 Cor 15:28). People enter into the saving life of Christ by faith in him, a faith created by God in them by God's Spirit.

Paul's regular confession of Jesus Christ as "Lord" is rich in meaning. In its Hebrew Bible background, it identifies Jesus Christ as the God of Israel. But Paul uses the title "Lord" for Jesus as God's Son, while making clear that Jesus is in some way subordinated to God (1 Cor 11:3; 15:28). In its Roman-Hellenistic background, so important for most of Paul's readers, "Lord" was a title of respect for the gods and goddesses. It was used for rulers like Augustus and the other emperors, especially when they were deified after their deaths. It also expressed honor to anyone in a higher social position in everyday society. Paul followed earlier church tradition when he called Jesus "Lord," and he used the title especially to denote Jesus as the conqueror of death and evil. Paul contrasts Christ with the symbol of earthly humanity, Adam: God's first human creation in the Hebrew Bible book of Genesis, and a person symbolic of all humans. Before Jesus' coming, humans lived only in Adam's perishable image, victims of sin and death (Rom 5:12–21). Despite the notable goodness and accomplishments of both Gentiles and Jews, their lives were distorted and ultimately destroyed by evil. By contrast, believers are now "in Christ," living with him and by his power. They belong to him, and his life has become theirs by means of God's Spirit living in them. At the end of time, they will also share in the glorified Christ's eternal life (1 Cor 15:21–24, 45–49).

Christ as Savior from the Power of Sin and Death

Paul believes that all human beings, Gentiles and Jews, are under the domination of sin and thus are alienated from God (Rom 1–3, 7). Paul views sin not just as individual and social wrongdoing, but also as a cosmic force that oppresses humans.

Sin's consequence for humans is death, a human condition we share with Adam (Rom 5:12–21). Christ's faithfulness to his Father and his death on the cross, in which he self-sacrificially took upon himself the penalty for sin, liberates those who trust in him. His death gives them life. It frees them from the power of sin, from death, and from the Torah's curses upon sinners (Gal 3–5, Rom 3–7). For Paul, "freedom in Christ" means deliverance from the "present evil age" of sin and punishment, including the Torah's power to condemn, and brings the believer into the "coming age" of God's perfect life (Gal 1:3–4). This freedom *from* sin leads to freedom *for* responsible, creative love. Jesus' sacrificial death, resurrection, and present reign have totally changed humans' relationship to God and have brought faith, life and hope to the world. Christ is the definitive and only means of destroying the powers of sin and death and making things right. Because Christ has now reconciled humanity to God, and is the only Lord, other supernatural beings such as angels or the spirits of the stars cannot rescue humanity.

Christ as the Center of Eschatology

This salvation in Christ is seen in an eschatological framework. Like many first-century adherents to the Jewish **apocalyptic** worldview, Paul sees human history as separated into two ages of different qualities. The **present evil age** is even now being replaced by a **new age/age to come,** a new creation characterized by perfect life. Paul believes that God will soon bring this new age in its fullness (Gal 1:3–4; 1 Cor 15:20–28; 2 Cor 5:17). Paul does not often use the phrase "kingdom/rule of God," but his thoughts on the new age closely parallel this leading teaching of Jesus. The old age is characterized by disobedience to God, faithlessness, death, and the oppressive rule of the Law of Moses. The new age is characterized by the dualistic opposites of these: obedience, faith, eternal life, and free life in the Spirit. Because the Messiah has arrived, died, and risen from the dead, Paul believes that the new age is present in significant part, and will come in its fullness when Jesus returns. In Christ, the two ages overlap in the present time. This overlap distinguishes Paul's apocalyptic thought from other apocalyptic of the day, Jewish and Christian. Paul's letters thus burn with special moral urgency, because he believes that the present time marks the crucial transition period between the two ages. This apocalyptic theology can be charted as follows:

Table 11.2 *Paul's Apocalyptic Theology*

The Present Evil Age	The Age to Come
Sin	Obedience
Flesh	Holy Spirit
Death	Eternal Life
Law	Grace
Slavery	Freedom
Life in Adam	Life in Christ

Paul's conviction that the Messiah's appearance has inaugurated the end of time permeates his teaching on morality. Paul's instruction on marriage, divorce, slavery, celibacy, and human behavior in general is shaped to some extent by his expectation of the impending end of the world. In his oldest surviving letter, he states that he expects to witness the **Parousia,** the return of Jesus Christ in glory: "We who are left alive until the Lord comes . . . [will be] caught up in the clouds to meet the Lord in the air" (I Thess. 4:15–17). In 1 Corinthians, his expectation to live until the End is equally certain; hence, he advises his people that "the time we live in will not last long" (1 Cor 7:29). He also writes, "We shall not all die, but we shall all be changed . . . For the trumpet will sound, and the dead will rise undying, and we [the living] shall be changed" (1 Cor 15:51–52). This imminent expectation leads at times to an **interim ethic,** moral guidance for Christians in the short time that the world has left but perhaps not applicable if the end is not near. For example, in 1 Corinthians he counsels Christians not to marry or remarry, because the end of time is near. In 1 Thessalonians he tells his church to keep busy and not to idle away the time because the end is near.

www   Follow the link to an excellent essay by Dr. Judith Stevens, "Paul and the New Creation."

Union with Christ

Paul's gospel and the life of his churches are not only a matter of what Jesus as Savior did, is doing, and will do at the end of time. Just as important for Paul's thought—found in all his letters—is a present spiritual relationship established by Christ and sustained by the Spirit between believers and God. Paul regularly addresses his letters to those "in Jesus Christ" (1 Cor 1:2; Phil 1:1, 1 Thess 1:1, and the rest). They were "baptized into Christ" and had "put on Christ" (Gal 3:26–28). In their baptism, they also "died with Christ" (Rom 6:1–14). Paul bases his authority as an apostle, and the validity of his distinctive gospel to the Gentiles, on his experience of a dramatic revelation of the resurrected Jesus (Gal 1:11–12, 15–17; 1 Cor 15:8–9). This experience tells him that Jesus Christ now exists as Lord in two interrelated ways, cosmic and personal. He is Lord of the cosmic spiritual domain, because Paul's revelation of Jesus came from heaven. He is Lord of the individual life of the believer, because the heavenly Jesus spoke to him as an individual to end his rebellion and call him to be an apostle. Christ is both the divine Son of God who will come from heaven with overwhelming power to recreate the world and a divine Son who lives within his earthly communities and in each individual believer through the Holy Spirit.

Paul's **mysticism,** union with an unseen spiritual person, is an important part of his thought. Paul's belief is similar to other religious systems of the time that promised living connection to the divine, especially the mystery religions. However, it is always connected with his Jewish eschatology, which in turn is grounded in the death and resurrection of the historical Jesus. Paul had recurring spiritual experiences that no doubt encouraged him in his apostolic career, but his ministry and theology did not depend on them. For example, Paul tells the Corinthians that he speaks to God in heavenly, spiritual tongues more than all of them but does so only privately, because speaking in tongues does not build others up in faith as much as plain speech does (1 Cor 14:1–19). To take another example, Paul says that he was "caught up as far as the third heaven, into paradise," where he "heard words that humans may not repeat"; he does not reveal these words but ministers only out of the weakness of the death of Christ (2 Cor 12:14–19). He adds that, to prevent him from becoming over-confident from such revelations, God gave him a chronic "sharp physical pain" to teach him that his apostolic abilities came from God, not from himself (2 Cor 12:7–8).

Believers Together in the Church, the Body of Christ

To judge from his letters, Paul was a strong individual, and he centered his life and thought on another individual, Jesus Christ. However, this must not allow us to conclude that he saw the Christian faith as something basically for individuals. Rather, in line with his Jewish heritage and the social ethos of the Mediterranean world, human life for Paul was first and foremost a social, group matter. For example, Paul's sense of union with Christ is expressed in the metaphor of the church as the "body of Christ." Using this image to identify the believing community as the earthly expression of Christ, Paul states that the faithful collectively are Christ's "body," of which he is the "head" (1 Cor 10:16–18; 12:12–30; Rom 12). The church lives and functions in union with Christ so fully that it reveals him to the world. Paul always stresses that within this whole body each believer is like a part of the human body, with her or his own individual function and gifts to be employed for the good of the whole. Individuality is acknowledged, and its strengths are encouraged, but only as a part of the whole earthly body as guided by its heavenly head, Christ himself. To put it another way, we find in Paul's letters *individuality* but not *individualism*.

Justification by Faith

How can a holy, righteous God "justify" (save by welcoming them as God's own people at the end of time) human beings whose unrighteous behavior makes them enemies of God? This question was no doubt raised in Paul's mind by his conversion/call on the road to Damascus. Paul experienced divine mercy, expressed through an unexpected revelation of Jesus to him, even as he was killing those who believed in Jesus. This experience convinced him that Christ had "justified" or "made him right" before God. This conviction became the basis of his ministry to the Gentiles: Paul believed that if God could save him, God could save anyone! This teaching of **justification by faith,** that faith in Christ delivers one from sin, and that (in retrospect) obedience to the Mosaic Law cannot, placed Paul at odds with most of Judaism. It characteristically held that obedience to the Law is essential to enter and stay in a relationship with God. Just as important for Paul's ministry, this teaching also put him at odds with many Jewish Christians of the first century C.E. For them, to accept Jesus as Israel's Messiah (Christ) was to observe the Jewish law just as Jesus had done. Some of these Jewish Christians visited Paul's churches to persuade these Gentile believers to be circumcised and keep at least some important Torah obligations. Paul argues strongly against them in letters like Galatians, 2 Corinthians, and Philippians. For observant Jews, the Law provides a valid means of maintaining a right relationship with the Deity. The Torah is clear and is clearly able to be kept, and the gift of the covenant empowered the Jewish people to follow God's law in a positive, joyful way.

Paul's encounter with Jesus gave him a new perspective. Although Paul claims that he kept God's law fully and well (Phil 3:6), after his encounter with the risen Jesus he knew that the Mosaic Covenant was no longer the means by which God restored humans to himself. Christ has created a different way to belong to God: by his sacrificial death, Jesus paid the Law's penalty for all human sin, thereby ending Law keeping as a path to God. Through belief in Christ, which God creates by the work of the Spirit, believers are incorporated into Jesus' self-sacrifice (they "die with Christ"), are brought back into God's family, and receive eternal life. God's **grace** (God's undeserved mercy and love) brings salvation to Jews and Gentiles alike. All this enables us to understand Paul's insistence on the equal inclusion of the Gentiles, and his career-long efforts to bring the Gentile world into the heritage of Judaism.

www   Follow the link to the recent Lutheran-Catholic joint statement on justification, which deals extensively with Paul's theology and its meaning for Christian churches today.

The New Perspective on Paul

This discussion of justification by faith in Paul leads us to an important issue in contemporary NT scholarship. The publication in 1977 of E. P. Sanders's *Paul and Palestinian Judaism* marked a turning point in Pauline interpretation. Sanders sharply attacked the portrayal of Judaism as a religion of "works righteousness" that generations of Christians had mistakenly derived from Paul, referring to the portrayal as a caricature. That caricature stemmed largely from the sixteenth-century Protestant reformer Martin Luther. Luther identified the personal battle in which he saw himself engaged with what he believed to be Paul's struggle in the mid-first century. Both, he thought, were confronting a religion of "works righteousness," earning one's own salvation by faithful deeds, exemplified in the one case by certain tendencies of late medieval Catholicism and in the other by Judaism. Luther's ideas of justification continued into the modern world by mainstream Protestants and evangelical Christians alike. Though Sanders had predecessors who tried to promote the same message, none managed to bring about the turn around that he achieved.

Three full post-Holocaust decades seemingly had to elapse for a total reconsideration of the way Judaism was portrayed in Christian scriptural interpretation. We now have, in the phrase coined by James D. G. Dunn, a **new perspective on Paul.**

Within that new perspective, as it has evolved over the years, there is considerable variety. The moderate view of the British NT scholar James Dunn has won wide acceptance (Dunn 1999). Dunn has helpfully explained the difference of the new perspective as being a matter of "staying in" the people of God, not primarily of "getting in." Within this variety of viewpoints, however, it is possible to list certain common characteristics of the new perspective.

- The new perspective stresses the continuities between Paul and Judaism, seeing him within the broad range of Second Temple Judaism rather than as a "convert" from it to a completely different religion. Paul is more "Jewish" than "Christian," as those terms are used of people today.
- It emphasizes the occasional nature of Paul's letters, including the letter to Rome. The letters explain the terms upon which Gentile converts should be admitted to the community of faith and allowed a full share in its life along with believers of Jewish background.
- A strong current has flowed into the new perspective on Paul from social scientific study of the early Christian communities. Christian teaching of salvation is seen more as a matter of "belonging" than of "getting in."
- Gentile Christians are the primary addressees of Paul's letters. When Paul addresses Jewish issues, especially those of the Torah, he does so for the benefit of Gentiles and with their concerns chiefly in mind. Any anti-Jewish sounding polemic principally targets Jewish-Christian missionaries who would seek to impose upon Gentile converts practices that were never intended for them. Therefore, Paul's attack on law observance in Gentile churches is a matter of inner Jewish argument, not an attack on a completely different religion.
- The failure of Israel does not consist so much in being bound up with the sinful state of humankind, though this is not denied. More so, the fault lies in Israel's ethnic pride and exclusivism, which fails to recognize God's grace to Gentiles as the fulfillment of the covenant promises to Abraham.

www Follow the link to an online presentation of the new perspective on Paul.

The Pauline Tradition

The analysis of Paul offered here is based on his seven generally accepted works: Romans, 1 and 2 Corinthians, Galatians, Philippians, 1 Thessalonians, and Philemon. These letters are *generally accepted* by NT scholars as authentic, and are often thus referred to as the **undisputed Pauline letters.** The six other books with Paul's name on them are **disputed Pauline letters;** that is, either the majority of scholars reject their authenticity or there is a good deal of debate about them. Two cautions must be sounded here. First, some leading scholars conclude that works like the Pastorals, Colossians, and 2 Thessalonians are genuine Pauline letters. Second, by using terms like "disputed" and "undisputed" most NT scholars do not mean to imply that the truth about whether or not Paul wrote these letters is determined by majority vote. The labels are merely a shorthand way to indicate where most scholarship lies on the question.

Although Paul probably did not write these letters, his influence can be seen in many passages that contain Pauline concepts. Such passages are now combined with other material that seemed to be appropriate for the conditions that existed in the churches at the time the letters were written. The **Deutero-Pauline letters** or epistles are Colossians, Ephesians, 2 Thessalonians, 1 and 2 Timothy, and Titus; the latter three letters are also known as the Pastoral Epistles because they deal with leading the church. (The Latin word *pastor* means "shepherd," a common biblical image of leadership.) Although we will discuss matters of authorship in subsequent chapters, we should indicate briefly here why most scholars conclude that these are later works in the Pauline tradition.

Colossians and Ephesians

The literary style of Colossians and Ephesians is significantly different from that of Paul's undisputed letters. Most scholars conclude that the difference is much greater than can be accounted for by Paul's old age, emprisonment, use of a liturgical or hymnic style, or giving to his secretary a wider freedom to compose the exact wording of his general ideas. In Colossians and especially Ephesians, for example, the sentences are long and complex; Ephesians 1:3–14 is one sentence in Greek, which English translations obscure by breaking into smaller sentences. Paul's usual style in his undisputed letters is to write more conversationally; his sentences there are shorter and livelier.

In matters of content, certain key words in Colossians and Ephesians are not found in Paul's authentic letters but are found frequently in the later New Testament writings and writings of the Church Fathers. Examples from Ephesians include: "commonwealth of God" (2:11); "likeness of God" (4:24), and "debauchery" (5:18). Also, the author of Ephesians used a different term or phrase in place of the one that would be expected from the unquestioned letters. For example, the writer often used "heavenly places" (Eph 1:3, 20; 2:6; 3:10; 6:12), but Paul generally refers to "heaven" (Rom 1:18; Gal 1:18; Phil 3:20). Also, the household code (Eph 5:21–6:9; Col 3:18–4:1) is not found in the unquestioned letters.

Some distinctive aspects of Colossians are a factor in questioning its authorship:

- Concern for the authority of Paul's unique position, which goes beyond Paul's regular defense of his apostleship (1:24–25)
- Stress on knowledge, wisdom, and correct teaching (1:9–10)

- Absence of central Pauline concepts such as the Holy Spirit, the law, and justification by faith
- The notion that believers have already been raised with Christ, which Paul denies in 1 Cor 15:2, 13.

In Ephesians we note the following main differences with Paul's undisputed letters:

- Disappearance of the expected imminent end of the world
- A household code more socially conservative than Colossian's (5:22–33) and much more conservative than social ethics in the undisputed letters
- Rising appreciation of the apostles (2:20; 3:5)
- Believers already share not only Christ's death, but his resurrection and even his ascension (2:5–6)
- The obvious use of Colossians as a source by the writer of Ephesians. By contrast, Paul's letters are always freshly written, even when he is talking on the same topic.

2 Thessalonians

Like Colossians and Ephesians, 2 Thessalonians is written in a style and content different from Paul's own. If we compare 2 Thessalonians to 1 Thessalonians, which was surely written by Paul, these differences are apparent:

- 2 Thessalonians is impersonal in comparison with the earlier letter to this church. No details of Paul's relationships with the Thessalonian Christians or his past and future travel plans are mentioned.
- 1 Thessalonians speaks of the salvation of Christians when Christ comes in judgment (1:10, 4:17–18); 2 Thessalonians is more concerned with the punishment that will come upon nonbelievers (1:6–9, 2:8–12).
- As much as a third of 2 Thessalonians consists of sentences and phrases from 1 Thessalonians. As we saw earlier, Paul does not recycle his earlier writings.
- Some terms and words that Paul used in his authentic letters occur in 2 Thessalonians with a very different meaning. To take one example, "standing firm" means standing firm "in the Lord" in 1 Thess 3:8, but in 2 Thess 2:15 it means holding on to the traditions that have been taught in the word and in the letters of the apostle.

The Pastoral Epistles

The Pastoral Epistles (1–2 Timothy and Titus) were probably written between 90 and 110 C.E. They are valuable from a historical perspective, since they reveal the beginnings of a type of church organization that, with modifications, has persisted to the present. They also testify to a struggle with Gnosticism that was to intensify in the second century. The Pastoral Epistles are different at key points with Paul's undisputed letters:

- Faith is not so much a personal commitment as it is a body of propositions to be believed (1 Tim 1:19). The value of good works is stressed (1 Tim 2:10; 5:10;

6:8; 2 Tim 2:21; Titus 2:14). Justification is the outcome of both faith and works (Titus 3:5–6).

- "Savior" is a title used for God as well as for Christ (1 Tim 1:1; 2:3; 4:10; Titus 1:3; 2:10; 3:4).
- The Pastorals lack or undervalue key Pauline concepts. For example, the phrase "in Christ" is not used, and the indwelling Spirit occurs in only two places: 2 Tim 1:14 and Titus 3:5.
- In vocabulary and style, 360 words contained in the Pastorals do not appear in the authentic letters, a much higher proportion of unique words than in any of the commonly accepted letters.

For these reasons, most NT researchers today do not consider the Pastorals to be genuine Pauline letters.

The Problem of Pseudonymity

The author of 2 Thessalonians tells his readers not to become overly excited if they receive a letter falsely bearing Paul's name, indicating that the practice of circulating forged documents purportedly by apostolic writers had already begun (2 Thess 2:1–3). To some modern readers, the notion that unknown Christians wrote in Paul's name is ethically unacceptable because such "forgeries" could not be part of the New Testament. In the ancient world, however, twenty-first-century ideas about authorship would have been irrelevant, for it was then common for disciples of great thinkers to compose works perpetuating their masters' thoughts. They wrote about contemporary issues as they believed their leader would have if he were still alive. However, there is some debate on whether early Christians appreciated these "blessed deceptions" (Achtemeier 1996).

This practice of creating new works under the identity of a well-known but deceased personage is called **pseudonymity.** Intending to honor an esteemed figure of the past rather than necessarily to deceive the reading public, both Jews and early Christians produced a large body of pseudonymous literature. In an attempt to apply the teachings of a dead prophet or spiritual mentor to current situations, Jewish authors wrote books ascribed to such revered biblical figures as Daniel, Enoch, Noah, David, Isaiah, Ezra, and Moses. Some, such as the book of Daniel, were accepted into the Hebrew Bible canon; others, such as 1 Enoch (quoted as scripture in the New Testament letter of Jude), were not. Still others, including the apocalyptic 2 Esdras, became part of the Apocrypha. The precise motives inspiring pseudonymous Christian writers are unknown, but some may have wished to obtain a respectful hearing for their views that only a work purportedly by Paul, Peter, or another authority in the early church could command. During the first three centuries C.E., numerous works, including Gospels, apostolic Acts, letters, and apocalypses, became associated with the names of Peter, John, James, Barnabas, and Paul. One, the letter to the Hebrews, was anonymous originally and stayed anonymous because no one tried to attach a name to it.

Some of these anonymous and pseudonymous books conveyed a message persuasive enough to gain a place in the Pauline tradition, and then in the New Testament. In other words, they were viewed as *apostolic* in content. In the last chapter of this book, we will examine the process of how and why certain documents entered the canon and others did not.

Key Terms and Concepts

amanuensis • apocalyptic structure of Paul's thought • benediction (section of letter) chronology of Paul (traditional and revisionist) • circular letters • Deutero-Pauline letters disputed/pseudonymous Pauline letters • grace • interim ethic • justification by faith mysticism • new age/age to come • new perspective on Paul • occasional writings parenesis • Parousia • present evil age • pseudonymity • salutation thanksgiving (section of letter) • undisputed/authentic Pauline letters

Questions for Study, Discussion, and Writing

1. One often hears the comment, "Paul was the real founder of Christianity, not Jesus." To what degree is this statement accurate, to what not?
2. Compare the genre of personal letters today—"snail mail" and e-mail—with Paul's letters. What are the similarities and differences, and why?
3. Give your own explanation for why Paul changed his name from Saul to Paul. Note carefully how his name shifts in Acts 13:9, and consider why in his letters he always calls himself "Paul."
4. We read these letters silently and individually today, but what would be some of the dynamics of reading these letters out loud to the whole congregation? For example, how does Paul's advice to or about particular people (e.g., Phil 4:2–3; 1 Cor 5:1–5) change when it is read out loud to the whole congregation?
5. It is sometimes said that Acts does not portray the importance to Paul of his conversion/call by the risen Jesus. In light of the three times in Acts where this event is narrated, how accurate is this idea?
6. Explain in your own words Table 11.2 on the structure of Paul's apocalyptic eschatology. Explain also the overlap in apocalyptic that Paul features.
7. What are your own thoughts on the issue of pseudonymity in the Bible? Do you regard it as a problem? Why, or why not?

Further Reading

Cousar, Charles B. *The Letters of Paul*. Nashville, TN: Abingdon Press, 1996. Places the letters in their historical and theological context.

Dunn, James D. *Theology of Paul the Apostle*. Grand Rapids, MI: Eerdmans, 1999. An excellent overview of Pauline theology, using Romans as an organizational pattern.

Horrell, David G. *An Introduction to the Study of Paul*. New York: Continuum, 2001. Introduces students to the differing methods and positions of contemporary scholars in Pauline studies, especially social scientific and feminist approaches.

Jewett, Robert. *A Chronology of Paul's Life*. Philadelphia: Fortress Press, 1979. Evaluates earlier systems of dating events in Paul's career and provides a new, revisionist chronology.

Murphy-O'Connor, Jerome. *Paul. A Critical Life*. New York: Clarendon, 1996. Explores psychological motivations for Paul's persecution of Christians, his Pharisaic background, and his missionary tours.

Neyrey, Jerome H. *Paul, in Other Words: A Cultural Reading of His Letters*. Louisville, KY: Westminster Press/John Knox Press, 1990. An analysis of Paul's writings to discover the underlying cultural and social assumptions on which Paul bases his worldview and theology.

Roetzel, Calvin. *The Letters of Paul: Conversations in Context*, 3rd ed. Atlanta: John Knox Press, 1991. Provides excellent introductions to each Pauline letter.

Sanders, E. P. *Paul, the Law, and the Jewish People*. Philadelphia: Fortress Press, 1983. An exploration of Paul's Jewish heritage by a leading expert.

Segal, Alan. *Paul the Convert: The Apostolate and Apostasy of Saul the Pharisee*. New Haven and London: Yale University Press, 1990. Examines Paul's views of the Christ event in the light of his Jewish heritage.

Chapter Twelve

1 Thessalonians, 1 and 2 Corinthians: Paul's Letters to Greek Churches

In this chapter we begin our study of Paul's letters with three of the earliest generally accepted letters, 1 Thessalonians and 1 and 2 Corinthians. 1 Thessalonians serves as a good point of entry to Paul's letters. It is a relatively short, happy, and uncomplicated epistle compared to Paul's other letters. 1 Thessalonians was written to draw its listeners closer to Paul as their leader, give them directions for a moral life, and solve a problem they had with Christ's return to earth. 1 Corinthians is one of Paul's longest letters but proceeds topically through many different problems at Corinth that Paul is trying to solve, giving us the most revealing look at a single Christian church that we have in the NT. Most critical approaches find reading 2 Corinthians a more complicated matter than reading 1 Corinthians or 1 Thessalonians. But even here we have something unique: a genuine Pauline letter that takes a follow-up look at a congregation in changing circumstances.

1 THESSALONIANS: Faithful Life and the Near Return of Christ

1 Thessalonians is chronologically first among Paul's letters that have come into the NT and the first document of the NT to be written. It provides rich insight into Paul's heartfelt relationship with one of his churches, the difficulties church members faced in an often-hostile environment, and the eschatological dimensions of their life. The writing of this letter seems to have been triggered by a particular twist in the **delay of the Parousia:** believers had died before the coming of the Lord, producing a crisis. Had these dead believers lost their place in salvation when Jesus would return? This letter, like all of Paul's letters, is well understood in the context of his situation and the situation of his audience, and thus historical reading has been important for many interpreters. But this letter is interesting, and important, for the other methods of reading as well.

1 Thessalonians in Brief: Outline of Structure and Contents

I. **Opening** Paul, Silvanus and Timothy to the Thessalonian believers; blessing (1:1)

II. **Thanksgiving** Remembrance, commendation, and implicit instruction for the recipients (1:2–10)

III. **Body** Strengthening the relationship of Paul and the readers; faithfulness in persecution; living well until the coming of Christ (2:1–5:22)

   A. Paul and the Thessalonian believers (2:1–3:12)

     1 Paul's faithfulness to them and their receptivity (2:1–16)

     2. Paul's desire to return to them, and his joy in their work (2:17–20)

     3. Timothy's follow-up visit and return to Paul (3:1–7)

     4. Paul's satisfaction and sentiments for them (3:8–13)

   B. Parenesis: Living faithfully until Christ comes (4:1–5:22)

     1. The importance of sexual purity, especially within the church (4:1–8)

     2. Love for fellow believers; good relations with outsiders (4:9–12)

     3. Instruction on the coming of Christ (4:13–5:11)

     4. Brief instructions: Respect leaders, build faith, abstain from evil (5:12–22)

IV. **Conclusion** First blessing, final instructions, concluding blessing (5:23–28)

Developing Your Skills

Read through 1 Thessalonians to get an initial impression of its contents and how the different methods of reading might approach this letter. Keep in mind the letter structure as you read. Take your time—it's a short letter!

A Guide to Reading 1 Thessalonians

In a short opening, Paul addresses the Thessalonians and gives them a blessing (1:1). He includes Silvanus (the Roman name of Silas in Acts) and Timothy, and the rest of the letter is largely written in the first person plural ("we/us"). But the real voice behind the written words is Paul's. Paul calls Jesus here, as in the rest of the letter, the "Lord" (Greek *kyrios* [KOO-ree-oss]), a term Romans used quite differently to refer to their dead-but-deified emperor. Use of this title makes a religious point with political consequences: for believers in Jesus, he is their only Lord.

In his thanksgiving section, Paul expresses thanks to God for the spiritual growth of the Thessalonians (1:2–10). This section, like every thanksgiving section in Paul's letters, hints encouragingly about the themes of the letter: the Thessalonians' relationship to Paul, the importance of living a good Christian life, and the coming of Jesus at the end of time. Paul begins by commending them to God because of their spiritual productivity, their present conduct as believers, and their hope of glory (1:3). The apostle reminds them that he proclaimed to them the gospel with full conviction in the power of the Holy Spirit (1:4–5). They accepted the gospel and followed Paul's instruction (1:6–8). They remained steadfast in the faith by turning from their Gentile religious life, with its many gods and no hope for a better world, to serving the one true God and awaiting his Son from heaven (1:9–10).

Next, Paul sets forth his relationship to the Thessalonian believers in order to defend the genuineness of his apostleship and apostolic relationship with them (2:1–16). The moving emotional power of this section is meant to counteract any remaining doubts the Thessalonians might have about Paul. To judge from the contents of Paul's statements here, the Thessalonian believers had heard others say two negative things about Paul designed to separate them from their leader and weaken them as a social organization. First, some charged that Paul peddled his message for his own monetary profit. This was a common way for people in the ancient Mediterranean (and today!) to attack a religious leader, because sometimes it is a valid criticism. Second, some charged that he did not really care for this church in Thessalonica, because he left in a hurry and has not bothered to visit them again. After dealing with these charges, Paul develops a positive argument. His apostleship and the Thessalonians' faith are genuine because: (1) Paul's message was from God (2:3–4); (2) his motives as he lived among them were pure, as they themselves knew (2:5–8); and (3) he worked self-sacrificially with hard manual labor while he was with them and did not take their money (2:9–12). Paul presents three kinship metaphors to describe their relationship; they are dear as his children, and he is both their nurse and father.

Paul now renews his thanksgiving for their reception of the gospel and their life in it (2:13). He defends his apostleship and the Thessalonians' faith by arguing that those who maligned the Thessalonians' faith reject the truth and will be rejected by God (2:14b–16). Paul reminds the Thessalonians that they have suffered at the hands of their neighbors, who are just like the Jews in Judea: they reject the truth. The eschatological wrath of God will certainly come on them because of this. (Historical readers of the NT debate the authenticity of 2:14–16.) Paul then expresses his deep desire to visit them again, a desire designed to create good feelings (2:17–3:10). Paul has not returned to Thessalonica because Satan has prevented him (2:17–20); what exactly this means is not explained, but it is designed to take blame off Paul. Of the three charges leveled against Paul, he evidently feels most defensive about his prolonged absence from the Thessalonians. Paul then recounts how he sent Timothy (mentioned in 1:1) to them to strengthen their faith in the midst of their persecutions (3:1–5). The result of Timothy's visit and return is that Paul now has a renewed desire to visit the Thessalonians and is much encouraged about their faith (3:6–10). In v. 8, the reader can almost hear Paul's happy sigh of relief that Timothy returned with a good report. The resulting confidence that Paul has about them is the emotional center from which he has written the whole letter. At this point (3:11) the first major section of the epistle body concludes with a transitional blessing of his audience, which introduces three ideas that will be important in the section to follow. Paul confidently prays that God will bring him back to the Thessalonians and bless them until they are fully mature in (1) love and (2) holiness/goodness at (3) the coming of Christ (3:11–13).

Having defended himself and the validity of the Thessalonians' conversion, Paul now turns to the moral exhortation section of the epistle (4:1–5:22). This is put last (note Paul's "finally" to begin this section) in the letter body for emphasis, but it is grounded on what goes before. As social scientific study of the Mediterranean world reminds us, belonging leads to proper behavior, not the reverse. Here belonging to God through Paul as apostle leads to good Christian conduct. First, Paul commands that the believers' lifestyle should feature proper, loving relationships with fellow Christians (4:1–12). He summarizes this by stating that their acts should be continually pleasing to God (4:1–2). (Note how Paul often gives the main point first and then the specifics). The believers' lifestyle should shun lust and the sexual immorality it produces, especially adultery (4:3–8). Perhaps the Thessalonian believers were especially tempted because of the city's prominence as a center for the worship of Dionysus and Cabirus, whose cults included sexual practices. Paul's audience would understand that he is talking here primarily to men, who have much more opportunity for adultery than women do in this society. The double standard was codified in both Jewish religious law and in Greco-Roman social codes—married men could have sexual intercourse with their own slaves or with prostitutes, but wives had to be absolutely faithful to their husbands. More positively, the Thessalonians should encourage each other to faithful living and to a work ethic that improves the nonbeliever's view of the church (4:9–12). This method of exhortation, dealing with the negatives first and then the positives, is typical of Paul.

The second moral exhortation is found in the middle of the letter body. Paul encourages the Thessalonians with his assurance that dead believers will be resurrected at the return of Jesus, so that they will participate fully in it (4:13–5:11). Evidently some members of the church have died since becoming believers, and other members are worried that they have lost their kinship place in salvation. Paul states that he has received an especially authoritative message, which he calls a "word of the Lord," that both living and dead saints will be together with the Lord at his return (4:14–17). God will "bring with Jesus" those who have died, so that the whole church will be together at the end and participate together in the church's eternal life. In 5:1–11 Paul exhorts the saints to be alert for the return of Jesus since they are children of light; the day of the Lord, he says, will come suddenly. This return will be abrupt and unexpected, even to believers. Paul follows this challenge with a promise: just as the nonbelievers are destined for God's wrath (1:10 and 2:16), God's children are destined for escape from God's wrath because they belong to Christ (5:9). At the end of this section, Paul reiterates his point with powerful simplicity: because Christ died for us, we will live with him whether we are alive or dead (5:10). Paul concludes this eschatological section with a final instruction to "encourage and build each other up" (5:11), which repeats the command to encouragement in 4:18.

Paul's third section of moral exhortation comes as he concludes the body of this letter, which he does with miscellaneous parenetic material in short commands. He often does the same in his later letters. Believers should respect their leaders within the church (5:12–13); this implies that they have not been giving due honor to leaders, which in an honor-shame society would cripple the leader's work. They all must be patient with imperfect believers, enabling them to become more mature (5:14). Echoing the teaching of Jesus, Paul commands members not to retaliate against those who do them wrong (5:15). They are to rejoice always (5:16, the shortest verse in the Greek NT), pray constantly (5:17), and give thanks to God at every situation (5:18). Finally, they must honor prophecy, which is preaching more than predicting, but keep a discerning attitude toward it. This instruction implies some conflict among the believers over prophecy (5:19–22).

The closing section of the letter in 5:23–28 is framed by a blessing at its beginning and its end. Paul prays for the believers' complete maturity and faithfulness at the return of Christ—in "spirit, soul and body," perhaps relating to their concerns about personal and social wholeness at the end of time. Paul assures them this prayer will be answered, a rhetorical move that will become typical in his other letters. Paul then requests that they pray for him, which will of course bond them closer to him in an environment that tries to split them. He commands that they greet each other with "a holy kiss," a symbol of Christian love. Paul solemnly commands "by the Lord" that the letter be read aloud to the whole church; his shift to the first-person "I" may indicate that he pens this sentence and the following in his own hand, but this is not certain. He then offers a final blessing, that the "grace of our Lord Jesus Christ" be with them.

Historical Reading of 1 Thessalonians

Historical-critical interpretation of 1 Thessalonians has had an important role since the recognition that it is the first of Paul's letters and the earliest document of the NT. It contains the first written use of early Christian creedal formulas (1:10; 4:14; 5:9–10). It shows that early Christians gave strong attention equally to gospel proclamation and moral exhortation—in other words, to both "talking the talk" and "walking the walk." It also shows that apocalyptic theology was strong from the first in Paul's communities and that the resurrection of Jesus and his anticipated coming at the end of time had become the center of early Christian eschatology. In sum, 1 Thessalonians gives good insight into an important Pauline community, especially its struggles to live and believe faithfully.

> ## 1 Thessalonians in Brief: Summary of Historical Reading
>
> **Author** Paul (undisputed today). Silas and Timothy, mentioned in the opening as authors, do not seem to play a role in the writing.
>
> **Date** 50 or 51 in the traditional chronology, written from Corinth within a few months of Paul's departure from Thessalonica.
>
> **Audience** Believers, mostly Gentiles, in the Thessalonian church that Paul founded.
>
> **Unity** Affirmed by almost all scholars today.
>
> **Integrity** Some serious dispute over 2:14–16; its seeming anti-Judaism is unusual for Paul.
>
> **Purpose** To reassure the believers about the unity of the church at the near end of time, to strengthen them against persecution, and to guide them in faithful life.

Author

Virtually all NT scholars today accept 1 Thessalonians as an authentic letter of Paul. In the external evidence from the second and third centuries, 1 Thessalonians is found as a letter of Paul in Marcion's canon and the Muratorian canon. It is quoted by name as a Pauline letter by Irenaeus, Clement of Alexandria, and Tertullian. In the internal evidence, however, two arguments are sometimes used against authenticity. First, in Acts 17:2 Paul's stay in Thessalonica is "three sabbaths," but the general impression given in 1 Thessalonians is that he must have stayed much longer. Second, Acts 17:4 seems to indicate that the makeup of the church was primarily Jews and "God-fearing" Gentiles, while 1 Thess 1:9 implies that most had come out of paganism. These historical problems are not unsolvable. Despite the record of Acts, it is quite possible that Paul had stayed in Thessalonica longer than three weeks and thus developed the deep relationship with his new converts that 1 Thess 1–3 implies. Moreover, if the church grew in numbers after Paul left, it is likely that many of these new members would be Gentiles, whether "God fearers" or not. In sum, most scholars do not find these arguments against authenticity convincing. The great majority, if they recognize a problem in reconciling Acts and 1 Thessalonians, usually incline toward the evidence in Paul himself.

1 Thessalonians is also accepted as genuine because it fits closely the style and content of the other generally accepted Pauline letters. First, this letter has a personal, conversational tone characteristic of Paul's undisputed letters. It reflects Paul's own experience, beliefs, and emotions. Second, in 5:12 the apostle calls their leaders merely "those who are over you." Someone writing in Paul's name after his death would know a more developed form of church order from that time and would perhaps use terms of church office such as "overseer" or "bishop" on one hand or "elders"

or "presbyters" on the other for these leaders. Third, no one in the 80s or 90s would have represented the apostle as hoping to be alive at the Parousia when it was known that he was already dead. In sum, the external and internal evidence points to the inescapable conclusion that 1 Thessalonians is a genuine letter from Paul himself.

Date

1 Thessalonians was written shortly after Paul's arrival in Corinth, the third stop after Thessalonica in his travel through Greece (see Acts 17). Paul was eager to correspond with the new church as soon as possible after Timothy had returned from visiting them. Although chronological arrangements of Paul's life vary a bit, most would date this event in 50 or 51 C.E. (We have more certainty about dating 1 Thessalonians because we know that Gallio was the Roman consul in Corinth between 51 and 53 C.E. and that he was consul when Paul was there.) Thus, 1 Thessalonians is chronologically the first of all Paul's letters that have found their way into the NT canon.

Audience

In 1:1 the apostle addresses "the church of the Thessalonians," that is, those Thessalonians who belong to the church that he founded. Many of these believers would have known Paul, but some would have been converted to the new faith after he left. According to Acts 17, Paul spent a short time there and all the while preached in the Jewish synagogue. Given this account, we can ask, was the congregation primarily Jewish or Gentile? 1 Thess 1:9–10 and Acts 17:1–10 both indicate that the church had a strong majority of Gentiles. We cannot tell how many had been attached to the synagogue as God fearers or how many had no background at all with Judaism. Although 1 Thessalonians makes no mention of it, according to Acts 17:4 the church at Thessalonica had a noticeable number of the "leading women" of the city. These were Gentile women who were socially and economically prominent.

Unity and Integrity

Some features of 1 Thessalonians may cast doubt on its literary unity—that is, whether it is one letter from Paul or more than one letter that has been put together here. The letter has two thanksgivings (1:2–10; 2:13–16) and two blessings (5:23, 28). Nevertheless, almost all interpreters today see these as minor points and hold to the unity of this letter. On its integrity, whether later wording has been added to this letter, there is some significant doubt about 2:14–16. Nowhere else does Paul speak like this, and many hold that what is said about the Jews here is so much more negative than Romans 9–11 that it could not have been written by Paul.

1 Thess 2:14–16 seems to paint all Jews as persecutors of Christianity and promises that God will punish them at the end. However, textual criticism argues for its authenticity: all ancient manuscripts contain this passage. Moreover, Paul's words, as harsh as they are, fall within the range of acceptable inner-Jewish criticism as found in other Jewish writings of the time. Here we must remember that Paul did not see himself as a promoter of a new religion called "Christianity"; rather, he was a Jewish rabbi called by God to spread the news of the Jewish Messiah to Gentiles and bring them into the people of God. In sum, the arguments for and against the authenticity of 2:14–16 are roughly balanced, and scholars remain sharply divided over it.

Occasion and Purpose

This chronological reconstruction of the occasion of 1 Thessalonians is based on Acts and altered in light of 1 Thessalonians. First, Paul and Silas had visited Thessalonica in late 49 or 50 C.E. After starting a church in Philippi (Acts 16), they passed through Amphipolis and Apollonia, since there was no synagogue in either town (Acts 17:1). Second, the apostle preached in Thessalonica for at least "three Sabbath days," between fifteen and twenty-seven days, in the Jewish synagogue (Acts 17:2). To judge from 1 Thessalonians, it was probably longer, similar to the amount of time Paul seems to have spent at Philippi. However, Paul worked at his tent-making trade to support himself, and "During the long hours at his workbench . . . Paul would have had opportunities to carry on his missionary activity" by sharing the Gospel and making both Jewish and Gentile converts (Hock 1979, 449–450). Third, some Jews were angry that Paul was drawing off some Jews and many Gentile God fearers from their synagogue. They gathered a Gentile mob and started a riot by claiming that Paul and Silas were promoting another king besides Caesar (Acts 17:7; compare 1 Thess 1:1 on Jesus Christ as Lord, and 2:14–16 on Jewish persecution). Thessalonica was a "free city" in the Roman Empire; if its people were to welcome another lord, Thessalonica would be in danger of losing this high status. Paul was forced to leave Thessalonica and was unable to return. To judge from Thessalonians, this persecution continued after Paul left. Fourth, Paul left for Beroea, Athens, and then Corinth (Acts 17:10–18:1). In Athens, he sent Timothy to Thessalonica to see them (1 Thess 3:1–2). When Timothy returned and reported to Paul, Paul wrote 1 Thessalonians to encourage the believers he knew he had left too quickly, and instruct them about several matters.

The exact purpose of this letter is debated. Some argue that 1 Thessalonians is rhetorically a letter of praise meant to persuade, or **epideictic rhetoric;** others see it as **judicial rhetoric** to defend Paul against charges made against him; still others see it as **deliberative rhetoric,** persuading its audience to reflect on and follow a course of action. Although elements of all three are visible, the last of these seems more likely to most interpreters today. Paul seems to have three main deliberative purposes in 1 Thessalonians. First, he seeks to vindicate his ministry and the Thessalonians' conversion, keeping them cohesive and connected to him in the face of persecution that sought to drive them apart and thus weaken their faith (chapters 1–3). This persecution did not involve death but did probably entail social and economic pressure to leave the faith. Second, Paul writes to reinforce proper standards of morality, especially sexual morality (4:1–8). Third, he corrects a misunderstanding about eschatology. After Paul left, some of the Thessalonian believers had died, leaving nagging questions about when they would be reunited with living believers; Paul answers that the church will be unified at the end. Although Paul probably writes for these three main persuasive purposes, he also takes the opportunity to instruct them in other moral matters. Some interpreters have argued that these instructions were necessary to include because of Paul's short stay in Thessalonica, but other letters written to churches with whom he stayed longer have the same "miscellaneous" instructions.

www For the best point of entry into Web resources on Paul, follow the link to the "Text This Week" site.

Doing Historical Criticism Yourself

Read Acts 17 carefully. Compare it to the situation indicated in 1 Thessalonians, both its similarities and differences.

---

1 Thessalonians in Brief: Summary of Newer Readings

Social Scientific 1 Thessalonians clearly draws on main categories of honor and shame, kinship, insiders and outsiders.

Feminist This letter poses an interesting challenge in that it does not explicitly mention specific women by name, which is unusual for Paul's letters. This may be due to the situation and purpose of this letter, and at any rate Paul does use some feminine imagery in interesting ways.

Cross-Cultural 1 Thessalonians presents major cultural boundaries of Jew and Gentile in the crossing.

Social Scientific Reading of 1 Thessalonians

The pages of 1 Thessalonians brim with key social scientific matters. *Kinship* runs through it as Paul reminds believers that God is their Father, and they are God's children forever. Paul gives them God's fatherly blessing at the beginning and end of this letter. Jesus Christ is God's unique Son, and he is the Thessalonians' new Lord to whom they belong. Paul defends his role as apostle by calling himself both their nurse and father. Reversing the image of Paul as their father, he even calls himself an "orphan" because of his unwilling separation from them (2:17). He repeatedly calls them "brothers [and sisters]" of each other and himself. No doubt the house church setting where 1 Thessalonians was read, similar to the settings of all Paul's letters, served to promote the use of this kinship language. Paul used such language to reinforce the close connections between himself and this church and the believers' connections with each other as a group. Finally, he commands that members greet each other with a "holy kiss," which normally in the Roman world was for family members only. Paul's ideal community is based on "mutual dependence and sharing among members" (Richard 1995, 221–222).

The *honor-shame* paradigm of social values is also prominent. Paul begins by honoring his audience with strong praise in the thanksgiving section (1:2–10). Paul defends his honor against the shaming attacks of opponents who are attempting to cut his church off from him (chapter 2). Even as he does this, he claims that honor or shame from people does not concern him, only the honor that comes from God (2:6). His urgings to proper Christian conduct are meant to inculcate a lifestyle that will bring eternal honor at the end of time. He urges that leaders and prophets be treated honorably so that the life of the church may be strengthened (5:12, 19–20).

Social Scientific Reading at Work
A Social-Rhetorical Reading of 1 Thess 1:1–10

In this reading Vernon Robbins develops the idea that a "new hermeneutical [meaning through interpretation] rhetoric" appears in Christianity with the beginning of Paul's letter-writing activity. This new interpretation entails turning the focus from what Jesus said and did (the Gospels) to the Christian faith and life of those whom Paul is addressing in letters.

In 1 Thessalonians, the new vehicle for Christian hermeneutical rhetoric appears in 1:2–3 where Paul gives thanks to God for the Thessalonians' "work of faith, labor of love and steadfastness of hope in our Lord Jesus Christ." The subject matter here is not anything Jesus said or did but what members of a community with whom Paul associates himself are doing. Paul evokes the validity of his hermeneutical rhetoric with a claim that "God has chosen" the Thessalonians (1:4). The initial move, then, is to confirm the members of the Thessalonian congregation . . . through God's action rather than anything Paul has done. In 1:5, Paul introduces himself and his associates as a correlative to the Thessalonians: "We" brought you the gospel "not only in word, but also in power and in the Holy Spirit with full conviction." God's power and the Holy Spirit accompanied the activity of Paul and his associates in such a manner that Paul is also not choosing himself and his associates of his own volition; . . . God has chosen them, and God and the Holy Spirit work through them.

Source: Vernon Robbins, "Socio-Rhetorical Hermeneutics and Commentary," in J. Mrazek, R. Dvorakova, and S. Brodsky, eds., *Studies in Honour of Petr Pokorny on His Sixty-Fifth Birthday* (Prague: Mlyn, 1998), pp. 284–297.

Then 1:6 adds "the Lord [Jesus]" to the circle of people: the Thessalonians became imitators of Paul and his associates, "and of the Lord," when they "received the word in much affliction, with joy inspired by the Holy Spirit." Now a hermeneutical circle emerges in which Paul, his associates, the Thessalonians, and the Lord Jesus all received the word of God in much affliction and joy inspired by the Holy Spirit. Paul does not rehearse any specific story that exhibits Jesus' acceptance of God's word in affliction and joy. Nor does Paul attribute to Jesus any saying in which Jesus expresses his joy at receiving the word and wisdom of God. . . . Rather, Paul evokes a confirmation of his assertion by appealing to the Lord Jesus and the Holy Spirit without using either a story or a saying of Jesus as a vehicle for his argumentation. In 1:7–9 Paul announces the Thessalonians as the focal point of his discourse and supports their central place with a rationale (v. 8) and a confirmation of the rationale (vv. 9–10). The Thessalonians have become an example to all believers in Macedonia and Achaia, *because* (the rationale) the world of the Lord has sounded forth from them and their faith in God has gone forth everywhere and *because* (the confirmation of the rationale) the people in Macedonia and Achaia know and tell the story that the Thessalonians welcomed Paul and his associates among them and turned from idols to serve a living and true God and to wait for God's Son from heaven, whom God raised from the dead.

www   You can read the whole article online.

Question

Give your evaluation of Robbins's "new hermeneutical rhetoric" in 1 Thessalonians. For example, just how far into the "background" does Jesus go?

Doing Social Scientific Reading of 1 Thessalonians Yourself

1. *Skim through 1 Thessalonians, noting all the words and phrases that denote or imply the insider/outsider group dynamic. What do you make of these references?*

2. *How does Paul's family language in this letter relate to the house church setting of the church?*

Feminist Reading of 1 Thessalonians

At first glance, 1 Thessalonians looks as if it has little about women, and what little there is appears patriarchal. No named women appear in its pages. Paul consistently addresses the "brothers" there, but not the "sisters" (the NRSV adds "and sisters"). In warning men against adultery, Paul refers to women as "vessels" in 4:4. In 5:5 he compares the suddenness of troubles at the end of time with a woman's labor pains that cannot be stopped. Most of 1 Thessalonians is not concerned with issues that, at first glance, are open to a gender-sensitive analysis, and it certainly does not advance the social status and roles of women in any explicit way.

However, a closer look at this letter shows a more nuanced picture. Although no named women among the Thessalonians appear in its pages, neither do any named Thessalonian men appear. Paul's use of "brothers" is used in an admittedly patriarchal way to mean his whole audience, so the NRSV decision to add "and sisters" is a good one. The comparison of eschatological troubles with a woman's labor pains has a hidden point, that a new world is being birthed in this process. Considering this letter's eschatological orientation, this metaphor is no small use of positive feminine imagery. Paul's talk about a wife as a body or "vessel" in 4:4 is indeed offensive to many modern readers. The source of this metaphor, however, is likely the Hebrew Bible's Prov 5:15–20, and the intertextuality may ameliorate this offense. Proverbs warns men against adultery by speaking of their wives as the fountains or vessels from which they should drink the pleasures of love. Moreover, Paul implicitly puts the blame for adultery on males, not, as is common in the wisdom literature of the Hebrew Bible, on wanton women preying on weak men. The clearest use of positive feminine imagery is in 2:7, where Paul stunningly compares himself to a nurse who tenderly cares for her children. In the ancient Mediterranean, "wet nurses" were regularly employed to breast-feed children whose mothers were unable to nurse, and literary works and gravestone inscriptions testify to the strong bond that developed between nurses and children. We can conclude that this letter was on the whole meant for both men and women in the Thessalonian church, and that although this letter did not explicitly try to advance the position of women there, neither did it hold Thessalonian women in low esteem.

Feminist Reading at Work
Holiness on the Day of the Lord (4:1–12, 5:12–22)

In this selection Pheme Perkins relates the moral exhortation at the end of 1 Thessalonians to the life of women in that congregation. Note how she reads gender issues from the wording of the various commands.

The expectation of the coming end of this age governs Paul's ethical exhortation as well. The Christians who have died—possibly victims of persecution—will come with the Lord and be reunited with the community (4:13–18). The admonitions to holiness in 4:2–8 are formulated with males in view. They are to discipline unruly sexual urges by an honorable marriage. They are not to defraud their brothers "in this manner," an ambiguous expression that could refer either to sexual or business affairs (4:6). It may be the sudden death of male members of the community that has led to the questions about the dead. Women were too constantly victims of early death in childbirth for their fate to cause much comment.

1 Thess 5:12–22 speaks in more general terms of relationships within the community, respect for its officials, encouragement and mutual support, prayer, prophesying,

Source: Pheme Perkins, "I Thessalonians," in Carol A. Newsom and Sharon H. Ringe, ed., *Women's Bible Commentary* (Louisville, KY: Westminster John Knox, 1992), p. 441.

and "doing good." There are no clues to indicate the extent to which women participated in these activities in Thessalonica. Since no women are mentioned anywhere, the community's leaders may have been all male. The poverty and largely artisan population of Thessalonica would make it less likely to have had women of sufficient wealth or education to act as patrons such as we find in other Pauline churches.

Questions

1. *Do you think that Perkins makes a good conclusion from her comment that "Women were too constantly victims of early death in childbirth for their fate to cause much comment"?*

2. *Explain the connection between the ability to be a patron and the likelihood of being a leader. Does the ability to be a patron also relate to the other activities mentioned, such as mutual support, prayer, prophesying, and doing good?*

Doing Feminist Criticism Yourself

1. *Put yourself in the situation of a woman in the Thessalonian church. Then read this letter to see what Paul has to say to you.*

2. *What does this letter have to say to women today, in your opinion?*

Cross-Cultural Reading of 1 Thessalonians

The main cross-cultural feature of 1 Thessalonians is the crossing of the Jew-Gentile barrier, the main cultural and religious divide in the NT. Paul is the "Apostle to the Gentiles," and this first of his letters is to a predominantly Gentile church. The members of this church have turned from worshipping idols to worshipping the one true God and awaiting the return of God's Son from heaven. Local synagogue authorities perhaps working in tandem with civil authorities are persecuting this church, as Acts 17 suggests. Paul urges them to stand fast against Jewish opposition (2:14–16, of disputed integrity). In chapter 4, Paul reinforces basic Jewish morality, especially sexual morality: believers must turn from Gentile ways, shun fornication, and be true to their spouses (4:3–5).

The second main feature of cross-cultural reading is dealt with in the reading that follows, on Paul's churches as anti-imperial organizations with an anti-imperial ideology. The reign of Caesar is being replaced by the reign of the one God and will be fulfilled at the Parousia of Christ. So, then, one could claim that early Christians believed in the replacement of human imperial ideology with divine "imperial" theology. The effect of this replacement is that, in God's rule, all people are true brothers and sisters. Slavery and subjugation are done away with, and injustice is burned away by God's wrath.

Cross-Cultural Reading at Work
The Rule of God and the Rulers of This World in 1 Thessalonians

In this reading Richard Horsley argues that Paul's apocalyptic theology provides a strong anti–Roman Empire stance that guides and motivates his readers/ listeners.

The most significant way in which a postcolonial reading of Paul disrupts the standard individualistic and depoliticized Augustinian-Lutheran Paul, consists in the rediscovery of the anti-imperial stance and program evident in his letters – for those with "eyes to see." For his discourse about Christ, Paul has invaded the very emperor cult by which imperial power relations were constituted in the cities such as Corinth and Ephesus, the two metropolitan bases from which he staged his mission in the provinces of Achaia and Asia. Some of the most basic symbols of his discourse, including "gospel" itself, "Savior/salvation," the *parousia* and "faith," he took, almost certainly on purpose, directly from the emperor cult, which, like Christmas in the United States, simply pervaded the public space in the form of festivals, temples, shrines, inscriptions and ubiquitous images. The true Lord (the true emperor of the world), Jesus Christ, has been enthroned in heaven and is imminently to return to earth in a dramatic *parousia,* as when the emperor pays a state visit to a city, at which point Roman imperial rule will be finally terminated (I Thess. 2:19; 3:13; 4:14–18; 5:23) . . . Paul has combined key imperial language with his Jewish apocalyptic discourse in an uncompromising opposition to the imperial order.

Questions

1. *What evidence is there that Paul, as Horsley asserts, took terms like* gospel, savior, parousia, *and* faith *directly from the emperor cult?*
2. *If you do not agree with Horsley on this direct borrowing, and perhaps see parallels to the imperial ideology but no borrowing, can you still affirm his main point? Why, or why not?*

Doing Cross-Cultural Reading Yourself

Read through 1 Thessalonians with an eye to the Jewish-Gentile divide. In what ways does Paul implicitly accept features of Gentile culture, and in what ways does he not?

Source: Richard A. Horsley, "Submerged Biblical Histories and Imperial Biblical Studies," in R. S. Sugirtharajah, ed., *The Postcolonial Bible* (Sheffield, UK: Sheffield Academic Press, 1998), pp. 167–168. Reprinted by permission of the Continuum International Publishing Group.

1 CORINTHIANS: Unity, Wisdom, Love, and Hope in a Dynamic Church

Although called "First Corinthians," this was not Paul's first letter to the Corinthian church (1 Cor. 5:9–13); the name comes from the letter's position before 2 Corinthians in the NT canon. 1 Corinthians gives us a fuller insight into the actual life of a first-century church than any other NT letter, which enriches its reading by every method used today. The church at Corinth was a virtual cross-section of Greco-Roman society, with a very few people who were rich and powerful, a majority of people who were poor and/or enslaved, and a small group of "middle-class" people. This church was beset by a multitude of problems but had no lack of dedication to the Christian faith. Paul sorts through these problems one by one in the letter body. At some points Paul is harsh and demanding, at other points he is conciliatory and tender. To judge from his varying emotional tone, Paul had some difficulty in writing this letter. 1 Corinthians affords us a full look not just into a first-century church but also into the life and belief of the Apostle Paul.

1 Corinthians in Brief: Outline of Structure and Contents

I. **Opening** Paul to the Corinthians, blessing (1:1–3)
II. **Thanksgiving** For the spiritually rich Corinthians (1:4–9)
III. **Body** Unity, wisdom, love, and hope (1:10–chap.15)
  A. Paul corrects divisiveness in the Corinthian church:
    1. Human wisdom divides the church and opposes the wisdom of God (1)
    2. The gospel owes nothing to human wisdom (2)
    3. Christian service and its reward; testing at the last judgment (3)
    4. Judgment of Christians not committed to other people (4)
    5. The peril of indifference to evil in the church (5)
    6. Christians forbidden take each other to court; sanctity of the body (6)
  B. Paul answers assorted questions they have raised in a letter:
    1. Christian marriage and singleness (7)
    2. Eating food offered to idols (8)
    3. Paul's apostolic rights (9)
    4. Warnings against idolatry (10)
    5. Disorders at the Eucharist; its order and meaning (11)
    6. Spiritual gifts explained and regulated (12–14)
    7. Resurrection of Christ and believers (15)
IV. **Conclusion** Instructions and personal greetings; blessing (16)

A Guide to Reading 1 Corinthians

The opening (1:1–3) mentions Sosthenes, Paul's scribe for the letter, as a co-sender (but not necessarily a co-author) with Paul. In the thanksgiving section (1:4–9), Paul gets the audience "on his side" with praise so that they will more willingly accept the strong corrections to come. He mentions Christ several times, anticipating the way he will try to correct the first problem, Corinthian factionalism. He reminds them that they were baptized in the name of Christ and find their unity in him. He also gives thanks that the Corinthians have been given grace, enriching them in speech and knowledge, and that they were not lacking in any **charism** (a spiritual gift that brings with it an ability). This is a positive but ironic touch since he will chastise them in the letter for abusing their speech, knowledge, and charisms. The thanksgiving section also anticipates the letter's contents by referring to the day of the Lord, the topic in chapter 15.

The long body of the letter (1:10 through at least the end of chapter 15) treats a series of problems in the Corinthian church. The first main part of the letter body (1:10–chapter 4) addresses the problem of factions in Corinth, about which members of Chloe's household have informed Paul. The divisions were not present when Paul was there, but now conflicting loyalties among the Corinthian Christians have evolved. They have grouped themselves according to leading figures in the church known to them: "I belong to Paul," or "I belong to Apollos," or "I belong to Cephas [Peter]," or "I belong to Christ" (1:12). Paul asks, "Is Christ divided? Was it Paul who was crucified for you or was it in Paul's name that you were baptized?" (1:13). These divisions reflected different personal loyalties among the Corinthian Christians. These loyalties may in turn connect with other problems Paul deals with in 1 Corinthians, but this is not clear or certain. In choosing a particular preacher, like Apollos, some Corinthians may have been opting for what sounded like greater wisdom, whereas Paul had preached a crucified Christ without relating it to human or divine wisdom (1:18–2:5). Paul now proclaims the mysterious wisdom of God hidden from the rulers of the present age who crucified Jesus (2:6–16). The Corinthians are not ready for wisdom, as their divisions show (3:1–9). Paul laid down a solid foundation, the only possible foundation, Jesus Christ. On the Day of Judgment everything else that is insubstantial will be shown up and burned off (3:10–15). The Corinthians ought to realize that they are God's temple in which the Spirit lives and they ought to despise the wisdom of this world as foolishness in God's sight (3:16–23).

With biting sarcastic rhetoric Paul contrasts "us apostles" to the Corinthians, who in their religious stance are falsely proud over nothing (4:7–9). "We are fools for Christ, while you are so wise in Christ" (4:10–13). This letter is a warning from a father to his children, and Timothy is sent to Corinth to correct their foolish divisions before Paul himself comes to punish the arrogant (4:14–21).

In the second part of the letter body (5:1–11:34), Paul turns to a variety of problems of Christian behavior among the Corinthians. Chapters 5–6 involve things he has heard about the Corinthians' behavior, and issues of sex and marriage come up frequently. The first instance addressed by Paul is to him the most egregious error, which he is clearly angry about, a believer sleeping with his stepmother (5:1–5). Paul does not give the details, but the Corinthians would know full well about it. (Remember that when we read the letters of the NT, we are in essence reading other people's mail!). Perhaps this man cited his freedom in Christ to justify his behavior, a freedom Paul had preached to them (6:12). Paul's attitude to this behavior probably comes from his Jewish roots; marriage with one's father's ex-wife was forbidden by the Mosaic Law as incestuous (Lev 18:8; 20:11) and was condemned by the prophet Amos (Amos 2:7). However, he bases his explicit appeal on the claim that such behavior was not tolerated even among the unbelieving Greeks (it may have been uncomfortably close to the story in which Oedipus unwittingly and tragically marries his mother), implying that it would cause scandal in the city. Paul issues an excommunication even from a distance in 5:4–5. What follows shows that his main concern is not about the immorality of the world outside the community but sinfulness within the community that might harm it if left uncorrected (5:9–13).

In the next topic, Paul insists that legal disputes between believers are to be settled by having fellow Christians act as judges rather than going before Gentile courts (6:1–8). This follows Jewish practice of the time and even of today. Paul then lists the vices in which the Corinthian believers formerly engaged, but now have left behind in Christ and the Spirit (6:9–11). In 6:12 we hear a slogan about moral freedom in circulation at Corinth that presumably is at the root of much of what Paul condemns: "For me everything is permissible." Paul agrees with it, and perhaps they originally heard it from him; but now he tempers it by insisting that not everything brings about good and that no choice should lead to loss of self-control. People do not live in a neutral environment: To indulge in immoral behavior is not freedom, but bondage to compulsions that enslave. Sexual permissiveness affects the Christian's body, which is a member of Christ's body (6:15) and is the temple of the Holy Spirit (6:19–20). Physical union of a member of Christ with an unworthy partner, like a prostitute, disgraces Christ. But marital union glorifies God.

Turning from what he has heard about the Corinthians, in chapter 7 Paul begins to answer questions that have been posed to him in a letter from the Corinthians. His lively pattern of citing statements or slogans and then discussing them has often been seen as Paul's imitation of the Cynic **diatribe** (sharp conversation) pattern. The first involves their statement, "It is good for a man not to touch [have sexual intercourse with] a woman." Although abstention from sex is laudable in itself,

Paul does not encourage it for married believers because it could create temptations to infidelity. He encourages marriage for those who cannot practice abstinence, although "I would like everyone to be as I am myself"—Paul seemingly means without a wife and, he implies, practicing abstinence (7:2–9). To those already married Paul repeats the Lord's ruling against divorce and remarriage as found in the Synoptics, but then he permits separation when one of the partners is not a Christian and does not wish to live with a believer (7:10–16). In 7:17–40 Paul shows the extent to which his thinking is affected by the imminent expectation: he would have all people stay in the state in which they were when called to Christ because the time of Christ's return is soon. This includes circumcised Jew, uncircumcised Gentile, slave (but see the alternate translation in the NRSV footnote—Paul is ambiguous about slaves, holding open the option of freedom), celibate, married, and widow.

In chapter 8 Paul answers questions about food that had been sacrificed to other gods and then offered for sale in the meat markets. Since there are no gods other than the one God, eating food that has been offered to these "gods" is morally neutral. So Christians have freedom, but this freedom itself is not intrinsically valuable: "We are no worse off if we do not eat [this food], nor better off if we do" (8:8). Yet Paul is concerned about the **weak in faith**, believers whose understanding is imperfect and who might think that eating food offered to a false god involves worship of that god. The **strong in faith** must in conscience be careful not to scandalize the weak. Paul's opening statement in 8:2 governs his stance: Knowledge can make one proud, but love builds others up and thus puts constraints on self-serving behavior. So if eating harms other believers, it is better not to eat (8:13).

In chapter 9, Paul offers himself (in typical fashion) as an example: he has rights as an apostle, but out of concern for others he does not exercise them. Paul has seen the risen Lord and was commissioned for his work by the risen Lord; this work is the practical proof of his apostleship. Paul does not pass over his rights as an apostle, in particular his right to be paid by his churches, because he is unsure of his apostolic role. Rather, he supported himself and preached the gospel free of charge lest a request for money put an obstacle to belief—people would think he was preaching for money, a complaint in 1 Thessalonians 2. Two rhetorically powerful passages (9:15–18, 19–23) show how persuasive a preacher Paul could be. He is clearly proud of what he has accomplished through his sacrifices, and yet in another sense he was under divine compulsion in his mission: "Woe to me if I do not proclaim the gospel!" In this proclamation he became "all things to all people," the ultimate cross-cultural person, so that he might win over socially and religiously diverse people. In 9:24–27 he ends with a fascinating use of imagery from athletic competitions that would be very familiar to the Corinthians. He has subjected himself to punishing disciplinary training so that, after proclaiming the gospel to others, he himself should not lose the contest.

Chapters 10–11 deal with problems affecting community worship. In 10:1–13 Paul cites the Exodus, where many Israelites received divinely supplied nourishment but still disobeyed God, and warns the Corinthians against sexual immorality, discouragement, and worship of false gods. All these offenses are examples from the testing of Israel that "were written as a lesson to us on whom the culmination of the ages has come." In 10:2, 14–22 Paul writes about baptism and about the Eucharistic cup of blessing that is a sharing in the blood of Christ and bread-breaking that is a sharing in the body of Christ (10:16). Here Paul makes it clear that through baptism and the Eucharist God delivers and sustains Christian believers, yet also shows that such exalted help does not immunize those who receive the sacraments from sin or exempt them from divine judgment. Since the many partakers are one body, participation in the Eucharist is irreconcilable with direct participation in pagan sacrifices that are in fact offered to demons and making people partners with demons. One cannot sit at both the table of the Lord and the table of demons. Paul interrupts the issue of the Eucharist to supply directions for community behavior at worship (11:1–16): A man must pray or prophesy with head bared, while a woman must have her head covered. The two theological reasons offered for this demand (a man is the glorious reflection of God while the woman reflects the man; "because of the angels," which Paul does not explain, the woman ought to have a sign of authority on her head) may not have been deemed fully persuasive even by Paul himself, for at the end (11:16) he resorts to asserting the authority of his own custom and those of the churches.

In 11:17–34 Paul returns to the Eucharist and the regular meal in which it was set, bluntly expressing his displeasure with Corinthian behavior. Divisions are being carried over to "the Lord's Supper" or Eucharist, where the Corinthians meet together as a church (11:18) to reenact a remembrance of what Jesus did and said on the night he was betrayed. Some have a full meal that precedes the Eucharist, while the poor ("those who have nothing") go hungry. Evidently all Christians, including the poor and slaves, are accepted into the house for worship, but the householder is inviting to his table only well-off friends who have brought good food for the main meal. Paul sharply instructs that either all should come together to share the same food or they should all eat first in their own homes (11:33–34). The whole purpose of the sacred meal is sharing (10:16), not division of the community. One also sins against the body and blood of the Lord if one eats the bread and drinks the cup unworthily (11:27), that is, by failing to discern that it is the body and blood of the Lord and by not acting in love toward the body of Christ, that is the church (11:29). Indeed, Paul contends that judgment is already falling on the Corinthians, for some have died and many are sick (11:30). This treatment of eating and drinking reminds us of the powerful social importance of dining in the ancient world.

In chapters 12–14, Paul deals with the spiritual gifts or charisms given in such abundance to the Corinthian Christians. Paul stresses equally the diversity of spiritual gifts and the unity of how they are to be used in love to serve others. Some Corinthians had evidently made claims to a higher honor status because they possessed a "superior" gift, but Paul rules this out. All gifts come from the same Spirit and are to be directed by the Spirit (12:1–11). The church is like a human body, in which all parts have an important place; there is no room for pride or jealousy. Because 12:28 lists apostles, prophets, and teachers as the first charisms, those who possessed these charisms may have administered the Corinthian community. Yet the picture is complicated because a different charism of "administration/leadership" is also listed in 12:28. Chapter 13, sometimes called "a hymn to love," corrects any covetousness about charisms. It poetically exalts loving service to others as more important than spiritual gifts; all spiritual gifts must be exercised in the Spirit for the good of all believers. Chapter 14 concludes this section by urging those exalting speaking in tongues to pursue instead the gift of prophecy, which builds others in the faith in ways that speaking in other tongues cannot. Paul lays down limits for speaking in tongues during services, because "If . . . all speak in tongues, and outsiders or unbelievers enter, will they not say that you are out of your mind?" (14:23). In 14:34–35, a passage that interrupts the treatment of prophecy, women are excluded from speaking at all in churches, yet 11:5 allows women to pray or prophesy with their head covered. Paul urges them to enforce his instructions in chapters 12–14 as the "command of the Lord" by refusing to have anything to do with those who do not accept them. He closes this topic by endorsing prophecy, urging a limited place for speaking in tongues, and commanding that in Christian worship "all things should be done decently and in order" (14:37–40).

In chapter 15, the final main part of the letter body, Paul describes the resurrection of Jesus and then draws out its implications for the eternal life of Christians. Some Corinthian Christians have been saying that there is no resurrection of the dead (15:12). They evidently believed that God raised Jesus from death, but they did not think that what happened to Jesus will happen to those who believe in him. The Corinthians may have thought that the resurrection had been accomplished already by the coming of the Spirit, which brought a life so full that nothing else was to be expected; at their deaths their spirits/souls would go to be with God, and their bodies go back to the earth forever. So Paul retells the story of Jesus: he died, and on the third day he rose from the dead and appeared to such known figures as Cephas, the Twelve, James (the brother of the Lord), and Paul himself (15:3–8; see also 9:1). Basing himself consistently on what happened to Christ, Paul asserts that all the dead are to be raised (15:12–19), that the resurrection is future (15:20–34) and bodily (15:35–50). Indeed, Christ is the "first fruits" of the dead: "As in Adam all died, so in Christ all shall be made alive" (15:20–22). An eschatological sequence is now in process: first, Christ is resurrected; at his return, those who belong to Christ are resurrected; then at the end, when he has destroyed death and all opposition to God, Christ hands over to the Father the kingdom; finally, the Son himself will be subjected to God and God may be all in all (15:23–28). Resurrection is not an abstract issue for Paul; it confers an eternal significance not only on matters of the spirit but also on the human body and the fullness of human life. The hope of being raised explains his willingness to suffer physically (15:30–34). In 15:35–58, Paul addresses another objection probably raised at Corinth to the resurrection of the dead: How are the dead raised, and what kind of body do they have? Paul has a nuanced answer: Resurrection will involve a transformed body, as different as the grown plant is from the seed—a body imperishable, not perishable; powerful, not weak; spiritual, not physical; of heavenly origin, not from the earth. At the end, whether alive or dead, "we shall all be changed" and be clothed with an undying body (15:51–54). Paul asserts that death has lost its sting only in Jesus' victory over death in his bodily resurrection (15:55–58).

The closing of 1 Corinthians instructs the Corinthians how to take up the collection for Jerusalem and outlines Paul's stay at Ephesus, where he writes this letter. He plans to come to Corinth via Macedonia and perhaps to spend the winter there. Whenever Timothy and Apollos come, they must be treated well (16:10–12). Although the concluding greetings (including those from Aquila and Priscilla) are warm, when Paul "signs" in his own hand, he curses any believer at Corinth "who does not love the Lord," by which he probably means those who refuse to heed his letter and thereby damage the church (16:21–22). But his last words are positive, not only extending love to all, but also uttering a prayer that evidently even the Corinthians know in the mother tongue of Jesus, Aramaic: *Marana tha,* "Our Lord, come."

Historical Reading of 1 Corinthians

1 Corinthians offers a fascinating description of what Wayne Meeks has called the "first urban Christians" (Meeks 1983). It provides rich insight into their life as a community and their relationship with the outside world, the fullest view of a NT church that we get in the NT. This is true not simply because of its quantity—it is a long letter—but because of the quality of Paul's description of this community's life. Most matters of historical introduction treated here are relatively uncomplicated. This allows historical study to concentrate on the content of the letter and what it shows about Paul, about the Corinthians, and about their relationship with each other.

www For an excellent website introducing current study of 1 and 2 Corinthians, follow the link to "Conflict and Community in the Corinthian Church."

---

1 Corinthians in Brief: Summary of Historical Reading

Author Paul, with authenticity undisputed.

Date 54–55, from Ephesus; in the revisionist chronology, 46–49.

Audience Corinthian believers, a predominantly Gentile church.

Unity Affirmed by almost all scholars today; a few see composition in stages or two different letters joined.

Integrity 14:33b–35, where women are commanded to be silent and submissive in church, may be a later interpolation.

Purpose To instruct the Corinthians on a wide variety of problems and issues, especially true wisdom, unity in the church, moral living, and eschatology.

Author

Although there is no dispute today about Pauline authorship, it may be helpful to state briefly the main arguments for it. The external evidence for the authenticity of 1 Corinthians is strong. Clement of Rome (around 95 C.E.) in his own letter to the Corinthians states explicitly that 1 Corinthians is by Paul. The *Didache* and *Barnabas* seem quite familiar with it; Ignatius and Polycarp know it intimately; Justin Martyr, Irenaeus, Marcion, and others all refer to it as Paul's. The internal evidence for authenticity is equally strong. In the controversy this letter contains, Paul defends himself and his gospel as though both were doubted; later pseudonymous works hardly recognize this doubt and instead put Paul on a pedestal. Finally, there are no historical discrepancies, differences in expression, or theological development between this letter and the other uncontested Pauline letters to cast any doubts on 1 Corinthian's authenticity.

Date

Paul had visited the Corinthians on his second missionary journey, and he was able to stay there eighteen months (Acts 18:10–11). This was in 50–51 C.E.—that is, up until some months after Gallio began his proconsulship. Most likely, Paul left Corinth in the fall of 51 C.E. After concluding his second missionary journey, Paul returned again to the Roman province of Asia (today western Turkey) on his third journey. This time he settled down in Ephesus for almost three years (Acts 19:10; 20:31)—that is, from the fall of 52 until the spring of 55 C.E. While Paul was in Ephesus he had some contact with the Corinthians, for he says they misunderstood his "previous letter" (1 Cor. 5:9). The apostle had to clear up the misunderstanding, as well as address other issues. Hence, "First" Corinthians was written from Asia, most likely Ephesus (1 Cor. 16:8–9, 19), and probably around 54 C.E. A minority revisionist position holds that Paul's first visit to Corinth was in 41–42, which Acts confuses with a later visit, and 1 Corinthians was written between 46 and 49.

Audience

The letter was written to the relatively new converts at Corinth (1:2). The church at Corinth was composed of both Jews and Greeks (Acts 18:4), though it was predominantly Gentile, to judge from the contents of 1 Corinthians.

Occasion

Three things apparently occasioned the writing of 1 Corinthians. First, Paul had written a previous letter to the Corinthians (1 Cor 5:9). In that letter he told them not to associate with immoral persons, and they took this to mean all immoral

Bema in Corinth The Roman structure where Paul was brought before the Roman proconsul Gallio (Acts 18:12) was at the center of the agora. This was the bema (BAY-muh), where Roman officials appeared before the public. An inscription mentioning Gallio enables us to date his proconsulship in Corinth to between 51 and 52 C.E. In the background is Acro-("High") Corinth, the first area of settlement in ancient times, now with visible remnants of a medieval fortress. Used by permission of BiblePlaces.com.

persons, while he meant only immoral believers (5:10–13). The matter needed to be cleared up. Second, the apostle also got news from members of Chloe's house that there were divisions arising among the Corinthian believers (1:11). Presumably the report included other problems such as attitudes toward the apostles (4:1–21), incestuous behavior (5:1–5), and lawsuits between Christians (6:1–11). Third, the beginning of chapter 7 indicates that Paul also received a letter from the Corinthian congregation detailing a number of problems. 1 Cor 7:1 begins "now about," which is repeated in 7:25, 8:1, 12:1, and 16:1. This sounds very much as though Paul is responding to questions that may or may not be intrinsically related to the preceding section.

www For a chart comparing the positions of Paul and the Corinthians, see the website.

1 Corinthians in Brief: Summary of Newer Readings

Social Scientific 1 Corinthians draws strongly on main categories of honor and shame, kinship, insiders and outsiders. Paul is particularly concerned to maintain his authority as their leader and use it to solve their many problems.

Feminist Corinthians seems to take a divided position about the status and role of women. Several passages are remarkably liberationist, others are repressive.

Cross-Cultural 1 Corinthians presents major cultural boundaries of Jew and Gentile in the crossing, but not in the problematic way that 2 Corinthians does.

Social Scientific Reading of 1 Corinthians

Because 1–2 Corinthians deal with a host of actual social and relational problems, they afford excellent opportunities for social scientific reading. The honor-shame structure of life is utilized on every page: the honor of Paul as an apostle and the honor of the Corinthian believers among themselves. In 1 Corinthians, matters of insiders and outsiders surface in what Paul says about outsiders coming into the Corinthian's worship services. **Commensality,** or social issues in table fellowship, is important as Paul writes about equality at the Eucharist and the issue of eating food offered to idols. Kinship affects the many things Paul says about marriage and children in chapter 7 and the way "brother and sister" language plays out in the text, the subject of the next reading.

Social Scientific Reading at Work
The Sibling Role in 1 Corinthians 6:1–11

Aasgaard examines the impact of Mediterranean sibling (brother/sister) role thinking in Paul's letters. He argues that Paul's nature and frequency in using sibling terminology reinforces and broadens the motivational basis for his moral exhortation.

In 1 Cor 6:1–11, as in 1 Cor 8, we encounter one of the cases of conflict in the Corinthian communities; it is literally a *case* that is involved, since Christians are taking one another before worldly courts of justice. Paul finds this unacceptable, and argues strongly against it: those who do so are failing to live up to the standards of prudence in judgment and wisdom appropriate for those who are holy (vv. 2–4, 5b). Instead, Paul proposes [among other things] that they should renounce their rights, preferring to suffer injustice or loss (v. 7). . . .

Source: Reidar Aasgaard, "'Role Ethics' in Paul: The Significance of the Sibling Role for Paul's Ethical Thinking," in *New Testament Studies* 48 (2002): 513–530.

Paul describes the conflict as a case between brothers (v 5b), and he underscores the sibling relationship even more strongly in the following verse: "a brother goes to court against a brother" (v. 6). The use of the metaphor culminates in v. 8b: "But you yourselves wrong and defraud—and brothers at that." It cannot be by chance that Paul gives such emphasis to the sibling metaphor in this text; it is clear that this is a part of his rhetorical strategy: the fact that the Christians are "siblings" makes this conflict even worse, even less acceptable. Why does Paul employ this as an argument? The most probable answer lies in the realities of family life and court cases in antiquity. Statistical investigations indicate that between 65 and 80 percent of all cases were connected to family disputes; most of these (58–65 per cent of all cases and 80 per cent of family disputes) concerned conflicts about dividing inheritances . . . Although cases involving family conflicts, especially questions of inheritance, were frequent, this was perceived as a very delicate matter. It was dishonorable to go to court, and all the more so if a family feud was involved. While harmony and loyalty were the main ideals in the family and sibling relationship, conflicts (sometimes very serious) were also common.

Paul's presentation of the situation in 1 Cor 6:1–11 seems to reflect the same kind of ideas. The fact that Christians are called siblings makes it all the worse that they take each other to court: such a thing ought not to happen among siblings. Thus, Paul is here employing general ideals regarding the sibling relationship as one element in his ethical argumentation, indeed as one of the most important elements. At the same time, we must also ask whether something further underlies this particular conflict. Statistically speaking, it is very possible that the dispute in Corinth concerned a family conflict, perhaps also a conflict about an inheritance within one household or between related households; the conflict may even have been between persons who were not only Christian "siblings," but also social siblings! This is suggested by the text itself, when Paul warns the parties in the conflict that those who behave in this way "will not *inherit* the kingdom of God" (v. 9)! This is one of the rare instances where Paul uses this traditional expression (cf. also Gal 5:21). In the type of conflict that we may presume occurred at Corinth, this may be taken as biting sarcasm: Christians (whether members of the one family, or indeed siblings) who engage in strife about earthly inheritances are at risk of losing their heavenly inheritance, the kingdom of God! Thus there is all the more reason to come quickly to an agreement, and to do so within the four walls of the house.

Question

Describe how sibling relationships make getting along in the church "family" both easier and more difficult.

Doing Social Scientific Criticism Yourself

Pick one of the leading social scientific paradigms, such as honor-shame or kinship, and use it to explain another one of the Corinthian's problems.

www   See the website for a link to an article on honor and shame in 1–2 Corinthians.

Feminist Reading of 1 Corinthians

1 Corinthians is read today as both the most pro-feminist and anti-feminist of Paul's generally accepted letters. To many women, his teaching on marriage in chapter 7 lowers gender equality to an interim ethic: "Let those with wives be as though they had none" (7:29). Women may speak in church, but they must wear head coverings or their hair "up" while doing so (11:2–16). Later Paul seems to correct himself in 14:33b–36, and his call for the silence and subordination of women in church seems downright misogynistic. On the other side, Paul is also friendly to women. He can use a mothering image, "I fed you with milk," in 3:2. In chapter 7, he can speak of mutuality in marriage, especially in regard to sexual intercourse (vv. 3–4) and abstention from it to spend time in prayer (v. 5). Paul counsels widows to remain single and independent (v. 8). His policies for marriage and divorce apply equally to husband and wife (vv. 10–16). Even the strictures of 14:33b–36 are ameliorated when we recognize that these verses may well be an interpolation from a later time, from someone trying to make Paul more conservative.

Feminist Reading at Work
Women as Witnesses of the Risen Christ (1 Cor 15:6)

Of the many places where the NRSV introduces the translation of the masculine plural adelphoi *by the gender-inclusive "brothers and sisters," this passage is one of the most significant and the most problematic. Here Ross Kraemer puts forward her view that* adelphoi *may include women in 1 Cor. 15:6.*

In 1 Cor. 15:5–8, Paul lists, in apparent chronological order, those to whom the resurrected Christ appeared: to Cephas, then "the twelve"; to five hundred *adelphoi* at one time; to James, and then to "all the apostles"; and last of all, to Paul himself. Although the canonical Gospels themselves differ significantly in their accounts of who saw the risen Jesus and in what order, none agrees with Paul's version. The shorter (and probably earliest) version of Mark contains no resurrection appearances. John 20:14–18 unambiguously states that Jesus appears first to Mary Magdalene, whereas according to Matt 28:9, Jesus appears first to Mary Magdalene and "the other" Mary (possibly, but by no means definitely, his mother). In Luke, Jesus appears first either to a man named Cleopas and his unidentified companion walking to the village of Emmaus (24:13–31) or to Simon (24:33–34). Subsequent to these appearances, Jesus appears again, to the eleven and their companions (24:36), among whom are almost certainly the women of the group who discovered the empty tomb earlier that same morning.

Paul, in short, relates a tradition of resurrection appearances in which no named women are said to have seen the risen Christ, although the masculine plural *adelphoi* might conceivably include women such as [the apostle] Junia (Rom 16:7). This tradition is seriously at odds with other early Christian traditions, including the narratives of Matthew and John. Accounting for these differences is difficult, especially since 1 Corinthians is one of the earliest Christian writings we have, earlier by as much as several decades than any of the Gospels. There are some possible explanations: Paul was ignorant of the traditions narrating an appearance to Mary (and other women); Paul intentionally omitted those traditions; those traditions had not yet been formulated or were not yet circulating among Christians.

For the translation of *adelphoi* in 1 Cor15:6, we need not resolve these difficult questions. We need only recognize that the translation "brothers and sisters" makes this passage an unambiguous description of Christ appearing to a mixed group of five hundred women and men. The appeal of such a reading for many contemporary Christian communities is obvious. Nevertheless, given the discrepancies between Gospel narratives of appearances to women, including Mary, and Paul's otherwise men-only list of appearances, it seems appropriate to be cautious in concluding that Paul here uses *adelphoi* to designate women as well as men.

Question

Explain in your own words why the question of women witnesses of the resurrection of Jesus is important in 1 Corinthians.

Doing Feminist Criticism Yourself

1. *Use historical and/or feminist criticism to relate the more balanced things said about women's participation in church in 11:2–16 with the command to silence in chapter 14.*

2. *Relate the spiritual gifts/charisms in chapter 12 to the role of women in the church.*

2 CORINTHIANS: Paul Defends His Apostolic Calling

2 Corinthians is a demanding letter to read. Although 1 Corinthians is a single letter and proceeds in an orderly topical way, 2 Corinthians with its probably several letters put into one is a literary archaeological dig. It has so many difficult shifts of topic and mood that most scholars see 2 Corinthians as a composite letter. Yet oddly enough, some thematic unity can be found in 2 Corinthians as it now stands, especially as Paul

defends against Jewish-Christian **superapostles** (missionaries from Judea attempting to make the Corinthians into Jewish Christians) his apostolic calling and mission as a "ministry of reconciliation." Despite these problems of reading, 2 Corinthians is a fascinating letter affording deep insight into Paul's ministry and theology.

---

2 Corinthians in Brief: Outline of Structure and Contents

I. **Opening** Paul to the Corinthians, blessing (1:1–2)

II. **Thanksgiving** The comfort of God in affliction (1:3–11)

III. **Body** Paul defends his apostolic calling, conduct, and authority (1:12–13:10)
- A. Defense of his conduct in the "tearful letter" and deferred visit (1:12–2:13)
- B. The nature of a true apostle (2:14–7:16)
- C. Two appeals for the collection for the believers in Judea (8–9)
- D. Defense of Paul's apostolic authority against challenges (10:1–13:10)

IV. **Conclusion** Final exhortation and greetings, blessing (13:11–14)

Developing Your Skills

Read quickly through 2 Corinthians and see if you can discover for yourself the main sections that may denote different letter bodies.

A Guide to Reading 2 Corinthians

Paul writes to Christian believers in the Corinthian church and "in the whole of Achaia" (the southern half of Greece). Perhaps he mentions Achaia to prepare the church for the collection that will be taken up throughout Achaia (2 Cor 9:2), but the contents of the letter are addressed to the Corinthians. In 1:3–11 Paul does not offer a formal thanksgiving for his audience, which indicates that his relationship with the Corinthians is strained. Instead, he uses a formal blessing of God to highlight God's goodness in the trials he suffered at Ephesus. This experience showed Paul his own weakness and Christ's comfort. Mention of this experience anticipates an important theme of this letter.

The first part of the letter body (1:12–7:16) discusses Paul's past dealings with the Corinthians by narrating these dealings and looking at them theologically. First, Paul explains his change of plans after the painful visit he had paid the Corinthians from Ephesus. The change was not simply an issue of human preference, but part of the positive plan that God has for the Corinthians and for Paul himself. Instead of subjecting them to another difficult confrontation that might make him seem too domineering (1:23–24), he wrote a letter "with many tears" to change their minds, so that when he did come it might be a joyful experience. In chapter 2 we learn that the problem during the painful visit had centered on a confrontational individual. In response to Paul's "tearful" letter, the Corinthians have disciplined this person, but now Paul urges mercy and forgiveness. He tells the Corinthians that to heal his relations with them he interrupted his preaching ministry at Troas (after leaving Ephesus) and crossed over to Macedonia to hear from Titus the effect of the tearful letter (2:12–13).

Paul then relates his apostolic ministry as a whole to the Corinthian crisis. That crisis wrings out of Paul passages of remarkable rhetorical power. If his thoughts seem to ramble, in part that is because he is responding to the activity of would-be apostles at Corinth and their attacks on Paul (of which he will say more in chaps. 10–12). Stressing that he is no hawker of God's word (2:17), Paul insists that he, unlike the others, should need no letter of recommendation to the Corinthians—they themselves are his letter (3:1–3). Paul then argues that a ministry of the Spirit is superior to a ministry of law engraved on stone (is Paul thinking of Jewish tombstones?) that brought death (3:4–11). Moses put a veil over his face in dealing with Israel, and the veil still remains when Israelites read the old covenant. However, when one turns to Christ, the veil is taken away because the Lord who spoke to Moses is now present in the Spirit (3:12–18). Paul's gospel is not veiled except to those who are perishing because the god of this world has blinded their minds (4:3–4). Paul's power is from God, although this treasure is carried in an "earthen (cheap clay) vessel" (4:7). In a masterpiece of irony (4:8–1 2), and drawing upon his theology of union with Christ, Paul links his physical suffering to his apostolic status in Christ, for "we always carry in our body the death of Jesus so that the life of Jesus may also be revealed in our body." Some may claim that an apostle's physical sufferings show that he or she is not a good apostle; Paul claims his sufferings as a badge of honor to show his living link with the death of Christ.

In 4:16–5:10, a series of opposites (outer/inner; seen/not seen; naked/clothed) explains why Paul does not lose heart. His troubles—physical, relational, spiritual—are momentary compared to eternal glory. When the earthly tent (his body?) is destroyed, there is an eternal, heavenly dwelling from God. Although Paul stresses that he is not commending himself to the Corinthians, he is clearly trying to get them to appreciate his ministry for them (5:11–15), which others among them denigrate. God "gave us the ministry of reconciliation . . . so we are ambassadors of Christ" (5:18–20). This passage describes the vocation that Paul wants to share with them. Appealing to the Corinthians not to receive God's grace in vain (6:1), Paul assures them that God would put no stumbling block in anyone's path (6:3). In a moving list of hardships showing the highs and lows of his career (6:4–10), Paul bares his soul to the Corinthians and challenges them to open their hearts to him (6:11–13). Shifting to dualistic contradictions (6:14–7:1:

righteousness/wickedness, light/darkness, etc.), Paul urges them not to become tied to unbelievers. In 7:2 he picks up again from where he left off in 6:13, explaining his behavior to the Corinthians, with a few remaining comments about the theme of reconciliation. He tells them how happy he was when Titus brought the news that his "tearful" letter had produced a good effect. He is glad that now he can have complete confidence in them (7:16), which serves as a good lead-in to the fund-raising sections to come.

In the next major section of the letter, chapters 8–9, Paul deals with his collection for the church in Jerusalem. These two chapters seem to overlap in such a way that some historical reading sees them as two separate fundraising letter bodies. Paul dares to request money from the Corinthians for his collection, a project they had already begun in the past but now are ignoring, probably due to difficult relations with Paul (8:10; 9:2). He holds up the example of the Macedonian Christians, who are being generous despite their poverty (8:1–5), as well as that of Jesus Christ himself "who, though he was rich, for your sake became poor, that you might become rich by his poverty" (8:9). Paul is sending Titus and two others to arrange the collection and probably to carry this letter, or at least the fund-raising part of it, from Paul. The collection for Jerusalem is also the subject of chapter 9, which seems to speak specifically to Achaia. Just as Paul is boasting about the generosity of the Macedonians to the Corinthians, he has been boasting about the Corinthians (Achaia) to the Macedonians, cleverly and shamelessly playing them against each other in a social contest designed to raise as much money for Jerusalem as possible. Paul's pronouncement, "God loves a cheerful giver" (9:7), has understandably been an ageless favorite with money raisers since Paul uttered it.

Chapters 10–13 contain Paul's more detailed response to challenges to his apostolic authority. Whereas chaps. 8–9 were optimistic and enthusiastic about the Corinthian response, in the next four chapters Paul turns more pessimistic and defensive as he voices uncertainty about his reception when he comes a third time. Indeed, he has to threaten to be as severe when he comes as he has been in his writing. Nevertheless, Paul wants to stress that the authority given him by the Lord is primarily for building up, not for pulling down in sharp criticism, which Paul can do masterfully (10:8; 13:10). "Apostles" and "super-apostles" (11:5; 12:11) have been undermining Paul at Corinth, arguing that the Gentile Corinthian believers should adopt more Jewish ways. They argue, among other things, that Paul's letters are strong, but his personal presence is weak and his speech is contemptible (10:10). As far as Paul is concerned, they are masqueraders and false apostles (11:13–15) who in the end will be punished. They have drawn forth from Paul here in 2 Corinthians 10–13 the longest and most impassioned description of his own apostolic service. Paul lists signs, wonders, and miracles that he had wrought among the Corinthians as "signs of an apostle." (12:12). However, the times he was imprisoned, whipped, stoned, shipwrecked, imperiled, hungry, thirsty, and stripped naked (this passage is another "catalogue of suffering") are more important to him as an expression of his apostolic concern for all the churches (11:23–29). Paul is willing to take the risk of boasting so that he may show the sincerity of his challenge to the Corinthians: "I will most gladly spend and be spent for your souls. If I love you more, will you love me less?" (12:15). Using this impassioned rhetoric, he persuades the Corinthians to rid themselves of divisions and corruptions before he comes so that he might not need to be harsh, but rather can build them up (12:20–13:10).

Paul's conclusion is brief but comprehensive: "Mend your ways, heed my appeal, think alike, live in peace." Did this happen, and was Paul's third visit peaceful? We cannot completely know. Acts 20:2–3 devotes only one sentence to the three months that he stayed in Achaia (of which Corinth was the capital); typically, Luke does not speak of conflict, so perhaps conflict continued and went unmentioned in Acts. Neither do passages in Rom 16:1,21–23 tell us much about Paul's later time in Corinth, from which he wrote Romans. At any rate, Paul's triadic blessing on the Corinthians in 13:13 serves as a fitting conclusion and as a model benediction even today.

Historical Reading of 2 Corinthians

In its present form the third-longest letter of Paul, 2 Corinthians is a literary, social, historical, and theological challenge to the modern reader. It contains some appealing themes of Pauline theology, such as reconciliation and power in weakness. Its history is a challenge because of the different literary layers, and the social situation is a difficult one. Now, after 1 Corinthians, the congregation seems to be more united, but it is at loggerheads with Paul as Jewish-Christian missionaries try to bring the Corinthians from law-free Gentile Christianity closer to their own form of Jewish Christianity. Second Corinthians is the most personal of Paul's letters, but most readers find it the most difficult.

---

2 Corinthians in Brief: Summary of Historical Reading

Author Paul, undisputedly.

Date: 57, from Macedonia; in the revisionist chronology of Paul, 55–56.

Audience Paul's Corinthian congregation, already recipients of 1 Corinthians.

Unity Most scholars hold that anywhere from two to five different letters (all from Paul) have been put together to form our 2 Corinthians.

Integrity Some conclude that 6:14–7:1 is a later, non-Pauline insertion.

Purpose To repair damaged relations with the Corinthians, to raise money for Paul's offering for Jerusalem, and to defend his apostolic authority.

Author

The opening of this letter names Paul and Timothy (1:1), but Timothy seems to disappear and Paul takes over as the real author. In general, the external and internal evidence for Pauline authorship of 2 Corinthians are the same as for 1 Corinthians. Three brief comments should be made here. First, the external evidence is strong for 2 Corinthians, though not as strong as for 1 Corinthians. It is not quoted by Clement but is quoted as a Pauline letter by Polycarp, Irenaeus, Clement of Alexandria, and Tertullian. Second, the internal evidence for 2 Corinthians, using 1 Corinthians as a benchmark of authenticity, is persuasive. The literary style, form of argumentation, and basic theological outlook are the same. Third, another significant piece of internal evidence is telling against a later pseudonymous authorship: a pious imitator would be most unlikely to portray Paul as an apostle in danger of losing his authority at Corinth.

Date

For reasons of literary unity to be discussed below, no single date can be given to 2 Corinthians. All scholars date all the various parts of 2 Corinthians soon after 1 Corinthians, ranging (in the traditional chronology) from 54 to 57. But the evidence does not allow us to be precise or certain.

Audience

The same audience is in view as in 1 Corinthians, but now in a different situation. 2 Corinthians is clearly a sequel to 1 Corinthians, as a whole and in its parts. Most of the moral issues addressed there have disappeared, or at least Paul puts them in the background until he can reestablish his authority (2 Cor 12:21). A new main issue has become important that is only mentioned in 1 Corinthians, that of Paul's apostolic authority.

Unity and Integrity

The unity of 2 Corinthians should be set in the whole context of the Corinthian correspondence. A few scholars, most recently Frank Matera, maintain that it is a single letter. Matera argues that Paul is addressing two crises at Corinth, one that has been resolved (the crisis of the painful visit), dealt with in chaps. 1–9, and one that still needs to be resolved (the presence of intruding apostles), dealt with in chaps. 10–13 (Matera 2003). However, the overwhelming majority argue that it is a composite of at least two Pauline letters. Although many reconstructions of this correspondence differ at points, we can present here one of the most common.

1. Paul's first letter to Corinth dealt with associating with sexually immoral people (1 Cor 5:9). This letter, usually called "Letter A" or the "Previous Letter," is almost certainly lost, but some believe that a fragment is preserved in 6:14–7:1.

2. 1 Corinthians basically as we have it today was written next. Paul sent Timothy to deliver this letter, and he probably reported back that not only were some old problems continuing but new ones were arising.

3. Paul paid them a "painful visit" (2 Cor 2:1–5). Soon after, he wrote a "letter of tears" or a "severe letter" (2:3–4, 7:8–12). As soon as it was sent, Paul regretted it and was filled with anxiety about how it would be received. But Titus reported to him that it was received well (7:15–16).

4. Paul then wrote a fourth letter, expressing his joy. Most scholars hold that this is basically canonical 2 Corinthians, minus traces of the other letters. But a substantial minority argues that 1–9 and 10–13 are different letters, and some that 8 and 9 are separate, fundraising letters coming at a joyful time. These arguments are becoming more widely accepted today than the view that 2 Corinthians is basically a unified letter.

5. Paul came to Corinth not long after writing the last of his letters to them. During this third visit, he wrote Romans and finalized his plan to go to Jerusalem to present his offering for the saints there.

6. Sometime after Paul's death, someone took all the Pauline correspondence to Corinth that was not already in what we call 1 Corinthians. This person or persons assembled the correspondence into a new letter to match 1 Corinthians' size, scope, and influence. This collection of correspondence was then "published" throughout the church and is now 2 Corinthians.

As for the integrity of 2 Corinthians as it stands today, 6:14–7:1 has often been called a non-Pauline interpolation. Many commentators see the strong theme of separation from unbelievers to be very unlike Paul (cf. 1 Cor 5:12–13); all commentators see this passage as a sharp digression. However, others argue that keeping worship pure of contamination and seeing the church as the temple of God (1 Cor 5:9–10; 3:16, respectively) fit with this passage, as does the series of OT quotations in its second half on the theme of keeping in a holy kinship with God.

Purpose

It is difficult to specify a single purpose for the letter as it stands now. We can be more certain about the purposes of its different parts. Chapters 1–7 were written to promote reconciliation between Paul and the Corinthian church. Chapters 8–9 were written to raise funds for the offering for Jerusalem. Chapters 10–13 were written to counterattack the superapostles who had been denigrating Paul.

www   See the website for a chart illustrating the positions of Paul and his opponents. Also, follow the link to resources for the study of 2 Corinthians.

2 Corinthians in Brief: Summary of Newer Readings

Social Scientific 2 Corinthians draws strongly on main categories of honor and shame, kinship, insiders and outsiders. Paul is particularly concerned to maintain his authority as their leader, and their standing as Gentile Christians, against Jewish Christian missionaries calling themselves "superior" or superapostles.

Feminist Unlike 1 Corinthians, 2 Corinthians does not deal with explicitly gender-related issues, and it makes little mention of women.

Cross-Cultural 2 Corinthians presents major cultural boundaries of Jew and Gentile in a problematic way, because Paul writes to maintain their Gentile cultural self-understanding against the incursions of Jewish-Christian missionaries who are trying to bring them into Judaism.

Social Scientific Reading at Work
Honor and Shame in Generosity (2 Corinthians 8–9)

Perhaps the most powerful social value in the ancient word was honor: life was a process of collecting and maintaining honor while keeping away shame. In this reading David deSilva explains Paul's use of the avoidance of shame as a motivating factor in raising money for the Judean churches.

These same oracles display another important strategy being used throughout the New Testament: they intentionally direct the hearers and channel their ambitions for honor toward the honors bestowed by God or by the group for having embodied God's values . . .

Fear of shame before one's fellow Christians in the local assembly or concern about loss of honor in the eyes of the trans-local Christian group now becomes a powerful motivation for investment of oneself in the activities and processes that sustain the minority culture. Paul, for example, uses this fear of being dishonored with a view to securing maximum participation in the relief efforts for the sisters and brothers in Judea: Openly before the churches, show them the proof of your love and of our reason for boasting about you . . . to the people of Macedonia, saying that Achaia has been ready since last year; and your zeal has stirred up most of them. But I am sending the brothers in order that our boasting about you may not prove to have been empty in this case, so that you may be ready, as I said you would be; otherwise, if some Macedonians come with me and find that you are not ready, we would be humiliated–to say nothing of you–in this undertaking. (2 Cor 8:24–9:4)

The Corinthians have already won a reputation for generosity among the churches (a desirable honor, to be sure) thanks to Paul's boasting about them, but this reputation

Source: David A. deSilva, *Honor, Patronage, Kinship, & Purity: Unlocking New Testament Culture* (Downers Grove, IL: InterVarsity, 2000), pp. 80–81.

is now on the line: the Corinthians must put their money where Paul's mouth is, as it were, if they are to confirm their honor in the sight of their Macedonian sisters and brothers. If they fail to support this relief effort generously, their reputation among the churches will suffer loss.

Question

Do you think that raising money this way was ethical for Paul?

Feminist Reading at Work
A Pure Bride or Deceived Eve? (11:2–3)

In this reading, Jouette Bassler examines the powerfully mixed feminine symbolism Paul uses to refute his opponents.

Paul's obvious concern throughout this letter is that "false" apostles have undermined the Corinthians' loyalty to him and have drawn them away from the gospel that he preached and thus (in Paul's view) from Christ. He expresses his concern here through the familiar metaphor of marriage. Just as the prophets often portrayed Israel as the bride of Yahweh (Isa 54:4–6; Jer 2:2; Hos 2:19–20), so Paul describes the church as betrothed to Christ. He himself is the "father" of the bride . . . The prophets often denounced Israel's infidelity to God with graphic descriptions of the behavior of the adulterous wife (Hos 2:2–3; Jer 3:1–5; 13:25–27; Ezek 23:1–21). Paul uses somewhat more restraint when he introduces the figure of Eve.

In Genesis both Adam and Eve are culpable in the tragic events of the garden, but only Eve admits to having been deceived (Gen 3:13). It is this idea that Paul uses, leaving the sexual overtones of the word "deceive" undeveloped. Unlike the author of the Pastoral Epistles, who equates only women with Eve's deception (1 Tim 2:11–15), Paul sees the issue in broader terms. The whole church is being exposed to "deceitful workers" (11:13), and Paul fears that the church, like Eve, may succumb. When Paul focuses in other letters on Adam's role, the emphasis is quite different: the universal consequences of the fall are described, not the moral flaw that permitted it (Rom 5:12–21; 1 Cor 15:42–49). In using the figures of Adam and Eve in these different ways, Paul follows–and perpetuates–sexual stereotypes. Clearly the whole church, comprising both men and women, is in danger of being deceived, but it is Eve who is for Paul the paradigm of susceptibility.

Question

Explain why this metaphor is important for women in Corinth and today.

Source: Jouette M. Bassler, "2 Corinthians," in Carol A. Newsom and Sharon H. Ringe, eds., *Women's Bible Commentary.* (Louisville, KY: Westminster John Knox, 2000), p. 498.

Key Terms and Concepts

charism • commensality • delay of the Parousia • deliberative rhetoric • diatribe
epideictic rhetoric • imminent expectation • judicial rhetoric • resurrection
strong/weak in faith • superapostles • unity of 2 Corinthians

Questions for Study, Discussion, and Writing

1 Thessalonians

1. What kind of persecution or opposition are the Thessalonians encountering?
2. Describe carefully the eschatological problem the Thessalonians had. Why was it such a pressing problem for them?
3. Explain 5:27, "I solemnly command that this letter be read [out loud] to all of them," in terms of the reception of this letter and how it would be understood. Who would read it, and when? What kinds of follow-up to this initial reading might there have been?
4. Read through the moral commands Paul makes in this letter, and explain how some are gender specific and many are not. Do the ones that are not apply to men and women equally?
5. Does Paul's exhortation to "greet each other with a holy kiss" at the end of 1 Thessalonians have a connection with the problems over sexual immorality in chapter 4? In other words, does this "holy kiss" counteract "unholy kisses"?

1 Corinthians

1. Recall as many separate issues as you can in 1 Corinthians. Why does this letter sometimes look like a laundry list of problems?
2. Do you think that there is one underlying problem in Corinth that this letter addresses? If so, what is it?
3. Describe Paul's teaching on sexual morality in chapters 5–7. How applicable is it to people today?
4. In a recent article, a NT scholar suggested that some members of the Corinthian church could well have been slaves forced into prostitution by their masters. How do you think such a moral problem would be handled in the Corinthian church?
5. Why is the "Love Chapter" (13) so well known today? Do you think that Paul wrote it or adapted it? Give your reasons.
6. Skim through this letter and pick out the passages in which Paul mentions how outsiders perceive and evaluate Christians. Why does Paul do this?

2 Corinthians

1. Give your own explanation of the different letters from which this document may be constructed.
2. Explain Paul's idea of "strength in weakness," relating it to his christology and his view of the Christian life.
3. Give your own explanation of what Paul's opponents in 2 Corinthians believed and were doing.

4. Read chapters 8–9 from the perspective of a modern fundraiser for a charity. What would work to raise money today, and what would not? How can Paul be so bold in raising money for others, but not himself?

For Further Reading

Best, Ernest. *Second Corinthians.* Interpretation Commentary Series. Atlanta: John Knox, 1987. A standard commentary, accessible to beginning students.

Donfried, Karl P. *Paul, Thessalonica and Early Christianity.* Excellent essays on many important aspects of the Thessalonian correspondence.

Donfried, Karl P., and I. H. Marshall. *The Theology of the Shorter Pauline Letters.* Cambridge: Cambridge University Press, 1993. Good discussion of key theological issues.

Furnish, Victor Paul. *II Corinthians.* Anchor Bible, volume 32A. Garden City, NY: Doubleday, 1984. Probably the best commentary on 2 Corinthians.

Keck, Leander E., and Victor P. Furnish. *The Pauline Letters.* Nashville, TN: Abingdon Press, 1984. Good treatment of Corinthians and Thessalonians.

Richard, Earl. *First and Second Thessalonians.* Collegeville, MN: Liturgical Press, 1995. An excellent recent commentary; considers 1 Thessalonians to be composite, 2 Thessalonians as pseudonymous.

Talbert, Charles H. *Reading Corinthians.* New York: Crossroad, 1989. Accessible treatment of both 1 and 2 Corinthians.

Theissen, Gerd. *The Social Setting of Pauline Christianity.* Philadelphia: Fortress Press, 1982. A study of the social dynamics operating in the church at Corinth; a most illuminating study of primitive Christianity.

Wanamaker, Charles, *The Epistles to the Thessalonians.* Grand Rapids, MI: Eerdmans, 1990. A commentary that focuses on historical, social scientific, and rhetorical methods; although based on the Greek text, it is accessible to beginning students.

Witherington, Ben. *Conflict and Community in Corinth.* Grand Rapids, MI: Eerdmans, 1995. A social scientific and rhetorical commentary.

Chapter Thirteen

Galatians and Romans: Believers Live by Faith

Among the NT documents accepted as genuinely Pauline, Galatians and Romans are leading letters. Both give insight into Paul's main religious themes, his persuasive skills as a letter writer, his missionary career, and his personality. In both, the theme of how one belongs to God's people figures prominently, as does the topic of the moral life of the believer who is justified by faith. A strong debate is brewing in NT scholarship about whether "justification by faith" means one's acceptance by God (the old view) or one's membership in the people of God. However, Galatians and Romans are different in audience, tone, and rhetorical purpose. In Galatians Paul is visibly upset, even angry, about what he sees as his churches' defection to Jewish Christianity, supposedly to make their faith complete. In Romans, however, Paul writes carefully and calmly to a church not his own, his only surviving letter of this type.

GALATIANS: Stand Firm in Christ's Freedom

Because of its teaching on salvation, Paul's letter to the Galatians has proven to be one of the most significant writings in the NT. It was used in the Protestant Reformation in the sixteenth century to establish an early modern variation on Paul's teaching of **justification** (right standing before God or belonging to God's people) by faith, and even today Galatians is a focus of happier discussion between Protestants and Roman Catholics on this doctrine. But Paul did not write Galatians to teach a doctrine. Rather, he was responding to a crisis caused by Jewish-Christian missionaries who were leading his Gentile Christians off into Jewish Christianity. He writes "to the churches of Galatia," a group of communities in the Galatian region or in the larger province of Galatia. Galatians is thus a **circular letter,** one that goes to more than one congregation in more than one city. (Romans may have gone to multiple house churches in one city, and the same may be true of 1–2 Corinthians, but they are not considered circular letters because they stayed in one city.) Paul is the target of attack in Galatia, and he makes a strong personal response, stronger even than that in 2 Cor 10–13. Although this letter is carefully structured and intentionally argued at every point, Paul's strong emotions pour through it like a musician's emotions pour through a symphonic composition. In its historical dimensions, its social scientific aspects, and its cross-cultural and feminist readings, Galatians is a powerful letter, reminding people everywhere that human relationship with God and with each other is based on God's love active in Jesus, not on one's own religious accomplishments.

Galatians in Brief: Outline of Structure and Content

I. **Opening** Paul to Galatian believers, blessing (1:1–5; no thanksgiving follows)

II. **Body** Stand firm in Christ's freedom (1:6–6:10)
  A. Accusation (1:6–10)
  B. Paul defends his apostleship and law-free gospel (1:11–2:21)
  C. Six arguments in defense of justification by faith (3:1–4:31)
    1. Galatians received the Spirit while outside the Law (3:1–5)
    2. God gave the Spirit to them through faith, not works (3:6–14)
    3. The Law came after the promises to Abraham, as a temporary custodian until Christ came (3:15–25)
    4. Galatians experienced freedom apart from the Law (3:26–4:11)
    5. How can Paul, formerly their friend, now be their enemy? (4:12–20)
    6. Hagar represents the enslaving covenant of the Law, Sarah the covenant of promise to Abraham (4:21–31).
  D. Moral exhortation: Live responsibly in your freedom, through the Holy Spirit and in love (5:1–6:10)

III. **Conclusion** Main point repeated in Paul's own hand, benediction (6:11–18; note lack of personal greetings).

Developing Your Skills

Read through Galatians carefully, noticing both the arguments and the emotions.

A Guide to Reading Galatians

The opening of Galatians, when compared with Paul's other letters and the typical secular letters of the time, indicates that this will be no happy document. Paul begins—before he even mentions the recipients!—by asserting that his own apostolic calling is from God through the risen Jesus Christ. Galatians is also the only authentic Pauline letter to his own church in which Paul does not name a co-sender. After naming his recipients as "the churches of Galatia," his blessing asserts his own understanding of the Christian message: God determined that only the death of Jesus frees people from evil.

The body opens in 1:6–10 with a biting tone of astonishment and distress. Paul omits the traditional thanksgiving section—which the audience certainly would have noticed—in a way that comes across well in English translations; instead of "I am thankful," he says "I am astonished." The Galatians have been "bewitched" by people teaching false doctrine; this is a metaphor drawn from other religions. Paul will soon use arguments that, if accepted, will end this delusion. Paul quickly lays out the issue, the adversaries, and the seriousness of the case. There is no other gospel than the one proclaimed by Paul when he called the Galatians in the grace of Christ; God curses (excludes from kinship with God) those who preach something different. Then, using the judicial rhetorical pattern, Paul begins with a self-defense (1:11–2:2), employing an effective sequence of arguments. In an implied courtroom setting, the Jewish-Christian missionaries who have come to Galatia are the accusers, Paul is the defendant, and the Galatians are the judges. As the letter is read, the Galatians hear Paul's testimony and are called to respond to it; and the accusers may be there during the reading, too! Paul's main point is that the gospel he proclaims came through divine revelation and not from any human source (1:11–12). To establish this point, Paul relates the main lines of his conversion: his initial divine revelation from Jesus Christ and the commission Jesus gave him to preach the gospel to the Gentiles, which entails Paul's independence from the Jerusalem apostles. Paul then relates the main lines of his career: his first challenge from Christian Jews (whom Paul calls false brothers) who were insisting on circumcision for the Gentiles; the resulting agreement between Paul and the Jerusalem authorities rejecting that challenge; and acknowledgment by the Jerusalem authorities that Paul was a valid apostle to the Gentiles (1:13–2:10). Paul then describes those who came to Antioch from Jerusalem and claimed to represent James to cause Jews and Gentiles to act against the agreement in hypocrisy. Paul implies that those men prefigure those who have come now to compel Gentiles to live like Jews. Even Peter ("Cephas") and Barnabas fall prey to the message of the Jewish-Christian missionaries for a while, so perhaps it is not such a surprise that the Galatians now do the same (2:11–14). As he continues in 2:15–21 into his main argument, that Christians are saved by faith in Christ and not by doing the works of the law, Paul movingly expresses his union with Christ: he has died to the law because "I have been crucified with Christ; and it is no longer I who live, but Christ who lives in me" (v. 20).

Paul now advances six arguments to convince the "bewitched" Galatians to come back to the **law-free gospel** based on faith in the crucified Christ (3:1–4:31). These arguments are based on the common experience of Paul and the Galatians and on Scripture. (1) When Paul first proclaimed the crucified Christ to them, the Galatians received the Spirit without observing the works of the Law, so how can those works be necessary now? (3:1–5). (2) Against the insistence of Jewish-Christian opponents that Abraham's circumcision is an example for them, Paul cites God's covenantal promise that in Abraham all the nations would be blessed. In giving the Spirit to believing but uncircumcised Gentiles, God is fulfilling the promise to Abraham, whose faith made him right in God's sight before he was circumcised (3:6–14). (3) A legally binding will cannot be annulled by a later addition. The Law came 430 years after the promises to Abraham, so how can his inheritance of those promises depend on observing the Law? The Law was only a temporary custodian or pedagogue until Christ came. Now there is no longer Jew or Greek, slave or free, male or female; all believers belong to Christ, and therefore all believers are Abraham's children by faith, not by works (3:15–29). (4) The Galatians, who had been slaves to the elemental spiritual powers of the universe, have experienced the freedom of the children of God through redemption by God's Son and divine adoption. Why do they want to become slaves again, this time to the demands of the Law? (4:1–11). (5) The Galatians formerly treated Paul extremely well, like an angel; how can he have become their enemy, as his opponents would make him? (4:12–20). (6) Paul closes his series of arguments with an allegorical illustration involving two women. Hagar, the slave woman who was Abraham's surrogate wife, does not represent the Gentiles (as Paul's opponents may have argued). She does represent the earthly Jerusalem and the enslaving covenant of the Law given on Mt. Sinai. Sarah, the free and full wife of Abraham, represents the heavenly Jerusalem and the covenant of God's promise to Abraham. She is the mother of all who are in Christ (4:21–31).

Paul finishes the body of Galatians (5:1–6:10) with a passionate exhortation against his opponents and warns that being circumcised and keeping the Law will not help the Galatians to become better people. This final section combines moral exhortation with Paul's main rhetorical point against his opponents in Galatia, and it indicates that his opponents probably promoted law observance as a way to moral self-improvement. Paul says with stinging irony that circumcision means being cut off from Christ (5:4), but he also makes a more nuanced affirmation in 5:6, "In Christ Jesus neither circumcision nor uncircumcision counts for anything, but faith working through love." Paul does not consider circumcision something evil; rather, it has no power to bring justification or moral strength to Gentiles. As he appeals to the Galatians to come to their senses and back to his way of seeing things, Paul ends with an insult to his opponents that the Galatians would certainly remember: "I wish that those who unsettle you [by urging circumcision] would [go all the way and] castrate themselves!" (5:7–12). This may seem harsh to us today, but in the ancient Roman world it was common rhetorical practice to end an appeal with a strong emotional statement.

In 5:13–14, Paul begins a more positive presentation of the moral structure of his law-free but love-filled Gospel. A believer who is justified by faith does not live in any sort of way but is directed and empowered by God's Spirit to serve ("become slaves to") each other. This is summed up in a commandment that resonates with Jesus' affirmation of Jewish piety: "Love your neighbor as yourself." Life in the Spirit is opposed to life in the "flesh" (fallen human nature). Typically, Paul first urges rejecting evils and then urges adopting the good. Paul lists fifteen "works of the flesh" in a lengthy **catalogue of vice** designed to identify evils and lead people to reject them. He then lists nine "fruit[s] of the Spirit" in a **catalogue of virtue** to identify and promote good things. The basis for turning away from moral evils is dying with Christ, not serving under the law. Those who come to new life by the Spirit must live this life by the Spirit (5:22–26). Paul's opponents may speak of the "law of Christ"; that, however, is not the Law of Sinai but the obligation to bear one another's burdens (6:2). He closes by urging candid self-examination of all believers to avoid hypocrisy (6:3–5), a willingness to pay their teachers well (6:6), and a renewed dedication to follow the Spirit in doing what is right to believers and all people (6:7–10).

Paul writes the lengthy conclusion (6:11–18) with his own hand in big letters, so that the Galatians can see his point and his passion one last time. Paul refuses to "boast" (honor himself in the sight of others) in anything except the death of Jesus, "by which the world has been crucified to me and I to the world" (v. 14). The Jewish-Christian missionaries praised the superiority of Israel, but Paul proclaims the true "Israel of God," a "new creation" so powerful that it makes circumcision irrelevant. As for the attacks on him, "From now on let no one make more trouble for me, for I bear the marks [Greek *stigmata*] of Jesus on my body." Just as this letter began without a thanksgiving, so too it ends without any personal greetings or a final indication of the depths of his feeling, which is unusual for Paul's letters. However, Paul's blessing of them with the grace of Jesus Christ affirms that they are in fact his "brothers and sisters."

Historical Reading of Galatians

Galatians in Brief: Summary of Historical Reading

Author Paul (undisputed).

Date 54–55; less likely is the revisionist dating of 57.

Audience Paul's churches in north-central ethnic Galatia, or his churches in the province of southern Galatia (the cities of Pisidian Antioch, Lystra and Derbe).

Unity and Integrity Not disputed by the vast majority of scholars.

Purpose To bring the Galatians back to Paul's Law-free gospel of salvation by grace through faith and life in the Spirit.

Author

The authenticity of Galatians as a genuine Pauline letter is secure in scholarship today. We will examine in brief the reasons given for such acceptance. In the external evidence, Galatians is quoted or alluded to as Paul's own letter in first-, second-, and third-century writings: Barnabas, 1 Clement, Polycarp's letter to the Philippians, Justin Martyr, Irenaeus, Clement of Alexandria, and Origen. Both Marcion's canon and the Muratorian canon list it. In the internal evidence, the typical grounds for asserting authenticity are three: (1) Galatians is so painfully personal that only a genuine historical situation involving Paul accounts for it. (2) Several coincidences of ideas, wording, and history match what we know of Paul from his other letters, and there are no discrepancies. (3) Paul defends himself and his gospel as though both were doubted. Followers of Paul after his death had a high view of him—for example, the writers of Ephesians and the Pastorals—and would be most unlikely to invent such an embarrassing situation for him!

Date

Uncertainty about the identity of the audience (dealt with in the next section) leads to uncertainty about its date. If the South Galatian theory is correct, the letter would come around 49 or 50, when Paul revisited the cities in his "Second Missionary Journey." In the more accepted North Galatian theory, the dating of the letter has two main options. The first is 54 or 55, assuming that the letter worked to persuade the Galatians to return to Paul and that Paul was successful in his plan to include the Galatians in his offering for Jerusalem (1 Cor 16:1). The second option is 57 or 58, argued by those who think that Galatians was not successful and that the plan of 1 Cor 16:1 comes before Paul knew about his failure. The first dating is followed by a majority of those who adopt the North Galatian theory, and we will follow it here, but given the slimness and uncertainty of the evidence, it is by no means certain.

Audience

A contested issue in the historical study of Galatians is the identity of the audience. Was this epistle sent to the churches in the *geographical region* known as Galatia, where the ethnic Galatians of Celtic origins settled in north central Asia Minor (*Gal*atians is related to *Gaul*, the Roman word for modern France)? This is the **North Galatian hypothesis.** Or was it sent to the Roman *province* of Galatia, which included the just-mentioned northern territory but extended south to the Mediterranean Sea? In this case, the audience would include churches in cities with Mediterranean peoples where Paul and Barnabas founded churches on the "second missionary journey" (Acts 13–14). This is known as the **South Galatian hypothesis.** Although there is still a good deal of debate over this issue, not least because it impacts the dating of the letter, most scholars incline toward the North Galatian hypothesis. Their main reason is that Paul calls his audience "Galatians," by which he probably refers to ethnic Galatian people in the center of the Asia Minor peninsula; this ethnic name would not have applied to his churches in the south.

Occasion and Purpose

Despite uncertainties of audience and date, scholars agree on the main lines of the situation that occasioned this letter. Acts 15:1 relates that Judean visitors came to Syrian Antioch. There they started to teach the Christians that those who were not circumcised in accordance with the Law of Moses could not be saved. This was the basic message; a whole theological system no doubt accompanied it. Others with the same message visited the daughter-churches of Antioch, not only in Syria and Cilicia, as the apostolic letter indicates (Acts 15:23), but also in Galatia. This was evidently the kind of mission that had reached the churches of Galatia and was making headway there. The purpose of this letter was obviously, then, to refute these Jewish-Christian teachers' gospel, in which circumcision was a sign of identity with Abraham's people and law observance and was essential to becoming a part of the people of God. Paul wrote to remind the Galatians of the real basis of their salvation and new life, and to bring them back from what he considered to be apostasy.

Social Scientific and Cross-Cultural Readings of Galatians

Galatians is nothing more or less than a social and religious struggle for the validity of cross-cultural Christianity. Must all "Christians" (to use our word that Paul did not use) be Jews as well, so that the church can be united in this way? This seems to have been the rationale of the Jewish-Christian missionaries in Galatia, who argued that to be a disciple of Jesus Christ, one had to be a child of Abraham. Paul argues for the validity of Gentile Christianity and its appropriateness for his Gentile churches. Often it is said that the Jewish-Christian missionaries' position is that one must become a Jew *before* one can become a believer in Jesus. Rather, they believe that all Christians should be Jewish Christians, a "Jew" and a "Christian" *simultaneously*. In this letter Paul's counterattack on these seems to rule out the possibility of any form of Jewish Christianity. However, it is important to keep the context in mind: Paul is saying that Jewish Christianity must not be imposed on *Gentiles,* but he says nothing explicit about its appropriateness for *Jews.* Judging by what he says in Romans, a more peaceful letter, Paul believes that it is indeed appropriate for Jews.

Social Scientific and Cross-Cultural Reading at Work
Redemption from a Curse (Galatians 3:13)

This reading from central Africa shows the deep social and cultural revulsion against hanging, especially in suicide. The authors use this to show in parallel the revulsion Jews of the Common Era would have felt toward the preaching of a crucified messiah.

"Christ redeemed us from the curse of the Torah, having become a curse for us–for it is written–'Cursed be every one who hangs on a tree'" (Galatians 3:13). By the first century of the Common Era it is likely that every Jew who witnessed a crucifixion interpreted that hanging in the context of Deuteronomy 21. Indeed, the pre-Christian Paul hearing the story of the cross of Jesus is likely to have thought of Jesus as cursed by God. The very idea of such a one being the Messiah would have been viewed as absurd . . .

In common with many African peoples the Babukusu acknowledge the immanent reality of ancestral spirits. . . . Included among malevolent spirits are those who have committed suicide. Suicide, especially suicide by hanging, is considered abhorrent. That a member of the Babukusu would be so unable to cope with life is considered a judgment on the society for not caring for one of its members. . . . The entire tribal unit shares in the shame and all become the object of the curses from God and the ancestral spirits, as well as the derision of the living. . . . Curses are usually passed within families related by blood, and are thought to have great power. . . . Because of the threat of the curse, extreme measures are taken in order to deflect its power. . . . The relatives hire strangers to take the body down. These people are provided with a sheep to be used in a sacrificial ritual of cleansing from any evil influence. . . . A cow is slaughtered, but not as a gift for the dead relative as would be customary, but as an appeasement to the spirit in order to prevent trouble for the survivors. . . .

There are remarkable similarities between the biblical tradition preserved in Deuteronomy 21:22–23 and ideas concerning hanging preserved in Babukusu oral traditions. . . . For our purposes the important issue is that both first century Judaism and the Babukusu people conceive of a connection between hanging on a tree and a curse which is attached to death by hanging. . . . It stands to reason that people within both cultures would conceive of Jesus' death as cursed and, therefore, would have difficulty understanding how the crucified Jesus could be of any benefit. . . . Paul came to understand the curse of hanging on a cross as an exchange curse which was capable of bringing redemption and blessing to those who believe. The logic which Paul invokes is the logic of sacrifice: an innocent victim can represent and take the place of one who is guilty; a curse can be removed from one by being transferred to another. The some logic is at work in the popular theology of the Revival movement among the Babukusu: in dying on the cross, Jesus became the

Source: Grant LeMarquand and Eliud Wabukala, "Cursed be Everyone Who Hangs on a Tree," in Musa W. Dube and Gerald O. West, eds., *The Bible in Africa: Transactions, Trajectories and Trends* (Boston and Leiden: Brill Academic, 2001), pp. 353, 354–355, 356–357, 358.

lamb of God who takes the world's sin so that the world can go free; the curse of sin and guilt is transferred to another. This logic of an exchange curse allows Paul to view the curse of the cross as God's way of giving life to people previously living under the curse of the Torah. The same logic has allowed Babukusu Christians to sing and preach about the cross as a life-giving tree. . . . The idea of the hanged Christ has the potential to be a cause of offense to Babukusu people. The cross could have been considered a source of cursing. Instead the logic of sacrifice has allowed the cross to be for the Babukusu a sign of life and blessing.

Question

If a culture does not have, like the Babukusu, a strong acceptance of sacrifice, what sense can be made of the curse of the cross?

www　Read another social scientific cultural analysis of cursing and bewitching in Galatians.

Doing Social Scientific and Cross-Cultural Reading Yourself

1. *Reflect on the ethnic and religious implications of this well-known hypothetical puzzle: If Paul had a son (with a Jewish wife, of course), would he have him circumcised and raise him as a Jew? Give your reasons.*
2. *Examine kinship language in Galatians and how Paul uses it to persuade his readers.*
3. *Examine the language of honor and shame in Galatians. What are the main verses where Paul focusses on this?*

Feminist Reading of Galatians

The main problem in Galatians is between Jewish Christianity and Gentile Christianity, and the issue of the role of women is in the background. It comes to the foreground in 3:28, "There is no longer male and female, for all of you are one in Christ Jesus." Being drawn into kinship with Christ erases the human differences that used to divide people. Paul also draws repeatedly on feminine imagery to make his case. Paul speaks of himself as being in labor pains with the Galatians, who must come to birth again as Christians (Gal. 4:19). Even if he is employing a typical expression, Paul thinks of himself not only as a father to believers but also as a mother. In 4:21–31, Paul uses feminine imagery to describe two covenants: Hagar the slave surrogate wife of Abraham, and Sarah his main wife. He argues that believers are children of Sarah. This even-handed use of feminine imagery suggests that Paul has achieved—or is at least working toward—a more balanced view of women and men together in the church.

Feminist Reading at Work
Human Unity and Diversity in Paul's Gospel (Gal 3:28)

Pamela Eisenbaum, a Jewish feminist NT scholar, answers the question in this article's title in the negative—Paul does not oppose women, nor is he biased against Jews. As a part of her argument, she critiques the standard liberal view of Gal 3:28, questioning its implications for cross-cultural concerns.

Interpreting Gal. 3:28 has become complicated in our modern context. Modern liberal commentators, particularly those influenced by recent scholarly trends, see in Gal. 3:28 three primary categories of human classification—race, class, and gender—and understand it as a call to break down the barriers that divide and exclude people. Enacting such a call would mean the liberation of peoples of color, poor people, and women. This liberal tradition goes back at least as far as the abolitionists, but it recently has been bolstered by the work of new-perspective scholars. Many new-perspective scholars claim that the issue fundamentally pre-occupying Paul is the seemingly impenetrable boundaries human beings erect between themselves, and that Torah ("law") constitutes one of these boundaries. . . . Although I generally position myself with liberal commentators and am profoundly influenced by the new perspective in my reading of Paul, I am troubled by the inclusive reading of Gal. 3:28 . . . I imagine that most Americans would agree that the elimination of slavery and the obliteration of all master-slave distinctions between people is a social good, such that we feel no ambiguity about proclaiming "no longer slave or free" and meaning it literally. But how about "no longer male and female"? Do we feel the same unambiguous enthusiasm for collapsing those distinctions? . . .

If by "no longer male and female" we mean equal political, social, and vocational opportunity for all women and men, then perhaps we might find it easy to subscribe to the dictum. But Paul does not use the language of equality; rather, he issues a call for erasing the distinguishing marks between people (if one accepts the liberal reading). Some liberal intellectuals, many who identify themselves as feminist, believe there are essential differences between men and women, differences which may or may not be complementary but which in any case cannot be transcended. In other words, erasing the distinction between women and men is neither attainable nor desirable. Do we really want a world in which there is neither Jew nor Greek? Certainly not from a Jewish perspective! But even, I imagine, from a Christian one. It seems to me that the value of the slogan "no longer Jew or Greek" as a broad universalist claim has become compromised. While perhaps at an earlier time people desired human homogeneity, most Americans have now come to embrace multiculturalism. We recognize there are profound differences between people, and furthermore we do not lament these differences but celebrate them. But if we follow the liberal reading of Gal. 3:28, which calls for the breaking down of barriers as a precondition for liberation, then, ironically, Gal. 3:28 undermines the goal of liberation, insofar as our contemporary understanding

Source: Pamela Eisenbaum, "Is Paul the Father of Misogyny and Anti-Semitism?" *Cross-Currents* 50, 4 (Winter 2000–01): pp. 258–270.

of liberation includes an appreciation of cultural difference, rather than a desire to eradicate it.

www Follow the link to the entire fascinating article.

Questions

1. *Explain your own conclusion on the topic that Eisenbaum discusses: Is Paul a misogynist?*
2. *What exactly, in your opinion, does Paul mean by saying "There is no longer male and female in Christ?"*

> **Doing Feminist Reading Yourself**
>
> *What might the fact that circumcision, a sign Jews perform only on males, is a leading issue in Galatians do to marginalize women in this letter?*

ROMANS: Paul Explains His Gospel to an Independent Church

Put first in the canonical order of Paul's letters in part because it is his longest letter, Romans has had a large influence in Christian history, from the first century until today. Several new Christian reform movements have started with a fresh reading of Romans, and debates over it have divided Christians as well, especially in the western churches. This letter is Paul at his calmest and most reflective, writing to a church independent of him and therefore to which he is not directly responsible. Newer methods of reading are beginning to be applied to Romans—they often are applied to Galatians and 1 Corinthians first—and repay the effort of reading with new insights.

> ### Romans in Brief: Outline of Structure and Contents
>
> I. **Opening** Paul to the Romans (1:1–7)
> II. **Thanksgiving** and wish to visit the Romans (1:8–15)
> III. **Body** God makes people righteous (in a right relationship with God) by the faith of Jesus Christ (1:16–15:14)
>   A. The need of righteousness by both Gentiles and Jews (1:18–3:20)
>   B. God's establishment of righteousness by the death of Jesus, and how faith taps into this righteousness (3:21–5:11)
>   C. The working of righteousness in the Holy Spirit (5:12–8:39)
>   D. God's continuing relationship with Israel (Chapters 9–11)

E. Moral exhortation (12:1–15:13)
  1. Conduct in the church, and toward the government
     (Chapters 12–13)
  2. How "weak" and "strong" believers should relate
     (14:1–15:13)
IV. **Conclusion** Paul's travel plans, recommendation of Phoebe, greetings
    to many believers in Rome (15:14–16:27)

Developing Your Skills

Romans is a long, complicated letter. Read through it quickly in one sitting, getting as much as possible of the overall flow of the letter.

A Guide to Reading Romans

Paul opens his epistle to the Romans with the longest introduction of any of his letters (1:1–17). He greets the saints whom he has heard of but never met (1:1–7) and expresses both thanks for them and a deep desire to visit them (1:8–15).

The body of the epistle begins with what is arguably its theme, the righteousness of God established in the work of Christ and appropriated by faith (1:16–17). Paul first elaborates on the sinfulness of humanity (1:18–3:20), demonstrating the universal need of righteousness. He begins by picking what to his readers is the most obvious example: the guilt of Gentiles who do not believe. The reasons for this guilt are first mentioned: the Gentiles have suppressed the knowledge of God and prefer serving false gods, even idols and animals (1:18–23). Therefore, God has released them to the consequences of their diverse sins, of which same-sex intercourse is for Paul the main example (1:24–32). Lest the Jews think that they are any less guilty, Paul turns the tables on them, addressing them in a sharp diatribe fashion (2:1–3:8). They are more culpable than the Gentiles because they have revelation from God and are God's covenantal people (3:1–8), yet they are hypocritical about true righteousness and have refused to share God's covenant blessings with the nations. Paul concludes this first section of the letter body by citing OT scripture that "Jews and Gentiles alike are all under sin" (3:9–20).

Now that Paul has established that all people need righteousness, he demonstrates how people can become righteous (3:21–5:11). First, righteousness has been revealed through the faithfulness of Jesus Christ and has been granted to all who put their trust in him (3:21–26). Second, the basis for righteousness is faith, which is the same for all, because God is One (3:27–31). Third, Paul argues from the life of Abraham (4:1–25). In a striking reversal of ethnic and religious ideas, Abraham is the father both of the Jews and the Gentiles, of all those who are saved by faith. This is illustrated by evidence that Abraham was not justified by works (4:1–8), nor by circumcision

(4:9–12), but only by faith in the promises of God (4:18–25). So too his descendants, both physical and spiritual, are justified by faith rather than by law (4:13–17, 23–25). After discussing the faith of Abraham, Paul turns to discuss the Roman's faith in Christ (4:23–25). He then concludes the section on justification by implying its results. If one has Christ, one has peace with God now, and the Law adds nothing to salvation (5:1–2). Consequently, one has great joy in the hope of sharing the glory of God and having eternal honor in God's presence (5:3–5). Christ came at the right time and died for us, and the eschatological result is that the righteous escape God's wrath, which will punish the wicked with eternal shame (5:6–11).

Paul now discusses the *granting* of righteousness, the third major section of the letter body (5:12–8:39). He lays out his views using the twin themes of reigning and slavery. He begins by contrasting the reign of grace with the reign of sin. In 5:12–21 Paul moves to union with Christ. In an argument based on **typology,** a contrast between two individuals representing two groups, Adam was humankind's representative in sin, bringing death to all (5:12). Christ is its representative in righteousness, bringing life to all (5:18). Since believers are in Christ, and therefore they are assured of their salvation, why should they not continue sinning? Paul likely had heard this distortion of his gospel before, and he answers to this in the second portion of this section (6:1–23). First, believers should not continue in sin because of their union with Christ—union in his death and his life (6:1–14). Second, they should not continue in sin because it leads to enslavement to sin (6:15–23).

Paul now turns to the issue of *how* not to sin (7:1–8:17). Chapter 7 is notoriously difficult to interpret. Is Paul using the word *I* in an autobiographical sense? If so, is he speaking about his former life as an unbeliever, his present life as a Christian, or both? Or is he speaking figuratively—either of believers in general or unbelievers in general? Although no one can be certain and opinions on this chapter vary, Paul is probably using the perspective of believers dealing with present sin. Two reasons point to this option: first, Paul's unusual present-tense language in this section probably indicates discussion about a present situation; second, Paul does not elsewhere speak of his past experience as frustrating, but with pride and confidence in the Law (Gal 1:14; Phil 3:4–6). He begins chapter 7 by reminding believers that they are dead to the Law (Rom 7:1–6). Does this mean that the Law is bad? No, it is simply powerless over sin (7:7–13). The law does not *produce* sin; rather, it merely reveals it (7:13). The Law is good, but the "flesh"—fallen human nature as a whole, not just its physical side—is evil (7:14–25). It is powerless to obey the Law. The point of 7:7–25 is that regardless of who attempts to fight sin—believers or unbelievers—if their method is to use the Law, they will fail and achieve nothing but frustration. Focusing on the Law necessitates subjecting the flesh to it, because the Law is the handmaiden of the flesh. But since believers are dead to the Law because they are united with Christ, they are able to gain victory over the flesh (7:6, 24–25).

Paul now turns to the good news. Those who are in Christ are not only forgiven eternally by God (8:1), but also are set free from the Law that produces sin and death (8:2). Believers live correctly through the power and direction of the Spirit in them (8:1–17). The Spirit of God enables believers to gain progressive victory over sin (8:1–8), death (8:9–11), and slavery (8:12–17). The Spirit is an internal witness to the believers' hearts that God is their Father (8:14–17). Finally, Paul concludes this section by discussing the goal of **sanctification**, moral purity produced by a strong kinship connection to God (8:18–39), which brings glory in the New Age (8:28–30). This glory needs to be kept in mind especially during the present sufferings that believers face (8:18–27). But lest anyone give up, thinking that their participation in glory is in jeopardy, Paul concludes with a movingly poetic hymn of assurance: God in Christ is eternally "for us," so no other force or event "can separate us from the love of God in Christ Jesus our Lord" (8:31–39).

The fourth major section turns to an issue that would be in the back of readers' minds, especially the Jewish believers in Christ at Rome. If God is so righteous, how could God give ancient Israel and contemporary Jews unconditional promises and then seemingly reject these people? After all, if God can do this to Israel, God can do the same to believers in Christ. Although Paul's primary concern in chapters 9–11 is to vindicate God's conduct toward God's people, he prefaces his remarks by expressing his own deep anguish over Israel's unwillingness to believe in Jesus as Messiah (9:1–5). Then he details how God has dealt with Israel in the past (9:6–33). In essence, God's choice was completely gracious (9:1–29), as can be seen in Israel's very history (9:6–13), especially when we remember that God is sovereign (9:14–29). Further, they have rejected their Messiah by clinging to the Law (9:30–33). God's present dealings with Israel, then, can only be interpreted on the basis of the past (10:1–21). Once again, Paul prefaces his remarks by yearning out loud for Israel's salvation (10:1). For the present time, Jew and Gentile have equal access to God (10:1–13). Yet the Jewish people as a whole are still unrepentant even though they repeatedly heard the message (10:14–21). Will Israel persist in its disobedience, or will there come a time when they will repent? Paul answers this in chapter 11. He points out, first, that God's rejection of the nation is not complete, for God still has a remnant in the nation (11:1–10). Further, the rejection is not final; God still keeps covenants with the Jews, and they are still God's people (11:11–32). Indeed, the present "grafting in" of Gentiles not only brings salvation to Gentiles but also should arouse the jealousy of the Jews, even prompting them to seek Christ (11:11–24). Once the number of Gentiles is full, then Israel will turn back to God and "all Israel will be saved" (11:25–32). (Remember that in the social mindset of the times, "all Israel" does not necessarily mean every Jewish person, but enough Jewish people to represent the whole.) All this is a part of God's inscrutable plan for the salvation of humankind. At the end of this topic, Paul can only break out in a short hymn of praise for God's infinite wisdom (11:33–36). Romans 9–11 is something unique in the NT—a view of the Jewish people that affirms that they are still God's people and that God has a plan for them.

Now Paul turns, as he often does, to the conduct of believers in the last major section of the letter body (12:1–15:13). First, he deals with conduct among fellow believers; the way the in-group behaves is important to a healthy church. He uses sacrificial language to describe his main point: believers are to be a "living sacrifice" to God (12:1–2). Because they are living sacrifices to God, they should live sacrificially for others. Service to others should be done by the employment of spiritual gifts for the benefit of the body (12:3–8) and with an attitude of sincere love and morality for both believers and unbelievers (12:9–21). Much of Paul's language here echoes, but does not quote, the teaching of Jesus on love for enemies and non-retaliation against evil, something that would be especially relevant to believers in the city of Rome, where officials kept an especially close eye on "foreign" religious movements. Second, believers should be good citizens of the Roman state. They demonstrate God's righteousness by submitting in obedience to divinely appointed authority (13:1–7) and by loving their neighbors (13:8–10). Such action is urgent because "our salvation is nearer now than when we first believed"—that is, the Lord's return is imminent (13:11–14). Third, Paul turns in a lengthy section to the problem of freedom in Christ, and how people of different cultural and religious backgrounds can get along with each other in the church. Those believers whose faith is "strong," that is, who see themselves as free of religious obligations such as keeping Sabbath and eating only kosher food, should not judge those who are "weak," that is, those who keep obligations (14:1–15:13). Neither the weak nor the strong should condemn the other, but instead should recognize the freedom that all have in Christ (14:1–12). But his freedom should not become a stumbling block to the weak: liberty must be guided by love (14:13–23). One believer's freedoms should not cause another to sin by influencing the other to act against her/his conscience (14:23). Ultimately, the strong believer (as well as the weak) should imitate Christ in his selflessness (15:1–13), rather than use liberty only to please him/herself.

Just as Paul opens Romans with a lengthy introduction, Paul concludes his epistle as it stands today (15:14–16:27) in a lengthy way. He gives an explanation of his mission, both in general (15:17–21) and specifically with reference to the Romans (15:22–33). He hopes to visit them, give and receive encouragement, and then travel west to Spain. In chapter 16 he gives final greetings to twenty-nine people, the longest list of names for personal greetings in any of his letters. One third of these are women, and three prominent women are given special attention: Phoebe, who is likely carrying this letter (16:1–2); Prisca (Priscilla), who is named before her husband Aquila (vv. 3–4); and Junia, who is called an apostle, the only woman in the NT to be so named (v. 7). After a final exhortation to avoid dissent and work for harmony, Paul assures them of success and gives them Jesus Christ's blessing (vv. 17–20). Timothy sends his greetings, as does Tertius, the scribe for this letter (vv. 21–22). Paul also sends greetings (v. 23) from Corinth, from Gaius and Erastus the city treasurer. Paul concludes with a lengthy ascription of praise to God that happily sums up this letter (vv. 25–27).

Romulus and Remus Statue at Night Roman legend states that a Vestal Virgin conceived twin boys, Romulus and Remus, by the god Mars. Accused of breaking her vow of chastity, she was ordered to abandon her babies. Left at the Tiber, these boys were found and nursed by a she-wolf in a cave on the Palatine Hill. When the boys grew up, they decided to found a new city, which they began on the Palatine Hill c. 753 B.C.E. After eventually killing his brother Remus, Romulus founded the city of Rome, named after himself. This statue is the most common artistic expression of the origins and nature of Romans: bold, enterprising, and ferocious. The people who follow Jesus trace their origins to a different kind of story, that of a suffering savior; their symbol would become the cross. Used by permission of BiblePlaces.com.

Historical Reading of Romans

Romans in Brief: Summary of Historical Reading

Author Paul (undisputed)

Date Between 55 and 58, from Corinth; in the revisionist chronology, 51–52.

Audience Believers in the city of Rome, with a strong mixture of Jews and Gentiles.

> **Unity and Integrity** A majority sees one continuous letter, with a substantial minority arguing that chapter 16 was added later from another Pauline source.
>
> **Purpose** The "Romans debate" puts forth several options: to express Paul's "last will and testament"; to create a new base for further work in Spain; to introduce and defend his controversial message to a conservative church; and so on.

Author

Romans is everywhere today viewed as a genuine Pauline letter. In the external evidence about its author, ancient writers regularly included Romans as a Pauline document. Marcion, the Muratorian fragment, and second-century writers such as Ignatius, Polycarp, Justin Martyr, and Irenaeus all affirm its Pauline authorship. More important, the internal evidence indicates a genuine Pauline letter. Despite being written in a more systematic organization than Paul's other letters, Romans echoes the theology and style of earlier writings such as Galatians and 1 Corinthians.

Date

Romans can be dated with relative certainty to between 55 and 58. Paul states in 15:26–28 that he has just completed the raising of funds for the poor believers in Jerusalem after visiting the believers in Macedonia and Achaia. This corresponds to Acts 20:1–2, identifying the time of composition as the year after Paul left Ephesus on his third missionary journey. Fixed dates for the span of Paul's labors are few, but one of them is the summer of 51 C.E., when Gallio arrived in Corinth to serve as proconsul of Achaia. When Paul wrote Romans, the collection for the Jerusalem church seems to have been completed (Rom 15:25–28). This may indicate a date in or around 57 for the writing of the letter. Paul was in Greece when he wrote, most likely in Corinth. This is seen in two incidental comments: (1) Phoebe of neighboring Cenchrea was apparently the letter bearer (16:1–2), and (2) Gaius, who is Paul's host (16:23), was a prominent Christian leader at Corinth (1 Cor. 1:14).

Audience

Romans 1:7, 15 identify this letter as being sent to the Christians at Rome. The founding of the Roman church is shrouded in the mists of history. Although later church tradition claims that Peter founded it, this cannot be demonstrated from evidence that survives from the first century. Neither did Paul found it, making this letter the only generally accepted Pauline letter written to a non-Pauline church. The Roman Christians were predominantly Gentile, as evidenced by Paul's statements in 1:5, 12–14 and 11:13. In 49 C.E., the Emperor Claudius expelled all Jews (including Jews who believed in Jesus) from Rome, so the church there must have been exclusively Gentile until Jews started trickling back in a few years. The Roman author Suetonius explains that Claudius expelled Jews because of rioting over "Chrestus," probably "Christ." But it is likely that there was a strong Jewish element as well, suggested in Romans by the heavier-than-normal use of the OT, use of traditional Jewish Christian wording in key doctrinal statements (1:3–4; 3:21–26), and the thematic treatment of the relationship of the Jewish people to Christ (chaps. 9–11).

www See the enrichment material for Chapter 20 of this book for a discussion of Suetonius' mention of the expulsion of Jews from Rome in 49.

Unity

There has been some debate about whether Romans ended with chapter 15 (or 14) rather than with chapter 16. The reasons are, first, that even though Paul had never visited Rome, chapter 16 is filled with personal greetings. These greetings suggest to some that chapter 16 was part of a letter originally sent to Ephesus, where Paul had ministered for three years. Second, Paul greets Priscilla and Aquila (16:3), who shortly before Romans was written were in Ephesus (1 Cor 16:19). Further, when Paul wrote to Timothy, the two are again in Ephesus (2 Tim 4:19). Third, Rom 15:33 seems to be a letter conclusion ("The God of peace be with you all. Amen."). Fourth, the earliest Pauline manuscript of Romans, P[46], places the doxology of Rom 16:25–27 after 15:33. Not only this, but the doxology is found in other MSS at the end of chapter 14. Finally, Marcion's text apparently did not contain chapters 15 and 16. These five data can be variously interpreted. Some suggest that the end of a letter to Ephesus somehow has been appended to Romans and that the list of names was originally meant for Ephesus. Others have suggested, primarily from the various locations of the doxology, that Paul had published two editions of Romans—the longer one sent to the Romans, the shorter one sent out as a circular letter. Again, although this is possible, the textual evidence is against it because every known manuscript has all 16 chapters of Romans. The best conclusion is that chapter 16 belongs to Romans, and Paul may be listing as many names as possible to show his connection with the Roman church.

Purpose

The purpose of Romans is so highly argued in recent scholarship that it has come to be known as the **Romans debate** (Donfried 1991). Here are the main options for reasons Paul wrote Romans (keep in mind that there may be more than one purpose):

- To get down his theological "last will and testament." As it turns out, Romans is probably the last letter we have from Paul. But he wrote it fully expecting to continue his ministry, and probably the letter writing that went with it, in the western Mediterranean (Rom 15:28).

- To establish a new base of operations in Rome and then go west all the way to Spain (15:23–29). Since he had already proclaimed the gospel in the major centers in the east, it now seemed good to Paul to go west. Antioch had provided a base of operations in the east, and Ephesus had in Asia Minor; Paul was hoping that Rome would be his new base in the west.

- To introduce himself and his gospel to the Christian church in Rome in advance of his visit. He did not found the church in Rome, but members had heard rumors about him, so he wrote to clear up misunderstandings.

- To ask for prayers and support from Roman Christians, especially Jewish Christians there, for his journey to Jerusalem and collection for Jerusalem's impoverished church (15:25–27, 30). He does not seem to be soliciting a contribution from the Romans for his collection, but he is clearly worried that Jerusalem Christians may not welcome his collection.

- To mediate between the "strong" and the "weak" in Rome (chapters 14–15). That this topic is placed last may indicate its importance. Paul himself sides with the "strong" but urges that each side respect and cooperate with the other.

www Follow the link to the recent Lutheran-Catholic joint statement on justification, which deals extensively with Paul's theology and its meaning for Christian churches today. See also the link to a list of resources for Romans.

Social Scientific and Feminist Reading of Romans

Social scientific reading of Romans is still in its beginning stages. This is probably the result of the lack of social description in Romans compared to the other Pauline letters. Nevertheless, Romans does hold great promise for social scientific study. As an example of its potential, we could examine issues of the "strong" and the "weak" in chapters 14:1–15:13. If Paul is so concerned in Romans with difficulties between Jews and Gentiles, why does he refer to each group with loaded terms that seem to approve of one group and denigrate the other? Probably the boundaries between the "strong" and the "weak" did not fall along strictly ethnic lines of Jews and Gentiles. Though a Jew, Paul identifies himself as one of the strong. Moreover, Gentiles who had been synagogue-attending God fearers may well have continued as Christians to adhere to some aspects of the Jewish Law. The "weak" maintained what might be termed a traditional Jewish attitude towards the Law of Moses, because they continued to regard it as binding and thus condemning to those who disregarded it. The "strong," on the other hand, were like Gentiles in their disregard for the Law and held Torah observance to be of no consequence because of their faith in God. This applied especially, or perhaps exclusively, to ethnic matters that divided one people from another, such as dress, language, food, and holy days.

Paul strongly cautions the "strong" that disregard for the Law should not be interpreted as a license to sin (Rom 6:1–23). Paul's use of these social terms may have a rhetorical point: he mainly addresses himself in this section to the "strong," and his use of that honoring title should encourage the "strong" to act more generously and responsibly toward the "weak."

In the feminist reading of Romans, its topic of righteousness and faith is gender neutral and does not cause gender issues to arise as explicit topics. Women appear as a part of Paul's main thematic arguments. For example, in 1:26 Paul argues even-handedly that same-sex intercourse is morally wrong for women just as it is for men (v. 27). In 7:2–3, Paul makes an analogy of a marriage ending in the death of the husband. He compares such a marriage with obligation to the Jewish law, which ended in the death of Christ. Paul's argument assumes that the Jewish wife cannot divorce her husband. Some have argued that this assumption smacks of patriarchy, but one should keep in mind that in 1 Corinthians Paul gives Christian wives freedom to divorce unbelieving husbands. In 8:22, Paul writes, "the whole creation has been groaning in labor pains until now." In this vivid use of imagery that derives from the experience of giving birth, Paul draws on the Hebrew Bible, where birth pains can serve as a metaphor for the period of strife and travail that ushers in a new age (Isa 13:8; Jer 4:31). In 9:10 Paul mentions Rebecca as the wife of Isaac. The most notable gender topic appears in chapter 16, where about one-third of the personal greetings involve women, some of them socially or religiously prominent: Phoebe the deacon and patron, Prisca/Priscilla the missionary, and Junia the apostle.

Social Scientific and Feminist Reading at Work
Phoebe as Patron (Rom 16:1–2)

The patron-client relationship was an important feature of the ancient Mediterranean world. In Rom 16:1–2, Paul commends Phoebe to the Romans, urging them to accept and help her in her work, perhaps among them on Paul's behalf. Phoebe may carry Paul's letter to the Romans, a symbol of her status.

Paul commends Phoebe to the Christians in Rome at the conclusion of his letter to them and provides, in two brief verses, just enough information to indicate her significant role in the early church. . . . If the purpose of Phoebe's trip to Rome is not specifically stated, her status in her home church is somewhat clearer. She is identified as a *diakonos* [dee-AH-kuh-noss, deacon] of the church of Cenchreae,

Source: Jouette M. Bassler, "Phoebe," in Carol Meyers, ed., *Women in Scripture*, pp. 134-135. Copyright © 2000 by Houghton Mifflin Company. Reproduced by permission of Houghton Mifflin Company. All rights reserved.

the eastern port of Corinth. . . . It is the same title (with no gender distinctions) that Paul applies to himself and to others engaged in a ministry of preaching and teaching (1 Cor 3:5; 2 Cor 6:4; Phil 1:1). The way the title is introduced suggests a recognized office, though doubtless not as well defined as it later became in the church (1 Tim 3:8–13). Phoebe is thus a church official, a minister of the church of Cenchreae.

She is also described as a *prostasis* [proh-STAH-sis], the feminine form of a noun that can denote a position as leader, president, presiding officer, guardian, or patron. . . . Because she is presented as *prostasis* "of many and of myself as well" (v. 2), and not specifically *prostasis* of the church, the emphasis is probably on her role as patron or benefactor, though the title also reinforces the concept of authority conveyed by her position as deacon. As a patron she would, of course, have provided funds for the church and probably publicly represented it when necessary. She would also have used her influence—derived from her wealth and social standing—to resolve any difficulties that might arise for the congregation. Paul himself is personally indebted to her in some way (that is, he is her "client"), and he asks the Roman church to help him repay that debt by providing her with a generous welcome and whatever support she requires.

Paul thus recommends Phoebe as his coworker, as a leader of an established church, and as a generous benefactor of many Christians. She is obviously an independent woman (she is not defined in terms of husband, father or family) of considerable means. . . . Paul's acknowledgment of her in this letter is brief, but it offers a tantalizing glimpse of the leadership of women in early Christianity.

Questions

1. *How does this reading combine feminist and social scientific methods?*

2. *Patrons were usually tied to the social networks in their home areas. What do you think that Phoebe might want to do as a patron in Rome?*

Doing Social Scientific and Feminist Reading Yourself

1. *Read Paul's presentation of the Adam-Christ typology in Rom 5:12–21. What might it mean for feminist criticism that the two representatives of humankind are male?*

2. *Read one section of Romans quickly using the honor-shame paradigm. What main issues emerge for you as important?*

 Follow a link to a succinct outline on the social aspects of the Pauline churches.

Cross-Cultural Reading of Romans

Romans, like Galatians, deals with the broad issues of Jews and Gentiles. Because we today often have a truncated idea of religion, confining it to individual matters of personal choice, it is sometimes hard to understand that "Jews" and "Gentiles" are cultural, ethnic terms as well as religious designations. Romans deals with all aspects of "Jews" and "Gentiles" as it sorts out how both groups need salvation in Christ (chapters 1–2), how the salvation of Christ reaches both on the basis of faith (3–8), how the unbelieving Jews still belong to God and God's plan (9–11), and how Jews and Gentiles can obey God and get along together in the church (12–15). Moreover, Paul assumes the validity of both Jewish and Gentile Christianity. As we discussed earlier, in Galatians Paul seems to be so harsh toward Jewish Christianity that he all but rules it out as a valid religion. Judging by what he says here in Romans, Paul believes that Jewish Christianity is indeed appropriate and expected for Jews. He affirms cultural diversity in the church, even as he realizes that it is no easy thing to maintain. The cultural diversity affirmed in Romans has made it a favorite letter for peoples of various cultures today to examine. The readings presented here and on the website provide two examples of how this is carried out.

Cross-Cultural Reading at Work
Torah and Spirit in Chinese Perspective (Romans 8)

What is the relationship of Jewish Law and teaching to the teachings of other cultures, especially to Christians in those cultures? In this reading, a leading Chinese NT scholar discusses this relationship in terms of Torah and Spirit.

The Pauline discussion of Torah and Spirit in terms of Pharisaic and Christian perspectives for both Jewish and Gentile audiences is a cross-cultural endeavor. The law of the Spirit ushers in a divine energy for the cross-cultural enterprise, and the Christ event provides a hermeneutical paradigm for the Chinese-Pauline interaction . . .

Confucius wants to preserve the traditional value and culture of knowing and doing the T'ien Ming; on the other hand, he wants each person to be renewed by the power of that mandate which had been long established by the sages in past dynasties . . . What Confucius is doing here is transferring the *Ming* of T'ien ("mandate of Heaven") from a highly political claim of the ruling family to a universally appropriated claim for all. That is, Confucius seeks to popularize that same mandate of Heaven so that everyone can cultivate selfhood and attain the wholeness of life.

Confucius could not have been a mere transmitter of tradition in its outer form, for that would never have sustained and forged a way of life which has exerted its influence on the Chinese society for the last two millennia—and likely for more to come. . . . What Confucius intended was to reinterpret his ancestral tradition in light of its meanings and moral principles for the sake of creative and lively appropriation.

Paul, too, is interested in reinterpreting tradition. In Romans, Paul is not seeking to eliminate the Torah. In fact, he affirms that the Torah is holy and good. But Paul's interpretation of the Torah in the light of the Spirit and the Christ event in Romans 7–8 does not merely accept the Torah as it is. Certainly, his view of Torah is not the same as that of his contemporary Jewish friends. More important, the age of the Spirit and *T'ien* compels one not to absolutize his beliefs (culturally or religiously) and to create an idol of them, but to examine the truth afresh always as the creative One reveals and intervenes in the eschatological moment.

Question

Explain in your own words how this passage illustrates the importance of reading communities as they encounter the NT from their own cultural perspective. What are the strengths and weaknesses of such an approach?

www See the website for another cross-cultural reading of Romans, on cross-cultural reading in North American ethnic minority communities.

> **Doing Cross-Cultural Criticism Yourself**
>
> *Read and respond to a Jewish reflection on Romans 7:10 linked at the website.*

Key Terms and Concepts

catalogues of vice and virtue • circular letter • justification by faith
law-free gospel • new perspective on Paul • North Galatian hypothesis
Romans debate • South Galatian hypothesis • strong/weak in faith
typology

Questions for Study, Discussion, and Writing

Galatians

1. Mark Nanos has argued recently that the situation of Galatians does not involve Jewish-Christian missionaries from Judea, but rather local Jewish "influencers" who sought to bring Paul's Gentile believers into their own synagogues as honored proselytes. Using your knowledge of Galatians, offer a critique of his thesis.

2. Why does the situation of the Galatians make Paul's moral-exhortation section in chaps. 5 and 6 even more important than what it usually is?
3. Examine all the possible evidence on the question, "Was Galatians successful in bringing the Galatians back to Paul's way?" Give and defend your answer to this question.
4. Some commentators have taken to using the phrase "Christian Jews" instead of "Jewish Christians." What do you see as the difference between these terms?

Romans

1. What is your own position on the Romans debate, and why?
2. What is Paul's analysis of the human condition in chapters 1–2? Explain how Paul's analysis of sin comes from his experience of salvation.
3. Imagine yourself as a member of the Roman church when this letter was read out loud for the first time. Would you have trouble following it? What would your main impression be?
4. What is your own position on the identity of the *I* of chapter 7?
5. Explain in your own words what the idea of justification means in Romans.
6. Read Romans 13 carefully and discuss how the experience of Roman Jewish Christians in the expulsion of 49 C.E. may be addressed here. Is it possible that Paul counsels believers not to spread the faith in ways that provoke riots?

For Further Reading

Galatians

Barclay, J. M. G. *Obeying the Truth: Paul's Ethics in Galatians*. Minneapolis: Fortress, 1991. Good treatment of a neglected topic.

Kern, Philip. *Rhetoric and Galatians: Assessing an Approach to Paul's Epistle*. Cambridge: Cambridge University Press, 1998. A thorough challenge to the interpretation of Galatians in light of Greco-Roman rhetorical handbooks.

Koperski, Veronica. *What Are They Saying about Paul and the Law?* Mahwah, NJ: Paulist Press, 2001. Student-friendly discussion of current interpretation of Paul's views on Law and faith.

Martyn, J. Louis. *Galatians*. Anchor Bible Commentary. Garden City, NY: Doubleday, 1997. An excellent commentary treating Paul from an apocalyptic viewpoint.

Nanos, Mark. *The Irony of Galatians*. Minneapolis: Augsburg-Fortress, 2002. Nanos, a Jewish scholar of the NT, offers an intra-Jewish reading, exploring several social scientific dimensions.

Matera, Frank. "Galatians in Perspective: Cutting a New Path through Old Territory," *Interpretation* (July 2000): 233–245. The "new perspective" on Paul as applied to Galatians, in a well-written article.

Romans

Carter, T. L. *Paul and the Power of Sin: Redefining "Beyond the Pale."* Cambridge: Cambridge University Press, 2002. Seeks to ground Paul's language of sin in its sociocultural context, with especially good treatment of Romans.

Donfried, Karl P. *The Romans Debate*, rev. ed. Peabody, MA: Hendrickson, 1991. Excellent essays on issues pertaining to the purpose of Romans.

Dunn, James D. G. *The Theology of Paul the Apostle*. Grand Rapids, MI: Eerdmans, 1998. An excellent in-depth treatment of Paul's "theology" using the outline of Romans as an organizational pattern.

Fitzmyer, Joseph A. *Romans*. Anchor Bible 33. New York: Doubleday, 1993. Perhaps the best single-volume commentary on Romans accessible to beginning students.

Heil, J. P. *Paul's Letter to the Romans: A Reader-Response Commentary*. New York: Paulist, 1987. Treats both historical and contemporary reader response criticism.

Chapter Fourteen

Philippians and Philemon: Two Letters from Prison

Letters from an author in prison hold a valued place in Western culture. The isolation and suffering endured by prisoners often seems to make their words more poignant and powerful. In the twentieth century, Martin Luther King, Jr.'s "Letter from a Birmingham Jail" penetrated the conscience of American southerners at the beginning of the civil rights movement, and Dietrich Bonhoeffer's letters and essays from prison helped to steady Christian resistance to the Third Reich at the end of World War II.

Paul's two letters from prison (from his undisputed letters) also are valuable for that reason. He writes Philippians as one suffering imprisonment, and his readers are acutely aware of the threat his imprisonment poses to him, and also to them if their leader should be put to death. His letter to Philemon also commends the slave Onesimus to his master Philemon, asking Philemon to receive him back mercifully.

PHILIPPIANS: Joy in the Lord

Paul's letter to the Philippians is his happiest and most positive letter, although he wrote it from prison and was facing possible execution. Even though he warns against people who he contends are preaching a false Christian message, such people are not yet present in the Philippian church, and Paul seems to think that they can be warded off. A careful reading of Philippians reveals Paul's own struggles and his ongoing relationship with this key church.

Philippians in Brief: Outline of Structure and Content

I. **Opening** Paul to the Philippian church, blessing (1:1–2)
II. **Thanksgiving** Paul's gratitude to God for the Philippians' partnership with him (1:3–11)
III. **Body** (1:12–4:9)
    A. Paul's present imprisonment and positive attitude to his possible death (1:12–26)

      B. Various commands for living faithfully based on Christ's example of humble love (1:27–2:16)

      C. Renewed statement of concern for Philippians, and sending of Epaphroditus (2:17–3:1)

      D. Warning against Jewish-Christian teachers (3:1–4:1)

      E. Final exhortations, especially to Euodia and Syntyche (4:2–9)

    IV. **Conclusion**

      A. Thanks for the Philippians' gift (4:10–20)

      B. Final greetings and blessing (4:21–23)

Developing Your Skills

In Philippians, as in I Thessalonians, Paul's thought shifts back and forth from topic to topic. Go through the letter quickly to get an initial impression of the contents, then turn to the Guide to Reading section.

A Guide to Reading Philippians

Paul and Timothy greet the saints and their leaders, the **bishops** (administrative overseers) and **deacons** (ministerial assistants) at Philippi. Paul blesses them with grace and peace (1:1–2). He continues with his customary thanksgiving (1:3–11), here the longest of his undisputed letters. First, he thanks God for the Philippians' participation with him in the gospel and expresses confidence in their continued perseverance in the faith. God is at work in their hearts, and will bring this work to completion by "the day of Christ," i.e., when he returns in glory (1:3–8). Then he prays that they will grow in a discerning love; this perhaps foreshadows his discussion of the opponents in chapter 3 (1:9–10). He ends his prayer with another expression of confidence of their continued growth until the return of Christ (1:11).

    The apostle now turns to his own circumstances, about which the Philippians had been anxious (1:12–26). First, Paul boldly states that his circumstances have advanced the gospel (1:12). He is obviously more concerned about the gospel than about his own life, and thus he illustrates the effect that the gospel has had on him and should be having on the readers/listeners. The **praetorian** (imperial) **guard** has heard Paul's good news (1:13) and many have responded (cf. 4:22), and other evangelists have been emboldened by Paul's continued effectiveness in spreading the message of Christ even while under arrest (1:14). Although some brothers have rightly gained courage in their preaching (1:15, 16), others preach Christ for the wrong reasons (1:15, 17). The mention of this latter group prepares the listeners/readers for Paul's attack on more serious misrepresentation of Christ later in the letter, in chapter 3.

What is Paul's attitude toward all this? First, Paul is pleased that the gospel is being proclaimed, regardless of the motive (1:18). Second, he longs to be with Christ, his reason for living and dying. He is torn between living and dying; dying would bring him into the presence of Christ, but living would mean that he could continue his ministry for the Philippians (1:19–23). Paul wrestles with himself briefly over this point but quickly comes to the conclusion that he will indeed live and see the Philippians again (1:19–26). In this personal reflection, Paul not only renews and reinforces his relationship with the Philippians, but he also provides a moral model for what he will stress later in the letter: the way of following Christ is the way of giving up one's personal preferences in order to serve others.

The heart of the epistle is 1:27–2:30, where Paul instructs the Philippian believers in their Christian life. First, Paul draws on the political background of Philippi as a free city and encourages the believers to live boldly as free citizens of heaven (1:27–30). In a city where so many patriotically revere Caesar as their lord, Paul points them to serving Jesus as the real Lord. Such bold living in the face of (imminent?) opposition will be a sign to their opponents that God is with believers and that opposing them is misguided. Second, the apostle exhorts them to live humbly as servants of Christ (2:1–11). He appeals to them on the basis of membership in the body of Christ (2:1–4), reminding them that selfishness hurts everyone.

Then he weaves an early Christian hymn (which they perhaps know and had used in worship) into the fabric of his argument. The "Christ hymn" (2:6–11) functions as a reminder for them to follow in the steps of Christ. If he who was in the "form of God" could humble himself to be like others and take on the shameful death of the cross, what right do believers have to refrain from doing the same thing? Further, after Christ "emptied himself" (by adding humanity, 2:6–8) God exalted him (2:9–11). The implication is that God will also exalt ("honor") believers who humble themselves (take on "shame"). This Christ hymn is one of the earliest poetic statements of the significance of Jesus Christ. The traditional interpretation, which most still hold to, is that "equal to God" refers to Christ's preexistence and that "he emptied himself" to the status of a slave refers to incarnation and death. This would give the hymn two stanzas, the first tracing Christ's movement from a position of exalted honor, to his time on earth being human, to death and burial—in other words, from heaven to under the earth (2:6–8). The second stanza would be the reversal, from under the earth by resurrection to heaven, there to be recognized and worshiped as Lord. A more recent interpretation is that the equal status with God refers to the immortality God originally gave to humanity that was lost when sin led to death. This immortality belonged to the sinless Christ, who nevertheless emptied himself and became a "slave" in his death on the cross and regained immortality for those who belong to him in his resurrection and exaltation to heaven. This second interpretation does not posit preexistence. Whatever view is adopted, the use to which Philippians puts this hymn—serving others in humble love—is the same.

Paul next skillfully weaves this principle of self-emptying into 2:12–30. In 2:12–18 he exhorts believers to live obediently as children of God. As is typical of Paul in his moral exhortations, he first states the **indicative**—"God is at work in you" (2:12–13)—then gives the **imperative,** the effect it should have on believers, that they should be blameless and pure (2:14–18). Paul encourages them here to obey and not to complain or grumble (2:14). Then he tries to cushion a blow: their beloved Timothy cannot return as they wanted and expected, but Epaphroditus can (2:19–30). The command to uncomplaining obedience between the hymn to Christ and the news about Timothy and Epaphroditus is well positioned. Paul does not want them to grumble about Epaphroditus' return and Timothy's staying with Paul, but to recognize that both men are following Christ's example of humble service by giving up their personal preferences. A further implication seems to be that just as God has highly exalted Christ, so also the Philippians should honor Epaphroditus for his sacrificial, life-risking service: "honor people like him" (2:29–30). Paul closes this section with a renewed mention of joy: "Finally, my brothers and sisters, rejoice in the Lord."

Then the tone changes as Paul instructs the Philippians about an impending visit of Jewish-Christian missionaries who will urge them to be circumcised and keep the Law of Moses. Paul first warns of these opponents (3:1–4a), then presents his own story as an example against them (3:4b–14), and finally issues moral exhortations based on this example (3:15–4:1). Paul attacks his Jewish-Christian opponents, not because they were present in Philippi, as they had been in Corinth, Galatia, and possibly Rome, but because he had gotten wind of their possible visit to Philippi. Perhaps Epaphroditus had brought news of them, or else (and this is less likely) Paul was simply making a kind of preemptive strike against them. Paul first insults them with invective: they are "dogs," "workers of evil," and "mutilators of the flesh" (3:2). (Some houses of the time had mosaic floors in the entryway depicting a fierce dog with the saying Paul uses here, "Beware of the dog.") He claims that his Gentile-Christian audience is the true circumcised people because they serve in the Spirit and do not put confidence in human marks made in the flesh (3:3). Paul then points out that he would have a greater claim to boast in the flesh than his opponents since he had impeccable Jewish credentials and had kept the Law of Moses "blamelessly" (3:4–6). Yet Paul does not boast; in fact, he says that he has given up all this for the sake of knowing Christ, considering all the value of his past life as mere "rubbish" (3:8). The term rendered as "rubbish" in the NRSV is a crude Greek word that can also be translated "excrement"; the French NT scholar Ceslaus Spicq argues that a good translation would be "It's all crap" (Danker 2000, 932). The basis of Paul's righteousness is not his accomplishments in Judaism but comes "through the faith of/in Christ," a common Pauline phrase understood today either as the faithfulness of Christ to God or human faith in Christ as Savior (3:9). Paul's goal is to participate in the power of Christ's resurrection even as he now participates in Christ's death (3:10–11). Paul then compares the Christian life to a footrace. It involves forgetting the past, always pressing on to the goal of maturity and the heavenly call.

To finish his polemics, Paul offers himself as an example of proper conduct (3:17–4:1). Once again he speaks first about his own conduct, then about that of his opponents, a pattern already seen in 1:12–26 and 1:27–4:1. Although their conduct is shamefully set on "earthly things," Paul reminds the Philippians that their citizenship is in heaven and that Jesus will return from heaven to transform their human bodies into a body like his, fit for heavenly glory. Paul urges the Philippians to stand firm in Lord.

Paul now ends the body of the letter with three exhortations and a note of thanks. He exhorts them, and Euodia and Syntyche especially, to get along with each other (4:2–3). What these two women's problem was, Paul does not have to say, but he urges a "loyal companion" to assist them in mending their rift. He also urges the Philippians to rejoice over God's provision without being anxious (4:4–7) and to think and act about honorable things (4:8–9). Then he thanks them once again for their sacrificial monetary help in his ministry (4:10–20). Philippians was the only church from which Paul was willing to take money for himself (as opposed to money for the Jerusalem relief fund). In this note of thanks, Paul expresses his own contentment in God's provisions (4:10–13). Here Paul's language parallels the Stoic idea of "self-sufficiency": he is free to enjoy what he has, but not in such a way that he suffers if he loses it. Paul may be tactfully releasing them from further obligation, since their generous giving had apparently caused hardship to them (4:14–18). Then to relieve their consciences about God's provision—especially if they had to stop helping Paul—Paul gives them the assurance that God provides for all believers' needs (4:19–20). The wording of this passage is difficult at points, but the overall message is clear.

Paul closes the letter with final greetings from the "saints" (believers), "especially those of the emperor's household." This reminds the Philippians that Paul and his gospel are making headway in the upper reaches of Roman society. Paul gives them a simple blessing, that the grace of the Lord Jesus Christ be with them (4:21–23).

Historical Reading of Philippians

Philippians in Brief: Summary of Historical Reading

Author Paul (almost unanimously undisputed), in prison (1:7, 12–14, 17, 19; 2:17).

Date If from Rome, which is most likely, 61–63; if from Ephesus, about 56; if from Caesarea, 58–60.

Audience Believers in Paul's church in Philippi in Macedonia (northern Greece), mostly Gentiles.

Unity Most scholars today hold it to be one letter; a strong minority holds that two letters were joined (1:1–3:1a; 3:1b–4:23).

Integrity No later additions to the letter are generally accepted today.

Purpose To build the faith and life of the Philippian church in the face of Paul's imprisonment, their persecution, and possible future Jewish-Christian incursions.

Author

Philippians enjoys virtually full acceptance as an authentic Pauline letter. Apart from some radical skepticism in the nineteenth century, its status has been unassailed. The external evidence is quite strong, beginning in the early second century with Ignatius, who alludes to 4:13 and other places. Polycarp refers to Paul's letter to the Philippians in chapter 3 of his own letter, which is written a half-century later to the same church. Irenaeus toward the end of the second century quotes from every chapter and calls Philippians a Pauline letter. Internally, it is authentically Pauline in style and content; Paul's personality and beliefs come through clearly.

Paul was in prison when he wrote this letter (1:7, 13, 16), but where? Until modern times, a Roman imprisonment at the end of Paul's life was almost universally accepted. But in the last two centuries, Paul's earlier imprisonments in Ephesus and Caesarea have become rivals to the traditional view.

The most substantive argument for Ephesus revolves around the issue of its proximity to Philippi. Since several letters went between Paul and the Philippians while he was in prison, and since Rome was so far away, there may not have been enough time for such correspondence during a Roman imprisonment. If Paul were in prison in Ephesus, there would be no problem with the number of communications. Two arguments weigh against Ephesus as the point of origin. First, Acts records no Ephesian imprisonment. Many scholars consider the silence of Acts to be decisive against this view. But Luke is sometimes selective, and to judge from Paul's own words, he was imprisoned more times than Luke records (cf. 2 Cor 6:5; 11:23). Second, there is no evidence of a praetorian guard in Ephesus during Paul's day (cf. Phil 1:13). Therefore, although Ephesus is *possible* as the city of Paul's imprisonment while he wrote Philippians, it is not plausible.

Some scholars, especially in light of the weaknesses of the Ephesian hypothesis, have proposed a Caesarean imprisonment. There was an imperial palace at Caesarea, and the mention of the praetorian guard in Phil 1:13 may be referring to this location. Moreover, Acts records Paul as in prison in Caesarea for two years. Still, there is nothing to commend this view over the traditional Roman one, and there is much evidence against it. Philippians gives indication that Paul's trial for his life is going on. This could apply only to a trial from which no appeal could be made, thus not to the Caesarean imprisonment, during which Paul appealed to Caesar. Also, the trial seems in Philippians to be nearing its completion. Further, Paul expects to be set free: he expresses strong conviction that he "shall remain and continue with you all" (1:25; cf. also 2:24). This refers best to the Roman imprisonment, for Acts shows that toward the end of Paul's Caesarean imprisonment he appealed to Caesar and would stay in custody (Acts 25:11). These two reasons seem decisive against a Caesarean imprisonment. Since the external evidence in Acts makes Rome the best choice, and since the internal evidence can harmonize with Rome as well as any place else, this tradition must still be given preference.

www Follow the link to read the witness to Philippians in Polycarp.

Date

Since we have placed the writing of this epistle within Paul's Roman imprisonment, it can be dated during his stay there in 61–64 C.E. If it was written from his imprisonment in Ephesus, it would be dated in the mid-50s; if it comes from his two-year imprisonment in Caesarea before he was transported to Rome, about 58–60.

Audience

This letter was written to the church that Paul founded at Philippi, the first (Pauline) church of Europe, although neither Paul nor Acts makes a great point of this. Philippi was a leading city on the Via Egnatia, the main trade route of the area. It was founded as a Roman colonia and had a large number of retired Roman army personnel in it. To judge from Acts, although there was a Jewish presence there, it was very much in the minority (Acts 16:13–14). Most of the congregation was Gentile, to judge from the letter itself.

Unity

Many commentators regard 3:1b as part of a different letter that Paul sent to the Philippians, probably earlier than 1:1–3:1a. Four arguments are advanced for this fragmentary view.

- The angry tone of chapter 3 is different from the joyous tone that precedes it, indicating that this material may be from a different letter.
- 3:1 begins with "finally," but Paul goes on for two chapters.
- Why would Paul wait until the end of his letter (4:10–20) to thank the Philippians for their generous gift?
- Polycarp in his *Letter to the Philippians* 3:2, 11:3 speaks of Paul's "letters" to the Philippians, not "letter."

In response, these arguments do not seem persuasive to most readers.

Philippi Public Latrines This latrine in the city center dates to the second century C.E.; once seating 42 people, it is one of the best-preserved in all of Greece. Water ran through the system to flush out the wastes. Roman-Hellenistic social mores made this shared latrine possible, but Semitic society shunned such exposure. Paul makes a striking reference to Greek *skubalon* ("rubbish, waste, excrement") in Phil 3:7–10, where he compares his old life outside Christ to this waste. Used by permission of BiblePlaces.com.

- Paul's tone does change in his other undisputed letters, but this is not a certain sign of a different document. Besides, Paul is not angry with the Philippians, but rather with Jewish-Christian missionaries.
- "Finally" in Paul's letters can signal its end (as in 2 Cor 13:11), but it also can signal that the last main issue in the letter body has begun, not the end of a letter as a whole (1 Thess 4:1). It could also refer to the final question that Epaphroditus raised, on how to deal with the Jewish-Christian missionaries.
- Paul alludes to the Philippians' gift in 1:5–7, and to finish the letter with a warm note of thanks would thus form an **inclusion** and also be literarily appropriate.
- Polycarp's use of the plural could be a citation from 2 Thess. 1:4, used as if the Philippians were addressed in that epistle. This would support the suggestion that in Polycarp's collection the Macedonian epistles to the Thessalonians and Philippians were united.

Furthermore, two other arguments weigh against this fragmentary theory. First, no textual evidence supports it. In particular, P[46] (c. 200 C.E.)—our earliest manuscript of the Pauline corpus—has Philippians intact. Second, several striking parallels tie together the two halves of this epistle, such as the self-emptying of Christ in 2:6–11 and the self-emptying of Paul in 3:4–14. This could be the result of skillful editing, but it is more likely to indicate a unified letter. Rarely are Christian copyists as skilled as the writers they edit, especially writers such as Paul! In sum, the fragmentary theory, as appealing as it is to some, fails to convince most scholars today.

Purpose

As we can see from its contents, this letter has several purposes. First, it is designed to reassure the Philippians that Paul's imprisonment is about to end. Second, it is a response to the various questions and problems that Epaphroditus brought back to Paul from his visit there, including issues of quarrelsomeness, selfishness, and especially Jewish-Christian opposition to Paul's gospel. Third, the letter is a diplomatic reintroduction of Epaphroditus in light of the Philippians' hope that Timothy would be sent. Finally, it is a "thank you" to the Philippians for their most recent gift, with a reminder that God will take care of Paul and them.

www   Follow the link to an article on the historical background and antecedent of the Philippians hymn.

We should say a bit more here about Paul's potential Jewish-Christian opposition in Philippi. Paul mentions his opponents in 1:15–17; 1:27–28; 3:2; and 3:18–19. Although some would like to believe that all these texts refer to the same group of opponents, others see four distinct groups. One of the overlooked items in this discussion is the *location* of the opponents: some are in Rome, others are in Philippi. It seems quite clear the group in 1:15–17 is true believers in *Rome* who are merely jealous of Paul's success, for he does not condemn the message, just their motives. In the other passages (except, perhaps, 3:18–19), the enemies are all in *Philippi*. In 1:27–28, Paul is responding to opponents in Philippi, though the reference is quite vague. They are certainly outsiders, but they could be Gentiles or Jews. Further, there is no hint about whether they ever were part of the church or are now attempting to infiltrate it. Very little more than this can be said. In 3:2 Jewish-Christian missionaries are the opponents in view, while in 3:18–19 it seems that Gentiles are the opponents—that is, those who had been part of the church but had defected. In short, there is at least one group in Philippi (Jewish-Christian missionaries), which is attacking (or about to attack) the church.

> ### Philippians in Brief: Summary of New Readings
>
> **Social Scientific** Paul writes to a predominantly Gentile Christian church who are confessing Christ as Lord in a city where many retired Roman army personnel and their families believe Caesar to be the only Lord and benefactor. Other social scientific dynamics at play are honor and shame in the imprisonment of Paul; the impending arrival of Jewish Christian missionaries can potentially raise social and religious boundary issues.
>
> **Feminist** As in Paul's other generally accepted authentic letters, here women have a good standing alongside men. Their status is not compromised by the fact that the only explicit mention of women is Paul's attempt to mediate in the spat between Euodia and Syntyche, whom he praises as valuable workers.
>
> **Cross-Cultural** The chief cross-cultural issue is the call to follow Christ as Lord in a city made up predominantly of Roman citizens, unusual outside Italy. This leads to suffering for Christ, but a firmer commitment to citizenship in heaven.

Social Scientific Reading of Philippians

The prominent "brother and sister" language of Philippians invites us to consider its social scientific meaning. Our mainstream North American system emphasizes the nuclear family to the exclusion of remoter family or kin. The nuclear family is a small, compact group of two generations, parents and their children, brought together by ties of diffuse loyalty and by parents' care of the young until they reach maturity and can repeat for themselves the process of family rearing. In this system, there are no intricate economic, political, or religious ties based on kinship; no ancestor worship or even veneration; and no formal connection with remoter kin.

In the first-century Mediterranean world, the tightest unit of diffuse loyalty is brothers and sisters. Their spouses enter the kin as strangers and always remain somewhat so. The affection we today expect of the husband and wife relationship was normally not a part of the husband-wife relationship in the Mediterranean world, but rather a mark of brother-sister and mother-son relationships. The kin group frequently shares economic, political, and religious ties, with an awareness of and formal connection with remoter kin. This last point is illustrated by Paul's awareness of his being "of the people of Israel, of the tribe of Benjamin, a Hebrew born of Hebrews; as to the law a Pharisee" (Phil 3:5). In this system, close relatives concealed each other's offenses and shortcomings from the outside and worked to protect family honor. For Paul to give up this social system in favor of his "fictive kin," his "brothers and sisters" in the church, is a sacrifice indeed.

Social Scientific Reading at Work
Paul Thanks the Philippians for Their Gift (4:10–20)

The end of Philippians has always puzzled interpreters. Why does Paul speak so convolutedly and apologetically about their monetary gift to him? A. W. Peterman answers this question by pointing to a little-known rhetorical convention of thanking people in writing for an unexpected gift.

In our study we shall use the term social reciprocity to refer to a convention that operates in the interpersonal relationships of some societies. Speaking generally, this convention dictates that when a person . . . is the recipient of good in the form of a favour or a gift, the receiver is obligated to respond to the giver with goodwill and to return a counter-gift or favour in proportion to the good received . . . .

It has long been known among classicists that social reciprocity operated at many levels of Greek and Roman society. . . . [I]n ancient societies, there is an economic element in every social relationship and a social element in every economic relationship.

In view of the reciprocal character of gift and service relationships in the Greco-Roman world, perhaps we should now ask to what extent an expression of verbal gratitude would be consistent with Paul's purpose in Philippians. It is commonly asserted that Paul mixes his appreciation for the gift with statements of independence. Must these statements be understood as displaying Paul's embarrassment over money matters, as some scholars contend? Rather, should not these statements at least in part be understood as reflecting Paul's desire to avoid the assumption that he has contracted a personal social obligation by accepting this gift? Instead of an expression of debt or of his intention to repay, the apostle relates his personal reflection, gives moral commendation and offers a theological interpretation of the gift. From this it should be clear that the purpose of Phil 4:10–20 is not simply to offer a personal response to financial support, but rather to offer instruction on the place of such sharing in the life of the Christian community . . .

In the light of Greco-Roman social expectations, Paul's response takes on fresh meaning. In each point of his response the apostle corrects a possible Greco-Roman understanding of it. The Philippians stand alongside the apostle as those suffering and working for the defense and confirmation of the gospel (1:7). Paul has not become socially obligated, and thereby he has accepted their gifts, they have been elevated to the place of partners in the gospel. Though Paul is in receipt of their gift and can mention his own benefit from it (4:18a), in 4:17b he rather makes it appear that they are actually the ones benefited. Their gift does bring them a return. It is an investment that reaps spiritual dividends. But ultimately the responsibility to reward them rests not with Paul, but with God (4:19).

Source: A. W. Peterman, *Paul's Gift from Philippi* (Cambridge: Cambridge University Press, 1997), 3, 4–5, 158, 159.

www   Examine a fascinating reader-response treatment of Philippians that puts you in the minds of two members of this church as the letter is read aloud to the congregation.

Feminist Reading of Philippians

The issues Paul addresses in Philippians are not gender related. As far as we can tell, Paul's approach to the women in this audience is generally encouraging and liberating. The main points of the letter are addressed to them just as much as to the men. Women are quite possibly among the "bishops and deacons" addressed in 1:1. This positive approach is not compromised by the fact that the only explicit mention of women is Paul's attempt to mediate between Euodia and Syntyche; he praises them as valuable workers, which is more than simple rhetoric. The implication that their difficulty is having a significant impact on the church may also imply that they are notable women in the congregation.

Feminist Reading at Work
On Euodia and Syntyche (Phil 4:2–3)

In this reading D'Angelo teases out the elusive meaning of these two women's experiences in Philippi.

Euodia was a coworker of both Paul and another woman named Syntyche; they are described in 4:3 as "having struggled beside me . . . with Clement and the rest of my coworkers." The athletic image ("struggled" or "co-contested") portrays their earlier missionary endeavors with Paul in a heroic vein. . . .

In Phil 4:2, Paul formally appeals to the two women "to be of the same mind in the Lord"; the usual interpretation depicts the two women in conflict with each other, and, because of their status as leaders in the community, causing dissention. . . . But when Paul asks the Corinthians to be of the same mind, he means the same mind with him (1:10; compare 4:14–21). The estrangement may thus have been between the two women and Paul; his complaints about preachers who proclaim Christ out of rivalry (1:15) and his elaborate appeal for agreement (2:1–11) and obedience (2:12) may have been directed to or against them.

Euodia and Syntyche may have functioned as a missionary couple; Romans 16 includes a pair of missionary women, Trypheana and Tryphosa (16:12), as well as female-male pairs (16:3–5, 7, 16), whose partnerships may reflect commitments to each other as well as to the mission. Perhaps Euodia and Syntyche belong on a "lesbian continuum," a prehistory of women's same-sex commitments.

Source: Mary Rose D'Angelo, "Euodia," in Carol Meyers, ed., *Women in Scripture*, p. 79. Copyright © 2000 by Houghton Mifflin Company. Reproduced by permission of Houghton Mifflin Company. All rights reserved.

Questions

1. *Give your own critique of the conclusions that the author of this selection draws.*

2. *How might the honor-shame structure of life be operating in Phil 4:21–3 as Paul first mentions trouble and then praises these women?*

Cross-Cultural Reading of Philippians

Paul writes to predominantly Gentile-Christian church members who are confessing Christ as Lord in a city where many retired Roman army personnel and their families believe Caesar (along with the official Roman pantheon) to be the world's true Lord and benefactor. These retirees would be Roman citizens, though it is likely that the church was largely made up of noncitizens. Even though their relationship with outsiders is a matter of Gentiles relating to Gentiles, this relationship is indeed cross-cultural as they follow Christ as Lord in a city strongly attached to Roman ideology. This leads to suffering for Christ, but a firmer commitment to citizenship in heaven.

Cross-Cultural Reading at Work
Christian Citizenship in 3:20–21

Superficial reading of Philippians may not reveal it, but Paul is writing a seditious letter: the Philippians do not belong to Rome, but they belong to God who will soon send Jesus as Savior to replace the salvation/safety of Rome.

Perhaps the clearest indication of Paul's that the Roman imperial order stands under divine condemnation (and immanent termination!) while he and his movement already live under a new government or polity comes in Phil. 3:20–21: "But our government/constitution is in heaven, and it is from there that we are expecting a Savior, the Lord Jesus Christ. He will transform the body of our humiliation that it may be conformed to the body of his glory, by the power that also enables him to make all things subject to himself."

That is indeed an apocalyptic statement, but contrary to the depoliticization of apocalyptic by Western biblical scholarship, it is also thereby a thoroughly political statement. The fact cannot be avoided that the context was the Roman Empire. According to the imperial ideology (or "gospel"), Jupiter/Zeus and the other gods had given over all their power to Augustus (and his successors), who in establishing "Peace and Security" (cf. 1 Thess. 5:3!) had become the Savior of the world. Paul stands diametrically opposed to the imperial order and ideology. The true God has certainly not given over power to the Roman emperor. Just the opposite: in the Christ-event

Source: Richard A. Horsley, "Submerged Biblical Histories and Imperial Biblical Studies," in R. S. Sugirtharajah, *The Postcolonial Bible* (Sheffield: Sheffield Academic Press, 1998), pp.168–169. Reprinted by permission of the Continuum International Publishing Group.

God is accomplishing the termination of the Roman imperial order. According to his counter-imperial "gospel," while he and the "assemblies" of his movement remain in the imperial order, *their* government is in heaven, from which the true, counter-emperor/Savior is soon to come. Meanwhile, known only to the movement, it is Christ who has been invested with power by God to subject all things to himself.

How seriously Paul took this counter-imperial "gospel" of the counter-imperial "Savior" and the counter-imperial "government" is indicated in his almost obsessive "building" of "assemblies" and his instructions to them on their relations with "the world." Paul was more of an activist movement-builder than an intellectual.

Questions

1. Explain Horsley's statement that Phil 3:20–21 is a "thoroughly political statement."

2. With all this emphasis on counterimperialism, how does Paul expect his listeners to live so as to carry this out? See especially 4:8.

PHILEMON: Paul's Intervention for a Christian Slave

Philemon is the shortest of Paul's letters, but it has stirred one of the largest controversies over how it should be read. Unlike his other letters, it is addressed to an individual, Philemon [figh-LEE-muhn], who owned a slave, Onesimus [oh-NESS-ih-muhs]. Onesimus somehow had attached himself to Paul, and Paul was now sending him back. This letter seems to give a tacit approval to slavery and has been widely quoted in times past to justify slavery; in the United States before 1860 it was called the "Pauline Mandate" for the institution of slavery. Many interpreters, however, have argued that this letter actually works against slavery, which would make it rhetorically subtle and socially powerful. Of course, feminist and cross-cultural readers, given as they are to liberationist aims of reading, tend to look at Philemon with a hermeneutic of suspicion: Why does not Paul take this opportunity to make a strong, categorical stance against the institution of slavery itself? All this makes for powerful, controversial readings of this short document. Although it might be put last in the Pauline letter collection of the NT because of its size, Philemon looms large in modern reading because of its topic.

Philemon in Brief: Outline of Structure and Contents

I. **Opening** Paul to Philemon, Apphia, Archippus, and "the church in your house"; blessing (1–3)

II. **Thanksgiving** Thanks for Philemon's faith, and prayer that he may "perceive all the good that we may do" (4–7)

III. **Body** Paul's plea for Onesimus (8–22)
  A. Paul's Return of Onesimus (8–16)
  B. Paul's hopes for Philemon's reception of Onesimus (17–22)
IV. **Conclusion** Greetings from five others and blessing on the whole church (23–25)

Developing Your Skills

Read this short letter very slowly and carefully, looking for Paul's main persuasive purpose.

A Guide to Reading Philemon

Paul opens this, his most personal letter in the canon, with a greeting to Philemon, Apphia, Archippus, and the church that meets in Philemon's house (1–3; note here that Philemon has only one chapter, so the numbers refer only to verses). Apphia and Archippus may be Philemon's wife and son, respectively; or they could be other leaders in the church, but this is less likely given the phrase "the church in your [plural] house" (2). This gives this "private" letter a more public audience and hence puts more pressure on Philemon to follow Paul's wishes. He then gives his customary thanks for the addressee, here only Philemon, and offers a prayer on his behalf (4–7; from 4 through 21, every "you" is singular, referring to Philemon). Although the thanksgiving in this letter contains an assurance that Philemon already shares Paul's faith and love (7), Paul asks him to deepen his perception of the good that "we may do for Christ" (6). So, like most thanksgiving sections in Paul's letters, this one anticipates the body of the letter and serves to soften up the possibly severe attitude of Philemon to Onesimus.

Paul appeals in the letter body directly to Philemon, in the hearing of the whole church, to take back Onesimus—but as a brother rather than as just a slave (8–22). Paul begins the appeal with a reminder that his apostolic authority to command such a thing extends even to Philemon (8), but then alters his tone from expecting strict obedience to love (9). Only at this stage in the letter does Paul mention Onesimus as the object of the appeal but does not yet say what he expects Philemon to do for Onesimus. Paul calls Onesimus "my child," and reiterates this for effect by saying that during his imprisonment Paul has become Onesimus' "father." With an allusion to Philemon's changed character—his name, which means "useful," fits him now—Paul's persuasive force gains momentum (10–11). Until this point Paul has still not yet specified the *content* of the appeal for Onesimus, but now he plainly states, "I am sending him, my very heart, back to you" (12). Then he boldly suggests that Philemon might consider sending him back to Paul so that Onesimus can work with him again "in place of you." (The idea that a slave can take the place of his owner is a bold social statement indeed!) Paul wants Philemon to do the right thing so that he will get the credit for it from God (13–16). The language in verse 16 implies that Onesimus was converted while with Paul; Onesimus is not just Philemon's slave, but a "beloved brother." Now Paul turns up the persuasive heat by reminding Philemon of his own (spiritual) debt to Paul and by volunteering to pay for any debt owed by Onesimus from damage or theft (17–21). Paul would not have made such an offer unless he knew that Onesimus owed a debt to Philemon. "You owe me your very self," Paul says. But now Paul reverts to more authoritative language, saying that he is confident of Philemon's "obedience" and that Philemon will in fact "do even more than I say" (21).

Paul concludes with a clever afterthought, a favorite device of modern detectives and ancient rhetoricians alike to catch one's listener off guard after the main points have been discussed. "One thing more," he says as if he forgot it earlier: he hopes "through your prayers" to return to Philemon in a personal visit. From this remark Philemon should certainly read between the lines that it would be most prudent to heed Paul's advice since Paul will follow up on the suggestion in person (22).

The letter concludes with greetings to Philemon from those with Paul, invoking their names on Paul's purpose in this letter (23–24). In a final benediction upon the whole congregation, Paul blesses Philemon and the whole congregation (plural "you") listening to the letter with him.

Historical Reading of Philemon

Philemon in Brief: Historical Reading

Author Paul (undisputed).

Date Around 55 if from Ephesus; 61–62 if from Rome.

Audience Philemon and the church in Philemon's house.

Unity and Integrity Not disputed.

Purpose To secure a safe reception for Onesimus, a slave whom Paul is sending back to Philemon, and to obtain the return of Onesimus for further service in Paul's missionary activities.

Author

Contemporary scholarship is virtually unanimous in accepting Philemon as a genuine letter of Paul. The external evidence for this assumption is strong. Even though the letter is a brief, personal letter to a friend, it is cited as Pauline in the second and third centuries and shows up in Marcion's and the Muratorian canons as a letter of Paul. Internally, nothing linguistic, historical, or theological points to pseudonymity, despite the fact that it is not easy to compare Philemon with the other Pauline letters because of its unique topic.

Date

This letter was sent while Paul was in prison (v. 10). Once the occasion for the writing of Philemon is established, it can be reasonably supposed this letter was written sometime during the middle of Paul's Roman imprisonment, about 62–63. Although we cannot be sure, it is possible that Philemon was written before Philippians. First, the statement of coming soon to see Philemon in verse 22 may be exaggerated for rhetorical effect, intended to reflect Paul's positive expectation of his release from prison more than its imminence. If Paul was in Rome, it would take him several weeks to travel to Asia Minor. Second, Epaphras is mentioned in v. 23 as someone known to Philemon without any mention of his illness (Phil 2:25), even though this passage says that Christians outside Rome knew of his illness. Third, only Timothy is mentioned as being with Paul when he wrote Philippians (Phil 2:19–21), whereas Luke, Demas, Aristarchus, Mark and Epaphras are with him when he wrote Philemon (vv. 23–24). The final piece of evidence is that Paul sends Epaphroditus to the Philippians (Phil 2:25–30) with the epistle, a journey that would take some time, while he is still with Paul when the apostle wrote Philippians. All of this evidence suggests, but cannot demonstrate, that Philemon was written before Philippians. How long before, we cannot say.

The traditional view that Paul wrote this letter while in Rome has been questioned from two corners: some claim Ephesus is a better starting point, others Caesarea. (This is similar to the debate over the origin of Philippians, earlier.) First, a Roman imprisonment may be improbable; Paul would not likely return to the east after arriving in Rome, because his previous intention was to go from Rome to Spain in the far west (Rom 15:23–24). But this assumes that Paul's arrest and long court case have not changed his plans after he wrote Romans. Some argue that both Ephesus and Caesarea are likely, given their closeness to Colossae. However, Onesimus would most likely not have had good access to Paul in a regular prison. Paul's Roman imprisonment of house arrest with privileges to receive visitors would give Onesimus the personal access to Paul that this letter seems to presuppose. Moreover, Onesimus would want to travel to Rome *because* it was far away—why would he run to Ephesus when it was so close to his master? In conclusion, the view that Paul was in Rome when he wrote Philemon is the most probable and has a plurality of assent among scholars, even though the evidence does not allow us to make a firm conclusion.

Audience

The letter is mainly addressed to Philemon, the owner of the slave Onesimus. It is also addressed to "Apphia our sister," "Archippus our fellow soldier," and the "church in your [plural] house." So we can say that it is addressed to Philemon in the hearing—literally—of the whole church to which he belonged. Similarities between parts of Philemon and Colossians, especially that Col 4:9 speaks of an "Onesimus" as a "beloved brother who is one of you," lead most to conclude that Philemon lived in Colossae; this is the case whether or not Colossians is genuine.

Purpose

Onesimus apparently ran away from Philemon, with a bag containing some of Philemon's possessions, and headed for Rome to join up with Paul. While he was with Paul, Onesimus became a Christian (v. 10) and proved himself "useful" (a word play on his name, Greek for "useful") to Paul. Now Onesimus is going back, for a reason Paul does not state in the letter. The apostle wrote this letter to Philemon, asking Philemon to reinstate Onesimus—this time as a "dear brother" (v. 16) rather than as (just?) a slave. Although Paul could command Philemon to do so, he urges him instead, hoping that Philemon will be willing to do so without coercion. The reader, understanding this occasion, is led to ask for more details: Under what circumstances did Paul meet the slave Onesimus? Why did he run away to Paul, and how did he become converted? Why is he going back? Unfortunately, neither the letter itself nor other early Christian literature provides much data for answers. However, as Morna Hooker states, the preservation of this letter suggests that Philemon responded positively to Paul's requests (Hooker 2003; 1448).

Occasion

The precise circumstances that occasioned this letter are not completely clear. The letter itself would not have had to explain them because its recipients would know what they were, but we today do not. Four main scenarios have been suggested:

1. Onesimus had run away; Paul writes to Philemon in sending him back, expecting that he will not punish Onesimus. This is the traditional interpretation.
2. Philemon had sent Onesimus to help Paul in prison; Paul is now writing Philemon to free Onesimus and send him back to be a full co-worker with Paul.
3. Onesimus committed some offense against Philemon and went to Paul to ask for help. Paul writes to Philemon expecting he will not only pardon and free Onesimus, but also return him to work for Paul. This most recent of scenarios fits well with

what we know about slaves, slave owners, and third-party mediators between them in the first century.

4. Onesimus did not run away from his master, who is Archippus of Philem 1 and Col 4:17, not Philemon. Instead, he had been delegated by his church to bring a message or gift to Paul and to be one of his co-workers for a time. Paul then sent Onesimus back with this letter as his reintroduction to the Colossian church. The letter asks that Onesimus be freed from slavery and sent back to Paul, and when this did not happen he wrote Colossians in part to complain that Archippus had not fulfilled this expectation (Col 4:17). Although this reading proposed by Sara Winter (Winter 1987) is *possible,* it is unlikely. This letter clearly implies throughout that Philemon is addressed as Onesimus' master, and the vast majority of NT scholars read it this way.

www Follow the link to leading Web resources on Philemon.

Doing Historical Reading Yourself

What does it mean in the reading and reception of this letter that Paul addresses the whole congregation in Philemon's house at the beginning and the end of the letter (you plural), but the body of the letter is addressed to Philemon (you singular)? How might this framing serve to persuade Philemon to follow Paul's requests?

Social Scientific Reading of Philemon

The social scientific reading of Philemon has of course been concerned with its main theme of slavery. Paul uses kinship language extensively in describing his relationship to both Onesimus and Philemon as well as their relationship to each other that Paul would like to see established. Paul puts his own honor on the line by writing this letter, especially with its promise to repay anything that Onesimus owes. In this way Paul seeks to heal a broken relationship that is impacting not just these two men, but the whole church of which they are members.

Social Scientific Reading at Work
Paul's "Gentle Compulsion" in Philemon

Frilingos argues that Paul uses his paternal relationship with Philemon to argue for lenient, perhaps liberating, treatment for the returning Onesimus.

Source: Chris Frilingos, "'For My Child, Onesimus': Paul and Domestic Power in Philemon," *Journal of Biblical Literature* 119 (2000): pp. 91–104.

Philemon, as Paul's "child," is subject to the will of the apostolic *paterfamilias* ["father of the family"]. The indirect annexation of Philemon in this parent-child imagery indicates apprehension on the apostle's part. Perhaps Paul feels some trepidation about his brazen challenge to Philemon's [power] and honor. In view of the authority that the Roman household assigned to the *paterfamilias,* this is a reasonable conjecture. I do not wish to understate, however, the force of the epistle's formidable rhetoric. The letter's family imagery generates a complex mixture of affectionate and authoritative claims. Moreover, the public nature of the [household] heightened the effect of such language. By emphasizing his total control over the situation, Paul shames Philemon in his own house: "I wanted to keep him with me . . . but I preferred to do nothing without your consent, in order that your good deed might be voluntary and not something forced" (v. 13–14).

The apostle simultaneously subverts Philemon's "right" to the slave and provides him with a "face-saving" response: Philemon's submission should be viewed (by the household) as an honorable act of free will. The challenge remains shaming, nevertheless, for it publicly questions Philemon's ability to manage his own household. Another example of epistolary audacity occurs in Philemon's final lines. The letter's conclusion, its "apostolic *parousia,*" weaves together intimidation and tenderness: "One thing more—prepare a guest room for me, for I am hoping through your prayers to be restored to you" (v. 22). In other words, whether or not Philemon agrees to the apostle's conditions, Paul himself will soon return to set the record straight. The apostle also projects his own desire (i.e., to visit Philemon's household) onto his audience.

The verse reminds Philemon of the apostle's divinely ordained mission and his authority, granted by the prayers of the *domus* [household] itself, to interfere in Philemon's household operations. Despite its threatening undercurrents, however, the travelogue maintains a warm and familiar tone. It does not command obedience but expresses the hope for a family reunion. This "gentle compulsion" contrasts sharply with other, less subtle disciplinary moments within the Pauline corpus: "What would you prefer? Am I to come to you with a stick, or with love in a spirit of gentleness?" (1 Cor 4:21). Paul's epistle to Philemon is not meant to frighten (see 2 Cor 10:9). The letter, then, is concerned less with Onesimus's situation than with Paul's own status. This assessment of the epistle resolves somewhat the tension between Paul's ostensible goal of helping Onesimus and his decision to send the slave back to an angry Philemon. If Philemon accepts Onesimus in accordance with the apostle's terms, then the slaveholder must also acknowledge Paul's authoritative presence in his family affairs. Onesimus will remain "forever" in Philemon's household as a sign of Paul's domestic power.

Question

Do you concur with the statement: "The letter, then, is concerned less with Onesimus' situation than with Paul's own status"?

www   Follow the link to read the whole article online.

> **Doing Social Scientific Reading Yourself**
>
> *Read carefully through this letter, noting the different uses of kinship language. How does Paul use kinship ideas to strengthen the persuasive power of his argument?*

Feminist Reading of Philemon

Philemon is the only undisputed Pauline letter to be addressed to an individual. Since this individual (Philemon) and the slave in question (Onesimus) are both male, this letter does not explicitly address women's concerns. However, women figure as a part of its audience, since "the church in your house" (v. 2) certainly contained women. Their presence is confirmed by the mention of the woman Apphia (also in v. 2); she, with Archippus, was a leader of this church.

Feminist Reading at Work
Appeal for Onesimus (vv. 8–22)

Although the letter to Philemon does not seem to have feminist concerns, Pheme Perkins here points out that the parallel between issues about slaves and issues about women is important.

Paul opens the body of the letter by claiming the authority to command Philemon (v. 8). Paul grounds this authority in his own public status. He is an ambassador . . . and now a prisoner for Christ (v. 9). Instead of commanding, he appeals to Philemon. Paul offers Philemon an opportunity to demonstrate the love for which he is renowned (v. 14).

Paul makes Philemon's compliance more socially acceptable by changing the way in which his action is described. Paul does not ask Philemon to free a runaway slave. Instead, Paul provides a series of new names for what Onesimus now is: "my child"; "once useless, now useful to us both"; "my own heart"; "beloved brother . . . both in the flesh and in the Lord"; a 'stand-in' for Paul himself (vv. 10, 16–17, author's translation). Though he promises to repay anything that Onesimus owes his master, Paul reminds Philemon that Philemon is indebted to him for much more than any material gain or loss. Just as Onesimus became Paul's "son" when he was converted (v. 10), so Philemon owes the apostle his "self," that is, his Christian faith and life (v. 19).

This appeal demonstrates the significance of publicly shared language. The renaming of the relationships among Onesimus, Paul, and Philemon that takes place opens up the possibility of a response to Onesimus different from that anticipated on the basis of common social practice. Philemon is not asked to "free a bad slave." He is

Source: Pheme Perkins, "Philemon," in Carol A. Newsom and Sharon H. Ringe, eds., Women's Bible Commentary (Louisville, KY: Westminster John Knox, 1992), p. 454. Used by permission of Westminster John Knox Press.

asked to confirm his own reputation for love, for comforting fellow Christians, and to show both his gratitude toward Paul and his own participation in Paul's mission. This example demonstrates the need for new patterns of naming as the basis for changing deeply ingrained patters of domination. Women struggle with this problem today as sexist and racist stereotypes make it difficult to see "the other" as a "beloved sister or brother."

Question

Reflect for yourself on how cross-cultural bias today relates to bias against women.

Doing Feminist Criticism Yourself

Study the feminine name "Apphia" and Paul's designation of her as "sister." What are the options for interpretation about who Apphia is? What difference does it make?

Key Terms and Concepts

bishops • deacons • imperative (moral exhortation) • inclusion indicative (moral exhortation) • pretorian guard

Questions for Study, Discussion, and Writing

Philippians

1. Why is it difficult to know where Paul was imprisoned when he wrote Philippians? How much difference does this make in the historical interpretation of the letter? in the other methods?
2. Consider why "bishops and deacons" are addressed in this letter. Why do we see them here when we haven't in Paul's other letters?
3. Explain why this letter's initial emphasis on "joy" makes the change of mood in 3:1b even more striking.
4. What might Euodia and Syntyche be arguing about? Would historical, feminist or social-scientific criticism offer any clues?

Philemon

1. Evaluate this statement by Raymond Brown: "In every line just beneath the surface is the basic challenge to the societal rank of master and slave offered by the changed relationship introduced by the gospel" (Brown 1997, 502–503).
2. Which one of the four scenarios about the occasion of this letter do you prefer, and why?

3. Paul seeks the return of Onesimus to himself for further service. Would this include Onesimus' being freed from slavery by Philemon? State your reasons, and also give your conclusion on if this question has an answer from Paul's letter.
4. Can any conclusions be drawn from Paul's plea for Onesimus to his general attitude to Christian slaves, or non-Christian slaves, in his time? In particular, why doesn't Paul come out forthrightly against slavery?
5. Some interpreters have argued that Philemon is too short a letter for a serious treatment of the institution of slavery. What is your conclusion on this argument? Give reasons based on Philemon and outside this letter.

For Further Reading

Philippians

Beare, F. W. *A Commentary on the Epistle to the Philippians.* New York: Harper & Row, 1959. A concise, excellent commentary.

Fee, Gordon. *Paul's Letter to the Philippians.* Grand Rapids, MI: Eerdmans, 1994. A thorough, up-to-date commentary.

Martin, Ralph P. *Carmen Christi: Philippians 2:5–11 in Recent Interpretation and in the Setting of Early Christian Worship,* 2nd ed. (Grand Rapids, MI: Eerdmans, 1983).

Oakes, Peter. *Philippians: From People to Letter.* Cambridge: Cambridge University Press, 2001. Excellent treatment of Philippians against its historical-cultural background.

Philemon

Barclay, J. M. G. "Paul, Philemon and the Dilemma of Christian Slave-Ownership," *New Testament Studies* 37 (1991): 161–186. Good discussion of its topic.

Barth, Marcus, and Helmut Blanke. *The Letter to Philemon.* Grand Rapids, MI: Eerdmans, 2000. Full commentary on the letter, prefaced by an extensive treatment of slavery in the ancient world and early Christianity.

Lewis, Lloyd A. "An African-American Appraisal of the Philemon-Paul-Onesimus Triangle," in Cain H. Felder, ed., *Stony the Road We Trod: African American Biblical Interpretation.* Minneapolis: Fortress, 1991, pp. 232–246. Fascinating cross-cultural perspective.

Nordling, J. G. "Onesimus Fugitivus: A Defense of the Runaway Slave Hypothesis in Philemon," *Journal for the Study of the New Testament* 41 (1991): 97–119. Maintains the traditional view.

Petersen, N. R. *Rediscovering Paul: Philemon and the Sociology of Paul's Narrative World.* Guides to Biblical Scholarship. Philadelphia: Fortress, 1985. Excellent, concise social scientific treatment of Philemon.

Chapter Fifteen

2 Thessalonians, Colossians, and Ephesians: The Pauline Tradition

Paul's continuing influence on the church was so great after his death in the middle 60s that various disciples probably composed letters in his name, claiming his authority to settle new issues troubling the Christian community in 80s and 90s. Six canonical letters in which the author explicitly identifies himself as Paul contain features that cause many scholars to question their authorship. These features raise questions not only in historical criticism, but in the newer methods of criticism as well. The authorship of two of the letters—2 Thessalonians and Colossians—is still vigorously disputed, with a substantial minority championing their authenticity. However, a majority of scholars today denies that Paul wrote the other four others—Ephesians, 1 and 2 Timothy, and Titus.

2 Thessalonians adapts Paul's eschatology in 1 Thessalonians to a new situation, asserting that a number of traditional apocalyptic signs must precede the end. Colossians identifies Jesus with the cosmic power and wisdom by and for which the universe was created. The "divine secret" is revealed as Christ's Spirit dwelling in the believer. Ephesians contains ideas similar to those in Colossians, revising and updating Pauline concepts about God's eternal plan of salvation for Jews and Gentiles and about believers' spiritual warfare with supernatural evil. The author warns his readers against false teachings (**heresy**), and urges them to keep to the original apostolic traditions. Despite the contested issues of author, date, and audience, these three letters have had an important role in the history of Christianity. Ephesians, for example, has been long regarded as a capstone of Paul's letters.

2 THESSALONIANS: Awaiting the End of Time Faithfully

Whatever one concludes on the authenticity of 2 Thessalonians, one must admit that its tone and some contents differ from 1 Thessalonians. It appeals to tradition in a way that 1 Thessalonians does not. Although both letters have an **apocalyptic** eschatology, 2 Thessalonians is much more apocalyptic in style, with imagery such as the "man of lawlessness" from the OT apocalyptic book of Daniel and with a sequence of events at the end of time. 2 Thessalonians repays a careful reading with good insight on how a Pauline church and Pauline theology can be addressed by apocalyptic.

---

2 Thessalonians in Brief: Outline of Structure and Contents

I. **Opening** Paul, Silvanus (Silas) and Timothy to "the church of the Thessalonians"; blessing (1:1–2)

II. **Thanksgiving** The author thanks God for the Thessalonians' love for each other, and faith during persecutions (1:3–4)

III. **Body** The end of time in teaching and exhortation (1:5–3:13)

  A. Salvation for God's people and punishment for opponents at the end of time; renewed prayer (1:5–12)

  B. Signs that precede the coming of Jesus (2:1–12)

  C. Renewed thanksgiving, teaching on salvation (2:13–17)

  D. Request for prayer from audience, prayer for them (3:1–5)

  E. Moral exhortation, especially against idleness and disobedience (3:6–15)

IV. **Conclusion** First blessing, final greeting from the author, final blessing (3:16–18)

Developing Your Reading Skills

Read through 1 Thessalonians, and then more carefully through 2 Thessalonians, noticing both the similarities and differences in content.

A Guide to Reading 2 Thessalonians

"Paul, Silas, and Timothy" greet "the church of the Thessalonians" and offer them God's blessing (1:1–2). The thanksgiving for the believers comes next, at least in 1:3–4, and perhaps extends all the way through v. 12. In vv. 5–10, apocalyptic touches clearly introduce (not just hint at, as in Paul's earlier, undisputed letters) the theme of the letter. Jesus will appear to save his persecuted people and inflict strong vengeance on those who do not know God or obey the gospel. This vengeance entails their eternal destruction, being banished forever from the Lord's presence; in the social world of the times, salvation is an honoring presence with God that comes from kinship with the Father and destruction is banishment from that presence. All this is meant to strengthen believers with the assurance that God will give them justice at the end of time. Chapter 1 concludes with a prayer that the Thessalonians will serve God faithfully and glorify Jesus Christ (vv. 11–12).

The author (note that we will try not to prejudice in this section the historical issue of whether or not Paul wrote this letter) now gets to the heart of the letter, correction of eschatological belief and practice in the audience. The occasion for 2 Thessalonians arises from a letter purportedly written by Paul saying "the coming of our Lord" and "our being gathered to him" is now present (2:1–2). The author also disqualifies "spirit" and "word" as sources of the idea that the Lord's coming is present. The author then says why the Thessalonians should stop thinking this way and acting on such belief. The signs of the arrival of the day of the Lord have not appeared yet (2:3–12): "the rebellion" has not started; the "man of lawlessness" is presently "being restrained" (2:6–7), but if Christ's coming were here, the "man of lawlessness" would be cut off by Christ himself (2:8–9) and those whose lives are characterized by evil would be facing judgment (2:10–12). God confirms the hostility that the evildoers have toward the good by sending on them a "powerful delusion, leading them to believe what is false" (v. 11). The author's affirmation of the divine plan and activity is a common feature of apocalyptic writings.

The author then discusses the destiny of the righteous in a renewed thanksgiving (2:13–17; compare the renewed thanksgiving in 1 Thess 2:13–16). The renewed thanksgiving here is in the form of a prayer that the Thessalonians stand firm to the promise of sharing the glory of Jesus Christ and to the "traditions that you were taught by us, either by word of mouth or by our letter" (2:13–15), and a benediction invoking God to comfort and strengthen "your hearts" (that is, your will) in good deeds and words (2:16–17).

The author begins the final main topic of the letter body ("Finally," 3:1) with exhortations related to prayer and eschatology (3:1–15). First, he requests that the Thessalonians pray for the spread of the gospel through Paul's efforts and assures them that, despite all that he has corrected them for, they are on the right track to salvation (3:1–5). If this author is not Paul, he has learned one of Paul's effective rhetorical devices: heavy correction followed by a quick reassurance. (Compare our practice of passing judgment and then saying, "Present company excepted!")

The author then rebukes the idle or unruly (3:6–15), expanding on a rebuke initiated in 1 Thess 5:14. The expansion of the warning is the result of a report that these vices were increasing among them (3:11). The author appeals to Paul's example of constant work to pay his own way (compare 1 Thess 1:6) and reminds the Thessalonians of something Paul said when he was with them: "Anyone unwilling to work should not eat" (v. 10). Being "unwilling to work" may entail only general unruliness or disorder, as some commentators have suggested, but probably in the heavily apocalyptic context of this letter it is both "busybodiness" and "not doing any work" (v. 11). This vice springs from an improper imminent expectation: if the end of the world will happen soon, why work? The author pointedly reduces this argument to absurdity: if the end is so close that there is no need to work, then there is no need to eat (3:10)! Evidently those who were refusing to work in the normal course of life were being supported by the common funds of the church or (less likely) by the private funds from other believers. The author then urges the church to ostracize those who disobey this letter so that they will feel shame and repent. But the author qualifies this ostracizing in a way that may make readers wonder how it can be done or how it will work: do not regard them as "enemies," as opposing outsiders, but "warn them as believers" (3:14–15).

The letter concludes with a final greeting in which the author reminds the Thessalonians of a built-in safeguard against forgeries: he writes a final note in his own hand in all his letters, and evidently they know his handwriting! (3:17). This note is bracketed by two benedictions, both of which invoke the Lord's presence for the believers as a further comfort to them as it gives them grace and peace (3:16, 18).

Historical Reading of 2 Thessalonians

2 Thessalonians in Brief: Summary of Historical Reading

Author Scholars are sharply divided on whether 2 Thessalonians was written by Paul or by one of his unidentifiable followers (but not necessarily one of his close colleagues) after his death; a preference for pseudonymity is gaining momentum.

Date If by Paul, it would come shortly after 1 Thessalonians, about 51 or 52; if pseudonymous, probably in the 90s.

Audience A few who hold the letter to be inauthentic doubt that it was written to Thessalonica, but most who hold it inauthentic argue for Thessalonica. All who argue that it is genuine see a Thessalonian destination.

Unity and Integrity Maintained almost by all.

Purpose To urge readers or listeners to eagerly await the return of Christ in proper understanding and living, but to caution that this was not going to happen immediately.

Author

The opening of this letter names Paul, Silvanus, and Timothy as authors, but its closing names only Paul, and this letter does look like the work of one person. As stated earlier, scholarship is sharply divided over whether Paul or one of his later followers wrote this letter. Scholars defending Pauline authorship of 2 Thessalonians advance several arguments, which can be summed up as follows.

- This letter is attested as Paul's in other Christian writings as early as the second century C.E., and it appears in the early canonical lists.
- The close literary relationship between 1 Thessalonians and 2 Thessalonians is the result of common recipients, common Pauline authorship, and closeness in time, perhaps only a few months.
- The situation of 2 Thessalonians could have resulted from a misinterpretation of 1 Thessalonians. There, Paul says that the coming of Jesus is near (4:17). In 2 Thessalonians, Paul writes to correct the Thessalonians' misconceptions about his earlier emphasis on the nearness of the end.
- Trouble has come to Thessalonica between the time of 1 Thessalonians and 2 Thessalonians. If the persecution Paul talks about in 1 Thessalonians increased, it could have led to a deeper yearning for Jesus' return. Some, claiming that "the Day of the Lord is already here" (2 Thess 2:2), were upsetting others with their otherworldly enthusiasms. In their state of apocalyptic fervor, some even scorned everyday occupations and refused to work to support themselves. It is possible that the visionary Spirit of prophecy that Paul encouraged the Thessalonians to cultivate (1 Thess 5:19–22, yet while urging discernment against abuses) had led to this development.
- The apocalyptic "timetable" of 2 Thessalonians does not necessarily mean that the end is not immediate.
- To argue that phrasing unique to 2 Thessalonians, and the absence of certain characteristic Pauline emphases, means that Paul did not write this letter assumes wrongly that Paul has to say the same thing in the same way in all his letters.

Although this is a plausible view, and Paul *could* have changed his mind and altered his style for 2 Thessalonians, the majority view is skeptical about its authenticity.

- If Paul actually composed it, why does he repeat—almost verbatim—so much of what he had already just written to the same recipients? This is not Paul's usual method of writing, as the Corinthian correspondence shows. Rather, this indicates that someone who knows 1 Thessalonians may be using it to write 2 Thessalonians.
- The style of 2 Thessalonians is rather formal and wooden, unlike the personal, vivid style of 1 Thessalonians. For example, 2 Thessalonians almost completely lacks the expressions of warm affection that are plentiful in 1 Thessalonians.
- The author presents an eschatology different in key aspects from that presented in the first letter. In 1 Thessalonians, the Parousia will occur stealthily, "like a thief in the night." In 2 Thessalonians, a number of apocalyptic signs will first advertise its arrival. Also, the mysterious events between the writer's time and that of the Parousia have the effect of placing the end further into the future.
- The author of 2 Thessalonians reverts to the cryptic language of apocalyptic discourse, referring to mysterious personages and events that may have been understood by the letter's recipients but that are largely incomprehensible to others of the time or later readers. The end of time cannot come before the final rebellion against God's rule, when evil is revealed in human form as a demonic enemy who desecrates the Temple and claims divinity for himself. In this passage, Paul's

terminology resembles that contained in the book of Daniel and other Jewish Second Temple apocalyptic writings (see Chapter 3). This is found infrequently, if at all, in Paul's undisputed writings; they are apocalyptic in *theological content,* but not in *literary style.*

- In Paul's other undisputed letters, he grounds his eschatology in the death and resurrection of Jesus. Where Paul has an eschatological sequence of events, it starts with the resurrection of Jesus and goes immediately to Jesus' coming at the end (1 Cor 15:23–28). Here there is little of Paul's characteristic emphasis on Jesus' cross and resurrection and the Holy Spirit.
- 2 Thess 2:2 and 3:17 imply that other letters of Paul, some even forged, were circulating by 50 C.E. Most scholars view this scenario as highly unlikely, although the evidence we have for the time when Paul began his letter-writing activities is spotty.

Date

Those scholars who argue that Paul wrote 2 Thessalonians date it c. 51–52, less than a year or at most two years after 1 Thessalonians. They conclude that it was meant for the same Thessalonian congregation that received 1 Thessalonians, now with a changed situation of end-time belief. If it is pseudonymous, the letter could be dated anytime from 80 to 100, with the usual dating in the 90s, when apocalyptic was strong (Revelation is usually dated in the 90s).

Audience

A few who hold that this letter is **pseudonymous** ("with a false name," written by someone other than the person whose name is on it) argue that it was written to another destination than Thessalonica, but most argue for Thessalonica. All who argue that it is genuine see a Thessalonian destination.

Purpose

If Paul wrote 2 Thessalonians, he wrote to sort out problems relating to misunderstandings of eschatological hope. If some other writer is writing in Paul's name, he does so to update Paul's teaching on the coming of Christ. With the waning of the **imminent expectation,** the hope that Jesus' coming was very soon, Paul's belief that some Thessalonians alive in the early 50s would live to see Christ return had to be reinterpreted. In either scenario of authorship, the author takes on the difficult task of urging Christians to be prepared for the Lord's return and achieves this delicate balance partly by insisting on an orderly, practical approach to life as believers await the Parousia.

Doing Historical Reading Yourself

1. In 3:10, the author states, "Even when we were with you, we gave you this command: Anyone unwilling to work should not eat." How likely is it, in your view, that Paul actually said this during his first visit to Thessalonica?

2. In 3:17, the author says, "I, Paul, write this greeting in my own hand. This is the mark in every letter of mine; it is the way I write." Examine the endings of the generally accepted Pauline letters on this point. Some have explicit Pauline penmanship, others do not, but could Paul have written the final part in his own hand without calling attention to it?

Social Scientific and Feminist Readings of 2 Thessalonians

The apocalyptic fervor behind 2 Thessalonians deals with how the imminent Parousia impacts the everyday life of the church as a whole and individual believers. Social scientists today study modern apocalyptic groups to discern their basic features: sectarianism over against the rest of society, breaking off of the patterns of ordinary daily life to prepare for the end, and a tendency to social disorderliness and sometimes even violence. In the face of these features in Thessalonica, the author attempts to reorder the life of the community by pushing the expected Parousia farther into the future.

In feminist reading, 2 Thessalonians contains no references to named women and, in most English translations, no references to unnamed women. Because it is so closely related to 1 Thessalonians, which has no explicit gendered issues, 2 Thessalonians might be the same. In the NRSV, the Greek "brothers" is rendered "brothers and sisters," giving the appearance that women are explicitly present, but this is not the case. How 2 Thessalonians relates to women, therefore, must be deduced from what is said in the letter to all believers.

Social-Scientific and Feminist Readings at Work
Silent Women in 2 Thessalonians?

Here Ross Kraemer analyzes the problem of idleness or unruliness at Thessalonica with social scientific methods, and she brings out its relevance for feminist reading.

Source: Ross S. Kraemer, "2 Thessalonians: No Women Mentioned?" in Carol Meyers, ed., *Women in Scripture*, pp. 486–487. Copyright © 2000 by Houghton Mifflin Company. Reproduced by permission of Houghton Mifflin Company. All rights reserved.

It seems reasonable to ask whether the problem of believers who fail to earn their own living is, in fact, gender-specific. . . . In 1 Thess 2:9, Paul reminds the Thessalonians that he, Timothy, and Silvanus "worked night and day, so that we might not burden any of you while we proclaimed to you the gospel of God"; in 4:11, he urges them to work with their hands, so as to be independent. In 2 Thess 3:9, the writers . . . contend that they have previously instructed the Thessalonians that "anyone unwilling to work should not eat" (3:10).

Does "anyone" include women as well as men? . . . . If by "work" the author(s) of 2 Thessalonians envision any productive labor, compensated or not, we may well expect that this injunction could easily be directed to both women and men. Many women in the Roman period engaged in commercial labor for which they received compensation, in varied occupational roles. . . . Elite women are less likely to have labored for financial gain. Enslaved women could expect no financial compensation from their owners, but could, and sometimes did, earn money on their own, often through prostitution. Whether free non-elite women labored for financial compensation probably depended on whether they were married, widowed, or divorced, and on their access to financial support from husbands and male kin. But if labor that produces financial remuneration is at stake, as 2 Thess 3:8 suggests, it becomes harder to imagine that 3:10 is directed equally to men and to women, many of whom would not have labored for direct financial compensation. In that case, 2 Thess 3:6–12 might be directed primarily, if not entirely, at men who now refrain from productive labor and expected support from the community.

Question

To judge from the last sentence in this reading, 2 Thessalonians' problem is largely with males who are wrongly awaiting the end of time. Does this mean that the women in this congregation are more mature than the men?

Doing Social Scientific and Feminist Reading Yourself

1. What does it mean for the social status of the audience if they are to "work with their hands"?

2. Do you think it is necessarily a negative thing for the importance of this letter today that it does not mention women explicitly? Why or why not?

COLOSSIANS: Following the Cosmic Christ

Colossae, Laodicea, and Hierapolis were cities located close together on the Lycus River, about a hundred miles upstream from Ephesus. This letter, addressed to the Pauline church in Colossae, was intended by its author to go to the Laodicean church also. Colossians has historical links with the letter to Philemon and connections in themes and wording with Ephesians. Many scholars believe that a follower of Paul wrote Colossians after his death, but others think that Paul is indeed the author. This letter often stands in the shadow of Ephesians, but it deserves to be read on its own merits.

Colossians in Brief: Outline of Structure and Contents

I. **Opening** Paul the sender, Colossians the recipients, blessing (1:1–2)

II. **Thanksgiving** Prayer of thanks and blessing (1:3–8)

III. **Body** Supremacy of the Cosmic Christ (1:9–3:4)

    A. Prayer for growth in faith (1:9–14)

    B. The sufficiency of Christ explained (1:3–2:7)

    C. Argument against error (2:8–3:4)

    D. Proper Christian action (3:5–4:6)

        1. Putting off the old ways (3:5–11)

        2. Putting on the new ways (3:12–17)

        3. Life in the Christian household (3:18–4:1)

    E. Final exhortations (4:2–6)

V. **Conclusion** Travel plans, final greetings, blessing (4:7–18)

Developing Your Reading Skills

Read Colossians carefully, noting the main argument and literary style.

A Guide to Reading Colossians

The apostle Paul, with Timothy, begins the letter with a greeting to the saints at Colossae (1:1–2). The author offers thanksgiving for the Colossians' positive response to the gospel (1:3–8), coupled with a prayer for them to grow in knowledge and productivity (1:9–14). This prayer hints very subtly at the errorists' claim to have a superior knowledge.

The author continues by reciting an early Christian hymn in which Christ is magnified as the image of God in the flesh, the Creator incarnate (1:15–20). The hymn ends with Christ as reconciler of "all things," serving as a bridge to the author's next theme: Christ has reconciled the Colossians to God, and Paul has ministered this reconciliation (1:21–23). He has been commissioned with proclaiming "the mystery of Christ in you, the hope of glory" (1:27), that "we may present everyone perfect in Christ" (1:24–29). The author is concerned about the believers in the Lycus Valley to whom he writes, especially that they are not "deceived by fine-sounding arguments" (2:4) which deny the sufficiency of Christ (2:1–7).

After having established both the supremacy of Christ and the author's commission and concern, the author now turns to the heart of his letter. False teachers in Colossae have denied the supremacy and sufficiency of Christ, and this heresy has already affected his audience (2:8–3:4). The author restates the supremacy of Christ (2:8–15) in the light of his opponents' wrong views, which he calls "philosophy and empty deceit" (2:8). Christ is both a divine and human person ("in Christ all the fullness of the Deity lives in bodily form," 2:9). He has ultimate cosmic authority (2:9–10). The power of God that raised Christ from the dead is available to believers. The author strongly implies that baptism now takes the place of circumcision (2:11–12). The death of Christ is not defeat, but triumph—over the human heart, over the Jewish Law, and over "powers and authorities" (2:13–15).

The author now turns to the influence that the false teachers have had on the Colossians (2:16–3:4). The Colossians deny Christ's supremacy by practicing mysticism and observing the Law of Moses—keeping kosher in some ways, celebrating Jewish festivals, and observing the Sabbath (2:16–19). The church that engages in these practices has lost its connection with the Head, Jesus Christ (2:19). Believers have died with Christ to any "elemental spirits of the universe," spiritual powers opposed to God (2:20–23). The author goes on to affirm that believers have also risen with Christ (3:1–4), so they should live only in him. Their return to human regulations (2:20–23) and their lack of real appreciation for the true mystery, Christ himself (3:1–4), are a contradiction of true life in Christ. The author's command to "set your mind on things above, not on things that are on earth" (v. 2) makes a transition to the next section.

In the last major section of the letter body, the author addresses parenetic concerns (3:5–4:6). These are directly connected to the preceding doctrinal section, because the author shows here that Christ is sufficient and supreme not only for salvation, but also for proper growth in Christian living. This entire section is packed with imperatives. Beneath the surface of all these imperatives, however, is the fact of Christ's cosmic sufficiency. This fact is a simple Pauline indicative on which all the imperatives are built. Because believers have already put off the "old self" (3:5–11; cf. 3:9), they must continue to do so and keep turning away from the practices of their former lives. The author gives two short catalogues of vice to remind believers of what these practices are (3:5, 8). They have put on the "new self" (3:10, 12–17; cf. 3:10), and their continuing battle against sin is rooted in their changed nature. The "new self" has a corresponding catalogue of virtues (3:12), to which the author adds love as the behavior that leads to harmony and peace (3:14–15). This new creation has strong cross-cultural implications: "there is no longer Greek and Jew, circumcised and uncircumcised, barbarian, Scythian, slave and free; but Christ is all and in all!" (3:11). All things should be done in the "name of the Lord Jesus," that is, in Christ himself (3:17).

Believers are to act responsibly in the household, and the author gives a **household code** of moral duties for people (parents, children, slaves) in a household. This literary form was common in the Greek world, and the author adapts it here for Christian use in two ways: by addressing the inferior partner in the pairs and by tempering custom with the love of Christ. To the ideal reader, the code given here may seem a comedown from the heights of the letter so far. In the paired relationship the household code mentions, the first person is to receive submission/obedience from the second, and the second is to receive kindness from the first. Wives should submit to their husbands (3:18), and husbands should love their wives (3:19). Children should obey their parents (3:20), and fathers must not embitter their children (3:21). Slaves should obey their masters and serve them wholeheartedly (3:22–25), and masters should treat their slaves humanely, realizing that even as masters they too are slaves to a Master in heaven (4:1).

The author then offers further moral instructions. Believers should devote themselves to prayer, being alert and thankful at all times (4:2–6). They are to pray for Paul and his companions, especially that the "mystery of Christ" might spread through their evangelistic efforts (4:3–4). Believers should make the most of their opportunities in relating wisely toward "outsiders" to the faith; this especially involves a gracious, seasoned response to those who ask about their faith (4:5–6).

The epistle closes with final greetings in which the letter bearer, Tychicus, is commended (4:7–9). Onesimus, no doubt the same Onesimus of the letter to Philemon, is accompanying Tychicus. Paul's co-laborers are mentioned, many of them notable NT figures (4:10–14). The author commands that greetings be given to the church in Laodicea and to the woman in whose house it meets, Nympha. This letter is to be shared with that church, and the letter addressed to that church must be read in Colossae (4:15–16). After commanding Archippus to complete the task given to him (which may relate to freeing Onesimus if this is the same Archippus of the opening of Philemon) Paul himself sends handwritten greetings, commands believers to "remember my chains" (imprisonment), and gives a remarkably short blessing that does not explicitly mention God: "grace be with you."

Historical Reading of Colossians

Colossians in Brief: Summary of Historical Reading

Author A substantial minority now holds for Paul; a majority holds for an unknown member of a Pauline church after his death.

Date If by Paul, 61–63; most who hold for pseudonymity place it in the 80s.

Audience Those who hold for authenticity argue that this letter was written to the church at Colossae in the Roman province of Asia. Founded by Paul's co-worker Epaphras, it is a Pauline church. Those who hold for pseudo-nymity place it around Colossae, which was largely abandoned after an earthquake somewhere between 60 and 64 C.E.

Integrity and Unity Not questioned.

Purpose To motivate believers to hold to Christ and his cosmic power, putting away both false teaching about salvation and immoral practices carried over from their Gentile past.

Author

If Paul is the author of Colossians, as a sizeable minority of scholars believes, he had not yet visited the city when he wrote this letter. If Colossians is genuine, it was probably composed at about the same time as Philemon, to which it is closely related. In both letters, Paul writes from prison, includes Timothy in the salutation (1:1), and adds greetings from many of the same persons such as Onesimus, Archippus, Aristarchus, Epaphras, Mark, and Luke (4:9–18). If Philemon's was the house church at Colossae, it is strange that Paul does not mention him, but his absence from the letter does not necessarily discredit the case for Pauline authorship. (Arguments based on silence—that something or someone is not mentioned—are particularly slippery.)

In the case against Paul's authorship, many sentences are longer and more flowery than in the undisputed Pauline letters. The tone of the letter is less personal and more formal than the personal conversational tone in the other letters. The theological ideas are similar to those in Paul's authentic letters, but the emphasis on Christ as the head of the church is new. Also striking is Colossian's idea that believers in Christ have already "risen" with him; this emphasis on realized eschatology is new. Also, the household code marks this letter as different from the undisputed letters. Some have tried to place this letter in Paul's time, but not written by Paul; for example, Eduard Schweizer argues that Timothy wrote it while Paul was in prison and for some reason could not, and had Paul "sign" it at its conclusion (Schweizer 1982). However, most scholars who hold to pseudonymity believe that an unknown follower of Paul wrote this letter.

Date

If Paul wrote this letter, he would have done so during his Roman imprisonment, somewhere around 61–63. If someone else wrote it after his death in 64, it would probably come in the 80s, since some time would have to elapse for Ephesians to use this letter in the 90s. The place of writing would then be unknown, but Rome and Ephesus have often been mentioned as likely possibilities.

Audience

Epaphras, one of Paul's missionary associates, had founded the church, perhaps only a short time prior to Paul's writing (1:7). Colossae, being a relatively small and remote town, would be unlikely to have Jewish residents. To judge from the contents of this letter, the church was predominantly, if not exclusively, Gentile Christian. This is confirmed because the letter nowhere cites the Jewish Bible and makes only a few allusions to it. Another factor identifying the date and audience of Colossians is that the city of Colossae was devastated by an earthquake sometime between 61 and 64, and largely abandoned. Therefore, if Paul wrote this letter, it could go to this city; if the letter were written later, it would go to Laodicea alone (see 4:16) or to a wider destination.

Purpose

Paul or one of his later disciples writes to the Colossian congregation to correct some false teachings prevalent there. These beliefs apparently gave undue honor to angels or other invisible spirits inhabiting the universe. Some Colossians may have worshiped angels. The author refutes these "hollow and delusive" notions, which they seem to have characterized as "philosophy," by emphasizing Christ's uniqueness and supremacy. Christ alone is their spiritual reality; lesser spirit beings are merely Christ's "captives" and are not worthy of worship. The author writes to make sure that the Colossians clearly recognize who Christ really is, and this gives the letter a christological center. The author stresses two themes: (1) Christ is supreme because God's power now manifested in him was the same power that created the entire universe, including those invisible entities the false teachers mistakenly worship; and (2) when they realize Christ's supremacy and experience his Spirit living in them, the Colossians are initiated into Christ's mystery, harmonizing their lives with the cosmic unity he embodies.

The false teachings that the author writes to correct bear on the dating of Colossians. In the opinion of some, both the complex nature of the false teachings, which seem to blend pagan and marginally Jewish ideas into a Gnostic synthesis, and the christology of Colossians seem too advanced for the letter to have originated in Paul's day. Perhaps, as some critics point out, the letter was written late in Paul's career to meet a situation significantly different from others he had encountered. If this is true, the letter could well have stimulated the apostle to produce a more fully developed expression of his views about Christ's nature and function.

www   See the website for a brief essay on the Christ hymn in Colossians 2.

> **Doing Historical Reading Yourself**
>
> *Examine the possibility that the remarkably lengthy instructions for slaves in the household code (3:22–25) are related to the situation of the letter to Philemon.*

Social Scientific and Feminist Readings of Colossians

In Colossians, the social world of early Christianity seems to most scholars today to turn more conservative. The Pauline tradition seems to challenge accepted social mores of the Roman Empire less and seek to conform more. This is not to say that the tradition lost its distinctively Christian features, but that it took how it looked to the wider world more seriously than before. Factors probably include the delay of the Parousia, the rapid growth of the church, and the rise of more internal diversity and dissent in the church that leaders of the Pauline tradition sought to correct by emphasizing traditional values. Although this can be seen throughout Colossians, it is most evident in the household code, where Christian women are urged to be submissive to their husbands and Christian slaves to their masters.

Social Scientific and Feminist Readings at Work
The Social Context of Submission in Household Duties (3:18–4:1)

In this essay, Professor Sheila McGinn explores the meaning of this household code in the context of Colossian's theme of the cosmic Christ and particularly how this limitation of freedom and power can be reconciled with the cosmic Christ.

There were many similar lists of household duties in the ancient world–called "household codes"–so the interesting features of this list pertain to how the traditional formula has been adapted for a Christian household. The basic schema involved the duties of wives, children, and slaves. This list devotes four times as much attention to the duties of slaves, which suggests that slavery was a troublesome issue for the author (or editor) and he wants to use this code to resolve the problem. His solution is to tell Christian slaves to obey their masters even better than they did before their conversion, knowing that they will be rewarded

Source: Sheila E. McGinn, "Colossians," an Internet essay: *http://www.jcu.edu/Bible/Paul/Pauline Traditions/Coloss_comm.htm*, Jan. 13, 2004. Copyright © Sheila McGinn.

by the Lord Christ, not simply their earthly masters (3:22–25). The other remarkable feature of this schema is that it includes duties for husbands, fathers, and slave-masters, not just for their subordinates. The duties of each pair are not equivalent, nor are the paired relationships egalitarian; there is no glossing over this. However, it is a significant innovation to find any explicit duties whatsoever of the superior party toward his inferiors. Much attention has been given to the submission of wives and obedience of children and slaves, but very little has been devoted to the duties of husbands to love their wives and treat them with kindness (3:19). Nor has there been much discussion of how fathers ought to treat their children so that they will not "lose heart" (3:21). Rather than eliminating the prerogative of the male householder to abuse his wife and children, as this expression of the code would do, this very text has been used to support the abusive impulses of male family heads. . . .

Still, this code accepts a Greco-Roman pattern of domination/submission as normative not only for the wider society but also for the Christian community–or, at least, for the Christian household. In so doing, it inevitably conflicts with earlier segments of the letter which insist that the gospel sets one free of control by the "principalities and powers" because of the universal Lordship of Christ (cf. 2:15). . . . While this household code, in comparison with others of the time, limits the power of human lords, conversely it also uses the power and authority of the Lord Christ to reinforce what remains of the power of those very human lords (3:18, 20, 22–25). The household code directly contradicts the author's claim that there is no longer slave or free in Christ (3:11). Even more, it undermines the letter's central message that Christ is Lord and there is no other Power over those who belong to Him. Why would the author–or even a later editor–have included something in this letter which contradicts its central point? Colossians portrays baptism as the event when Christians die to sin and death and also are raised up with Christ (2:11–13). Christians no longer "belong to the world" (2:20), so they should focus on heavenly rather than earthly things (3:1–3). . . . These freedoms from earthly habits apply precisely to Christians who live *in* this material world. The "hope in the heavens" provides the motivation for behavioral and attitudinal changes in this present world–including the overcoming of racial, ethnic, and class prejudices (3:11), acceptance of women as leaders (4:15), and reciprocity in communal life and worship (3:1–17). The household code presumes an alternate view of this heavenly hope, one which postpones its applicability to the life to come. It assumes that life in this world remains the same, not simply in terms of how outsiders perceive believers, but also in terms of how Christians treat each other. If the heavenly hope breaks into this life at all, it does not prevent Christians being chattels of one another because they all belong to Christ (cf., e.g., Gal 3:26–29; Philemon 15–20). Rather, this future hope is used to justify heightening Christian wives', children's, and slaves' responsibility toward their husbands, fathers, and masters–and perhaps softening the hearts of Christian husbands, fathers, and masters toward their chattels. In the world to come, this may change, but not yet.

Questions

1. *Is McGinn correct, in your view, when she argues that this household code contradicts the religious message of the rest of Colossians?*

2. *McGinn urges after this excerpt that this passage not be read or proclaimed in Christian liturgical services. Do you agree? Why, or why not?*

www   Follow the link to read this whole essay on line.

Doing Social Scientific and Feminist Reading Yourself

1. *Compare Col 3:11 to Gal 3:28. What do you make of the fact that "male and female" is not present in Col 3:11?*

2. *What might the fact that two (freed?) slaves, Tychicus and Onesimus, are sent to deliver this letter, relay greetings from Paul, and "encourage the hearts" of the recipients mean for this letter's attitude to slavery?*

3. *Give your critique of this statement on household codes in Colossians and Ephesians: "The writer's intent is not to universalize Greco-Roman household management. The passage teaches that all Christians are under Christ's lordship and are to 'submit' to one another for Christ's sake."*

Cross-Cultural Reading of Colossians

With their emphasis on the cosmic Christ and the cosmic church, one might think that cross-cultural issues take a back seat in Colossians and Ephesians. Actually, the message has the effect of drawing Gentile and Jewish believers in Christ closer together as the author of Colossians emphasizes that the cosmic Christ is sufficient for the faith and life of believers. Devotion to spiritual powers and beings (such as angels) other than Christ, whether done by Jewish or Gentile believers, is strongly cautioned against here. This basic tenet of monotheism—worship of only one God— has been challenging to maintain from the first century to the twenty-first, as Christianity spreads to peoples whose cultures recognize a plurality of gods, spiritual beings, and cosmic forces.

Cross-Cultural Reading at Work
Salvation from the Cosmic Powers

In this short selection the authors draw attention to the parallel between cosmic powers in traditional African religions and in the NT, particularly in Colossians.

Source: John R. Levinson and Priscilla Pope-Levinson, "Global Perspectives on New Testament Interpretation," in Joel B. Green, ed., *Hearing the New Testament* (Grand Rapids, MI: Eerdmans, 1995), p. 337.

African theologians discern a "kindred atmosphere" connecting African traditional religion to the Hebrew Bible, with its emphasis on the pervasiveness of religion in all activities of life, the preponderance of rites and rituals, the importance of oral tradition, and the centrality of solidarity and group loyalty. Elements from the NT also resonate with African traditional religion. For example, the African emphasis on community illuminates the communal dimension of the NT. In a pioneering attempt to interpret the NT from the perspective of African culture J. S. Mbiti interpreted the resurrection as a communal event in which individuality is subsumed by a corporate resurrection body. Other central NT concepts such as salvation are also understood in light of the African emphasis on the need for equilibrium in community and cosmos. In this context the NT discussion of cosmic powers from whose negative influence people must be saved (e.g., Col 2:20) has a place in African theology.

Question

How might Christ's conquering of spiritual powers bring the "equilibrium" to community and cosmos of which the authors speak?

Doing Cross-Cultural Reading Yourself

Do you think that the concept of the "cosmic powers" of evil has any relevance to North American culture(s) today? If so, how?

EPHESIANS: Following Christ in a Cosmic Church

Ephesians is a masterpiece of devotional literature despite its long sentences and formal tone. Much of this structure has been rephrased into shorter units in English translations, but the reader of Ephesians still must take special care not to be lulled by its style into inattentiveness to the meaning! Unlike Paul's undisputed letters, it has a quiet and meditative tone, with no temperamental outbursts or attacks on the writer's enemies. Although it imitates the letter format by including a brief salutation, a brief thanksgiving, and a final greeting and blessing, Ephesians is a sophisticated theological essay. Rich in spiritual insight, Ephesians is a creative summary of some major Pauline concepts. Even if it is not by Paul, as a strong majority of NT scholars conclude, it is a significant statement of Pauline Christian ideals. Virtually every sentence resonates words and concepts from Paul's authentic letters, now reapplied to a new situation for many, if not all, of Paul's churches.

Ephesians in Brief: Outline of Structure and Contents

I. **Opening** Paul the sender, to saints "in Ephesus" (uncertain), blessing (1:1–2)

II. **Thanksgiving** for the blessedness and blessings of God (1:3–14)

III. **Body** God's plan of salvation in Christ through the unified, obedient body of the Church (1:15–6:20)

    A. God's eternal plan of salvation in Christ (1:15–3:21)

        1. The individual Christian in Christ: From death to life (2:1–10)

        2. The Christian community: one in Christ (2:11–22)

        3. The mystery of God's plan made clear by Paul; prayer and doxology (chapter 3)

    B. Moral exhortation on living in the world while united to Christ (4:1–6:20)

        1. Maintaining unity in diversity (4:1–16)

        2. Morality in relationship to believers (4:17–32)

        3. The believers' relation to unbelievers (5:1–14)

        4. Life in the Spirit (5:15–21)

        5. Table of household duties (5:22–6:9)

        6. Spiritual warfare and the armor of God (6:10–20)

IV. **Conclusion** Final greetings, commendation of Tychicus, blessing (6.21–24)

Developing Your Skills

Since Colossians and Ephesians are closely related in wording, read rapidly through Colossians and then Ephesians in one sitting, noticing the connections between the two.

A Guide to Reading Ephesians

Paul, or someone writing in his name, opens with a blessing to the "saints who are faithful" (1:1–2). Immediately he launches into praise for God as a theological preface to the body of his letter (1:3–14, one long sentence in the Greek original!) The author blesses God for several things that will be treated thematically in this letter: blessing with Christ in the heavenly places (v. 3), redemption by God's grace acting in Christ (vv. 5–7), God's mystery made known (vv. 8–10), and living for God's glory (vv. 13–14). This replacement of an initial thanksgiving for the faith of the recipients with a blessing of God should not, to judge from the contents of this letter, be considered a rebuke.

With this as a backdrop, the author now prays that his readers will understand what God has done for them (1:15–23). This prayer features a short thanksgiving for the audience (vv. 15–16). Basically, it functions as a prayer for understanding the contents of the next two chapters: God's great power for believers shown in Christ, who is the head of his cosmic church.

The author once again speaks to his audience about the great things God has done, this time with more detail (2:1–22). He begins by discussing individual reconciliation (2:1–10). First, he paints a dark picture of the former state of his Gentile readers/listeners: they were controlled by Satan and destined for destruction, "the children of [God's] wrath" (2:1–3). Then the author shows how God delivered people from this fate when God mercifully saved them (2:4–10). Not only did Christ's people die with him to secure their salvation (as Paul's undisputed letters state) and rise with him (as Colossians states), but God also made them ascend to heaven with Christ and caused them to reign with the heavenly Christ in the present (vv. 5–6). The author reaffirms a key Pauline notion, that "by grace you have been saved through faith, and this is not your own doing; it is the gift of God" (v. 8). All this is in God's plan. The way of life of God's people is "good works" (v. 10).

God has also reconciled Jew and Gentile as groups to each other by creating a new spiritual community in Christ's church (2:11–22). The author describes the Gentiles' former state. They were under Satan's control (2:1–3) and isolated from God's people (2:11–13). Now both Jews and Gentiles constitute a new spiritual community (2:14–18). The apostles are the foundation of this new spiritual community and Christ is the cornerstone (2:20–22). To make sure that the Gentile audience does not see the author as replacing the apostles—and they themselves as replacing the Jews—he explains that his gospel is new in the sense that it was not revealed in the OT. But yet his gospel is not different in kind from the gospel of the other apostles (3:1–7). The author emphasizes the importance of Paul's calling and how it revealed the mystery of salvation for the Gentiles to him: "I wrote this above in a few words, a [second?] reading of which will enable you to perceive my understanding of the mystery of Christ" (3:3–4). Further, the content of the new spiritual community is now made clear: Jew and Gentile are fellow heirs, fellow members of the church, and fellow partakers of the promise (3:5–6). The Gentiles have been incorporated into the body of Christ, or the church, not for their sake only, but so that even the cosmic powers may know of their incorporation into Christ (3:10).

Having completed his major treatment on the "indicatives of the faith," the author prays once again for his audience (3:14–21). As with the first prayer, this one is a hinge between two sections, an introduction to the last three chapters in which he turns from the indicative to the imperative. "Maintain the unity of the Spirit in the bond of peace" is the opening statement of its theme (4:3). The author gives a theological example of how unity and diversity are possible: in the Spirit, the Lord Jesus, and the Father there is oneness (4:4–6). There is one Lord, one faith and one baptism, and one God the Father who is above, through, and in all things (4:5–6). This leads the author to develop his argument in relation to the varied gifts that God has given to the church. In the genuine Pauline letters, these are gifts given to every church member; in Ephesians, they are gifts creating leadership in the church. Leaders must use them to promote unity in the church and equip the saints for their own ministry in daily life (4:7–16). Not all members have the same gifts, but all are to grow together in unity. Now the author deals with more concrete issues of morality. He reminds his readers what they were before they believed in Christ (4:17–19), how they have put off the "old man" and put on the "new man" (4:20–24). Since they are new creatures in Christ, they ought to act like it; further, since they are organically connected (i.e., members of one another), they ought not to go back to the old ways of hostility (4:25–32). Do not conform to outsiders' sinful ways (5:1–7), the author says, but tell outsiders the truth of the gospel (5:8–14). After exhortations to be filled by the Spirit (5:18–21), the author turns to life in the Christian household (5:22–6:9). In a household code, the author gives instruction: Wives must submit to their husbands (5:22–24); the husband must love his wife (5:25–33; this is the longest, most emphatic section of the household code in Ephesians). Children are to obey their parents (6:1–3); fathers are to raise their children in the discipline and admonition of the Lord (6:4). Slaves are to obey their masters (6:5–8), and masters are to treat their slaves humanely (6:9).

The body of his epistle concludes ("Finally," 6:10) with a treatise on spiritual warfare that draws on an extended analogy with Roman military equipment (6:10–20). The author presents an ongoing cosmic conflict between good and evil with no end in sight. He describes two levels of evil cosmic powers: the earthly rulers of the present evil age and the invisible forces of evil in "heavenly places," not God's residence but a place between earth and God's heaven (6:10–12). The author knows that the second evil, invisible forces, is so powerful that mere human wickedness cannot explain it (Wink 1998). Instead of despairing, however, the author rejoices that God provides ammunition with which to successfully defeat even supernatural evil. According to Ephesians, each article of God's armor is a Christian virtue; cultivated together, qualities like truth and faith offer full protection from even the devil's worst attacks.

The author concludes the epistle with a commendation of Tychicus (6:21–22) and a blessing (6:23–24).

www Follow the link to examine Professor Felix Just's table on the household codes in Colossians and Ephesians.

Historical Reading of Ephesians

Ephesians in Brief: Summary of Historical Reading

Author A strong majority holds that Ephesians is pseudonymous; a small but persistent minority holds for Paul.

Date If authentic, 60–64; if pseudonymous, probably in the 90s.

Audience "In Ephesus" (1:1) is not in the best manuscripts and is likely a later addition. Most scholars hold that the audience is Christians in various Pauline churches, perhaps in western Asia Minor, where Ephesus is located.

Unity and Integrity Not questioned.

Purpose To keep its audience loyalty to the heights of Pauline Christianity, especially to faith in Jesus Christ alone as sufficient for salvation and the basis of a faithful life.

Author

Although Paul's authorship of Colossians is seriously doubted by a bare majority of scholars today, a much stronger majority rejects the claim that he wrote Ephesians. Although it closely resembles Colossians, Ephesians differs from the undisputed Pauline letters in three ways. First, its vocabulary contains over ninety words not found elsewhere in Paul's writings. Second, its literary style features long—sometimes extremely long—convoluted sentences, in contrast to Paul's direct, forceful statements. Paul's style is conversational, but Ephesians is formal. This difference in literary style is perhaps the difference most noticeable to beginning students of the NT. Ephesians also borrows wording from Colossians, which Paul does not do in his authentic letters; 75 of Ephesians' 155 verses are paralleled in Colossians. Third, the theology of Ephesians lacks emphasis on typical Pauline doctrines such as justification by faith and the nearness of Christ's return. It contains a more conservative household code or house table than Colossians. Despite its similarity to Colossians, it presents a different view of the "mystery" (divine secret) revealed in Christ. In Colossians, God's long-kept secret is Christ's mystical union with his followers (Col. 1:27), but in Ephesians, it is the union of Jew and Gentile in one church (Eph. 3:6).

Date and Audience

If Ephesians is by Paul, he probably wrote it during his Roman imprisonment in the early 60s. But if it is by a later Pauline disciple, Ephesians was probably written when the author's letters first circulated as a unit, perhaps about 90. More than any other disputed Pauline letter (except those to Timothy and Titus), Ephesians seems to

Library of Celsus in Ephesus According to an inscription on the front, the consul Gaius Julius Aquila built the library in 110 C.E. as a tomb for his father, Gaius Julius Celsus, who had been governor of Asia. Twelve thousand scrolls once filled the halls of the library, stored in niches in the walls. Although the library did not stand in the first century, it certainly testifies to the love of learning and letters that is evident in the NT letter to the Ephesians. Used by permission of BiblePlaces.com.

reflect a time in church history significantly later than the author's day. References to "apostles and prophets" as the church's foundation imply that these figures belong to the past, not the author's generation (2:20; 3:5). The Gentiles' equality in Christian fellowship is no longer a controversial issue but an accomplished fact; this strongly suggests that the letter originated after the church had become largely non-Jewish (2:11–22). Jewish-Christian intruders no longer question the author's stand on circumcision, again indicating that the work was composed after Jerusalem's destruction had lessened the influence of the Jewish mother church. When Paul uses the term *church* he always refers to a single congregation (Gal 1:2; 1 Cor 11:16; 16:19, etc.). By contrast, Ephesians' author speaks of the church collectively, as a universal institution encompassing individual groups. This view of the church as a worldwide, even cosmic entity also points to a time after the apostolic period.

The accumulated evidence convinces most scholars that Ephesians is a deutero-Pauline document, a secondary work composed in the author's name by an admirer thoroughly steeped in the apostle's thought and theology. The close parallels to Colossians, as well as phrases taken from Romans, Philemon, and other letters, indicate that unlike the author of Acts this unknown writer was familiar with Pauline correspondence. Some scholars propose that Ephesians was written as a kind of "cover letter" or essay to accompany an early collection of the author's letters. Ephesians, then, can be seen as a tribute to Paul, summarizing some of his ideas and updating others to fit the changing needs of a largely Gentile and cosmopolitan church.

Purpose

Ephesians relays no explicit purpose, and nowhere does it explicitly correct errors, so we are left to deduce its purpose from its main theme. Ephesians' theme is the union of all creation with Christ, manifested on earth by the church's international, intercultural unity (1:10–14). Echoing Romans' concept of predestination, the author states that before the world's foundation God selected Christ's future "children" (the church) to be redeemed by Jesus' blood, a sacrifice through which their sins are forgiven. According to his preordained plan, God has placed Christ as head of the church, which is his cosmic body. The Spirit of Christ now fills the church as fully as God dwells in Christ (1:22–23). This mystical union of the human and divine is God's unforeseen gift, his grace that saves those who trust him (2:1–10). God's long-hidden secret is that Gentiles, previously under divine condemnation, can now share in the biblical promises made to Israel. This divine purpose to unite Jew and Gentile is the special message that the author is commissioned to preach (3:1–21). Ephesians' last three chapters are devoted to instructions on living properly in the world while remaining united to Christ. The author reinterprets the concept of Jesus' descent from and ascension to the spirit realm of heaven to be a cosmic military campaign in which he made lesser spirits his prisoners and filled the universe with his presence. From heaven he gave leadership gifts to the church, and the proper exercise of these gifts knit the people of God together and fit them for service to others.

The Christian faith requires the highest ethical conduct, Ephesians states, so the author contrasts Greco-Roman vices with Christian virtues and urges believers to continue transforming their lives to fit God's new creation (4:17–5:20). Home life is to be as reverent and orderly as behavior in church. While insisting on a domestic hierarchy—"man is the head of the woman, just as Christ . . . is head of the church"—the writer reminds husbands to love their wives and thus to honor them (5:21–6:9). Ephesians endorses the rigid domestic hierarchy of Greco-Roman society but makes the system more humane by insisting that Christian love apply to all public and private relationships. In adapting the household code to do this,

Ephesians (and Colossians) show that the gap between the best of Greco-Roman values and life in Christ is not so large after all.

www Read an essay on 4:2, the only place in the NT where any explicit reference to humor occurs, and follow a link to an excellent essay on the Ephesian household code by Professor Carolyn Osiek.

Cross-Cultural Reading of Ephesians

Of all NT documents, Ephesians stresses most fully the cross-cultural unity of the church. It does this by emphasizing how the death of Christ and his cosmic reign has broken down the division between Jew and Gentile, the paradigmatic cultural division in the NT. But hidden in Ephesians is evidence that cross-cultural freedom is still to be fully won—slaves that come at this time from other cultures are given a better standing, but not yet a good one (in the eyes of most contemporary readers, that is).

Cross-Cultural Reading at Work
The Problem of Masters and Slaves (Eph 6:5)

In this selection a prominent Hispanic cross-cultural reader of the NT reminds us that the "social location" of the reader can play a large role in how one reads the Bible.

Because the master controlled what portions of the Bible would be taught to slaves, most of the biblical stories and teaching selected attempted to justify the master's self-interest. Most sermons were based on passages like Ephesians 6:5, which states, "Slaves, obey your masters according to the flesh, with fear and trembling, and in singleness of heart, as unto Christ." The interpretations from the center of slavocracy urged slaves to fulfill God's will by being docile and obedient so that they could be blessed by God with eternal salvation.

Yet, whenever the Bible is used to justify oppression, the [people on the] margins read the Bible to understand their oppression and to seek their liberation. While white preachers in the employ of the masters interpreted the biblical stories spiritually and metaphorically, black slaves interpreted these same stories materially and literally (i.e., God's liberation of the Hebrew slaves in Egypt was a physical, not just a spiritual, liberation). Such readings reserved the right to resist passages within the text that had been historically used by the dominant culture to justify the dehumanization of oppressed groups. For this reason, one would be hard pressed even today to find sermons within the African American community based on Philemon

Source: Miguel De La Torre, *Reading the Bible from the Margins* (New York: Orbis, 2002) 62–63.
Copyright © 2002 by Miguel A. De Le Torre. Used by permission of the publisher.

(where the author sends a runaway slave back to his master) or to hear any Negro spirituals honoring the author, who penned passages such as Ephesians 6:5.

Question

If Philemon were to appear in a spiritual, how might the song treat that letter?

> **Doing Cross-Cultural Reading Yourself**
>
> *Why is it that modern readers of the NT household codes, including readers from a variety of cultures, assume that slavery is an absolute evil and should never be practiced but are sometimes hesitant to assert the same about submission of wives to their husbands?*

Key Terms and Concepts

apocalyptic • household code • imminent expectation • pseudonymous

Questions for Study, Discussion, and Writing

2 Thessalonians

1. What is your conclusion on the authorship of 2 Thessalonians, and why?
2. Where does the thanksgiving section of 2 Thessalonians end? Does it make a difference in the interpretation of this letter?
3. Describe in your own words the problem with eschatology in 2 Thessalonians and how the author tries to solve it. How persuasive is the author, do you think?

Colossians

1. What is your conclusion about the authorship of Colossians, and why?
2. Analyze the similarities between the two Christ hymns in Philippians 2 and Colossians. What different uses are they put to by their author(s)?
3. Describe carefully the problem to which Colossians is written. What might be the origin of this situation?

Ephesians

1. What is your conclusion about the authorship of Ephesians, and why?
2. What is the significance of Ephesians' emphasizing warfare with unseen spirits rather than the Parousia? Is the hope for the Parousia given up?
3. Describe the "armor of God" at the end of Ephesians, and relate it to what you know of Roman military armor. Keep in mind a fact that this passage does not mention: Roman foot soldiers had very little armor on the back of their torso and legs, to keep them going forward instead of running away–to turn back is to be unprotected.

4. Critique the following short analysis of the social ethic adopted in Colossians and Ephesians: "What the Pauline tradition seeks is not social revolution, but social reform."

For Further Reading

2 Thessalonians

Donfried, Karl P., and I. H. Marshall. *The Theology of the Shorter Pauline Letters.* Cambridge: Cambridge University Press, 1993. Superb, succinct treatment of the thought of 1–2 Thessalonians.

Krentz, Edgar. "Through a Lens: Theology and Fidelity in 2 Thessalonians," in Jouette M. Bassler, ed., *Pauline Theology* (Minneapolis: Fortress, 1991), vol. 1, pp. 52–62. Short treatment of the theology of 2 Thessalonians.

Levine, Amy-Jill, ed. *A Feminist Companion to the Deutero-Pauline Epistles.* London: T. & T. Clark, 2003. Contains nine accessible essays on 2 Thessalonians, Colossians, Ephesians and the Pastorals.

Marshall, I. Howard. *1 and 2 Thessalonians.* Grand Rapids, MI: Eerdmans, 1983.

Richard, Earl. *First and Second Thessalonians.* Collegeville, MN: Liturgical Press, 1995. An excellent recent commentary; considers 1 Thessalonians to be composite, 2 Thessalonians as pseudonymous.

Wanamaker, Charles. *The Epistles to the Thessalonians.* Grand Rapids, MI: Eerdmans, 1990. A commentary that focuses on historical, social scientific, and rhetorical methods; although based on the Greek text, it is accessible to beginning students.

Colossians

Barth, M., ed. and trans. *Colossians and Philemon.* Vol. 34a of the Anchor Bible. Garden City, NY: Doubleday, 1974. A scholarly translation and analysis.

Lohse, Eduard. *Colossians and Philemon.* Hermeneia Commentary. Philadelphia: Fortress Press, 1971. A scholarly analysis concluding that a disciple of Paul wrote Colossians.

O'Brien, P. T. *Colossians, Philemon.* Word Biblical Commentary 44. Waco, TX: Word Books, 1982. Defends the Pauline authorship of Colossians; includes author's translation.

Martin, Clarice. "The Haustafeln (Household Codes) in African American Biblical Interpretation: 'Free Slaves' and 'Subordinate Women,' in Cain H. Felder, ed., *Stony the Road We Trod: African American Biblical Interpretation* (Minneapolis: Fortress, 1991), pp. 206–231. Fascinating treatment by a feminist African American NT scholar.

Schweizer, Eduard. *The Letter to the Colossians: A Commentary.* Minneapolis: Augsburg, 1982. Less technical than works by Lohse and O'Brien; suggests that Timothy played a role in writing Colossians.

Ephesians

Barth, Markus, ed. and trans. *Ephesians.* Vols. 34 and 34a of the Anchor Bible. Garden City, NY: Doubleday, 1974. This extensive commentary defends Pauline authorship.

Furnish, V. P. "Ephesians, Epistle to the." In D. N. Freedman, ed., *The Anchor Bible Dictionary*, vol. 2, pp. 535–542. Garden City, NY: Doubleday, 1992. An excellent overview of current scholarship on Ephesians.

Mollenkott, Virginia Ramey. "Emancipative Elements in Ephesians 5:21–33: Why Feminist Scholarship Has (Often) Left Them Unmentioned, and Why They Should be Emphasized." In Amy-Jill Levine, ed., *A Feminist Companion to the Deutero-Pauline Epistles*. London: T. & T. Clark, 2003, pp. 37–58. A moderate defense of a more traditional reading of the Ephesian household code from a prominent feminist.

Mitton, C. L. *Ephesians*. New Century Bible. Grand Rapids, MI: Eerdmans, 1981. A brief study of Ephesians as a work produced by one of the author's disciples.

Quinn, J. D., ed. and trans. *1 and 2 Timothy and Titus*. Vol. 35 of the Anchor Bible. Garden City, NY: Doubleday, 1976. A recent translation with commentary.

Wink, Walter. *The Powers That Be: Theology for a New Millennium*. Garden City, NY: Doubleday, 1998. Connects Pauline talk of supernatural forces—angels and demons—with sociocultural assumptions and practices that inhibit God's rule in human society.

Chapter Sixteen

1–2 Timothy and Titus: Pastoral Letters to Guide the Pauline Churches

The Pastoral Letters seemingly deal with leadership and doctrine in Paul's churches at the end of his life and immediately after his death. They present a more developed form of church leadership than earlier Pauline letters, and they provide a structure that starts Christians on the way to creating the **threefold office** of bishop, elder/presbyter, and deacon that was to become important in all three main branches of Christianity (Eastern Orthodox, Roman Catholic, and Protestant). The Pastoral Letters also have a second main purpose, to direct the church's growing struggle with the form of false teaching known as Gnosticism.

The **Pastoral Letters,** 1–2 Timothy and Titus, obtained that name in early modern times. The Latin word *pastor* means "shepherd," a common ancient metaphor for a leader. The first two Pastorals are addressed to **Timothy,** the son of a Jewish mother and a Greek father (Acts 16:1), who served as Paul's missionary companion (1 Cor 4:17; 16:10). According to Acts and Paul's authentic letters, Timothy was an important contributor to Paul's evangelism in Greece and Asia Minor, a co-founder of churches in Macedonia, and later Paul's representative to Philippi, Thessalonica, and Corinth. In listing him as a coauthor of as many as six different letters, Paul and disciples who wrote in Paul's name after his death affirm Timothy's vital role in the Christian mission (see the first verses of 2 Corinthians, Philippians, 1 and 2 Thessalonians, Philemon and Colossians). Titus was only a slightly less important colleague of Paul's. He was a Gentile convert to Paul's gospel. In Gal 2:1, he went with Paul to the "Jerusalem Conference," and he served as Paul's representative to the Corinthian church, especially in 2 Corinthians. In the Pastorals, however, Timothy and Titus are no longer historical characters but now are literary symbols. They represent a new generation of church leaders to whom the task of preserving the apostolic church is entrusted. A new generation of Christians must take on the job of defending true church teaching against falsehood (1 Tim 4:2, 11–12). Titus resembles 1 Timothy more than 2 Timothy in its style and contents. We will consider the pastorals in their canonical order—1 Timothy, 2 Timothy, and

Titus—although many scholars conclude that they were written in the order of Titus, 1 Timothy, and 2 Timothy.

1 TIMOTHY: Combating False Teaching and Setting Up Church Leadership

The longest of the Pastoral Letters, 1 Timothy is a letter of exhortation to combat the teachings of insiders that the author considers false. It defines the boundaries of the faith against this false teaching, and it considers any departure from the true teaching it lays down as heresy. It urges good behavior by Christians to outsiders in order to advance the church's image—and therefore its mission—in the world. In line with this exhortation, 1 Timothy draws on Roman-Hellenistic household codes to define and regulate the life of its churches. Written in a formal, businesslike style, the letter transmits the main aspects of Paul's theology and applies them to a changing situation after his death.

I Timothy in Brief: Outline of Structure and Contents

I. **Opening** Paul to Timothy, blessing (1:1–2; no thanksgiving follows)
II. **Body** Stop false teaching and promote good order (1:3–6:19)
   A. Beware of false teaching (1:3–11)
   B. Paul's pastoral example for Timothy (1:12–20)
   C. Good order for worship, especially men and women (chap. 2)
   D. Qualifications for bishops and deacons (chap. 3)
   E. Correcting false teaching (4:1–5)
   F. Timothy as teacher of good doctrine (4:6–5:2)
   G. Instructions for widows, elders, slaves (5:3–6:2)
   H. Instructions against false teaching and the love of money (6:3–10)
   I. Final instructions to Timothy (6:11–19)
III. **Conclusion** the author's blessing on Timothy (6:20–21)

Building Your Skills

Read the letter carefully in one sitting, noting how the author presents his material by oscillating between two main themes: Timothy's duty to repress false teachings; and church order in structure (bishops, deacons, and elders) and conduct (social roles, especially of women).

A Guide to Reading 1 Timothy

After a brief opening and blessing to Timothy (1:1–2), Paul's "loyal son in the faith," the author omits a thanksgiving in order to move directly into the body of his epistle. This indicates a businesslike, even urgent attitude; it does not indicate that the author is upset with the recipients.

The first major section of the body is a reminder of why Paul left Timothy in Ephesus: to stop false teachers (1:3–20; this probably indicates the audience's locale). These people were preoccupied with the OT Law and also with "myths and endless genealogies that promote speculations." The author attacks them for not knowing what they are so confidently talking about (vv. 6–7). He explains the proper use of the Law: it is for sinners, to lead them to repentance (vv. 8–11). In a short catalogue of vice illustrating and discouraging sinful behavior, the author includes "slave traders" as part of this more traditional list. These false teachers were probably forcing the Law on believers (v. 9). Then "Paul" follows with a personal illustration showing the true purpose of the Law: it taught him that he was a sinner, but Christ showed him grace (vv. 12–17). The first of many **faithful sayings** in the Pastoral Letters comes in v. 15, "Christ Jesus came into the world to save sinners." These sayings are short affirmations that have an authoritative, almost creedal role in teaching what the true faith believes. The author then repeats his charge to Timothy (vv. 18–20), although this time the emphasis is on Timothy's perseverance and godliness in the face of opposition and the importance of keeping a clear conscience. The charge concludes with a note about the author's removing two church leaders, Hymenaeus and Alexander, by "turning them over to Satan" (1:20).

The doctrinal controversies promoted by the false teachers had evidently created a factional spirit within the congregation, so the author lays down important guidelines for church life, especially worship. He commands the church to pray for all people, especially those in governmental authority, so that Christians may live a quiet, respectable life that will gain a hearing for the faith. The author affirms that God appointed Paul an apostle to the Gentiles to teach these things and implies that those who do not follow them are not faithful and true members of Paul's churches (2:1–7). With this note on "authority" still sounding in the ears of the audience, the author addresses social roles within the church using ideas adapted from pagan household codes (2:8–15). The false teachers had perhaps persuaded women to follow them (in some second-century Christian groups, women had a prominent role as teachers), so 2:8–15 reminds the women of the proper order in worship. Men are to pray, seemingly not women (v. 8). Wealthy Christian women are to dress modestly in church, not parade their wealth; instead, they are to be rich in "good works" (vv. 9–10). Women (probably only wives is meant, but the Greek is ambiguous) are to be fully subject to men; they are not to teach or have any authority over men in the church (vv. 11–12). The author mentions Eve's deception in the Garden of Eden

(v. 14), causing her to teach Adam, for this is probably what had happened at Ephesus—women were being deceived by false teachers and were becoming teachers of men themselves. Women are prohibited from teaching men as a reversal of God-ordained order (vv. 12–13). As the NRSV footnotes indicate, the Greek word for "women" can be translated as "wives," thus limiting the author's instructions to married women in the congregation; but would this author let single women and widows teach men? Godly women will be kept safe through the perils of childbirth if they continue in "faith, love and holiness"; the author adds one last time, "with modesty" (v. 15).

Regarding church leadership (3:1–13), the author emphasizes the ethical qualifications of overseers (bishops, elders) (vv. 1–7) and deacons (vv. 8–13). The fact that he does not describe the duties of these offices may indicate that they already exist but need better men to serve in them. Bishops must be "the husband of one wife" (the meaning of which is disputed, but it must refer to more than just monogamy!), sober, apt teachers, hospitable, good family men, and so on. Deacons must share many of the same qualities, which may indicate that some deacons moved from that office to the office of bishop. Church leaders must be male, but in v. 11 we may have a tantalizing reference to women deacons. The author then summarizes the need for good conduct in the church (vv. 14–15), followed by a short hymn to Christ that celebrates the progress of the gospel in the world (v. 16).

Next, Timothy is charged with guarding "the truths of the faith" against false teaching (4:1–16). Apostates had crept into the church, just as the Spirit had predicted they would. They embraced a mixture of Jewish legalism and Greek asceticism, forbidding both marriage and diets that are restricting (vv. 2–5). Timothy must warn the church to stay away from them (vv. 6–7). Further, Timothy is urged to "train yourself to be godly" (v. 7), to gain honor from his people even though he is "young," to set forth the true gospel of Jesus Christ before the congregation (v. 13), and to make progress in his own leadership (v. 16).

Next, Timothy is given instructions in addressing certain groups in the church (5:1–6:10). The instructions are related especially to Timothy's "youthfulness" and his inexperience in pastoral duties. As a young man, he needed guidance in how to address the various age and gender groups of the church (5:1–2); this is in line with the social system of the times, where young men (or older men, unless they were the head of a household) would not have had experience in guiding older males or females of any age. Timothy gives priority to the widows (5:3–16), especially regarding the church's provisions for them (5:5, 9), though certain qualifications had to be met. In particular, young, able-bodied widows and those whose children could take care of them should not be helped out by the church (5:4, 7, 11–16). Elders who have remained faithful to the gospel should receive a "double honor," including financial remuneration (vv. 17–18). ("Honor" in the Mediterranean world always has a practical, tangible component.) But those who have sinned (provided the sin is proved by at least two witnesses) earn a shaming rebuke instead of honor (5:19–20). Prospective elders need to be screened carefully, because they could be motivated by greed (5:21–25; cf. 6:3–10). Slaves are mentioned last (6:1–2). Rather than having the church supply their needs, they are to serve their masters well since, by implication, their needs will be met by their masters. Some "think that godliness is a means to financial gain" (v. 5). Greed had motivated the false teachers and caused them and others to wander from the faith, so the leaders Timothy appoints must keep clear of it (vv. 6–10). The author strongly affirms the social idea of "limited goods" and its pressure against becoming rich by taking the goods of others: "those who want to be rich fall into temptation" and then spiritual ruin (v. 9). There follows what is perhaps the most misquoted verse in the NT: the *love of money*, not money itself, is the root of all kinds of evil (v. 10).

The epistle concludes with more personal and pastoral instructions to Timothy (6:11–21). He is to shun riches, "pursue godliness . . . [and] fight the good fight of the faith" (vv. 11–12), a theme repeated throughout this epistle. But before the author can finish the letter, he turns to those who are both already wealthy and godly in the church (vv. 17–19). Those who are wealthy ought to be rich in good deeds as well (v. 18) and thus by their generosity lay up treasures for themselves, probably in heaven (v. 19). The epistle closes with a final reminder to Timothy to guard the gospel entrusted to him and avoid the contradictions of "what is falsely called knowledge [Greek *gnosis*]," then a short blessing (vv. 20–21).

Historical Reading of 1 Timothy

The Pastorals in Brief: Summary of Historical Reading

Author A strong majority of scholars concludes that the Pastorals were written by one leader in a Pauline church after Paul's death; a small minority holds that Paul wrote them.

Date If by Paul, in the 60s; if pseudonymous, probably in the 90s.

Audience If written by Paul, Timothy and Titus are its recipients in Ephesus and Crete, respectively. If pseudonymous, the Pauline churches in and around the western Mediterranean.

Unity and Integrity Not questioned today.

Purpose To strengthen churches by laying down qualifications for special church offices and order in the church, and to put down false teaching of Gnosticism.

Author

This letter bears Paul's name, and some NT scholars believe that Paul did in fact write it during his final imprisonment to guide Timothy and Titus in a new generation as they carried on after his death. It is filled with Pauline words and ideas. However, the vast majority of NT scholars today, probably 80–90 percent, hold that 1 Timothy and the other two Pastoral Letters are written by the same person, but pseudonymously. (Here we must remember that the importance of a NT document is not determined by whether it was written by the person whose name it carries. The Pastorals have been valuable in the Christian church for almost two thousand years, whoever their author was.) The following four main reasons are often given for concluding that the Pastoral Letters are not by Paul.

- *Vocabulary*. Although scholars debate the validity of vocabulary statistics in determining authorship, the numbers are nonetheless impressive. Of 848 words (beside proper names) found in the Pastorals, 306 are not in the remainder of the Pauline corpus, even including 2 Thessalonians, Colossians, and Ephesians. This is far beyond the proportion of unique words in Paul's undisputed or even disputed letters. Of these 306 words, 175 do not occur elsewhere in the New Testament, but 210 are part of the general vocabulary of Christian writers of the second century. What is more significant, the Pastorals use Paul's key words in a non-Pauline sense. For example, "righteous" in Paul means primarily "justified" by God's gift, but in the Pastorals the emphasis is on being morally "upright" (1 Tim 6:11; 2 Tim 2:22); "faith" in Paul is a noun of action, "active trust," but in the Pastorals has become "the Christian faith" (1 Tim 3:9; 6:20; Titus 1:13; 2:1; 2 Tim 1:14; 4:7); "church" is no longer individual congregations but the one church universal; and despite what Paul said about faith and works, the Pastorals continually praise good works with no nuance. Differences in vocabulary also appear in small words; some nineteen conjunctions and adverbs that appear throughout each undisputed Pauline letter are absent from the Pastorals.
- *Literary style*. Paul writes a conversational, lively Greek, with gripping arguments and emotional flare-ups, and he introduces real or imaginary opponents and partners in dialogue. When Paul's letters were read to their audience, they must have felt like Paul himself was there. The Pastorals, however, are in a formal, meditative style more like Ephesians but quite unlike Romans, to say nothing of the Corinthian correspondence or of Galatians.
- *The situation of the church witnessed in the letters*. The letters reflect the characteristics of what has been called **early Catholicism.** This includes emphasis on the church universal; the importance of defining and keeping the true faith, especially against heretical challenges; establishing offices, which Paul mentions only occasionally in the undisputed letters (Phil 1:1; 1 Thess 5:12; Rom 12:8; Paul's churches have elders in Acts 14:23); and putting women into roles that are generally far less participatory and equal to men's roles than in Paul's letters.
- *The situation of Paul implied in the letters*. The Pastorals present this situation for Paul: (1) Paul had left Timothy in Ephesus, while he moved on to Macedonia (1 Tim 1:3);

(2) Paul likewise left Titus in Crete, after having spent some time with Titus on the island evangelizing (Titus 1:5); (3) Paul is a prisoner in Rome when he writes 2 Timothy (2 Tim 1:8, 16–17; 4:16). This situation does not easily fit into any reconstruction of Paul's life and work as we know it from his other letters, nor can it be deduced from the Acts of the Apostles. If Paul wrote these letters, then he must have been released from his (first) Roman imprisonment and have traveled to Crete to set up a mission there, and thus the Pastorals would come after Acts ends its story of Paul. Although this is *possible,* the scanty information we have about this matter seems to be derived from his plans in Romans 15, not based on solid information.

From the contents of the Pastorals, we can deduce the following about the author. First, the author was a man; a woman with the ability to exercise the authority of these letters would not tell other women to keep silent and be submissive! Second, he was well educated, as he writes in a formal style and has knowledge of Roman-Hellenistic writings. Third, and most important, he was a "student" of Paul or a member of his circle, one who probably had known Timothy and Titus. He was intent on applying Paul's theology, as he understood it, to the new situation in Paul's churches about thirty years after Paul's death. He probably addressed his letter to two trusted companions of Paul (who themselves may have been deceased) to show how Paul would have instructed them about their conduct as church leaders in the last third of the first century. In this way, he applied Paul's heritage to the type of issues that were arising as the Pauline churches grew and changed.

Date

If the Pastorals are by Paul, they are to be dated in the 60s, shortly before his death. If they are pseudonymous, they probably come from the 90s, to judge by the situation of the church with respect to the challenge of Gnosticism, the rise of church office, and the rest.

Audience

The literal addressees of the Pastorals are two co-workers of Paul, Timothy and Titus, who appear here as Paul's relatively youthful successors. Timothy is located in the established church in Ephesus, and Titus is setting up new churches on Crete. These letters are most probably aimed at the Pauline churches as a whole, expecting that they will follow their advice to strengthen church organization and put down false teaching, things that all Pauline churches were busily engaged in during the second century.

Purpose

In 1 Tim 3:14–16, the author says, "I am writing these instructions to you so that, if I am delayed [in coming to you], you may know how one ought to behave in the household of God, which is the church of the living God, the pillar and bulwark of the truth." This stresses behavior in the church as a well-ordered household of which God is the Father, and God's children are well behaved. In particular, the author is concerned to refute false teachings and false practices of his opponents, and this purpose probably extends to the other two Pastorals. Because the author does not offer an objective, explicit description of his opponents' errors, or even describe them in any detail when he refutes them, we do not know the exact nature of the beliefs that the Pastorals attack. From the author's language, it does appear that these false teachers are *inside* the church and have not left it to form an oppositional outside group. Some commentators suggest that the false teachers practiced an early form of **Gnosticism,** a movement of secret, saving "knowledge" holding that the physical world was irredeemably evil, mentioned in 6:20, but the letter reveals too little about the heresies involved to confirm this suggestion. Because the author describes his opponents as teaching the "moral law" and being wrongly preoccupied with "interminable myths and genealogies" (1:3–4, 7–9), many critics suppose that some form of Hellenistic Judaism is under attack. Practicing an extreme asceticism (severe self-discipline of the physical appetites), these persons forbid marriage and abstain from various foods (4:1–3). Gnostic practices took diverse forms, ranging from the kind of self-denial mentioned here to the open sexual immorality Paul rebuked in Corinth. Timothy must correct this by transmitting the authorized teachings (4:11), thereby saving both himself and those who obey his orders (4:16). Probably some combination of gnostic and Jewish practice is in view.

Invoking Paul's authority, the author is eager to preserve sound doctrine through a stable church organization. His list of qualifications for **bishops** (overseers), **deacons** (assistants), and **elders** (the religiously mature leadership) implies a hierarchy of church offices much more rigidly stratified than was the case in Paul's day. Paul once used the terms *bishops* and *deacons* (Phil. 1:1), but perhaps as designating areas of service more than the specific ecclesiastical offices enumerated here. Although the author says that church officials must demonstrate all the virtues typical of Hellenistic ethical philosophy (3:2–23), he says nothing in these lists about their intellectual qualifications or possession of the Spirit. Rather than the spiritual gifts that Paul advocated, the Pastoral Letters' standards for church offices include hallmarks of social respectability.

www Follow the link to good resources on the historical and feminist study of the Pastoral Epistles.

> ### Doing Historical Reading Yourself
>
> *Imagine that you are a member of the group that the author of the Pastorals opposes. What would you say in response to his attacks?*

> ### The Pastoral Letters in Brief: Summary of Newer Methods
>
> **Social Scientific** Virtually every major aspect of social scientific study is relevant to the Pastorals. Kinship values are stressed as the church is consolidated as a "fictive" household. Purity is a matter of separation from the world but is not emphasized. Honor and shame are stressed as the church seeks some social respectability to forestall persecution and continue conversions. The idea of "limited goods" is prominently affirmed. As the church grows rapidly and faces more internal dissent, its need for organization increases.
>
> **Feminist** The Pastorals intensify the patriarchal attitude to women in the church that is found in Colossians and Ephesians. Women are seemingly barred from church office, told not to talk or show their wealth in church services, and urged to attend to more domestic duties. The reasons for this return to patriarchy are debated but likely have to do with the internal fight with false teaching and the church's standing with outsiders.
>
> **Cross-Cultural** The issues dealt with in the Pastorals do not emphasize matters important to cross-cultural reading. Still, cross-cultural readers of the NT are beginning to look to the Pastorals as they reflect on their own patterns of church organization and struggles over what constitutes true Christian teaching and life.

Feminist Reading of 1 Timothy

Paul recognized women as prophets and speakers (1 Cor. 11:5) and as deacons, patrons, and apostles (Romans 15), but the author of 1 Timothy does not permit women (perhaps only wives are meant) to teach or hold any position of authority over a man. The detailed instruction on women's dress and conduct in 1 Timothy probably applies to public worship and parallels the restricted position assigned women in Greco-Roman society. Christian churches today differ about whether this is a timeless prescription that permanently limits women's roles in the church or a time-bound prescription limited to the author's situation, where the faith is threatened by heresy spread in part by women. Feminist reading, of course, keeps to the latter position. The author also issues instructions for the church's treatment of widows. He distinguishes between "true widows" who do "good deeds" and women who are unqualified for that status because of their youth or inappropriate conduct. Following Jewish law (Exod 22:22; Deut 24:17–24), the church assumed responsibilities early for supporting destitute widows (Acts 6:1), but the author stipulates that widows must be sixty years old before they can qualify for financial assistance.

Feminist Reading at Work
Men and Women at Worship (1 Tim 2:8–3:1a)

In this reading Pheme Perkins discusses the most (in)famous passage in 1 Timothy on the status and role of women. Note how she uses a combination of feminist and social scientific methods.

1 Timothy sketches a conventional picture of the virtuous woman. Her deportment is that of the female counterpart to the male, with hands raised up in the traditional *orans* [praying] posture. Does this segment have anything at all to do with women at prayer? That they were expected to devote themselves to prayer is clear in the description of the real widow in 5:9, though the activities of younger women are connected with their activities as mistress of the household, not prayer (5:10, 14; Titus 2:4–5). Good works are the deeds of charity and hospitality appropriate to female benefactors.

The only possible connection between this section and worship occurs in the prohibition against women teaching or having authority over males (2:11). That reading assumes that the teaching took place in the context of a community gathered for worship rather than at some other time. Nothing in the Pastorals makes that link explicitly. Teaching as evangelization took place in households, workshops, and various public spaces. . . . We have seen that those who defended teaching women philosophy had to counter the objection that such education would make them figures of ridicule, neglecting home and family, seeking quarrels with men. The false teachers are described as upsetting entire households (Titus 1:11). As we have seen, women constituted a higher proportion of the early Christian churches that of the larger society. The wealth attributed to the woman in this passage suggests that she was also a person capable of exerting the influence of a rich benefactor.

To which audience is this depiction of the godly and dignified Christian woman directed? To outsiders, including pagan husbands and family, who suspect that Christianity is another oriental cult likely to involve women in the disorderly and anti-authoritarian behavior often depicted in [contemporary] comedy? Or to insiders, caught in the asymmetries of wealth, status, and influence that would pressure lower-status males to defer to their female patroness? The letter does not say. Women are not permitted to engage in the verbal give-and-take characteristic of the instruction

Source: Pheme Perkins, "Pastoral Epistles," in James D. G. Dunn and John W. Rogerson, eds., *Eerdmans Commentary on the Bible* (Grand Rapids, MI: Eerdmans, 2003), p. 1434.

of males in a rhetorical culture. To remain silent while learning automatically insures that they cannot become teachers in that setting. But 1 Tim 2:9–12 does defend instructing women. It will provide the clothing of virtue, especially modesty and self-control, to replace that of wealth (v. 9; cf. 1 Pet 3:3–6).

Question

What is your own answer to the questions that Perkins poses at the beginning of the last paragraph? Could it be both?

Doing Feminist Criticism Yourself

1. *What are some of the factors that make the Pastorals turn more patriarchal than the historical Paul? In your view, is this change justified?*

2. *Puzzle out this interpretive problem: Are women in general restricted here, or just wives of husbands who are church members?*

---

2 TIMOTHY: Personal Advice for Church Leadership

Second Timothy is the most personal of the Pastoral letters, personal in the sense of Paul's life coming through. Although most scholars hold for pseudonymity, a strong minority of scholars believes that the author of the Pastorals used fragments of previously unpublished Pauline writings to compose this letter.

---

2 Timothy in Brief: Outline of Structure and Contents

I. **Opening** Paul to Timothy, blessing (1:1–2)
II. **Thanksgiving** for Timothy (1:3–7)
III. **Body**
   A. The power of God in Paul and Timothy (1:8–18)
   B. Exhortation to be a good soldier and approved worker (2:1–26)
   C. Against false teachers, especially those who prey on women (3:1–9)
   D. The gospel in the light of the end of time (3:10–4:8)
      1. The example of Paul (3:10–13)
      2. Instructions for Timothy (3:14–4:5)
      3. Paul's impending death (4:6–8)
IV. **Conclusion** (4:9–22)
   A. Personal instructions and information (4:9–18)
   B. Final greetings and blessing (4:19–22)

A Guide to Reading 2 Timothy

In a brief opening (1:1–2), "Paul" calls himself "an apostle of Christ Jesus by the will of God," to spread "the promise of life," anticipating the correction of false teaching that life has already come in its fullness (2:18). Timothy is "my beloved child," and this letter will bear out this affectionate relationship. The author blesses Timothy with grace, mercy, and peace.

In the thanksgiving section, the author assures Timothy that he prays for him constantly. He remembers happily the faith of Timothy's grandmother Lois and his mother Eunice, and urges Timothy to rekindle the "gift of God that is within you through the laying on of my hands" (compare 1 Tim 4:14). This gift brings power, love, and self-discipline.

The body of the letter begins by encouraging Timothy with the example of Paul's own courage (vv. 8–12) and commitment to the firm teaching of the gospel (vv. 13–14). Timothy is exhorted to be brave in the face of opposition to his ministry. This first section is concluded with an emotional explanation of the author's present situation (vv. 15–18). When he was arrested in Asia Minor, no one came to his aid (v. 15), since they apparently were ashamed of his imprisonment (cf. 1:8, 16). When Onesiphorus got to Rome, perhaps only to see Paul, he was not "ashamed of my chain" and faithfully searched until he found the author (vv. 16–17).

The author now exhorts Timothy in his own ministry with some specifics. First, he urges him to a life of perseverance. He must pass on the faith to other faithful people who will themselves be able to pass it on (2:1–2). He is to endure hardship like a good soldier (2:3–4), compete according to the rules like an athlete (2:5), and work hard like a farmer (2:6). He is commanded to "remember Jesus Christ"—at first blush an odd thing to say, as if Timothy would ever forget him!— and goes on to explain that Paul is a prisoner for Jesus, "but the word of God is not chained" (vv. 8–9). A hymn is cited next, celebrating the faithfulness of Christ in the face of human fickleness but warning believers to stand true to the gospel (vv. 11–13). The second specific exhortation is to a life of faithfulness in Timothy's teaching and personal conduct (vv. 14–26). Timothy must be faithful in his teaching (vv. 14–19), especially as he explains "the word of truth" (v. 15) to those who "wrangle over words" to the ruin of others (v. 14) and engage in "profane chatter" (v. 16), no doubt a reference to false teachers. These people teach that "the resurrection has already taken place" (v. 18). Timothy must be faithful in his conduct, a "special utensil" in God's house, shunning "youthful passions" and pursuing righteousness (2:20–26). Once again the author condemns his opponents, those who engage in "stupid and senseless controversies" (v. 23). If true Christian teachers are kind, apt teachers, correcting opponents with gentleness, God may grant opponents repentance from error and escape from the devil (v. 24).

In the last major section the author charges Timothy to pursue his ministry well in light of the approaching end of time (3:1–4:8). He begins with an explicit prediction of godlessness and distress in the last days (3:1–9). Because of this over-all context and especially from 3:6, we can see that the author has in mind godless *teachers* when he catalogues their vices (vv. 1–5). They enter some households and gain control of "silly" (weak-willed) women (vv. 6–7), just as the false teachers mentioned in 1 Timothy apparently had. They are like Jannes and Jambres, leaders of the opposition against Moses (v. 8). The author concludes this eschatological warning with the firm conviction that the false teachers' folly will be exposed (v. 9). This warning then becomes the framework for urgency in the proclamation of the word in the next subsection (vv. 10–4:8). The author uses Paul as a model of how one ought to persevere in faithful teaching and life despite persecutions. Timothy had witnessed this faithful perseverance in the past (vv. 10–11). In fact, the meas-ure of one's godliness is seen by the level of persecution he or she is subject to (v. 12). The author's instruction to Timothy now becomes more direct (vv. 14–4:5). Timothy must proclaim the word of God fervently and frequently (4:1–5). Again, this charge is given in light of eschatological realities, both positive in the coming of Christ (v. 1) and negative in the rise of people with "itching ears" who wander from the truth into myths (vv. 3–4). The occasion for such somber instruction to Timothy is now stated clearly and poignantly: Paul is about to die, and he anticipates receiv-ing the "crown of righteousness" from the Lord in company with all the people of God (vv. 6–8). Thus the author's instruction to Timothy is framed by Paul's exam-ple. He closes with lengthy personal instructions and information (vv. 9–18), fol-lowed by final greetings and a blessing upon "you" plural, on all the letter's audience (vv. 19–22).

Historical Reading of 2 Timothy

Our remarks here assume the historical treatment of all the Pastorals given earlier, and only new information on the author will be noted.

Author

Of the three Pastorals, 2 Timothy most closely resembles Paul's genuine letters. Although this letter, like the other Pastorals, is concerned with refuting false teach-ings, its tone is more intimate and personal. Especially poignant are several pas-sages in which the author depicts himself as abandoned by former associates and languishing alone in prison except for the companionship of Luke (1:15; 4:9–11, 16). These and other flashes of the author's characteristic vigor and emotional fire (see 4:6–8, 17–18) lead some scholars to speculate that the work contains fragments of otherwise lost letters from Paul. These scholars, however, are in the minority.

The part of 2 Timothy with the best claim to Pauline authorship is the section ending the letter (4:6–22), in which the writer emulates the fluctuations between lofty thoughts and mundane practicalities so typical of the apostle. In the beginning of this section, he compares himself to a runner winning the athlete's coveted prize—not the Greek competitor's laurel crown, but a "garland of righteousness" justifying him on God's Judgment Day (6:6–8). Switching abruptly to practical matters, the author asks the recipient to remember to bring his books when he comes. In another quick change of subject, he complains that during his court hearing nobody appeared in his defense and that the testimony of one "Alexander the coppersmith" seriously damaged his case. Then, in a seemingly contradictory about-face, the writer states that he has (metaphorically) escaped the "lion's jaws" and expects to be kept safe until the Parousia (6:13–18). Although such rapid changes of subject and shifts from gloom to optimism characterize Paul's genuine correspondence, most scholars believe that the entire document is the Pastoral writer's work. The more vivid passages may be simply the writer's most successful homage to the apostle's memory.

Social Scientific and Feminist Readings of 2 Timothy

Social scientific reading of 2 Timothy emphasizes the kinship language in this letter. In contrast to 1 Timothy and Titus, which are formal in tone and content, the author speaks warmly and personally to the audience, building its ability to set up church offices and fending off false teaching by appealing to a "father-son" relationship. This is fictive kinship, but effective nonetheless. In feminist reading, 2 Timothy shares the same position toward women that the other Pastorals have. In 2 Tim 3:6, in a list of vices that draws on traditional Greco-Roman material, the author complains about "silly" women. Under the influence of the false teachers, they have been "overwhelmed by their sins" and "swayed by all types of desires." Even though women are under constant instruction, they cannot seem to hold onto the truth. This may draw on ancient traditions that consider women less rational than men, more "flighty" and emotional; at any rate, it indicates that these women are being instructed in various behaviors that the author considers contrary to the gospel.

Social Scientific and Feminist Reading at Work
The Mother of Timothy (2 Tim 1:5)

In this selection, James Arlandson discusses the social background of Timothy.

According to 2 Timothy 1:5, [Timothy's mother's] name was Eunice, and Timothy's believing grandmother's name, incidentally, was Lois. As was true for Elizabeth and

Source: James Malcolm Arlandson, *Women, Class, and Society in Early Christianity: Models From Luke-Acts* (Peabody, MA: Hendrickson, 1997), p. 135.

her son, Timothy's mother enjoys the privilege of having a spiritual and celebrated son. The people of Lystra and Iconium attest to his character (Acts 16:2). His mixed heritage does not detract from his popularity. But it was Eunice and Lois who instructed their son and grandson in the Scriptures, a nurturing process that gave him the opportunity to become a popular and recognized leader (2 Tim. 3:15). Because of their apparent knowledge of the Scriptures, these two women may be Christians, although this is tentative because of lack of information. The occupation of Timothy's Greek unbelieving (?) father is unknown, however. F. F. Bruce, following Ramsay, makes the enticing observation that in Phrygia (and the same is true for Lycaonia) "the Jews married into the dominant families." This implies that Eunice (and Timothy) is well-off, but this is only a guess. It may be assumed that she is paired with her husband and is exalted more highly than he . . . because she is a believer.

Question

Discuss the various social scientific dimensions of this selection.

TITUS: False Teaching and Church Office

Like the other Pastoral Letters, Titus focuses on making converts and on sound Christian teaching, especially for use in combating false teaching. The historical **Titus,** a Greek youth whom Paul refused to have circumcised (Gal 2:1, 3, 10), accompanied Paul on his missions in Greece. He acted as Paul's representative to the troublesome Corinthians (2 Cor. 8:6, 16–23), where he was instrumental in reconciling them to Paul. Like the Timothy of the other Pastorals, Titus also represents the postapostolic church leadership and is the model of those preserving Paul's gospel in a new generation. Consequently, the instruction to "Titus" here is to establish an orthodox and qualified ministry. The letter's chief purpose is to outline the requirements and some of the duties of church presbyters and bishops.

Titus in Brief: Outline of Structure and Contents

I. **Opening** Paul to Titus, blessing (1:1–4; no thanksgiving follows)
II. **Body** Appoint qualified Christian leaders, put down false teaching, and encourage good conduct (1:5–3:11)
    A. Appointing presbyter/bishops (1:5–9)
    B. The threat of false teaching (1:10–16)
    C. Conduct and teaching in Titus' churches (2:1–3:11)
III. **Conclusion** Personal greetings and blessing (3:12–15)

A Guide to Reading Titus

"Paul" begins this short letter to Titus with a blessing, emphasizing God's faithfulness (1:1–4). Then he introduces the first theme of his letter and the reason why he left Titus in Crete: to put unfinished business in order and appoint qualified presbyters or elders in every town (1:5). Titus was to leave Crete (3:12) when other apostolic delegates arrived. But the elders would of course stay on Crete and continue Titus' ministry. So this letter is directed to Titus, but it is also directed to the elders of the church (see the plural greeting and blessing in 3:15). The first instruction, regarding the appointing of church officers, is a list of ethical and doctrinal qualifications (1:6–9). The author now suddenly begins speaking of "bishops/overseers," which leads us to believe that the later separate offices of bishop and presbyters had not yet been distinguished from each other. Another list of moral qualifications for the bishop is given; all items on the list point to his (and it is a "he") ability to preach with sound doctrine and refute those who oppose it (v. 9). The author then points to some of these rebellious people who are Jews or (more likely) Jewish Christians on Crete ("those of the circumcision"), false teachers who attempt to ruin many households of the church (vv. 10–11). He quotes an **invective** (clever insult) against them from a Cretan poet: "Cretans are always liars, vicious brutes, lazy gluttons," and then to hammer home the point he adds, "That testimony is true"! Some hope is held out that they may become sound in the faith and turn from "Jewish myths or commandments (vv. 13–14), but then this hope is virtually taken away by reiterating how "detestable, disobedient, and unfit" they are for good works (v. 16).

The author now gives moral instructions for the church so that it may lead a godly and commendable life (2:1–15). The thrust of his instruction is moral standards for various groups in the household (vv. 2–10). This section resembles to some extent 1 Tim 2:8–3:13. Older men are given a general catalogue of virtue to follow (2:2). Older women, on the other hand, are specifically commanded to avoid slander, being "slaves to drink" (probably alcoholics), to encourage young women to love their husbands, to love their own children, to be good managers of their households, and to be submissive to their husbands, all so that "the word of God may not be discredited" among outsiders (vv. 3–5). Younger men, like Timothy, must be self-controlled; Timothy is to be a model of good work and effective teaching. Once again the author probably makes this statement with outsiders in view: "any opponent" will not be able to make slander stick (vv. 6–8). Slaves must be submissive to their masters, showing full respect and fidelity, for this "ornaments" the teaching of "God our Savior" (vv. 9–10). At the end of these instructions, the author reminds Titus of the Lord's return as a motivation to do good right now; this is what Jesus Christ gave himself to death for (vv. 11–14). This section ends by exhorting Timothy to "declare these things" by exhorting and correcting with all authority; in a culture that respects old age and suspects youth, Titus is to "let no one look down on you" and avoid following his instructions (v. 15).

The last part of the body deals with doing good deeds (once again!) as a positive witness to unbelieving neighbors (3:1–14). In particular, the audience should respect governmental authorities (vv. 1–2), especially because the grace of God has changed the condition of their hearts from disobedience to obedience (vv. 3–4). The author reminds his audience of their own conversion experience, phrasing it in typically Pauline terms (vv. 5–7). Part of the way in which the Cretan believers could show that God was in them was to avoid silly controversies, genealogies, dissentions, and quarrels about the law, most probably the Law of Moses. People who keep causing dissent are to be warned twice if necessary, and if they continue in their socially deviant ways, they are to be shunned (vv. 9–11). Another way for believers to live out their conversion is to provide for God's people. This is the purpose of work, to be able to provide for the needs of others (vv. 12–14).

The epistle concludes with a short general greeting and a short blessing upon "all of you" (3:15).

Historical Reading of Titus

See the discussion of historical-critical reading of the Pastorals at the beginning of this chapter.

Social Scientific Reading of Titus

Social scientific reading of Titus notes that it combines strong attention to in-group identity and life (correct doctrine, sound leadership) with out-group concern for the conversion of others. This concern is to be carried out not only by spreading the Christian message, but also by lifestyle. Christians are to live as good citizens and practice "every good work" (3:1). Christian slaves and women are to live faithfully and give full respect to masters and husbands so that the church may have honor, here a good reputation, among outsiders.

Social Scientific Reading at Work
Group Honor and Shame (Titus 1:12)

A part of ancient training in rhetoric was invective, the ability to insult one's opponent effectively. In this reading Bruce Malina relates it to notions of collective honor and dishonor. Note how these notions can be extended to other things the author of the Pastorals uses to identify people teaching error and distance his people from them.

Since first-century Mediterranean societies did not consider individualism a pivotal value as we do, collective or corporate honor was one of their major focuses. Social groups, like the family, neighborhood, village, or region, possessed a collective honor in which the members participated (. . . Titus 1:12: "Cretans are always liars, evil beasts, lazy gluttons."). This perception might be expressed as "I am who I am and with whom I associate." Depending on the dimensions of the group, which can run a replicating range from the single nuclear family to kingdom or region, the *head* of the group is responsible for the honor of the group with reference to outsiders and symbolizes the group's honor as well. Hence members of the group owe loyalty, respect, and obedience of a kind that commits their individual honor without limit and without compromise.

Questions

1. *How well do you think such invectives worked in the ancient world? Do invectives such as the ethnic slurs in Titus 1:12 have any place today?*

2. *What kind of invectives might the group under attack in the Pastorals have used on the author and his followers in the churches to which he writes?*

Feminist Reading of Titus

Like the other Pastorals, Titus has a more traditional, patriarchal attitude to women than the undisputed Pauline letters. The offices in the church that Titus sets up are for men only. Older women are to live soberly and teach younger women to love their husbands and children and practice the virtues that flow from this love. Their good lives and especially their submission to their husbands will bring honor, not shame, to the whole Christian community (2:2–5). This will silence the occasional slander of outsiders and will give the church a better standing that will result in more conversions. There is no indication in this letter, as in the other Pastorals, that women are a part of the Gnosticizing movement that the author opposes.

Source: Bruce J. Malina, *The New Testament World: Insights from Cultural Anthropology* (Louisville, KY: Westminster John Knox, 2001), pp. 43–44.

Feminist Reading at Work
Older Women and Younger Women (Titus 2)

In most societies, especially traditional ones like Mediterranean cultures, the dividing line between "young women" and "older women" was menopause, the time at which child-bearing ability ceases. In this reading, Maxine Hancock explains how this demarcation relates to roles in the church.

In the New Testament "older women," probably post- or perimenopausal, are given a specific role in teaching younger women in the church (Titus 2:3). There is also an ethic of care for senior widows, the church perpetuating the dying Christ's concern for the care of his mother in caring for widowed, postmenopausal women.

In the New Testament, interest in women's reproductive capacity is replaced with an interest in their spiritual fruitfulness. Priscilla teaches in her home without any hint given of her age; since no children are mentioned, it might be possible that Priscilla is either postmenopausal or, in Old Testament terminology, barren. Yet she is fruitful in her ministry. Under the new covenant, women are to be valued not for their reproductive capacity but for their ability to "bear fruit in every good work" (Col 1:10).

Contemporary secular authors have written about menopause and post menopause as a time when women are no longer defined societally by their sexual attractiveness and can be valued for other attributes. Christian women find their worth throughout their lives in the knowledge that they have been created lovingly and are embraced by God's love from conception to death. They can see menopause as marking the commencement of a new season of maturity and serenity and be secure in the promise, "The righteous flourish like the palm tree. . . . In old age they still produce fruit; they are always green and full of sap, showing that the Lord is upright; he is my rock" (Ps 92:12, 14–15).

Question

Give your own reflections on this reading. In particular, reflect on what Titus says about the responsibility of older women to encourage young women to be good wives and mothers (Titus 2:3–5).

Key Terms and Concepts

bishop/overseer • deacon • early Catholicism • Gnosticism • invective
Pastoral Letters • presbyter/elder • threefold office • Timothy (historical person)
Titus (historical person)

Questions for Study, Discussion, and Writing

1. 1 Timothy and Titus have no thanksgiving section, but 2 Timothy does. Explain why.
2. Explain the rhetorical point and effect of 1 Timothy's alternating between the two topics of establishing order in the church (structure of offices and behavior of Christians) and putting down false teaching.
3. Explain the Pastoral Letters' views about wives, children, and slaves. How do these views both differ from and agree with the position of the "historical Paul"?
4. Is it fair to say that the Pastorals have a threefold office of bishop, presbyter, and deacon, or a fourfold office of bishop, presbyter, deacon, and widow?
5. What do you make of the fact that the sections of the Pastorals that deal with bishops, elders/presbyters, and deacons speak explicitly about their qualifications but hardly ever about their duties? Go through 1 Timothy 3 to draw up a list of their duties based on your inferences from their qualifications.
6. How do you explain the fact that 2 Timothy is so much more personal than the other two Pastoral letters?
7. Why, in 2 Timothy 2, is the author so insulting to his opponents but urges Timothy to be kind, gentle, and patient with them (vv. 23–26)?
8. Describe the evidence that persuades most scholars that the Pastorals were written by a later churchman. In what specific concerns do the Pastorals reflect church organization and administration that are different from those obtaining in the author's time? Why are these letters so concerned about holding to tradition and combating heresy?

For Further Reading

Collins, Raymond F. *1 & 2 Timothy and Titus: A Commentary*. Louisville, KY: Westminster John Knox, 2002. The most recent commentary on the Pastorals, excellent for beginning students of the NT.

Dibelius, Martin, and Conzelmann, Hans. *The Pastoral Epistles*. Hermeneia Commentary. Philadelphia: Fortress Press, 1972. Conzelmann's updating of Dibelius's famous commentary first published in German in 1913; more challenging for beginning students.

Hanson, A. T. *The Pastoral Epistles*. New Century Bible. Grand Rapids, MI: Eerdmans, 1982. A brief but helpful treatment.

Johnson, Luke T. *Letters to Paul's Delegates: 1 Timothy, 2 Timothy, Titus*. Valley Forge: Trinity Press International, 1996. Expert commentary by one who holds to Pauline authorship of the Pastorals.

Quinn, Jerome D. *Titus*. Anchor Bible Commentary. Garden City, NY: Doubleday, 1990. Close analysis of the least-studied Pastoral letter.

Quinn, Jerome D., and William C. Wacker. *The First and Second Letters to Timothy*. Eerdmans Critical Commentary. Grand Rapids, MI: Eerdmans, 2000. Comprehensive treatment.

Young, Francis. *The Theology of the Pastoral Letters*. Cambridge: Cambridge University Press, 1994. Excellent treatment of the religious thought of the Pastorals.

Part V

General/Catholic Letters and Revelation

Chapter Seventeen

Hebrews, James, 1–2 Peter, and Jude: The General Letters

In this chapter we will consider Hebrews, James, 1 and 2 Peter, and Jude. These documents, along with the Letters of John that we will consider in the next chapter, are traditionally known as the **General** or **Catholic Letters** or epistles. (*Catholic* here means "universal," not Roman Catholic.) This name arose in the church because it was thought that they were written to the whole church, unlike the Pauline letters, which were written to specific congregations or people. However, this assumption is obviously incorrect, as can be seen in the opening addresses of some General/Catholic letters, which are indeed addressed to specific churches. The contents of the letters we consider in this chapter also show that they are addressed to situations that are just as specific as the situations addressed in the Pauline letters. Thus, church tradition and NT scholarship may call them the General Letters, but there is nothing general about them.

The General/Catholic Letters as a group are historically the most neglected books of the NT canon. NT study has too often ignored them, mostly out of a preference for the Pauline letters, and so has the Christian church. Many reasons explain this neglect, including uncertainty in the ancient world and today about their authors and audiences as well as difficulties in interpreting certain passages. That James, Jude, and 2 Peter may address a Jewish-Christian audience has also caused some feeling against them, because a predominantly Gentile Christianity has marginalized these books with Jewish Christian features. Nevertheless, the careful interpreter of the NT will recognize great value in these works. The NT—not to mention early Christianity—would not be the same without them. Now all these books are receiving good attention from a variety of methods, with Hebrews, 1 Peter, and James leading the way.

THE LETTER TO THE HEBREWS: Stay True to Christ

The Letter to the Hebrews is one of the most remarkable documents in the NT. It is rhetorically powerful, written in a stylish Greek that comes through well in English translation, and it is long without being tiresome. However, it is also a mystery. Hebrews is the only document in the NT with no author's name in or on it, and it has the best chance of any NT document to have been written by a woman. The church put it first in canonical order after the Pauline letter collection, thinking that Paul may have written it, but this attribution is almost universally rejected today. Although it is traditionally called a "letter" or a more formal "epistle," Hebrews is almost completely nonletter in format; rather, it is a sermonic essay with some final letter material at the end. Despite these mysteries—or perhaps because of them—Hebrews is a fascinating and unique document for all contemporary ways of reading.

Hebrews in Brief: Outline of Structure and Contents

I. **Teaching** Christ is superior to the Old Covenant (1:1–10:18; no letter opening)
   A. Christ is superior to the prophets (1:1–4)
   B. Christ is superior to the angels (1:5–2:8), with first of several admonitions to stay true to the faith (2:1–4)
   C. Christ is superior to Moses; second admonition (3:1–4:13)
   D. Christ is superior to Aaron; third admonition (4:14–7:28)
   E. Christ's ministry is superior to the Old Covenant, to the old temple, and to the Jewish system of sacrifice (8:1–10:18)
II. **Moral Exhortation** Faithful life while under persecution (10:19–13:17)
   A. Enter the new sanctuary, with fourth admonition (10:19–31)
   B. Endure persecution (10:32–39)
   C. Examples of faith in the old covenant (11:1–40)
   D. Endure persecution, with fifth admonition (12:1–29)
   E. Conduct toward believers and leaders (13:1–17)
III. **Conclusion** Fitting for a letter: prayers, instructions, Timothy's release, farewells and blessing (13:18–25).

Developing Your Skills

Read Hebrews quickly while still being careful to notice: the overall structure; the interspersed admonitions to stay faithful; and the many quotations from the Hebrew Bible and how they are used.

A Guide to Reading Hebrews

The author begins by pointing to recent, full revelation of God's Son. First, God is superior to the Hebrew prophets (1:1–4). The prophets were servants or spokesmen (1:1), but the mediator of God's revelation is a Son (1:2–4). That this point is so quickly dealt with is an indication that the audience did not seriously doubt it.

Second, Christ is superior to the angels (1:5–2:18). The author transitions into the section on angels by showing that, as God's Son (in contrast to the prophets), Christ "has obtained a more excellent name than [the angels]" (1:4). This is demonstrated by a **catena** (collection in chainlike form, from the Latin word for "chain") of OT quotations (1:5–14). At this point the author inserts the first admonition that is the rhetorical purpose of the letter (2:1–4): stay true to the faith and do not "drift away." Whoever rejects the message of salvation in favor of a message of judgment mediated through angels will face strong judgment. The argument about Christ's superiority over angels is resumed in 2:5–18. Christ is superior to the angels not by his divine nature, but by his human nature. This may seem odd to us, as it may have to the first readers of Hebrews, but Jewish thought saw humans as beings superior to angels. The scriptures that describe Christ's exaltation over the angels demonstrate this point of view (vv. 5–9), and it is even shown by the necessity of his suffering (vv. 10–18), for by this he brings us salvation. Third, Christ is superior to Moses (3:1–4:13). The author bridges the topic by showing how, by Christ's full humanity, he has become a sympathetic high priest (2:17–18). The author, not wishing to alienate the audience, points out that Moses, like Christ, was indeed faithful to God (3:1–2). Unlike Christ, Moses was merely part of the house that Christ built (3:3–4) and a servant in the house in which Christ was the Son. The author gently commands the readers to "hold firm" to their confidence in order to be a member of that household (3:5–6).

This discussion about Moses leads into the second warning against unbelief, this time based on Israel's wilderness experience (3:7–4:13). The author is careful here: only once does he/she implicate Moses in Israel's unbelief in the wilderness (3:16; the reason for referring to the author as "he/she" will become clear in the section on historical criticism). Unlike the first warning, which dealt with Christ's superiority to the angels' message, this warning has to do with the nation's failure to believe in God, which led to disobedience to God (3:7–11). The readers are urged to believe in the promise of God to give them the Sabbath rest of refreshment and renewal that Israel never obtained (3:12–4:11). What is at stake, however, is not a temporary rest, but an eternal rest. This warning concludes with a somber note about God's piercing Word (4:12–13).

The transition from God's piercing word to the topic of Christ's superiority over Aaron (4:14–7:28) is made by way of a gentle reminder: although God's word is sharp and harsh, cutting through to the intentions of the heart, Christ our high priest understands our weaknesses (4:14–16). At this point the author begins what will become a regular rhetorical maneuver: immediately after a strongly negative warning section, he/she softens the tone so as to encourage the readers positively. The priesthood of Aaron is first mentioned (5:1–5), followed by scriptural argument (based especially on Psalm 110) for the priesthood of Christ (5:6–10) after the order of **Melchizedek,** the mysterious priest of Salem to whom Abraham offered tithes (5:6, 10). The third warning then begins as the author challenges the readers to a more mature understanding of the faith (5:11–6:8). Dealing with **typology,** the often complex comparison of personages from the past and present, may be too much for the letter's readers, for they are still immature in the faith (5:11–14). They must move forward in their spiritual growth if the seed of salvation is ever to take root (6:1–3). In light of the exposure they have had to the truths of salvation, it had better take root—or else they are in danger of apostasy (6:4–8). The author supposes that one is either moving forward in the faith, or falling back. Next comes the harshest warning in Hebrews: If any of the audience, who had seen God's Spirit working in their lives, fall away, they "crucify again the Son of God" and subject him to shame (6:4–6), making **second repentance** (the regaining of salvation after leaving the faith) impossible. The main rhetorical point of this warning is to keep the audience inside the faith, not to shut them out as outsiders when they have left. An indication of this intent is that the author's tone softens after this warning. In 6:9–20 he or she reminds the recipients of the promises of God and tells them that they are among the productive seed.

The discussion about the Aaronic priesthood is then resumed with an elaboration on the order of Melchizedek (7:1–28). (Note that all through Hebrews the discussion is about the tabernacle of Israel, not the Temple of Jerusalem.) Melchizedek was greater than Abraham and, by implication, so are all his descendants including the tribe of Levi (7:1–10). But Melchizedek's priestly order is greater than the Aaronic order (7:11–28) because its rise was predicted while the Levitical order was in effect (7:11, 17). The superiority of Melchizedek's order is seen in that it involves one priest, but the Levitical priesthood involved many, since death prevented them from continuing (7:23–24). Moreover, this new order involves a single, perfect sacrifice, the death of Jesus as a Melchizedek-order priest, whereas the old order involved daily sacrifices (7:26–27).

The final main section of the first half of Hebrews argues that Christ's ministry is superior to the old covenant ministry (8:1–10:18). The transition between the Jewish priesthood and the discussion of the covenants is hinted at in 7:12: "When there is a change in the priesthood, there is necessarily a change in the Law as well." Christ's ministry is superior to the old covenant ministry in three ways: in its covenant, in its sanctuary, and in its sacrifice. After a brief introduction of these three elements (8:1–6), the author begins by contrasting the old covenant with the new (8:7–13). The inadequacy of the old covenant is demonstrated by scripture, as is the adequacy of the new covenant (8:7–13). In essence, the new covenant involves knowing God internally because of the indwelling Spirit rather than knowing God by external means, which looks back to Jeremiah 31:31. The implications of the new covenant are two: (1) believers are now organically united to God in the body of Christ, and (2) the end of this age has dawned and the kingdom has been inaugurated in the first coming of Christ. The author will develop these two implications in the parenetic (moral exhortation) section (cf. 12:28; 13:3, etc.). Next, the two sanctuaries—earthly tabernacle and heavenly pattern—are contrasted (9:1–12) in terms of imperfection versus perfection and

Model of the Tabernacle This full-size model of the Tabernacle in ancient Israel is located in the south of modern Israel. Although no original materials (e.g., gold, silver, bronze) have been used, the model is accurately based upon the biblical description. Note the exterior fence, the altar of sacrifice, the bronze laver (washbasin for priests), and tent housing the altar of incense, showbread, and the Ark of the Covenant. The letter of Hebrews links the tabernacle to Jesus Christ. It was divinely ordained but only a shadow of what was to come in him (Heb 8:5). Used by permission of BiblePlaces.com.

original pattern versus replica (9:11; cf. v. 24). Such a discussion draws on Greek philosophical ideas of this world as a copy of the ideal heavenly world. This portion of Hebrews concludes by contrasting the old sacrifice with the new (9:13–10:18). Though both sacrifices required blood (9:13–22), Christ's sacrifice is better because it has purified the original, heavenly sanctuary (9:23–28) and it was done once and for all (10:1–18).

Having completed the first section of Hebrews on a strong note with the capability of Christ's death to save his people, the author now turns to the effects that Christ's superiority should have in the believer's life. This section includes exhortations, with a warning and the great "Hall of Faith" chapter wedged in between. The audience is exhorted to enter the new sanctuary completely (10:9–31). The idiom is not necessarily meant to indicate that the readers were unbelievers, but that their faith needed strengthening (10:19–22). A fourth warning section (10:26–31) follows this exhortation, sounding very much like the admonition in 6:4–8, though this time the point is related specifically to desecrating the blood of Christ (10:29). Next, the readers are exhorted to endure persecution (10:32–39), especially in light of the promises of God (10:36). There follows a typical reassurance: "we are not of those who shrink back and are destroyed, but of those who have faith and keep their souls" (10:39). Having just argued that the readers should endure as they had in the past (10:32), the author reminds them of others who have endured and kept the faith (cf. 10:39). Chapter 11 has often been called "The Hall of Faith"—and with good reason. In this chapter the author shows how God's people in the past had endured hardship, pain, and death. Yet they kept the faith, and their faith kept them going. As he or she proceeds chronologically, the bulk of the author's illustrations are about pre-Law individuals (prepatriarchs in 11:4–7; Abraham, Isaac, and Jacob in 11:8–22). In fact, when the author discusses Moses (11:23–29), Moses' faith is seen up until the time of the crossing of the Red Sea (11:29), though nothing is said about him after the giving of the Law. In the space of two verses (11:30–31), the author addresses the faith of the Israelites when Jericho fell (11:30) and Rahab's faith that helped the event to take place (11:31). Thus, even though the *period* of the Law is dealt with, the author produces no example (outside of Moses keeping the Passover in v. 28) of anyone's demonstrating faith in relation to the Israelite sacrificial system— a subtle argument that following this system is not the way for the audience to go. The chapter is then hastily concluded with a mere mention of names, mostly of prophets and warriors (11:32–33), followed by a striking summary of the sufferings they faced (11:34–39).

Now the readers are encouraged to endure the chastening experience of persecution (12:1–29). The author begins with a metaphor from the spectator sport of Greek foot races to drive home the point: the crowd of chapter 11 is on both sides as the audience of Hebrews runs its race, so they must lay aside the weight and clinging clothing of sin in order to keep running the race of the Christian life "with perseverance." Then comes one of the most poignant NT statements on the death of Christ utilizing the honor-shame system: Jesus "for the joy that was set before him endured the cross, disregarding [shaming] its shame, and has taken his seat [in honor] at the right hand of the throne of God" (v. 4). Kinship ideas follow: just as Christ is God's Son, so are believers (12:5)—that is to say, because he is a Son, so are they. God will deal with them as a Father does his own children (12:5–11). In the midst of the severe warnings comes this note of encouragement: even though the readers are suffering, they will be saved in the end because they are God's children. This discipline from God is a proof that they are indeed sons and daughters (12:8)—in fact, unless they are disciplined they will not grow in grace (12:12–17). (This passage draws on the role of the Mediterranean father in occasionally dealing out strong discipline to his children.)

The fifth and final warning of the book now occurs. The author implores the readers not to deny God by refusing to heed God's voice (12:18–29). Once again, as with previous warnings (2:1–4; 10:26–29), the author argues from the lesser to the greater, a common Jewish rhetorical device: from the minimum punishment (physical death) for disobedience in the OT to the maximum punishment for disobedience now (hell). He or she contrasts Mount Sinai with Mount Zion (12:18–24), showing that the awesome power of God shakes mountains, but it cannot shake the kingdom in which true believers dwell (v. 28). The warning is concluded with the somber note that "our God is a consuming fire" (v. 29). The readers are then exhorted in pragmatic ways about the community of believers (13:1–17). The author instructs them to show love for one another in welcoming strangers, in avoiding adultery, in not loving money, and in honoring their leaders (vv. 1–14); this love is grounded in the sacrifice of Christ. Sharing goods with others is a sacrifice pleasing to God (vv. 15–16). The author admonishes the audience to "obey your [church] leaders" (v. 17), asks for prayer, and with a beautiful blessing aimed at their completion in faith ends the body of this epistle (vv. 20–21).

In the letter-format conclusion, the author appeals to the readers to "bear my word of exhortation," because "I have written to you briefly." Although this may seem a bit tongue in cheek after a long document, mention at the end of a letter of its "brevity" was common in ancient letters whether they were long or short (see 1 Peter, 2 and 3 John). Then the author gives the good news that Timothy is free and if possible is coming with the author to visit the recipients. After commanding greetings to "all your leaders and all the saints," and conveying greetings from "those from Italy," the author gives a short blessing (13:22–25).

Historical Reading of Hebrews

The historical study of Hebrews is full of uncertainties. Its author is anonymous to this day, its dating and place are uncertain, and so is the situation of the audience. Are they from a Jewish background and now tempted to return to Judaism, or are they Gentiles looking to combine their belief in Jesus with membership in the people to which he belonged? Despite these uncertainties, the historical reading of Hebrews is fascinating and rewarding.

Hebrews in Brief: Summary of Historical Reading

Author An anonymous Jewish Christian, well acquainted with the Jewish Bible and Greek philosophy. Later church identification of Paul as the author is no longer maintained. Of all NT books, this has the strongest claim to the possibility of female authorship.

Date Some place this letter in the 60s, but the majority favor the 80s or 90s.

Audience Not identified, but the implied readers are Christians who are attracted to Judaism. They have been surmised to be in various places, with Alexandria, Jerusalem and especially Rome most prominent.

Unity Not in significant doubt.

Purpose To keep its audience true to the Christian faith, specifically to prevent them from going into Judaism.

Author

The author of this work writes anonymously, though the audience knows him or her (13:19, 22–23). The first author to cite this epistle was Clement of Rome (around 96 C.E.), although he does not say who wrote it. The Marcionite canon and the Muratorian canon omit it. From the earliest times in church history, whenever Hebrews' authorship was mentioned there has been great dispute about it. Tertullian (in the second century) was the first to suggest Barnabas as its author. The Protestant reformer Martin Luther in the sixteenth was the first to suggest Apollos, and this is a common conclusion today. Adolf von Harnack, the greatest church historian of the nineteenth century, proposed that Priscilla was the author, which if true would make Hebrews the only NT book to be written by a woman. (This makes an intriguing explanation for Hebrews' anonymity.) All in all, the argument about authorship is full of conjectures. Oddly enough, the most common ancient conjecture was that Paul wrote Hebrews, and it was made from Clement of Alexandria at the end of the second century on. The letter does have occasional Pauline touches, such as viewing faith as dynamic trust, and Timothy as the author's co-worker (13:23). However, Paul's literary style and theology differ so much on the whole from Hebrews that he cannot be the author of this document. Besides, it is almost impossible to imagine Paul writing a document and not putting his name on it! Origen's often-quoted words from the early third century are still true: "Whoever wrote this letter, God only knows." We can safely surmise from internal evidence that the author is a skilled rhetorician of the second or third Christian generation, well acquainted with Judaism and Greek philosophy, acquainted with Paul's theology but not bound to it. The mention of Timothy makes it possible that this author is in, or on the fringe of, a Pauline circle.

www   Follow the link for a listing of the main possibilities for authorship.

Date

The earliest possible date of Hebrews is the death of Paul (the middle 60s). That Paul is dead can probably be inferred from 13:7, 23. Further, the audience is now at least second-generation Christians (2:3), which also points to the 60s as the earliest date. Because the Temple is assumed to be still standing, Hebrews is often dated before its destruction in 70, but Jewish and sometimes Christian documents written after 70 can speak of the Temple as standing. The latest possible date is around 96, set because 1 Clement frequently uses Hebrews. So the range is 65–95, and most scholars date this document around 90.

Audience

Palestine and Rome are the most popular suggestions. But others have been made: Alexandria, Colossae, Ephesus, the Lycus Valley in Asia Minor, Cyrene, Antioch, Syria in general, Corinth, and Cyprus. Against Rome is the following evidence: The best interpretation of 13:24, "those from Italy send you their greetings," is that the *author* is somewhere in Italy; it is harder to make sense of this statement if the *audience* is there. Also, churches of the western Mediterranean were the last to accept Hebrews into the canon, and if Hebrews was written to Rome, the leading church in the west, its late acceptance there is more difficult to explain. However, Clement of Rome knew this book in 96 C.E., an argument for a Roman destination if Hebrews was written in the 90s. Against a Palestinian destination is the following evidence: The statement in 2:3 could not easily apply to the audience, for some Palestinian believers could have heard Jesus in the flesh. The Jerusalem church had already lost a number of its leading members to persecution: Stephen (Acts 8:59–60), James, the brother of John (Acts 12:2), and probably James, the brother of the Lord (died around 62 C.E.) The statement in 12:4 does not fit them. Many interpreters suggest that this letter was written for the church in Alexandria, Egypt because its philosophic style would be at home there; this is possible but not demonstrable. In sum, the author has hidden the location of the audience as well as she or he has hidden her or his own identity.

If we cannot know *where* the audience is, at least we can know something about what kind of people they are. The traditional view, still held by the majority for good reasons, is that the audience is Jewish Christian. The main point of external evidence for this conclusion is that the title "To the Hebrews," that is, "To the Jewish Christian believers," is found as early as the middle of the second century. Those who were already convinced of the greatness of Judaism would see the point of the author's attempts to show the supreme worth of Christianity by means of its superiority to Judaism. This would fit a Jewish Christian audience. However, Hebrews contains no specific language about "returning/relapsing/going back" to Judaism. The author's description of the condition of the readers indicates that the crisis being written to is not the problem of readers' temptation to return to Judaism.

Nothing in Hebrews *requires* its audience to be Jewish Christians. It could just as well be, as some more recent researchers have argued, that the audience was Gentile Christians who were being tempted to turn to Judaism as a superior religion, more ancient and honorable and with a well-developed system for handling human sins, and also one more protected from the persecution they were suffering.

Purpose

The language of Hebrews implies that the readers had faced some persecution in the past (10:32–34), and the threat of renewed persecution is present. However, the source of the immediate threat of defection to Judaism lay not in persecution, but in the community's own inattention and indifference. The writer warns of "drifting away" (2:1), "neglect" (2:3), and "sluggishness" (6:12); the audience is "dull in understanding" (5:11) with "drooping hands" and "weak knees" (12:12). They must stop absenting themselves from the church services, the only time the NT has to make such a command (10:25). They must pay closer attention (2:1), exercise vigilance (3:12), be firm in their faith (3:6; 4:14), and show earnestness (6:11) and endurance (10:36, 38; 12:1). This exhortation is more than mere rhetoric; it indicates something new in early Christianity—a loss of intensity of belief and action in a formerly high-intensity movement.

This loss of intensity brings the opportunity to go over into Judaism, perhaps encouraged by mild to moderate persecution. From the way the author argues so extensively about sacrifice for sin, it seems that the audience desires to "resort to Jewish customs to come to terms with their sense of sin against God and need for atonement" (Lindars 1991, 10). To counteract this tendency, Hebrews presents a starkly realistic portrayal of the humanness of Jesus, including his weakness, tears, temptation, genuine need to trust God, and acceptance of abuse and shame (2:11–18; 4:15; 5:7–10; 13:12–13). It does this in close conjunction with what is probably the "highest" christology in the NT: Christ is God's agent in creating all that exists, the exact imprint of God's very being, and is explicitly addressed as "God" (1:3–13; 4:14; 7:17; 12:2) (Thistleton 2003, 1453). This Jesus, so human and divine, died, rose, and ascended to deal fully and finally with human sin. Hebrews was written to call believers to stay true to this Christ and the way of forgiveness and restoration to God that he has fully accomplished.

Social Scientific Reading of Hebrews

Hebrews is rich in material for social scientific reading. It uses kinship language to try to keep its readers in the family of God, emphasizing their brotherhood with Christ and the fatherhood of God. It uses honor and shame language extensively to urge them to persevere in the faith. Jesus endured the shame of persecution and even death on the cross, so they should be willing to do the same. Hebrews also is an interesting example—and the only one in the NT—of a Christian community that is not so intense and intentional as it once was.

Social Scientific Reading at Work
Kinship Ethos in Hebrews (Hebrews 13:1–3)

David deSilva, a leading interpreter of Hebrews and a social scientific reader of the NT, introduces here the important topic of the role that kinship plays in the rhetoric of Hebrews.

The Christian group is called to share, to serve, to support one another as Jesus gave himself for them–unselfishly and without reservation. Writing to addressees who had known the full range of society's deviancy-control techniques (short of mob lynching or legal execution; Heb 12:4), the author of Hebrews captures even more completely the essence of the kind of community that enables its members to withstand social pressure: Let mutual love . . . continue. Do not neglect to show hospitality to strangers, for by doing that some have entertained angels without knowing it. Remember those who are in prison, as though you were in prison with them; those who are being tortured, as though you yourselves were being tortured (Heb 13:1–3).

The author invokes the ethos of kinship, specifically the love characteristic of siblings, which represented the pinnacle of friendship and the most enduring and intimate of relationships. Adopting a kinship ethic meant mutual sharing of resources as any had need, as well as a firm commitment to one another. They were to be family, a call that was all the more essential given the networks of relationships that a believer could potentially lose in the ancient world. This kinship was to extend beyond the local group to the provision of hospitality to traveling sisters and brothers. Hospitality in the early church served to create strong bonds between local churches, facilitating communication and mission work between churches and allowing an itinerant leadership to keep linking local cells together. The love of sisters and brothers of Christ is most needed where the censure of society is most keenly felt. The author therefore urges the hearers to reach out to those most acutely targeted by the society for deviancy-control techniques, letting them know that the family they joined will not desert them, and letting each other know at the same time that their bond is stronger than society's hostility.

Questions

1. *What does the author mean by "deviancy-control techniques"?*

2. *Explain in your own words how kinship relates to hospitality here and how the author uses this to advance the purpose of his book.*

Source: David A. deSilva, *Honor, Patronage, Kinship, and Purity: Unlocking New Testament Culture* (Downers Grove, IL: InterVarsity, 2000), pp. 59–60.

Doing Social Scientific Reading Yourself

Skim through Hebrews to pick out items relevant to the honor-shame paradigm. Then choose one of these to analyze more closely.

Feminist Reading of Hebrews

Women are mentioned explicitly only in chapter 11, the heroes of faith, where they receive a brief treatment. The main point of Hebrews does not seem to be gender related and would apply equally to the men and women of the audience. Recent feminist criticism has reopened the question of possible female authorship of this letter, but as Cynthia Briggs Kittredge remarks, "Just as it is problematic today, it is impossible to describe what a 'feminine mind' would have been in the ancient world," and feminine authorship in itself would not assure that the content of the letter would be liberating for women today (Kittredge 1994, 450.)

Feminist Reading at Work
Rahab and Sarah (Hebrews 11)

Hebrews mentions two women by name. This selection puts the reader employing feminist methods further toward understanding why.

Women are included in Hebrews, but only marginally. Hebrews 11:1–40 remembers a series of elders attested by the scriptures as examples. Only two women, Sarah (11:11–12) and Rahab the harlot (11:31) are remembered by name. . . . Thus Hebrews seems not merely to neglect to provide women examples but almost to avoid them. Both Rahab and Sarah appear to represent Gentiles rather than women. Rahab's dubious sexual status renders her problematic as an example to women who also hear, "Let marriage be held in honor by all and let the marriage bed be kept undefiled, for God will judge fornicators and adulterers" (13:4). Does the author then seek to exclude women, to discourage the women of the community from "drawing near"? If Sarah is presented as a woman who has attained the perfection of maleness, then perhaps the women of the community are included by being invited to look only to the "manly" heroes of the past.

Questions

1. *Why might Hebrews avoid the example of women in chapter 11 and not pick up women's issues elsewhere?*

2. *Why do you think Rahab, a morally problematic figure, is included in this list?*

Source: Mary Rose D'Angelo, "Hebrews," in Carol A. Newsom, and Sharon H. Ringe, eds., Women's Bible Commentary, (Louisville, KY: Westminster John Knox, 1992), pp. 456, 457.

> **Doing Feminist Reading Yourself**
>
> *Read Hebrews 11:35–36, about unnamed women receiving their dead by resurrection, in the light of its probable OT references: the widow of Zarephath and the Shunammite woman, and also the mother of the seven martyrs in 2 Maccabees 7 (cf. also 4 Maccabees 14:11–18:24). What light do these intertextual references shed on feminist reading of Hebrews?*

Cross-Cultural Reading of Hebrews

The single explicit cross-cultural issue in Hebrews is the Gentile-Jewish question. This issue is important for cross-cultural reading today, affirming the importance of staying with one's origins in the faith when attracted to something else. Like the Pauline letters, Hebrews is a ringing defense of the validity and growing importance of Gentile Christianity.

Cross-Cultural Reading at Work
Hebrews and Yin-Yang

Here Professor Yeo relates Hebrew's ideas of cosmology (the structure of the universe) with the cosmic dualist cosmology of the Chinese yin-yang concept.

The author of Hebrews assumes that the eons in the cosmos are in constant flux or movement. . . . He accepts this truth and takes the further step of describing the life of faith as a life of pilgrimage, that is, a life of process and change, with seemingly endless challenges on the way. This understanding of cosmology and human experience is quite similar to yin-yang philosophy. In *I Ching* (the *Book of Changes*) and *Tao Te Ching*, the earliest books of cosmology, the concept of change is depicted as the essence of the cosmic process. . . . Yin and yang respectively signify rest and movement, being and becoming, responsiveness and creativity, and so forth. Ultimate reality is to be understood in terms of change, rather than merely as a static, deterministic state. It is change that produces ontology, pilgrimage that produces rest, process that produces existence, and suffering that produces perfection. It is change that produces creativity through the process of becoming.

The *Tao Te Ching* says, "Essential nature [the Tao] is ever changing and changeless." In other words, change, or even chaos, is not to be disliked, manipulated, or feared. Change produces a life of pilgrimage. It is in that change and pilgrimage that one finds his being, the meaning of existence, just as the pioneer of faith and salvation who is the "ever changing and changeless," did. According to the author the preexistent Jesus brought forth the cosmos and controls it (Heb 1:2–3, 2:8b), yet he

Source: Yeo Khiok-khng, *What Has Jerusalem to Do with Beijing? Biblical Interpretation from a Chinese Perspective* (Harrisburg, PA: Trinity Press, 1998), pp. 97–98. Copyright © 1998 Yeo Khiok-khng. Used by permission.

partakes of our human nature in flesh and blood (Heb 2:9–10) and shares obediently our suffering and death (Heb 2:10–11). In the midst of change, chaos, and entropy, Christ has expiated human sin, accomplished atonement, been exalted to glory and honor, and has become the Great High Priest (2:17–18; 4:14–15). Thus, the yin-yang nature of the cosmos and life is to be accepted. That is, one has to accept change and chaos as edifying components of the whole cosmos, as designed by God.

Question

Give your own reflection on this selection. In particular, how well does Chinese thought about the universe as expressed in yin-yang illustrate Hebrews?

www   Follow the link for more information on the yin-yang concept.

Doing Cross-Cultural Reading Yourself

What difference might it make for cross-cultural reading if one adopts the idea that Hebrews is written to Jewish Christians?—to Gentile Christians?

JAMES: Faith and Justice in Keeping God's Law

After Hebrews in the canonical order of the NT comes James, a work famously called by the sixteenth-century Protestant reformer Martin Luther an "epistle of straw," almost worthless because it seemed to argue against Paul's teaching of justification by faith, a most important teaching to Luther. Much scholarly reading of the NT between Luther's time and the twentieth century has also seen James as less valuable and interesting than Paul, but today the situation is changing. James is now seen as one of the most sophisticated and powerful statements of personal and social ethics in the NT. Feminist and cross-cultural methods of reading appreciate its emphasis on *doing* what is right. Moreover, in modern times when Jewish Christianity is seen as one of the legitimate varieties of early Christianity, this letter is a vital, important source for our knowledge of Jewish Christianity.

James in Brief: Outline of Structure and Contents

I. **Opening** Author "James" to "the twelve tribes in the dispersion"; greetings (1:1)
II. **Body** Various themes of faith, works, wisdom and obedience
   A. Enduring trials as faith is tested (1:2–18)
   B. Avoiding anger, passivity, foolish speech, and partiality to the rich (1:19–2:13)

C. Faith and works (2:14–26)
D. Speech and obedience (3:1–12)
E. The wisdom of obedience (3:13–18)
F. The power of faithful prayer (4:1–3)
G. Friendship with the world to be avoided (4:4–6)
H. The humility of faith (4:7–10)
I. Avoiding slander in the community, boasting; warning to the wealthy (4:11–5:6)
J. The patience of faith; prayer for healing (5:7–18)
K. Bring back wandering persons to the faith (5:19–20; note: no formal letter ending)

Developing Your Skills

Of all the documents of the NT, James seems to be the most scattered in organization. A handful of themes are continually treated, in no apparent order. Read through this letter in one sitting, with special attention to the themes and their possible interrelationships (for example, what does wisdom have to do with keeping the Law of Moses, or Law keeping to treatment of the poor?).

A Guide to Reading James

James opens his letter addressed to "the twelve tribes in the Dispersion," probably Jewish Christians scattered throughout the world, with a brief greeting (1:1). The rest of the letter is all body, with no thanksgiving, no final greeting, and no benediction. It gives the appearance of an essay, but an essay to a specific audience in a more or less specific situation.

In the first section, James speaks about enduring trials (1:2–18). He begins with a lengthy statement on the testing of one's faith (1:2–8). In this statement James touches on four points: (1) trust God in trials (1:2); (2) trials produce perseverance and perseverance produces maturity (1:3–4, a **catena** [chain-linked list] of virtues); (3) God gives wisdom and all good things to the one who believes (1:5); and (4) genuine faith must remove doubt (1:6). James then develops these points in a roughly **chiastic** (reverse) order. First, the one who doubts is unstable and will receive nothing from the Lord (1:7–8). Second, God has given the doubter hope—the lowly will be lifted up (1:9–11). Third, the one who perseveres in his faith in the face of adversity will be blessed and rewarded with the crown of life (1:12). Finally, the believer ought never to blame God for temptations or trials (1:13–15) but instead should thank God for God's goodness and sovereign care (1:16–18).

The second major section deals with life within the community. James begins with a summary statement in which he articulates four characteristics of obedient faith: (1) not quick-tempered (1:19–21); (2) not passive (1:22–25); (3) not uncontrolled in speech (1:26); and (4) not partial towards the rich, but helping the marginalized poor like widows and orphans (1:27). James then develops these themes. First, he addresses the sin of partiality. Rather than helping the poor, his audience has been catering to the rich (2:1–13). James portrays a memorable scene of two men entering their assembly (in Greek, "synagogue"), one poor and one rich, in which the church shows partiality to the rich man and treats the poor person as shabbily as he is dressed (2:2–4). The audience is then rebuked both for partiality and for its naiveté about the wealthy (2:5–7). Then James gives a biblical argument for showing no partiality (2:8–11) and finishes this section with a restatement of a biblical principle: one cannot pick and choose between God's requirements. Therefore, the audience is to "speak and act as those who are going to be judged by the law that gives freedom."

James now turns to the issue of faith and works in justification (2:14–26). James has just warned against partiality toward the wealthy. James argues that one who lives by the slogan of "faith alone," if one does not care for the unfortunate within the believing community, cannot be saved. He does not yet explain what he means by faith, which comes in the next section. In **diatribe** (sharp conversational) style, James poses a possible objection from someone who believes in "faith alone," and answers it. The objector may be arguing that one can be saved either by faith or by works. James rebuffs this view (v. 18b) by saying that it is impossible to divorce the two, as some people in his audience do. A faith that is doctrinally correct (as the demons' monotheistic "belief") but does not lead to faithful acts cannot save anyone; it shows itself to be false faith. What, then, is true faith? For its positive definition, James uses two illustrations from the OT. First, Abraham was justified by works when he offered up Isaac (2:21). His faith could not be divorced from works but cooperated with it (2:22). His works perfected his faith (v. 22), his faith was completed by his works (v. 23; Gen 15:6). His faith and his works culminated in his being called "a friend of God." James summarizes by saying that "a man is justified by works and not by faith alone" (2:24). Lest one conclude from this statement that heaven is reserved only for those who are morally perfect or near to it, James hastens to add the striking illustration of Rahab. She too was justified by her "works" (i.e., deeds) when she helped the Israelite spies get away from Jericho (2:25). James explicitly reminds his audience that Rahab was a prostitute, yet she was justified. Rahab had a genuine faith because she acted on it. Both illustrations explain faith and works in such a way that it is unthinkable that one could please God and do justice without both. James concludes with an analogy to illustrate his point (2:26).

Next, James addresses the issue of controlling one's speech (3:1–12), a prominent theme in OT wisdom literature. The author has just finished arguing that faith entails correct deeds; now faith entails being obedient to God in what one says (3:1–12). Even teachers need to control their tongues (3:1); hence, one whose tongue is kept in check—probably against angry speech—is mature (3:2). Then James begins a series of analogies. First, even though the tongue is small, it can have a power over one's whole person. Horses' bits, ships' rudders, and sparks in the forest are also small, yet they have great power (3:3–6). Second, even though human beings have tamed all kinds of animals, ironically we cannot tame our own tongues (3:7–8). Third, it is just as inconsistent for the tongue to praise God and curse people as it is for fresh and salt water to come from the same spring or for the same tree to produce two different kinds of fruit (3:9–12). James next notes the wisdom of obedience (3:13–18). This paragraph nicely caps this section: just as faith must be impartial, and productive in deed and word, it must also be *wise*. This *wisdom motif* has been seen before in the talk about trials in 1:5, but the real content of wisdom in 3:13–18 is not related to trials as much as it is to community relationships. Thus James uses wisdom as a character goal that comes about by ridding oneself of bitterness, envy, and selfishness—all outgrowths of anger (3:13–14). Indeed, the proper kind of wisdom is from heaven (compare 1:16–18), not from earth, and produces a harvest of good deeds (3:17–18). This description of wisdom as divine and practical is particularly Jewish, not Hellenistic.

Without any transitional statement, an omission typical of James, the author begins the next major section: the carrying out of faith before the world (4:1–5:20). He characteristically begins with a summary statement on the reward of faith (cf. 4:10). This statement includes three points: first, the prayer of faith is strong (4:1–3); second, friendship with "the world" is to be avoided (4:4–6); third, humility is most important: "Humble yourselves before the Lord and he will lift you up" (4:7–10). James then fills in the specifics as he urges the recipients to avoid evil influences (4:11–5:6). First, believers are not to speak evil against and judge each another, for only God can judge, and when believers judge they break God's Law (4:11–12). Second, they must not boast about their plans for the future, for such boasting reveals a foolish and presumptuous spirit (4:13–17). Third, the author condemns wealthy landowners for oppressing the poor; since no alternative behavior is proposed, they are most likely not Christians (5:1–6).

James now turns to oppressed farmers in his audience (probably landless peasants) and commands them to be patient (5:7–12). The Lord's return is a message of hope to the oppressed (5:7–8) just as it is a message of doom to the rich oppressor (5:1). A patient faith refrains from judging (5:9; cf. 4:11–13). James concludes with the legendary "patience of Job" as a biblical illustration (5:10–11), and then tells the recipients to avoid oaths (5:12), for such swearing is presumptuous (cf. 4:13–18). James then gives instruction about believing prayer (5:13–20). He urges prayer for the sick, saying that, "the prayer of a righteous person is powerful and effective" (5:16). He gives a biblical illustration of Elijah as a man of faith and effective prayer, whom the audience would recognize as one who healed the sick (5:17–18). James began with this theme (1:2–8), and now it is mentioned near its end. Finally, James urges its audience to bring back one who is wandering from the faith, thus affirming the possibility of a second repentance. This is effective for the wandering sinner, and will "cover a multitude" of the rescuer's sins, an expression drawn from sacrificial language to imply a particularly good deed (5:19–20).

Historical Reading of James

> ### James in Brief: Summary of Historical Reading
>
> **Author** The letter claims to be written by James, most likely the brother of Jesus, and some scholars conclude that it is authentic. Much more common is the view that this letter is pseudonymous, written by an unknown Jewish Christian from the Diaspora.
>
> **Date** If authentic, before the death of James in 62; if pseudonymous, anywhere from 70 to 100, with the latter half of that period more likely.
>
> **Audience** "The twelve tribes in the dispersion," probably Jewish Christians outside Palestine.
>
> **Unity and Integrity** Not questioned today.
>
> **Purpose** To inculcate a renewed obedience to the Law of Moses.

Author

In 1:1 the author identifies himself only as "James, the servant of God and of the Lord Jesus Christ." The NT mentions at least four men, and possibly as many as seven, bearing the common name of James (Hebrew, "Jacob"). It is probable, but not certain, that the writer of this epistle is to be identified with one of them. By far the most likely candidate is James the brother or near relative of Jesus (Matt 13:55; Mark 6:3; Acts 12:17; 15:13; 21:18; 1 Cor 15:7; Gal 1:19). James became the leader of the Jerusalem church sometime before 44 C.E. and was one of two leaders Paul met within Jerusalem three years after his conversion (Gal 1:19). James's martyrdom in 62 increased his standing in the church. That this James (also known in later church traditions as "James the Just") is the author of the letter has been the traditional view and is stoutly defended today by some. The most persuasive reasons for this letter's authenticity are:

- *The authority assumed by the author.* A well-known, respected James must have been intended, having the status to speak to "the twelve tribes in the dispersion."

In the NT, Jesus' close relative is the only James who appears to have played a sufficiently prominent part in early Christian history to meet this requirement.

- *The author's Jewish background.* The author comes from Judaism, whether from Palestine or the Hellenistic Diaspora. This is seen in his use of the OT that includes a few quotations, numerous allusions, and several illustrations, and in other, more subtle ways such as traces of Hebrew idioms behind his polished Greek, strong presence of wisdom traditions, and Hebrew prophetic style.

- *Acquaintance with the teaching of Jesus.* The parallels to the Sermon on the Mount are especially notable; this author seems to have assimilated the form and content of Jesus' wisdom teaching. A few today conclude that the author even heard Jesus himself. However, this would not prove that James, the Lord's brother, was responsible for the letter, because James the son of Zebedee would be just as likely a candidate. Moreover, ample evidence in the Gospels shows that Jesus' family did not follow Jesus during his lifetime.

- *General agreement with the NT account of James.* Not only is James the leader of the Jerusalem church in Acts, but he also promotes the continuing validity of the law, although in a moderate way. This portrait of James in Acts 15 corresponds with James's statements in this letter about the law (cf., e.g., 1:22–25; 2:8–13). Richard Bauckham boldly argues that the passages in James that seem to argue against Paul are wholly intelligible from James' situation in the 50s, without reference to Paul or Paulinism (Bauckham 2003, 1487–1488).

In the external evidence from the third and fourth centuries, the letter of James is first mentioned by name by Origen, who apparently regards it as scripture. Eusebius and Jerome also cite it as scripture and apparently accept that it is from James, the Lord's brother. However, Eusebius classes it among the disputed books, and Jerome implies that another wrote in James's name or later edited the work. Before Origen, however, there may be allusions to James in some late first-century Christian writers, especially Clement of Rome and Hermas. However, whether these writers allude to James or whether all three borrow independently from a common pool of wisdom motifs cannot be demonstrated either way.

www   For a chart illustrating the connections between the Sermon on the Mount in Matthew 5–7 and James, see the website.

In the last one hundred years, scholars have developed arguments against the traditional view. Now most conclude that the letter of James is pseudonymous for these reasons:

- *Excellent Greek style.* Among the most refined Greek in the New Testament, the style is far too good for an Aramaic-speaking Galilean peasant, James's background. The sentence structure and vocabulary are sophisticated, and the author is expert at using Greco-Roman rhetorical devices such as the diatribe. James *could* have learned Greek this well, or written through a very literate scribe, but most scholars doubt this.

- *A different concept of the Law.* The concept of the law in this writing differs in some ways from what might be expected from James. Circumcision is not mentioned here, and given that James is an advocate of circumcision for Jews, this omission is peculiar. Of course, this is an argument from silence; other reasons could account for such a silence, including a common understanding between the author and audience that circumcision is still binding on Jewish Christians.
- *Literary parallels with the rest of the NT.* James has many parallels with other NT books, especially the Sermon on the Mount in Matt 5–7. The majority of scholars believe that James depended on other works and hence was written later than during the lifetime of the Lord's brother.
- *Argument with Paulinism, not Paul personally.* The type of Paulinism opposed in James probably comes not from Paul and James's time, but after their deaths in the 60s.

In sum, most scholars today conclude that James is pseudonymous. The letter points to James of Jerusalem as its supposed author, but its style and (more important) its content indicate that James probably is not the real author. Although we cannot be certain, and widely respected NT scholars like Luke Timothy Johnson (Johnson 1995) and Richard Bauckham (Bauckham 2003) argue for its authenticity, the letter seems to be at home in a time after the death of James in 62. To judge from the letter's contents and style, the author seems to be a Jewish Christian living outside Palestine, fully acquainted with the heritage of Judaism and Hellenism. He writes in James's name to perpetuate his heritage as an advocate of Jewish Christianity.

Date

If this letter is by James, the brother of Jesus, then it came sometime before 62 C.E., when James died. Those who embrace authenticity advocate two dates: either early (late 40s, but before the Jerusalem Council in 49) or late (between 50 and 60). Those who conclude that James is pseudonymous mostly place it in the 80s or 90s, with enough time after the death of Paul to allow disputes over the correct interpretation of Paul's teaching on faith and works to develop, disputes that this writing may address.

Audience

The contents of the letter point to a Jewish Christian audience in several churches; thus, this is a circular letter. The recipients of the letter meet in a "synagogue" (2:2, usually translated as "assembly"), and the only creedal statement in the letter is about

Torah Scroll Being Lifted at Sukkoth Orthodox Jews at the Sukkoth ("Booths") festival lift a Hebrew Torah scroll in its box. The devotion of observant Jews and Jewish Christians to the Law is an important part of the background of the book of James. Used by permission of BiblePlaces.com.

Jewish monotheism (2:19). That James's audience is made up largely of poor people is obvious from his warnings in 2:1–13 (especially v. 5). The recipients are likely either poor tenant farmers who worked the land of the rich (5:1–6), or lower class merchants (4:13–17). The wealthy are on the fringes of James's audience, either actually or rhetorically, serving primarily as a foil for his ethical instructions. James's audience was also an oppressed group, marginalized because of their poverty and their Christian conviction. Peter Davids explains this well: "On the one hand, the church naturally felt resentment against the rich. They had 'robbed' many of the members of their lands; they probably showed discrimination against Christians in hiring their labor; and they . . . were the instigators of attempts to suppress the church. On the other hand, if a wealthy person entered the church or was a member, there would be every reason to court him. His money was seen as a means of survival. . . . [T]heir inappropriate response to the oppression, rather than the oppression itself, is what James condemns, pointing out that they should seek in such circumstances the wisdom and gifts of God" (Davids 1983, 33).

Purpose

James was written to reinforce Law observance in Jewish Christian churches (or as he would say, "synagogues"). It seeks to end what it considers wrong ideas about faith and law probably originating in Pauline churches and now found in James' churches, and its vision of Law-observance takes in a strong concern for what we today would call social justice. Throughout the letter, the author speaks as an authoritative wise man, a teacher of wisdom attempting to increase the wisdom of his audience in following the Law to live good Christian lives and strengthen them against various types of adversity.

www   See the website for a short essay comparing James's and Paul's views of faith and works.

Social Scientific Reading of James

James is rich in social scientific perspectives. It uses kinship language to keep its readers in the family of God, with the exalted leader James repeatedly calling his audience "my brothers and sisters." James uses honor and shame language to urge them to persevere in the faith. James seeks to bring a harmony between believing and acting, particularly in ways consistent with the best of the Jewish Law. Its championing of the believing poor against rich oppressors marks it as the NT document most concerned about social justice.

Social Scientific Reading
The "Health Care System" of the Letter of James (5:13–18)

In this conclusion to his journal article, Albl states the social-spiritual dimensions of sickness and healing in the Letter of James, which of course reflects the wider Mediterranean-Jewish culture.

"Are any among you sick?" James's question and subsequent instructions for healing challenge the community to respond not merely to the bodily needs of the patient but also to help the patient make sense out of his or her experience of illness.

Source: Martin C. Albl, "'Are Any among You Sick?' The Health Care System of the Letter of James," *Journal of Biblical Literature* 121 (2002): 123–143.

Studying a community's response to illness as a health care system provides a particularly useful avenue for analyzing the profoundly holistic shape that this response takes in the community addressed by James.

The health care system in James provides meaning to the patient by situating the illness within the community's dualistic symbolic world. In this world, the patient's illness is seen not as an isolated incident, a "natural" occurrence, or a merely "physical" problem. Instead, illness is understood as a demonic disturbance of the godly integrity of the person's body. This conflict is a microcosm of larger struggles between division and integration, between life and death, between the demonic and the divine that play out both in the community body and in the cosmos as a whole.

The patient thus does not experience healing as an isolated individual. The community body, led by the elders, must gather and show its united support through prayer, confession, and public ritual. As integrity is restored to the individual body, so it is reinforced in the community body. Beyond the community level, the individual healing has cosmic significance. Healing of a single person does not merely "symbolize" or "foreshadow" his or her eschatological salvation. Rather, the ritual anointing and community prayers move the patient into the realm of *both* bodily healing *and* eschatological salvation. The system does not separate the two.

The health care system, as presented in James's ideal symbolic world (and as manifested to a greater or lesser extent in social reality), is radically integral. Individual, social, and cosmic levels interpenetrate. Boundaries between present "physical" healing and future "spiritual" salvation do not exist. Distinctions between the sick who are poor and those who are rich are erased. God is one, and both the healed individual and the healed community participate in God's oneness.

Questions

1. *Compare this "health-care system" with our health care system today, especially the move today toward more holistic care that can make room for psychological and spiritual concerns.*

2. *A theme in Jesus' miracles in the Synoptics is the connection between faith and healing. How might the communities of James's letter have used these miracle accounts in their own "health-care system"?*

Cross-Cultural Reading of James

Because Jewish Christianity was an ethnic as well as a religious phenomenon, cross-cultural issues abound in James. Its readers today must always keep in mind that the audience is Jewish, seeking to live out Jewish Christianity in a Gentile world and perhaps over against a Gentile church (Paulinism or distorted Paulinism). Also, its orientation to praxis makes it attractive to readers from the margins today.

Cross-Cultural Reading at Work
"Faith without Works" (James 2)

James is oriented toward the practice (praxis) of faith, and methods of reading like the cross-cultural approach seem particularly suited to bring out its meaning. Because praxis must be done today in order to understand the text for what it is, cross-cultural reading also challenges the modern person of faith to practice it more fully.

Believing in Jesus is insufficient for obtaining salvation. Does not the author of the letter of James warn us that even the demons believe in Jesus and tremble at his name? "My brothers and sisters, what profits those who say they have faith but do not have works? Is faith able to save them? If a brother or sister is naked and lacking daily food, and any one of you says, "Go in peace, be warmed and filled," but does not give them the necessities of the body, what is the profit? So also faith, if it has no works, is dead by itself. Yet one will say, "You have faith and I have works." Show me your faith without your works and I will show you my faith by my works. . . . For the body without spirit is dead, so also faith without works is dead" (2:14–20, 24, 26).

Concentrating solely on personal faith in Jesus Christ, divorced from actions of loving justice, encourages cheap grace. People from the margins insist that Christians move beyond an abstract belief in Jesus to a material response to those who are hungry, thirsty, naked, alien, sick, and incarcerated. The task for those seeking eternal life must go beyond an intellectual understanding of Jesus Christ to the actual doing of Christ-like actions—not because salvation is achieved by those actions but because they serve as witness to the empowering grace given by God. To continue worshiping Christ apart from any commitment to those who are the least contributes to maintaining our present structures of oppression along gender, race, and class lines. To ignore the cry of those who are marginalized is to deny Christ's message, regardless of whether or not we confess our belief in him and proclaim his name with our lips.

Question

What does the author mean by "cheap grace," and why would NT readers "from the margins" be especially concerned about it?

www The Letter of James has played a large role in the debate on salvation between Protestant and Roman Catholic Christians, with Roman Catholics frequently taking a position that resembles James's, and Protestants one that resembles Paul's. Follow the link on the website to read the joint statement on justification by the Lutheran churches and the Roman Catholic Church.

Source: Miguel A. De La Torre, *Reading the Bible from the Margins.* Copyright © 2002 by Miguel A. De La Torre. Published by Orbis Books, Maryknoll, New York. Used by permission of the publisher.

1 PETER: Faithful Life under Persecution

Of all the General Letters, 1 Peter is probably the most well known and influential. It bears the name of Peter, the main disciple of Jesus and a leader of the early church, and as we would expect from a letter written by a key church leader, 1 Peter addresses several issues important for Christianity. It is rhetorically powerful, often sermonic and poetic. As a letter to Christians under the threat of persecution, it exhorts them to stay faithful to Christ, and to live lives worthy of their standing as God's children.

1 Peter in Brief: Outline of Structure and Contents

I. **Opening** Peter to the dispersed people of God, salutation (1:1–2).
II. **Thanksgiving** Praise to God for new birth and guiding through persecution (1:3–9).
III. **Body** (1:10–5:11)
  A. The identity of the people of God: new life, priesthood (1:10–2:10)
  B. The responsibilities of the people of God (2:11–5:11)
   1. Their mission in the world (2:11–12)
   2. Honor all people (2:13–17)
   3. Household duties (2:18–3:7)
   4. Do good in mutual love; vindication at the end of time (3:13–5:11)
IV. **Conclusion** Purpose of the letter, final greetings and blessing (5:12–14).

A Guide to Reading 1 Peter

Peter opens with a greeting to "exiles of the Dispersion" in Roman provinces in the northern half of Asia Minor (1:1–2). They have been "chosen and destined" by God the Father, made holy in the Spirit, and are obedient to Jesus Christ. This hints at themes to follow. He blesses them with grace and peace (v. 2).

The author then presents an expansive blessing of God that functions as a thanksgiving section (1:3-12). Its theme is that the Christian's hope is founded on the death and resurrection of Jesus. Believers have a precious salvation that gives them hope (vv. 3–5) and joy (v. 6). Their suffering "for a little while" will result in the refining and strengthening of their faith (vv. 6–9). Their salvation was predicted by the OT prophets (vv. 10–11) and even desired by angels (v. 12).

In its letter body, 1 Peter turns quickly to matters of holiness, not sinless perfection but separation from this world to be a part of God's family and kingdom.

Note that unlike Paul, this writer goes straight to moral exhortation. Believers have been given a new way of life (1:13–25), which requires the holiness of "obedient children" (1:13–16). They must respect their heavenly Father, and they are strangers in this world (1:17–21). They must show genuine love toward brothers and sisters in the faith (1:22–25). They are a chosen priesthood (2:5, 9), so they must desire the word (2:1–3) and come to Christ in worship by offering a spiritual sacrifice that is acceptable to God (2:4–5). Further, this new identity ("spiritual house") is based on the precious stone that the builders rejected, a reference to the death of Jesus (2:6–8). The author summarizes the status of his audience eloquently: they are a people chosen by God, a royal priesthood, a holy nation, a people of God's own possession (2:9), all to the praise of God's glory (2:10).

Next, 1 Peter develops further how God's people should act. He first summarizes believers' responsibilities in the world by saying that they must abstain from sin (2:11) and live "honorably" before non-Christians (2:12). Then he goes into detail, explaining what for him seems to be the key to the Christian life, a key closely related to social scientific reading giving honor to those who deserve it (2:13–25). This practice is for every Christian, and the author proceeds to categorize groups of people who should give and receive honor. First, all Christians should respect all people (v. 17), especially the emperor and provincial governors, but the author distinctly calls them "human authorities" (2:13–14, 17). Respect should not be given in a powerless, subservient way but rather by people whose slavery to God makes them free in this world (2:16). Then, in a **household code** that runs from 2:18 to 3:7, the author urges the audience to show honor to all honorable people and to members of the Christian household. Christian slaves must submit to their masters, whether the masters are good or evil (2:18–20); this follows Christ's example, whose suffering brought believers salvation (2:21–25). This is well-developed instruction for slaves, but this household code (unlike Colossians' and Ephesians') does not have any commands for masters, which may indicate that there were few slave owners in Peter's audience. Wives likewise must submit to their husbands, even unbelieving husbands, with a gentle and quiet spirit (3:1–4); this may lead to a husband's conversion. The author makes a strong plea for women to avoid outer beauty and rich adornment of their hair and clothing, but to cultivate the inner beauty that pleases God and will attract their husbands to their faith (3:3–5). Women must follow the example of OT saints, especially Sarah, in dressing modestly and accepting the authority of their husbands (3:5–6). Husbands must honor their wives "as the weaker vessel/sex" so that the husbands' prayers may be answered (3:7). If this (in)famous "weaker sex" reference is to the physical strength of a woman compared to a man, which many scholars conclude today, then honoring one's wife probably includes the idea of not physically overpowering or abusing her, just as much a problem in the ancient world as today.

The household code concluded, the author continues the theme of nonretaliation against persecution, especially the command to bless others who oppose believers (3:8–12). The author encourages not just passive suffering for right-eousness' sake, but actively doing good (3:13–4:6). Believers are to do good even if they should suffer for it, and avoid suffering for doing wrong (3:13–17). Once again, 1 Peter points to the example of Christ's sufferings, which brought believ-ers their salvation (3:18–22). As a part of this discussion, the author mentions Christ's proclamation to the "imprisoned spirits" of Noah's generation, one of the most puzzling texts of the NT. Three main interpretations have been offered: (1) preaching by the preexistent Christ through Noah to the "imprisoned" wicked gen-eration before the flood; (2) preaching of the risen Christ to spirits in hell to show that no one of any generation is beyond the reach of salvation; (3) announcement by the risen Christ to the imprisoned evil angels that his death and resurrection has won a triumph over all rebellious spiritual forces (the preferable view, in my opinion). At any rate, believers should follow Christ's example (4:1–2), avoid their former lifestyle (4:3), and look forward to gaining their heavenly hope (4:4–6). The author admonishes his audience to band together in order to face their suf-ferings better, commending mutual love, hospitality, and faithful use of gifts that serve to build up the group (4:7–11). Because Christ's return is imminent, believ-ers should pray with a clear mind (4:7), love with deep affection (4:8), show hos-pitality (probably to traveling Christians) without grumbling (4:9), and exercise spiritual gifts with faithfulness (4:10–11). A brief blessing of God concludes this segment of the letter (v. 11).

In the next major section, the author addresses suffering in the midst of fiery trials (4:12–19). He encourages the believers in light of the sufferings of Christ to suffer in the name of Christ (vv. 12–14), and even uses the name "Christian" to describe them (v. 16). They are not to suffer for doing crimes large or small, but only as innocents, which suggests that some Christians were indeed punished by Rome for good reasons. Then he reminds them that even the house of God needs some housecleaning, since the end of time is very near (v. 17). The author ends this section by reiterating its basic point: those suffering because they do good should entrust themselves to God and keep on doing good (v. 19).

In the final part of the letter body, the author gives commands for community life. First, speaks to the elders/presbyters, urging them to be faithful shepherds of God's people. They are to avoid being overbearing and greedy (5:1–4). He then addresses the rest of the congregation, "you who are younger" (5:5), urging them to honor their leaders. All believers should humble themselves (5:6) and cast their cares on God (5:7). The author concludes this section with a further reason why believers need to depend on God: the devil, a supernatural enemy, is prowling around to devour them. The author links the devil's presence to the worldwide suf-fering he sees all Christian believers going through (5:8–9). This supernatural oppo-sition should not cause undue fear, for God is greater than the devil (5:10–11).

First Peter concludes with an explicit statement of its purpose, made here for persuasive effect. The author has written "through Silvanus," most probably the

Silvanus/Silas who is a co-worker of Paul, this "short letter." He writes to encourage the recipients to stand firm in the true grace of God as they undergo trials. Then greetings are given from "she who is in Babylon," probably a "sister" church, and from "my son Mark." The author commands them to greet each other with "a kiss of love," in the Mediterranean normally shared by close kin, and closes with a blessing for their peace (5:12–14).

Historical Reading of 1 Peter

1 Peter in Brief: Summary of Historical Reading

Author Traditionally, Peter the main disciple of Jesus; today a majority of interpreters hold that an unknown Jewish Christian member of the Pauline circle wrote the letter.

Date If authentic, 60–64; if pseudonymous, in the 80s or 90s.

Audience Gentile Christians in provinces in northern Asia Minor.

Unity and Integrity Unquestioned by the majority of scholars today.

Purpose To encourage Christians to live confidently and faithfully in the face of persecution.

Author

The opening verse indicates that "Peter, an apostle of Jesus Christ" is the author, clearly meaning Simon Peter, Jesus' leading disciple. Today, however, most scholars dispute Peter's authorship. We will begin with external evidence. In the early second century, 1 Peter has verbal parallels in the writings of Clement of Rome, Ignatius, Barnabas, Hermas, and Polycarp, but these works do not mention Peter as the author. In the middle of the second century, Irenaeus does quote from 1 Peter and regards it as a work of Peter. From the end of the second century on, this letter is regularly regarded as Petrine. In spite of this external evidence in favor of Petrine authorship, scholars have noted internal difficulties that tend to outweigh the early church's testimony. In general, three types of objections have been put forth: linguistic, historical, and literary.

- *Linguistic objections.* The Greek of 1 Peter seems too good for Peter, a Galilean fisherman. It ranks, in terms of vocabulary and sentence style, just below James. The author of this letter surpasses Paul in his skill in Greek, yet Paul had much better training in Greek than Peter.

- *Historical objections.* First, the historical situation presupposed is that of widespread persecution (cf. 1:6–7; 4:12, 14–16). This was not true at the end of Peter's life, probably in the 60s. Nero persecuted Christians only in Rome (as far as history records), although during Domitian's reign persecution spread in the 90s to the eastern Mediterranean. Second, Peter has no known relationship with the churches of Asia Minor. Indeed, as these seem to be Gentile churches, one wonders why Peter as the "apostle to the circumcision" would be writing to predominantly Gentile churches. Third, in the closing of 1 Peter the author seems to put himself in a Pauline circle, which the historical Peter most probably was not.
- *Literary objections.* This letter is parallel to, and probably dependent on, Paul's letters for some of its contents, Romans and Ephesians in particular. For example, compare 1 Pet 2:6–8 with Rom 9:32–33; 1 Pet 2:13–17 with Rom 13:1–7; 1 Pet 1:3 with Eph 1:3; and 1 Pet 2:4–6 with Eph 2:20–22. The letter also shows more distant affinities to Hebrews. If Ephesians was written sometime after Paul's death, then of course Peter could not have written 1 Peter, since Peter likely died in the middle 60s at roughly the same time as Paul. The reasons for an apostle of Peter's stature to borrow so heavily from Paul seem difficult to grasp. As several commentators have written, if this letter did not have Peter's name on it, we would be debating if it might be from Paul! For these reasons, most scholars today view 1 Peter as a pseudonymous work by an unknown Jewish Christian in the Pauline tradition.

Date

If Peter is genuinely the author, then a date up to around 64 C.E. is possible. However, if this letter is pseudonymous, as most believe, it is best placed in the 90s, during the reign of Domitian, when persecution occurred in the area to which the author writes. This dating also makes sense of the author's knowledge of Romans, Ephesians and Hebrews.

Audience

This letter is addressed to Christians in the modern-day Turkish peninsula. First Peter refers to the geographical, rather than political, districts in using the terms "Pontus, Galatia, Cappadocia, Asia and Bithynia." We know this because Pontus and Bithynia were one Roman province politically but were separate areas geographically.

What does the author mean by "to the exiles of the Dispersion" (1:1)? Three main ideas are current in scholarship. First, some think it refers to all Christian believers, who are spiritually exiled from the full reign/kingdom of God (Best, 1971). Second, John Elliott and others understand it literally as "resident aliens and visiting strangers" in the Roman provinces they inhabit, probably a status they gained before, not after, conversion (Elliott 1981, 48). Third, the most preferred view takes this phrase as an example of the author's adaptation of a Jewish term to apply to Gentile Christian believers (Achtemeier 1996, 56). But are these believers Jewish or Gentile Christians? A view for a Jewish-Christian audience is based on the Jewish overtones of "exiles in the Dispersion" and the heavy use of the Jewish Bible by the author— he cites the LXX nine times, and alludes to it in more than thirty other places. However, a few passages in 1 Peter point decisively to a Gentile audience. Specifically, in 1:18 the author reminds the audience that "you were ransomed from the futile ways inherited from your fathers," something that no one would say about Jews; in 2:10, he says, "once you were no people, but now you are the people of God"; in 4:3, he says, "the time is gone for doing what the Gentiles like to do." So a Gentile audience is in view, but it is also possible that the audience was predominantly Gentile with a significant Jewish element. The references to their pagan background would still be appropriate if the majority were Gentiles, and the particularly heavy use of the OT would be meaningful to the Jewish members of the churches and somewhat intelligible to Gentile members when we remember that the Septuagint was used every week in their religious services.

Place

In 5:13, the author sends a greeting from the church "in Babylon." Assuming as most readers do that he is writing from "Babylon," two main possibilities present themselves: Mesopotamian Babylon, a literal use of the name, and Rome, a symbolic use. Four reasons argue against the literal Babylon: (1) Peter is nowhere else associated with this region; (2) the Eastern church did not claim any association with Peter in its church origins until a late period; (3) the area was very sparsely populated, and the city itself still in a state of destruction; (4) early tradition centered the activities of Peter in the West and not the East. This leads us to Rome. The only real problem with Rome as the place of writing is the reason for the symbolic term Babylon. But in 5:13 we have two other symbolic expressions, that Mark is "*my son,*" and "*She* who is at Babylon, who is likewise chosen," a reference to the church. The cryptogram "Babylon" was possibly used to protect the Roman church in case the letter fell into the wrong hands during times of persecution; ironically, it suggests that Rome will go the way of Babylon. In sum, Rome seems to be the best location for the writing of this letter.

Unity

Several scholars see the doxology in 4:11 and the supposedly different emphasis on persecution after 4:11 as indications two letters may have been joined at this point. But most scholars see no clear seam here, because the whole letter from beginning to end talks about endurance under one kind of persecution. Therefore, the great majority of scholars today holds to the literary unity of 1 Peter.

Purpose

The ending of 1 Peter gives the author's general reason for writing: "to encourage you and to testify that this is the true grace of God; stand fast in it" (5:12). Specifically, the "true grace of God" of which the author speaks is rooted in the death, and resurrection and glorification of Jesus that has made them God's people. This grace is meant to empower and direct the way they live in the world, especially as this Christian way of life brings them social alienation and suffering.

Feminist and Cross-Cultural Readings of 1 Peter

Feminist reading of 1 Peter notes how closely it resembles the disputed Pauline letters. It has a conservative but still Christian approach to the status and role of women, expressed like the disputed Pauline letters in a household code (3:1–7). Cross-cultural reading sees the crossing of the cultural barrier between Jew and Gentile as important in 1 Peter. This letter emphasizes how believing Gentiles have become the new people of God, a people who suffer for and with Christ so fully that they are known by his name: they are "Christians" (4:16).

Feminist and Cross-Cultural Readings at Work
Women as "Living Stones" (1 Pet 2:1–8)

First Peter's metaphor of the people of God as "living stones" is striking but difficult to grasp. In this reading from Africa, Grace Eneme explains this in terms of the "living stones" of her culture.

Among the Bakossi people in the forest region of the southwest province in Cameroon, stones are classified into two main groups: living stones and dead stones. Living stones are stones that are movable, portable, and usable. . . . Of the living stones, tripod stones for cooking have great significance to the Bakossi women. These stones serve a vital purpose in the life of the family and the community. Around them people meet for family discussions. Here is where moral instruction takes place and folk tales are told, a place of warmth and a refuge for strangers.

When a man takes a bride, one of the ceremonies that integrates her into the family is the laying of the tripod stones. The first stone is pitched by the bride and her

Source: Grace Eneme, "Women as Living Stones," in John S. Pobee and Bärbel von Wartenburg-Potter, eds., *New Eyes for Reading* (Geneva: WCC Publications, 1986), pp. 28–32.

husband, signifying oneness in building up their home. The second stone is pitched by the bride and the eldest woman in the family, signifying her acceptance and integration into the family and village community. It also symbolizes her active participation in family affairs, mutual respect, and sharing with others. The third stone is pitched by the bride and her chaperon (sister or aunt). It symbolizes a bridge of contact for the two families, the husband's and the wife's. That stone assures the bride of solidarity by her family members in both good and bad times.

From that moment on the stones assume their functions and the wife feels integrated in the family. Is the image of tripod stones the same as the image of living stones? Certainly not, but there is some similarity between them. The image of living stones as presented to us by Peter signifies the Church as a community of believers whose main function is service and witness. The community is compared to a building, having Christ as the foundation stone and Christians as stones in the edifice. As each stone is important in erecting the walls, so is each Christian in the community of believers. The appeal to build up Christ's Church is an open invitation to all, male and female, young and old.

As the tripod stones integrate the bride into the family, so does Christ, the foundation stone, integrate each Christian into the family of God. Christ's family is bigger than any human family. It includes people of all races and colors, and it is bound together by his Spirit.

Doing Feminist and Cross-Cultural Reading Yourself

1. *Examine the household code section on wives and husbands (3:1–7). To what degree is it influenced by a desire to see conversions continue and persecution kept away?*

2. *In 1 Pet 2:12, "Gentiles" does not refer to non-Jews. Rather, "Gentiles" is a metaphor for nonbelievers to highlight their distinction between Christians as the chosen people, whatever their race or ethnicity. Discuss the cross-cultural and social scientific implications of this use of the term.*

3. *Reflect on how the encouragement given to slaves to "suffer for doing right" (2:20) is generalized to all Christians in 3:14, 17 and in 4:19. What are the social and ethnic implications of this?*

JUDE: Contending for the True Faith

This brief letter exhorts its audience to remain true to the traditional Christian faith, rejecting the immoral lures of false teachers. The difficulty of establishing the author, date, and location of its audience complicates the historical interpretation of this letter, but other methods are more certain.

Jude in Brief: Outline of Structure and Contents

I. **Opening** Jude to "those who are called," blessing (verses 1–2)
II. **Body** Keep to the one true faith, and stay clear of false teaching (3–23)
  A. Occasion for writing: to oppose licentiousness and denial of Jesus Christ (3–4)
  B. The judgment of the ungodly (5–19)
    1. God's judgment of the ungodly in the Hebrew Bible (5–7)
    2. The false teachers' slanderous speech and evil character (8–13)
    3. The destruction of the false teachers predicted by Enoch and apostles (14–19)
  C. Exhortation for believers to keep true faith and show mercy (20–23)
III. **Conclusion** Doxology of praise to God; no greetings or formal blessing (24–25)

Developing Your Skills

In one sitting, read through first Jude and then 2 Peter. What is the relationship between the two letters in terms of overall themes and specific wording?

A Guide to Reading Jude

Jude, "a slave of Jesus Christ and brother of James," greets his audience with three positive statements: they have been "called" and "loved" by God and "kept safe" by Christ (v. 1). He blesses them with "mercy, peace and love in abundance" (2).

The author first expresses his reason for writing in order to stress its importance. He wanted to write to these believers a perhaps happier letter about salvation, but news of false teaching infiltrating the church changed his plans. Now he writes to tell them to stand their ground and fight for the faith they had learned, a faith "once for all entrusted to the saints" (3). Heretics are present among them, perhaps wandering Christian teachers, who abuse God's grace in "licentiousness," that is, unrestrained evil, and thereby deny Jesus Christ (4). Then the author launches into a short but pointed attack on these teachers. He points out that this kind of false teacher is not new; the character of such teachers was exposed and condemned in the OT. The author gives three examples of false belief and false action: unbelievers among Israel who doubted God's promise to bring them into Canaan (5), angels who rebelled against God and are now kept in darkness until the final judgment (6), and the citizens of Sodom and Gomorrah who engaged in sexual immorality (7). The false teachers Jude is dealing with act "in the same way" by "defiling the flesh" (acting immorally), rejecting authority of others in the churches (as wandering teachers often do), and slandering the angels (8). The author strongly implies that they will receive the same fate of condemnation as rebellious people and angels in the past. Their rejection of authority and slanderous speech is contrasted with Michael, one of the archangels, who according to a nonbiblical Jewish tradition refused to slander even the devil (8–9). But these false teachers slander all authority, suffering the consequences of the "very things that destroy them" (10). Once again, Jude links them to OT evils: they resemble Cain's selfish hatred of authority, Balaam's greed, and Korah's rebelliousness (11). The false teachers are "blemishes [or "reefs"] at your **love feasts**," communal meals perhaps associated with the Eucharist. They are only concerned to feed themselves, not (he implies) to share love by feeding others. In rapid succession of invectives, he heaps up images from nature to describe them and their corrupting influence in the community (12–13). They are waterless clouds who promise satisfaction of one's spiritual thirst but cannot deliver; they are trees without nourishing fruit because they are spiritually dead; they are wild waves of the sea casting up the polluted foam of their own shameful immorality; they are "wandering stars" kept in darkness like the fallen angels in v. 6, suggesting that their "light" cannot guide others.

In its rhetorical effort to distance the audience from these opponents, Jude now addresses their fate (14–19). First, Enoch predicted that the day would come when the ungodly would be judged (14–16). They are "grumblers and malcontents," and they flatter people to convince them. In what may be an act of chutzpah—audacity—for this author so given to overblown invective, he charges that they "are bombastic in speech" (16). The apostles had even predicted these believers. They are "worldly people, devoid of the Spirit," and they are causing divisions in the church (17–19). Jude now returns at the conclusion of the letter body to the positive note with which the letter began, reminding the audience to continue in faith, prayer, love, and the hope of Christ's mercy at the last judgment (20–21). Even this language is an appeal to the preservation of tradition: "Build yourself up *on* your most holy faith," not *in* it (20); "keep yourselves" in God's love (21). Jude gives final instructions on how to deal with those in the community influenced by the false teachers, but not the teachers themselves, because they are eternally lost. Those "wavering" under their influence are to receive direct mercy (note the connection between trusting in Christ's mercy in 21 and extending mercy to others in 22 and 23), others who have fallen into the "fire" of error are to be snatched out of it before they are consumed, and those deeply influenced by error are to receive mercy from believers, who should have a distancing "fear" to avoid any contaminating influences that might lead them into sin (22–23). The epistle concludes with a beautiful blessing of God that emphasizes God's grace for the believers' perseverance, displaying Jude's confidence that God "is able to keep you from falling" and bring them, holy, honored and happy, into God's presence (24–25).

Historical Reading of Jude

Jude in Brief: Summary of Historical Reading

Author Jude, the brother of James, most likely James of Jerusalem. Most scholars today view the letter as pseudepigraphical.

Date If authentic, the 60s; if not, anywhere from 80–120, with most accepting a date around 100.

Audience Probably a Jewish Christian church or churches in an unknown location.

Unity and Integrity Unchallenged today.

Purpose To warn against the moral and doctrinal errors of gnosticizing Christians, keeping readers "true to the faith that was once for all delivered to the saints" (v. 3).

Author

Verse 1 introduces the author as "Jude, a servant of Jesus Christ and a brother of James." In Greek, this name is "Judas," but Christians soon restricted that to Jesus' betrayer. But which good Jude in the NT is meant? Is the work really by a Jude, or is it pseudepigraphical?

Apart from Jude the brother/close kinsman of Jesus, only one other candidate has any plausibility: Jude the apostle, son of James (Luke 6:16; Acts 1:13). The strongest reason on behalf of identifying the author as Jesus' brother is that Jude identifies himself as "the brother of James." A well-known James is presupposed, and the only one that fits is James, the brother of the Lord. But why then does Jude call himself "the brother of James" rather than "the brother of Jesus"? As Bauckham explains, "Palestinian Jewish-Christian circles in the early church used the title 'brother of the Lord' not simply to identify the brothers, but as ascribing to them an authoritative status, and therefore the brothers themselves, not wishing to claim an authority based on mere blood-relationship to Jesus, avoided the term" (Bauckham 1983, 21).

In the external evidence, patristic literature in the late first century and early second century gives Jude modest confirmation. Clement of Rome, Shepherd of Hermas, Barnabas, and the Didache may allude to it, and more probable allusions are found in Polycarp. The Muratorian canon mentions it, as does Clement of Alexandria. Tertullian comments on its use of 1 Enoch, Origen speaks of the doubts of some, Didymus the Blind defended its authenticity, and Eusebius classified it with the disputed canonical books. We see that as time progressed doubts about Jude's authenticity/canonicity became articulated, principally because of its use of apocryphal material. Some scholars today accept Jude as both authentic and written by Jude, the brother of Jesus. A growing number today, however, regard it as pseudepigraphical, principally because there are internal features that suggest a date after the death of Jude.

Date

Proposed dates for Jude currently vary between 50 and 140 C.E.., which shows that where solid evidence is lacking opinions multiply. A number of issues impinge on the dating of this letter: the relation of Jude to 2 Peter, the question of authenticity, and the type of false teachers in view. The three main dates proposed for Jude are (1) sometime during the apostolic age (50s–60s), (2) the last decade of the first century, and (3) the first two decades of the second century. If Jude is dated in the apostolic age, it would be an authentic letter from the Jude who was the brother of the Lord. Those who hold this dating also normally assume the priority of Jude over 2 Peter. Those who date it in the second century use two arguments: references in Jude (vv. 3, 17) that seem to indicate that the apostolic age had now passed and the identification of the false teachers with Gnosticism. However, that the apostolic age is past does not necessitate a date in the second century. Such a date is chosen based on the time the main apostles died, which started in the 60s and probably concluded by 90. Concerning the connection with Gnosticism, some scholars note that Jude lacks any mention of the cosmological dualism or other features of Gnosticism. However, the author of Jude does not say anything about the *content* of the error; he only condemns the immoralities it leads to, so it is entirely possible that Gnosticism is present. Moreover, the early and widespread second-century external attestation of this epistle is hard to explain if it did not come into existence until the second century. Most probable, and accepted by most scholars, is a date in the middle of the range of possibilities, at the end of the first century, in the 90s.

Audience

The letter uses the Jewish Bible extensively and also the nonbiblical Jewish books the *Assumption of Moses* and *1 Enoch* in vv. 14–15. This heavily Jewish character of argumentation indicates that the letter was addressed to a predominantly Jewish Christian church or group of churches from a prominent leader of the Jewish Christian church.

Purpose

Wording and tone suggest this was a letter directed to a specific audience for a specific purpose, not a letter for general circulation. The purpose of Jude is stated at the beginning: to urge recipients to stand true to their traditional faith against the incursion of false teachers. Standing true involves three things: rejecting the teachers themselves just as God has eternally rejected them; identifying their teaching as a false form of the faith; and attempting to save from error those in the churches who have fallen to their teachings. Commentators often overlook this more positive last item as a reason for this letter.

2 PETER: Contending for the True Faith Reiterated

The last of the seven General or Catholic letters to be considered in this chapter, 2 Peter is a letter with a literary testament inside, and its relationship to Jude figures large in historical criticism. Like Jude, 2 Peter attacks false teachers spreading dissent and immorality in the churches. Along with 1 Peter and a body of works in the second century ascribed to Peter, 2 Peter illustrates that the personage of Peter grew in importance as the first century ended and the second began. Peter is one of the main witnesses of Jesus' life and resurrection, and one of the leading (if not the leading) apostle.

A Guide to Reading 2 Peter

"Simeon [or Simon: the textual evidence is divided] Peter" opens this letter by calling himself both a "slave and apostle" of Jesus Christ. He greets believers "who have received a faith as precious as ours" and by implication share an opposition to false teaching. He blesses them with grace and peace (1:1–2).

The body of this letter begins immediately. It opens with positive statements about what God has done, then discusses what believers should do. The author organizes the material around salvation rather than, as 1 Peter does, suffering. The certainty of believers' salvation is grounded in God. Based on this divine empowerment, which promises "sharing in the divine nature" (an ambiguous phrase, but probably meaning eternal life), believers ought to live a certain way (1:5–9). They must grow in grace as directed by a catena of virtues that stretches from faith to love (1:5–7) and be productive for God (1:8). Those who do not grow in grace and virtue are "blind" and have forgotten the effect of their baptism (1:9). Growth will prove to believers that their election has resulted in salvation (1:10), and ultimately an entrance into Christ's kingdom will be richly provided for them (1:11).

The author now suggests the purpose of the letter: to remind believers, even though he reassures them that they do not need it, of the "truth that has come to you" (1:12) so that they will continue to stand firm in it. Then the immediate occasion for the writing of this letter is stated, Peter's impending death (1:12–15). This announcement adds solemnity to the words that will follow, making this part of 2 Peter a "last will and testament" in literary purpose, if not in form. After his departure, Peter's audience will have a permanent memorial—this letter. The author now defends his message about their salvation (1:16–21). He wants to ground his audience in his understanding of Scripture—not yet the NT, but the Jewish Bible—to combat "cleverly devised myths" (1:16). The apostles were eyewitnesses of the transfiguration of Jesus (1:16–18), and the writings of the Hebrew prophets are inspired by God's Spirit, because both men and women prophets spoke by the Spirit (1:20–21). The clear implication is that both apostles and prophets are against these false teachers.

In the next section, the author deals with the falsehoods of the "coming" heretics and their punishment (2:1–3:16; note that the future tenses soon become present tenses). The false teachers are discredited because of their character (2:1–22). They "deny the Master," Jesus Christ. They are **antinomian** (against the very idea of law) and greedy. After warning the believers of the heretics' imminent arrival, Peter reveals their future condemnation (2:3b–9). Then he illustrates this condemnation by several biblical analogies, showing how God deals with sinful beings who challenge the truth. God did not spare angels who sinned (2:4), the world in Noah's day (2:5), or Sodom and Gomorrah (2:6), but the righteous at the time were spared (Noah and Lot). The author again reiterates the certainty of the coming condemnation, coupled with God's protection of the righteous (2:9). He characterizes those he attacks as "those who indulge the flesh in depraved lust, and who despise authority" (2:9). The author now launches into a discussion of their character: they slander and speak against others to a degree that even angels dare not do. They are low on the cosmic range of beings: lower than angels, they are animals empty of reason (2:10–12). They "party" in the daytime, a sure sign of complete evil in the Mediterranean world (2:13). They practice drunkenness, adultery, and greed (2:13–16), and they are enslaved to sin even though they promise freedom in their antinomianism (2:19). No second repentance is possible for them (2:20–22).

The author continues his testament by speaking of future attacks on the teaching of the Lord's return (3:1–16). He begins with a reminder that he has written before about the coming of the Lord (3:1, a reference to 1 Pet 1:13). Their own apostles had also revealed to them both the coming of the Lord and the rise of false prophets (3:2). After Peter makes this reminder, thus rhetorically increasing the authority of his current letter, he attacks what the false teachers will believe about the coming of Christ (3:3–7). They deny it using probably the sharpest statement of the "delay of the Parousia" in the NT: to paraphrase it, "Despite this promise, nothing has changed with the world, so when is Jesus returning, anyway?" Here the author implicitly links the two OT motifs with the coming destruction of the world: the world was destroyed by flood (in Noah's day) and will be destroyed by fire (as were Sodom and Gomorrah in Lot's day) (3:5–7). In 3:8–10, the author counters this crisis of faith over the delay by saying that God's perception of time ("soon") is not a human understanding, and furthermore God is patiently delaying the end to allow more people to repent. But he reaffirms standard Christian teaching: when the end comes, it will come suddenly (3:10). The whole universe will be destroyed by fire, and God will make a new heaven and a new earth "where righteousness is at home." The author uses this prophecy to appeal to holy living (3:11, 14). He once again reminds his audience that none of this is new. Paul himself had written to this same audience before concerning these truths (3:15–16). Included in this reminder is a statement that the opponents in view distort Paul's words, as they do "the other scriptures" (3:16b).

2 Peter concludes with a final command that summarizes this letter: avoid false teaching and grow in grace and knowledge (3:17), followed by a blessing of Jesus Christ that looks to eternity (3:18).

Historical Reading of 2 Peter

2 Peter in Brief: Summary of Historical Reading

Author Traditionally, Simon Peter the disciple of Jesus. Today a strong majority of scholars holds that the work is pseudonymous.

Date If authentic, 60–64; if pseudonymous, anywhere from 100 to 130, with around 120 the most likely.

Source Chapter 2 of 2 Peter is widely seen as a revision of Jude.

Audience Christians, probably Jewish in background, in Asia Minor or the eastern Mediterranean in general, who would know of Peter and Paul's writings.

Unity and Integrity Generally unquestioned today.

Purpose To encourage Christians to stay true to traditional forms of Christian belief and practice, especially to shun heretics and their misuse of Paul's letters.

Author

Peter, who is presented as the author of this book, could have been martyred in Rome around 65, or he could have been imprisoned there shortly after the outbreak of the Jewish revolt and killed around 66 or 67. If this letter was authentic and written from prison, the change in circumstance could arguably account for some of the differences between this letter and 1 Peter (on the assumption that 1 Peter is genuine). However, several factors militate against the authenticity of 2 Peter. To judge from the unique Greek vocabulary and relatively sophisticated rhetoric of this book, the author of 2 Peter was probably a strongly Hellenized Jew, not a Palestinian Jew like Peter. It is easiest to read this book as a look back at Peter and application of his authority to the situation in the early second century, not as a look forward. Indeed, the literary genre of the testament was completely identified in the first century with pseudonymity. The external evidence also confirms pseudonymity: no NT document is as weakly confirmed among the church fathers or was as slowly accepted into the NT canon as 2 Peter.

Date

2 Peter is dated in a range from 60 to 160. It knows the Pauline letters, which were collected after Paul's death around 64. The first generation of apostles is dead (2 Pet 3:4). The best piece of evidence for dating is that 2 Peter uses Jude as a source, and therefore must be dated at least some years after it. Since most scholars place Jude around 90 to 100, 2 Peter is often dated from 100 to 120. We should not go too far into the second century, however, since the mid-second century work the *Apocalypse of Peter* knows it.

Audience

The same audience is assumed in 2 Peter as in 1 Peter (2 Pet 3:1). That 2 Peter did in fact have the same audience is likely even if it is pseudonymous.

Source

Jude and 2 Peter share a common overall theme and vocabulary. Although it was once thought that Jude drew on 2 Peter as a source, now it is common to view 2 Peter as drawn on Jude. A majority of scholars concludes that 2 Peter as a whole is a reapplication of Jude.

Purpose

The author writes to convince his audience of three closely related things: to hold fast to the faith taught since the days of the apostles (1:12–21; 3:1–2); to live a life of holiness and love (1:3–11; 3:11–18); and to shun those who have repudiated the true faith (2:1–22).

Cross-Cultural Reading of 2 Peter

Along with Jude, 2 Peter does not raise explicit cross-cultural issues. However, cross-cultural readers today find especially in 2 Peter, with its command to work faithfully in a world that seems to last for a good deal longer, a resource for liberative reading.

Cross-Cultural Reading at Work
Utopia and Resistance in 2 Peter

Lugo Rodríguez, a Roman Catholic parish priest in Mexico, relates 2 Peter's hope for the end of time to its call for "active waiting" that makes life in the present more like God's future reign.

Although 2 Pet 2:5–7 reveals to us a cosmological conception that is quite confused, in which the author makes allusion either to the stories of Genesis or to diffuse mythological legends or to originally Stoic beliefs, the doctrine of the author is certainly clear: God rules over everything with God's word and directs history in order to prepare for a radical renewal of the universe. In a second moment (2 Pet 3:8–9, 11–14) the same author gives greater precision to his proposal: God's apparent slowness to fulfill God's promise is due to the complexity of the work of salvation that is not accomplished without the collaboration of men and women and, more than anything else, is due to God's desire to save everyone. Thus the idea of the Parousia and its proximity is not abandoned. There will be a second coming that will bring with it the destruction of everything that is defective and wicked and, at the same time, will bring to infinity everything that is good. . . .

It is precisely at this level that the text most clearly acquires the characteristics of resistance literature. In the face of emerging realities, the author's proposal is that Christians change the tenor of their hope: emphasis should be placed on an active waiting that contributes to the realization of that kingdom which has already begun, but is also still to come. . . . Active waiting signifies a life of holiness and righteousness. . . . Through the mediation of a personal and social life lived in accordance with the kingdom, the time of the Parousia is advanced.

At the base of the entire exhortation . . . we find the promise of "the new heaven and the new earth." This expression, taken from Isaiah (65:17; 66:22), refers to the radical and complete messianic renovation to which history will irreversibly come. There will be perfect harmony between humans and God, among human beings themselves, and between humans and the natural world. Justice will then be the fundamental characteristic of creation. But it will only be possible to live in the land where justice shall rule (2 Pet 3:13) if we have known and practiced beforehand "the way to justice" (2 Pet 2:21). The way, then, to nurture community resistance is to derive from the eschatological hope, the utopian kingdom, the energy needed for here and now.

Question

Explain in your own words how this vision of a "utopian" future directs and empowers the "here and now."

Source: Raúl Humberto Lugo Rodgríguez, "'Wait for the Day of God's Coming and Do What You Can to Hasten It . . .' (2 Pet 3:12): The Non-Pauline Letters as Resistance Literature," in Leif Vaage, ed., *Subversive Scriptures: Revolutionary Readings of the Christian Bible in Latin America* (Valley Forge, PA: Trinity Press International, 1997), pp. 202–203.

Key Terms and Concepts

antinomianism • catena (of virtues) • Catholic Letters • chiastic order
diatribe • General Letters • household code • Melchizedek
second repentance • typology

Questions for Study, Discussion, and Writing

1. What do you make of Harnack's suggestion that Priscilla may be the author of Hebrews? How might your reading of this letter change if you believed that Priscilla was its author?
2. Do you think that Hebrews was written to Jewish Christians or Gentile Christians? Why?
3. Compare and contrast the theology of Hebrews to that of Stephen's speech in Acts 7.
4. Can Hebrews' denial of second repentance, and James's advocacy of it, be explained by their different situations and persuasive purposes?
5. Explain the relationship of wisdom and Law observance in James.
6. What is your conclusion on the faith and works discussion in James? Is it aimed at a situation before Paul, Paul himself, or post-Paul?
7. What vision of social justice does James try to promote?
8. How do you explain 1 Peter's close similarity to Paul?
9. Describe the sort of persecution that the readers of 1 Peter may be going through.
10. Explain the ways that 2 Peter is literarily dependent on Jude.
11. What rhetorical use of invective do Jude and 2 Peter make? How can this be understood today in North American culture when invective is considered "politically incorrect"?
12. Why do you think that this group of General/Catholic Letters has so often been on the margins of NT study?

For Further Reading

Achtemeier, Paul. *1 Peter*. Hermeneia Commentary Series. Minneapolis: Fortress, 1996. The most comprehensive recent commentary on 1 Peter.

Bauckham, Richard. "James," in James D. G. Dunn and John W. Rogerson, eds., *Eerdmans Commentary on the Bible*. Grand Rapids, MI: Eerdmans, 2003. Succinct introduction and commentary.

Bauckham, Richard. *Jude, 2 Peter*. Word Biblical Commentary. Waco, TX: Word, 1983. Excellent comment by a leading NT interpreter.

Bechtler, Steven R. *Following in His Steps: Suffering, Community and Christology in 1 Peter*. Atlanta: Scholars Press, 1998. A historical-critical and social scientific approach to 1 Peter, arguing that Christ's suffering and glorification are the key to 1 Peter's response to the sufferings of the recipients of the letter.

Chester, Andrew, and Ralph P. Martin. *The Theology of the Letters of James, Peter, and Jude*. Cambridge: Cambridge University Press, 1994.

Daryl, Charles J. *Virtue amidst Vice: The Catalog of Virtues in 2 Peter 1*. Sheffield, UK: Sheffield Academic Press, 1997. Despite its title, this is a wide-ranging study of the whole of 2 Peter, emphasizing its role as a parenetic document.

Elliott, John H. *A Home for the Homeless: A Sociological Exegesis of 1 Peter, Its Situation and Strategy.* Philadelphia: Fortress, 1981. The most influential social scientific treatment of 1 Peter.

Eisenbaum, Pamela. *The Jewish Heroes of Christian History: Hebrews 11 in Literary Context.* Atlanta: Scholars Press, 1997. Fascinating commentary on Hebrews 11 by a Jewish expert in the NT.

Johnson, Luke T. *James.* Anchor Bible Commentary. Garden City, NY: Doubleday, 1995. An excellent commentary that treats James as the genuine author.

Lindars, Barnabas. *The Theology of the Letter to the Hebrews.* Cambridge: Cambridge University Press, 1991.

Perkins, Pheme. *First and Second Peter, James and Jude.* Interpretation Commentary. Louisville, KY: Westminster John Knox, 1995. A fine commentary for students of the General Epistles, especially accessible to beginners.

Tamez, Elsa. *The Scandalous Message of James.* New York: Crossroad, 1992. Treatment of the social ethics of James by a Jewish NT scholar.

Thistleton, Anthony. "Hebrews," in James D. G. Dunn and John Rogerson, eds., *Eerdmans Commentary on the Bible.* Grand Rapids, MI: Eerdmans, 2003. Concise, incisive commentary.

Watson, Duane F. *Rhetorical Criticism of Jude and 2 Peter.* Atlanta: Scholars Press, 1988. Discusses both theological and literary concerns.

Chapter Eighteen

1, 2 and 3 John: The Johannine Community in Conflict

As the Christian movement grew rapidly in the Roman world of the first century, it struggled to define itself against other religions and philosophies. Early Christianity was also no stranger to internal conflict. Growth—especially the growth across lines of culture, class, and gender that Christianity experienced—brings change, and change commonly brings conflict. As we see in the Acts of the Apostles and the Pauline letters, conflicts often arose over correct Christian beliefs and practices. The three letters of John show that internal conflict arose in the Johannine community of churches as well. These letters deal with an argument within the Johannine community that can be studied historically and social scientifically: how to define and maintain group identity when it is threatened by internal conflict. Which group was the true successor of the Gospel: the author of 1–3 John and his audience in these letters, or a group that seceded from them? In 1 John, the author who calls himself **the Elder** explains his group's identity by treading the heights of the Gospel of John's theology. In 2 John, he tries to enforce this distinction of his own group by instructing his addressees to keep secessionists out of their churches. In 3 John, this same author attempts to correct an over-enforcement of the message of 2 John. Although it is not always possible to trace the background and meaning of these letters as fully as we would like, they do afford a fascinating glimpse into the history of the Johannine church. The newer methods of reading the NT give some additional insight into these three letters, especially 1 John.

1 JOHN: Love and Community

The Gospel of John and 1 John share so many similarities in style and content that no one can doubt that they are from the same tradition, if not the same author. First John makes more sense if it was written after the emergence of the Fourth Gospel; this is how the vast majority of interpreters take it. To judge from 1 John, the struggles of the Fourth Gospel, especially with the synagogue, were no longer the major issue. Now a division among Johannine Christians had occurred, with the two groups having different views of Jesus. Although both groups accepted the Gospel and its profession that Jesus the Word was God, they disagreed about the importance of what kind of being that Jesus the Word was on earth and what he had done. One group believed that the Son of God had been fully incarnated in Jesus and that his actions set a moral standard to be followed; the other seems to have believed that the Son of God was not fully incarnated in Jesus and that believing in the Word was what mattered most. The author writes to point out and reinforce that difference and to urge his audience to live a life that was pleasing to God.

---

1 John in Brief: Outline of Structure and Content

I. A theological prologue: "We proclaim eternal life to you" (1:1–4)
II. Living faithfully in God's light (1:5–2:27)
   A. Forgiveness of sin (1:5–2:2)
   B. Obedience to God's commands (2:3–14)
   C. Not loving the word (2:15–17)
   D. Avoiding false prophets, relying on the Holy Spirit (2:18–27)
III. Walking together in the church (2:28–3:24)
   A. Being God's children by mutual love (2:28–3:3)
   B. A call to uprightness (3:4–10)
   C. Avoiding divisions in the community (3:11–17)
   D. Living in love and faith (3:18–24)
IV. Basic commands reiterated: believe and love (4:1–5:12)
   A. The Spirit's witness to the incarnation (4:1–6)
   B. The people of God are known for their mutual love (4:7–12)
   C. Live in faith and love (4:13–5:5)
   D. A final statement of Jesus as the incarnate Son (5:6–12)
V. Concluding summary and commands (5:13–21)

Developing Your Skills

Read through 1 John in one sitting, noting the oscillation of the different themes. Because this book is written in a formal and poetic (almost convoluted) style, you will have to keep alert and not let the rhythm lull you.

A Guide to Reading 1 John

Although 1 John is called a "letter," it starts not with the customary letter opening, but with a theological statement (1:1–4). The short theological prologue to 1 John in these first verses is modeled after the prologue of the Gospel of John and implicitly claims the truth of that Gospel against those who claim otherwise. Its theme is

Jesus as the life of the world. The "word of eternal life," made possible only in Christ, is found in **fellowship** (community in a close-knit organization of common belief and sharing) with God and in fellowship with the Johannine community. This writing seeks to strengthen the fellowship between the writer and his audience.

First John opens with the theme of light (1:5–7), a key theme in the Fourth Gospel. The author restates the Johannine view of a world separated into light and darkness. "Walking in light" means doing what is right; it comes from fellowship with one another and with God, because the blood of Jesus—the power of his death—cleanses believers from sin. Then 1 John 1:8–2:2 turns to the topic of those who refuse to acknowledge any sin, probably the opponents of the author. True Christians, he says, acknowledge their sins, for which Jesus is **expiation** (reconciling sacrifice). The saving value of Jesus' death has become more important in the community's present situation. To claim sinlessness is to make God a liar, an act of darkness. In chapter 2, the author does not intend to encourage sin and says that one of his purposes in writing is "that you may not sin" (2:1). But he tells his audience that, when "we do sin," we have a helper or advocate (the **Paraclete**) with the Father, "Jesus Christ the righteous one, the atoning sacrifice for our sin." Thus forgiveness of individual and group sin is grounded on the death of Christ and brought about by the intercession of the living Christ in heaven. In 1 John 2:3–11 we see a common theme in the moral structure of early Christianity: the call to full obedience, to "walking the walk," is coupled with the realization that Christians still sin, and they must know and confess their sin. But the promise of easy forgiveness should not make people morally lax or arrogant (as in our contemporary saying, "The best thing about being forgiven is sinning beforehand"). The author's opponents may have charged his churches with this very thing. The "whoever says" of 2:4 is likely directed against opponents of the author; they claim to know Jesus but do not obey God's commandments, at least in the way that the author approves. In 2:6 we find another "whoever says": "Whoever says, 'I abide in him,' ought to walk just as Jesus walked." In particular, the author emphasizes an "old" commandment: love for other Christians ("brother or sister"), rather than for one's enemies or the world in general. Although Johannine Christians knew this "old" commandment "from the beginning" of the coming of Jesus, it is "new" because it has yet to be fulfilled in a world Jesus came to free from darkness and death. The author implies here that the opponents who have left his churches do not love their brothers and sisters.

A powerful but mysterious passage is next in 2:12–14. Twice this passage uses three enigmatic kinship terms—children, fathers, and young people—for the audience and describes them with honor. "Children" may be a general term for all Johannine Christians; it is commonly used this way in the letter. "Children" so understood includes "fathers," males and females who have been Christians for some time, and "young people," Christians new to the faith. Mention of the struggle against the Evil One (the Devil) elicits a censure of the world that the Evil One controls and its dangerous attractions: sensual desires, enticements to do wrong, and attraction to gaining riches (2:15–17).

The struggle with the agent of the Evil One, the antichrist, is discussed in 2:18–23. The author begins this theme on an eschatological note: "Children, it is the last hour!" This struggle is already going on, especially in the opposition to the author and the true Johannine Christians. These opponents are the real **antichrists** (note the plural, otherwise unknown in the Bible, showing that this author is reinterpreting this tradition). They "have gone out" from the author's churches (v. 19). That they have left the churches and "gone out" into the world is social proof that they belong to the world and not "to us." The doctrinal content of this anti-Christian denial seems to have a particular meaning that comes clear in 4:3; here the author is content to describe them as those who deny that "Jesus is the Christ" and who deny "the Father and the Son" (v. 22). Yet the writer does not need to say this to his audience, because they have the anointing from the Holy One. This came "at the beginning"—probably the Spirit coming upon them at baptism—and now they do not need any teachers. True believers have both eternal life and the truth, and they remain in them (2:24–27).

The next section of this letter, 2:28–3:3, deals with the Parousia of Christ. This section ends the section on the last hour and anticipates the treatment of union with God. Although there is little emphasis in the Gospel of John on the **Parousia,** the return of Jesus in glory at the end of time (see 5:26–29; 14:1–3), it is important now in 1 John. The connection between the mostly **realized eschatology** of the Gospel and the mostly **final eschatology** of 1 John is this: Jesus, who was righteous, is already present to all believers who do what is right (realized), but the fullness of his presence is possible only with his return (final). Present fellowship/abiding with Jesus enables one to face confidently his return in judgment: "See what love the Father has given us that we may be called the children of God" (3:1). The children of God act in righteousness and love their brothers and sisters, but the children of the devil do not. The author exhorts his audience to "abide in him," so that when Jesus returns they may be honored and not be put to shame. (Note the rich combination of kinship language and the honor-shame paradigm.)

In his prologue to this letter, the author used the metaphors of *life* and *light* to explain the gospel to believers. Now 3:1–18 proclaims that the gospel message is *love.* God's love has made them his children (3:1). In a moving passage that taps into human uncertainty about the afterlife that all people and even his Christians share, the author says, "We are God's children now; what we will be has not yet been revealed. What we do know is this: when he is revealed [at the Parousia], we will be like him." Being children of God is eternal, and the Mediterranean social axiom holds true: children are like their father. The author turns from this reassurance to urge his readers not to presume upon this status by being morally lax: those who have this hope for Christ's return purify themselves, because God (their father) is pure (3:3). Then the author strengthens this idea: sin is not just individual acts of wrong, but an attitude and lifestyle of "law-lessness." Christ came to do away with this; there is no sin in Christ, so believers must not abide in sin (3:4–6). Urging them not to be deceived by opponents, the author insists on a basic distinction: those whose lives are characterized by sin do not abide in God; those who do abide in God do not sin. It is a matter of relationship—those who sin are children of the devil and act like their father; those who do what is right are the children of God and act like him (3:7–8). Jesus came as the Son of God to destroy the devil and his works. Once again the author states his **perfectionism:** those who are born of God, God's children, "do not sin, because God's seed abides in them"; indeed, "they cannot sin" (v. 9). These sharp distinctions between the children of God and the children of the devil (v. 10) are meant to draw a bright line between God and his opponents, and keep the author's audience on the right side.

The author now reemphasizes that the characteristic Johannine message is "we should love one another" (3:11). As the example of Cain shows, hatred is a form of murder; indeed, it is especially terrible when brother murders brother (3:12–15). The world hates the believers (v. 13), but their experience of love in the Christian fellowship brings strong assurance that they already have eternal life. Christ laid down his life for us, and so "we ought to lay down our lives" for brothers and sisters (3:16). Those who have means to help a "brother or sister in need" but refuse to stand condemned. This may be an instruction for the whole church, but is likely pointed at opponents as an example of their lovelessness (v. 17). We can assume, therefore, that at least some of them were socially prominent and perhaps left John's church financially the worse when they left. John warns his children that true love is a matter of action, not just of words (v. 18). Now, after stressing perfect mutual love that brings complete assurance of salvation, John alternates with a more realistic theme. Sometimes "our hearts condemn us," that is, the human conscience feels guilt, "but God is greater than our hearts," and God forgives. True to form, John stresses moral earnestness next. It is better "if our hearts do not condemn us" because this leads to boldness before God (3:19–22). We must keep God's commandments, specifically to love: "We should believe in the name of God's Son, Jesus Christ, and love one another as he [Jesus] commanded us" (3:23–24)—the two points of belief and practice on which the author attacks his opponents. Then John gives a final indication of how Christians know that God is in them: "by the Spirit that he has given us" (v. 24).

This leads to the next section in 1 John, in which the author begins to give some concrete advice about carrying out conflict with opponents. 4:1–6 sets down a test to discern false prophets (moral leaders) with their hollow claim of being led by the Spirit. Every person who acknowledges that Jesus Christ came "in the flesh" belongs to God, and those who do not believe in this **incarnation** do not belong to God. Belief in the heavenly Jesus alone, or an earthly Jesus in whom God did not fully and/or truly dwell, is not good enough. The follow-up principle "Anyone who knows

God listens to us" becomes a way of distinguishing the truth from deceit. We may surmise that the secessionists are directing the same charges against the author and his followers; for the secessionists, the *author* has the spirit of deceit, and *he* does not listen to *them*! Brusquely, 4:7–21 resumes the theme of love with the affirmation, "God is love." We know this not because we loved God first, but because God took the initiative and sent God's Son into the world so that believers might have life and that their sins might be expiated in Jesus' death. : "We love [God and other people] because he first loved us" (v. 19). The simplicity of this thought is developed in 4:12: "No one has ever seen God," yet if we love one another, God remains in us and "God's love is brought to perfection in us." To make this beautiful but abstract statement real, the writer specifies a test aimed at his opponents and all believers: Anyone who claims to love God while hating a fellow believer is not true to God (v. 20). For John the Elder, love first happens in the community of the church; if it is not there, it does not exist.

As the author builds to the conclusion, he treats faith, love, and obedience together in 5:1–5. Everyone who believes that Jesus is the Christ is begotten by God and conquers the world by faith. The statement about the three who testify in 5:6–8 (i.e., the Spirit, the water, and the blood) is unclear. It may draw on John 19:34, in which the blood flowing from the side of Christ comes out with water, a traditional sign of the Spirit (John 7:38–39). Of course, it could also be a sacramental reference. This emphasis on Jesus' death as saving is aimed at the secessionists, who perhaps emphases Jesus' baptism and receiving the Spirit as salvific; the author, in contrast, stresses that the Spirit comes with both the water and blood of Jesus. This section ends in 5:9–12 by underlining that faith in this divine testimony about Jesus' death leads to true belief in God's Son and true life.

As the author concludes this "letter," he allies himself one last time with the Gospel of John by imitating it (John 20:31). The Evangelist wrote his book so "That you may believe that Jesus is the Christ, the Son of God, and that believing you may possess life in his name"; the writer of 1 John writes so "That you may know that you possess this eternal life, you who believe in the name of the Son of God" (1 John 5:13). He urges prayer, saying once more that God hears and answers prayers, but this time adding that believers need to "ask according to his will" (v. 14). He also urges his audience to pray that sinners among the "brothers and sisters" may receive life, and he says that God will hear such prayers. However, in the light of the situation of this letter, the writer discourages believers from praying for those who commit "deadly/mortal sin," probably the sin of denying the incarnation of Christ. Such sin shows that life is not in that person. The letter has taken a firm position on such people, and the boundaries between the two competing communities have been made steady and certain. The ones "who have left" may be coming back to try to make converts, but the community of John is not to missionize among them. This charge reflects a theological division and a practical one—lack of contact will stem any further defections to error.

Three "We know" proclamations are made in 5:18–20 as the writer once again expresses his dualistic view in which God and God's children are opposed to the Evil One and the world that lies in his grasp. We know that those born of God do not sin (v. 18); we know that we are God's children and that the whole world is in the power of the devil (v. 19); we know that God's Son has given us the understanding to know him (v. 20). Jesus Christ is "the true God and eternal life" (v. 20). Just as 1 John began by quoting the beginning of John's Gospel, it also ends as John did (20:28); it affirms the divinity of Christ. The concluding command of 1 John, "Little children, guard yourselves against idols" (5:21), probably has the secessionists in mind, for their false christology is to the Elder a form of idolatry.

Historical Reading of 1 John

The historical study of 1 John, like all three Johannine letters, is first concerned with how these letters relate to the Gospel of John. Some continuing history of the Johannine community seems to be present here, and is important in understanding the situation of 1-3 John and their religious message.

---

1 John in Brief: Summary of Historical Reading

Author Anonymous. Because all three Johannine letters were probably written by the same person, and in 2 and 3 John the author calls himself "the Elder," it is likely that 1 John was written by this elder.

Date Around 100 C.E.

Audience The congregations in the Johannine circle of churches, probably in and around Ephesus. Although 1 John is a timely communication from one author to an audience, it is not a letter in literary format.

Unity Not questioned today.

Author

First John does not name either the author or the recipients. Traditionally it was assumed before the rise of historical scholarship that the same writer composed John and the three Letters of John. Since the name of John the son of Zebedee was attached to the Gospel, the same name transferred over as the author of these three letters because it was recognized in the ancient world that the same person wrote all three letters. Remarkable similarities between 1 John and the Gospel of John are found in both content and style, enough to say that they belong to a **Johannine School** or **Circle,** a group of tradition bearers and teachers working together to guide the churches of John. Yet there are also some important differences between 1 John and the Gospel of John:

- The opening of 1 John does not emphasize the preexistence of the personified Word, as does the Prologue of John. While it keeps the style of John 1, it testifies to the human life of Jesus, the word of life that was seen, heard, and felt. In other words, 1 John talks about the incarnate One, the prologue of the Gospel of John about the incarnation.
- First John talks proportionally more about God than the Gospel of John does, even though both writings are christologically centered. First John assigns to God features that the Gospel assigns to Jesus. For example, in 1 John 1:5 God is light; in John 8:12; 9:5 Jesus is the light. In 1 John 4:21 God gives the commandment to love one another; in John 13:34 this is the command of Jesus.
- First John lays proportionally much more stress on Jesus' sacrificial death, and less on his mediation between God and believers, than the Gospel does.
- First John emphasizes the Holy Spirit much less than the Gospel, and the characteristic Gospel term *Paraclete* is never used of the Spirit. Instead, Christ is the paraclete or "advocate" in 2:1.
- Future eschatology is stronger than realized eschatology in 1 John, although both are present; in the Gospel, this is reversed.
- The Gospel uses irony and multiple layers in the same symbol; 1 John is much simpler (and sometimes unclear, at least to us), and its symbols seem to have only one meaning.
- The historical situation behind the fourth Gospel and 1 John are different.

Overall, these differences suggest to most scholars that the same person did not write the Epistles and the Gospel. At most, we have three important figures in the Johannine School: the Beloved Disciple (who was the source of the tradition), the evangelist who wrote the body of the Gospel, and the "Elder" who wrote the Epistles. This title comes, of course, from 2 and 3 John, and it suggests someone in a position of honor and authority in the Johannine churches. However, its lack of a proper name has no parallel in early Christian literature.

Date

Dating of the Johannine letters is usually done together, in relation with the dating of John's Gospel. To almost all interpreters today, 1 John clearly presupposes the existence and influence of the fourth Gospel. The debate between its two groups may well be an argument over how to interpret the fourth Gospel. Since John is usually dated in the 90s, 1 John is put around 100 C.E., on the supposition that it took some time for conflict to develop after the Gospel was written. Second and

Sidewalk Advertisement for Brothel This inscription on a sidewalk in Ephesus, the traditional center of Johannine Christianity, showing a foot (for direction), a heart, and a woman's head, was an advertisement for a brothel. Although prostitution was culturally acceptable in Roman-Hellenistic society, early Christians strongly forbade sexual intercourse outside marriage. In the words of 1 John 2:15–16, this "desire of the flesh" belongs to a world opposed to God. Used by permission of Bibleplaces.com.

Third John follow shortly after. (A few scholars hold that the order is 1, 3, and 2 John.) Perhaps it took no more than two or three years for the three Johannine letters to be written.

Audience

Scholarship has largely followed church tradition in placing all the Johannine writings in or around Ephesus. Nothing in the letters themselves confirm or contradict this attribution; there simply is no hard evidence about the location of the audience. The only wisp of evidence we have is that Christian writers in the Roman province in which Ephesus is located, Asia, are the first to show knowledge of them.

Purpose

First John is obviously a response to a crisis in the Johannine churches. The author speaks of certain people who "went out" from this community; he calls them antichrists, deceivers, and false prophets. They do not believe that Jesus is the Christ and the Son of God, particularly that "Jesus Christ is come in the flesh" (2:18–27; 4:1–6). They are probably those who claim to have no sin, or (perhaps its equivalent) to be the children of God even though they do sin in a serious way (1:5–2:2; 2:28–3:10). These opponents are usually considered to be early **docetists,** those who believe that Jesus was a completely divine person who only "seemed" (Greek *dokeo*) to be human; some consider docetists to be related to the early Gnostic teacher Cerinthus. The evidence in 1 John may be too slim to make these precise identifications, but the opponents do seem to have devalued the physical aspect of Jesus' humanity in some way. They may have distinguished the human nature of Jesus from the divine Christ, and argued that the revelation Christ brought is more significant for salvation than his death. Perhaps they had therefore refused to couple "Jesus" and "Christ" in their belief and worship, preferring the latter. It also appears, to read between the lines of John's criticism of his opponents, that faith in Christ and possession of the Spirit gave them an eternal nature incapable of sin in the here and now. Rejecting the human Jesus as a sacrificial offering for their sin, they saw no need to show sacrificial love to others. This conviction led to their leaving the Johannine fellowship, and many others may have gone with them. Now they may be making efforts to convince still others from the Johannine churches to join them, and the author writes to end this appeal. To judge from the intense, sometimes passionate way he writes, this continuing appeal was a significant threat. The author reaches back to the Johannine tradition to stress loyalty to "what was from the beginning," the confession that the Word became flesh (John 1:14) in Jesus Christ. The author may also be reaching out to other types of Christians at the turn of the century, affirming the importance of such common apostolic teachings as the atoning death of Jesus, his return at the end of time, and the importance of dealing with sin in the church. In sum, 1 John says that relationship with God requires both mutual love and belief in a Christ who died *for* humans as a full human, things that are two sides of the same coin for this author.

www For a figure illustrating Raymond Brown's influential reconstruction of the entire history of the Johannine community, see the website.

Social Scientific Reading of 1 John

Social scientific reading of 1 John notes its strong kinship language, typical in the NT, but unusually powerful here. The author also rhetorically uses in-group and out-group ideas to keep his own group loyal to him. In fact, these in- and out-group ideas are so prevalent here that many scholars see the Johannine community as sectarian, cut off from the world and from the wider church.

Social Scientific Reading at Work
The Sense Zones of 1 John 1:1–3

In this selection Bruce Malina shows how the prologue of 1 John draws on Semitic Mediterranean ways of speaking of human behavior to reinforce the fullness of the revelation that the author of 1 John claims in 1:1–3.

Semitic descriptive approaches tend to be highly synthetic rather than analytic—more like floodlights than spotlights. . . . Similarly, specific words covering one of the three zones [of human activity] would stand for the whole zone, while always keeping the total functioning human being in view. Here is a representative list of such words and the zones to which they refer:

1. *Zone of emotion-fused thought:* eyes, heart, eyelid, pupil . . . to see, know, understand, think, remember, choose, feel, consider, look at. . . . In our culture, this zone would cover the areas we refer to as intellect, will, judgment, conscience, personality . . . , affection, and so forth.
2. *Zone of self-expressive speech:* mouth, ears, tongue, lips, throat, teeth, jaws . . . to speak, hear, cry, question . . . instruct, praise, listen to, blame, curse, swear, disobey, turn a deaf ear to. . . . In our culture this zone would cover the area we refer to as self-revelation through speech. . . . .
3. *Zone of purposeful action:* hands, feet, arms, fingers, legs . . . to do, act, accomplish, touch . . . walk, stand, sit. . . . In our culture, this zone would cover the area of outward human behavior [in actions]. . . .

The idea is that all human activities, states, and behaviors can be and are in fact chunked in terms of these three zones. Now, when all three zones are explicitly mentioned, then the speaker or writer is alluding to a total and complete human experience. For example, it is to such a total and complete experience that "John" alludes when he writes, "That which was from the beginning, which we have *heard*, which we have *seen* with our *eyes*, which we have *looked* upon and *touched* with our *hands*, concerning the word of life . . . that which we have *seen* and *heard* we *proclaim* also to you, so that you may have fellowship" (1 John 1:1–3).

Questions

1. *Explain in your own words the three "zones of human activity" that Malina lays out here.*

2. *State as fully as you can how 1 John 1:1–3 is worded to reflect a full and complete human experience, and how this full human experience might relate to how the author describes his opponents.*

Source: Bruce J. Malina, *The New Testament World: Insights from Cultural Anthropology* (Louisville, KY: Westminster/John Knox, 2001), pp. 69, 70.

Doing Social Scientific Reading Yourself

1. Describe the kinship language of 1 John. How does it reinforce the author's religious message?

2. Read through this letter to list the different ways in which the author maintains the boundary between his group and the "deceivers."

Feminist Reading of 1 John

First John contains no references to any named women or men, and has no issues that are explicitly related to gender. Its terms "beloved" and "young people" can (and probably should) be understood inclusively to refer to both males and females. The author's message in all likelihood applies equally to the males and females of this audience.

Feminist Reading at Work, 1
Staying Strong through Knowing the Father (1 John 2:12–17)

This brief selection from Catherine Clark Kroeger and Mary Evans suggests the implication of the kinship language of the letters of John for feminist reading.

John is able to give some praise and reassurance to the community. He uses terms of endearment and family–"little children," "fathers" and "young people." "Children" refers to the whole community, male and female. If women were excluded, it would have been more natural to commence with fathers. John writes that the sins of children are forgiven and that they know the Father, something that is true of men and women (2:12, 14). The second letter of John, addressed to the elect lady and her children (1:1), suggests that the letter was written to a particular lady, probably the leader of a house church, and the children were the members of that community. If 1 John is written to the same community (and there is no reason to doubt that), then the use of "children" in 1 John 2:12 and 1 John 2:14 would refer to the whole community of believers that remain in fellowship in the Johannine community. In a similar manner the term father refers to mature adults, male and female, who have known him who is from the beginning. Therefore, they provide a foundation for the young people in the community.

Question

In your opinion, how likely—or unusual—is it that "father" can be used for adult females?

Source: From *The IVP Women's Bible Commentary* edited by Catherine Clark Kroeger and Mary J. Evans. Copyright © 2002 by InterVarsity Christian Fellowship/USA. Used by permission of InterVarsity Press, P.O. Box 1400, Downers Grove, IL 60515. *www.ivpress.com*.

Doing Feminist Reading Yourself

1. *Why is it that no women are named in 1 John and there are no explicitly gender-specific issues?*

2. *In 2 and 3 John, the terms "elect lady" and "elect sister" are used, probably for churches. How appropriate do you think this is? Give your reasons.*

Feminist Reading at Work, 2
Raising Feminist Concerns about 1–3 John

In this reading Margaret Hutaff presents an "against the grain" feminist reading of the Johannine letters, employing a "hermeneutic of suspicion" to read one element of the text against the rest of it.

Feminist readers who value texts that can serve as models for creating inclusive community and honoring diversity will have obvious differences with 1 John. Its author affirms the command to "love one another" as the essence of the Christian "message," but turns this injunction away from being a constructive challenge addressed to everyone (including him) and uses it as his criterion of judging others. He diverts love from the hard work of fostering openness and tolerance and uses it for exclusionary purposes. . . . We might also raise questions . . . about Johannine Christianity's limited application of the love command as an inner-Christian ethic, casting others as outsiders.

Another major area posing difficulties for feminist readers is 1 John's view of theology and "the spirit." By constructing theology in terms of truth versus error and defining it in dogmatic terms, he opens the way for historically and culturally conditioned interpretations to the elevated to the level of ahistorical timeless truths. . . . 1 John's association of "the spirit" with correct theology, dogmatically defined, also raises questions about how theologies are to be "tested" or verified. A hermeneutic of suspicion rightly questions any claim that an individual, institution or theological position represents truth or God or is exclusively motivated by or in possession of "the spirit." . . .

In conclusion, reading these epistles raises questions about how we view theology, create hospitable communities, and deal with diversity, not only in our churches but in all aspects of life. From my perspective, to the degree that 1 and 2 John construct a rhetorical of intolerance, they have misused the ethical and theological resources available to them: a strong tradition of hospitality and generosity, and emphasis on the primacy of love as the basis of Christian self-understanding, and a more inclusive, noncoercive appeal to "the spirit." On the other hand, by reading with a "hermeneutic of suspicion," we can recover these basic early Christian resources and use them ourselves to construct meaningful theologies and build communities that teach tolerance—an important component of "love"—by practicing it.

Source: Margaret D. Hutaff, "The Johannine Epistles," in Elisabeth Schüssler Fiorenza, ed., *Searching the Scriptures,* vol. 2 (New York: Crossroad), pp. 442, 426.

Question

Give your own critique of this selection.

2 JOHN: Keep False Teachers Away

Unlike 1 John, 2 John is a true letter in its literary form, content, and rhetoric. Already in the second century it was connected with 1 John, and through 1 John to the fourth Gospel. The author calls himself "the Elder" and therefore is not to be identified with the author of the fourth Gospel or even 1 John. Like other Christian works around the end of the first century, 2 John stresses proper doctrine and defends the borders of true teaching against false teaching. Although this is a short letter—it probably fit on one page of papyrus—it gives us good insight into the theology and history of the continuing Johannine tradition.

---

2 John in Brief: Outline of Structure and Contents

I. **Opening** The "Elder" to the "Elect Lady and her children"; blessing on "us" (1–3)

II. **Body** Do not receive anyone who denies that Christ came in the flesh (4–11)

    A. Love one another and walk in God's commandments (4–6)

    B. Do not receive into the house-church those who deny that Christ "came in the flesh"; they are deceivers and antichrists (7–11)

III. **Conclusion** Apology for such a short letter, with promise to visit soon; greetings from others (12–13)

Developing Your Skills

Read 2 John carefully, trying to discern what the underlying social and religious situation might be.

A Guide to Reading 2 John

The letter opens in verses 1–3 with the author calling himself "the Elder" (or *presbyter*). This term for a leadership official has not been seen before in the Johannine writings, but the author writes to another church with an authority over a local church that an elder would have. The addressee section is symbolically worded: "To the elect lady and her children." To judge from the following contents, especially verse 13 understood as a reference to a "sister" church, this probably means an unnamed local church and its members. The fact that the Elder will give that church instructions and send along greetings from the children of "your elect sister" (13), perhaps his own congregation, suggests he is an authoritative figure in the latter church. The fairly common Christian greeting "Grace, mercy, peace" is followed by the addition of the more particularly Johannine "truth and love," a veiled claim here that the author stands in the true Johannine tradition and his instruction should be heeded (3).

Next comes a transitional statement of joy (4). In the ancient letter format, a statement of joy (which, when more fully developed, becomes a thanksgiving section) is often employed as a transition to the body of the letter. Here it is marked by a "commandment by the Father" in 4 that is developed in 5. The main message of the letter comes in 5–12: the audience must "walk" in love and believe in the full humanity of Christ. The commandment of love and the necessity of "walking" in this commandment (5–6) repeat the main parenetic point of 1 John. Similarly, the christological point of 1 John is echoed by the insistence in 2 John 7 on acknowledging Jesus' coming in the flesh as the dividing line between those whom the Elder acknowledges as his (and God's) beloved children and the "antichrists" and "deceivers" who have gone out into the world. These deceivers, already clearly present in 1 John, are probably only about to arrive at the church addressed in 2 John. The author warns his recipients to look to themselves as this threat approaches (8). The adversaries are described as "going ahead and not remaining in the teaching of Christ" (9). This difference is fundamental: whoever has the wrong teaching does not have God! (9). At the end of the letter body, the author gives concrete advice to his recipients for protecting themselves from this error: they must not receive into their "house" (probably the house church meeting, or the household as a haven during the week for traveling preachers) those who bring another doctrine. To do so is to share in evil and go over into false teaching (10–11).

In closing the letter in verse 12, the Elder adds a customary apology for writing too little (also in 3 John 13–14). His expressed hope to visit soon should also be understood as a literary custom, but coupled with the apology for a short letter it functions to remind the audience as they finish listening to this letter that it is a substitute for the author's personal presence. "That our joy may be complete," echoes 1 John 1:4, where joy stems from the fellowship of Johannine Christians with one another and with God and Jesus Christ. It is this fellowship of mutual love and true faith that the author is writing to preserve. As the Elder concludes, he sends greetings to them from "the children of your elect sister," members of a fellow Johannine church. The lack of a concluding blessing, while unusual, should not be read as meaning that the author is upset with his audience.

Historical Reading of 2 John

> ### 2 John in Brief: Summary of Historical Reading
>
> **Author** "The Elder," probably the author of all three Johannine letters.
>
> **Date** Around 100 c.e., shortly after 1 John and shortly before 3 John.
>
> **Audience** One congregation in the Johannine circle of churches, probably around Ephesus, threatened by the "deceivers" who have left the Johannine church. This church had perhaps not received 1 John.
>
> **Unity and Integrity** Unquestioned in current scholarship.
>
> **Purpose** To keep Johannine Christians unified and dedicated to the distinctives of the Johannine tradition against the threat of those who have left it. This is to be accomplished in this church by refusing entrance to them.

The historical information for 2 John is the same as 1 John, with these brief differences. First, the date is probably later, perhaps not by more than a year or two. Second, the purpose of the letter is different, because here the author writes to propose a more specific and drastic solution to the problem of his opponents: refusal of hospitality to traveling teachers who do not espouse traditional Johannine christology. In all likelihood, 2 John was addressed to a church that the opponents had not yet visited.

Its purpose is to tell its audience briefly of the main teaching of the first letter (which they may or may not have received): they should confess faith that Jesus Christ came in the flesh and show love for each other, all the while keeping false teachers at an arm's length. On the basis of this teaching, the author commands them to refuse entrance into the church meetings, and its platform to speak, to those who do not share this main teaching.

3 JOHN: Let Faithful Teachers In

When we turn from 2 John to 3 John, christology and how to walk in Christ's way is no longer the explicit topic, but rather the practical implications of how to carry it out. In 3 John, matters of church authority have taken over from theology, and the theology of 1 and 2 John have given way to difficult relationships between four persons: John the Elder, the author of the letter; Gaius, whom John addresses and supports; Demetrius, whom the author recommends; and Diotrephes, whom the author opposes. How this fits into Johannine community history is difficult to diagnose. (Once again, we see that reading other people's mail—with the difficulties of "filling in the gaps" in the situation of the letters—is not always easy!) But a common scholarly reconstruction goes something like this: In one church, Diotrephes, who has emerged as a leader, has decided to keep all traveling missionaries out of his church, probably in an attempt to exclude all false teaching. Hospitality, a prime social virtue that Christianity shares with the Mediterranean world, has been refused. If Diotrephes had excluded those sent by John the Elder, this would be a double difficulty for the Elder. This situation causes the Elder to write a letter to Gaius, seemingly a wealthy person in a neighboring church. Gaius has been providing hospitality on a temporary basis, but the Elder wants him to take over larger responsibility for helping the missionaries, including the well-known Demetrius, who will soon arrive.

---

3 John in Brief: Outline of Structure and Contents

I. **Opening** The Elder to the beloved Gaius (1)
II. **Thanksgiving** A prayer for Gaius's health and joy that he is "walking in the truth" (2–4)
III. **Body** Support faithful wandering preachers, avoiding the example of the disobedient Diotrephes (5–12)
IV. **Conclusion** Apology for the shortness of the letter, wish to visit soon; blessing and greetings (13–15)

Developing Your Skills

Read 3 John carefully, noticing the different characters named in this short letter.

A Guide to Reading 3 John

The opening section is very brief, with "the Elder" addressing "the beloved Gaius, whom I love in truth" (v. 1). A health wish (2) is close in form and content to health wishes at the opening of secular letters, but the Elder also expresses his fitting concern for Gaius' spiritual health.

As with 2 John , an expression of joy introduces the body of this letter (3–4). The author praises Gaius for "walking in the truth" because he is implicitly contrasting Gaius with Diotrephes (9). "Brothers" who have come to the author had conveyed news about Gaius. Seen with 5–6, this shows that the Elder may be in charge of a group of traveling missionaries and/or prophets. The "brothers" of 5–6, among whom Gaius has a reputation of being hospitable, are coming from the Elder's community to that in which Gaius lives. The author asks Gaius to help them on their way. Like almost all traveling missionaries in early Christianity, they depend on the assistance of generous local Christians and accept no support from "nonbelievers" (in the Greek "Gentiles") (5, 8). In the Elder's encouraging expression, those who help them will become "co-workers in the truth" (8).

Now in 9–10, without any warning or transitional device, a conflict situation is revealed. A certain Diotrephes "likes to be first," that is, he is asserting a leadership role in the church and does not pay attention to the Elder's authority over it. Besides that, Diotrephes is spreading "false charges" about the Elder; what these are is not stated. He also refuses to receive "brothers" (missionaries sent by the Elder, or perhaps under his general authority), hindering those who wish to do so, and expelling them from the church. The author does not order Diotrephes to be removed or ostracized, but takes the mild path of urging his audience not to imitate this evil example (11). The author directly labels Diotrephes as evil (12). Then he recommends to them a figure named Demetrius (12), perhaps a missionary for whom this letter serves as a recommendation. The author does not say, but the commendation of Demetrius immediately after the condemnation of Diotrephes may imply that Demitrius is the author's emissary to tackle this problem in person.

As in 2 John 12, the Elder closes the Body or message of the letter in 13–14 with an apology for brevity and the hope to see Gaius soon. Third John closes by having "the beloved here" (i.e., in the Elder's church) send greetings to Gaius and to the beloved there, "each by name."

Historical Reading of 3 John

3 John in Brief: Summary of Historical Reading

Author "The Elder," probably the author of all three Johannine letters, and certainly the author of 2 John.

Date Around 100 C.E., shortly after 2 John and as a follow-up to it.

Audience One congregation in the Johannine circle of churches, probably around Ephesus, threatened by those who have left the Johannine church.

Unity and Integrity Unquestioned in current scholarship.

Purpose To urge one congregation to admit visitors and not to bar their meetings to all outsiders in order to keep themselves "pure."

Third John shares the same historical issues as 1 and 2 John. As for its date, it is almost certainly after 2 John, because it seems best to read it as a follow up to 2 John. But the time of 3 John could be as little as a few months to a few years later. Third John is imprecise (for us, that is—the original audience would be able to understand it quite well) about how its figures are related to one another and the Elder. For example, does Gaius offer hospitality to those who have recently been rejected by Diotrephes, or does Diotrephes refuse hospitality to those whom Gaius was helping? Or was there no connection between their actions? Next, the author blames Diotrephes for liking to make himself first in a church, shown in a series of things: paying no attention to the Elder; refusing to welcome "brothers"; and hindering and expelling those who extend that hospitality. (Wanting to be first was often anathema in the Mediterranean world, where leadership is inherited or given by others; seeking to leave one's social place is not done.) Many have suggested that Diotrephes was, by title or not, an example of the emerging presbyter-bishop as found in the Pastoral Letters and endorsed by Ignatius of Antioch in the 110s. His emergence would be very troubling on the Johannine scene, where so little emphasis had been placed on church structure. By contrast, the Elder would represent the older Johannine situation, wherein there might be a "School" of tradition bearers but where there were no authoritative community administrators. Demetrius was a prominent missionary (receiving "a good report from all"). He was coming to Gaius, carrying 3 John, or arriving shortly after it would have been received. The seriousness of the testimonial to him reflects the Elder's view that hospitality must be extended so that his message can get out.

What was the reason(s) for the conflict between the Elder and Diotrephes? The letter did not have to, and perhaps even want to, spell this out. Perhaps Diotrephes was a secessionist leader who took over a church in the Johannine orbit; this would make sense of the Elder's implication that Demetrius "has not seen God" (12), perhaps leaning toward secessionists. Demetrius would then have a theological reason to keep out the friends and emissaries of the Elder. But the letter makes more sense if both Demetrius and the Elder were opposed to secessionist missionaries. If we assume that the Elder wrote 1 John as well, he thought that there was no need for human teachers: Those who have the anointing with the Spirit are automatically taught what is true, and so all believers together must test the spirits to detect false prophets (1 John 2:27; 4:1–6). But Diotrephes knew that the secessionists also claimed that they had the true spirit, making it impossible for people to know who was speaking the truth. Diotrephes may have decided that authoritative human teachers were needed, namely, those who had the background to know what was erroneous and the authority to keep false teachers away. He took on that role for his local church, keeping all missionaries out, including those of the Elder. He may have reasoned, as we say, "It's better to be safe than sorry." In the Elder's view of things, Diotrephes was arrogant in departing from the traditional way of doing things. In Diotrephes' outlook, the Elder was naive and impractical. If this is the case, John 21 *may* indicate that Diotrephes' view of what would save Johannine Christianity ultimately won. There Jesus gives Peter pastoral authority over the sheep, effectively modifying the thrust of John 10, that Jesus' followers do not need human leaders.

Key Terms and Concepts

antichrists • docetists • the Elder • expiation • fellowship • final eschatology incarnation • Johannine School/Circle • Paraclete • Parousia • perfectionism realized eschatology

Questions for Study, Discussion, and Writing

1. Describe what you believe to be the historical situation behind 1, 2, and 3 John.
2. Do you think that the author of 1 John or his opponents were correct about what the Gospel of John meant? Give your reasons.
3. Describe the relationship in 1 John between belief in Jesus and moral conduct toward other Christians.
4. What do you think about the issue of authority in 2–3 John? Was the Elder too heavy handed in asserting his authority in 3 John? Analyze this issue historically, and also analyze it using social scientific ideas of hierarchy and leadership in the Mediterranean.

For Further Reading

Brown, Raymond E. *The Epistles of John*. Anchor Bible. Garden City, NY: Doubleday, 1982. The most comprehensive, authoritative commentary on the letters of John.

Lieu, Judith. *The Second and Third Epistles of John: History and Background*. Edinburgh: Clark, 1986. Excellent treatment of issues in historical reading.

Lieu, Judith. *The Theology of the Johannine Epistles*. Cambridge: Cambridge University Press, 1991. A survey of the thought of 1–3 John.

Perkins, Pheme. *The Johannine Epistles*. Wilmington: Michael Glazier, 1984. An excellent commentary for students.

Smalley, Steven S. *1, 2, 3 John*. Word Bible Commentary. Waco, TX: Word, 1984. Full, careful treatment.

Thompson, Mariann Meye. *The Johannine Letters*. Downers Grove, IL: InterVarsity, 1992. Concise historical and theological commentary.

von Wahlde, Urban C. *The Johannine Commandments: 1 John and the Struggle for the Johannine Tradition*. New York: Paulist Press, 1990. Good treatment of the historical and theological dimensions of 1 John.

Chapter Nineteen

Revelation: The Flowering of Christian Apocalyptic

The last book in the NT is the most challenging to read. The author of Revelation (more fully known as "The Revelation to John" or sometimes as "The Apocalypse") shows his readers a series of visions unveiling the conflicted spiritual realities of the universe that lead toward a happy ending. Events on earth are a part of a universal, cosmic drama in which good and evil violently contend. The violence depicted here is meant as a reassurance to those under persecution but is often off-putting to readers today. However, the basic message of Revelation is a positive, hopeful one—God will triumph over sin and death, so God's followers should stay true to the faith in the face of deadly persecution. John writes his visions in a deeply dramatic way, touching both the reader's mind and emotions.

Many people think of Revelation as unique. As noted in Chapter 3, however, Revelation is only one of many similar apocalyptic works that Jewish and early Christian writers produced between about 300 B.C.E. and 200 C.E. These apocalyptic books not only employ the same kinds of imagery used in Revelation, but they point to the same triumph of God. Although their depiction of the end of human history is difficult to grasp, their portrayals of the afterlife have been particularly influential on Christian thought. Almost two millennia after they were written, they continue to shape popular beliefs about divine judgment, heaven, and hell. The persistence of these popular beliefs results, at least in part, from the incorporation of their views of the afterlife into later masterpieces of Western literature, such as Dante's *Divine Comedy* and Milton's *Paradise Lost*. Modern literature and film often portray the afterlife apocalyptically as well; the astonishing 1998 film *What Dreams May Come* (directed by Vincent Ward) powerfully depicts the joys of heaven and the despair of hell. In sum, Revelation is perhaps the hardest book in the NT to interpret using any method, but certainly one of the most fascinating if the reader can accept it on its own terms, let go of the impulse to understand every metaphor as symbolic, and gain an overall appreciation of its message.

www Follow the link to excellent information on this film at hollywooodjesus.com.

Revelation in Brief: Outline of Structure and Contents

I. **Prologue** The author and the divine revelation given to him (1:1–20)

II. Jesus' letters to the seven churches of Asia Minor (2:1–3:22)

III. Visions of the end (4:1–22:5)

    A. A scroll with seven seals; seven trumpets (4:1–11:19)

    B. Signs in heaven: Visions of the woman, the Dragon, the beast, the Lamb, and the seven plagues (12:1–16:21)

    C. The "Great Whore" and the fall of Babylon (Rome) (17:1–18:24)

    D. Heavenly rejoicing, the warrior Messiah, the imprisonment of the beast and Satan, judgment of the dead, and the final defeat of evil (19:1–20:15)

    E. The "new heaven and new earth" and the establishment of a new Jerusalem on earth (21:1–22:5)

IV. **Epilogue** Authenticity of the author's prophetic visions and the nearness of their fulfillment; final blessing (22:6–21)

Developing Your Skills

Read through Revelation quickly, noticing the distinctiveness of its apocalyptic style and the overall structure of the book. Don't get bogged down trying to figure out the symbolic language as you read; instead, go for an overall impression of them.

A Guide to Reading Revelation

The book of Revelation opens by calling itself that—a revelation (Greek *apokalypsis*, from which we get **apocalypse**) from Jesus Christ, "which God gave him to show his servants" through John. The one who reads aloud the words of this "prophecy," probably in the church service, is blessed, and especially blessed are those who hear and keep it, for "the time is near" when the contents of this book will happen (1:1–3). Entering now a letter format, John names himself and addresses this book to the "seven churches in Asia," that is, the Roman province called Asia located east of the Aegean Sea. He blesses them and then offers a blessing from Jesus Christ. Jesus is coming "with the clouds of heaven"; those who persecute him (and his people) will see him, and "all the tribes of the earth will wail." The last word in the opening is God's: God is the beginning and the end of all things, eternal and all powerful (1:4–8).

In common with other apocalyptic writers, John claims divine inspiration for his work, which he calls a "prophecy." He reports that on the **"Lord's Day"**—Sunday, the day when Jesus' resurrection brought life to the world—he "was caught up by the Spirit" to hear and see heaven's unimaginable grandeur (1:9). All the visions of this book are depicted as given to John on this one day. His message derives from God's direct revelation to Jesus Christ, who in turn transmits it through an angel to John (1:1–2). John's visions generate an intense urgency, for they reveal the immediate future; the "imminent expectation" is prominent in this writing (1:1). Visionary previews of Jesus' impending return convince the author that what he sees is about to happen, and this is repeated at the book's conclusion when Jesus proclaims that his arrival is imminent (22:7,10, 12).

In his first symbolic depiction of the risen Christ in heaven (1:12–16), John describes a male figure with snow-white hair, flaming eyes, shining brass feet, and a sharp sword in his mouth. These images derive largely from Daniel's depiction of God (Daniel 7 and 10) and are common in apocalyptic writings of the time. The first two items in the description—a man with long white hair—have for better or worse become the depiction of God (the Father) in Western art and imagination, but here John applies them to Jesus. To universalize this figure, John adds astronomical features to his biblical symbols, describing him as holding seven stars in his hand and shining like the sun. As the "first and the last" who has died but now lives forever, he is the crucified and risen Christ. John further explains his symbols in 1:20. The stars represent angels, and the lampstands nearby are the seven churches of John's home territory. This identification reassures the author that his familiar earthly congregations do not exist solely on earth, but are part of a larger reality in which angelic spirits protectively oversee assembled Christians. The symbols also serve John's characteristic purpose in uncovering the spiritual reality behind physical appearance. Like the eternal stars above, the lamps shed Christ's light on a benighted world.

John now surveys the churches of Asia Minor, the seven lamps that shine light into heaven and earth. Like the contemporary author of 2 Esdras (14:22–48), John presents himself as a secretary recording dictation, in his case Christ's dictation in the seven letters to follow. Christ's letters to the seven communities all follow the same pattern. First, Christ commands that a letter be written to the angel of a particular church, and then describes some aspect of his own power. Then he employs the formula "I know," followed by a description of the positive aspects of the church's spiritual condition. A second formula, "but I have it against you," then introduces a summary of the particular weaknesses of the church. Each letter also includes a prophetic call for repentance, a promise that the Parousia will occur soon, an exhortation to maintain integrity, a command to "hear" (understand and obey), and a final promise that God will reward those who keep the faith. In this way, the rhetorical point of these seven letters is much like that of Revelation as a whole. The letters also serve to show that the grand cosmic Revelation to follow has implications for the everyday life of Christians.

Jesus' messages to Ephesus (2:1–7), Smyrna (2:8–11), Pergamum (2:12–17), Thyatira (2:18–29), Sardis (3:1–6), Philadelphia (3:7–13), and Laodicea (3:14–22) provide insight into the author and the situation to which he writes. The letters describe each of these cities' churches in images that suggest the spiritual reality beneath them. For example, Laodicea's richness is corrected because its wealth is causing it to reject others, just as that city had refused Roman help to rebuild after a great earthquake in the 60s. Pergamum is labeled the site of Satan's throne (2:13), probably because it was one of the first centers of the emperor cult. In this setting, eating meat previously sacrificed to the gods is especially dangerous (2:14). John's refusal to tolerate Christians who eat idol meat is typical of his exclusivism and moral rigor. It contrasts sharply with Paul's more flexible attitude on the same issue (1 Cor 8:1–13), but it does adhere to the line against eating idol meat laid down in Acts 15:20. John's attitude speaks of a time when paganism enforced its power by killing those who were seen to undermine it and when Christians reacted by distancing themselves.

John's first vision made the heavenly Christ visible and audible for these seven churches; his second (4:1–11:19) opens the view into heaven itself. After the Spirit carries him to God's throne, John is to be shown dramatic portrayals of events soon to come (4:1–2). His first vision, however, is the happy sight of God's splendor and the joyous worship that all heavenly creatures give to God eternally (4:3–11). John's purpose is not merely to predict future happenings, but by doing so to remove the veil that shrouds heavenly truths and to assure his readers that God still controls the world. The author intends the visions that follow to reassure Christians that their sufferings are temporary but their salvation is certain, all because God is guiding the world to its conclusion. John conveys this assurance in two series of seven visions involving seven seals and seven trumpets (chapters 5–6). The opening of the seven seals reveals that the future course of events has already been recorded on a heavenly scroll. In John's vision, the Lamb (Jesus) opens each of the seven seals in sequence, disclosing either a predestined future event or God's interpretive viewpoint. Christ as the Lamb "standing as if it had been slaughtered" (5:6) becomes the model for Christian faithfulness in a world of conflict (Stuckenbruck 2003, 1536). When Jesus breaks the first four seals, this sends out four horses and riders— the famous "Four Horsemen of the Apocalypse"—representing military conquest, war itself, famine, and death by plague in the "sickly pale" rider. They are followed closely by Hades, the land of the dead (6:1–8). Breaking the fifth seal makes visible to John the souls of persons executed for their steadfast Christian faith, souls now kept under the altar of heaven. After crying to God for vengeance, they are given white clothing and told to rest peacefully until the full number of predestined martyrs has been killed (6:9–11). John indicates that believers' willingness to die for the faith earns them the white garment of spiritual purity—and that God soon will act to bring them justice. From this point on in Revelation, John repeatedly addresses the martyrs' demands for divine justice (see 8:3–4; 10:3–7; 11:1–2; 14:1–3, 9–11, 13, 18; 15:1–4; 16:5–7; 18:8, 20; and 19:3).

After the sixth seal is broken, John portrays this terrifying day of God's justice by relating astronomical catastrophes. He borrows from the same apocalyptic tradition that the Synoptic Gospel writers used to predict Jesus' coming (Mark 13;

Matt 24–25; Luke 21). John predicts that the sun will turn black, the moon will turn a bloody red, and the stars will fall to earth as the sky vanishes into nothingness (6:12–14). The population of the earth—every social class is mentioned—hides in fear, and angels appear with God's seal to mark believers on the forehead (chapter 7; see Ezekiel 9). The symbolic number of those marked for salvation is 144,000, a multiple of the number of the twelve traditional tribes of Israel. This probably indicates that John sees a full complement of his fellow Jews redeemed at the End (compare Paul's view in Rom 9:25–27). But because this is Revelation, other interpretations are possible! Later in Revelation, the 144,000 are designated the first ingathering of God's harvest, a sort of first fruits of the salvation of the world (14:1–5). This prophecy is hinted at here, because accompanying this numerable Jewish group is a vast, innumerable crowd from "all nations, tribes, peoples and languages" on earth, signifying the countless multitudes and varieties of Gentile believers. They too have passed through great persecutions. Both groups wear clothes previously stained by their own blood as they died, now "made white in the blood of the Lamb." They stand eternally before God, holding palm branches signifying their victory and singing the praise of God and the Lamb (7:9–17). When the seventh seal is finally opened, there is total silence in heaven for one-half hour as all worship and the visions given to John stop. This silence is reminiscent of the cosmic silence before creation—the silence before the "Big Bang," as we might say—and indicates that a new creation is coming soon. Then an angel carrying a golden censer stands at the altar and presents a large offering of incense to God, in which the prayers of the saints are mixed (8:1–5).

As if answering the churches' prayers for justice and peace on the earth, seven angels blow seven trumpets, and a new series of events begins to tell the story of the end in another way. The first six announce catastrophes similar to the ten plagues on Egypt in the Hebrew Bible book of Exodus. The initial trumpet blast triggers a hail of fire and blood, causing a third of the earth to burn (8:6–7). The second causes a fire-spewing mountain to be hurled into the sea (8:8–9). Volcanic eruptions like that of Mount Vesuvius near Pompeii, Italy in 79 C.E. were commonly regarded as expressions of divine judgment, and their devastating power makes a powerful image here. The third and fourth trumpets bring more astronomical disasters, including a blazing comet called "Wormwood," perhaps representing Satan's fall from heaven. The sun, moon, and stars lose a third of their light as the power of God's creation weakens (8:10–12). After the fifth trumpet blast, the fallen star opens the abyss (pit down to the land of the dead and Hell), releasing columns of smoke that produce a plague of locusts similar to those described in Exodus 10:12–15 and Joel 1:4; 2:10. Persons not marked as belonging to God (who in the dualist scheme thereby belong to the Devil) are tormented with unbearable agonies but are unable to die to end their pain (9:1–6). Despite the unleashing of further destructive hordes as the sixth trumpet sounds (9: 14–19), John does not believe that such afflictions will stop humanity's evil deeds. People who survive the plagues will continue

Prayers Collected in the Western Wall, Jerusalem The Jewish faithful visiting the Western Wall in Jerusalem today often place written prayers in the cracks of the wall. In this way, they are collected in a holy place. This parallels Rev 5:8 and 8:3–4, where the prayers of God's people are collected in golden bowls in heaven and then offered with incense before God's throne. Used by permission of BiblePlaces.com.

practicing their false religions and tormenting God's people, just like the ancient Egyptians did to the Israelites during and after the plagues (9:20–21).

John now draws upon Ezekiel again, this time to describe the symbolic eating of a little scroll that tastes like honey but turns bitter in the stomach (Ezek 2:8–3:3). The sweet-to-bitter scroll suggests the double-sidedness of John's message: sweet to the faithful but sour to the disobedient (10:8–11). The next section of Revelation in chapter 11 tells a bittersweet story indeed. The angel accompanying John in heaven instructs him to measure the Jerusalem Temple and those who worship there, the first time that John becomes a participant in the vision. The Temple will continue under Gentile (pagan) domination for three and a half years. In the meantime, two human witnesses are appointed to prophesy on earth for this period of time—the traditional period of persecution of God's people established in Daniel (7:25; 9:27; 12:7). As they prophesy in Jerusalem, the Beast (personification of cosmic evil) comes up from the abyss and kills them, but after three and a half days they are resurrected and taken to heaven. The executed prophets may refer to Moses and Elijah, to Peter and Paul, or more likely to all Christian martyrs in John's time. After the risen martyrs' ascension, an earthquake kills 7,000 inhabitants of their city, symbolically called "Sodom and Egypt." Sodom, guilty of violence, immorality, and inhospitality, was destroyed by fire from heaven; Egypt, which enslaved God's people, was devastated by ten plagues. The identity of this city is further confirmed by the author's tip "where also their Lord was crucified" (11:8). A tenth of its inhabitants die in the earthquake, but all the rest see what happens, are struck by fear, and "gave glory to the God of heaven," wording that indicates that they repent and now belong to God (cf. 11:18; 14:7; 15:4; 19:5). Evidently John wishes to convey that although the Gentiles will not repent however much they are punished (9:20–21), the Jewish people as a whole will.

The seventh trumpet does not introduce a specific calamity, but proclaims God's sovereignty and the eternal reign of his Christ. With the Messiah invisibly reigning in the midst of his enemies (Ps 2:1–12), God's heavenly sanctuary opens to view amid awesome phenomena recalling Yahweh's presence in Solomon's Temple (1 Kings 8:1–6).

Chapter 12 introduces a series of unnumbered visions dramatizing the cosmic battle between the Lamb and the Dragon. In this series (12:1–16:21), John once again links unseen events in heaven with their consequences on earth. The opening war in heaven where organized evil is born (12:1–12) finds its earthly counterpart in the climactic battle of Armageddon where it is destroyed (16:12–16). Between these two analogous conflicts, John mixes inspirational visions of the Lamb's domain with warnings about "the Beast" and God's strong judgment upon disobedient humanity. The first astronomical sign of this section reveals a woman dressed in the sun, moon, and stars. John probably means the figure to symbolize Israel, the people from whom Jesus Christ was born. However, like most of John's symbols, this figure can be interpreted in many ways, including the traditional Roman Catholic view that it represents Mary the mother of Jesus. Arrayed in "twelve stars" suggesting the traditional twelve tribes, the woman labors in great pain to give birth to the Messiah. Second Esdras also depicted Israel's holy city as a persecuted woman (2 Esdras 9:38–10:54). The Dragon/Devil, whom the archangel Michael hurls from heaven, wages war against the woman's children, identified as the faithful who bear witness to Jesus' sovereignty (12:13–17). However, John has already informed his hearers that this Satanic attack on the church is really a sign of the Dragon's last days. His expulsion from heaven and his wrathful conduct on earth signify that Christ has already begun to rule; the demonic power behind Rome has already been defeated but fights on as it brings hell on earth. His activities now limited to human society, the Dragon appears in the form of a monster with ten horns and seven heads. The reversed number of heads and horns shows the beast's kinship to the Dragon, who gives the beast his power (13:1–4). Most scholars believe that John intended the beast as a symbol of Rome, a government he regarded as Satanic in its persecution of the church (13:3, 5–8). The picture grows more complicated after the main beast is slain, only to revive unexpectedly. A second beast emerges, not from the sea but from the earth, to work miracles and enforce public worship of the first beast. In an evil reversal of the angelic sealing, the beast allows no one to conduct business unless he bears the beast's mark. John then adds a "key" to this bestial riddle: the beast's number is that of "a man's name," and the "numerical value of its letters is six hundred and sixty-six" (13:14–18). In the author's day all numbers were represented by letters of the alphabet. Thus, each letter in a person's name was also a number. By adding up the sum of all letters in a given name, we arrive at its "numerical value."

John's hint that the beast's cryptic number could be identified with a specific person has probably inspired more speculation than any other statement in his book. In every century until ours, apocalyptically minded Christians have found men or institutions that they claimed fit the beast's description and thus filled the role of Antichrist, whose appearance supposedly confirmed that the world was near its End. By contrast, most New Testament scholars believe that John (or the source he employs) refers to a historical person of his own time. Who that person might have been, however, is debated. Some historians believe that the man who best fit John's description of the beast was Nero, the first Roman head of state to torture and execute Christians. Following Nero's suicide in 68 C.E., popular rumors swept the Empire that he was not dead but in hiding and planned to reappear at the head of a barbarian army to reassert his sovereignty. (This view explains the Beast's recovery from its "death-blow" and his execution of those Christians who refused to acknowledge his divinity.) Proponents of this hypothesis point to the fact that in Aramaic the numerical value of the name "Nero Caesar" is "666." Although it is widely accepted, the theory identifying John's beast with Nero leaves much unexplained. Other historians suggest that John intended to imply that Nero was figuratively reborn in Domitian, his vicious spirit ascending "out of the abyss" (17:8) to torment Christians in a new human form. Still others argue that we do not have "the key" (13:18) necessary to understand John's meaning.

In surveying more quickly now Revelation's last chapters (17–22), we note that the ever-repeated struggle on earth is dramatized in a variety of ways. John's method in presenting his visions is to retell the same story in different terms, using different symbols to illustrate the same concept. Thus, to dramatize Christ's victory over evil, he does not proceed in a straight chronological line from the opening battle to the devil's final defeat, but turns back to narrate the same basic conflict between good and evil repeatedly. For example, after the seventh trumpet blast, John assures his readers that Jesus is victorious and now reigns as king over the world (11:15). However, another battle ensues in chapter 12, after which John declares that Christ has now achieved total power (12:10). Still another conflict follows, the Battle of Armageddon (16:13–16), after which the angel repeats, "'It is over!'" (16:18).

But it is not really over, because Satan's earthly kingdom—"Babylon," that is, Rome—is yet to fall (chapters 17–18). In 17:1–19:10, the punishment of Rome is dramatized in visions associated with the angels who pour out "bowls of wrath," plagues on the earth. Earlier in chapter 12 the people of God were portrayed as a woman and her children, but now Babylon is also a woman, the "great whore" who seduces the world with her wealth and power (17:1–18). When Babylon falls and a fourth victory is proclaimed (19:1–3), Christ must repeat his conquest again (19:11–21). Between these two events, John is so overcome by his angelic guide's message that he falls down to worship him. The angel rebukes him and tells him to worship only God, perhaps suggesting to John's audience that they are not to rely on angels as mediators of protection, but look for this only to God (19:9–10). In John's cyclic visions, evil does not stay defeated but must be fought continuously until the truly final end of time.

In contrast to the cyclic repetitions of earlier sections, in chapter 20 John apparently pursues a linear narration, presenting a chronological sequence of events that hurries in quick narrative pacing to the End. In this final eschatological vision (20:1–22:5), an angel hurls the Dragon into the abyss, the primordial void that existed before God's creative light ordered the visible world, and now the home of evil (20:1–3). With the Dragon temporarily imprisoned, Christ's reign at last begins. Known as the **millennium** because it lasts 1,000 years, even this triumph is impermanent because at its conclusion Satan is again released to wage war on the faithful, which is according to God's plan. The only New Testament writer to present a one-thousand-year prelude to Christ's full kingdom, John states that during the millennium the martyrs who resisted the beast's influence are resurrected to rule with Christ (20:4–6). The Dragon's release and subsequent attack on the faithful is based on prophetic drama of Ezekiel 38–39 involving **Gog** and **Magog**, symbols of Israel's enemies. The attack ends with fire from heaven destroying these enemies. A resurrection of all the dead ensues; released from the control of Death and Hades (death and the land of the dead personified), they are judged and rewarded according to their deeds. Even Death and Hades themselves are annihilated as they are thrown into the "lake of fire" (20:7–13).

John's primary purpose is to show that God will vanquish evil for all time and create the new universe described in chapters 21–22. He combines images from Isaiah and other Hebrew prophets to portray a universe of peace contrasting with the bloody violence in his previous visions. Borrowing again from ancient myth, in which epic conflict commonly ends with a new union of supernatural beings, John describes a sacred marriage of the Lamb with the holy city that descends from heaven to earth, symbolizing the perfect union of Christ with his people. The wedding of a city to the Lamb may strike readers today as a strangely mixed metaphor, even given the "strangeness" of Revelation's style. Readers will likely agree, however, that John attains great heights of poetic inspiration describing the brilliance of the heavenly Jerusalem. Rendered in terms of gold and precious stones, the jewellike city is illumined by the radiance of God himself. John draws again on Ezekiel's vision of a restored Jerusalem Temple to describe a crystal stream flowing from God's throne to water a new Tree of Life. Growing in a new Eden, the fruits of the tree restore humanity to full health. The renewed and purified faithful can now look directly upon God (21:1–22:5). However, the cowardly, the faithless, and all others whose lives were characterized by evil are excluded from heaven; their place is in the lake of fire (21:8; 22:15). John has finally completed his picture of a renewed creation. God's will is finally done on earth as it is in heaven, as the Lord's Prayer/Our Father asks, because heaven and earth are one.

The book ends in 22:8–21. John once again attempts to worship the angel, but the angel rebukes him sharply (22:8–9). Warning that the scrolls on which the revelations are written are not to be sealed because their contents will soon be fulfilled, John adds a curse upon anyone who changes the wording in his book, especially in the process of copying it (22:18–19). The practice of making such a curse was sometimes used in the Hebrew Bible (Deut 4:2; 12:32; Ezra 6:11) and was widespread in the Greco-Roman world, and the author borrows it here. (Of course, it applies only to the book of Revelation, not to the NT itself, which did not exist in John's time.) It makes for a somewhat anticlimactic conclusion to what is for many readers today the NT's most puzzling and fascinating book. But the end of Revelation is yet to come: Jesus assures the readers that "I am coming soon," and John invites his readers one last time to enter eternal life and avoid being put on the outside eternally with sinners of all sorts (22:15). Once again Jesus says, "Surely I am coming soon," and the reader is invited to add, "Amen. Come, Lord Jesus" (v. 20). The book of Revelation ends with a fitting blessing characteristic of NT letters: "The grace of the Lord Jesus be with all the saints."

Historical Reading of Revelation

A reading of Revelation challenges us to find a reliable method of understanding its complex system of images. There are **three ways to interpret Revelation.** The first approach, favored by scholars, assumes that Revelation was composed for a first-century C.E. audience familiar with apocalyptic imagery and that its chief purpose was to give an eschatological interpretation of then-current events. We are familiar with this method as the *historical* approach. Reasoning that the book would not have been preserved if it did not have immediate significance to its original audience, the reader looks to contemporary Roman history for primary meanings of John's symbols. According to this scholarly method, Babylon (18:2, 10) is Rome, the Beast personifies the Empire's blasphemous might (represented in human form by the emperors), and the various plagues are metaphorically intensified versions of wars, invasions, famines, earthquakes, and other disasters experienced (or feared) during this era. Viewed from the historical approach, this book speaks of the end of this world and the beginning of the next in order to encourage readers in the first century to be faithful under pressure.

According to a second view, favored by modern apocalyptically inclined Christians, Revelation should be read as *future predictive*. In this view, the visions had a contemporary application in Roman times, but John's main purpose was to prophesy about events far into the future. Apocalyptic interpreters generally regard their own time as that predicted by John. During the last several centuries, such interpreters, comparing Daniel's use of "times," "years," and "days" with similar terms in Revelation (12:6, 14; 13:5; etc.), have tried to calculate the exact year of the End. Thus far, all such groups have been wrong, which casts some doubt on whether apocalypses like John's were intended to be blueprints of the future. To try to construct a paradigm of End time from Daniel's or Revelation's chronological or numerical symbols, some argue, is to miss their purpose, as well as to ignore Paul's advice about computing "dates and times" (1 Thess. 5:1) and Jesus' statement that "No one knows about that day or hour." However, failures in the past are not likely to deter future apocalyptists from making predictions.

Although historians' attempt to correlate Revelation's images and symbols with conditions in the first-century Roman Empire is helpful, it does not exhaust the potential meaning of the book. A third method recognizes that John's visions have a vitality that transcends any particular situation, time or place, which we call here the *timeless* approach. John's lasting accomplishment lies in the universality of his symbols and dramas. His visions continue to have appeal today, not because they apply to any specific time, but because they reflect some of the deepest hopes and terrors of the human imagination at all times. As long as opposition to powerful evils and deep yearning for justice and peace motivate human beings, Revelation's promise of the triumph of God over evil will remain appealing.

www Follow the link to the Public Broadcast Service's website for their television broadcast on the book of Revelation.

Revelation in Brief: Summary of Historical Reading

Author Traditionally, John the apostle; most scholars today hold to an otherwise unknown Jewish-Christian prophet named John.

Date Around 95, at the end of Emperor Domitian's rule.

Audience Churches in western Asia Minor, particularly named in chapters 2–3.

Unity Not seriously questioned.

Integrity Not seriously questioned.

Purpose To encourage Christians under severe persecution to be faithful unto death and receive the crown of eternal life.

Author

The author of Revelation identifies himself as "John" (1:1), a name that implies Jewish descent. According to some late-second-century traditions, the author is the apostle John the son of Zebedee, one of Jesus' main disciples, the same person who supposedly wrote the Gospel and Letters of John. However, other early Christian sources recognized the immense differences in thought, language, and theology between Revelation and the fourth Gospel and concluded that they could not have originated with the same author. Eusebius suggests that another John, known only as the "Elder," an official of the late-first-century Ephesian church, may have written the Apocalypse (*History of the Church* 3.39.1–11). Virtually all modern scholars agree that the Gospel, the Letters of John, and Revelation stem from three different authors. Most prefer to accept no more than the writer's own self-identification: He simply calls himself John, a "servant" of Jesus Christ (1:2) who writes a "prophecy." Exiled by Rome to internal exile on the island of Patmos in the eastern Aegean Sea, he received his visions there (1:9). Although a common feature of Jewish apocalyptic works is the use of pseudonymity to place them in the pen of an ancient seer, the author of Revelation obviously does not do this, so we can conclude that Revelation is not pseudonymous.

By studying the contents of his work, scholars can infer something of John's background. He is familiar with internal conditions in the seven churches addressed (Rev 2:1–3:23), although he seems to belong to none of them. To some commentators, this indicates that John was an itinerant Christian prophet who traveled among widely scattered churches. Although he does not call himself a prophet, he does call his book a "prophecy," and his recognized stature as a prophet likely gave him considerable influence in the communities to which he wrote. Because he writes Greek as if it were his second language, phrasing idiosyncratically in a Semitic style, most scholars believe that John was a native of Palestine, or at least had spent much time there. A few suggest that he had some connection with the Johannine community, because like them he refers to Christ as Logos (Word), Lamb, Witness, Shepherd, Judge, and Temple. Also, Revelation and the Gospel of John both express a *duality* of spirit and matter, good and evil, God and the Devil. Important differences include the quality of the Greek—excellent in the Gospel and awkward in the Apocalypse—and the writers' respective eschatologies. The Gospel of John has the most "realized" eschatology in the NT, whereas Revelation has a future eschatology. In sum, John the Evangelist and John the Elder were not the author of this book; instead, we should call him John the Prophet.

Date

Writing about 180 C.E. the Christian leader and theologian Irenaeus stated that Revelation was composed late in the reign of Domitian, who was emperor from 81 to 96 C.E. Internal references to government hostilities toward Christians (1:9; 2:10,

13; 6:9–11; 14:12; 16:6; 21:4), policies associated with Domitian's administration, support Irenaeus's assessment. Most scholars date the work about 95 or 96 C.E. Others have proposed a time before or just after the destruction of the Jerusalem Temple in 70 C.E.

Style and Characteristics

Revelation's depiction of Jesus' character and function derives partly from the author's apocalyptic view of human history. The writer perceives a sharp contrast between the present world, which he regards as hopelessly sinful, and God's planned future world, a realm of ideal purity. The righteous new order can be realized only through God's direct intervention in human affairs. God's intervention requires that Jesus return to judge the world, so that the world order as we know it can be destroyed and a new world can be created. To understand Revelation's emphasis on violence and destruction, with its correspondingly harsh picture of Jesus' cosmic rule, we must examine briefly Jewish and Christian apocalyptic. **Apocalyptic literature** is distinguished by several characteristics, which are found in Revelation with some adaptation:

- *Cosmic dualism* **Apocalyptic theology** sees human society profoundly influenced by unseen spiritual forces—angels and demons—battling in a celestial realm. Events on earth, especially the persecution of God's people, are also the arena of these spiritual conflicts, and the Devil and his minions often act in concert with humans. Of course, Revelation, like all apocalyptic writings, sees God and the spiritual forces allied with God as superior; the cosmic dualism is not equal, so God must win the battle.
- *Temporal dualism* Apocalyptic regards all history as separated into two mutually exclusive periods of time, a current sinful age and a future age of perfection. Seeing the present world situation as too evil to reform, apocalyptic expects a sudden and violent change in which God or his Messiah imposes divine rule by force. Thus, Revelation depicts God's kingdom as suddenly interrupting the ordinary flow of human history. Moreover, this end is coming "soon," a feature Revelation shares with other NT writings (e.g., Mark 9:1; 13:30–31; Rom 13:11–12; 1 Thess 4:13–17; 1 Pet 4:7), but perhaps with greater urgency.
- *Moral dualism* In apocalyptic there are only two kinds of human beings, just as there are two levels of existence (heavenly and earthly) and two ages. Apocalyptic sees humanity as divided into two sharply opposing moral camps. Most people walk in spiritual darkness and are doomed victims of God's wrath against sin. The eschatological terrors God visits upon the earth, and the final punishment of the wicked, are an expression of John's sense of justice; only with cosmic justice can cosmic peace come. The group to which the writers belong and direct their message remains faithful and receives salvation. This moral dualism is reflected in Jesus and his dualistic opposite, the thoroughly evil Antichrist figure of the "Beast" in 12:18–13:10. Like Jesus as the Lamb, the Beast has horns and crowns (13:1; 5:6), can be pictured as a lion (13:2; 5:5), has

supernatural power (13:2; 5:12), is worshiped (13:4; 5:13), and (most important) appears "as mortally slaughtered," falsely imitating Jesus as the Lamb who stands "as slaughtered" (13:3 and 5:6; I have given a literal translation of the Greek which the NRSV obscures by translating "received a death-blow"). This moral dualism, which, applied to people, has often seemed simplistic both in the ancient world and today, can be traced to the main rhetorical purpose of apocalyptic authors. To keep God's people obedient in very difficult times, they draw a division between good and evil that is as sharp as possible, perhaps reasoning that only by knowing the difference between black and white can people recognize the shades of gray.

- *Predestination* Most biblical writers emphasize that historical events are the consequence of real moral choices by humans, but they also believe that God guides history in a general way, often seen best in hindsight. Apocalyptic views the course of history as predetermined by God. Just as the rise and fall of empires happens according to God's plan (Daniel 2, 7–8), so too the course toward the End will take place in a time God has already set. The book of Revelation dramatizes this idea with heavenly scrolls in which the future is laid out. Although human history is predetermined, human beings are still held fully responsible for their actions, both individually and socially.

- *Exclusivism* Many apocalypses, including Revelation, encourage the faithful to maintain their integrity and resist the ever-present temptation to compromise with evil and save their life. Apocalyptic associates faithfulness to God with a rejection of the ordinary goals, social attachments, and other pursuits of unbelieving society. Such separation from ordinary social structures often results when people running those structures are trying literally to kill off the people of God because they give allegiance to God. Regarding most people as condemned, apocalyptic commonly urges its audience to adopt a sectarian attitude, avoiding all association with unbelievers. In such a situation, sharing the Christian message with others in an effort to bring them into the people of God is not a prominent goal. However, the book of Revelation's exclusivism is not extreme; for example, sometimes persecutors repent (11:13), and the kings of the earth, portrayed as formerly acting with Rome to persecute the faithful, will bring the glories of their kingdoms into heaven (21:24).

- *The use of symbols and code* Almost all apocalypses contain obscure language that veils the authors' meaning to outsiders. Most were written during periods of persecution, which encouraged the practice of using terms and images that the intended audiences could understand but outsiders would not. Thus, it is quintessential in-group language. In Enoch, Daniel, Revelation, and other apocalypses, the authors employ symbols from a wide variety of sources, biblical and occasionally pagan. These symbols have both cognitive meaning and emotional power. Particular numbers, such as 4, 7, and 12, have special meanings. Both Daniel and Revelation depict Gentile nations as wild animals because, to the authors, their behavior resembles that of wild beasts. Emperors who demand worship are symbolized as idols, and worshiping them is idolatry. Using code words helps to hide the writer's politically seditious message. Despite the prevalence of this coded language, the general meaning and persuasive message of Revelation comes through to the ancient and modern reader.

www For a consideration of the genre of Revelation, see the short essay on the website. Follow a link to Professor Felix Just's interesting page on the use of numbers in Revelation.

Situation

Almost all interpreters trace this book to the situation in the Roman Empire in the 90s. Domitian, emperor at that time, was the son of Vespasian and the younger brother of Titus, the general who had crushed the Jewish revolt against Rome and destroyed the Jerusalem Temple. As emperor, Domitian accepted divine honors offered him during his lifetime (a new practice in Rome), and allowed himself to be worshiped as a god in various parts of the Empire. He grew to enjoy being addressed as "Our Lord and God." We have no real evidence that Domitian personally enforced a universal observance of the emperor cult, but in certain areas—especially Asia Minor, to which Revelation is addressed—some governors and local officials demanded public participation in the cult to prove one's patriotism. During this period, persecution of Christians for refusing to worship the emperor seems to have been local and sporadic but fierce. Despite the lack of a concentrated official assault on the faith, John clearly feels a growing tension between church and state. His sense of impending conflict makes him regard Rome as a new Babylon, destroyer of God's people. Although empirewide persecution to create a holocaust of Christians did not arise until the third century, John accurately saw it coming and portrays it in his apocalypse.

Because Rome had recognized the Jews' monotheism, and because with the crushing of the Jewish revolt the Jews no longer looked like an organized threat, Rome generally exempted Jews from the emperor cult. Gentile Christians, and perhaps increasingly Jewish Christians, were not exempt, and because their movement grew rapidly, Rome became increasingly hostile to it. To most Romans, their "stubborn" refusal to honor any of the many Greco-Roman gods or deified emperors was not only unpatriotic but was also likely to bring down the gods' wrath on the Empire. Christians became known as unsocial "atheists" for their rejection of other gods except their own, and intolerant "haters of humankind." Labeled as a seditious secret society dangerous to the general welfare, early Christian groups increasingly endured social ostracism and hostility. When they also refused to pledge their allegiance to the emperor as a symbol of the Roman state, many local governors and other magistrates had them arrested, imprisoned, tortured, and even executed. To cite the most famous example, Pliny the Younger, a Roman governor of Bithynia (the province next door to Revelation's seven churches), wrote to the emperor Trajan inquiring about the government's official policy toward Christians (Pliny, *Letters* 10.96–97).

Pliny's situation around 112 C.E. may be similar to Revelation's around 95. Pliny reports that he did not hesitate to torture two slave women, who were deacons in a local church, and execute other believers. Now he was having second thoughts: should he punish people just because they were Christians, or should he punish them only if they committed actual crimes? The Emperor replied that although his governors were not to hunt for Christians or accept anonymous accusations against them, those who were found out as Christians and did not "repent" were to be punished—a type of ancient "don't ask, don't tell" policy. Both the emperor and Pliny clearly regarded Christians as a threat to the empire's security and treated them accordingly (Van Voorst 2000, 23–29).

www See the website for more on Pliny's investigation and prosecution of Christians.

Purpose

The purpose of Revelation is suggested by its opening line: the author wants the audience to "keep" the words of this book, that is, obey them. Particularly, they must stand true to the faith, and the author calls repeatedly for the endurance of the saints. The Christians for whom John writes were in crisis. They were faced with a small amount of Jewish opposition, growing public suspicion, and sporadic but fierce Roman governmental persecution. Many believers must have been tempted to renounce Christ, as Pliny asked his suspected Christian prisoners to do, and conform to the norms of Roman society. Recognizing that the costs of remaining Christian were terribly high, John recorded his visions of cosmic conflict to strengthen those whose faith wavered, assuring them that death is not defeat but victory. Revelation has a Christ-centered pattern for this message: Jesus died for his faith, and now his followers must follow in his steps. Just as Jesus offered no violent resistance to evil and taught his disciples to do the same, so too Revelation encourages peaceful, nonviolent resistance to Rome. God vindicated Jesus by resurrecting him to eternal life, and John's audience is to be propelled by hope for eternal life for themselves and the whole creation. The purpose of Revelation comes through clearly in the words of Jesus: "Be faithful unto death, and I will give you the crown of life" (2:10).

Social Scientific Reading of Revelation

Revelation depicts its audience as an oppressed group struggling against the vast social, economic, and ideological forces of the Roman Empire. It uses apocalyptic theology and imagery (in-group language) to encourage deeper religious commitment as the way to deal with this oppression.

Social Scientific Reading at Work
The Early Christian Challenge to the Roman Empire

This selection gives a helpful summary of the challenge that Christianity presented to the Roman Empire.

The Roman Empire, with its power relationships structured to benefit the ruling elite at the expense of most of the population, while simultaneously trying to persuade that population that Rome sought their best welfare and offered them maximum benefit, was vulnerable to parts of the first-century Christian movement. . . . The empire's vulnerability lay not in a direct military attack, the threat of assassination or coup, the risk of economic boycott or strike, but in its inability to secure and maintain attachment and loyalty. The very existence of the early Christian communities and texts points to people who did not find the imperial system politically, economically, militarily or ideologically (theologically) compelling. They created new relationships between ruler and ruled by constructing alternative, inclusive, more egalitarian communities with a more plausible worldview that asserted God's sovereignty and the agency of Jesus, disclosed the limitations of imperial claims, envisioned the certain defeat of Rome, and required appropriate social practices and behaviors. . . . Accordingly their threat lay in a combination of theological sabotage, social outflanking, and eschatological extermination. There is nothing more dangerous to an ideology than the presence of those who no longer take it for granted. . . . Christianity was at a profound level a deeply subversive force within the empire, because it denied and then undermined the religious legitimation of the ideology upon which the whole system was erected.

But this does not go far enough. It is not only a matter of "thinking makes it so." . . . The early Christian movement organized in groups, religio-political assemblies (*ekklesiae,* "churches"), that constituted an inclusive, egalitarian, international movement with alternative social structures, rituals, and practices to embody these understandings. . . . In so thinking and living, they created an alternative empire that sought different social structures and a compelling understanding of the world.

Question

How much of this discussion fits Revelation?

www See the website for a review of Paul Duff's 2001 book *Who Rides the Beast?* which argues that the author of Revelation uses dramatic license to construct a symbolic world of persecution.

Source: Warren Carter, "The Roman Empire Challenged by the First Christians," in Anthony J. Blasi and others, eds., *Handbook of Early Christianity: Social Science Approaches* (Walnut Creek, CA: Alta Mira Press, 2002), p. 487.

Feminist Reading of Revelation

The main point of Revelation is not gender specific. True to his apocalyptic style, the author can depict women symbolically: the woman prophet referred to as Jezebel (2:20); the woman in labor, clothed with the sun (12:1–17); the "Great Whore" (17:3–18:24), and the bride (18:23; 19:7–8; 21:2, 9–11; 22:17). Two of these uses are positive, two negative.

Feminist Reading at Work
The "Great Whore" in Feminist Critique (Rev. 17:3–18:24)

In this reading the feminist scholar Tina Pippin summarizes the meaning of this passage for feminist readers and suggests at the end a feminist ambivalence to it.

The most notorious symbolic female in the New Testament is the great whore of Babylon. . . . The whore is the symbol of the city and empire of Babylon. . . . She symbolizes political power, and her reign is characterized by extreme political oppression, especially of the saints and believers in Jesus Christ. Thus her downfall and destruction are particularly graphic, and some scholars note the cathartic impact of this narrative for first-century Christians under Roman rule.

As in the story of the woman prophet referred to as Jezebel in Rev 2:20, the accusations against the whore include illicit sex or "fornication," this time with the kings of the earth (17:2). The believers are warned against fornicating with her, and those who have are instructed to "come out of her" (18:4). The whore is also accused of being drunk with a wine that consists of the impurities of her fornication (17:2, 4) and also the blood of the saints and martyrs (17:6). . . . The whore is simultaneously a beautiful and horrifying figure. On her forehead (in the manner of marking slaves) is her name: "Babylon the great, mother of whores and of earth's abominations" (17:5). The multiple characterizations of the whore have inspired much art: she is depicted as beautiful, drunk, seductive, and dangerous. . . . She is arrogant in her luxurious lifestyle and says to herself, "I will never see grief" (18:7). . . . But the scene in Revelation is primarily one of judgment, and the whore is quickly brought down by the beast and its ten horns (kings). . . . The stripping, making desolate, eating and burning of her flesh bring her to a grotesque, violent end. . . .

Biblical prophets often characterize cities as female. This tendency continues in Revelation, in the symbols of the whore and the bride. . . . Many scholars focus on the downfall of the city as the destruction of an evil political power, ignoring the gender dimensions of the narrative. Some feminist scholars find a liberating message in this story of the destruction of the whore; the evil imperial system has fallen. Others note a more ambiguous reading by pointing out problems with symbolizing the evil political power as a woman and then destroying the woman.

Questions

1. Fill in some detail on the two alternatives presented in the last two sentences. What in particular might the first group and the second group say about this passage?

2. Some current feminist critiques complain that this passage is "pornographic." Do you agree? (Keep in mind that the derivation of this word is from the Greek "writing about prostitutes.")

Doing Feminist Reading Yourself

1. Aside from four symbolic figures in Revelation (Jezebel, the woman who gives birth to the child, the Great Whore and the bride), women are not mentioned often in this rather long book. Why is that?

2. The NRSV and other translations render male-oriented words in inclusive ways where the translators think both women and men are meant. Sometimes the way that this is done can be questioned. What critique might you make of Rev 21:3, where the Greek "men" (anthropōn, "humans") is rendered as "mortals"?

Cross-Cultural Reading of Revelation

Revelation has a worldwide, even cosmic, vision that envisions all peoples of the earth represented in the new heaven and earth. Various cross-cultural readers use it today to further the struggle of marginalized people against modern systems, especially international economic systems, seen by many Christians to be oppressive or even demonic.

Cross-Cultural Reading at Work
The Significance of Revelation for a Twentieth-Century Church

Professor K.-K. Yeo draws a parallel between the growth of apocalyptic in twentieth-century Chinese Christian experience and the book of Revelation.

Source: Yeo Khiok-Khng, *What Has Jerusalem to Do with Beijing? Biblical Interpretation from a Chinese Perspective* (Harrisburg, PA: Trinity Press, 1998), pp. 227, 228–229, 233. Copyright © 1998 Yeo Khiok-Khng. Used by permission.

The growth of apocalyptic in China is especially remarkable because Chinese culture in general is not eschatologically oriented.

The persecution of Christians in the book of Revelation arose from their resistance to emperor worship, their exclusive loyalty to Christ without compromising with the synagogue, and their persistent adherence to a faith at odds with the syncretistic practices of pagan religions. . . . The persecution experienced by Chinese Christians during the Cultural Revolution had its ideological-political and religious-philosophical cause, as did the persecution suffered by Christians in Roman times . . .

However, during the ten catastrophic years of the Cultural Revolution [1966–1976, a time of social and political upheaval instigated and directed by Mao Tse-tung, the Communist leader of China, in order to eliminate remnants of precommunist China such as organized religion], when all the church [buildings] were closed, house churches kept functioning and blossoming. . . . Most of these groups have loved to study the book of Revelation, from which they derive strength, faith, and hope. They hold to this apocalyptic hope in the midst of turmoil and danger. A high view of Christology helps them to hold fast to their faith. . . . The important doctrines they hold dear center around the sacrificial death, resurrection, and second coming of Christ. All these doctrines grant hope and assurance to these Christians.

The Book of Revelation did not give Chinese Christians during the Cultural Revolution merely existential strength; the book also infused them with a view of history different from that of the communists. Unlike the communists, Chinese Christians are able to see the world from the transcendent perspective in the apocalyptic visions of Revelation. Chinese Christians counter the communist, socialist, and human construction of utopian society by opening the world to divine transcendence and the New Heaven. By means of the motifs of visionary transportation to heaven, visions of God's throne room in heaven, angelic mediators of revelation, symbolic visions of political powers, coming judgment, and new creation, Chinese Christians see the final destiny of this despairing world in the transcendent divine purpose.

Question

List all the parallels you see between the situation of Chinese Christians in this reading and the situation you see in Revelation. What are the important commonalities and differences?

Key Terms and Concepts

apocalypse • apocalyptic literary style • apocalyptic theology • cosmic dualism
Gog and Magog • Lord's Day • millennium • moral/ethical dualism
predestination • temporal dualism • three ways to interpret Revelation

Questions for Study, Discussion, and Writing

1. Identify and discuss the characteristics of apocalyptic literature. When and where did this type of visionary writing originate, and what is its main purpose?
2. Compare the letters of Revelation 2–3 with the typical letter format of the time as seen in Paul's letters. What similarities and dissimilarities do you see?
3. Martin Luther spoke for many "mainstream" Christians when he said that Revelation did not truly reveal the nature of God and Christ. On the other hand, many Christians today take Revelation as the key book of the NT. Discuss the ethical strengths and religious limitations of John's view of God and God's plans for the human future, keeping in mind some of the different perspectives that different times and cultures might have.
4. Give your analysis of the British novelist D. H. Lawrence's comment on Revelation: "It is a rather repulsive work, not content till the whole world be destroyed, except that lake of fire in which those who fail to get in line might suffer eternally."
5. One of the features of Jewish and Christian apocalyptic is that as the end of time approaches, evil will get increasingly stronger until God intervenes to save the righteous and the physical world itself from annihilation. Can this be reconciled with other NT ideas of the suddenness and unexpectedness of the end of time? Why/not?
6. How can Christianity's belief (along with traditional Judaism and Islam) in an infinitely loving God be reconciled with a doctrine of eternal punishment for sinners?
7. Evaluate this claim made on the Public Broadcast System (PBS) website for its television show on Revelation: "Of all the books in the Bible, none has fired the Western imagination more than this one."
8. Reflect on this saying made by an expert on Christian eschatology to explain its viewpoint on violence: "Evil itself cannot be corrected; it can only be destroyed." Or, do you see a possible objection that it is wrong to depict God using force to overcome anything?
9. What does Revelation say about the eternal destiny of the Jewish people? See especially 7:1–8 and 11:1–13.
10. Revelation has a notable stress on the idea that Jesus is coming "soon." Does the fact that Jesus did not come "soon" mean that the value of this book for Christians is lost?

For Further Reading

Aune, David. *Prophecy in Early Christianity and the Ancient Mediterranean World.* Grand Rapids, MI: Eerdmans, 1983. Places Christian apocalyptic in historical perspective.

Collins, Adela Yarbro. *The Apocalypse.* Wilmington, DE: Glazier, 1979. An excellent commentary by an expert in apocalyptic.

Collins, Adela Yarbro. *Crisis and Catharsis: The Power of the Apocalypse.* Philadelphia: Westminster Press, 1984. Analysis of the sociopolitical and theological dimensions of John's visions.

Hanson, Paul D. *The Dawn of Apocalyptic: The Historical and Sociological Roots of Jewish Apocalyptic Eschatology.* Philadelphia: Fortress Press, 1979.

Hill, Craig. *In God's Time: The Bible and the Future.* Grand Rapids, MI: Eerdmans, 2002. This fine introduction to biblical eschatology, especially written for the current North

American religious scene, has a chapter on the Hebrew Bible book of Daniel and Revelation.

Koester, Craig. *Revelation and the End of All Things.* Grand Rapids, MI: Eerdmans, 2001. Intelligently discusses common questions about Revelation based on current scholarship.

Malina, Bruce J., and John J. Pilch. *Social Scientific Commentary on the Revelation.* Minneapolis: Fortress, 2000. An excellent resource for social scientific reading.

Perkins, Pheme. *The Book of Revelation.* Collegeville, MN: Liturgical Press, 1983. A brief and readable introduction.

Ramírez Fernández, Dagoberto. "The Judgment of God on the Multinationals: Revelation 18," in Leif Vaage, ed., *Subversive Scriptures: Revolutionary Readings of the Christian Bible in Latin America*, Valley Forge, NY: Trinity Press International, 1997, pp. 75–100. Argues that Revelation critiques not only Roman imperial economic domination, but also the economic system of modern global capitalism.

Part VI

After the New Testament

Chapter Twenty

Christian Origins after the New Testament

In this chapter we will examine a few important issues in NT study that arise after the writing of the NT documents themselves is largely complete. We will examine the formation of the NT canon, some books that the ancient church considered "on the border" of the NT, the challenge of Gnosticism, and finally the Apocryphal New Testament.

The Formation of the NT Canon

Today, someone opening a copy of the New Testament for the first time might be disturbed to find no list of contributors or editor's name. A plethora of literature on the formation of the New Testament, and the research it represents, demonstrates that these are issues of concern also for NT scholarship. How it was that twenty-seven documents have come to be accepted as authoritative Christian scripture out of a much wider array of early Christian literature remains only slightly less mysterious than the authorship of a number of those twenty-seven documents.

In the history of NT scholarship, different theories have been proposed concerning the adoption of certain writings as **canon,** the sacred and authoritative texts, and the rejection of others. Some theories see the formation of the NT canon almost wholly as a move by early leaders of a developing mainstream church to exclude sects or groups holding alternative interpretations of Jesus along with the writings they employed to support their claims. Others maintain that as individual Christian congregations networked to become a "Great Church," the gospel or gospels and apostolic letters that individual congregations held in reverence were shared, resulting in a broader collection that eventually became the New Testament. Still others see canonization as the work of a patriarchal Church hierarchy that only counted as authoritative those writings supporting, or at least benignly indifferent to, their position of power within the Church. However, most of the evidence available to us indicates that the formation of the New Testament canon was a long process that we can attribute to many different factors. To focus too specifically on any single probable factor as the determining one is an oversimplification.

The Gospels

Earliest Christianity was a scriptural religion to the degree that it maintained that the Hebrew Bible supported its claim that the crucified Jesus of Nazareth was the promised Messiah. However, the remembered words and works of Jesus were probably regarded as highly as the scriptures that were understood to promise his coming. Remembrances of what Jesus said and did circulated orally among the early Christians before being written down as narrative accounts of his life or collections of his teachings. Even after written narratives came into circulation, they did not immediately replace orally transmitted traditions about Jesus. For some time, oral traditions concerning Jesus and written accounts lived side by side in the church. Evidence of continued preference for the authority of oral tradition over written accounts is found in the writings of the early-second-century Bishop Papias, which have been preserved by the early church historian Eusebius:

> If I met with anyone who had been a follower of the elders anywhere, I made it a point to inquire what were the declarations of the elders. What was said by Andrew, Peter or Philip? What by Thomas, James, John, Matthew, or any other of the disciples of our Lord? What was said by Aristion, and the presbyter John, disciples of the Lord? I do not think that I derived so much benefit from books as from the living voice of those that are still surviving. (*Ecclesiastical History* 3.39.5)

Eventually, written narratives and collections of Jesus' sayings gained preference over oral tradition. Time distanced the continuing Jesus movement from reliable recollections of the apostles, all of whom were dead by the beginning of the second century. These short written narratives and sayings collections were the primary source material for the later comprehensive narratives we call gospels.

One of our canonical gospels, the Gospel of Mark, was perhaps the earliest comprehensive narrative gospel. As discussed previously, the authors of Luke and Matthew probably appropriated Mark along with other written as well as oral sources. The author of the Gospel of John apparently used sources generally independent of the Synoptic writers. However, these four were not the only gospels produced. Christian writers of the second century testify to many other gospels in circulation at that time. Until recently all we knew about most of these other gospels were their names. However, modern manuscript discoveries have brought to light full or partial texts of some of the more important of these noncanonical gospels, which will be discussed later in this chapter. It was not until late in the second century that the four gospels that eventually came to have canonical status achieved a level of authority in the church above the others. Even then, gospels other than Matthew, Mark, Luke, and John retained regional authority and popularity.

A contributing factor to the acceptance of Matthew, Mark, Luke, and John as authoritative, and finally canonical, may have been the use of these gospels together by the end of the second century as a fourfold collection. The reception of the four together is contrary to their original intentions: it was the aim of each of the gospel authors to offer a comprehensive narrative with its own theological interpretation of Jesus for the use of a specific Christian community. Exactly how the four came to be regarded together as a collection and used as such remains a mystery. Perhaps as Matthew, Mark, and Luke circulated among the various Christian communities during the early years of the second century, they came to be received as reliable accounts based upon their corroborating testimony. The acceptance of the Gospel of John by most second-century Christians was more problematic because of its differing perspective and its employment by Christian groups outside the developing mainstream church.

The earliest testimony to the use of the four canonical gospels together comes, ironically, from an attempt to weave them together into a single reconciled document. About the year 170, Tatian, a Syrian converted to Christianity at Rome under the influence of Justin Martyr, composed the *Diatessaron,* a harmonization of Matthew, Mark, Luke, and John into a single coherent work. Tatian appropriately borrowed his title from a musical term designating a series of four harmonious tones. The *Diatessaron* became widely popular, demonstrating the unease many Christians felt over the use of multiple gospels. While the *Diatessaron* enjoyed immediate popularity, it was rather short lived and probably did more to promote the authority of Matthew, Mark, Luke, and John as a collection than to promote a single harmonized version. After composing the *Diatessaron,* Tatian returned to Syria, where he founded a sect of radical ascetics called the Encratites, who rejected marriage, eating meat, and drinking wine. The danger that Christianity would dissolve into syncretism put pressure on the church to firmly delineate what writings were and were not authoritative for Christian faith and practice. A singular gospel account, even a harmonized one such as the *Diatessaron,* was unacceptable given the diversity of contexts among the Christian communities that had formed by the end of the second century. But uncritical employment of every gospel circulating at that time was not an acceptable alternative.

Ten years after Tatian's *Diatessaron* (c. 180), Irenaeus, Bishop of Lyons, wrote in defense of accepting only the four gospels known today as canonical in *The Refutation and Overthrow of the Knowledge Falsely So Called,* later known popularly as *Against Heresies.* The bulk of Irenaeus' argument proceeds in elaborate allegory, comparing the fourfold nature of the gospel as presented in Matthew, Mark, Luke, and John to the four principal winds and the four creatures of Ezekiel's vision in Ezekiel 1. However, it is notable that Irenaeus promotes Matthew, Mark, Luke, and John also on the basis that the major heretical groups each employ one of these gospels, albeit wrongly interpreted, in defense of their teaching, and that each group can be refuted through a correct interpretation of the very gospel they each employ (*Against Heresies* 3.11.7–9). Certainly those groups coming to be identified as outside authentic Christianity employed other writings in defense of their teachings. But Irenaeus' comments in *Against Heresies* indicate that by the end of the second century, disputes focused as much upon interpretation of the later-canonized gospels as upon what gospels should or should not be accepted as genuine witnesses to Jesus Christ.

A further witness to the acceptance of Matthew, Mark, Luke, and John in lieu of all others comes from a manuscript fragment of an ancient list of authoritative Christian writings known as the *Muratorian canon*. The manuscript fragment is only partially preserved, beginning with a discussion of Luke as the third gospel. However, statements on the authority of Matthew and Mark may be safely presupposed. The Muratorian canon defends the fourfold gospel witness against the argument of discrepancies among the four, claiming that the Holy Spirit has inspired in each account everything essential to salvation and that any discrepancies are really inconsequential for the faith of believers. Traditionally the Muratorian canon has been dated to the late second or early third century. However, recent analysis of the fragment has argued for a much later dating, in the early to middle fourth century (Hahneman 1992).

Second-century Christianity found that a fourfold collection was the impetus from external challenges and from internal pressures for delineating from a broad field of gospel narratives. The fourfold collection became authoritative for the Great Church, although the four gospels were not recognized as the only canonical gospels until much later. Now that we have briefly considered the early history leading eventually to the canonization of the four gospels, we turn our attention to the making of the epistolary section of the New Testament.

The Pauline Epistles

Of the twenty-seven documents comprising the New Testament, thirteen are letters traditionally attributed to Paul. Although the earliest document in the New Testament is probably 1 Thessalonians, citations by second-century writers indicate that the gospels were accepted as authoritative before any of the Pauline letters. The question of authority regarding Paul's letters is not so much a question of which should be accepted and which should not, but rather why occasional letters to particular churches should ever have been collected and regarded as universally authoritative in the first place.

It is possible the Pauline letters first came to be esteemed not because of their theological content or their universal applicability but because of the reverence accorded Paul himself by early church leaders. A second possible influence may have been a "Pauline school"—a group of Paul's disciples who sought to preserve the legacy of his teaching by gathering and circulating his letters as a collection. Such a school may also have been responsible for generalizing redactions in ancient manuscripts of Romans, 1 Corinthians, and Ephesians that made the letters more universally appealing. Furthermore, the deutero-Pauline letters may be attributable to this theoretical school of disciples because they sought to expand the influence of the apostle's thought after his death. This school, if it indeed existed, may have also employed numerological considerations to bolster its efforts. Nine letters in the

Pauline corpus are addressed to seven churches. That seven is a number signifying completeness in the Old Testament was not lost on second-century Christians. This numerological connection with completeness was only further enhanced by including the Pastoral Epistles and attributing Hebrews to Paul, which brought the total number of epistles in the Pauline corpus to fourteen, or two times seven.

Another catalyst for including the Pauline letters in the New Testament canon came via the thought and work of **Marcion,** a heretical teacher of mid-second-century Rome. Marcion rejected the Old Testament, seeing it as a witness to an inferior deity or demiurge mistakenly worshiped by the Jews. Jesus was the messenger not of this inferior deity who had created the material realm, but of the great God of Goodness. He maintained that the twelve apostles had misunderstood Jesus completely, had mistaken him for the expected Messiah of the Jews, and thereby corrupted his teaching. Marcion was convinced that Paul alone had grasped the real identity of Jesus and the significance of his teaching. Marcion based this theory upon what he understood as Paul's rejection of the Jewish Law. Of the gospels circulating among the churches of the second century, Marcion accepted only the Gospel according to Luke—probably upon the understanding that Luke had been the traveling companion and disciple of Paul. Even this gospel Marcion edited extensively in order to purge from it what he maintained were Judaizing interpolations. To his edited version of Luke he then joined Paul's nine letters to the seven churches and the letter to Philemon to form a unified canon. This *Marcionite canon* provided a coherent text to serve as the basis for Marcion's own teaching.

Marcion's teaching spread rapidly across the Mediterranean world through the second half of the second century, becoming a formidable threat to mainstream Christianity. As Marcionite teaching challenged the church, the Marcionite canon exerted pressure upon the church to clearly define its own canon, but the exact nature of this interaction remains debated. Did Marcion develop his canon from a more comprehensive one already tacitly acknowledged by the church, or did his canon come first with the church following his lead (and including in its canon Petrine and Johannine writings in reaction to Marcion's Pauline emphasis)? This chicken-or-egg debate will continue. What can be said with some degree of accuracy is that Marcion's activity forced mainstream Christianity to articulate the faith more clearly and accelerated the already existing process of fixing a New Testament canon.

The Acts of the Apostles, the General Epistles, and Revelation

Christian writings other than gospels and the letters of Paul proliferated in the second century, yet only a few of these eventually came to be accepted as authoritative. Why and how those writings were included remains enigmatic. Even today, when canonical writings such as Hebrews and Revelation are compared with canonically excluded works such as *1 Clement* and *The Shepherd of Hermas,* one might wonder on what grounds some writings were accepted and others rejected.

The Acts of the Apostles, though written as a companion to the Gospel according to Luke, seems to have been neglected through the first half of the second century. It may have gained a broader readership as Christianity spread and later church leaders appealed to it as evidence for the unity of the apostles and their doctrine in confronting heterodox teaching. The Muratorian canon list, which may have been composed as early as the late second century, includes Acts as an authoritative book.

The Letter to the Hebrews enjoyed earlier popularity in the Eastern church, but there is little evidence that it was much regarded in Latin regions of the church through much of the second century. It is not included in the Muratorian list. The authorship of Hebrews has been debated since the time of Origen. However, it was theological content rather than the question of authorship that prevented widespread use of the Epistle. Statements in Hebrews were seen to promote a doctrine that sins committed after baptism cannot be forgiven—a position that did not favor the Latin church in its struggle against the morally rigorist Montanist sect during the second half of the second century. Eusebius, writing in the early fourth century, notes that some Christians of Rome even then did not consider Hebrews an authoritative work (*Ecclesiastical History* 6.20.3).

Like Hebrews, Revelation suffered from theological suspicion. It was, however, accepted earlier in the Christian West than in the East. In the East, millennialist groups interpreted the book literally in support of their views. We may illustrate the ambiguous canonical position of Revelation in early Christianity by noting that it was included in the Muratorian list and classified as disputed by Eusebius in his *Ecclesiastical History* (3.25.4).

The early history of the letters of James, Jude, 1 and 2 Peter, and 1, 2, and 3 John are almost completely unknown. The use of 1 Peter and 1 and 2 John by Christians of the second century is only sparingly attested. James, 2 Peter, and 3 John remain totally unattested until the third and fourth centuries. Like Hebrews and Revelation, the authority of these later epistles remained contested, even as late as the sixteenth century. Disputed authorship of these later epistles produced hesitation to accept them as authoritative. They gained status and approval regionally during the late third through the fourth centuries as they came to be employed by the mainstream church against divergent forms of Christian teaching.

By the middle of the fourth century, there seems to have developed a growing consensus concerning the Christian canon. The thirty-ninth **Festal Letter of Bishop Athanasius** of Alexandria names as authoritative the same twenty-seven books we find in the contemporary New Testament. Late in the fourth century, the Council of Hippo and Council of Carthage each published lists of exclusively authoritative Christian Scripture naming the 27 books of the current New Testament. These council lists were statements of agreement among church leaders about what writings already had de facto authority in the churches, but these were regional synods that could not speak for the church universally. The ancient church prepared no universally binding definition of a Christian canon, declaring once and for all the official contents of the New Testament. One could argue that the NT defined itself in the church, not the other way around.

www See the website for an essay on canonical criticism of the NT.

On the Borders of the New Testament

It is appropriate here to consider several significant early Christian works that lie just outside the margins of the New Testament. Three of the writings here considered were noted as authoritative by a number of early church leaders and were so employed in worship and in ordering congregational life. The other works we will survey here were never serious candidates for the canon but are mentioned as primary resources for the study of second-century church life.

www Follow the link to the writings discussed in this section and the following section at the excellent Early Christian Writings website.

1 Clement

1 Clement is a good example of the didactic epistles circulated in response to internal crises that faced the church in the late first and early second centuries. The name of Clement does not appear in direct connection with the text of this work as we have it. The letter was ascribed to Clement of Rome by very ancient church tradition. The exact nature of this Clement's position in the church at Rome is disputed. Early episcopal lists name him as the third bishop of Rome, but this may be reading back a later hierarchical development into the letter's provenance. Attempts to identify him with the Clement of Philippians 4:3 are conjectures. The letter is addressed to the church at Corinth and most probably dates to sometime between the years 95 and 100.

1 Clement was written by a church leader, or leaders, in Rome to the church at Corinth in response to a revolt there in which the ruling presbyters of the church had been deposed. The Roman church, having received indirect word on the matter, sought to intervene in order to set things right. Such intervention was not unusual. Local congregations did not see themselves as isolated, autonomous units but understood themselves as a part of the larger body of the greater church. As individual Christians maintained a feeling of responsibility for each other and accountability to one another, the same was true for congregations. Church leaders in Rome would have felt a natural responsibility to lovingly admonish and intervene at Corinth.

There is no indication that church leaders in Rome felt themselves in a superior position to the church at Corinth as was later the case.

Where *1 Clement* does foreshadow later hierarchical developments in the church is in the letter's view of the ministry. The letter presses the authority of the duly ordained presbyter-bishops (there is no clear distinction between these titles in *1 Clement*) and admonishes the dissidents at Corinth to submit to them. Supporters of the later-developed doctrine of apostolic succession point to the view expressed in *1 Clement* as a precedent. However, there remains disagreement about how some of the Greek phrasing of the passage used to support apostolic succession should be interpreted. Arguments for electing presbyters and for the right of presbyters to ordain have been advanced from the same passage in the letter. In either case, the submission of the congregation to the guidance and rule of the clergy, so long as the later are faithful in their ministry, is defended.

The author of *1 Clement* appeals to the orderliness of creation as an example for reestablishing proper church order at Corinth. He recommends faithfulness, hospitality, and humility based upon numerous examples drawn from the stories of the Hebrew Scriptures, the Jesus tradition, and the lives of the apostles. He cites the destructive consequences of envy and rivalry in the Cain and Abel story (Genesis 4), the revolt of Korah, Abiram, and Dathan against Moses (Numbers 16), and the troubled relationship between David and Saul (1 Samuel 18) in exhorting the Corinthians to desist from schism.

The Letter of Barnabas

The **Letter of Barnabas** was attributed by ancient tradition to the early missionary companion of Paul, but it is really the work of an Eastern Christian teacher of the early second century. It probably dates to sometime soon after 131, since it references the construction of a pagan temple in Jerusalem, reflecting the temple to Jupiter built by Hadrian after the Second Jewish Revolt. It is included in one of the oldest complete Greek manuscripts of the New Testament, and both Clement of Alexandria and Origen considered it scripture.

Barnabas does not resemble an ancient epistle, but rather is a treatise on the Christian allegorical interpretation of the Old Testament according to the method developed in Alexandria and employed in the Greek East. The letter derides the Jews as having misinterpreted their own scriptures, which led them to reject Jesus as the messiah to whom their scriptures pointed.

> But what do you think it typifies, that Israel was commanded that the men whose sins were full grown should offer a heifer, and slaughter it and burn it, and then boys should take the ashes and put them into bowls, and tie scarlet wool on a stick of wood (notice again the type of the cross and the scarlet wool) and take hyssop, and then the boys should sprinkle the people one by one, so that they

may be purified from their sins? Notice how plainly he is speaking to you. The calf is Jesus, the sinful men who offer it are those who brought him to be slain. Then they are no longer mere men, the glory no longer belongs to sinners. The boys who sprinkled are those who preached to us the forgiveness of sins and the purification of the heart. To them—they were twelve in number, as a testimony to the tribes, for there are twelve tribes of Israel—he gave authority to preach the gospel. But why are there three boys that sprinkle? To testify to Abraham, Isaac, and Jacob, for they were great in the sight of God. And why was the wool placed on the stick of wood? Because the reign of Jesus rests upon wood, and those who hope in him will live forever. And why the wool and the hyssop together? Because in his reign there will be evil and corrupt days, in which we will be saved, because he who suffers in body is cured through the juice of the hyssop. And that they happened for this reason is evident to us, but obscure to them, because they have not listened to the voice of the Lord.

Contemporary methods of biblical interpretation look askance at the allegorical method of interpretation, but it was an accepted method in antiquity. Furthermore, its accepted use in interpreting the Old Testament was important for the spread of Christianity among educated Gentiles and Hellenistic Jews in the first three centuries.

The Shepherd of Hermas

Notable early Christian leaders, such as Clement of Alexandria, Origen, Irenaeus, and, for a time, Tertullian, accepted *The Shepherd of Hermas,* a second-century apocalypse, as scripture. It probably received its final form some time around 150, although some scholars believe it may have originated in a primitive form in the early years of the second century.

The author of the book identifies himself as Hermas, a freed slave, who received a series of revelations. The revelations are first given to Hermas through an appearance by his former owner and later through the angel of repentance, whom Hermas identifies as the Shepherd. The form of revelation found in Hermas approximates that found in the apocryphal 2 Esdras, in which the Old Testament figure Ezra records his interview with the angel Uriel. Hermas understands himself as entrusted with these revelations in order to proclaim a time of rigorous repentance among believers.

The first set of visions, delivered by Hermas' former owner, Rhoda, presents a symbolic building up of the church as a stone tower. Different qualities of stone are representative of believers: some are already made part of the final structure, but others are not of appropriate quality to be included. Their fitness, or lack thereof, is demonstrative of their repentance and faithfulness. The second set of visions consists of twelve commandments, expostulated at length by the Shepherd to Hermas. They are moralistic prohibitions against sexual sins, the love of riches, and ill tempers as well as positive commandments to poverty, chastity, and rejoicing in suffering.

The final section of the book is made up of ten "parables," which are really extended allegories. These allegories hearken back to the earlier visions Hermas received from Rhoda, symbolically representing different categories of believers according to their level of repentance and their faithfulness in life.

The Shepherd of Hermas seems to be addressed to the doctrinal question about repentance from postbaptismal sin. In its extended exhortation to repentance before the imminent and rapidly approaching close of the age, the book holds that those who commit grave sins after baptism, such as apostasy, may be restored to communion, as illustrated by the allegorical Parable 9:

> So when the glorious man, the owner of the whole tower, had finished these things, he called the shepherd to him and turned over to him all the stones that were lying beside the tower, which had been removed from the building, and said to him, "Clean these stones carefully, and put the ones that fit the rest into the structure of the tower, and throw the ones that do not fit far from the tower." After giving the shepherd these orders, he left the tower, with all those with whom he had come, but the girls stood around the tower, guarding it. I said to the shepherd, "How can these stones go back into the structure of the tower after being rejected?" He answered me, saying, "Do you see these stones?" said he. "I do, sir," said I. "The largest part of these stones," he said, "I will shape and put into the building, and they will fit with the rest of the stones." (Goodspeed 1950, 179)

Like Revelation, *The Shepherd of Hermas* claims authority on the basis of being a heavenly vision mediated by a chosen seer. However, where Revelation is a vision delivered chiefly by the risen and ascended Christ to a recognized elder of the church, *The Shepherd of Hermas* is an apocalypse chiefly delivered by an unknown angel to an apparent lay Christian.

The Didache

The origination of the **Didache** is shrouded in mystery. At one time thought to be an ancient document contemporary with the canonical gospels, further study has determined the *Didache* to date sometime to the first half of the second century. *Didache* (Greek "teaching") is the common title for the book also known as *The Teaching of the Twelve Apostles*. It consists of two main parts. The first part is a sort of catechism or code of Christian moral conduct presented as a choice between "Two Ways": the Way of Life and the Way of Death. The second part is a manual of church order, dealing with sacramental administration, fasting, the treatment of itinerant prophets, and the ministry of bishops and deacons. The treatise concludes with a brief exhortation to faithfulness as the end of the age approaches.

It has been argued that the first part of the *Didache* is a Jewish catechism with Christian interpolations from the Gospel of Luke, the Gospel of Matthew, and even

The Shepherd of Hermas. Though whether or not the *Didache* is a reworked Jewish document remains disputed among scholars, it does demonstrate relationship with the documents here named. Furthermore, a slightly variant form of this portion of the *Didache* is found appended to *The Letter of Barnabas* in its final form.

The manual of church order, which makes up the second part of the *Didache,* represents a probable compilation of late-first- or early-second-century church practices, meant to guide rural congregations in the Christian East, probably Syria. As such, it reflects church life and administration at a very early date. References to the offices of bishops, or "overseers," and deacons indicate that the office of bishop was not yet separate from the presbyters. Itinerant "apostles and prophets" are recognized as a regular part of church life, with directions for welcoming them and testing their teaching for genuineness. Instructions for administration of the Eucharist, or Lord's Supper, indicate that the Christian sacred meal was still being conducted as a full meal rather than only the symbolic bread and wine and that the unbaptized were excluded from participation.

The Martyrdom of Polycarp

The Martyrdom of Polycarp is the narrative account of the death of the aged Bishop Polycarp of Smyrna, who was executed by local Roman authority in 155 or 156 for his confession of Christianity. The account was authored soon after the event as a letter from the church at Smyrna, along the Aegean coast of Asia Minor, to the church at Philomelium, some two hundred miles to the east. Replete with the miraculous signs attending the death of a Christian saint (notable in the stories of Christian martyrdom from the second and third centuries), *The Martyrdom of Polycarp* is a moving narrative that relates the arrest, trial, and execution of the eighty-six-year-old bishop of Smyrna. The actual cause of the outbreak of persecution in Smyrna leading to Polycarp's death is not told in the narrative, but much of the blame is laid to the city's Jewish population. The story is significant as a very early testimony to the practice of the veneration of the saints and martyrs and their relics.

The Martyrdom of Polycarp marks the beginning of a voluminous literature of martyrdom that has remained a significant genre of Christian literature even to the present day. Such stories echo the passion of Jesus and have inspired Christian fortitude and faithfulness everywhere in the face of hardship and persecution.

To conclude this section: The few extra-canonical writings we have surveyed here provide only a sampling of a large body of Christian literature produced in the second century, some of which, at least for a time and in a limited region, was regarded as authoritative. At a first reading, it may not be apparent what prevented some of these works from being included with the twenty-seven books of the New Testament. However with a deeper reading and analysis of the texts some conclusions may be deduced. In some cases, a work's **christology,** the understanding of the person and work of Jesus, is confused or not harmonious with the other writings fully accepted as authoritative. For instance, *The Shepherd of Hermas* sometimes favors an *adoptionist christology,* the idea that God adopted Jesus as God's son sometime during his life. At other times it presents Jesus as co-eternal with God. In some cases, the authorship and origination of a text was so dubious as to exclude it. Some documents were very early seen as profitable for reading, but lacking *apostolicity*: the witness to apostolic teaching that was necessary to be accepted as authoritative. Perhaps the single most important factor for understanding how some works became part of the New Testament and how some did not lies in the relationship between the development of the New Testament canon and the development of the church **catholic.** As is well known, *catholic* means not only "universal," but also "according to the whole." The majority church identified itself as catholic not only because of its universal nature, but also because it included the unified witness of all the apostles. Those books that came to be part of the canon were broad enough in their subject and outlook to qualify for inclusion. Works such as we have surveyed here that remained outside the canon were often excluded at the last because they failed the test of catholicity. Their focus and subject were too narrow, and they could not speak authoritatively to a "church catholic." In grasping something of this relationship, we can understand better how the New Testament formed the church while at the same time the church formed the New Testament.

The Challenge of Gnosticism

We have previously mentioned **Gnosticism,** but we have reserved our discussion of this religious movement until now in order to more fully treat its rise and challenge to Christianity. For it was Gnosticism more than any other system of teaching, group, or movement that posed the greatest threat to second-century Christianity.

The term *Gnosticism* comes from the Greek word *gnosis,* meaning "knowledge." Gnostic thought systems were based upon the notion that the reception of a body of secret knowledge, accessible only to the truly spiritual, is necessary for salvation. An exact definition of Gnosticism can be difficult. Gnostic systems varied, and there were Christian and non-Christian forms of Gnosticism. A brief review of its development in the ancient world may help us to understand Gnosticism without necessarily defining it.

Gnosticism arose at almost precisely the same time as Christianity, perhaps finding seminal form during, or in the years immediately following, the life of Jesus. Evidence suggests, and most scholars believe today, that it developed within the wisdom speculation and apocalypticism characteristic of the religious turmoil created by the intersection of Hellenism with Judaism (Perkins 1993). At the heart of all Gnostic teaching was a core myth concerning the regrettable creation of the material universe and the way in which individuals could find salvation out of their gross material existence.

Gnosticism posited a supreme god whose desire was for a spiritual reality only. Consequently, this god created only spiritual beings. One of these spiritual beings, ignorant of the supreme god, or jealous of the supreme god's creative powers, independently attempted to create and birthed the material world. Therefore creation, rather than being understood as something good, was considered by the Gnostics a horrible mistake, an "abortion" birthed by an inferior spiritual being, that was contrary to spiritual reality and the intentional will of the supreme god. Nonetheless, since the material world is the creation of a spiritual being, there exists within it "sparks" of spirit. These sparks have been imprisoned within human beings, though not all human beings. Some human beings are completely carnal, without redeemable spirit. They cannot spiritually apprehend the gnosis and thus are doomed to the eventual destruction awaiting the material realm. The spiritual, those who have a spark of spirit, can apprehend the **gnosis:** the secret spiritual knowledge necessary to free the spirit from its imprisonment in the material human body, where it is subject to the needs and passions of the flesh. However, the gnosis is not present in the material world. It must be delivered to the spiritual by a messenger-redeemer sent from the supreme god. Only those who are spiritual can apprehend from the messenger-redeemer the saving significance of the gnosis. With this gnosis, the spiritual can avoid the pitfalls and traps set by the evil spiritual powers ruling in the intermediate heavenly spheres between the material world and the supreme spiritual reality, and thus return to the bliss of their origin.

Gnostic speculation found an agreeable home within Christianity, interpreting Jesus as the spiritual messenger-redeemer. A Gnostic understanding and interpretation of the saving work of Jesus probably grew up side by side with what would eventually become orthodox teaching. In Christianity's earliest years, when it was a developing Jewish sect without its own sacred writings or established doctrine and relying upon oral tradition in following Jesus as the Messiah, the differences between the two were not clearly defined. As the first century passed into the second, eyewitnesses to Jesus died and later generation believers became the leaders of a markedly Gentile religion teaching less from oral tradition and more from written accounts. Christian teaching evolved from apostolic reminiscence of Jesus to interpretation of this apostolic witness. With this evolution, the difference between understanding Jesus as self-sacrificial messiah-redeemer or Jesus as Gnostic messenger-redeemer became more pronounced.

By the mid-second century, the didactic differences between Gnostic Christians and the majority church were clearly defined, and in critical conflict. The chief difference between the two was fundamental, lying at the core of theistic religion. This fundamental difference lay in their doctrines of God, which of course impacted all other doctrines, practices, and church life.

In most Gnostic teaching, the God of the Hebrew Scriptures was understood as the lesser creator deity, or **demiurge** (from the Greek *demiurgos* = "creator"), who sought to rule over human beings as a tyrannical lord and master through law and judgment. This god was not the father of Jesus, but rather Jesus was the messenger-redeemer sent from the supreme god and bearing the gnosis into the world. In fact, in Gnosticism the relationship of the messenger-redeemer Christ to the person of Jesus of Nazareth was complex. In some Gnostic teaching, the messenger-redeemer Christ "borrowed" the human Jesus until the crucifixion, then abandoned him to his grisly fate. In other Gnostic traditions Jesus only seemed to have a material body, which was really an illusion. This idea was labeled ***docetism*** (Greek *dokeo* = "to seem"). Gnosticism was forced to deal with the relationship between the divine Christ and the human Jesus in such manner because to have the messenger-redeemer suffer bodily would have meant that he, too, had been trapped in the material realm. Gnosticism had no need for the resurrection, since it was redemption *from* the body that was sought, not redemption *of* the body. What had saving import was not the death of the redeemer, but his teaching.

The gnosis, according to later Gnostic teaching, was passed from Christ (mostly after the crucifixion of Jesus, but before his return to the Gnostic **pleroma,** or highest spiritual realm) to the apostles, who in turn passed on the gnosis as secret revelation to a second generation of the spiritually elect. These disciples in turn became Gnostic spiritual masters teaching a succeeding generation, and so on. Gnostic Christians understood their initial salvation as having freed their spirits from the passions of the flesh and from bondage to the demiurge. Freedom of the spirit from the flesh led some to severe asceticism, punishing the body as a means of putting it under control of the spirit. Others, however, took a libertine route, claiming that the unbridled actions of the flesh were inconsequential since the liberated spirit was all that really mattered. Both responses were fostered by the devaluation of the material world. Freedom from the control of the demiurge put one on an individual spiritual journey meant to lead eventually toward final salvation in reunification with the pleroma. Thus Gnostic Christianity was highly individualistic.

Those who believed themselves enlightened by the gnosis tended also to see themselves as spiritually advanced beyond the level of "ordinary" Christians, who were still in need of the ordinances of the church and ministry of its clergy. Gnostic Christians generally did not acknowledge the authority of most clergy. For them, spiritual authority was a matter of one's spiritual advancement through the apprehension of the gnosis rather than church hierarchy and clerical order. Here is perhaps the area in which the conflict between Gnostic Christians and the rest of the church became the most pronounced.

Bishops sought to excommunicate and expel Gnostic Christians from the church catholic. This effort proved neither simple nor easy. History indicates that the Gnostics did not seek separation from their "fleshly" brothers and sisters, but desired to remain within the church. Furthermore, Gnostics could publicly profess the same beliefs as catholic Christians while privately maintaining a different interpretation of that profession. Some scholars have seen the movement to expel Gnostic Christians from the church as a political move of the established clergy, who felt their place and position of power threatened by these spiritual elitists. Such a proposition may be reading too much medieval clericalism back into the second century, when recognized clergy were more likely to be the first targets of persecution than to hold any position of public power or respect. It is just as likely that early church leaders saw the potential dangers posed to the church's sense of community and mission by Gnosticism, which could not, by its very nature, ever envision a community of the baptized as the body of Christ.

Another important dividing line between Gnostics and catholic Christians was the writings they each regarded as authoritative. Those gospels and other writings that the Gnostics employed relied upon the same sources as the works that came to be regarded as canonical for the church catholic, but with Gnostic theological interpretation given to the material. For many years, we knew little about these texts beyond quotations in writings by those who opposed the Gnostics. In 1945, however, near the Egyptian village of Nag Hammadi, a peasant accidentally unearthed from the desert a cache of buried codices containing Gnostic Christian texts, previously known only in fragments and by quotation and reference in the writings of the early church fathers. In the so-called Nag Hammadi Library were found copies of the *Gospel of Thomas*, the *Gospel of Philip*, the *Gospel of Truth*, the *Gospel to the Egyptians*, the *Secret Book of James*, the *Apocryphon of John*, the *Apocalypse of Peter*, the *Apocalypse of Paul*, and the *Letter of Peter to Philip*. Each of the texts found at Nag Hammadi expresses a theology amenable to Gnosticism. None of the Nag Hammadi texts enjoys a favorable ancient witness as authoritative scripture.

The Apocryphal New Testament

The church's exclusion of certain texts employed by Gnostic Christians and other groups to validate their own interpretation of Jesus is an example of the church's growing concept of catholicity. As we discussed early in this chapter, the fourfold Gospel, which eventually gained canonical status, was broad and included apostolic testimony to Jesus that reflected the continuing testimony to Jesus in the living church. This is true also for the letters of the New Testament attributable to a single apostle. The letters of Paul, for instance, complement the overall witness to Jesus in the Gospels and the rest of the New Testament. Gnostic teachers and sect groups, on the other hand, tended to employ a single gospel for which they claimed authority above, or in opposition to, other witnesses. Likewise, the Gnostic texts themselves often demonstrate a kind of theological particularism that is contrary to catholicity. Nonetheless, these excluded gospels and other literature can serve as important sources for gaining a deeper understanding of the early history of Christianity as it spread into the world.

The **Apocryphal New Testament,** or NT Apocrypha, is a large body of approximately ninety extra-NT Christian writings penned from the end of the first century to the ninth. Many scholars now prefer the term "Early Christian Apocrypha" because most of these writings are only remotely related to the NT and many of them were written before the NT canon was finalized. Here, however, we keep to the traditional term. These writings claim to have been written by the apostles or those close to them. A few, like the *Gospel of Peter,* were used in some mainstream Christian churches at first. Over time the Great Church rejected their canonicity, and these writings became "apocryphal," or hidden. Unlike the Old Testament Apocrypha, which many Christians accept as canonical, the NT Apocrypha is today universally rejected as a valid part of the canonical NT. The NT Apocrypha has been organized according to the NT genres that it contains: gospels, acts, letters, and apocalypses, but there is considerably more blending of genres than in the NT. The scholarly study of the NT Apocrypha is in an intermediate stage and still draws predominantly on the historical-critical method. Recently, the discovery of the Nag Hammadi literature has breathed new life into this study. The NT Apocrypha forms a main witness to Christian views of Jesus, approved and disapproved by the early mainstream church, in the formative centuries of the faith.

The Gospel of Thomas

The **Gospel of Thomas,** unknown except for citation by Hippolytus and Origen until its rediscovery at Nag Hammadi, contains 114 sayings of Jesus. The copy discovered at Nag Hammadi dates between 70 and 140. Most interpreters place it in the early second century, although the oral tradition behind this gospel is much older. The *Gospel of Thomas* is written in Coptic and titled only at the end. The text begins (without a title), "These are the sayings which the living Jesus spoke and which Didymus Judas Thomas wrote down."

The sayings recorded in the *Gospel of Thomas* are most often organized according to catchwords, which demonstrates a near proximity in time to an older oral tradition for the collection. They come in several forms: proverbs and other wisdom sayings, parables, prophetic sayings, and very brief "dialogues." About one-quarter of the sayings are nearly identical to sayings in the Synoptic Gospels. About one-half of the sayings have partial parallels in the canonical Gospels. The remaining one-quarter to about one-third of the sayings are undoubtedly Gnostic, with a different theological perspective than the rest. A sampling of the sayings in the *Gospel of Thomas* will demonstrate this internal diversity. First, here are sayings 20 and 54, which are nearly identical to sayings of Jesus found in the Synoptic Gospels:

20. The disciples said to Jesus, " Tell us, what is the Kingdom of Heaven like?" He said to them, "It is like a mustard seed, smaller than all seeds. But when it falls on plowed ground, it puts forth a large shrub and becomes a shelter for the birds of heaven."
54. Jesus said, "Blessed are the poor, for yours is the Kingdom of Heaven."

Sayings 89 and 102 have parallels in the canonical gospels:

89. Jesus said, "Why do you wash the outside of the cup? Do you not know that he who made the inside is also he who made the outside."

102. Jesus said, "Woe to the Pharisees; they are like a dog lying in the oxen's food trough, for he does not eat nor let the oxen eat."

Sayings 18 and 29 are "semi-Gnostic":

18. The disciples said to Jesus, "Tell us how our end will occur." Jesus said, "Have you found the beginning that you search for the end? In the place of the beginning, there the end will be. Blessed is he who will stand at the beginning, and he will know the end, and he will not taste death."

29. Jesus said, "If the flesh exists because of spirit, it is a miracle, but if spirit (exists) because of the body, it is a miracle of miracles. But I marvel at how this great wealth established itself in this poverty."

The Gospel of Thomas cannot be called Gnostic in the fullest sense, since it lacks a formal Gnostic mythology and other elements of formally Gnostic literature. However, it does present a "gnosticizing" interpretation of some Jesus material, as demonstrated in the preceding sample of sayings.

The *Gospel of Thomas* bears little resemblance to what we know as a gospel. It has, in fact, no narrative element at all. But its rich collection of sayings, many of which may go back to early stages of Jesus tradition, shed light on parallel passages in the Synoptic Gospels. Gnosticizing sayings must, of course, be ruled out in this comparison. However, the remainder of the collection has potential value for better understanding the teaching of Jesus.

The Gospel of Peter

Mention of a *Gospel of Peter* occurs in some of the church fathers from the early third century, but no other evidence for this gospel existed in modern times. Then, in 1886, a French archaeological team excavating at the ancient monastery of Pachomius, 250 miles south of Cairo, discovered in the grave of a monk a small book containing an account of the death and resurrection of Jesus. Scholarly examination soon concluded the account was a part of the long-lost *Gospel of Peter*.

At first the *Gospel of Peter* was labeled a popularized and docetic adaptation of the canonical Gospels, particularly reliant upon material from the Gospel of Matthew. However, extensive historical study and text analysis has demonstrated that it probably enjoyed brief favor among more orthodox Christian circles of the second century. The *Gospel of Peter* does share a number of characteristics with other popular Christian works of that period. It focuses more upon the efficacy of miracles than do the canonical Gospels. It has a rather strong anti-Jewish element about it. And the *Gospel of Peter* consistently uses "the Lord" rather than "Jesus" in devotional fashion. A minority of New Testament scholars have argued that the *Gospel of Peter* shares a source for its passion narrative with the passion narratives of the canonical Gospels (e.g., Crossan 1988). At this time, however, the majority consensus is that the passion narrative of the *Gospel of Peter* originates in the second century.

Although the *Gospel of Peter* may well have enjoyed popular favor among some catholic Christians of the second and third centuries, it also contains gnosticizing elements that would have had strong appeal for Gnostic Christians. Perhaps the most notable gnosticizing elements in the passion narrative are found in the account of Jesus being affixed to the cross and in the version of the cry of dereliction found in this noncanonical gospel, which present a somewhat docetic Christ:

(4:10)   And they took two evildoers and crucified the Lord between them. But he was silent as though he had no pain.
(5:19)   And the Lord cried out, saying, "My power, O power, you have forsaken me."

The eventual fate of the *Gospel of Peter* might be compared with that of the Gospel of John. Both were employed extensively by Gnostic as well as catholic Christians. However, the Gospel of John became included with the Synoptic Gospels as a part of the fourfold Gospel witness of the New Testament. The *Gospel of Peter,* perhaps originating not too many years after the composition of the Gospel of John, was rejected at the last and fell into obscurity—perhaps based upon the theological implication of a few verses.

Significant Second-Century Acts

In addition to gospels that remained outside the canon, there were several second-century works produced comparable to the canonical Acts of the Apostles. These other Acts focused upon one apostle as the main character, whose activities and teaching in the narrative often centered upon a single theological issue. Their use by catholic Christians as well as by other groups is well attested among the fathers of the early church. The noncanonical Acts appear to have enjoyed wide popularity beginning in the late second century and continuing for quite some time, even after the New Testament canon became somewhat fixed.

The *Acts of Peter* originated, perhaps in Asia Minor, probably between 180 and 190. Three passages from the original work have survived. One passage tells a story about Peter and his daughter, who is very beautiful but partially paralyzed. Since Peter is known to work miracles of healing, he is questioned about the continuing physical state of his daughter. Before his questioners, Peter commands the girl to arise whole, which she does. But then he commands her to return to her former state. He goes on to explain that her infirmity is a disguised blessing that has preserved her virginity—a main theological virtue for the work's author.

A second preserved passage tells the story of a peasant who asks Peter to offer a prayer for his only daughter, requesting that the apostle pray for what would most benefit the girl's soul. When Peter prays, the girl immediately falls down dead. According to the author/narrator, this was the most spiritually beneficial thing, since it prevented her from engaging in sexual activity. However, the girl's father subsequently entreats Peter to raise the girl, which he does. Not long afterward a passing stranger seduces her and the two disappear, never to be seen again.

The most extensive fragment preserved from the *Acts of Peter* is a tale pitting the apostle against Simon the magician, who we meet in the canonical Acts of the Apostles (Acts 8:9–25). The setting for this story is Rome. Following Paul's departure from that city for Spain, Peter receives a revelation directing him to go to Rome. In Rome Peter finds Simon corrupting the Roman Christians. The confrontation between Peter and the magician eventually leads to a miracle-working contest in the Roman Forum. Of course, Peter wins the contest and Simon is exposed as a worker of Satan. At the end of the story is appended the legend of Peter's martyrdom at Rome. In keeping with the author's theological preoccupation, Peter's preaching leads to the conversion of a Roman prefect's concubines, who subsequently renounce sexual intercourse. In retaliation, the prefect charges the apostle with irreligion and has him crucified. As the legend goes, Peter requests that his executioners crucify him head downward. He dies on an inverted cross after using the manner of his death to instruct the attending faithful.

The *Acts of Paul* also dates from near the end of the second century. The theologian Tertullian relates that a presbyter of Asia Minor composed this work out of love and respect for Paul. This unnamed presbyter probably edited and expanded upon a collection of legendary material on Paul to produce the work. Tertullian states that the presbyter was subsequently defrocked, probably because of some questionable, if not heretical, theology the work could be used to support. Our knowledge of the *Acts of Paul* is dependent upon fragmentary remains of several manuscripts preserving different legendary episodes from the life of the apostle. These include the legend of Paul's martyrdom at Rome, which, according to the *Acts of Paul,* was accompanied by miraculous portents. An apocryphal letter from Paul to the Corinthians, containing a forceful antidocetic polemic, has also been preserved. Perhaps the most interesting surviving segment is a narrative that had a long independent history as the *Acts of Paul and Thecla*. The story of Paul and Thecla, which focuses far more on the latter than the former, begins when Paul comes to preach at Iconium. Thecla, a woman of the city, is converted under Paul's preaching. She subsequently breaks her engagement to be married and adopts a life of chastity. This act provokes her fiancé to plot against Paul with the authorities and have him imprisoned. Thecla clandestinely visits Paul but is discovered. Paul is expelled from the city, but Thecla is sentenced to death. She is miraculously spared from death at the stake and escapes to follow Paul to Antioch. At Antioch, a man named Alexander falls in love with her. Of course, Thecla spurns his advances. In retribution, Alexander convinces the governor of the region to condemn Thecla to the arena. In the arena, Thecla casts herself into a pit of water filled with hostile seals. Upon entering the water, Thecla baptizes herself in the name of Jesus Christ (only), and a subsequent lightning flash miraculously kills the seals. She is likewise miraculously delivered from other vicious beasts in the arena and eventually set free by the governor. She follows Paul to Myra, but the apostle commissions her to return as a Christian teacher to Iconium. She complies with this commission before moving on to Seleucia, where she dies peacefully.

The different noncanonical *Acts* of the second century perhaps circulated in a collected *Acts of the Apostles* that may have been unfavorably compared to our canonical book of that name. As our brief survey has shown, the second century *Acts* were typically far more interested in telling miracle stories for popular consumption than relating historical facts about the first generation of Christian apostles. The understanding of discipleship they present has almost narrowed to an abstinence from sexual intercourse. If Gnosticism was the most serious challenge to Christianity's faithful witness to Jesus and his teaching that arose in the second century, the distortion of the body-spirit relationship and subsequent depreciation of human sexuality in the mainstream church has been the most enduring.

Key Terms and Concepts

Apocryphal New Testament • *1 Clement* • *Barnabas* • Canon • Catholic christology • demiurge • *Diatessaron* • *Didache* • docetism *Festal Letter of Bishop Athanasius* • gnosis • Gnosticism • *Gospel of Thomas* Marcion • *The Martyrdom of Polycarp* • pleroma

Questions for Study, Discussion, and Writing

1. What are the strengths and weaknesses of a canonical fourfold gospel witness over: (a) a singular canonical gospel, excluding others? (b) a harmonized account, such as produced by Tatian?
2. What factors were prominent in causing the early church's hesitation in acknowledging the authority of some of the General Letters?
3. How are the development of the church's understanding of itself as "catholic" and the formation of the New Testament canon interrelated?
4. Discuss the potential influence of Marcion and his canon on the formation of the New Testament canon.
5. Name at least three inadequacies found in various early Christian writings that contributed to their final exclusion from the New Testament.
6. Discuss the major doctrinal elements of Gnostic Christianity.
7. Discuss the dangers Gnosticism posed to Christianity in the second century. What might have been the impact on Christianity, and Western civilization, had Gnostic doctrine prevailed?
8. What do the commonly shared themes and narrative elements of the noncanonical *Acts* produced in the second century tell us about the popular Christianity of that period?

For Further Reading

Ferguson, Everett. *Backgrounds of Early Christianity,* 3rd ed. Grand Rapids, MI: Eerdmans, 2003. A thorough and readable survey for the beginning student.

Gonzalez, Justo L. *The Story of Christianity*, vol. 1: *The Early Church to the Dawn of the Reformation.* San Francisco: HarperCollins, 1984. A widely used resource for the introductory study of church history.

Goodspeed, Edgar J. *The Apostolic Fathers: An American Translation.* Harper & Brothers, 1950.

Hahneman, Geoffrey Mark. *The Muratorian Fragment and the Development of the Canon.* Oxford: Clarendon Press, 1992. A thorough study of the Muratorian fragment and scholarly argument for its dating in the fourth century.

Hall, Stuart G. *Doctrine and Practice in the Early Church.* Grand Rapids, MI: Eerdmans, 1991. A very readable history of the development of doctrine in the early church.

Hennecke, Edgar. *New Testament Apocrypha,* vol. 1: *Gospels and Related Writings.* Wilhelm Schneemelcher, ed. Trans. R. McL. Wilson. Philadelphia: Westminster Press, 1963. The premier scholarly treatment of this literature.

Hennecke, Edgar. *New Testament Apocrypha,* vol. 2: *Writings Relating to the Apostles; Apocalypses and Related Subjects.* Wilhelm Schneemelcher, ed. Trans. R. McL. Wilson. Philadelphia: Westminster Press, 1963. The premier scholarly treatment of this literature.

Metzger, Bruce M. *The Canon of the New Testament: Its Origin, Development, and Significance.* Oxford: Clarendon Press, 1987. A full scholarly treatment of the development of the New Testament canon.

Pagels, Elaine. *The Gnostic Gospels.* New York: Vintage Books, 1979. An interesting and readable study for the beginning student.

Perkins, Pheme. *Gnosticism and the New Testament.* Minneapolis: Fortress Press, 1993. A well-researched account of the interrelationship of Gnosticism and early Christianity.

Robinson, James M., gen. ed. *The Nag Hammadi Library in English.* 3rd ed. San Francisco: Harper & Row, 1988. Primary texts in translation.

Van Voorst, Robert E. *Jesus outside the New Testament: An Introduction to the Ancient Evidence.* Grand Rapids, MI: Eerdmans, 2000. Presentation and analysis of the sources outside the New Testament about historical Jesus.

Glossary

acts Greco-Roman literary genre narrating deeds of famous people.

Alexander the Great Macedonian conqueror of the Near East in the fourth century C.E., spreading Hellenism.

amanuensis One who wrote down a document by dictation and/or draft from the author.

Antichrist Apocalyptic figure who opposes God at the end of time.

antinomianism Religious system oriented against God's Law or any transcendent moral norms.

anonymous Document with no author's name in the work itself (as opposed to a later title that provides an author's name).

antitheses Literally, "opposing statements"; specifically, Jesus' sayings about opposites in his treatment of the Law of Moses in Matthew 5: "You have heard that it was said X, but I say to you Y."

apocalypse Literary genre in which an author, usually pseudonymous, reports dreams and visions telling of heavenly mysteries that explain present and future events on earth; as a proper noun, another name for the NT book of Revelation.

apocalyptic theology Worldview that sees a distinction between this sinful world controlled by evil forces and God's world to come.

apocryphal gospels "Hidden" gospels, term used for gospel books on the fringe of the NT canon.

Apocryphal New Testament Collection of documents from the first century through the ninth claiming to have been written by NT authors or others known to them.

apostles "Ones sent out" on a mission from God. In the Synoptic Gospels, the apostles are identical with the twelve disciples; in Paul's writings, apostleship is a wider concept.

ascension Jesus' departure from earth to heaven after his resurrection, dramatized in Acts 1.

asceticism Discipline of the body to promote the mind and/or soul.

augur Roman interpreter of omens seeking to foretell future events.

authentic The literary character of a document that was actually written by the person whose name it bears; opposite of **pseudonymous.**

authorial intent In historical reading, judging the meaning of a document by considering what the author intended to convey to the audience.

autograph Original manuscript, whether the author "signed" it or not.

Barnabas Early Christian leader in Acts, the first traveling companion of the apostle Paul.

beatitudes Generally, sayings pronouncing blessing on someone for some quality; used as a technical term for Jesus' blessings opening Matthew's Sermon on the Mount and Luke's Sermon on the Plain.

Beloved Disciple The "disciple Jesus loved," an unnamed figure in the Gospel of John, perhaps a founder of the Johannine community and the authority behind the fourth Gospel. Older tradition identified him as John the son of Zebedee, one of the Twelve.

benediction Formal blessing in religious services; in NT letters, author's blessing at the end to readers or listeners.

Beth Din (bait DEEN) the "house of judgment," a rabbinic law court.

Bible Name for scriptures of Judaism and Christianity, from the Greek word for "book." In Judaism, "Bible" is the books of the Hebrew Bible; in Christianity, it refers to the Old Testament (plus or minus the **deuterocanonical** books) plus the New Testament (the same for all Christians).

biblical criticism Careful, scholarly study of the Bible that seeks to understand it and reach informed, discerning conclusions about it.

bishop high office in church ministry and governance; the Greek original can also be translated "overseer."

Book of Glory Name often given to chapters 13–21 of the Gospel of John, in which Jesus is glorified by his death, resurrection, and return to his Father.

Book of Signs Name often given to chapters 1–12 of John because of the prominence of Jesus' miracles in it; not to be confused with the "Gospel of Signs."

canon Recognized collection of texts; in religion, a body of religious writings held as sacred and authoritative.

canticles Formal religious songs, especially those found in Luke 1–2.

catalogue of vice List of evil acts used to identify and instill avoidance of bad behavior.

catalogue of virtue List of good acts used to identify and instill moral behavior.

catena (kah-TEN-ah) "Chain" of virtues: A leads to B, B leads to C, and so on.

catholic "Universal" in time and space; later, a part of the name of the Roman church.

Catholic Letters The seven NT letters of James, 1–2 Peter, 1–2–3 John, Jude, and Hebrews, so called because they were thought to be addressed to the whole church, not to any one congregation. Also called **General Letters.**

celibate Not engaging in sexual intercourse, usually for religious reasons.

center section Middle of Luke's Gospel, featuring Jesus' journey to Jerusalem.

centurion A Roman army officer in charge of one hundred troops.

charism In Paul's letters, a gift by the Holy Spirit of an ability to be used for the good of the whole congregation.

Christian Scriptures Alternate name used by some for "New Testament" in order to avoid the perceived negative implications of that term; also called **Christian Testament.**

christology Teaching on the nature of Jesus Christ; high christology features a more exalted view of Jesus, low christology a less exalted view.

chiastic order "Cross-structured," a forward-and-reverse literary structure for listing of items, for example "He has love, faith, goodness, and she has more goodness, more faith, more love."

circular letters Letters meant by the author to be read in more than one congregation.

Circumcision Party Group of conservative Jewish Christians who opposed admitting Gentiles to the church without making them Jewish as well by circumcision.

civic magistrates Men of means in the towns and cities of the provinces of the Roman Empire, appointed to local offices to wield local power and patronage.

client The person in the lower half of the patron-client relationship, one who is obligated to serve a patron in return for income and social standing; see also **patron.**

1 Clement A letter written by Clement, bishop of Rome in the 90s, to the church at Corinth, Greece.

collegium (pl. **collegia**) Latin term for voluntary association, privately organized small groups who shared a common interest or task such as trade or craft associations.

commensality Table fellowship, with the social equality it usually implies.

covenant Relationship God has established with particular people, binding the future conduct of both parties in working out God's design for human life.

criteria of authenticity Guidelines by which scholars attempt to discern if sayings attributed to Jesus in the Gospels were actually spoken by Jesus.

criticism Scholarly activity of discerning the essential qualities of a writing or artistic product.

cross-cultural criticism Method of NT interpretation that reads from the social location of marginalized peoples, with a goal of promoting their liberation.

deacons Office in early church ministry and governance, often associated with serving a congregation or assisting a higher-level officer.

Dead Sea Scrolls Jewish documents discovered in the 1940s near Qumran at the northern end of the Dead Sea; contains manuscript copies of the Hebrew Bible and Qumran community documents.

delay of the Parousia Perception among early Christians that the return of Jesus has not come as soon as it should have; see **Parousia** and **imminent expectation.**

deliberative rhetoric Persuasion to convince an audience to follow a certain course of action.

demiurge (DEH-mee-uhrj) Literally, "maker," used in Gnostic texts for a powerful but lesser divinity who made the world.

deuterocanonical books Books in the **Septuagint** but not in the Hebrew Bible; Roman Catholic and Eastern Orthodox Christians consider them scriptural, but most Protestants do not.

deutero-Pauline letters Literally, "second-Pauline" writings, bearing Paul's name but thought by a significant number of scholars today to be written in his name after his death: 2 Thessalonians, Colossians, Ephesians, 1–2 Timothy and Titus; equivalent to the **disputed Pauline letters.**

Diadochi (dee-AH-duh-key) Rulers and their kingdoms that succeeded Alexander the Great.

Diaspora (dee-ASS-poh-rah) Greek, "dispersion" of a people from their native land; in Judaism, the dispersion of Jewish people throughout the ancient Mediterranean and Near Eastern world.

Diatessaron The harmony (combination into one account) of the Gospels written by Tatian in the second century.

diatribe Greek philosophical style of writing featuring sharp conversation between the speaker and the audience and/or an imaginary conversation partner.

Didache Second-century document on church life and order, thought to come from Syria; also known as the *Teaching of the Twelve Apostles.*

disciple "Student, learner"; the Gospels call all of Jesus' regular followers by this term, not just the (all-male) Twelve.

disputed Pauline letters Letters carrying Paul's name that a significant number of scholars today do not conclude are authentic: 2 Thessalonians, Colossians, Ephesians, 1–2 Timothy and Titus. Also called **post-Pauline letters;** opposite of **undisputed Pauline letters.**

docetism (DOSS-eh-tizm) Belief that Jesus was not human but only seemed to be.

double tradition Parallel passages in Matthew and Luke.

dualism Feature of apocalyptic thought in which life is divided into polar opposites: cosmic dualism (heaven and earth as separate realms), moral dualism (good and evil absolutely distinguished), temporal dualism (the present evil age and the age of God's reign to come).

dynamic equivalence translations Translations that try to remain close to the ideas expressed in the original language, not following its exact wording or word order.

early Catholicism Conclusion by some NT scholars that the end of the NT period, c. 70–110, sees a transitional period from the first and second generation of Christians to the Great/Catholic Church with its emphasis on correct doctrine and organization.

epideictic rhetoric A letter of praise meant to persuade.

eschatology Teaching about the "last things," the end of this world and the beginning of the next, perfect world.

Essenes An apocalyptic communal movement in Second Temple Judaism, c. 150 B.C.E. to 70 C.E., considering themselves the predestined remnant of Israel; produced the Dead Sea Scrolls.

expiation Atonement for sin, a sacrifice reconciling human(s) to God.

external evidence Evidence outside a document for its wording, authorship, audience, date, and so on; opposite of **internal evidence.**

faithful sayings Short sayings in the Pastoral Letters that begin or end with "This is a faithful saying"; these are often important statements about key beliefs.

Farewell Discourse The speech of Jesus to his disciples on the night before his death, in John 13–17.

fellowship Spiritual, social, and material sharing by early Christians.

feminist criticism Reading to identify and promote liberation of women; in NT study, it seeks to uncover and explain the varieties of women's roles, with a view to promoting the liberation of women in church and society today.

Festal Letter of Bishop Athanasius Names as authoritative the same twenty-seven books we find in the contemporary New Testament; written in 367 C.E.

final eschatology Belief that the end of the world is yet to come; opposite of **realized eschatology.**

form criticism Study of the structure and content of the different types of passages ("forms") of the written gospels and the history of their oral transmission.

formal correspondence translations Standard translations that keep as closely as possible to the original wording and word order of the Hebrew and Greek texts.

forum Central civic area in the Roman and Roman-Hellenistic city, featuring temples, other government buildings, and businesses. Also Greek **agora.**

Four-Document Hypothesis A solution to the Synoptic Problem that sees four sources behind Matthew, Mark, and Luke: (1) Mark, used by Matthew and Luke; (2) Q, used by Matthew and Luke; (3) M, the material found only in Matthew; (4) L, the material found only in Luke.

freedmen Former slaves, who often retained a close socioeconomic relationship with their former masters.

fulfillment quotations Formal citations of the OT used to argue that a NT person or event accomplishes an OT prediction; used especially in the Gospel of Matthew.

fundamentalism Conservative religious movement marked by a strongly negative reaction to modernity and religious change.

genealogy Formal list of one's ancestors, in the biblical tradition generally traced through the males.

General Letters James, 1–2 Peter, 1–2–3 John, Jude, and sometimes Hebrews, called this on the supposition that they were written for many or all churches; another term for **Catholic Letters.**

genius (plural **genii**) A person's supernatural guardian spirit.

Gentile Jewish religious and ethnic term for a non-Jew.

genre Overall literary form of a document, such as a letter or gospel.

geographic outline Pattern of the spread of Christianity "from Jerusalem and Judea to Samaria and to the end of the earth" that serves as the outline of the narrative in Acts; see Acts 1:8.

gnosis Greek word for "knowledge"; in Gnosticism, this knowledge brought salvation.

Gnosticism (NOSS-tih-sizm) Group of ancient religious and philosophical movements, some closely related to Christianity, that believed that elements of the divine had become entrapped in persons in this evil material world and could be released only when these persons gained knowledge (*gnosis*) of this divine origin, a knowledge generally brought by a divine figure.

God fearer Gentile who participates in synagogue services of worship and accepts the moral demands of Judaism.

Gog and Magog Symbolic names in Revelation for nations that oppose God's power.

gospel "Good news," the basic Christian message; when the term refers to the genre of the first four books of the New Testament, it is capitalized.

Gospel of Thomas Second-century book of sayings of Jesus, many of which are identical or nearly identical to sayings of Jesus in the Synoptics, especially the Q source.

grace God's free, unmerited saving love for humans.

Great Commission Jesus' command to the eleven disciples at the end of Matthew to take the Christian message into the whole world, baptizing converts and teaching them the Christian moral vision.

Griesbach Hypothesis Theory to solve the Synoptic Problem that the earliest Gospel was Matthew; Luke adapted Matthew, and Mark is a shortened combination of Matthew and Luke; proposed around 1800 by J. J. Griesbach, also known today as the **Two-Gospel Hypothesis.**

gymnasium "Place of naked" exercise for males in cities.

Hasidim (HAHS-ih-deem) "Separated ones" in the second century B.C.E. who opposed Hellenism and advocated strict observance of traditional Jewish religious practices.

Hasmonean Dynasty Alternative name for the Maccabeans, the family of Jewish priests that led the successful revolt beginning in 167 B.C.E. and ruled Israel until to the Roman takeover in 63 B.C.E.

Hebrew Bible The sacred scriptures of Judaism, composed of the Law, Prophets, and Writings; Christians often call it the **Old Testament** (minus the deuterocanonical books).

Hebrews Jews of the early Jerusalem community who spoke Aramaic as a first language and had more traditional attitudes to Judaism; headed by the Apostles; opposite of **Hellenists.**

Hellenism Ancient Greek culture spread throughout the eastern Mediterranean by Alexander the Great.

Hellenistic Greek Form of Greek language widely spread throughout the Roman Empire and used in the NT; also called **Koine** ("common") Greek.

Hellenistic Judaism The particular forms of Judaism found outside Palestine in the Greco-Roman environment; characterized by Greek language of the Bible and worship and some use of Greco-Roman philosophy.

Hellenistic Age The Greek-dominated eastern Mediterranean from Alexander the Great until the fall of Ptolemaic Egypt in 30 B.C.E.

Hellenists In the Acts of the Apostles, Jews of the early Jerusalem church who spoke Greek as their first language and were more attuned to Greco-Roman culture; headed by the Seven, they probably began the mission to non-Jews; opposite of **Hebrews.**

heresy Any unapproved form of faith or life; often refers to a movement opposed by NT writers or later church authorities.

hermeneutic of suspicion Type of critical interpretation that holds that the surface of the text is covering up an important truth deeper within it; practiced by feminist and cross-cultural reading.

hermeneutics "Interpretation," in its widest sense the meanings and methods of understanding a text.

Herod the Great Jewish client-king who ruled a greater Judea (the area of Palestine, including Galilee) from 37–4 B.C.E.

historical-critical method Scholarly attempt to understand what a document meant to its original writer(s) and audience.

historicity When an event actually happened more or less as it was written up.

honor-shame paradigm Social scientific concept that some societies are primarily motivated by the desire to accumulate and keep social honor and its power while keeping away shame and its loss of power.

household code Greco-Roman list of moral duties for people in a household (parents, children, slaves); also called "house table."

imminent expectation Belief that Jesus was soon returning in glory, at least within the lifetime of early Christians.

implied author Image of the author that readers create (infer) while reading the story.

implied reader Reader that the text shapes as it is read, the person who cognitively and emotionally enters the story and responds to it as the implied author intends.

incarnation Belief that the preexistent Son of God "became flesh (human)" in Jesus.

inclusion Literary device in which a document or section of a document ends with the same topic or wording with which it began; signals a full-circle conclusion.

indicative/imperative NT moral commands (the imperative) based on a new nature/character in Christ (the indicative).

infancy narratives Stories of the prediction, conception, birth, and infancy of Jesus in Matthew 1–2 and Luke 1–2.

infanticide Greco-Roman practice of killing unwanted babies, usually by abandoning them in desolate places.

intercalation Narrative arrangement in which the text tells two stories at once: the author initiates one story, interrupts it by another event that is then told in full, and then finishes the initial story; more popularly known as a **sandwich.**

interim ethic Christian moral instruction especially tailored for the short time before Jesus returns.

internal evidence Indications from inside a document about its author, audience, date, and so on; opposite of **external evidence.**

introduction Matters usually dealt with at the beginning of historical-critical study of a NT document: its author, audience and situation, date, purpose, etc.

invective Careful use of insults, name calling, and the like to persuade an audience.

Jerusalem Council In Acts 15, the meeting of the Jerusalem church's important figures with Paul to decide on what grounds the Gentiles were to be admitted to the church.

Johannine School Group of transmitters of the Johannine tradition about Jesus and leaders in the Johannine churches; called by some the **Johannine Circle.**

judicial rhetoric Persuasion used to enable an audience to come to a desired conclusion about right or wrong.

justification by faith Teaching in Paul's letters that a person is made right ("justified") with God only by trusting in the results of Jesus' sacrificial death, not by keeping the works commanded in the Jewish Law.

kinship A leading social scientific paradigm that stresses the importance in Mediterranean societies of values of families and wider kin relations.

L Material found only in Luke, thought by many to be a literary source of Luke.

lares (LAHR-ace) Roman gods of the hearth and home.

Latinisms Greek-language words that are derived directly from Latin.

law-free gospel Scholarly shorthand expression for Paul's idea that salvation in Christ is outside one's keeping of the Jewish Law.

lectionary System of reading set NT passages that arose in the early Greek church in the eastern Roman Empire.

legion Largest unit of the Roman army, comprising at least 6,000 soldiers.

letter Form of communication from one person or small group to another person or group; in NT times, had its own genre format of opening, thanksgiving/wish for health, body, and closing.

letters from prison   Letters composed and sent while their author is imprisoned; in the NT and elsewhere, they tend to have a different tone and content but not overall form.

limited goods   Social scientific concept that material wealth is limited in nature and society, so that anyone's attempt to get more wealth means that others must lose it.

lives   Greco-Roman type of writing focused on the deeds of a famous person; also called "biographies."

Lord's Day   In the book of Revelation, Sunday, the day of Jesus' resurrection and the revealing of the visions in this book; in Gentile Christianity it became the main day of worship.

Lord's Prayer/Our Father   Jesus' prayer, typically Jewish in content, given to his disciples as a model for their prayers.

love feasts   Ritual meals of social and material sharing in the early church, often connected with the Eucharist.

M   Document that no longer survives but that Matthew drew upon for material about Jesus not in Mark or Luke.

manuscripts   Handwritten documents, both original and copies.

Marcion   Second-century church leader later deemed false to the faith for his docetic Christology and his belief in two Gods, the harsh OT God of the Jews and the loving NT God of Jesus; the first to draw up a formal canon of the NT.

Markan appendix   The later endings of the Gospel of Mark, almost certainly not a part of the original Gospel.

Markan priority   View that Mark was the first of the Synoptic Gospels to be written and that Matthew and Luke used it as a source.

The Martyrdom of Polycarp   Second-century work telling the story of the martyrdom (death by persecution) of Polycarp, a bishop in Asia Minor.

Mediterranean person   Identified by anthropologists as a cultural prototype characteristic of NT peoples and times.

memoir   Type of Greco-Roman writing that contains individual stories about famous persons such as philosophers and national leaders, often including some of their teachings.

messiah   Hebrew for "anointed one," the promised deliverer that first-century C.E. Jews had a wide range of ideas about; translated into Greek as "Christ."

messianic secret   Hypothesis that although Jesus is the Messiah, he hides this fact and tells his disciples not to reveal his miraculous healings to others; the result is that only demons recognize his identity.

millennium   Thousand-year reign of Christ on earth in Revelation.

miracle story   Gospel form in which the healings, feedings, and other miraculous deeds of Jesus are told.

mixed metaphor   When two separate, conflicting metaphors are used to describe the same thing; typical of Hebrew poetry and often found in NT writings.

monotheism   Belief that only one God exists; usually accompanied by belief in God's holiness as well as creation and general governance of the world.

mujerista criticism   Feminist criticism as practiced by Latina women.

mystery religions   Ancient religious movements that featured initiation rites, cult secrets (mysteries), and the offer of hope for a better life after death.

mysticism In general, a close spiritual relationship with the divine that brings blessing; in particular, refers to the apostle Paul's spiritual relationship with God through Jesus Christ.

Nag Hammadi Village in southern Egypt where a collection of Gnostic writings, including the full *Gospel of Thomas,* was discovered in 1945.

narrative characterization In narrative method, how characters in a story are portrayed and act in the plot as well as the author's implicit attitude to them.

narrative conflict In narrative method, how different characters clash with each other, how this conflict propels the plot along, and how it is resolved.

narrative criticism A critical method for analyzing a literary narrative (story), including its structure, point of view, characters, plot, and audience.

narrative plot In narrative method, the path by which the story unfolds from introduction, conflict, resolution, to aftermath (denouement).

narrative point of view In narrative method, the character from whose perspective the story is told shapes the values implicit in the story.

new age/age to come In apocalyptic theology, the perfect world that God will bring at the end of time to replace its opposite, the "present evil age."

new perspective on Paul The recent rethinking of Paul's theology led by E. P. Sanders, James D. G. Dunn, and others, stressing that for Paul salvation is more a matter of "staying in" the people of God than "getting in"; counteracts what it sees as a Lutheran understanding of justification by faith.

New Testament The second, Christian half of the Bible, with twenty-seven documents written by early Christian leaders to guide members of the new faith in their common life.

NT introduction Matters of authorship, date, audience, literary unity, and the rest.

North Galatian hypothesis The theory that Galatians was addressed to believers in the north-central part of the modern Turkish peninsula; opposite of the **South Galatian hypothesis.**

occasional writings Documents written to deal with (and in the NT almost always correct) a specific situation among their recipients.

Old Testament The scriptures or canonical writings of the Jewish people, as labeled by Christians; also called the Hebrew Scriptures.

pantheon The Greek and Roman gods, considered as a group.

papyri Scrolls, a type of writing material common in the ancient Mediterranean, made from Nile river reeds.

parable Short comparison, usually in the form of a story, used to illustrate an aspect of life in the kingdom of God.

Paraclete In the Gospel of John, a technical term for the Holy Spirit meaning "advocate/counselor/comforter"; in 1 John, the role ascribed to Christ.

paraphrases Translations that take great freedom with the wording of a text in order to bring out its meaning more fully and expressively.

parenesis Moral exhortation, whether long (e.g., household codes) or short (two-word commands like "pray constantly").

Parousia Greek word for "presence/coming," used as a technical term for the return of Jesus in glory at the end of time. See also **delay of the Parousia.**

passion narrative The story of Jesus' suffering (Latin *passio*) that begins with his arrest and extends through his burial.

Pastoral Letters 1–2 Timothy and Titus, so called because they are thought to be letters for pastoral (church) leadership.

patriarchy Male rule in the home and society with the related repression of females, and the ideas that support this social order.

patrician class Highest class in Roman society, from which senators and (typically) emperors came.

patron One who from a position of social and financial power sponsors building projects, art works, and the like **(patronage)** to advance his or her own standing or that of his or her group. The persons employed in this activity are **clients.**

Pax Romana (pahks roh-MAH-nah) "Roman Peace" imposed on the Mediterranean world by Roman conquest.

pedagogue Slave assigned the role of guardian over male children in a household; responsible for seeing these children to and from schooling and regulating their behavior.

Pentecost Jewish feast that falls fifty days after Passover, on which in Acts 2 the Spirit descends upon the church.

perfectionism A feature of 1 John in which Christians are urged to live without sin.

pericope Small, independent unit of oral tradition now written down in the Gospels.

Pharisees Jewish sect that probably originated in the Maccabean revolt; they emphasized future eschatology and strict observance of the Law of Moses.

pleroma Greek "fullness"; used as a technical term in Gnosticism for the highest divine nature.

pontifex maximus High priest of the city of Rome.

Pontius Pilate Roman governor of Judea during the ministry of Jesus who ordered Jesus to be crucified.

preexistence christology Belief that the divine being in Jesus Christ existed as divine before Jesus.

prefect (PREE-fekt) Another word for a Roman governor of a province.

presbyter/elder Office of ministry and leadership in the synagogue and the early church.

present evil age In apocalyptic theology, the system of this world characterized by sin and death that God will end when the "Age to Come" arrives.

preunderstanding The knowledge, attitudes, and experience that one brings to a text and uses, often unknowingly, to interpret it.

pronouncement story In form criticism, a short story that ends in a typically one-sentence pronouncement that the story itself explains and seeks to make authoritative.

Prophets Second section of the Hebrew/Jewish Bible; prophets are spokespersons for God seeking to advance Israel's faithfulness to God.

pseudonymous When a document is not actually written by the person whose name it bears; opposite of **authentic.**

Ptolemaic dynasty (tahl-uh-MAY-ick) Successor dynasty of Alexander in Egypt begun by his Greek general Ptolemy, from the death of Alexander until 30 B.C.E.

purity and pollution Social scientific paradigm positing that purity is a state that prevails when things and people are what and where they are supposed to be, pollution prevails when they are not (e.g., dirt makes for purity in the garden, but it pollutes in the house).

Q Hypothetical "Synoptic Sayings Source" consisting of the material common to Matthew and Luke but not Mark; probably from the German word for source, *Quelle.*

Qumran Area in southern Judea along the Dead Sea at which a Jewish sectarian community, almost certainly of Essenes, was located; see also **Dead Sea Scrolls.**

realized eschatology Belief that the end of the world is being worked out in the present—for example, that believers already have eternal life in some way. The Gospel of John is typically thought to have a rich amount of realized eschatology.

redaction criticism Study of how Gospel authors used, and especially modified or edited ("redacted"), their sources in view of their own interests in presenting Jesus.

repentance Change of mind and behavior that reorients one to God.

resurrection Raising of a dead human being with a deathless body fit for heaven; should be distinguished from NT raisings of dead people with the same mortal body.

Romans debate Scholarly dispute over why Paul wrote his letter to the Romans.

Sabbath Jewish day of rest, from Friday sunset until Saturday sunset.

sacral manumission The process of depositing money in the temple of a Greco-Roman god until there is enough to buy the slave's freedom.

Sadducees (SAD-you-sees) Jewish party associated with the Temple and the leading Jewish priests who ran it; they comprised the Jewish aristocracy of Judea.

salutation Blessing on the audience, from God through the author, at the beginning of a letter.

salvation history The idea that salvation is revealed and established in human history by means of God's action, in the NT particularly through Jesus Christ.

Samaritans Descendants of Israelites who continued living in the region of Samaria in central Israel, despised by Jews for their mixed ancestry.

sanctification The process and resulting state of moral purity; may or may not entail sinlessness.

sandwich Narrative arrangement in which the author initiates one story, interrupts it by another event that is then told in full, and then finishes the initial story; more formally known as **intercalation.**

Sanhedrin Jewish governing council in Jerusalem headed by the high priest.

scripture Writings accepted and used by a religious community as especially sacred and authoritative.

second repentance Idea that restoration to the Christian faith is possible after one defects from it.

Second Temple period Period of Jewish history from about 520 B.C.E.–70 C.E., so called because the second Jerusalem Temple stood at this time.

Second Testament Alternate name for the "New Testament," used by some to avoid the perceived negative implications in that term; also called "Christian Testament."

secret disciple In John's Gospel, one who believes in Jesus but does not make that public in order to avoid persecution.

sectarianism Social and ideological separation from other groups in order to promote one's purity and effectiveness. Some NT interpreters hold that some first-century Christian churches—John's, for example—were sectarian.

Seleucid dynasty (sell-OO-sid) Successor dynasty of Alexander in Syria, Asia Minor, and Mesopotamia.

Septuagint (sehp-TOO-uh-jihnt) The Greek translation of the Hebrew Bible, with additional deuterocanonical books added; abbreviated LXX for the seventy people legend says translated it.

Sermon on the Mount In Matthew 5–7, his opening (and longest) discourse, with teaching on following Jesus.

Sermon on the Plain Luke's collection of Jesus' teaching in Luke 6:17–49.

sign Gospel of John's term for a miracle by Jesus; they point to his identity as God's Son.

Signs Gospel Jewish-Christian document used by the Gospel of John, focusing on Jesus' miracles.

Sitz im Leben (zits ihm LAY-ben) German for the social and religious "setting in life" of the first-century church where such oral forms originated and developed.

slaves Lowest social class in Roman society, consisting of those persons owned by Romans who were required to do a wide variety of manual, artistic, and intellectual labor.

social scientific criticism Method of reading NT and other texts in order to bring out the social scientific background, and sometimes the foreground, of the meaning of the text.

source criticism Study of if and how some NT documents draw on other sources either inside or outside the NT.

South Galatian hypothesis Theory that Paul wrote Galatians to believers in the south-central area of the modern-day Turkish peninsula.

spiritual powers and principalities Cosmic beings and their human associates who rule the present evil age to their own advantage and the suppression of God's purposes.

strong/weak in faith In Paul's churches, the "strong" saw themselves as free from the service of the Law of Moses such as kosher foods, observances of holy days, and the like; the "weak" in faith saw these practices as binding.

superapostles Paul's derisive name for his Jewish-Christian opponents in 2 Corinthians, mocking their claim to be apostles superior to him.

synagogue Jewish place of worship or prayer, or the assembly itself, from the Greek word for "gathering."

Synoptic Gospels First three gospels of the NT (Matthew, Mark, and Luke), so-called because one can survey their parallel passages in "one view" (Greek *synopsis*).

Synoptic Problem Task of explaining the reasons for the similarities and differences between the three Synoptic Gospels.

Table of Nations In Acts 2:9–11, the listing of different nationalities of Jewish listeners at Pentecost, perhaps symbolizing the future spread of the gospel.

tax farming Roman imperial system of contracting with local companies for the right to collect Roman taxes.

Temple of Jerusalem The Jewish house of God for sacrifice and other worship that stood in Jerusalem; the First (Solomonic) Temple was built by Solomon in the ninth century B.C.E. and was destroyed by warfare in the sixth century B.C.E.; the Second Temple stood from about 520 B.C.E. until 70 C.E.

testament In both Hebrew and Greek, *testament* also means "covenant." Christianity has attached this name to its "New Testament," but Judaism does not use it to describe its canon.

textual criticism The process of establishing as fully as possible the wording of the original text of a manuscript document; a part of historical criticism.

textual variants Different readings in the manuscripts of a word or phrase of the text.

thanksgiving Section of a Greco-Roman (and NT) letter following the opening, and gives thanks to God or the gods for the recipients.

theology Systematic academic study of the Christian faith, especially its beliefs, most often done by Christians in the service of the church.

theology of the cross Christology that says that Jesus came in large measure to die for people's sins and that the Christian life is therefore a difficult sharing in these sufferings; opposite of **triumphalist christology.**

threefold office The system of having three special ministries, the bishop/overseer, the elder/presbyter, and the deacon/assistant, work together in the church; its antecedents grew in the first century, but the system was not put together formally until the second century.

three ways to interpret Revelation Revelation is interpreted *historically* as a witness to the first century C.E., *future-predictively* as a witness to the end of time, and *timelessly* as a witness to all times.

Timothy Key co-worker of Paul, as a historical figure; also the one to whom two Pastoral Letters are addressed.

Titus Coworker of Paul, as a historical figure; also the one to whom one of the Pastoral Letters is addressed.

Torah Hebrew word meaning "guidance, teaching, law"; designates both the Law of God given to Moses and the first five books of the Hebrew Bible.

tradition Any idea, teaching, or practice handed down from one person to another; this process is called **traditioning.**

tradition criticism Study of how particular forms are transmitted, both orally and in writing; a part of historical criticism.

tradition of the elders Tradition of oral law passed down by Pharisees explaining and implementing the Law of Moses; later enters the Mishnah and the Talmud.

transfiguration Temporary change in the appearance of Jesus' earthly body.

triple tradition Closely related material in Matthew, Mark, and Luke.

triumphalist christology A Jesus with power to overcome his problems and to triumph over death to the exclusion of his suffering; understands the life of discipleship as so powerfully Spirit-filled that it overcomes virtually all human problems; opposite of **theology of the cross.**

Twelve Jesus' main disciples, signifying the renewal of all of Israel—the "Twelve Tribes"—in Jesus' movement.

Two-Document Hypothesis Theory that Matthew and Luke used the two documents Mark and Q as sources.

Two-Gospel Hypothesis Theory to solve the Synoptic Problem that the earliest Gospel was Matthew; Luke adapted Matthew, and Mark is a shortened combination of Matthew and Luke; also called the **Griesbach Hypothesis.**

typology Linking of personages from the past and present, such as Adam and Christ.

uncial Greek manuscripts written in upper-case, "inch-high" lettering.

undisputed Pauline letters Letters generally accepted today by most scholars as actually written by Paul: Romans, 1–2 Corinthians, 1 Thessalonians, Galatians, Philippians, and Philemon.

virginal conception The belief that Jesus was conceived by supernatural action of the Holy Spirit in Mary of Nazareth, not by a natural conception with a human father.

Way Earliest name of the Christian movement in Acts, probably referring to the Way of Jesus.

we sections In Acts, those passages that are narrated in the first-plural, "we/us" (16:10–17; 20:5–21:18; chapters 27–28).

woes Eschatological curses, usually meaning that the persons who receive them are deprived of God's blessing of eternity in God's presence.

womanist criticism Liberationist reading of the NT done by African American women.

Writings Third division of the Hebrew Bible after the Law and the Prophets, comprising miscellaneous genres such as the Psalms, wisdom writings, and so on.

Zealots Group of Galilean Jews who fled to Jerusalem in the revolt against Rome in 66–70 C.E., seized power there and led resistance to Rome to the end; it is disputed today if Zealots existed as a group before the Jewish revolt.

Bibliography

Achtemeier, Paul. "The Origin and Function of the Pre-Marcan Miracle Catenae." *Journal of Biblical Literature* 91 (1972): 198–221.

Achtemeier, Paul. "Toward the Isolation of Pre-Marcan Miracle Catenae." *Journal of Biblical Literature* 89 (1970): 265–291.

Achtemeier, Paul. *1 Peter: A Commentary*. Hermeneia Commentary. Minneapolis: Fortress Press, 1996.

Adler, Mortimer, and Charles Van Doren. *How to Read a Book*. New York: Simon & Schuster, 1972.

Alexander, Patrick H., and others. *SBL Handbook of Style*. Peabody, MA: Hendrickson, 1999.

Anderson, Janice C., and Stephen D. Moore. *Mark and Method: New Approaches in Biblical Studies*. Minneapolis: Fortress Press, 1992.

Aune, David E., ed. *The Gospel of Matthew in Current Study*. Grand Rapids, MI: Eerdmans, 2001.

Aune, David E. *Prophecy in Early Christianity and the Ancient Mediterranean World*. Grand Rapids, MI: Eerdmans, 1983.

Barclay, J. M. G. *Obeying the Truth: Paul's Ethics in Galatians*. Minneapolis: Fortress Press, 1991.

Barclay, J. M. G. "Paul, Philemon and the Dilemma of Christian Slave-Ownership." *New Testament Studies* 37 (1991): 161–186.

Barth, M., ed. and trans. *Colossians and Philemon*. Garden City, NY: Doubleday, 1974.

Barth, Markus, ed. and trans. *Ephesians*. Anchor Bible Commentary. Garden City, NY: Doubleday, 1974.

Barth, Marcus, and Helmut Blanke. *The Letter to Philemon*. Grand Rapids, MI: Eerdmans, 2000.

Bauckham, Richard. "James." In James D. G. Dunn and John W. Rogerson, eds., *Eerdmans Commentary on the Bible*, pp. 1483–1492. Grand Rapids, MI: Eerdmans, 2003.

Bauckham, Richard, ed. *The Gospels for All Christians*. Edinburgh/Grand Rapids, MI: T. & T. Clark/Eerdmans, 1997.

Bauckham, Richard. *Gospel Women: Studies of the Named Women of the Gospels*. Grand Rapids, MI: Eerdmans, 2002.

Bauckham, Richard. *Jude, 2 Peter*. Word Commentary. Waco, TX: Word, 1983.

Beare, F. W. *A Commentary on the Epistle to the Philippians*. New York: Harper & Row, 1959.

Bechtler, Steven R. *Following in His Steps: Suffering, Community and Christology in 1 Peter*. Atlanta: Scholars Press, 1998.

Beirne, Margaret M. *Women and Men in the Fourth Gospel: A Genuine Discipleship of Equals*. Sheffield, UK: Sheffield Academic Press, 2003.

Best, Ernest. *Second Corinthians*. Atlanta: John Knox, 1987.

Betz, Hans D. *Galatians*. Hermeneia Commentary. Philadelphia: Fortress Press, 1979.

Blount, Brian. *Go Preach! Mark's Kingdom Message and the Black Church Today.* New York: Orbis, 1998.

Blount, Brian. *Then the Whisper Put on Flesh: NT Ethics in an African American Context.* Nashville, TN: Abingdon, 2001.

Borg, Marcus. *Meeting Jesus Again for the First Time.* San Francisco: HarperSanFrancisco, 1995.

Bornkamm, Gunter, with Gerhard Barth and Heinz Held. *Tradition and Interpretation in Matthew.* Philadelphia: Westminster, 1963.

Braun, Willi. *Feasting and Social Rhetoric in Luke 14.* Cambridge: Cambridge University Press, 1995.

Brooks, Stephenson H. *Matthew's Community: The Evidence of His Special Sayings Material.* Sheffield, UK: JSOT Press, 1987.

Brown, Raymond E. *The Community of the Beloved Disciple.* New York: Paulist Press, 1979.

Brown, Raymond E. *The Epistles of John.* Anchor Bible Commentary. Garden City, NY: Doubleday, 1982).

Brown, Raymond E. *The Gospel According to John.* Anchor Bible Commentary. Garden City, NY: Doubleday, 1966, 1970.

Brown, Raymond E. *An Introduction to the Gospel of John*, ed. Francis J. Moloney. Garden City, NY: Doubleday, 2003.

Brown, Raymond E. *An Introduction to the New Testament.* Garden City, NY: Doubleday, 1997.

Brown, Raymond E., and John P. Meier. *Antioch and Rome.* New York: Paulist Press, 1983.

Bruce, F. F. *The Acts of the Apostles.* Grand Rapids, MI: Eerdmans, 1954.

Bultmann, Rudolf. *History of the Synoptic Tradition.* New York: Harper & Row, 1963 (German original, 1921).

Burridge, Richard. *What Are the Gospels? A Comparison with Greco-Roman Biography.* Cambridge: Cambridge University Press, 1992.

Byron, Gay L. *Symbolic Blackness and Ethnic Difference in Early Christian Literature.* London: Routledge, 2002.

Carson, Donald A. "Current Sources Criticism of the Fourth Gospel: Some Methodological Questions." *Journal of Biblical Literature* 97 (1978): 411–429.

Carter, T. L. *Paul and the Power of Sin: Redefining "Beyond the Pale."* Cambridge: Cambridge University Press, 2002.

Carter, Warren. *Matthew and the Margins: A Sociopolitical and Religious Reading.* Maryknoll, NY: Orbis, 2000.

Chancey, Mark A. *The Myth of a Gentile Galilee.* Cambridge: Cambridge University Press, 2002.

Chatman, Seymour. *Story and Discourse.* Ithaca, NY: Cornell University Press, 1978.

Chester, Andrew, and Ralph P. Martin. *The Theology of the Letters of James, Peter, and Jude.* Cambridge: Cambridge University Press, 1994.

Collins, Adela Yarbro. *The Beginning of the Gospel: Probings of Mark in Context.* Minneapolis: Fortress Press, 1992.

Collins, Adela Yarbro. *Crisis and Catharsis: The Power of the Apocalypse.* Philadelphia: Westminster Press, 1984.

Collins, Adela Yarbro, *The Apocalypse*. Wilmington, DE: Glazier, 1979.

Collins, John J., ed. *The Apocalyptic Imagination: An Introduction to the Jewish Matrix of Christianity*. Los Angeles: Crossroads, 1984.

Collins, Raymond F. *1 & 2 Timothy and Titus: A Commentary*. Louisville, KY: Westminster/John Knox, 2002.

Schmidt, Karl Ludwig. *The Place of the Gospels in the General History of Literature* Columbia, SC: University of South Carolina Press, 2002 (German original, 1927).

Conzelmann, Hans. *The Theology of St. Luke*. London: Faber & Faber, 1960 (German original, 1953).

Coogan, Michael D., ed. *The New Oxford Annotated Bible*, 3rd ed. New York: Oxford, 1999.

Corley, Kathleen. *Women and the Historical Jesus: Feminist Myths of Christian Origins*. Sonoma, CA: Polebridge, 2002

Cousar, Charles B. *The Letters of Paul*. Nashville, TN: Abingdon Press, 1996.

Crossan, John Dominic. *The Cross That Spoke: The Origins of the Passion Narrative*. San Francisco: Harper & Row, 1988.

Crossan, John Dominic, *The Historical Jesus*. San Francisco: HarperSanFrancisco, 1993.

Danker, Frederick, and others. *A Greek-English Lexicon of the New Testament and Other Early Christian Literature*, 3rd ed. Chicago: University of Chicago Press, 2000.

Daryl, Charles J., *Virtue amidst Vice: The Catalog of Virtues in 2 Peter 1*. Sheffield, UK: Sheffield Academic Press, 1997.

Davids, Peter H. *James*. New York: Harper & Row, 1983.

Davies, W. D. *The Setting of the Sermon on the Mount*. Cambridge: Cambridge University Press, 1977.

De La Torre, Miguel A, *Reading the Bible from the Margins*. Maryknoll, NY: Orbis, 2002.

deSilva, David A. *Honor, Patronage, Kinship, & Purity: Unlocking New Testament Culture*. Downers Grove, IL: InterVarsity, 2000.

Dibelius, Martin, and Conzelmann, Hans. *The Pastoral Epistles*. Hermeneia Commentary. Philadelphia: Fortress Press, 1972.

Dibelius, Martin. *From Tradition to Gospel*. New York: Scribner, 1965 (German original, 1934).

Dodd, C. H. *The Apostolic Preaching and Its Development*. London: Hodder and Stoughton, 1936.

Donfried, Karl P., and I. H. Marshall. *The Theology of the Shorter Pauline Letters*. Cambridge: Cambridge University Press, 1993.

Donfried, Karl P. *Paul, Thessalonica and Early Christianity*. Grand Rapids, MI: Eerdmans, 2002.

Donfried, Karl P. *The Romans Debate,* 2nd ed. Peabody, MA: Hendrickson, 1991.

Dube, Musa. *Other Ways of Reading: African Women and the Bible*. Geneva: World Council of Churches, 2001.

Dube, Musa. *Postcolonial Feminist Interpretation of the Bible*. St. Louis: Chalice, 2000.

Dube, Musa L., and Jeffrey L. Staley. *John and Postcolonialism: Travel, Space and Power*. London: Sheffield Academic Press, 2002.

Dube, Musa, and Gerald West. *The Bible in Africa*. Boston: Brill Academic, 2001.

Dunn, James D. G. *Jesus Remembered*. Grand Rapids, MI: Eerdmans, 2003.

Dunn, James D. G. *Theology of Paul the Apostle*. Grand Rapids, MI: Eerdmans, 1999.

Duruseau, Patrick. *High Places in Cyberspace*, 2nd ed. Atlanta: Scholars Press, 1998.

Efird, J. M. *Daniel and Revelation: A Study of Two Extraordinary Visions*. Valley Forge, NY: Judson Press, 1978.

Eisenbaum, Pamela. *The Jewish Heroes of Christian History: Hebrews 11 in Literary Context*. Atlanta: Scholars Press, 1997.

Elliott, John H. *A Home for the Homeless: A Sociological Exegesis of 1 Peter, It's Situation and Strategy*. Philadelphia: Fortress Press, 1981.

Elliott, John H. "Jesus Was Not an Egalitarian: A Critique of an Anachronistic and Idealist Theory," *Biblical Theology Bulletin* (Summer 2002). Online on April 20, 2004 at http://www.findarticles.com/cf_dls/m0LAL/2_32/94332342/p1/article.html.

Elliott, John H. *What Is Social-Scientific Criticism?* Minneapolis: Fortress Press, 1993.

Farmer, W. R. *The Synoptic Problem*. Dillsboro, NC: Western North Carolina Press, 1976.

Fee, Gordon. *Paul's Letter to the Philippians*. Grand Rapids, MI: Eerdmans, 1994.

Felder, Cain, ed. *Stony the Road We Trod: African American Biblical Interpretation*. Minneapolis: Fortress Press, 1991.

Ferguson, Everett. *Backgrounds of Early Christianity*, 3rd ed. Grand Rapids, MI: Eerdmans, 2003.

Fish, Stanley. *Is There a Text in This Class? The Authority of Interpretive Communities*. Cambridge, MA: Harvard University Press, 1980.

Fitzmyer, Joseph A., *The Acts of the Apostles*. Garden City, NY: Doubleday, 1998.

Fitzmyer, Joseph. *The Gospel According to Luke*. Garden City, NY: Doubleday, 1981, 1985.

Fitzmyer, Joseph A. *Romans*. Anchor Bible Commentary. Garden City, NY: Doubleday, 1993.

Fortna, Robert. *The Gospel of Signs*. Cambridge: Cambridge University Press, 1970.

Fredricksen, Paula. *Jesus of Nazareth, King of the Jews: A Jewish Life and the Emergence of Christianity*. New York: Vintage Books, 2000.

Furnish, Victor Paul. "Ephesians, Epistle to the." In D. N. Freedman, ed., *The Anchor Bible Dictionary*, vol. 2, pp. 535–542. Garden City, NY: Doubleday, 1992.

Furnish, Victor Paul. *II Corinthians*. Garden City, NY: Doubleday, 1984.

Gager, John. *Kingdom and Community: The Social World of Early Christianity*. Englewood Cliffs, NJ: Prentice-Hall, 1975.

Gaventa, Beverly. "Towards a Theology of Acts." *Interpretation* 42 (1988): 146–57.

Gold, Victor R., and others. *The New Testament and Psalms: A New Inclusive Translation*. New York: Oxford University Press, 1995.

Goodacre, Mark, *The Case against Q*. Harrisburg, PA: Trinity International Press, 2002.

Goodspeed, Edgar J. *The Apostolic Fathers: An American Translation*. New York: Harper & Brothers, 1950.

Green, Joel B. *The Gospel of Luke*. Grand Rapids, MI: Eerdmans, 1997.

Green, Joel B. *The Theology of the Gospel of Luke*. Cambridge: Cambridge University Press, 1995.

Gundry, Robert. *Matthew: A Commentary on His Literary and Theological Art.* Grand Rapids, MI: Eerdmans, 1982.

Hahneman, Geoffrey Mark. *The Muratorian Fragment and the Development of the Canon.* Oxford: Clarendon Press, 1992.

Hanson, A. T. *The Pastoral Epistles.* Grand Rapids, MI: Eerdmans, 1982.

Hanson, Paul D. *The Dawn of Apocalyptic: The Historical and Sociological Roots of Jewish Apocalyptic Eschatology.* Philadelphia: Fortress Press, 1979.

Harrington, Daniel J. *Interpreting the NT: A Practical Guide.* New York: Liturgical Press, 1990.

Hayes, John H., and Sara Mandell. *Jewish People in Classical Antiquity: From Alexander to Bar Kochba.* Louisville, KY: Westminster John Knox, 1998.

Heil, J. P. *Paul's Letter to the Romans: A Reader-Response Commentary.* New York: Paulist Press, 1987.

Hill, Craig. *In God's Time: The Bible and the Future.* Grand Rapids, MI: Eerdmans, 2002.

Hock, Ronald. "The Workshop as a Social Setting for Paul's Missionary Preaching." *Catholic Biblical Quarterly* 41 (1979): 438–450.

Hooker, Morna. "Philemon." In James D. G. Dunn and John W. Rogerson, eds., *Eerdmans Commentary on the Bible.* Grand Rapids, MI: Eerdmans, 2003, pp. 1447–1450.

Horrell, David G. *An Introduction to the Study of Paul.* New York: Continuum, 2001.

Horsley, Richard. *Hearing the Whole Story: The Politics of Plot in Mark's Gospel.* Louisville, KY: Westminster/John Knox, 2001.

Hultgren, Arland J. *The Parables of Jesus* Grand Rapids, NY: Eerdmans, 2000.

Ilan, Tal. *Jewish Women in Greco-Roman Palestine.* Peabody, MA: Hendrickson, 1996.

Jervel, Jakob. *The Theology of the Acts of the Apostles.* Cambridge: Cambridge University Press, 1996.

Jewett, Robert, *A Chronology of Paul's Life.* Philadelphia: Fortress Press, 1979.

Johnson, Luke T. *James.* Garden City, NY: Doubleday, 1995.

Johnson, Luke T. *Letters to Paul's Delegates: 1 Timothy, 2 Timothy, Titus.* Valley Forge, NY: Trinity Press International, 1996.

Jones, F. Stanley. *An Ancient Jewish Christian Source on the History of Christianity.* Atlanta: Scholars Press, 1995.

Kee, Howard C. *Understanding the New Testament.* Upper Saddle River, NJ: Prentice- Hall, 1993.

Kermode, Frank. *The Genesis of Secrecy.* Cambridge, MA: Harvard University Press, 1979.

Kilpatrick, G. D. *The Origins of the Gospel of St. Matthew.* Oxford: Oxford University Press, 1946.

Kingsbury, Jack D. *Matthew as Story.* Philadelphia: Fortress Press, 1988.

Kittredge, Cynthia Briggs. "Hebrews." In Elizabeth Schüssler Fiorenza, *Searching the Scriptures,* vol. 2, pp. 428–452. New York: Crossroad, 1994.

Klauck, Hans-Josef. *The Religious Context of Early Christianity: A Guide to Greco-Roman Religions.* Minneapolis: Augsburg Fortress, 2002.

Koester, Craig. *Revelation and the End of All Things*. Grand Rapids, MI: Eerdmans, 2001.

Koester, Helmut, and James M. Robinson, *Trajectories through Early Christianity*. Philadelphia: Fortress Press, 1979.

Koester, Helmut. *Introduction to the New Testament*, 2nd ed., 2 vols. Berlin and New York: de Gruyter, 1995.

Kopas, Jane. "Jesus and Women: John's Gospel." *Theology Today* 41 (1984): 201–205.

Kopas, Jane. "Jesus and Women: Luke's Gospel," *Theology Today* 43 (1986): 193–202.

Koperski, Veronica. *What Are They Saying about Paul and the Law?* Mahwah, NJ: Paulist Press, 2001.

Krentz, Edgar. "Through a Lens: Theology and Fidelity in 2 Thessalonians." In Jouette M. Bassler, ed., *Pauline Theology* (Minneapolis: Fortress, 1991), vol. 1, pp. 52–62.

Kurz, William S. *Reading Luke-Acts: Dynamics of Biblical Narrative*. Louisville, KY: Westminster/John Knox Press, 1993.

Kwok, Pui-lan. *Discovering the Bible in the Nonbiblical World*. Maryknoll, NY: Orbis, 1995.

LaGrand, James. *The Earliest Christian Mission to All Nations in the Light of Matthew's Gospel*. Grand Rapids, MI: Eerdmans, 1998.

Levine, Amy-Jill. *A Feminist Companion to the Deutero-Pauline Epistles*. Sheffield, UK: Sheffield Academic Press, 2003.

Levine, Amy-Jill. *A Feminist Companion to John*. Sheffield, UK: Sheffield Academic Press, 2003.

Levine, Amy-Jill. *A Feminist Companion to Luke*. London: Sheffield Academic Press, 2002.

Levine, Amy-Jill, ed., *A Feminist Companion to Matthew*. Sheffield, UK: Sheffield Academic Press, 2001.

Lewis, Lloyd A. "An African-American Appraisal of the Philemon-Paul-Onesimus Triangle," In Cain H. Felder, ed., *Stony the Road We Trod: African American Biblical Interpretation*. Minneapolis: Fortress Press, 1991, pp. 232–246.

Lieu, Judith. *The Second and Third Epistles of John: History and Background*. Edinburgh: Clark, 1986.

Lieu, Judith. *The Theology of the Johannine Epistles*. Cambridge: University Press, 1991.

Lindars, Barnabas. *The Theology of the Letter to the Hebrews*. Cambridge: Cambridge University Press, 1991.

Lohse, Eduard. *Colossians and Philemon*. Philadelphia: Fortress Press, 1971.

Lüdemann, Gerd. *Early Christianity according to the Traditions of Acts*. Minneapolis: Fortress Press, 1989.

Luz, Ulrich. *The Theology of the Gospel of Matthew*. Cambridge: Cambridge University Press, 1995.

Maddox, R. *The Purpose of Luke-Acts*. Edinburgh: Clark, 1982.

Malbon, Elizabeth S. *Hearing Mark: A Listener's Guide*. Harrisburg, PN: Trinity, 2002.

Malina, Bruce and Richard Rohrbaugh, *Social-Science Commentary on the Synoptic Gospels*, 2nd ed. Minneapolis: Fortress Press, 2003.

Malina, Bruce J., and John J. Pilch. *Social Scientific Commentary on the Revelation*. Minneapolis: Fortress Press, 2000.

Malina, Bruce. *Social Scientific Commentary on the Gospel of John*. Minneapolis: Fortress Press, 1998.

Malina, Bruce. *The New Testament World: Insights from Cultural Anthropology*, 3rd ed. Louisville, KY: Westminster/John Knox, 2001.

Malina, Bruce. *Windows on the World of Jesus: Time Travel to Ancient Judea*. Louisville, KY: WestminsterJohn Knox, 1993.

Manson, T. W. *The Teachings of Jesus,* 2nd ed. Cambridge: Cambridge University Press, 1935.

Marcus, Joel. *Mark 1-8*. Garden City, NY: Doubleday, 1999.

Marshall, I. Howard, and David Peterson, eds. *Witness to the Gospel: The Theology of Acts*. Grand Rapids, MI: Eerdmans, 1998.

Marshall, I. Howard. *1 and 2 Thessalonians*. Grand Rapids, MI: Eerdmans, 1983.

Martin, Clarice. "The Haustafeln (Household Codes) in African American Biblical Interpretation: 'Free Slaves' and 'Subordinate Women.'" In Cain H. Felder, ed., *Stony the Road We Trod: African American Biblical Interpretation* (Minneapolis: Fortress Press, 1991), pp. 206–231.

Martin, Ralph P. *Carmen Christi: Philippians 2:5–11 in Recent Interpretation and in the Setting of Early Christian Worship,* 2nd ed. Grand Rapids, MI: Eerdmans, 1983.

Martyn, J. Louis. *Galatians*. Garden City, NY: Doubleday, 1997.

Martyn, J. Louis. *History and Theology of the Fourth Gospel,* 2nd ed. Nashville, TN: Abingdon, 1979.

Marxsen, Willi. *Mark the Evangelist: Studies on the Redaction History of the Gospel*. Nashville, TN: Abingdon, 1969 (German original, 1954).

Matera, Frank. *II Corinthians: A Commentary*. Louisville, KY: Westminster John Knox, 2003.

Matera, Frank. "Galatians in Perspective: Cutting a New Path through Old Territory," *Interpretation* (July 2000): 233–245.

McKenzie. Steven L., and Stephen R. Haynes. *To Each Its Own Meaning: An Introduction to Biblical Criticisms and Their Application,* 2nd ed. Louisville, KY: Westminster John Knox, 1999.

Meeks, Wayne. *The First Urban Christians*. New Haven, CT: Yale University Press, 1983.

Meier, John. *A Marginal Jew: Rethinking the Historical Jesus,* 3 vols. New York: AnchorDoubleday, 1991, 1994, 2001.

Metzger, Bruce. *Textual Commentary on the Greek New Testament,* 2nd ed. New York: United Bible Societies, 1994.

Mitchell, Joan L. *Beyond Fear and Silence: A Feminist-Literary Approach to the Gospel of Mark*. New York: Continuum, 2001.

Mitton, C. L. *Ephesians*. New Century Bible Commentary. Grand Rapids, MI: Eerdmans, 1981.

Murphy-O'Connor, Jerome, *Paul. A Critical Life*. New York: Clarendon, 1996.

Nanos, Mark, *The Irony of Galatians*. Minneapolis: Augsburg-Fortress, 2002.

Neyrey, Jerome H. *Paul, in Other Words: A Cultural Reading of His Letters*. Louisville, KY: Westminster/John Knox, 1990.

Nickelsburg, George W. E. *Ancient Judaism and Christian Origins: Diversity, Continuity and Transformation*. Minneapolis: Fortress Press, 2003.

Nilsson, Martin. *Greek Folk Religion*. Philadelphia: University of Pennsylvania Press, 1987.

Nordling, J.G. "Onesimus Fugitivus: A Defense of the Runaway Slave Hypothesis in Philemon." *Journal for the Study of the New Testament* 41 (1991): 97–119.

O'Brien, P. T. *Colossians, Philemon*. Waco, TX: Word Books, 1982.

Oakes, Peter. *Philippians: From People to Letter.* Cambridge: Cambridge University Press, 2001.

Paffenroth, Kim. *The Story of Jesus according to L.* Sheffield, UK: Sheffield Academic Press, 1997.

Pagels, Elaine. *The Gnostic Gospels.* New York: Vintage Books, 1989.

Painter, John, and others. *Word, Theology, and Community in John.* St. Louis: Chalice, 2002.

Perkins, Pheme. *The Book of Revelation.* Collegeville, MN Liturgical Press, 1983.

Perkins, Pheme. *First and Second Peter, James and Jude.* Louisville, KY: Westminster/John Knox, 1995.

Perkins, Pheme. *Gnosticism and the New Testament.* Minneapolis: Fortress Press, 1993.

Perrin, Norman. *What Is Redaction Criticism?* Philadelphia: Fortress Press, 1969.

Pervo, Richard I. *Profit with Delight.* Philadelphia: Fortress Press, 1987.

Petersen, N. R. *Rediscovering Paul: Philemon and the Sociology of Paul's Narrative World.* Philadelphia: Fortress, 1985.

Peterson, Eugene. *The Message: The Bible in Contemporary Language.* Colorado Springs: Navpress, 2002.

Powell, Mark A. *What Are They Saying about Acts?* New York: Paulist Press, 1991.

Powell, Mark A. *What Are They Saying about Luke?* New York: Paulist Press, 1989.

Powell, Mark A., *What Is Narrative Criticism?* Minneapolis: Fortress Press, 1990.

Quinn, Jerome D., ed. and trans. *1 and 2 Timothy and Titus.* Anchor Bible Commentary. Garden City, NY: Doubleday, 1976.

Quinn, Jerome D., and William C. Wacker. *The First and Second Letters to Timothy.* Grand Rapids, MI: Eerdmans, 2000.

Quinn, Jerome D. *Titus.* Garden City, NY: Doubleday, 1990.

Rhoades, David, Joanna Dewey, and Donald Michie. *Mark as Story: An Introduction to the Narrative of a Gospel,* 2nd ed. Minneapolis: Fortress Press, 1999.

Richard, Earl. *First and Second Thessalonians.* Collegeville: Liturgical Press, 1995.

Robbins, Vernon K. *The Tapestry of Early Christian Discourse: Rhetoric, Society and Ideology.* London: Routledge, 1996.

Robinson, James M., and Helmut Koester. *Trajectories through Early Christianity.* Philadelphia: Fortress Press, 1971.

Roetzel, Calvin. *The Letters of Paul: Conversations in Context,* 3rd ed. Atlanta: John Knox Press, 1991.

Rohde, Joachim. *Rediscovering the Teaching of the Evangelists.* London: SCM/Philadelphia: Westminster Press, 1968.

Rohrbaugh, Richard, ed. *The Social Sciences and New Testament Interpretation.* Peabody, MA: Hendrickson, 1996.

Saldarini, Anthony J. *Pharisees, Scribes and Sadducees in Palestinian Society: A Sociological Approach.* Grand Rapids, MI: Eerdmans, 2001.

Sanders, E. P. *Paul, the Law, and the Jewish People.* Philadelphia: Fortress Press, 1983.

Sanders, E. P. *Paul and Palestinian Judaism.* Philadelphia: Fortress, 1977.

Sanders, E. P. *The Historical Figure of Jesus.* London: Penguin, 1993.

Santos, Narry. *Slave of All.* London: Sheffield Academic Press, 2003.

Schaberg, Jane. "Luke." In Carol Newsome and Sharon Ringe, eds., *Women's Bible Commentary*, pp. 275–292. Louisville, KY: WestminsterJohn Knox, 1999.

Schmidt, Karl L. *The Place of the Gospels in the General History of Literature.* Darmstadt: Wissenschaftliche Buchgesellschaft, 1964 (German original, 1919).

Schnelle, Udo. *The History and Theology of the New Testament Writings.* Minneapolis: Fortress Press, 1998.

Schweizer, Eduard. *The Letter to the Colossians: A Commentary.* Minneapolis: Augsburg, 1982.

Segal, Alan. *Paul the Convert: The Apostolate and Apostasy of Saul the Pharisee.* New Haven, CT and London: Yale University Press, 1990.

Segovia, Fernando. *Decolonizing Biblical Studies: A View from the Margin.* Maryknoll, NY: Orbis, 2000

Selvidge, Marla. *The New Testament.* Upper Saddle River, NJ: Prentice-Hall, 1999.

Senior, Donald, and others. *The Catholic Study Bible*, 2nd ed. New York: Oxford University Press, 1990.

Smalley, Steven S. *1, 2, 3 John.* Waco, TX: Word, 1984.

Smith, D. Moody, Jr. *Johannine Christianity: Essays on Its Setting, Sources, and Theology.* Columbia, SC: University of South Carolina Press, 1984.

Smith, Morton. *Clement of Alexandria and a Secret Gospel of Mark.* Cambridge, MA: Harvard University Press, 1973.

Soards, Marion L. *The Speeches in Acts: Their Content, Context and Concerns.* Louisville, KY: Westminster John Knox, 1992.

Stanton, Elizabeth Cady. *The Woman's Bible.* Seattle: Coalition Task Force on Women and Religion, 1974. (Original, 1891).

Stibbe, Mark W. G. *John as Storyteller: Narrative Criticism and the Fourth Gospel.* Cambridge: Cambridge University Press, 1992.

Streeter, B. H. *The Four Gospels.* London: Macmillan, 1924.

Stuckenbruck, Loren. "Revelation." In J. D. G. Dunn and J. Rogerson, eds., *Eerdmans Commentary on the Bible,* pp. 1535–1572. Grand Rapids, MI: Eerdmans, 2003.

Sugirtharajah, R. S. *The Postcolonial Bible.* London: Sheffield Academic Press, 1998.

Sugirtharajah, R. S. *The Bible and the Third World.* Cambridge: Cambridge University Press, 2001.

Talbert, Charles H. *Reading Corinthians.* New York: Crossroad, 1989.

Taylor, Kenneth. *Living Bible.* Wheaton, IL: Tyndale House, 1971.

Taylor, Vincent. *The Gospels.* London: Epworth, 1930.

Theissen, Gerd, *The Social Setting of Pauline Christianity.* Philadelphia: Fortress Press, 1982.

Theissen, Gerd. *Sociology of Early Palestinian Christianity.* Philadelphia: Fortress Press, 1978.

Theissen, Gerd, and Annette Merz. *The Historical Jesus: A Comprehensive Guide.* Minneapolis: Fortress Press, 1998.

Thompson, Mariann Meye. *The Johannine Letters.* Downers Grove, IL: InterVarsity, 1992.

Tolbert, Mary Ann. *Sowing the Gospel: Mark's World in Literary-Historical Perspective.* Minneapolis: Fortress Press, 1989.

Trible, Phillis. "Feminist Hermeneutics and Biblical Studies." *Christian Century,* February 3, 1982, p. 116.

Tuckett, Christopher M. "Introduction to the Gospels." In J. D. G. Dunn and J. Rogerson, eds., *Eerdmans Commentary on the Bible.* Grand Rapids, MI: Eerdmans, 2003, pp. 989–999.

Tuckett, Christopher. *Reading the New Testament: Methods of Interpretation.* Philadelphia: Fortress Press, 1987.

Van Unnik, W. C. "Luke-Acts, a Storm Center in Contemporary Scholarship." In Leander Keck and J. Louis Martyn, eds., *Studies in Luke-Acts,* pp. 15–34. Nashville: Abingdon, 1966.

Van Voorst, Robert E. *Ascents of James: History and Theology of a Jewish-Christian Community.* Atlanta: Scholars Press, 1989.

Van Voorst, Robert E. *Jesus Outside the New Testament.* Grand Rapids, MI: Eerdmans, 2000.

Vanderkam, James C. *An Introduction to Early Judaism.* Grand Rapids, MI: Eerdmans, 2001.

Vanderkam, James C. *The Dead Sea Scrolls Today.* Grand Rapids, MI: Eerdmans, 1994.

Vermes, Geza. *The Dead Sea Scrolls in English,* 3rd ed. Harmondsworth, UK: Penguin, 1984.

Vielhauer, Philip. "On the 'Paulinism' of Acts." In Leander Keck and J. Louis Martyn, eds., *Studies in Luke-Acts.* Philadelphia: Fortress Press, 1980.

Von Wahlde, Urban. *The Earliest Version of John's Gospel.* Wilmington, DE: Glazier, 1989.

Wanamaker, Charles. *The Epistles to the Thessalonians.* Grand Rapids, MI: Eerdmans, 1990.

Watson, Duane F. *Rhetorical Criticism of Jude and 2 Peter.* Atlanta: Scholars Press, 1988.

Weeden, Theodore, and Werner Kelber. *The Christology of Mark's Gospel.* Philadelphia: Fortress Press, 1983.

Wimbush, Vincent. *African Americans and the Bible: Sacred Texts and Social Textures.* New York: Continuum, 1999.

Wink, Walter. *The Powers That Be: Theology for a New Millennium.* Garden City, NY: Doubleday, 1998.

Winter, Bruce. *Roman Wives, Roman Widows: The Appearance of New Women and the Pauline Communities.* Grand Rapids, MI: Eerdmans, 2003.

Winter, Sara. "Paul's Letter to Philemon." *New Testament Studies* 33 (1987): 1–15.

Witherington, Ben. *The Acts of the Apostles: A Socio-Rhetorical Commentary.* Grand Rapids, MI: Eerdmans, 1998.

Witherington, Ben. *Conflict and Community in Corinth: A Socio-Rhetorical Commentary on 1 and 2 Corinthians.* Grand Rapids, MI: Eerdmans, 1994.

Witherington, Ben. *The Gospel of Mark: A Socio-Rhetorical Commentary.* Grand Rapids, MI: Eerdmans, 2001.

Wrede, William. *The Messianic Secret.* Cambridge, UK: J. Clarke, 1971. (German original 1901.)

Wright, N. T. *The Original Jesus.* Grand Rapids, MI: Eerdmans, 1996.

Yeo, Khiok-khng. *What Has Jerusalem to Do with Beijing? Biblical Interpretation from a Chinese Perspective.* Harrisburg, PA: Trinity Press International, 1998.

Young, Francis. *The Theology of the Pastoral Letters.* Cambridge: Cambridge University Press, 1994.

Index

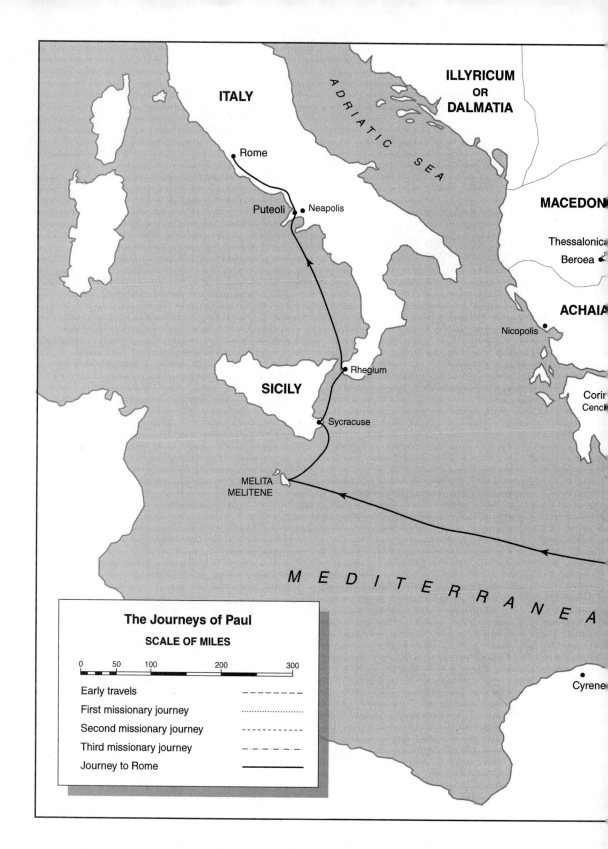

ITALY

• Rome

Puteoli • • Neapolis

Rhegium •

SICILY

• Sycracuse

MELITA
MELITENE

ADRIATIC SEA

ILLYRICUM
OR
DALMATIA

MACEDON

Thessalonica
Beroea

ACHAIA

• Nicopolis

Corin
Cench

MEDITERRANEA

• Cyrene

The Journeys of Paul

SCALE OF MILES

0   50   100   200   300

Early travels	– – – – –
First missionary journey	....
Second missionary journey	– – – – –
Third missionary journey	–·–·–·–
Journey to Rome	———